T0235914

Lecture Notes in Computer Science   8814

Commenced Publication in 1973
Founding and Former Series Editors:
Gerhard Goos, Juris Hartmanis, and Jan van Leeuwen

Editorial Board

More information about this series at http://www.springer.com/series/7412

Aurélio Campilho · Mohamed Kamel (Eds.)

Image Analysis and Recognition

11th International Conference, ICIAR 2014
Vilamoura, Portugal, October 22–24, 2014
Proceedings, Part I

 Springer

Editors
Aurélio Campilho
Faculty of Engineering
University of Porto
Porto
Portugal

Mohamed Kamel
Department of Electrical and Computer
  Engineering
University of Waterloo
Waterloo, ON
Canada

ISSN 0302-9743   ISSN 1611-3349 (electronic)
ISBN 978-3-319-11757-7   ISBN 978-3-319-11758-4 (eBook)
DOI 10.1007/978-3-319-11758-4

Library of Congress Control Number: 2014950801

LNCS Sublibrary: SL6 – Image Processing, Computer Vision, Pattern Recognition, and Graphics

Springer Cham Heidelberg New York Dordrecht London

Printed on acid-free paper

Springer is part of Springer Science+Business Media (www.springer.com)

Preface

This is the 11th edition of the ICIAR series of annual conferences offering an opportunity for the participants to interact and present their latest research in theory, methodology, and applications of image analysis and recognition. ICIAR 2014, the International Conference on Image Analysis and Recognition, was held in Vila Moura, Portugal, October 22–24, 2014. ICIAR is organized by AIMI – Association for Image and Machine Intelligence, a not-for-profit organization registered in Ontario, Canada.

For ICIAR 2014, we received a total of 177 full papers from 39 countries. Before the review process all the papers were checked for similarity using a comparison database of scholarly work. The review process was carried out by members of the Program Committee and other reviewers. Each paper was reviewed by at least two reviewers, and checked by the conference chairs. A total of 107 papers were finally accepted and appear in the two volumes of this proceedings. We would like to sincerely thank the authors for responding to our call, and we thank the reviewers for the careful evaluation and feedback provided to the authors. It is this collective effort that resulted in the strong conference program and high-quality proceedings.

Each year we attempt to focus on a specific topic for the keynote speeches and conduct a panel discussion on the topic.

This year, the conference theme was focused on the topic "Sparse Representations for Image Analysis and Recognition." We were very pleased to include three outstanding keynote talks on this topic: "Optimization Algorithms for Sparse Representations: Some History and Recent Developments" by Mário Figueiredo, Instituto Superior Técnico Portugal; "Morphological Diversities in Astrophysics" by Jean-Luc Starck, CosmoStat Laboratory, France; and "Sparse Stochastic Processes with Application to Biomedical Imaging" by Michael Unser, Ecole Polytechnique Fédérale de Lausanne, Switzerland. The keynote speakers also participated in the panel "Sparse Representation for Image Analysis and Recognition: Trends and Applications." We would like to express our gratitude to the keynote speakers for accepting our invitation to share their vision and recent advances in their areas of expertise, which are at the core of the topics of the conference.

We would like to thank Khaled Hammouda, the webmaster of the conference, for maintaining the Web pages, interacting with the authors, and preparing the proceedings.

As all conferences, the success of ICIAR 2014 is attributed to the effort and work of many people, including members of the Organizing Committee, staff, and volunteers. We gratefully acknowledge their support and efforts.

We are also grateful to Springer's editorial staff for supporting this publication in the LNCS series. We also would like to acknowledge the professional service of Viagens Abreu in taking care of the registration process and the special events of the conference.

Finally, we are very pleased to welcome all the participants to ICIAR 2014. For those who were not able to attend, we hope this publication provides a good view into the research presented at the conference, and we look forward to meeting you at the next ICIAR conference.

October 2014   Aurélio Campilho
                                                                            Mohamed Kamel

ICIAR 2014 – International Conference on Image Analysis and Recognition

General Chairs

Aurélio Campilho	University of Porto, Portugal
Mohamed Kamel	University of Waterloo, Canada

Local Organizing Committee

Ana Maria Mendonça	University of Porto, Portugal
Jorge Alves Silva	University of Porto, Portugal
João Rodrigues	University of the Algarve, Portugal
José Rouco Maseda	Biomedical Engineering Institute, Portugal
Jorge Novo Buján	Biomedical Engineering Institute, Portugal

Conference Secretariat

Viagens Abreu	SA, Portugal

Webmaster

Khaled Hammouda	Waterloo, Ontario, Canada

Advisory Committee

M. Ahmadi	University of Windsor, Canada
P. Bhattacharya	Concordia University, Canada
T.D. Bui	Concordia University, Canada
M. Cheriet	University of Quebec, Canada
E. Dubois	University of Ottawa, Canada
Z. Duric	George Mason University, USA
G. Granlund	Linköping University, Sweden
L. Guan	Ryerson University, Canada
M. Haindl	Institute of Information Theory and Automation, Czech Republic
E. Hancock	University of York, UK
J. Kovacevic	Carnegie Mellon University, USA
M. Kunt	Swiss Federal Institute of Technology (EPFL), Switzerland

J. Padilha	University of Porto, Portugal
K.N. Plataniotis	University of Toronto, Canada
A. Sanfeliu	Technical University of Catalonia, Spain
M. Shah	University of Central Florida, USA
M. Sid-Ahmed	University of Windsor, Canada
C.Y. Suen	Concordia University, Canada
A.N. Venetsanopoulos	University of Toronto, Canada
M. Viergever	Utrecht University, Netherlands
B. Vijayakumar	Carnegie Mellon University, USA
R. Ward	University of British Columbia, Canada
D. Zhang	Hong Kong Polytechnic University, Hong Kong

Program Committee

A. Abate	University of Salerno, Italy
M. Ahmed	Wilfrid Laurier University, Canada
L. Alexandre	University of Beira Interior, Portugal
J. Alirezaie	Ryerson University, Canada
G. Andreu-Garcia	Universitat Politècnica de València, Spain
H. Araújo	University of Coimbra, Portugal
Emilio Balaguer-Ballester	Bournemouth University, UK
T. Barata	University of Coimbra, Portugal
J. Barbosa	University of Porto, Portugal
J. Batista	University of Coimbra, Portugal
R. Bernardes	University of Coimbra, Portugal
A. Bezerianos	National University of Singapore, Singapore
J. Bioucas	Technical University of Lisbon, Portugal
I. Bloch	Télécom ParisTech, France
T.D. Bui	Concordia University, Canada
C. Busch	Gjøvik University College, Norway
F. Camastra	University of Naples Parthenope, Italy
J. Cardoso	University of Porto, Portugal
G. Carneiro	University of Adelaide, Australia
M. Coimbra	University of Porto, Portugal
M. Correia	University of Porto, Portugal
J. Debayle	Ecole Nationale Supérieure des Mines de Saint-Étienne, France
J. Dias	University of Coimbra, Portugal
G. Doretto	West Virginia University, USA
H. du Buf	University of the Algarve, Portugal
J. Fernandez	Centro Nacional de Biotecnología – CSIC, Spain
I. Fondón	University of Seville, Spain
A. Fred	Technical University of Lisbon, Portugal
G. Freeman	University of Waterloo, Canada

D. Frejlichowski	West Pomeranian University of Technology, Poland
G. Giacinto	University of Cagliari, Italy
M. Giger	University of Chicago, USA
B. Gosselin	University of Mons, Belgium
G. Grossi	University of Milan, Italy
M. Grzegorzek	University of Siegen, Germany
M. Haindl	Institute of Information Theory and Automation, Czech Republic
A. Hernandez	Universitat Autònoma de Barcelona, Spain
L. Heutte	Université de Rouen, France
C. Hong	Hong Kong Polytechnic University, Hong Kong
L. Igual	University of Barcelona, Spain
M. Khan	King Saud University, Saudi Arabia
A. Kong	Nanyang Technological University, Singapore
M. Koskela	Aalto University, Finland
A. Kuijper	Fraunhofer IGD and TU Darmstadt, Germany
J. Liang	Simon Fraser University, Canada
L. Liu	McGill University, Canada
N. Lomenie	Paris Descartes University, France
L. Lopes	University of Aveiro, Portugal
J. Lorenzo-Ginori	Universidad Central "Marta Abreu" de Las Villas, Cuba
R. Lukac	Foveon, Inc., USA
A. Marcal	University of Porto, Portugal
F. Marcelloni	University of Pisa, Italy
U. Markowska-Kaczmar	Wroclaw University of Technology, Poland
J. Marques	Technical University of Lisbon, Portugal
M. Melkemi	Univeristé de Haute Alsace, France
A. Mendonça	University of Porto, Portugal
J. Meunier	University of Montreal, Canada
M. Mignotte	University of Montreal, Canada
M. Mirmehdi	University of Bristol, UK
A. Mohammed	Imam Muhammad Ibn Saud Islamic University, Saudi Arabia
A. Monteiro	University of Porto, Portugal
M. Nappi	University of Salerno, Italy
M. Nixon	University of Southampton, UK
H. Ogul	Başkent University, Turkey
M. Pelillo	University of Venice, Italy
M. Penedo	Universidade da Coruña, Spain
F. Pereira	Technical University of Lisbon, Portugal
E. Petrakis	Technical University of Crete, Greece
P. Pina	Technical University of Lisbon, Portugal
A. Pinho	University of Aveiro, Portugal

Reviewers

Supported by

AIMI – Association for Image and Machine Intelligence

Center for Biomedical Engineering Research
INESC TEC – INESC Technology and Science
Portugal

Department of Electrical and Computer Engineering
Faculty of Engineering
University of Porto
Portugal

CPAMI – Centre for Pattern Analysis and Machine Intelligence
University of Waterloo
Canada

Contents – Part I

Image Restoration and Enhancement

Feature Detection and Image Segmentation

Classification and Learning Methods

Document Image Analysis

Image and Video Retrieval

Remote Sensing

Applications

Contents – Part II

Action, Gestures and Audio-Visual Recognition

Biometrics

Medical Image Processing and Analysis

Medical Image Segmentation

Computer-Aided Diagnosis

Retinal Image Analysis

3D Imaging

Image Representation and Models

Path Descriptors for Geometric Graph Matching and Registration

Miguel Amável Pinheiro$^{(\boxtimes)}$ and Jan Kybic

Center for Machine Perception, Department of Cybernetics, Faculty of Electrical
Engineering, Czech Technical University in Prague, Prague, Czech Republic
amavemig@cmp.felk.cvut.cz

Abstract. Graph and tree-like structures such as blood vessels and neuronal networks are abundant in medical imaging. We present a method
to calculate path descriptors in geometrical graphs, so that the similarity between paths in the graphs can be determined efficiently. We show
experimentally that our descriptors are more discriminative than existing alternatives. We further describe how to match two geometric graphs
using our path descriptors. Our main application is registering images
for which standard techniques are inefficient, because the appearance
of the images is too different, or there is not enough texture and no
uniquely identifiable keypoints to be found. We show that our approach
can register these images with better accuracy than previous methods.

1 Introduction

Blood vessels, nerve fibers or pulmonary airways are examples of biological structures that can be represented as *geometrical graphs* with nodes corresponding
to branching points and edges corresponding to curves connecting the branching
points (Fig. 1). We consider the problem of registering two 2D or 3D images
based on a common geometric graph structure both images contain and which
we assume to be already extracted (e.g. [1]). This approach has the potential of
being much faster than standard pixel-based image registration techniques [2]
and tolerate very different image appearances. With respect to key point registration methods [3], registering geometric graphs provides more clues.

Unlike most existing approaches, our method can in a reasonable time handle
rather general transformations and large displacements, as well as partial overlaps. The key contribution over our previous work [4,5] is an alternative coarse
alignment step based on finding similarities between *path descriptors* to restrict
the set of possible correspondences and thus make the matching more efficient.

2 Related Work

Ignoring edges, the geometric graph registration becomes a point cloud matching
problem, which can be solved by RANSAC-like approaches [6,7] These methods

© Springer International Publishing Switzerland 2014
A. Campilho and M. Kamel (Eds.): ICIAR 2014, Part I, LNCS 8814, pp. 3–11, 2014.
DOI: 10.1007/978-3-319-11758-4_1

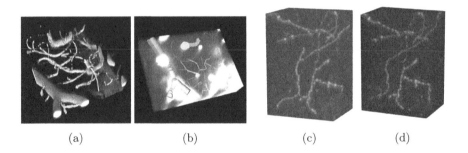

(a)   (b)   (c)   (d)

Fig. 1. Example registration problems with prominent geometric graph structures: Blood vessels in brain tissue acquired using **(a)** two photon microscopy and **(b)** bright-field optical microscopy; two-photon microscopy images of axons in the brain **(c,d)**

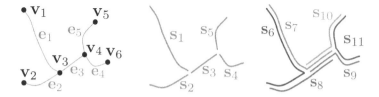

Fig. 2. Example of the representation and notation for a graph with $K = 2$

do not need initialization but only work for restricted class of transformations, such as rigid or affine. On the other hand ICP-like approaches [8,9] can handle nonlinear transformations but require a good initialization. Finally, the matching can be viewed as a discrete optimization problem with cost functions assigned to node or edge pairings [10–12], which is very powerful but computationally demanding. Pruning the search space is important to increase efficiency [4,5] and node and edge descriptors [13,14] can be used for that purpose.

3   Problem Definition

Let us have an undirected graph $\mathbf{G}^A = (\mathbf{V}^A, \mathbf{E}^A)$ with nodes $\mathbf{V}^A = \{\mathbf{v}_1^A, \ldots, \mathbf{v}_{|\mathbf{V}^A|}^A\}$ and edges $\mathbf{E}^A = \{e_1^A, \ldots, e_{|\mathbf{E}^A|}^A\}$. We represent each edge $\mathbf{e}_k^A \in \mathbf{E}^A$ as a cubic B-spline [15], limiting the generality of the representable shapes in exchange to better robustness with respect to noise. In doing so, we now have a continuous representation of each edge, which can be represented by a mapping $\xi_{\mathbf{e}_k^A} : [0,1] \to \mathbb{R}^D$, where if $\mathbf{e}_k^A = (\mathbf{v}_i^A, \mathbf{v}_j^A)$, then $\xi_{\mathbf{e}_k^A}(0) = \mathbf{v}_i^A$ and $\xi_{\mathbf{e}_k^A}(1) = \mathbf{v}_j^A$.

We define *superedges* $\mathbf{S}^A$ of graph $\mathbf{G}^A$ as paths of at most K consecutive edges. Similarly to edges, we can now define a mapping $\xi_{\mathbf{s}_k^A} : [0,1] \to \mathbb{R}^D$, which will define the path of each superedge. Superedges are needed to deal with the case of approximative matching, where some nodes and edges are detected only in one of the graphs. Our graph can then be represented by $\mathcal{G}^A = (\mathbf{V}^A, \mathbf{S}^A)$, i.e. a set of nodes and a set of superedges.

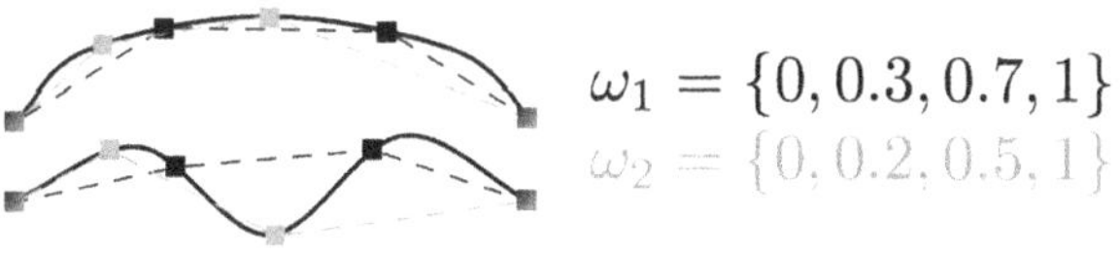

$$\omega_1 = \{0, 0.3, 0.7, 1\}$$
$$\omega_2 = \{0, 0.2, 0.5, 1\}$$

Fig. 3. Example of sampling vectors on two curves

Let us now introduce a second graph $\mathcal{G}^B = (\mathbf{V}^B, \mathbf{S}^B)$, which is related to $\mathcal{G}^A$ by a matching $\mathcal{M}_{A \to B} = (M_{\mathbf{V}}, M_{\mathbf{S}}, T)$, where $M_{\mathbf{V}} \colon \mathbf{V} \to \mathbf{V}$ is a mapping between nodes and $M_{\mathbf{S}} \colon \mathbf{S} \to \mathbf{S}$ is a mapping between superedges. The transformation T provides us a mapping of both $\mathbf{V}^A$ and $\mathbf{S}^A$ to $\mathbf{V}^B$ and $\mathbf{S}^B$ respectively, in $\mathbb{R}^D$. The elements of $\mathcal{M}_{A \to B}$ are not independent. In fact, if one of them is given, it is possible to at least approximate the remaining two. The task is therefore to find $\mathcal{M}_{A \to B}$. We will solve this task by finding similarities between the superedges $\mathbf{S}^A$ and $\mathbf{S}^B$, using path descriptors to be defined in Section 4.

4   Path Descriptors

The geometrical transformation between images in biomedical applications can usually be decomposed into a rigid motion plus a mildly non-linear component. Typically, the scale is known from the acquisition parameters and we can consider it is equal to zero, without loss of generality. Due to mechanical properties of the tissue, the nonlinear component is small and we therefore assume that for all $\mathbf{x}, \mathbf{y} \in \mathbb{R}^D$, there is a bound ε_T on the relative length change, such that

$$\frac{1}{1 + \varepsilon_T} d(\mathbf{x}, \mathbf{y}) \le d\big(T(\mathbf{x}), T(\mathbf{y})\big) \le (1 + \varepsilon_T) d(\mathbf{x}, \mathbf{y}), \tag{1}$$

holds for a transformation T, where $d(\mathbf{x}, \mathbf{y})$ is the Euclidean distance and ε_T is a *deformation parameter*, i.e. it is bi-Lipschitz.

We propose to use *path descriptors* – a vector characterizing each curve associated with a geometric graph edge. Unlike previously suggested curve descriptors [13,14,16], we have a good estimate of the change of descriptor values under our transformation model. Let us have a *sampling vector* $\boldsymbol{\omega} = (\omega_0, \dots, \omega_{n_\omega+1})$, such that $0 = \omega_0 < \omega_1 < \cdots < \omega_{n_\omega} < \omega_{n_\omega+1} = 1$. Given a geometric path $\xi_{\mathbf{s}_k} \colon [0,1] \to \mathbb{R}^d$ (Section 3) of a superedge $\mathbf{s}_k$, we calculate its descriptor parameterized by $\boldsymbol{\omega}$:

$$h_{\boldsymbol{\omega}}(\mathbf{s}_k) = \sum_{i=0}^{n_\omega} d\big(\xi_{\mathbf{s}_k}(\omega_i), \xi_{\mathbf{s}_k}(\omega_{i+1})\big) = \sum_{i=0}^{n_\omega} \|\xi_{\mathbf{s}_k}(\omega_{i+1}) - \xi_{\mathbf{s}_k}(\omega_i)\|. \tag{2}$$

In plain words, we resample the path in $n_\omega + 2$ points, pass a piecewise linear approximation through the points and calculate the length of this approximation. For an allowable transformation (1), we assume that

$$\frac{1}{1 + \varepsilon_h} h_{\boldsymbol{\omega}}(\mathbf{s}_k) \le h_{\boldsymbol{\omega}}\big(T(\mathbf{s}_k)\big) \le (1 + \varepsilon_h) h_{\boldsymbol{\omega}}(\mathbf{s}_k), \tag{3}$$

for an ε_h close to ε_T. This holds as long as the transformation T is not too far from a rigid body transformation. Given a set of sampling vectors $\mathbf{\Omega} = (\boldsymbol{\omega}_1, \ldots, \boldsymbol{\omega}_{|\Omega|})$, we can calculate a vector of descriptors $\mathbf{h}_\Omega(\mathbf{s}_k) = \big(h_{\boldsymbol{\omega}_1}(\mathbf{s}_k), \ldots, h_{\boldsymbol{\omega}_{|\Omega|}}(\mathbf{s}_k) \big)$. Given a large enough size of $\mathbf{\Omega}$, the value of the vector $\mathbf{h}_\Omega(\mathbf{s}_k)$ will describe the geometric disposition of the superedge in $\mathbb{R}^D$.

Given two geometric graphs $\mathcal{G}^A = (\mathbf{V}^A, \mathbf{S}^A)$ and $\mathcal{G}^B = (\mathbf{V}^B, \mathbf{S}^B)$, we say that two superedges $\mathbf{s}_k^A \in \mathbf{S}^A$ and $\mathbf{s}_l^B \in \mathbf{S}^B$ are *compatible* with respect to $\mathbf{h}_\Omega$, if (3) holds for all $\boldsymbol{\omega} \in \mathbf{\Omega}$,

$$\frac{1}{1 + \varepsilon_h} \mathbf{h}_\Omega(\mathbf{s}_k^A) \leq \mathbf{h}_\Omega(\mathbf{s}_l^B) \leq (1 + \varepsilon_h) \mathbf{h}_\Omega(\mathbf{s}_k^A), \tag{4}$$

where the multiplication and comparison is done element by element.

5   Finding a Global Solution

To find a solution based on our descriptors we formalize our problem as an integer quadratic program (IQP) [10,17]. Given the graphs $\mathcal{G}^A = (\mathbf{V}^A, \mathbf{S}^A)$ and $\mathcal{G}^B = (\mathbf{V}^B, \mathbf{S}^B)$ we define an affinity matrix $\mathbf{W}$ with size $|\mathbf{V}^A| \cdot |\mathbf{V}^B| \times |\mathbf{V}^A| \cdot |\mathbf{V}^B|$ and elements $W_{ik;jl} = \exp(-\|\mathbf{h}_\Omega(\mathbf{s}_a^A) - \mathbf{h}_\Omega(\mathbf{s}_b^B)\|/\sigma^2)$ similarly as in [10,17], if $\mathbf{s}_a^A = (\mathbf{v}_i^A, \mathbf{v}_j^A) \in \mathbf{S}^A, \mathbf{s}_b^B = (\mathbf{v}_k^B, \mathbf{v}_l^B) \in \mathbf{S}^B$ and the superedge pair $(\mathbf{s}_a^A, \mathbf{s}_b^B)$ is compatible, i.e. if eq. (4) holds. Otherwise $W_{ik;jl} = 0$. If matching node $\mathbf{v}_i^A$ with $\mathbf{v}_k^B$ is consistent with matching node $\mathbf{v}_j^A$ with $\mathbf{v}_l^B$, $W_{ik;jl}$ is high and vice versa.

The matching is represented by a binary vector $\mathbf{x}^*$, such that $\mathbf{x}_{ij} = 1$ iff nodes $\mathbf{v}_i^A$ and $\mathbf{v}_j^B$ match, maximizing the total affinity

$$\mathbf{x}^* = \arg \max_{\mathbf{x}} \mathbf{x}^\mathsf{T} \mathbf{W} \mathbf{x} \quad \text{s.t.} \quad \mathbf{x} \in [0, 1]^{|\mathbf{V}^A||\mathbf{V}^B|}, \tag{5}$$

$$\forall j \sum_{i=1}^{|U|} \mathbf{x}_{ij} \leq 1, \quad \forall i \sum_{j=1}^{|V|} \mathbf{x}_{ij} \leq 1.$$

Furthermore, there are constraints on node positions:

$$\forall \mathbf{x}_{ik}, \mathbf{x}_{jl} \neq 0, \quad \frac{1}{1 + \varepsilon_T} \|\mathbf{v}_i^A - \mathbf{v}_j^A\| \leq \|\mathbf{v}_k^B - \mathbf{v}_l^B\| \leq (1 + \varepsilon_T) \|\mathbf{v}_i^A - \mathbf{v}_j^A\|. \tag{6}$$

We use the Reweighted Random Walks method [17] to find an approximate solution $\tilde{\mathbf{x}}^*$ of this NP-hard problem [18]. In order to find the required binary vector $\mathbf{x}^*$, we use the Hungarian algorithm [19] to calculate the best assignment using the weights of $\tilde{\mathbf{x}}^*$. We iteratively select the best individual assignment which does not contradict the previously selected ones and also (6).

This may give us a partial mapping $M_\mathbf{V}$, with only a subset of the nodes matched. In order to complete and refine $M_\mathbf{V}$ and also to match the paths between nodes, we use a fine alignment algorithm described in [5]. This technique first uses $M_\mathbf{V}$ to predict the elastic transformation T represented by a Gaussian process model. Given T, it then uses the Hungarian algorithm to calculate the optimal matching $M_\mathbf{V}$ between nodes as well as the matching between other points on the edges, repeating until convergence.

6   Experiments and Results

6.1   Datasets

We test our path descriptors and global matching with datasets from various applications in medical imaging, featuring graph-like structures to be registered. In retinal fundus imaging (see Fig. 4(a)), the registration of different frames taken from various views helps build a single view of the retinal fundus [20].

In neuroscience, to better understand the learning of cognitive functions, images in vivo of the axons in the brain of a mouse are acquired before and after a learning task using 2-photon microscopy [21]. Due to the complexity and small (but crucial) changes in the images (see Fig. 4(b)), the registration procedure helps identifying the differences between the structures. The registration of images acquired with different modalities such as electron and light microscopy (see Fig. 4(c)) is helpful to have a better understanding of the neuronal network [12].

In angiography (see Fig. 4(d)), image registration helps tracking the displacement of the blood vessels in the heart, during heart cycle. The registration of images of blood vessels in the brain acquired using different imaging techniques, such as optical and 2-photon microscopy (see Fig. 4(e)) helps find details which are present in only one of the acquisition techniques [4].

6.2   Path Descriptors

To validate the path descriptors, we take two graphs, $\mathcal{G}^A = (\mathbf{V}^A, \mathbf{S}^A)$ and $\mathcal{G}^B = (\mathbf{V}^B, \mathbf{S}^B)$ and calculate the path descriptors $\mathbf{h}_\Omega$ for all superedges in both graphs. For each pair of superedges $\mathbf{s}_k^A \in \mathbf{S}^A$ and $\mathbf{s}_l^B \in \mathbf{S}^B$ we determine if they are compatible (eq. (4)) with respect to $\mathbf{h}_\Omega$ for different ε_h.

In Fig. 4, we show the ROC curves for various previously described datasets. To obtain the ground truth, we assume a superedge $\mathbf{s}_k^A$ is a true match of $\mathbf{s}_l^B$ if both their end nodes match. Apart from the proposed path descriptor, we tested 3-D Curve Matching [16], Determining the Similarity of Deformable Shapes [13], and Curve Matching using Fast Marching [14]. We have varied ε_h for the proposed method, the deformation cost for [13,14] and the residual Euclidean distance between the matched curves for [16]. Clearly, the proposed descriptor obtains the best performance in all tested datasets.

6.3   Global Matching

We used the methodology described in Sec. 5 to find the match $\mathcal{M}$ between the given graphs $\mathcal{G}^A$ and $\mathcal{G}^B$. In Fig. 5, we depict the results of applying this final alignment, based on the proposed path descriptors.

In Table 1, we show the average Euclidean distance between true matches of the registered graphs and the respective processing times using different approaches, namely CPD [9], IPFP [10] and ATS [5], with recommended parameters. In most cases, our proposed method presents the smallest error of all tested methods. The average error is close to the performance of ATS, however accomplished in a much faster time.

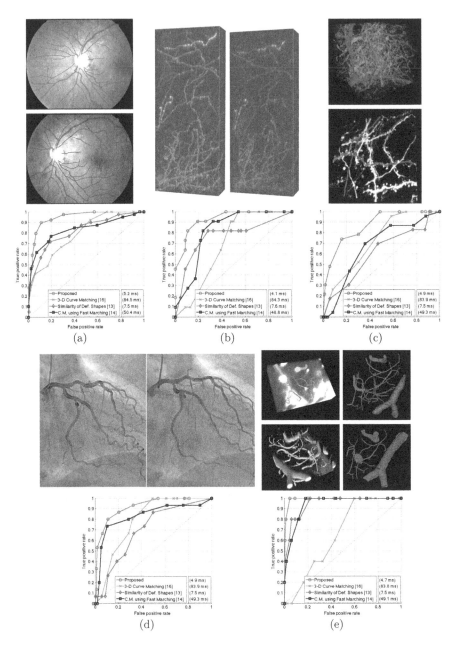

Fig. 4. ROC curve of the performance and average processing times for each of the descriptors in (**a**) retinal fundus [20], (**b**) 2-photon microscopy of neuronal network [21], (**c**) electron (top) and light (bottom) microscopy of neuronal network, (**d**) angiography and (**e**) optical (top) and 2-photon (bottom) microscopy of brain blood vessels

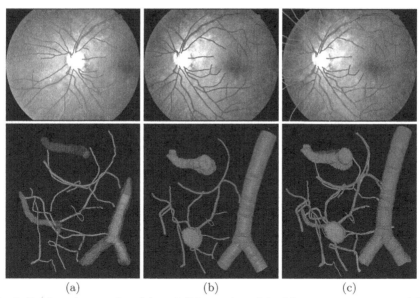

(a)   (b)   (c)

Fig. 5. Registration results. **(a)** and **(b)** are the original images or structures. **(c)** is the obtained alignment with the proposed approach.

Table 1. Average distance between true matches of registered graphs and processing times in seconds separated by a backslash for proposed approach and other methods. Graphs were normalized s. t. $\mathbf{V}^A, \mathbf{V}^B \in [-1, 1]^D$.

Datasets	Proposed	CPD[9]	IPFP[10]	ATS[5]
Retina (Fig. 4(a))	**0.012** / 173.7	0.327 / 6.0	0.540 / 7.0	0.015 / 1155.8
Axons (Fig. 4(b))	**0.013** / 106.5	0.014 / 17.4	0.770 / 57.0	0.087 / 4172.5
EM/LM (Fig. 4(c))	0.053 / 12.8	0.449 / 0.2	0.191 / 0.2	**0.035** / 49.2
Angiography (Fig. 4(d))	**0.024** / 12.6	0.065 / 0.8	0.067 / 0.4	0.026 / 308.7
Brain vessels (Fig. 4(e))	**0.028** / 18.6	0.108 / 1.4	0.542 / 0.6	0.052 / 615.7

7   Conclusion

We presented an approach for matching geometric tree-like structures using path descriptors. The descriptors were shown experimentally to have a better performance than similar methods and the derived graph matching also performs well. The path descriptors are fast to compute and compare, and are usable for robust registration of large 3D images such as those coming from electron microscopy.

Acknowledgments. This work was supported by the Grant Agency of the Czech Technical University in Prague, grant SGS12/190/OHK3/3T/13, the Czech Science Foundation project P202/11/0111 and the Fundação para a Ciência e Tecnologia grant SFRH/BD/77134/2011.

References

1. Türetken, E., Benmansour, F., Fua, P.: Automated reconstruction of tree structures using path classifiers and mixed integer programming. In: IEEE ICCV, pp. 566–573 (2012)
2. Zitová, B., Flusser, J.: Image registration methods: a survey. Image and Vision Computing **21**, 977–1000 (2003)
3. Can, A., Stewart, C.V., Roysam, B., Tanenbaum, H.L.: A feature-based, robust, hierarchical algorithm for registering pairs of images of the curved human retina. IEEE Trans. on Pattern Analysis and Machine Intelligence **24**, 347–364 (2002)
4. Serradell, E., Głowacki, P., Kybic, J., Moreno-Noguer, F., Fua, P.: Robust non-rigid registration of 2D and 3D graphs. In: IEEE CVPR, pp. 996–1003 (2012)
5. Pinheiro, M.A., Sznitman, R., Serradell, E., Kybic, J., Moreno-Noguer, F., Fua, P.: Active testing search for point cloud matching. In: Gee, J.C., Joshi, S., Pohl, K.M., Wells, W.M., Zöllei, L. (eds.) IPMI 2013. LNCS, vol. 7917, pp. 572–583. Springer, Heidelberg (2013)
6. Torr, P.H.S., Zisserman, A.: MLESAC: A new robust estimator with application to estimating image geometry. Computer Vision and Image Understanding **78**, 138–156 (2000)
7. Chum, O., Matas, J.: Matching with PROSAC - progressive sample consensus. In: IEEE CVPR, pp. 220–226 (2005)
8. Besl, P.J., McKay, N.D.: A method for registration of 3-D shapes. IEEE Trans. on Pattern Analysis and Machine Intelligence **14**(2), 239–256 (1992)
9. Myronenko, A., Song, X.: Point set registration: Coherent point drift. IEEE Trans. on Pattern Analysis and Machine Intelligence **32**(12), 2262–2275 (2010)
10. Leordeanu, M., Hebert, M., Sukthankar, R.: An integer projected fixed point method for graph matching and map inference. In: NIPS (2009)
11. Zaslavskiy, M., Bach, F., Vert, J.-P.: A path following algorithm for the graph matching problem. IEEE Trans. on Pattern Analysis and Machine Intelligence **31**(12), 2227–2242 (2009)
12. Serradell, E., Moreno-Noguer, F., Kybic, J., Fua, P.: Robust elastic 2D/3D geometric graph matching. In: SPIE Medical Imaging, vol. 8314(1), pp. 831408-1–831408-8 (2012)
13. Basri, R., Costa, L., Geiger, D., Jacobs, D.: Determining the similarity of deformable shapes. Vision Research **38**, 135–143 (1998)
14. Frenkel, M., Basri, R.: Curve matching using the fast marching method. In: Rangarajan, A., Figueiredo, M.A.T., Zerubia, J. (eds.) EMMCVPR 2003. LNCS, vol. 2683, pp. 35–51. Springer, Heidelberg (2003)
15. Unser, M.: Splines: A perfect fit for medical imaging. Progress in Biomedical Optics and Imaging **3**, 225–236 (2002)
16. Pajdla, T., Gool, L.V.: Matching of 3-D curves using semi-differential invariants. In: IEEE ICCV, pp. 390–395 (1995)
17. Cho, M., Lee, J., Lee, K.M.: Reweighted random walks for graph matching. In: Daniilidis, K., Maragos, P., Paragios, N. (eds.) ECCV 2010, Part V. LNCS, vol. 6315, pp. 492–505. Springer, Heidelberg (2010)
18. Sahni, S.: Computationally related problems. SIAM Journal on Computing **3**(4), 262–279 (1974)

19. Kuhn, H.W.: The Hungarian method for the assignment problem. Naval Research Logistics **2**(1–2), 83–97 (1955)
20. Deng, K., Tian, J., Zheng, J., Zhang, X., Dai, X., Xu, M.: Retinal fundus image registration via vascular structure graph matching. Journal of Biomedical Imaging (2010)
21. Holtmaat, A., Randall, J., Cane, M.: Optical imaging of structural and functional synaptic plasticity in vivo. European Journal of Pharmacology **719**(1–3), 128–136 (2013)

A Method to Detect Repeated Unknown Patterns in an Image

Paulo J.S.G. Ferreira and Armando J. Pinho[✉]

IEETA/DETI, Universidade de Aveiro, Aveiro, Portugal
{pjf,ap}@ua.pt

Abstract. Consider a natural image that has been manipulated by copying, transforming and pasting back fragments of the image itself. Our goal is to detect such manipulations in the absence of any knowledge about the content of the repeated fragments or the transformations to which they might have been subject. The problem is non-trivial even in the absence of any transformations. For example, copy/paste of a textured fragment of a background can be difficult to detect even by visual inspection. Our approach to the problem is a two-step procedure. The first step consists in extracting features from the image. The second step explores the connection between image compression and complexity: a finite-context model is used to build a complexity map of the image features. Patterns that reappear, even in a somewhat modified form, are encoded with fewer bits, a fact that renders the detection of the repeated regions possible.

Keywords: Tampering detection · Finite-context models · Kolmogorov complexity · SIFT

1 Introduction

Finding repetitions of exact or approximate *unknown* patterns in images can be a difficult problem even for a human observer. This paper addresses the problem and proposes an approach that combines feature extraction with information-theoretic analysis.

Consider a natural image that has been manipulated by copying, transforming and pasting fragments of the image itself. Our goal is to detect such manipulations in the absence of any knowledge about the content of the repeated fragments, or the transformations that they might have undergone.

We stress the fact that the repetitions are *unknown*. There is an important difference between known repetitions and unknown ones. Given one pattern (i.e. a fragment of an image), it is easy to find matching patterns. However, if the

---

Funded in part by National Funds through FCT - Foundation for Science and Technology, in the context of the project PEst-OE/EEI/UI0127/2014.

A. Campilho and M. Kamel (Eds.): ICIAR 2014, Part I, LNCS 8814, pp. 12–19, 2014.
DOI: 10.1007/978-3-319-11758-4_2

nature of the repeating pattern is totally unknown, the problem becomes much harder (even for exact or almost exact repeats).

The first step in our approach consists in extracting as many relevant features from the image as possible, bearing in mind one crucial condition: the features must be invariant to any transformations that the manipulations might have introduced. For example, if the transformations include rescaling, then the feature extraction step should yield scale-invariant features.

In the examples the feature extraction step is performed using SIFT, a well known method that provides invariance with respect to a number of transformations (see [1], also [2]). However, our approach is not tied to SIFT and the feature extraction step could in principle be performed using other appropriate techniques — either SIFT variants or refinements or totally distinct approaches. The feature extraction step is followed by an analysis step which uses information-theoretic tools. The goal of this second step is to determine the complexity of the features using a class of compression algorithms able to approximate the Kolmogorov complexity of the target. The key insight is that the Kolmogorov complexity of a repeated pattern is essentially that of the pattern itself. Repetitions or quasi-repetitions are associated with low-complexity data regions. To turn this idea into practice we use finite-context models that can capture, in a compact form, the most relevant content in the set of features.

In the absence of any transformations the problem is simpler but still non-trivial. The feature extraction step can then be omitted, and a complexity map of the image itself is known to lead to interesting and useful results [3,4].

2   The Method

2.1   Feature Extraction and Quantization

As stated, the features can be extracted using SIFT or other methods, provided that they are invariant to the transformations used during the image manipulations. We assume that each feature extracted from the image is associated with an image coordinate. For example, in SIFT there are at least four natural parameters: the coordinates, the scale σ and the angle θ. It is also assumed that each feature is a vector with fixed dimension (dimension 128 for SIFT feature vectors). At the end of this step one has a collection of features or vectors, associated with a specific image coordinate. The ith feature will be denoted by $f_i(x, y)$, where (x, y) denotes the associated image coordinate pair. The feature vectors are stored as columns in a data matrix, in no particular order.

It is advisable to go through the set of features and discard those of limited usefulness. This depends on the features and on their parameters. For example, if one is interested in detecting *small* repeated unknown fragments, SIFT features associated with smaller scales σ are probably more relevant than those associated with larger scales. We found that SIFT features with σ greater than $5 - 6$ have a negligible impact on the results. The elements of SIFT feature vectors are integers in the range 0-255, but in general they may be real numbers. Even in the case of integers, one could wish to reduce the number of amplitude levels, for reasons that will become clear later.

We subject the elements of all non-discarded feature vectors to scalar quantization. Our implementations have used Lloyd-Max quantization or the well known K-means method. The main parameter is the number of clusters, which determines the number of distinct intensities, the initialization policy (typically random) and the overclustering factor (typically 1.0, meaning that no overclustering is performed). In the case of K-means, we used the implementation in the `mlpack` [5] C++ library.

2.2 Sorting

The quantization step yields a collection of quantized feature vectors, stored as columns in a data matrix in no particular order. Before the complexity analysis stage we need to convert the vectors into a single bitstream. First, we sort the feature vectors. Then, we create the bitstream by vectorizing the sorted vectors, i.e. by stacking the columns of the sorted data matrix. Sorting impacts the performance significantly. We tried the following approaches:

1. Sort the features $f_i(x,y)$, $i = 1, 2, \ldots N$ by considering their coordinates (x,y) on the image, in row-major order.
2. Idem, but use column-major order.
3. Sort the features $f_i(x,y)$, $i = 1, 2, \ldots N$ by the Euclidean (L^2) distance to the origin of (x,y).
4. Idem, using a zig-zag scan (essentially, the L^1 distance to the origin of (x,y)).
5. Order the feature vectors by L^2 norm.
6. Order the feature vectors by L^1 norm.
7. Order the feature vectors by L^∞ norm.
8. Cluster the features by proximity and sort them by cluster. Within the same cluster, scan row-by-row.

Clustering the features by proximity leads to good results, since it tends to keep any features that are close to each other on the image close to each other on the sorted data matrix.

Consider an image that includes three features A, B and C, one at position (x,y), another at $(x+1, y)$ and a third at $(x, y+1)$. Row-major or column-major scans of the image are unlikely to preserve the proximity between these three features. At least one of the three features is likely to end up in a distant column of the sorted data matrix. By contrast, when clustering by distance, A, B and C will be assigned to the same cluster with overwhelming probability. Sorting by cluster creates a data matrix in which features close to each other on the image tend to be assigned to columns that are also close to each other on the matrix. The advantages of this will become clear later.

2.3 Finite-Context Encoding

The input to the finite-context encoders is the bitstream obtained by stacking the columns of the sorted, quantized data matrix. A finite-context model provides

Fig. 1. Left: the original image. Center: the manipulated image. Right: The manipulated image, with the edited regions outlined.

an information measure of the number of bits required to represent the current symbol, conditioned on the accumulated knowledge of all past symbols. We use this information to build a complexity profile of the bitstream, in which the bitrate at one point of the bitstream indicates how complex it is. Since any given point in the bitstream can be mapped to a feature vector and hence to an image point, the complexity profile can be related to the complexity of the image itself.

The data are scanned symbol by symbol. When a pattern is found for the first time, the encoder assigns to it a certain complexity, i.e. number of bits needed to represent it. When the pattern is seen again, the number of bits needed will be smaller. The complexity assigned to a pattern therefore depends on the order by which the stream is scanned, a fact that could mask the first occurrences of some patterns.

To remove this dependency, we scan the sorted data twice, once in the forward direction and once in the backward direction. The two complexity profiles obtained are then combined to produce the final complexity profile, $p_i = \min(d_i, b_i)$, where d_i and b_i denote the profiles in the forward and backward directions. This prevents the masking of the first occurrence of a repeating pattern (in forward scans) or the masking of its last occurrence (in backward scans).

To encode the data we use a set of competing finite-context models as described in [6]. The probability estimates provided by each model are averaged using weights updated by a recursive procedure. We used models of depth 3, 5, 8, 10 and 15. As for the parameter α, we took $\alpha = 1$ for the lower order models and $\alpha = 0.05$ for the models of order 10 and 15. A description of all the parameters and their roles can be found in [6].

3   Why Finite-Context Models

The Kolmogorov complexity [7–12] of A is denoted by $K(A)$ and represents the size of the smallest program that produces A and stops. $K(A)$ is not computable, and so it has to be approximated by a computable measure, such as

Lempel-Ziv based complexity measures [13], linguistic complexity measures [14] or compression-based complexity measures [15], which provide approximations and hence upper bounds on the Kolmogorov complexity.

The bitstream produced by a lossless compression algorithm, together with the appropriate decoder, enables the reconstruction of the corresponding original data. Thus, the number of bits required for representing the decoder and the bitstream can be viewed as an estimate of the Kolmogorov complexity of the data. Lossless compression methods thus provide approximations to the Kolmogorov complexity, with better compression algorithms yielding tighter bounds.

Kolmogorov theory can be used to measure object similarity. Li et al. proposed a similarity metric [16] based on an information distance [17], defined as the length of the shortest binary program that transforms A and B into each other, and a practical analog based on standard compressors, called the normalized compression distance [16]. These ideas have been successfully applied in astronomy, genomics, handwritten digits languages, literature, music and virology [18], but are less used in images for one reason. According to Li et al. [16], a compression method needs to be "normal" in order to be used as a normalized compression distance. This means that compressing the concatenation of A with itself should generate essentially the same number of bits as compressing A alone [18]. To satisfy this requirement, the compression algorithm needs to accumulate knowledge about the data as the compression proceeds. It has to collect statistics, i.e., it has to create an internal model of the data.

The Lempel-Ziv algorithms create internal data models and are among the most often used compression algorithms in compression-based complexity applications, including those reported in the imaging field [19–21]. Unfortunately, although they are quite effective for 1D data, they do not perform as well in the case of images or multi-dimensional data. State-of-the-art image compressors, such as JPEG2000 or JPEG-LS, perform better but are not normal. They decorrelate the data using either a transformation or a predictive method, and assume an *a priori* data model that remains essentially static during compression. The decorrelating step destroys most of the data dependencies, leaving to the entropy coding stage the mere task of encoding symbols from an (assumed) independent source. As a result, they cannot be used for conditional complexity estimation. These obstacles lead us to propose compression algorithms based on finite-context models that are both normal and adequate to images [22–25].

The fact that finite-context models are normal and show good performance on images makes them useful to build compression-based image complexity measures. We used them to find unknown (non-transformed) repeated patterns in images [3,4] and again in the present, more challenging application.

4 Results and Discussion

Fig. 1 shows the original image and the manipulated image, formed by copying, translating and rotating a fragment of the image and pasting it back. The regions are not immediately obvious under visual inspection. For convenience, they are outlined in the image on the right.

Fig. 2. Detected regions (squares) and SIFT features (circles). The manipulated regions are outlined for convenience only; the input to the algorithm was the image shown in Fig. 1 (center).

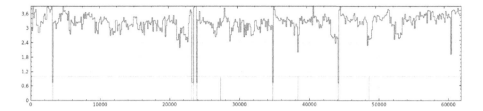

Fig. 3. The median of the complexity profile. The curve below it measures the balance between high and low complexity values in a running histogram of the profile (see text).

Fig. 2 shows the position of the SIFT features as circles (with $\sigma \leq 7$) and the low-complexity regions detected (the squares). In addition to the manipulated regions, the algorithm also marked certain other image regions as similar among themselves. This is unavoidable, since natural images may well contain such regions. Any reasonable algorithm designed to detect unknown repetitions or quasi-repetitions will very likely encounter and report both artificial repetitions, the result of introduced manipulations, and natural repetitions.

Fig. 3 shows the median value of the complexity profile, computed over segments of 128 symbols. This corresponds to the median value of the complexity over each feature (in the case of SIFT, over 128 symbols). The curve on the bottom is obtained by comparing the number of times that in each feature vector the complexity profile assumes small values with the number of times that it assumes large values. By small and large we mean, respectively, the bottom 4 and the top 4 bins in a 10-bin running histogram of the profile.

The quantization is necessary to reduce the number of intensity levels and therefore the alphabet size in the context models. We found that values of about

20 levels are adequate, but found different values (as small as 15) also useful. The sorting step is an important one. The optimal sorting strategy depends on the image and the location of the repetitions, but clustering the features by proximity appears to be the best general strategy. The reason is that it tends to keep features that are close to each other on the image close to each other on the sorted data matrix.

To fully appreciate the impact of this, consider an exact repeat of a region containing n features. Assume that the repeated part also contains n features, and that they are similar to the original ones, as one would expect. Sorting by proximity tends to keep the features of the first region together on the data matrix, forming a set of columns adjacent to each other. The same applies for the repetition. The bitstream will therefore present two identical segments, of size $128n$ symbols each. Other sorting strategies may lead to scattered identical pairs of segments of 128 symbols each, which are harder to detect.

Concerning the context models, we found that it is important to combine a number of models of different lengths, and it is important to use a smaller value of α (typically 0.05) for deeper models (say, above 10). We have obtained good results with 3, 4 and 5 models of depths between 3 and 15. It is important to implement the deeper models using e.g. hash tables, since a context array would require a prohibitive amount of memory.

The computational requirements depend mainly on the number of features and the dimension of each feature vector. An image of average complexity with several hundred features can be processed in a few seconds (this includes the time necessary to extract the features and quantize the data). In the example given there were 483 features and the total computation time did not exceed a couple of seconds, with the algorithm running on a laptop computer.

A limitation of the approach is that it is oblivious to tampering in regions for which SIFT returns no features. This is not a limitation of SIFT, but of the approach itself. Given any other feature extraction algorithm and a region S of the image, if there are no features $f_i(x, y)$ with $(x, y) \in S$, we will not be able to detect repetitions of subsets of S. This becomes more serious as the size of the edited regions decreases, since the probability of a feature lying on a region naturally decreases with its size. In general, however, SIFT seems appropriate and produces a sufficiently rich feature set, for all but the smallest edits. Despite the limitations, we feel that our approach provides an interesting solution to the challenging problem of detecting unknown repeats in images.

References

1. Lowe, D.G.: Distinctive image features from scale-invariant keypoints. International Journal of Computer Vision **60**(2), 91–110 (2004)
2. Otero, I.R., Delbracio, M.: The anatomy of the SIFT method. Image Processing On Line (2012), http://demo.ipo.im/demo/82
3. Pinho, A.J., Ferreira, P.J.S.G.: Finding unknown repeated patterns in images. In: EUSIPCO 2011, Barcelona, Spain, pp. 584–588 (2011)

4. Pratas, D., Pinho, A.J.: On the detection of unknown locally repeating patterns in images. In: Campilho, A., Kamel, M. (eds.) ICIAR 2012, Part I. LNCS, vol. 7324, pp. 158–165. Springer, Heidelberg (2012)
5. Curtin, R.R., Cline, J.R., Slagle, N.P., March, W.B., Ram, P., Mehta, N.A., Gray, A.G.: MLPACK: A scalable C++ machine learning library. J. of Machine Learning Research **14**, 801–805 (2013)
6. Pinho, A.J., Pratas, D., Ferreira, P.J.S.G.: Bacteria DNA sequence compression using a mixture of finite-context models. In: IEEE SSP 2011, Nice, France, pp. 125–128 (2011)
7. Solomonoff, R.J.: A formal theory of inductive inference. Part I. Information and Control **7**(1), 1–22 (1964)
8. Solomonoff, R.J.: A formal theory of inductive inference. Part II. Information and Control **7**(2), 224–254 (1964)
9. Kolmogorov, A.N.: Three approaches to the quantitative definition of information. Problems of Information Transmission **1**(1), 1–7 (1965)
10. Chaitin, G.J.: On the length of programs for computing finite binary sequences. Journal of the ACM **13**, 547–569 (1966)
11. Wallace, C.S., Boulton, D.M.: An information measure for classification. The Computer Journal **11**(2), 185–194 (1968)
12. Rissanen, J.: Modeling by shortest data description. Automatica **14**, 465–471 (1978)
13. Lempel, A., Ziv, J.: On the complexity of finite sequences. IEEE Trans. on Inf. Theory **22**(1), 75–81 (1976)
14. Gordon, G.: Multi-dimensional linguistic complexity. Journal of Biomolecular Structure & Dynamics **20**(6), 747–750 (2003)
15. Dix, T.I., Powell, D.R., Allison, L., Bernal, J., Jaeger, S., Stern, L.: Comparative analysis of long DNA sequences by per element information content using different contexts. BMC Bioinformatics **8**(Suppl. 2), S10 (2007)
16. Li, M., Chen, X., Li, X., Ma, B., Vitányi, P.M.B.: The similarity metric. IEEE Trans. on Inf. Theory **50**(12), 3250–3264 (2004)
17. Bennett, C.H., Gács, P., Li, M., Vitányi, P.M.B., Zurek, W.H.: Information distance. IEEE Trans. on Inf. Theory **44**(4), 1407–1423 (1998)
18. Cilibrasi, R., Vitányi, P.M.B.: Clustering by compression. IEEE Trans. on Inf. Theory **51**(4), 1523–1545 (2005)
19. Tran, N.: The normalized compression distance and image distinguishability. In: Human Vision and Electronic Imaging XII - Proc. of SPIE, p. 64921D (January 2007)
20. Mallet, A., Gueguen, L., Datcu, M.: Complexity based image artifact detection. In: DCC 2008, Snowbird, Utah, p. 534 (2008)
21. Gondra, I., Heisterkamp, D.R.: Content-based image retrieval with the normalized information distance. Computer Vision and Image Understanding **111**, 219–228 (2008)
22. Pinho, A.J., Neves, A.J.R.: Lossy-to-lossless compression of images based on binary tree decomposition. In: IEEE ICIP 2006, Atlanta, GA, pp. 2257–2260 (2006)
23. Pinho, A.J., Neves, A.J.R.: L-infinity progressive image compression. In: PCS 2007, Lisbon, Portugal (2007)
24. Pinho, A.J., Neves, A.J.R.: Progressive lossless compression of medical images. In: IEEE ICASSP 2009, Taipei, Taiwan (2009)
25. Neves, A.J.R., Pinho, A.J.: Lossless compression of microarray images using image-dependent finite-context models. IEEE Trans. on Medical Imaging **28**(2), 194–201 (2009)

Some "Weberized" L^2-Based Methods of Signal/Image Approximation

Ilona A. Kowalik-Urbaniak[1], Davide La Torre[2,3],
Edward R. Vrscay[1(✉)], and Zhou Wang[4]

[1] Department of Applied Mathematics, Faculty of Mathematics,
University of Waterloo, Waterloo, ON N2L 3G1, Canada
{iakowali,ervrscay}@uwaterloo.ca
[2] Department of Applied Mathematics and Sciences, Khalifa University, Abu Dhabi,
United Arab Emirates
[3] Department of Economics, Management and Quantitative Methods,
University of Milan, Milan, Italy
davide.latorre@kustar.ac.ae, davide.latorre@unimi.it
[4] Department of Electrical and Computer Engineering, Faculty of Engineering,
University of Waterloo, Waterloo, ON N2L 3G1, Canada
zhouwang@ieee.org

Abstract. We examine two approaches of modifying L^2-based approximations so that they conform to Weber's model of perception, i.e., higher/lower tolerance of deviation for higher/lower intensity levels. The first approach involves the idea of intensity-weighted L^2 distances. We arrive at a natural weighting function that is shown to conform to Weber's model. The resulting "Weberized L^2 distance" involves a ratio of functions. The importance of ratios in such distance functions leads to a consideration of the well-known logarithmic L^2 distance which is also shown to conform to Weber's model.

In fact, we show that the imposition of a condition of perceptual invariance in greyscale space $\mathbb{R}_g \subset \mathbb{R}$ according to Weber's model leads to the unique (unnormalized) measure in $\mathbb{R}_g$ with density function $\rho(t) = 1/t$. This result implies that the logarithmic L^1 distance is the most natural "Weberized" image metric. From this result, all other logarithmic L^p distances may be viewed as generalizations.

1   Introduction

In this paper we examine some methods of modifying, or "Weberizing," L^2-based approximations so that they conform as much as possible to Weber's model of perception. The term "Weberized" has been used in recent papers which have incorporated Weber's model into classical image processing methods, namely, total variation (TV) restoration [5] and Mumford-Shah segmentation [6].

For a long time, it has been recognized that the well known and very commonly used mean squared error (MSE) and PSNR – examples of L^2-based measures – perform poorly in terms of perceptual image quality [2,8]. Nevertheless,

© Springer International Publishing Switzerland 2014
A. Campilho and M. Kamel (Eds.): ICIAR 2014, Part I, LNCS 8814, pp. 20–29, 2014.
DOI: 10.1007/978-3-319-11758-4_3

L^2-based methods are still employed to a large degree, most probably due to their relative simplicity of computation. Other perceptually more meaningful image quality measures are generally more difficult to optimize. The Weberized L^2 methods examined in this paper are quite straightforward to compute.

That being said, the structural similarity (SSIM) image quality measure [8,9], which has demonstrated a superior performance in comparison with traditional quality measures such as MSE and PSNR, already has a "Weberized" component, namely, the luminance term, denoted as $S_1(\mathbf{x}, \mathbf{y})$, which characterizes the similarity between mean values, $\bar{\mathbf{x}}$ and $\bar{\mathbf{y}}$, of image patches/blocks $\mathbf{x}$ and $\mathbf{y}$, respectively. The fact that $S_1(\mathbf{x}, \mathbf{y})$ may be expressed as a function of the ratio $\mathbf{x}/\mathbf{y}$ (or $\mathbf{y}/\mathbf{x}$) accounts for its "Weberized" form.

Let us first recall Weber's model of perception which, for simplicity of treatment, will be restricted to the case of greyscale images: Given a greyscale background intensity $I > 0$, the minimum change in intensity ΔI perceived by the human visual system (HVS) is related to I as follows,

$$\frac{\Delta I}{I} = C, \tag{1}$$

where C is constant, or at least roughly constant over a significant range of intensities I [7]. Eq. (1) suggests that the HVS will be less/more sensitive to a given change in intensity ΔI in regions of an image at which the local image intensity $I(x)$ is high/low. As such, a Weberized L^2 distance between two functions u and v should tolerate greater/lesser differences over regions in which they assume higher/lower intensity values.

The basic mathematical ingredients of our formalism are as follows:

1. The **base (or pixel) space** $X \subset \mathbb{R}$ on which our signals/images are supported. Here, we assume, without generality, that $X = [0, 1]$. For images, $X = [0, 1]^2$. In the case of digital images, X can be the set of pixel locations (i, j), $1 \le i \le n_1$, $1 \le j \le n_2$.
2. The **greyscale range** $\mathbb{R}_g = [A, B] \subset (0, \infty)$.
3. The **signal/image function space** $\mathcal{F} = \{u : X \to \mathbb{R}_g\}$. Note that from our definition of the greyscale range $\mathbb{R}_g$, $u \in \mathcal{F}$ is positive and bounded, i.e., $0 < A \le u(x) \le B < \infty$ for all $x \in X$. A consequence of this boundedness is that $\mathcal{F} \subset L^p(X)$ for all $p \ge 1$, where the $L^p(X)$ function spaces are defined in the usual way. For any $p \ge 1$, the L^p norm can be used to define a metric d_p on $\mathcal{F}$: For $u, v \in \mathcal{F}$, $d_p(u, v) = \|u - v\|_p$. Our primary concern is the approximation of functions in the case $p = 2$, i.e., the Hilbert space, $L^2(X)$. In this case, the distance between two functions $u, v \in L^2(X)$ is given by

$$d_2(u, v) = \|u - v\|_2 = \left[\int_X [u(x) - v(x)]^2 \, dx \right]^{1/2}. \tag{2}$$

2   The Use of Intensity-Dependent Weighting Functions

The approximation of signals and images – and functions in general – must involve some mesaurement of "distance," as determined by an appropriate metric. In the usual L^2-based methods of approximation employed in signal and image processing, the L^2 metric in Eq. (2) is used. This metric, and indeed all other L^p- based metrics, $p \geq 1$, are not adapted to Weber's model of perception since they involve integrations over appropriate powers of intensity differences, $|u(x) - v(x)|$, with no consideration of the magnitudes of $u(x)$ or $v(x)$.

One way to "Weberize" this metric is to insert a weighting function in the integrand of Eq. (2). The use of weighting functions in metrics is, of course, not a new idea. In mathematics, they have generally been functions of the independent variable – in this case, the spatial variable x. In image processing applications, they have been employed for spatial weighting, for example, in foveated or region-of-interest image processing and coding [3] or frequency weighting in perceptual image quality assessment [10]. In our application, the weighting function should be dependent upon one or both of the intensities of the image functions $u(x)$ and $v(x)$. As such, the weighted L^2 metric may be written in the generic form,

$$d_{2W}(u, v) = \left[\int_X g(u(x), v(x))[u(x) - v(x)]^2 \, dx \right]^{1/2}, \tag{3}$$

where $g : \mathbb{R}_g \times \mathbb{R}_g \to \mathbb{R}_+$ denotes the intensity-dependent weighting function.

This leads to an interesting set of questions regarding the properties that must be satisfied by the weighting function g as well as the possible functional forms that it may assume, keeping in mind two important requirements:

1. $d_{2W}(u, v)$ should, if possible, satisfy the mathematical properties of a metric,
2. $d_{2W}(u, v)$ should, in some way, conform to Weber's model of perception.

A detailed discussion of these questions, many of which represent open problems, is well beyond the scope of this paper.

Perhaps one of the most fundamental properites that must be satisfied in order that Weber's model of perception can be accommodated is that $g(u, v)$ be decreasing in both of its arguments. This requirement is satisfied, for example, by the symmetric family of functions, $g(u(x), v(x)) = |u(x)v(x)|^{-q}$, where $q > 0$.

A simplification is achieved if we consider g to be a function of only one intensity function. Furthermore, if we assume that $g(u(x), v(x)) = g(u(x)) = u(x)^{-2}$, then the weighted L^2 distance in Eq. (3) becomes

$$d_{2W}(u, v) = \left[\int_X \left[1 - \frac{v(x)}{u(x)} \right]^2 \, dx \right]^{1/2} =: \Delta(u, v). \tag{4}$$

In this case, we consider the function u, which defines the weighting function g, to be the *reference function*. If we then consider v to be an approximation to u, then $\Delta(u, v)$ in Eq. (4) is the approximation error.

If we assume a weighting function of the form $g(u(x), v(x)) = g(v(x)) = v(x)^{-2}$, the weighted L^2 distance in Eq. (4) becomes

$$d_{2W}(u, v) = \left[\int_X \left[1 - \frac{u(x)}{v(x)} \right]^2 \, dx \right]^{1/2} =: \Delta(v, u). \tag{5}$$

Note that in general, $\Delta(u, v) \neq \Delta(v, u)$, which implies that Δ is not a metric in the strict mathematical sense of the term. This is the price paid for employing weighting functions $g(x)$ which are not symmetric in the functions $u(x)$ and $v(x)$. This complication, however, is not a serious limitation because of the following results that apply to our space $\mathcal{F}$ of image functions.

Theorem 1: Let $u, v \in \mathcal{F}$, with the assumption that the greyscale range $[A, B]$ is bounded away from zero, i.e., $A > 0$. Then

$$\frac{1}{B} d_2(u, v) \leq \left\{ \begin{array}{c} \Delta(u, v) \\ \Delta(v, u) \end{array} \right\} \leq \frac{1}{A} d_2(u, v),\tag{6}$$

where d_2 denotes the L^2 metric in Eq. (2) from which it follows that

$$\left[2 - \frac{B}{A} \right] \Delta(u, v) \leq \Delta(v, u) \leq \frac{B}{A} \Delta(u, v).\tag{7}$$

The proofs are rather straightforward and will be omitted.

A consequence of the above Theorem is that it it is sufficient to consider only one of these two distance functions, which will be the approach adopted for the remainder of this paper. Unless otherwise stated, the function u will be the *reference function* and v an approximation to it, in which case the approximation error will be given by $\Delta(u, v)$ in Eq. (4).

From Eq. (4), we see that for $\Delta(u, v)$ to be small, the ratio $v(x)/u(x)$ must be close to 1 for all $x \in X$. This already suggests that Weber's model of perception is being followed: Larger values of $u(x)$ will tolerate larger deviations between $v(x)$ and $u(x)$ so that the ratio $v(x)/u(x)$ is kept within a specified distance from 1. The following simple example illustrates this.

Example 1: Consider the "flat" reference image $u(x) = I$, where $I \in \mathbb{R}_g$. Now let $v(x) = I + \Delta I$, with $\Delta I > 0$, be the constant approximation to $u(x)$, where $\Delta I = CI$ is the minimum perceived change in intensity corresponding to I, according to Weber's model in Eq. (1). The L^2 distance between u and v is

$$d_2(u, v) = K \cdot \Delta I = KCI, \text{ where } K = \left[\int_X dx \right]^{1/2}.\tag{8}$$

A simple computation shows that the weighted L^2 distance in Eq. (4) is

$$\Delta(u, v) = K \frac{\Delta I}{I} = KC.\tag{9}$$

The L^2 distance in Eq. (8) increases with the intensity level I. This is expected since ΔI increases with I. However, the weighted L^2 distance in Eq. (9) remains constant. As such, we claim that $\Delta(u, v)$ can better accommodate Weber's model of perception: Perturbations ΔI of image intensities I according to Eq. (1) yield the same distance measure.

3   Best Approximation in Terms of $\Delta(u, v)$

Firstly, let $\{\phi_k\}_{k=1}^{\infty}$ denote a set of real-valued functions that form a complete orthonormal basis of $L^2(X)$, i.e., $\langle \phi_i, \phi_j \rangle = \delta_{ij}$, where δ_{ij} denotes the usual Kronecker delta. Now let $u \in \mathcal{F} \subset L^2(X)$ denote the reference signal/image function to be approximated. Given an $N > 0$, we are interested in best approximations of the form

$$u \approx u_N = \sum_{k=1}^{N} c_k \phi_k \, . \tag{10}$$

As is well known, the best L^2 approximation to u, which is the *minimizer* of the L^2 distance $\|u - u_N\|_2$, is yielded by the *Fourier coefficients* of u in the $\{\phi_k\}$ basis, i.e.,

$$c_k = \langle u, \phi_k \rangle = \int_X u(x)\phi_k(x)\,dx, \quad 1 \le k \le N \, . \tag{11}$$

We now wish to determine the "best Weberized" approximation, i.e., the expansion in Eq. (10) that minimizes the weighted L^2 distance $\Delta(u, u_N)$. For simplicity, we consider the squared distance $\Delta^2(u, u_N)$,

$$\Delta^2(u, u_N) = \int_X g(x) \left[u(x) - \sum_{k=1}^{N} c_k \phi_k(x) \right]^2 dx =: f(c_1, c_2, \cdots, c_N). \tag{12}$$

Here, the weighting function is $g(x) = 1/u(x)^2$ but the algebraic expressions presented below apply to any weighting function $g(x)$.

Imposition of the stationarity constraints $\frac{\partial f}{\partial c_k} = 0$, $1 \le k \le N$, yields a linear system of equations in the unknowns c_k of the form,

$$\mathbf{Ac} = \mathbf{b}, \tag{13}$$

where $\mathbf{c} = (c_1, c_2, \cdots, c_N)$,

$$a_{ij} = \int_X g(x)\phi_i(x)\phi_j(x)\,dx, \quad b_j = \int_X g(x)u(x)\phi_j(x)\,dx, \quad 1 \le i, j \le N. \tag{14}$$

Note that in the special case $g(x) = 1$, the matrix $\mathbf{A} = \mathbf{I}$, the $n \times n$ identity matrix, and the solution reduces to the Fourier coefficients in Eq. (11).

Note: In the examples that follow, we shall denote the "Weberized approximation" yielded by the solution of Eq. (13) as u_N^W in order to distinguish it from the best L^2 approximation, u_N, yielded by the Fourier coefficients Eq. (11).

Example 2: Consider the following step function on $X = [0, 1]$,

$$u(x) = \begin{cases} 1, & 0 \le x \le 1/2, \\ 3, & 1/2 < x \le 1. \end{cases} \tag{15}$$

The following set of $L^2[0, 1]$ basis functions was used: $\phi_1(x) = 1$, $\phi_k(x) = \sqrt{2}\cos(k\pi x)$, $k \ge 2$. In Figure 1 are presented plots of the best L^2 and best weighted/Weberized L^2 approximations to $u(x)$ using $N = 5$ (left) and $N = 10$ (right) basis functions. As expected, the Weberized L^2 approximations, u_N^W, yield a higher L^2 errors than their best L^2 counterparts, u_N. Also as expected, the approximations u_N^W yield better approximations of $u(x)$ than u_N over $[0, 0.5]$ and a poorer approximations over $[0.5, 1]$. The Logarithmic L^2 approximations u_N^L shown in the figure will be discussed in Section 5.

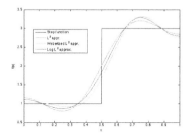 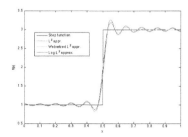

Fig. 1. Best L^2 (u_N, dotted), Weighted L^2 (u_N^W) and Logarithmic L^2 (u_N^L) approximations to step function in Eq. (15) using cosine basis functions. **Left:** $N = 5$. **Right:** $N = 20$. Approximation errors:

N	$\|u - u_N\|_2$	$\|u - u_N^W\|_2$	$\|u - u_N^L\|_2$
5	0.315	0.399	0.345
20	0.142	0.194	0.156

Example 3: The 512×512-pixel, 8 bits-per-pixel *Lena* image, partitioned into nonoverlapping 32×32-pixel blocks, with the first $N = 70$ standard 2D DCT basis functions used over each block (i.e., starting at $(0, 0)$, then $\{(1, 0), (0, 1)\}$, etc.. In Figure 2 are shown the best L^2 (left), Weberized L^2 (center) and Logarithmic L^2 (right) approximations to the shoulder region. The rather small value of N was chosen in order to demonstrate the significant differences as well as similarities between the L^2 and Weberized approximations in this region. The most significant differences occur in blocks containing edges that are formed between regions of low and high greyscale intensities, e.g., the edge defining Lena's shoulder. In each case, as expected, there is a ringing effect due to the low number of DCT basis functions employed ($N = 70$ out of a total of $32^2 = 1024$ functions). In the L^2 case (left), the error due to the ringing appears to be of similar magnitude in both light (shoulder) and dark (background) regions. In the Weberized L^2 cases, however, the ringing error appears to be larger over the lighter region (shoulder) than over the darker background (hair), which is consistent with the Weberized approximation method – a kind of two-dimensional analogy to the 1D step function in Example 2 above. As expected, blocks with little greyscale variation, e.g., the shoulder region without edges, are approximated equally well by the three methods.

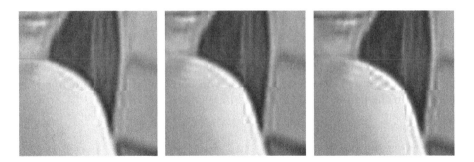

Fig. 2. Best L^2 (left), Weberized L^2 (center) and Logarithmic L^2 (right) approximations to *Lena* image using $N = 70$ 2D DCT basis functions over 32×32-pixel blocks comprising the shoulder region of *Lena* image

4   Logarithmic L^2 Metric

Looking back at Eqs. (4) and (5) for the weighted L^2 metrics $\Delta(u, v)$ and $\Delta(v, u)$, we see that their accommodation of Weber's model of perception comes from the fact that their integrands involve ratios of the signals/images u and v. Indeed, a ratio between signals/images can also be obtained if we consider their logarithms. This, of course, is the basis of homomorphic filtering [4] and, indeed, this portion of our paper may be viewed from such a perspective. In this study, however, logarithms of image functions are used for the purpose of image approximation as opposed to image enhancement.

Our choice of logarithms may appear *ad hoc* but can actually be justified mathematically. Only a brief account can be presented here. As introduced in [1], we consider a measure ν defined over the greyscale space $\mathbb{R}_g$. Then define the following intensity-weighted distance between two functions u and v:

$$D(u, v; \nu) = \int_{X_u} \nu(u(x), v(x)] \, dx \; + \; \int_{X_v} \nu(v(x), u(x)] \, dx \,, \tag{16}$$

where $X_u = \{x \in X \mid u(x) < v(x)\} \subset X$ and $X_v = \{x \in X \mid u(x) \geq v(x)\} \subset X$. This distance involves an integration of the sizes of the greyscale intervals $(u(x), v(x)]$ or $(v(x), u(x)]$ over X. Note that in the special case, $\nu = m_g$, uniform Lebesgue measure on $\mathbb{R}_g$, the distance $D(u, v; \nu)$ in Eq. (16) becomes the L^1 distance between u and v [1].

Theorem 2: The unique measure ν on $\mathbb{R}_g$ which accommodates Weber's model of perception over the greyscale space $\mathbb{R}_g \subset \mathbb{R}_+$ is (up to a normalization constant) defined by the continuous density function $\rho(t) = \frac{1}{t}$.

Sketch of Proof: For any two greyscale intensities $I_1, I_2 \in \mathbb{R}_g$,

$$\int_{I_1}^{I_1 + \Delta I_1} \frac{1}{t} \, dt = \int_{I_2}^{I_2 + \Delta I_2} \frac{1}{t} \, dt \implies \nu(I_1, I_1 + \Delta I_1) = \nu(I_2, I_2 + \Delta I_2) \,, \tag{17}$$

where $\Delta I_1 = CI_1$ and $\Delta I_2 = CI_2$, are the minimum changes in perceived intensity at backgrounds I_1 and I_2, respectively, according to Weber's model in Eq. (1). Eq. (17) is a kind of invariance result with respect to perception.

Using this measure ν, the distance between u and v in Eq. (16) becomes

$$D(u,v;\nu) = \int_{X_u} \left[\int_{u(x)}^{v(x)} \frac{1}{t} \, dt \right] dx + \int_{X_v} \left[\int_{v(x)}^{u(x)} \frac{1}{t} \, dt \right] dx$$

$$= \int_X |\ln u(x) - \ln v(x)| \, dx , \tag{18}$$

the logarithmic L^1 distance between u and v. All other logarithmic L^p distances, $p > 1$, may be viewed as generalizations of this result. This brief treatment hopefully shows why logarithms provide a natural representation for Weber's model.

We now outline the mathematical formalism for a logarithmic L^2-based approximation method. First define the space of functions $\mathcal{G}$ composed of the logarithms of all functions $u \in \mathcal{F}$, i.e.,

$$\mathcal{G} = \{ U : X \to [\log A, \log B] , \ U(x) = \log u(x), \ \forall x \in X \} . \tag{19}$$

Now consider the $L^2(X)$ distance between two elements $U, V \in \mathcal{G}$,

$$d_2(U,V) = \left[\int_X [U(x) - V(x)]^2 \, dx \right]^2 < \infty . \tag{20}$$

Use this distance to define the following "logarithmic L^2 distance" on $\mathcal{F}$,

$$d_{\log}(u,v) = d_2(U,V) = d_2(\log u, \log v) , \quad u, v \in \mathcal{F} . \tag{21}$$

Since $U = \log u$ implies that $u = e^U$ for all $U \in \mathcal{G}$, it can be shown that $d_{\log}$ is a metric on $\mathcal{F}$, i.e., it satisfies all of the properties of a metric, including the triangle inequality. From Eq. (21),

$$d_{\log}(u,v) = \left[\int_X [\log u(x) - \log v(x)]^2 \, dx \right]^{1/2}$$

$$= \left[\int_X \left[\log \frac{u(x)}{v(x)} \right]^2 dx \right]^{1/2} = \left[\int_X \left[\log \frac{v(x)}{u(x)} \right]^2 dx \right]^{1/2} . \tag{22}$$

The appearance of both ratios is a consequence of the symmetry of the metric.

Example 1 Revisited: The reference image $u(x) = I$ and constant approximation $v(x) = I + \Delta I$ as before. A quick calculation yields

$$d_{\log}(u,v) = \log\left(1 + \frac{\Delta I}{I} \right) = K \log(1 + C) , \tag{23}$$

where K is given in Eq. (8). As in the case of the weighted L^2 metric, $\Delta(u,v)$, the logarithmic L^2 distance is independent of the intensity level I.

As an interesting side note, in the case that the Weber constant C in Eq. (1) is small, then $\log(1+C) \approx C$, so that, from Eq. (9),

$$d_{\log}(u,v) \approx KC = \Delta(u,v)\,. \tag{24}$$

Experimentally, $C \approx 0.02$ [7] which justifies the above approximation.

5   Best Approximation in Terms of Logarithmic L^2 Metric

We shall now use the logarithmic L^2 distance to approximate a function $u \in \mathcal{F}$. As before, we consider, for an $N > 0$, an approximation u_N of the form in Eq. (10). The best approximation will minimize the squared $d_{\log}$ distance,

$$d_{\log}^2(u,u_N) = \int_X \left[\log u(x) - \log\left(\sum_{k=1}^{N} c_k \phi_k(x) \right) \right]^2 dx =: h(c_1,\cdots,c_N). \tag{25}$$

Unfortunately, application of the stationarity conditions $\frac{\partial h}{\partial c_k} = 0$, $1 \le k \le N$, yields an extremely complicated set of nonlinear equations in the unknown coefficients c_k. A huge simplification is accomplished if we consider the L^2 approximation of the logarithmic function $U(x) = \log u(x)$. The goal is then to approximate $U \in \mathcal{G} \subset L^2(X)$ as follows,

$$U \approx U_N = \sum_{k=1}^{N} a_k \phi_k\,. \tag{26}$$

The minimization of the squared L^2 distance, $d_2^2(U,U_N)$, is provided by the Fourier coefficients a_k of U in the ϕ_k basis, i.e.,

$$a_k = \langle U, \phi_k \rangle = \int_X U(x)\phi_k(x)\,dx\,. \tag{27}$$

We bypass some technical mathematical details and simply state that the logarithmic L^2-based approximations to u, which we shall denote by u_N^L, are given by

$$u_N^L(x) = \exp\left(U_N(x) \right) = \exp\left(\sum_{k=1}^{N} a_k \phi_k(x) \right)\,. \tag{28}$$

In summary, the logarithmic L^2 approximation method is seen to be much simpler than the weighted/Weberized L^2 method. One finds the Fourier coefficients of the logarithm U of the signal and then exponentiates to recover the approximation u_N. There is no system of equations to be solved.

Example 2 Revisited: We again consider the step function $u(x)$ in Eq. (15) and employ the same orthonormal cosine basis on $[0,1]$. The best logarithmic

L^2 approximations, u_N^L, to $u(x)$ using $N = 5$ basis functions (left) and $N = 10$ basis functions (right) are plotted in Figure 1 along with their L^2 and Weberized L^2 counterparts. As expected, the logarithmic L^2 approximations are seen to behave in a "Weberized" way. Note that the L^2 approximation errors associated with the logarithmic approximations are significantly lower than those of the weighted L^2 method.

Example 3 Revisited: The *Lena* image, approximated over 32×32 pixel blocks with $N = 70$ 2D DCT basis functions. The approximations afforded by the Logarithmic L^2 method are virtually identical to their Weberized L^2 counterparts. As such, they display the same kind of "Weberized ringing" over regions with edges separating high and low greyscale intensities, with lesser ringing error over the latter regions.

Acknowledgments. We gratefully acknowledge that this research has been supported in part by the Natural Sciences and Engineering Research Council of Canada (ERV,ZW) and the Ontario Centre of Excellence (ZW).

References

1. Forte, B., Vrscay, E.R.: Solving the inverse problem for function and image approximation using iterated function systems. Dynamics of Continuous, Discrete and Impulsive Systems **1**, 177–231 (1995)
2. Girod, B.: What's wrong with mean squared error? In: Watson, A.B. (ed.) Digital Images and Human Vision. MIT Press, Cambridge (1993)
3. Lee, S., Pattichis, M.S., Bovik, A.C.: Foveated video quality assessment. IEEE Trans. Multimedia **4**(1), 129–132 (2002)
4. Oppenheim, A.V., Schafer, R.W., Stockham Jr, T.G.: Nonlinear filtering of multiplied and convolved signals. Proc. IEEE **56**(8), 1264–1291 (1968)
5. Shen, J.: On the foundations of vision modeling I. Weber's law and Weberized TV restoration. Physica D **175**, 241–251 (2003)
6. Shen, J., Jung, Y.-M.: Weberized Mumford-Shah model with Bose-Einstein photon noise. Appl. Math. Optim. **53**, 331–358 (2006)
7. Wandell, B.A.: Foundations of Vision. Sinauer Publishers, Sunderland (1995)
8. Wang, Z., Bovik, A.C.: Mean squared error: Love it or leave it? A new look at signal fidelity measures. IEEE Sig. Proc. Mag. **26**, 98–117 (2009)
9. Wang, Z., Bovik, A.C., Sheikh, H.R., Simoncelli, E.P.: Image quality assessment: From error visibility to structural similarity. IEEE Trans. Image Proc. **13**(4), 600–612 (2004)
10. Wang, Z., Li, Q.: Information content weighting for perceptual image quality assessment. IEEE Trans. Image Proc. **20**(5), 1185–1198 (2011)

A New Compressor for Measuring Distances among Images

Armando J. Pinho$^{(\boxtimes)}$, Diogo Pratas, and Paulo J.S.G. Ferreira

IEETA/DETI, Universidade de Aveiro, Aveiro, Portugal
{ap,pratas,pjf}@ua.pt

Abstract. Ideally, we would like to have a measure of similarity between images that did not require a feature selection and extraction step. In theory, this can be attained using Kolmogorov complexity concepts. In practice, because the Kolmogorov complexity of a digital object cannot be computed, one has to rely on appropriate approximations, the most successful being based on data compression. The application of these ideas to images has been more difficult than to some other areas. In this paper, we suggest a new distance and compare it with two others, showing some of their relative advantages and disadvantages, hoping to contribute to the advance of this promising line of research.

Keywords: Finite-context models · Kolmogorov complexity · Compression-based distances · Image similarity

1 Introduction

In recent years, there has been interest in image similarity measures based on compression methods (see, for example, [1–8]). They rely on the notion of Kolmogorov complexity and opened a line of research that seems very promising.

Compression-based distances are tightly related to the Kolmogorov notion of complexity, also known as algorithmic entropy [9–14]. Without losing generality, let x denote a binary string of finite length. Its Kolmogorov complexity, $K(x)$, is the length of the shortest binary program x^* that computes x in a universal Turing machine and halts [15]. Therefore, $K(x) = |x^*|$, the length of x^*, and represents the minimum number of bits from which x can be computationally retrieved [16]. The conditional Kolmogorov complexity, $K(x|y)$, denotes the length of the shortest binary program that on input y outputs x. For $y = \lambda$ (where λ denotes the empty string) $K(x|\lambda) = K(x)$.

Bennett et al. proposed an information distance [17], based on the Kolmogorov complexity, that minorizes in an appropriate sense every effective metric [18]. It is defined as

$$E(x, y) = \max\{K(x|y), K(y|x)\}, \tag{1}$$

Funded in part by National Funds through FCT - Foundation for Science and Technology, in the context of the project PEst-OE/EEI/UI0127/2014.

A. Campilho and M. Kamel (Eds.): ICIAR 2014, Part I, LNCS 8814, pp. 30–37, 2014.
DOI: 10.1007/978-3-319-11758-4_4

and represents the length of the shortest binary program that computes x from y and y from x. Because $E(x, y)$ is an absolute measure, it is not appropriate to assess similarity. Hence, a normalized version was proposed, overcoming this limitation [18]. The normalized information distance (NID) is defined as

$$\text{NID}(x, y) = \frac{\max\{K(x|y), K(y|x)\}}{\max\{K(x), K(y)\}}, \tag{2}$$

and is a metric capable of measuring the similarity between two sequences. However, because $K(x)$ is noncomputable, alternatives have to be devised in order to be able to use it in practice.

One such alternative is the normalized compression distance (NCD) [18, 19], defined as

$$\text{NCD}(x, y) = \frac{C(x, y) - \min\{C(x), C(y)\}}{\max\{C(x), C(y)\}}, \tag{3}$$

where $C(x)$ and $C(y)$ represent, respectively, the number of bits of a compressed version of x and y, and $C(x, y)$ the number of bits of the conjoint compression of x and y (usually, x and y are concatenated). Distances near one indicate dissimilarity, while distances near zero indicate similarity.

Successful applications of the NCD have been reported, for example, in genomics, virology, languages, literature, music, handwritten digits and astronomy [19].

To be useful for computing the normalized compression distance, the compression method needs to be *normal* [19]. One of the most crucial conditions for a compression method to be normal is that the compression of xx (the concatenation of x with x) should generate essentially the same number of bits as the compression of x alone (i.e., the compressor should comply with the idempotency property [19]). This characteristic holds, for example, in Lempel-Ziv based compressors, making them a frequent choice [1, 2, 20]. However, generally speaking, Lempel-Ziv based compressors do not perform well on images. Most of the best performing image compression algorithms, in turn, are not normal [6].

A normal compression algorithm is able to collect knowledge of the data while compression proceeds. It finds dependencies, gathers statistical evidence, i.e., it creates a model of the data. Most state-of-the-art image compressors start by decorrelating the data using a transformation (for example, the DCT or DWT as in JPEG or JPEG2000) or a predictive step (as in JPEG-LS). This approach destroys most of the data dependencies, leaving to the entropy encoder the task of encoding symbols from a nearly independent source. In this case, the data model may remain unchanged during compression. The down side is that it also makes it unsuitable for measuring similarity.

In the normalized compression distance represented in (3), instead of the more obvious direct substitution of $K(x|y)$ by $C(x|y)$, a term corresponding to the conjoint compression of x and y, $C(x, y)$, was preferred. The main reason for adopting this form is that a direct substitution of K by C in (2) requires the availability of compressors that are able to produce conditional compression, i.e., $C(x|y)$ and $C(y|x)$. However, most compressors do not have this functionality and, therefore, the NCD avoids it by using suitable manipulations of (2) [19].

Usually, the $C(x, y)$ term is interpreted as the compression of the concatenation of x and y, but, in fact, it could adopt any other form of combination between x and y. Concatenation is often used because it is easy to obtain, but it is known that it may hamper the efficiency of the measure [21].

To overcome this limitation, a normalized conditional compression distance (NCCD) was proposed, using compressors based on sets of image transformations [22,23]. The NCCD is therefore computed using a direct substitution of $K(x|y)$ by $C(x|y)$ as follows:

$$\text{NCCD}(x, y) = \frac{\max\{C(x|y), C(y|x)\}}{\max\{C(x), C(y)\}}. \tag{4}$$

Because we wanted to compare the NCCD with the NCD and with an additional variant described below, using the same type of compressor in the three situations to leave out as much as possible the effect of the compressor in the comparison, we developed a special purpose image compressor. This compressor is able to work as usual, allowing to calculate $C(x)$ as well as $C(xy)$, but is also able to work in a conditional compression mode, in the following two modes.

In the first mode, it starts by building an internal model of y, using a combination of finite-context models of several orders (see below for more information regarding finite-context modeling). After processing y, these models are kept fixed. In the second phase, x is compressed using the (fixed) models of y and another set of finite-context models that learn the statistics of x as it is processed. Each symbol of x is encoded using a probability estimate that results from a mixture of the probabilities produced by each of the finite-context models (those modeling y and those assigned to model x). This setup implements the $C(x|y)$ required in (4).

The second mode of conditional compression differs in how the internal models of the conditional encoder are built. In this case, as in $C(x|y)$, a set of finite-context models are loaded with the information of y. However, contrarily to $C(x|y)$, there is no modeling of x during encoding, i.e., x is encoded exclusively using the statistics collected from y. In this case, we use a modified normalized conditional compression distance (NCCD'), given by

$$\text{NCCD}'(x, y) = \frac{\max\{C'(x|y), C'(y|x)\}}{\max\{|x|, |y|\}}, \tag{5}$$

where $C'(x|y)$ denotes the number of bit required by the compressor to represent x using exclusively the statistics of y, and $|x|$ denotes the uncompressed size of x.

2   The Encoder

We have developed an encoder that implements the running modes necessary to compute the three distances described in the previous section. It is similar in concept to that used in [6], although much more flexible for allowing the

Fig. 1. Context templates used by the encoder, corresponding to model orders of 2, 4 and 6

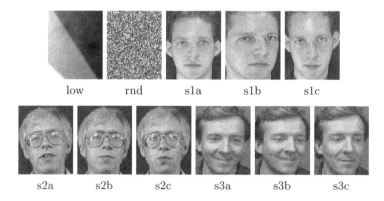

Fig. 2. Image set used: a low complexity image, a random image, and nine images from the ORL face database: the first three images of the first three subjects

different modes of operation. Next, we provide a brief description of the finite-context modeling concept used, because it is the core of the encoder.

Consider that n symbols of x have already been encoded, and that we want to represent efficiently the next symbol, x_{n+1}. Finite-context models assign probability estimates to the symbols of an alphabet $\mathcal{A} = \{s_1, s_2, \ldots, s_{|\mathcal{A}|}\}$, where $|\mathcal{A}|$ denotes the size of $|\mathcal{A}|$, according to a conditioning context computed over a finite and fixed number, $k > 0$, of the most recent past outcomes $c_{k,n} = x_{n-k+1} \ldots x_{n-1} x_n$ (order-k finite-context model) [24].

The probability estimates, $P(X_{n+1} = s|c_{k,n}), \forall_{s \in \mathcal{A}}$, rely on symbol counts that are accumulated while the image is processed, and are calculated using the estimator

$$P(X_{n+1} = s|c_{k,n}) = \frac{n_s^{c_{k,n}} + \alpha}{n^{c_{k,n}} + \alpha|\mathcal{A}|}, \tag{6}$$

where $n_s^{c_{k,n}}$ is the number of times that, in the past, a symbol s following $c_{k,n}$ has occurred and where

$$n^{c_{k,n}} = \sum_{a \in \mathcal{A}} n_a^{c_{k,n}} \tag{7}$$

is the total number of events that has occurred so far in association with context $c_{k,n}$. Parameter α allows balancing between the maximum likelihood estimator and a uniform distribution: When n is large, the estimator behaves as a maximum likelihood estimator, whereas for small n it behaves more as a uniform estimator.

The encoder was implemented using finite-context models associated with context templates as those shown in Fig. 1. For each symbol, the probability estimate given by each of the models is combined using averaging, according to

$$P(X_{n+1} = s) = \sum_{k=2,4,6} P'(X_{n+1} = s|c_{k,n})\, w'_{k,n} + \tag{8a}$$

$$+ \sum_{k=2,4,6} P(X_{n+1} = s|c_{k,n})\, w_{k,n}, \tag{8b}$$

where

$$w'_{k,n} \propto w'^{\gamma}_{k,n-1} P'(X_n = x_n|c_{k,n-1}) \tag{9}$$

and

$$w_{k,n} \propto w^{\gamma}_{k,n-1} P(X_n = x_n|c_{k,n-1}), \tag{10}$$

constrained to

$$\sum_{k=2,4,6} w'_{k,n} + \sum_{k=2,4,6} w_{k,n} = 1. \tag{11}$$

It can be shown that these weights favor the models that have provided better performance in the recent past of the sequence of symbols [25]. Parameter γ is usually very close to one (we used $\gamma = 0.99$).

To compute $C(x)$, we set $w'_{k,n} = 0$, i.e., the encoder delivers $C(x|\lambda)$. When computing $C(x|y)$, six finite-context models are involved, three modeling y (those are associated with weights $w'_{k,n}$) and three for modeling x (associated with weights $w_{k,n}$). Note that while encoding x in $C(x|y)$ all weights ($w'_{k,n}$ and $w_{k,n}$) are adjusted, respectively, using (9) and (10). However, whereas $P(X_{n+1} = s|c_{k,n})$ evolves as new data from x is processed, $P'(X_{n+1} = s|c_{k,n})$ is kept fixed. For computing $C'(x|y)$, only weights $w'_{k,n}$ are adapted when x is encoded, leaving $w_{k,n} = 0$.

3   Some Results and Discussion

In this section, we provide some experimental results with a set of eleven images. We calculated the distance between every pair in this set, including the distance from one image to itself, thus evaluating how well the idempotency property is respected by the distance. Nine of the images used were drawn from the ORL face database [26]: the first three images of the first three subjects. We added to the set a random image and an image with low complexity. The complete set is displayed in Fig. 2.

Before being processed by the encoder, the images are quantized to four levels, using a Lloyd-Max quantizer. The aim of this operation is to limit the size of the alphabet and hence reduce the number of conditioning contexts in the finite-context models.

Tables 1, 2 and 3 show, respectively, the distances calculated using the NCD, NCCD and NCCD'. Maybe the first aspect that comes to our attention is the wider range of values of the NCCD', compared to the other two distances. Also,

Table 1. Values of the normalized compression distance (NCD) computed between all images in the test set. Smaller values indicate higher similarity.

	low	rnd	s1a	s1b	s1c	s2a	s2b	s2c	s3a	s3b	s3c
low	0.740	1.026	1.047	1.025	1.030	1.025	1.023	1.030	1.027	1.037	1.030
rnd	1.094	0.656	1.111	1.114	1.114	1.120	1.121	1.121	1.120	1.123	1.121
s1a	1.041	1.062	0.786	0.941	0.935	0.974	0.962	0.965	0.962	0.966	0.960
s1b	1.019	1.068	0.925	0.785	0.920	0.960	0.955	0.960	0.957	0.960	0.951
s1c	1.029	1.069	0.933	0.929	0.763	0.961	0.954	0.962	0.971	0.970	0.963
s2a	1.029	1.081	0.966	0.964	0.959	0.742	0.937	0.927	0.980	0.978	0.971
s2b	1.025	1.081	0.958	0.959	0.951	0.932	0.770	0.928	0.963	0.965	0.963
s2c	1.033	1.083	0.965	0.968	0.967	0.933	0.937	0.749	0.978	0.977	0.973
s3a	1.022	1.077	0.960	0.965	0.968	0.984	0.972	0.981	0.852	0.926	0.922
s3b	1.035	1.078	0.967	0.970	0.975	0.985	0.976	0.983	0.934	0.848	0.930
s3c	1.024	1.074	0.961	0.959	0.964	0.979	0.972	0.975	0.918	0.922	0.837

Table 2. Values of the normalized conditional compression distance (NCCD) computed between all images in the test set. Smaller values indicate higher similarity.

	low	rnd	s1a	s1b	s1c	s2a	s2b	s2c	s3a	s3b	s3c
low	0.749	1.006	1.000	1.000	0.999	0.999	0.998	0.998	0.998	1.000	0.998
rnd	1.006	0.552	1.006	1.006	1.006	1.006	1.006	1.006	1.006	1.006	1.006
s1a	1.000	1.006	0.763	0.951	0.946	0.977	0.972	0.977	0.969	0.971	0.963
s1b	1.000	1.006	0.951	0.764	0.942	0.977	0.971	0.974	0.976	0.976	0.971
s1c	0.999	1.006	0.946	0.942	0.739	0.974	0.969	0.977	0.975	0.981	0.971
s2a	0.999	1.006	0.977	0.977	0.974	0.713	0.945	0.935	0.977	0.975	0.976
s2b	0.998	1.006	0.972	0.971	0.969	0.945	0.740	0.947	0.977	0.976	0.975
s2c	0.998	1.006	0.977	0.974	0.977	0.935	0.947	0.720	0.977	0.978	0.975
s3a	0.998	1.006	0.969	0.976	0.975	0.977	0.977	0.977	0.834	0.944	0.929
s3b	1.000	1.006	0.971	0.976	0.981	0.975	0.976	0.978	0.944	0.827	0.939
s3c	0.998	1.006	0.963	0.971	0.971	0.976	0.975	0.975	0.929	0.939	0.818

Table 3. Values of the modified normalized conditional compression distance (NCCD′) computed between all images in the test set. Smaller values indicate higher similarity.

	low	rnd	s1a	s1b	s1c	s2a	s2b	s2c	s3a	s3b	s3c
low	0.020	0.815	0.237	0.247	0.250	0.353	0.337	0.349	0.223	0.258	0.238
rnd	0.815	0.427	0.902	0.904	0.913	0.933	0.930	0.936	0.878	0.887	0.884
s1a	0.237	0.902	0.125	0.165	0.166	0.251	0.238	0.248	0.172	0.192	0.180
s1b	0.247	0.904	0.165	0.129	0.164	0.251	0.239	0.249	0.179	0.197	0.183
s1c	0.250	0.913	0.166	0.164	0.127	0.247	0.235	0.248	0.182	0.196	0.182
s2a	0.353	0.933	0.251	0.251	0.247	0.178	0.236	0.233	0.261	0.259	0.256
s2b	0.337	0.930	0.238	0.239	0.235	0.236	0.175	0.233	0.245	0.244	0.243
s2c	0.349	0.936	0.248	0.249	0.248	0.233	0.233	0.177	0.255	0.254	0.252
s3a	0.223	0.878	0.172	0.179	0.182	0.261	0.245	0.255	0.138	0.175	0.162
s3b	0.258	0.887	0.192	0.197	0.196	0.259	0.244	0.254	0.175	0.153	0.174
s3c	0.238	0.884	0.180	0.183	0.182	0.256	0.243	0.252	0.162	0.174	0.141

contrarily to the NCD and NCCD, and in this set of images, the NCCD$'$ always yields values smaller than one, as one would expect from a normalized distance. As can be observed and as expected, the NCD is not symmetric, a characteristic that may pose some problems, although it can be circumvented by using NCD$(x, y)/2$ + NCD$(y, x)/2$, at the cost of increased computation (in fact, it suffices to use $C(x, y)/2 + C(y, x)/2$ in (3)).

The values of NCCD$'(x, x)$ are generally much smaller than those obtained with the NCD or NCCD, suggesting a better compliance with the idempotency property. Whereas the distances from the low complexity image (low) and random image (rnd) to all others are maximal or close to maximal in the case of the NCD and NCCD, for the NCCD$'$ it is only close to maximal for the random image, remaining at a more lower (and, in our opinion, reasonable) level in the case of the low complexity image. Regarding the distances among the face images, all three distance measures tend to give smaller distances between images of the same subject. However, here the NCD and NCCD seem to have some more discriminative power than the NCCD$'$.

The research community is still looking for ways of putting the full potentiality of the theory behind Kolmogorov complexity at the service of effective image similarity metrics. Contrarily to other application areas, where very good results have already been attained, images pose additional problems that have to be solved. With this paper, we took some more steps in that direction, and hope to have motivated others to embrace this exciting field.

References

1. Gondra, I., Heisterkamp, D.R.: Content-based image retrieval with the normalized information distance. Computer Vision and Image Understanding **111**, 219–228 (2008)
2. Tran, N.: The normalized compression distance and image distinguishability. In: Human Vision and Electronic Imaging XII - Proc. of the SPIE, p. 64921D (January 2007)
3. Perkiö, J., Hyvärinen, A.: Modelling image complexity by independent component analysis, with application to content-based image retrieval. In: Alippi, C., Polycarpou, M., Panayiotou, C., Ellinas, G. (eds.) ICANN 2009, Part II. LNCS, vol. 5769, pp. 704–714. Springer, Heidelberg (2009)
4. Mortensen, J., Wu, J.J., Furst, J., Rogers, J., Raicu, D.: Effect of image linearization on normalized compression distance. In: Ślęzak, D., Pal, S.K., Kang, B.-H., Gu, J., Kuroda, H., Kim, T. (eds.) SIP 2009. CCIS, vol. 61, pp. 106–116. Springer, Heidelberg (2009)
5. Pinho, A.J., Ferreira, P.J.S.G.: Finding unknown repeated patterns in images. In: Proc. of the 19th European Signal Processing Conf., EUSIPCO 2011, Barcelona, Spain (August 2011)
6. Pinho, A.J., Ferreira, P.J.S.G.: Image similarity using the normalized compression distance based on finite context models. In: Proc. of the IEEE ICIP 2011, Brussels, Belgium (September 2011)
7. Cerra, D., Datcu, M.: A fast compression-based similarity measure with applications to content-based image retrieval. J. Vis. Commun. Image R. **23**, 293–302 (2012)

8. Besiris, D., Zigouris, E.: Dictionary-based color image retrieval using multiset theory. J. Vis. Commun. Image R. **24**, 1155–1167 (2013)
9. Solomonoff, R.J.: A formal theory of inductive inference. Part I. Information and Control **7**(1), 1–22 (1964)
10. Solomonoff, R.J.: A formal theory of inductive inference. Part II. Information and Control **7**(2), 224–254 (1964)
11. Kolmogorov, A.N.: Three approaches to the quantitative definition of information. Problems of Information Transmission **1**(1), 1–7 (1965)
12. Chaitin, G.J.: On the length of programs for computing finite binary sequences. Journal of the ACM **13**, 547–569 (1966)
13. Wallace, C.S., Boulton, D.M.: An information measure for classification. The Computer Journal **11**(2), 185–194 (1968)
14. Rissanen, J.: Modeling by shortest data description. Automatica **14**, 465–471 (1978)
15. Turing, A.: On computable numbers, with an application to the Entscheidungsproblem. Proc. London Math. Soc. **42**(2), 230–265 (1936)
16. Li, M., Vitányi, P.: An introduction to Kolmogorov complexity and its applications, 3rd edn. Springer (2008)
17. Bennett, C.H., Gács, P., Li, M., Vitányi, P.M.B., Zurek, W.H.: Information distance. IEEE Trans on Information Theory **44**(4), 1407–1423 (1998)
18. Li, M., Chen, X., Li, X., Ma, B., Vitányi, P.M.B.: The similarity metric. IEEE Trans. on Information Theory **50**(12), 3250–3264 (2004)
19. Cilibrasi, R., Vitányi, P.M.B.: Clustering by compression. IEEE Trans. on Information Theory **51**(4), 1523–1545 (2005)
20. Mallet, A., Gueguen, L., Datcu, M.: Complexity based image artifact detection. In: Proc. of the Data Compression Conf., Snowbird, Utah, p. 534 (2008)
21. Cebrián, M., Alfonseca, M., Ortega, A.: Common pitfalls using the normalized compression distance: what to watch out for in a compressor. Commun. in Information and Systems **5**(4), 367–384 (2005)
22. Nikvand, N., Wang, Z.: Generic image similarity based on Kolmogorov complexity. In: Proc. of the IEEE ICIP 2010, Hong Kong, pp. 309–312 (September 2010)
23. Nikvand, N., Wang, Z.: Image distortion analysis based on normalized perceptual information distance. Signal, Image and Video Processing **7**, 403–410 (2013)
24. Bell, T.C., Cleary, J.G., Witten, I.H.: Text compression. Prentice Hall (1990)
25. Pinho, A.J., Pratas, D., Ferreira, P.J.S.G.: Bacteria DNA sequence compression using a mixture of finite-context models. In: Proc. of the IEEE Workshop on Statistical Signal Processing, Nice, France (June 2011)
26. Samaria, F., Harter, A.: Parameterisation of a stochastic model for human face identification. In: 2nd IEEE Workshop on Applications of Computer Vision, Sarasota, Florida, pp. 138–142 (December 1994)

Perceptual Evaluation of Demosaicing Artefacts

Tomasz Sergej and Radosław Mantiuk[(⊠)]

Faculty of Computer Science, West Pomeranian University of Technology,
Szczecin, Żołnierska 52, 71-210 Szczecin, Poland
rmantiuk@wi.zut.edu.pl

Abstract. Most of the digital camera sensors are equipped with the
Colour Filter Arrays (CFAs) that split the light into the red, green, and
blue colour components. Every photodiode in the sensor is capable to
register only one of these components. The demosaicing techniques were
developed to fill the missing values, however, they distort a scene data
and introduce artefacts in images. In this work we propose a novel evaluation technique which judge a perceptual visibility of the demosaicing
artefacts rather than compares images based on typical mathematically-
based metrics, like MSE or PSNR. We conduct subjective experiments in
which people manually mark the visible local artefacts. Then, the detection map averaged over a number of observers and scenes is compared
with results generated by the objective image quality metrics. This procedure judges the efficiency of these automatic metrics and reveals that
the HDR-VDP-2 metric outperforms SSIM, S-CIELAB, and also MSE
in evaluation of the demosaicing artefacts.

1 Introduction

Contemporary digital cameras use the CFA (Colour Filter Array) filters to register colours. The photodiodes in the camera sensor measure the intensity of light
but the CFA filter splits the light into three red, green, and blue colour components. The most popular CFA pattern is the Bayer mosaic, which strengthens
the impact of the green colour by allocating twice more green filters than red
and blue ones. The *demosaicing techniques* were developed to fill the missing
colour channel values when converting from the Bayer mosaic to the RGB digital image. They use different strategies to find the missing information, however
in all of them, as the information is interpolated, the artefacts can occur in the
output image.

In this work we conduct a perceptual experiment to evaluate the quality of
images after demosaicing. We assess images generated using *bilinear interpolation* (BI), *Gradient-Based Interpolation* (GBI) [1], and *Adaptive Homogeneity-
Directed* (AHD) [2] techniques. However, our main objective is not to find the
best demosaicing algorithm but rather to propose an evaluation technique, which
could be efficient and perceptual, i.e. assess visibility of the demosaicing artefacts in the way a human would do. Authors of the most demosaicing algorithms

© Springer International Publishing Switzerland 2014
A. Campilho and M. Kamel (Eds.): ICIAR 2014, Part I, LNCS 8814, pp. 38–45, 2014.
DOI: 10.1007/978-3-319-11758-4_5

test the efficacy of their techniques comparing the reference undistorted image with an image after demosaicing. This evaluation is mainly based on typical mathematically-based metrics like *Mean-Square-Error* (MSE) or *Peak-Signal-to-Noise-Ratio* (PSNR). However, it is know that this type of metrics should not be used for perceptual image assessment, because the same error score is often measured for images of distinct different appearance [3].

In this paper we evaluate whether the advanced objective image quality metrics (IQMs), like S-CIELAB [4], SSIM [5], and HDR-VDP-2 [6] give results comparable with the subjective judgement. We conduct subjective experiments in which people manually mark the visible local artefacts [7,8]. Then, the detection maps averaged over a number of observers and scenes are compared with the results generated by IQMs. The results reveal which metric is the most suitable for detection of the demosaicing artefacts.

The paper is organised in the following way. In Sect. 2 the artefacts occurring after demosaicing are presented and discussed. Sect. 3 presents details about the conducted experiments. Their results are analysed in Sect. 4. The paper ends with conclusions and providing directions for further work in Sect. 5.

2 Demosaicing Artefacts

For our studies we chose three popular and representative demosaicing techniques that differ in complexity and principle of operation. The bilinear interpolation (BI) is one of the simplest techniques, in which missing colour values are filled by the interpolation of the neighbouring pixels. Due to low quality, BI is not used in practice but it is good point of reference for the evaluation of other algorithms. Better approach is to interpolate values along the edges of objects. To detect an edge the difference (gradient) between green colour components in horizontal and vertical direction is calculated. The smaller difference determine the course of the edge, and hence the direction of interpolation [9]. This edge-directed interpolation is implemeted in GBI [1]. In [2] the algorithm was proposed, in which the vertical or horizontal direction is chosen on the basis of local similarity between pixel values (so-called local homogeneity). This similarity determines the difference of luminance and chrominance in the immediate vicinity of the pixel. The technique is called *AHD* and is considered to be one of the best demosaicing algorithms. Among others, it is used in a popular *dcraw* program [10] converting images from the RAW format to the RGB image.

Demosaicing may result in visible artefacts in images. The most prominent one seems to be the *zippering effect* (see Fig. 1a) caused by choosing the wrong direction of interpolation. Similar artefact, but distorting also colours, is called the *false colour effect* (see Fig. 1b). The zipper and false colours mainly occur close to the strong edges. Accumulated false colour effect provides to the *Moire effect* (see Fig. 1c). The simple demosaicing algorithms (e.g. BI) are prone to a typical interpolation artefact - blurring (see Fig. 1d). In general, the demosaicing artefacts occur locally, as they result from interpolation of a small area around the pixel. The artefacts become clearly visible in the enlarged reproduction of deteriorated images.

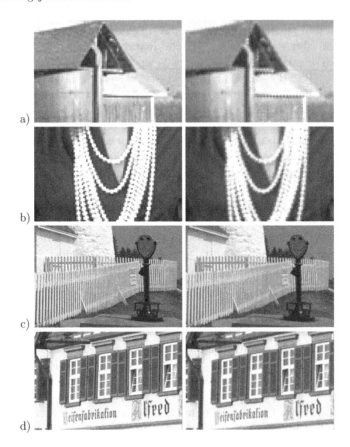

Fig. 1. Reference images (left column) and distorted images generated by the BI demosaicing (right column). Rows from top to bottom: a) zipper effect, b) false colour effect, c) Moire effect, d) image blur. To better depict the artefacts, the images was enlarged using the NNI (Nearest Neighbour Interpolation) method.

3   Experimental Evaluation

In the conducted experiments we evaluate which of the MSE, S-CIELAB, SSIM, and HDR-VDP-2 metrics is the most suitable for the perceptual assessment of the image deterioration caused by the demosaicing techniques.

The evaluation procedure is presented in Fig. 2. The reference difference maps are generated during the subjective experiments. The consistency of these maps is tested using Kendall's analysis and then averaged over a number of observers. Next, we compare the reference maps with the maps generated by the objective image quality metrics. The final score is expressed by the receiver-operator characteristic (ROC) [11] showing effectiveness of individual IQMs.

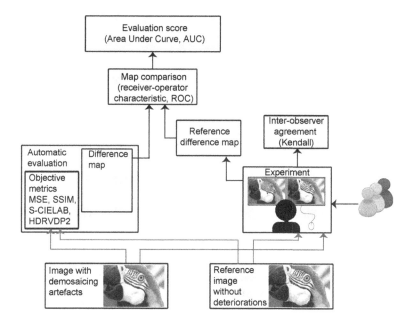

Fig. 2. The evaluation procedure

Stimuli. We used four images from the Kodak Image Suite as a stimuli. This dataset is commonly used to evaluate demosaicing algorithms, as it includes wide range of natural scenes, colours, and textures. The reference images were converted to the Bayer mosaic by removing appropriate colour components. Then, the demosaicing was applied for these mosaics using BI, GBI, and AHD techniques. Additionally, the resulting images were twice and four times enlarged. We preserved resolution of 768x512 pixels by choosing the most interesting areas (containing artefacts described in Sect. 2) and removing the remaining parts of images. To achieve the high quality of the magnification, for visualisation purposes the bicubic interpolation technique from Adobe Photoshop CS5 was applied (see examples in Fig. 3).

Subjective Experiment. We asked people to manually mark visible differences between the reference image and image distorted by a particular demosaicing technique. Observers used a custom brush-paint interface controlled by the computer mouse. The brush size could be reduced up to per-pixel resolution. This procedure was repeated for every scene/demosaicing pair, resulting in 36 comparisons and finally 36 binary difference maps generated per observer.

The experiment was performed in a darkened room. Images were displayed on 24" Eizo ColorEdge CG245W monitor with native resolution of 1920 x 1200 pixels. This display is equipped with the hardware colour calibration module and was calibrated before each experimental session to sRGB colour profile with the maximum luminance level increased to 200 cd/m2. During the experiment, an

Fig. 3. An example reference image taken from the LIVE database and its twice and four times magnified versions

observer was sitting in front of the display at a distance of 65 cm (this distance was stabilised by a chin rest).

We repeated the experiment for 14 observers (age between 20 and 26 years, 11 males and 3 females). They declared normal or corrected to normal vision and correct colour vision. The participants were aware that the image quality is evaluated, but they were naïve about the purpose of the experiment.

Objective Metrics. Objective Image Quality Metrics (IQM) deliver quantitative assessment of the perceptual quality of images [12][13]. In general, they are specialised in predicting the level of annoyance caused by globally present artefacts such as image blockiness, noise, or blur, rather than localised distortions caused by e.g. demosaicing [12]. In our studies we chose three representative IQMs: S-CIELAB [4], SSIM [5], and HDR-VDP-2 [6] that prove their efficacy in perceptual comparison of images. Additionally, we evaluated the results of the MSE metric to give a background for comparison. In particular, SSIM detects structural changes in the image. It is sensitive to difference in the mean intensity and contrast but the main factors are local correlations of pixel values. These dependencies carry information about the structure of the objects and reveal structural image difference between tested and reference images. HDR-VDP-2 predicts the quality degradation expressed as a mean option score of the human observers and visibility (detection/discrimination) of the differences between tested and reference images. It takes into account the contrast sensitivity function measured for variable background luminance and spatial frequencies. The sensitivity to light is modelled separately for cones and rods resulting in correct prediction for mesopic and scotopic light conditions. More complex IQMs exist like metrics based on the machine learning techniques in which various image feature descriptors like the SSIM index, computer vision bag-of-visual worlds, Spearman correlation and many others are used to assess the perceptual difference [14]. We address their application in our framework to future work.

For every metric, 36 difference maps were generated that we compare to corresponding reference maps achieved in the subjective experiments. To avoid any differences in the results generated by the selected objective metrics, we employed the original Matlab implementations of the subjective metrics provided by their authors and available in Internet.

4   Results

Inter-observer Agreement. The subjective experimental task of marking demosaicing artefacts seems challenging, so the variations between observers are expected to be high. To test the inter-observer agreement, we computed *Kendall's coefficient of agreement* (τ) per pixel [15]. An example map of τ values is presented in Fig. 4 (right). We achieved the average τ equal to 0.66, which denotes relatively high agreement. After removing pixels that was marked by less than two observers, the τ value decreased to 0.44. This more conservative measure makes sense because in the images there are many undistorted areas that were consistently left unmarked by most of observers, thus, they overestimate the τ value. However, even this second score τ=0.44 is acceptable and relatively high as compared to the values typically reported in such experiments [7,16].

Fig. 4. From left: an example reference image, the same image but with artefacts caused by the GBI demosaicing technique (see the Moire artefacts on the fence), a map of Kendall coefficients (brighter pixels denote higher agreement between observers)

IQMs Performance Comparison. The key question is whether any of the IQM performs significantly better than the others in terms of detecting demosaicing artefacts. In our experiment, observers binary classified pixels that contained artefacts. The performance of such classification can be analysed using the receiver-operator-characteristic (ROC) [11]. ROC captures the relation between the size of artefacts that were correctly marked by a IQM (true positives), and the regions that do not contain artefacts but were still marked (false positives). The metric that produces a larger *area under the ROC curve* (AUC) is assumed to perform better. The overall metric performance is presented in Fig. 5. Following the solution adopted in [7], the plot was drawn for image regions that were marked by 50% or more observers, i.e. we assume that 50% observers must mark an artefact to consider it noticeable and take into account during ROC

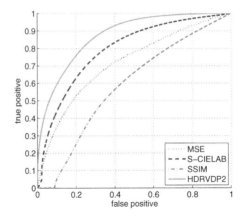

Fig. 5. The performance of IQMs shown as ROC plots

Table 1. AUC scores (higher value means better agreement with the reference data)

Objective metric	25%	50%	75%	Average
SSIM	0.6068	0.5854	0.6385	0.6102
S-CIELAB	0.7769	0.7923	0.7983	0.7891
MSE	0.6887	0.7170	0.7069	0.7042
HDR-VDP-2	0.8462	0.8734	0.8595	0.8597

analysis. Tab. 1 summarises the AUC values also for $\geq 25\%$ and $\geq 75\%$ criteria. The results are comparable showing that accuracy of the subjective experiment does not influence the findings significantly.

As can be seen the highest score was achieved for HDR-VDP-2 and this metric can be considered as the best analysis tool for the demosaicing artefacts. Comparable results were achieved for much simpler S-CIELAB. Both techniques analyse distortion on per pixel level, which reveals even small local artefacts. Interestingly, we achieved the worst result for SSIM, which seems to be the best metric for testing compression artefacts. Conclusion is that demosaicing deteriorations have different characteristic which makes SSIM ineffective for such kind of artefacts, however, further research on more images is needed to prove this statement.

5   Conclusions and Future Work

In this work we asked people to freely mark artefacts that they see in the images deteriorated by the demosaicing algorithms. The difference maps averaged over observers were compared to the difference maps generated by the advanced automatic image quality metrics. The results revealed that HDR-VDP-2 is the best technique for testing the demosaicing artefacts.

In future work we plan to repeat the subjective experiment for more images including the mosaics captured by contemporary camera sensors. The extended dynamic range of these sensors can be challenging for existing demosaicing techniques revealing their drawbacks.

Acknowledgments. The project was funded by the Polish National Science Centre (decision number DEC-2013/09/B/ST6/02270).

References

1. Laroche, M., Prescott, C.A.: Apparatus and method for adaptively interpolating a full color image utilizing chrominance gradients (1994) U.S. Patent no. 5 373 322
2. Hirakawa, K., Parks, T.W.: Adaptive Homogeneity-Directed Demosaicing Algorithm. IEEE Trans. Image Processing **14**, 360–369 (2005)
3. Wang, Z., Bovik, A.C.: Mean Squared Error: Love It or Leave It? IEEE Signal Processing Magazine **26**, 98–117 (2009)
4. Zhang, X.M., Wandell, B.A.: A spatial extension to cielab for digital color image reproduction. In: Proceedings of the SID Symposiums, pp. 731–734 (1996)
5. Wang, Z., Bovik, A., Sheikh, H., Simoncelli, E.: Image quality assessment: From error visibility to structural similarity. IEEE Transactions on Image Processing **13**, 600–612 (2004)
6. Mantiuk, R., Kim, K.J., Rempel, A.G., Heidrich, W.: Hdr-vdp-2: A calibrated visual metric for visibility and quality predictions in all luminance conditions. ACM Trans. Graph. **30**, 40:1–40:14 (2011)
7. Čadík, M., Herzog, R., Mantiuk, R., Myszkowski, K., Seidel, H.P.: New measurements reveal weaknesses of image quality metrics in evaluating graphics artifacts. ACM Transactions on Graphics (Proc. of SIGGRAPH Asia) **31**, 1–10 (2012)
8. Mantiuk, R.K., Tomaszewska, A.M., Mantiuk, R.: Comparison of four subjective methods for image quality assessment. Comput. Graph. Forum **31**, 2478–2491 (2012)
9. Hibbard, R.: Apparatus and method for adaptively interpolating a full color image utilizing luminance gradients (1995)
10. Coffin, D.: dcraw: camera RAW file format parser (2000)
11. Baldi, P., Brunak, S., Chauvin, Y., Anderson, C.A.F., Nielsen, H.: Assessing the accuracy of prediction algorithms for classification: an overview. Bioinformatics **16**, 640–648 (2000)
12. Wang, Z., Bovik, A.: Modern Image Quality Assessment. Morgan & Claypool Publishers (2006)
13. Wu, H., Rao, K.: Digital Video Image Quality and Perceptual Coding. CRC Press (2005)
14. Čadík, M., Herzog, R., Mantiuk, R.K., Mantiuk, R., Myszkowski, K., Seidel, H.P.: Learning to predict localized distortions in rendered images. Comput. Graph. Forum **32**, 401–410 (2013)
15. Salkind, N.: Encyclopedia of measurement and statistics. A Sage reference publication. SAGE, Thousand Oaks (2007)
16. Ledda, P., Chalmers, A., Troscianko, T., Seetzen, H.: Evaluation of tone mapping operators using a high dynamic range display. ACM Transactions on Graphics (Proc. of SIGGRAPH 2005) **24**, 640–648 (2005)

Multiscale Shape Description with Laplacian Profile and Fourier Transform

Evanthia Mavridou[1,2]([✉]), James L. Crowley[1,2], and Augustin Lux[1,2]

[1] University of Grenoble Alpes, LIG, 38000 Grenoble, France
[2] Inria Grenoble Rhône-Alpes Research Centre, LIG, 38000 Grenoble, France
{evanthia.mavridou,james.crowley,augustin.lux}@inria.fr

Abstract. We propose a new local multiscale image descriptor of variable size. The descriptor combines Laplacian of Gaussian values at different scales with a Radial Fourier Transform. This descriptor provides a compact description of the appearance of a local neighborhood in a manner that is robust to changes in scale and orientation. We evaluate this descriptor by measuring repeatability and recall against 1-precision with the Affine Covariant Features benchmark dataset and as well as with a set of textureless images from the MIRFLICKR Retrieval Evaluation dataset. Experiments reveal performance competitive to the state of the art, while providing a more compact representation.

Keywords: Robust image description · Scale invariance · Local appearance description · Compact descriptor · Variable vector length

1 Introduction

Robustness is fundamental for image description. While discriminative power has always been an important consideration, applications have increasingly imposed constraints on robustness, memory requirements and computation cost. In an effort to provide a compact robust descriptor, we have explored a new visual descriptor based on combining a Laplacian Profile with a Radial Discrete Fourier Transform (LP-RDFT) [13]. An interesting property of the LP-RDFT is that it has a adjustable description length, making it possible to tradeoff description length for discriminative power. In comparison with popular descriptors, we have found that at equivalent discrimination levels, the LP-RDFT descriptor provides a much smaller description length. We have also found that the LP-RDFT provides useful discrimination at even its smallest vector lengths [13].

To evaluate the utility of LP-RDFT, we compared its performance for repeatability and recall against 1-precision to other descriptors chosen from the state of the art using the Affine Covariant Features benchmark dataset and the MIRFLICKR Retrieval Evaluation dataset. The results show that LP-RDFT provides effective recall and repeatability at a substantial reduction in computational cost and memory requirements compared to other descriptors.

© Springer International Publishing Switzerland 2014
A. Campilho and M. Kamel (Eds.): ICIAR 2014, Part I, LNCS 8814, pp. 46–54, 2014.
DOI: 10.1007/978-3-319-11758-4_6

Chapter 2 reviews the existing state of the art for local appearance description in images. Chapter 3 describes how the proposed method combines a Laplacian of Gaussian with radial Fourier Transform to provide a local descriptor. Chapter 4 describes experiments with robustness and discusses the results. Chapter 5 summarizes our conclusions from this work.

2 Local Descriptors

Since its introduction in 1999, the Scale Invariant Feature Transform (SIFT) descriptor [12] has remained the reference in local image description. The SIFT descriptor uses local maxima in the Laplacian pyramid to determine a reference scale for local appearance, and then describes local appearance at this scale using local histograms of the orientation of image derivatives calculated within a grid of small windows. Despite many challengers, SIFT, and its numerous variations continues to dominate the state of the art. In [14] it is shown that SIFT and similar descriptors performed the best. Recently, SURF [2] has been shown to provide results that are similar to SIFT with a reduced computational cost. A number of other local descriptors have recently been proposed, including ORB [16], BRISK [10], FREAK [1], BRIEF [5] and NSD [4]. None-the-less, SIFT remains the reference for image description due to its repeatability and recall.

As embedded computing and mobile computing applications for computer vision increase in popularity, memory requirements have emerged as an important issue. In response, many researchers have investigated the use of binary descriptors [4,5,10,16]. As an alternative, we explore a compact descriptor with a variable vector length that can be adapted to meet the requirements of individual problems.

3 Creating the Proposed Descriptor

In order to create a robust multiscale descriptor, we investigated the use of two transformations with known invariant properties: the Laplacian of Gaussian Pyramid and the 2D Fourier Transform (figures 1 and 2). Both of these transformations are known to provide useful descriptions of local appearance. Our objective is to combine these two transformation to obtain a variable size image descriptor that preserves their invariant properties while improving discriminability.

A Gaussian pyramid is computed by convolving an image with Gaussian low pass filters with variances taken from an exponential series, such as 2^k [6]. Resampling each low pass image at a sample distance that is proportional to the standard deviation results in a set of images of exponentially decreasing size and identical impulse response. A Laplacian of Gaussian pyramid (or DoG pyramid) is created by subtracting each sampled low pass image from the next larger image in the pyramid. Each sample in the Laplacian Pyramid contains the value of the Laplacian (2nd derivative) of the image at a particular scale (variance) and position. Local maxima in the Laplacian of Gaussian can be used as keypoints for position and scale, as with the SIFT descriptor.

A Laplacian Profile (LP) is the vector of laplacian samples over an exponential set of scales at a specific image position. This vector is a co–variant with scale [7,11]. Changes in image scale due to optical zoom or changes in distance result in an exact translation of the Laplacian Profile in the scale direction. Local extrema in the Laplacian profile can be used to determine the characteristic scale for image description.

We use the Half-Octave Gaussian pyramid algorithm [6,17] to produce a Laplacian pyramid. The scaled images are convolved with a Gaussian filter $G(x, y, 2^k)$ for integer k and resampled with a sample distance of $s_k = 2^{(k-1)/2}$, keeping impulse response identical for each level. We then construct an LP vector for $p(x, y)$ collecting the Laplacian of Gaussian values for sample $p(x, y)$ from the k adjacent levels in the Laplacian pyramid. Although sampling results in some loss of invariance, this pyramid algorithm is highly efficient for computing LPs.

The LP can be computed at any image position. As with the Laplacian, the LP is also invariant to rotation. The length of the LP is variable and can be calculated on any height on the pyramid of scaled images.For example, an LP vector of length three can be collected in a six level pyramid at levels two-three-four and levels three-four-five. The top pyramid levels can be discarded because they are produced with an impulse response that is larger than the original image.

To improve the discriminative power, we use a Radial Discrete Fourier Transform (RDFT) around each sample of the Laplacian profile. In [13], the neighborhoods were either the 4 closest neighbors around each LP value, sampled on the Laplacian image pyramid (easily calculated by the Gaussian pyramid), or a disk of samples around each LP value, sampled on the Gaussian pyramid. We extended the approach by using 8 neighbors sampled on the Gaussian pyramid and calculate an 1D DFT linearly on them. This is an important extension from [13] as it works well with local description while keeping a small descriptor vector length. From the 8 neighbors $x_0, x_1, ..., x_7$, we take 8 Fourier coefficients $X_0, X_1, ..., X_7$. We keep the absolute value (magnitude) of X_0, the sign of X_4 and the magnitudes of X_1, X_2 and X_3. The absolute value of X_0 and the sign of X_4 are a measure of the sum of intensities of the 8 neighbors. The magnitudes of X_1, X_2 and X_3 provide frequency information. X_5, X_6 and X_7 provide similar information and are therefore discarded. Phase coefficients may be discarded or used to determine a characteristic orientation for the neighborhood.

In [13], an RDFT is computed around every element of an LP vector. This parameter can also be made variable to provide additional discriminative power. We concatenate the RDFTs to form a single description vector that is then normalized with the L_2-norm. The LP vector length, the LP elements around where the RDFT is computed and the radius where the 8 neighbors are taken, are all variable and can be selected according to the needs of an application.

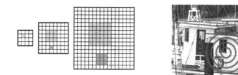

Fig. 1. A small neighborhood at a scale corresponds to a larger one at a lower scale. So, a multiscale vector captures information of increasingly larger areas on the image.

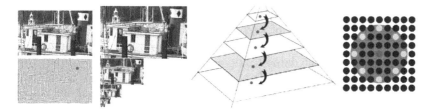

Fig. 2. Left: A Laplacian of Gaussian is easily computed on the levels of a pyramid of scaled images as a weighted difference of adjacent pixels. **Center:** Collecting a LP vector on the Gaussian pyramid. **Right:** Collection of 8 pixels around an LP element on a pyramid level for computing the RDFT. There is no limitation, concerning around which or how many of the elements of an LP, that the RDFT can be computed.

4 Experiments

4.1 Textured Images

We evaluate LP-RDFT against the well established local descriptors ORB, BRISK, FREAK, SIFT, SURF, BRIEF and the newly proposed NSD in its two forms, the Seed of Life (SOL) and the Binary Seed of Life (BinSOL). We use the Affine Covariant Features benchmark dataset [14] for the experiments. The test is keypoint matching between images. The testing protocol is proposed on the dataset web site: compare the first image in each case folder with the rest of the images in the same case folder. The images are highly textured, and thus result in variations in the image signal that provide rich information about content.

The measures we use for the evaluation are repeatability [9,15] and recall against 1 - precision [14]. Repeatability shows how good a method is at finding correct matches. Recall against 1-precision plots show how important is the quantity of correct matches found by a method considering the quantity of false matches. We use the Euclidean distance for matching the descriptor vectors. For all the descriptors except NSD, we use the OpenCV library [3]. For NSD we use the source code provided by the authors. The parameters for the descriptors are kept at their default values, trusting that their authors and developers have made the best choices.

For LP-RDFT, after some experimentation, we concluded that the best performance was given by creating LP vectors of length seven (seven exploited pyramid levels). The same experiments showed that for the computation of the RDFT, the best choice is to collect samples at a radius of five pixels around the LP coordinates for the highest four of the seven pyramid levels. These choices create a descriptor vector of 27 real valued elements. The smallest descriptors in the competing test set are the binary descriptors ORB and BRIEF with 256 binary elements (bits) stored in 32 bytes (OpenCV implementation).

For each descriptor we use the keypoint detector proposed by its authors and developers. For LP-RDFT, we collect keypoints using DoG to compute the Laplacian pyramid. The results of keypoint matching is shown in four figures, numbers 3 to 6. Each figure has two pairs of graphs, each pair corresponding to a particular case folder of the dataset. For each graph pair, one graph shows the repeatability measure for each couple of compared images (image 1 to another image in the same case folder, characterized by an index number) and one graph shows the recall against 1 - precision.

As we can see from the figure 3, for the cases of increasing blur ("bikes"and "trees"), LP-RDFT works very well compared to the state of the art, with very competitive rates for both correct and false matches as depicted by the repeatability and recall against 1 - precision plots. For the right pair of graphs in figure 3 for the case folder "trees", LP-RDFT outperforms the other methods. In both cases, LP-RDFT outperforms SIFT. The right pair of figure 6 for the case of increasing JPEG compression ("ubc") shows that LP-RDFT has a very competitive performance, with high readability and few false matches. For high values of JPEG compression, LP-RDFT outperforms all other descriptors. These results show that LP-RDFT performs well when information is lost due to bad resolution or image compression, regardless of its very small vector length.

Figure 4, for viewpoint changes ("graf"and "wall"), shows that the proposed method has a mediocre repeatability compared to the state of the art. It also provides comparable amount of false matches to the other descriptors as can be concluded by the recall against 1 - precision plots. Figure 5 for zoom and

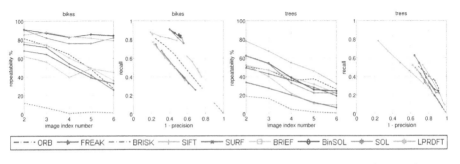

Fig. 3. Affine Covariant Features dataset. **Two left graphs:** Blur ("bikes"). **Two right graphs:** Blur ("trees"). Keypoint matching of image 1 to the rest.

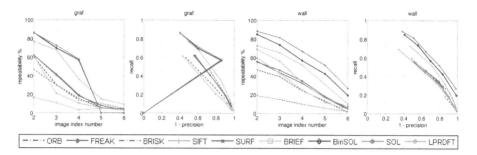

Fig. 4. Affine Covariant Features dataset. **Two left graphs:** Viewpoint ("graf"). **Two right graphs:** Viewpoint ("wall"). Keypoint matching of image 1 to the rest.

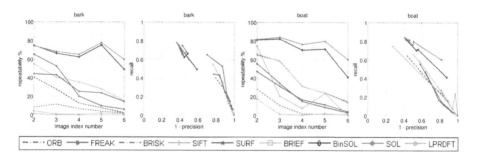

Fig. 5. Affine Covariant Features dataset. **Two left graphs:** Zoom + rotation ("bark"). **Two right graphs:** Zoom + rotation ("boat"). Keypoint matching of image 1 to the rest.

rotation changes ("bark"and "boat"), shows also lower performance than most of the state of the art. Again LP-RDFT provides comparable number of false matches. In figure 6, the left pair for the case of decreasing light ("leuven"), shows that the proposed method has a lower performance compared to the state of the art.

LP-RDFT performs very competitively to the state of the art with a very small vector of only 27 elements, especially when the higher frequencies are lost. The method works very well for blur and JPEG compression, which are relevant to image scaling, but it is weaker at viewpoint changes and light variations.

4.2 Textureless Images

Textureless images are more difficult to discriminate because they exhibit fewer visual features, smooth edges and large homogeneous areas. In order to make a more general testing, we collected a set of images (figure 7) from the MIR-FLICKR Retrieval Evaluation dataset [8] with these characteristics.

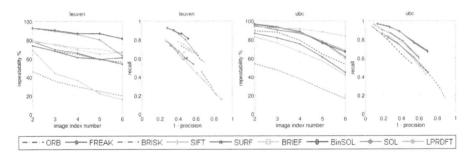

Fig. 6. Affine Covariant Features dataset. **Two left graphs:** Light ("leuven"). **Two right graphs:** JPEG compression ("ubc"). Keypoint matching of image 1 to the rest.

Fig. 7. The textureless images taken from MIRFLICKR Retrieval Evaluation dataset.

The tests include rotation of the images from $0°$ to $180°$ every $30°$ and scaling of the images from four times bigger to four times smaller with scale factor $\sqrt{2}$ (figure 8). The same measures are used for evaluation. All compared descriptors are used in the same way as before. Concerning the proposed descriptor, we use another shorter version of LP-RDFT due to the size of the images. Also, the radius, where we collect the samples for the RDFT, is a little bigger; six pixels instead of five. Again, the parameters are chosen after exhaustive tests. We use two element long LP vectors, so two exploited levels on the image pyramid, and the Fourier information from only the highest of the two used pyramid levels. The final vector is thus particularly small with only 7 elements!

From the plots we see that none of the methods give high performance, with low recall and repeatability. The low recall against 1-precision measures results from the small number of keypoints detected and used for matching. Surprisingly, for all descriptors except LP-RDFT, the matching performance on the same image (original image to its self) is very low. This can be explained by the lack of meaningful signal information in this images that causes many of the descriptor features to look alike and cause false matches. The proposed method performs almost perfectly for matching on the original image, which shows that it can handle low quality information. Its performance though deteriorates with rotation and scaling. For small rotations and scale changes the repeatability of LP-RDFT is the best among all descriptors.

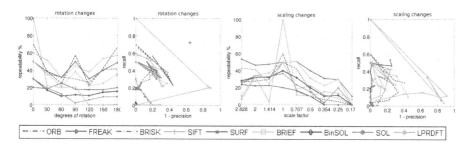

Fig. 8. Textureless images from MIRFLICKR Retrieval Evaluation dataset. **Two left graphs:** Rotation tests. **Two right graphs:** Scaling tests.

5   Conclusions

In this work, we proposed a method of image description by combining two transformations with interesting invariant properties with the goal of creating a very compact and robust image descriptor. The resulting LP-RDFT is a multiscale descriptor with variable vector size that can become very small if needed while remaining discriminative enough. The experimental results on keypoint matching for textured images showed that LP-RDFT works efficiently having a very small vector length. LP-RDFT outperforms the state of the art for scale changes and image changes relevant to scaling, like increasing blur and JPEG compression. Tests on textureless images showed that LP-RDFT beats the state of the art for small values of rotation and scaling but its performances deteriorates for larger values. The most important fact is that the vector size of LP-RDFT for the textureless images tests is particularly tiny, with only 7 elements. LP-RDFT is a proposition for very compact image description and especially suitable for cases where a large amount of information is unnecessary and large vector sizes can be a problem.

References

1. Alahi, A., Ortiz, R., Vandergheynst, P.: FREAK: Fast Retina Keypoint. In: 2012 IEEE Conference on Computer Vision and Pattern Recognition (CVPR), pp. 510–517 (June 2012)
2. Bay, H., Ess, A., Tuytelaars, T., Van Gool, L.: Speeded-Up Robust Features (SURF). Comput. Vis. Image Underst. **110**(3), 346–359 (2008). http://dx.doi.org/10.1016/j.cviu.2007.09.014
3. Bradski, G.: The OpenCV Library. Dr. Dobb's Journal of Software Tools (2000)
4. Byrne, J., Shi, J.: Nested Shape Descriptors. In: 2013 IEEE International Conference on Computer Vision (ICCV), pp. 1201–1208 (December 2013)
5. Calonder, M., Lepetit, V., Ozuysal, M., Trzcinski, T., Strecha, C., Fua, P.: BRIEF: Computing a Local Binary Descriptor Very Fast. IEEE Trans. on Pattern Analysis and Machine Intelligence **34**(7), 1281–1298 (2012)

6. Crowley, J.L., Stern, R.M.: Fast Computation of the Difference of Low-Pass Transform. IEEE Trans. on Pattern Analysis and Machine Intelligence PAMI **6**(2), 212–222 (1984)

7. Hall, D., Colin de Verdière, V., Crowley, J.L.: Object recognition using coloured receptive fields. In: Vernon, D. (ed.) ECCV 2000. LNCS, vol. 1842, pp. 164–177. Springer, Heidelberg (2000). http://dx.doi.org/10.1007/3-540-45054-8_11

8. Huiskes, M.J., Lew, M.S.: The MIR Flickr Retrieval Evaluation. In: MIR. ACM, New York (2008)

9. Juan, L., Gwon, O.: A Comparison of SIFT, PCA-SIFT and SURF. International Journal of Image Processing (IJIP) **3**(4), 143–152 (2009)

10. Leutenegger, S., Chli, M., Siegwart, R.: BRISK: Binary Robust invariant scalable keypoints. In: 2011 IEEE International Conference on Computer Vision (ICCV), pp. 2548–2555 (November 2011)

11. Lindeberg, T.: On the axiomatic foundations of linear scale-space: Combining semigroup structure with causality vs. scale invariance, Technical report, Department of Numerical Analysis and Computing Science, Royal Institute of Technology, S-100 44 Stockholm, Sweden, August 1994. (ISRN KTH NA/P-94/20-SE). Revised version published as Chapter 6 in Sporring, J., Nielsen, M., Florack, L., Johansen, P. (eds.): Gaussian Scale-Space Theory: Proc. PhD School on Scale-Space Theory, (Copenhagen, Denmark, May 1996), pp. 75–98. Kluwer Academic Publishers (1997)

12. Lowe, D.: Object recognition from local scale-invariant features. In: The Seventh IEEE International Conference on Computer Vision, vol. 2, pp. 1150–1157 (1999)

13. Mavridou, E., Hoàng, M.D., Crowley, J.L., Lux, A.: Scale normalized radial fourier transform as a robust image descriptor. In: ICPR (in press, 2014)

14. Mikolajczyk, K., Schmid, C.: A performance evaluation of local descriptors. IEEE Trans. on Pattern Analysis and Machine Intelligence **27**(10), 1615–1630 (2005)

15. Mikolajczyk, K., Tuytelaars, T., Schmid, C., Zisserman, A., Matas, J., Schafalitzky, F., Kadir, T., Van Gool, L.: A Comparison of Affine Region Detectors. International Journal of Computer Vision **65**(1–2), 43–72 (2005). http://dx.doi.org/10.1007/s11263-005-3848-x

16. Rublee, E., Rabaud, V., Konolige, K., Bradski, G.: ORB: An Efficient Alternative to SIFT or SURF. In: 2011 IEEE International Conference on Computer Vision (ICCV), pp. 2564–2571 (November 2011)

17. Ruiz-Hernandez, J.A., Lux, A., Crowley, J.L.: Face detection by cascade of Gaussian derivates classifiers calculated with a Half-Octave Pyramid. In: 8th IEEE International Conference on Automatic Face Gesture Recognition, FG 2008, pp. 1–6 (September 2008)

Structural Similarity-Based Approximation over Orthogonal Bases: Investigating the Use of Individual Component Functions $S_k(\mathbf{x}, \mathbf{y})$

Paul Bendevis and Edward R. Vrscay$^{(\boxtimes)}$

Department of Applied Mathematics, Faculty of Mathematics,
University of Waterloo, Waterloo, ON N2L 3G1, Canada
{ptbendev,ervrscay}@uwaterloo.ca

Abstract. We examine the use of individual components of the Structural Similarity image quality measure as criteria for best approximation in terms of orthogonal expansions. We also introduce a family of higher order SSIM-like rational functions.

1 Introduction

In this paper, we wish to examine further the idea of orthogonal expansions in $\mathbb{R}^N$ that are best approximations in terms of the Structural Similarity (SSIM) image quality measure [6]. This study represents a kind of followup of the work presented in an earlier ICIAR conference [3] in which the optimization was done with respect to the SSIM function, $S(\mathbf{x}, \mathbf{y})$, a product of three terms, namely, (i) luminance, (ii) contrast and (iii) structure. The luminance term, $S_1(\mathbf{x}, \mathbf{y})$ is a function only of the means of $\mathbf{x}$ and $\mathbf{y}$ and therefore cannot provide a nontrivial approximation. Here we examine whether either of the contrast or structure terms alone can be used as a criterion for best approximation determination and find that the answer is negative. At least two of the three components, one of which must be the luminance term, are necessary to provide a unique solution.

In the final section of this paper, we introduce a family of higher-order or "generalized" SSIM functions, using a method that is analogous to the construction of the rational function $S_1(\mathbf{x}, \mathbf{y})$.

2 SSIM and SSIM-Based Approximations of Signals/Images

In what follows, we let $\mathbf{x}, \mathbf{y} \in \mathbb{R}^N$ denote two N-dimensional signal/image blocks or local patches, i.e., $\mathbf{x} = (x_1, x_2, \cdots, x_N)$. The SSIM measure between $\mathbf{x}$ and $\mathbf{y}$ was defined originally as follows [6,7],

$$
\begin{aligned}
S(\mathbf{x}, \mathbf{y}) &= S_1(\mathbf{x}, \mathbf{y}) S_2(\mathbf{x}, \mathbf{y}) S_3(\mathbf{x}, \mathbf{y}) \\
&= \left[\frac{2\bar{\mathbf{x}}\bar{\mathbf{y}} + \epsilon_1}{\bar{\mathbf{x}}^2 + \bar{\mathbf{y}}^2 + \epsilon_1} \right] \left[\frac{2s_{\mathbf{x}}s_{\mathbf{y}} + \epsilon_2}{s_{\mathbf{x}}^2 + s_{\mathbf{y}}^2 + \epsilon_2} \right] \left[\frac{s_{\mathbf{xy}} + \epsilon_3}{s_{\mathbf{x}}s_{\mathbf{y}} + \epsilon_3} \right],
\end{aligned}
\tag{1}
$$

© Springer International Publishing Switzerland 2014
A. Campilho and M. Kamel (Eds.): ICIAR 2014, Part I, LNCS 8814, pp. 55–64, 2014.
DOI: 10.1007/978-3-319-11758-4_7

where

$$\bar{\mathbf{x}} = \frac{1}{N}\sum_{i=1}^{N} x_i, \quad s_{\mathbf{xy}} = \frac{1}{N-1}\sum_{i=1}^{N}(x_i - \bar{\mathbf{x}})(y_i - \bar{\mathbf{y}}), \quad s_{\mathbf{x}} = \sqrt{s_{\mathbf{xx}}}, \text{ etc..} \quad (2)$$

The small positive constants ϵ_k are added for numerical stability and can be adjusted to accomodate the perception of the human visual system.

The functional form of the component S_1 in Eq. (1), which measures the similarities of local patch luminances or brightness values, was originally chosen in an effort to accomodate Weber's law of perception [7]. The form of S_2, which measures the similarities of local patch contrasts, follows the idea of divisive normalization [5]. In the case that $\epsilon_3 = 0$, the component S_3, which measures the similarities of local patch structures, is precisely the correlation $C(\mathbf{x},\mathbf{y})$ between $\mathbf{x}$ and $\mathbf{y}$. We shall be taking a closer look at S_2 and S_3 below.

Note that $-1 \leq S(\mathbf{x},\mathbf{y}) \leq 1$, and $S(\mathbf{x},\mathbf{y}) = 1$ if and only if $\mathbf{x} = \mathbf{y}$. The component $S_1(\mathbf{x},\mathbf{y})$ measures the similarity between the means of $\mathbf{x}$ and $\mathbf{y}$: If $\bar{\mathbf{x}} = \bar{\mathbf{y}}$, then $S_1(\mathbf{x},\mathbf{y}) = 1$, its maximum possible value. We shall return to this idea in a later Section.

It is common practice to set $\epsilon_2 = 2\epsilon_3$, in which case the product of S_2 and S_3 in Eq. (1) collapses to a single term, namely,

$$S_{2'}(\mathbf{x},\mathbf{y}) = \frac{2s_{\mathbf{xy}} + \epsilon_2}{s_{\mathbf{x}}^2 + s_{\mathbf{y}}^2 + \epsilon_2}. \quad (3)$$

It was indeed this form of the SSIM, i.e., $S(\mathbf{x},\mathbf{y}) = S_1(\mathbf{x},\mathbf{y})S_{2'}(\mathbf{x},\mathbf{y})$, that was analysed in [3]. (In that paper, $S_{2'}$ was denoted as S_2.) In this paper, we wish to examine the roles of the individual terms S_2 and S_3, as opposed to their product.

In the discussion that follows, we consider $\mathbf{x}$ to be a given signal and $\mathbf{y} \in A$ to be an approximation to $\mathbf{x}$ where A is an M-dimensional subset of $\mathbb{R}^N$, with $M \leq N$. Of course, we shall be concerned with *best approximations* to $\mathbf{x}$, but not in terms of SSIM, as was done in [3]. Instead, we shall be determining best approximations with respect to each of the SSIM components S_2 and S_3.

As in [3], we work with a set of (complete) orthonormal basis functions $\mathbb{R}^N$, to be denoted as $\{\phi_0, \phi_1, \cdots, \phi_{N-1}\}$. We assume that only the first element has nonzero mean: $\overline{\phi_k} = 0$ for $1 \leq k \leq N-1$. We also assume that ϕ_0 is "flat", i.e., constant: $\phi_0 = N^{-1/2}(1, 1, \cdots, 1)$, which accomodates the discrete cosine transform (DCT) as well as Haar multiresolution system on $\mathbb{R}^N$. (If ϕ_0 were not constant, then the definitions of the mean $\bar{\mathbf{x}}$ in Eq. (2) can be modified accordingly.) The L^2-based expansion of $\mathbf{x}$ in this basis is

$$\mathbf{x} = \sum_{k=0}^{N-1} a_k \phi_k, \quad a_k = \langle \mathbf{x}, \phi_k \rangle, \quad 0 \leq k \leq N-1, \quad (4)$$

from which it follows that

$$\bar{\mathbf{x}} = a_0 N^{-1/2}. \quad (5)$$

The expansions of the approximation $\mathbf{y} \in A$ to $\mathbf{x}$ will be denoted as follows,

$$\mathbf{y} = \mathbf{y}(\mathbf{c}) = \sum_{k=0}^{N-1} c_k \phi_k, \tag{6}$$

where the notation $\mathbf{y}(\mathbf{c})$ acknowledges the dependence of the approximation on the coefficients c_k. It also follows that

$$\bar{\mathbf{y}} = c_0 N^{-1/2}. \tag{7}$$

Note that at this point, we do not assume a relationship between a_0 and c_0.

For simplicity of discussion, we consider the approximation spaces A to be

$$A_M = \text{span}\{\phi_0, \phi_1, \cdots, \phi_{M-1}\} \tag{8}$$

where $0 \le M \le N - 1$. The discussion which follows can easily be adapted to conform to the situation studied in [3] in which an arbitrary subset of distinct functions $\{\phi_{\gamma(k)}\}$, $0 \le k \le M - 1$ was chosen from the complete set of N functions. As is well known, the best L^2-based approximation of x in A_M is

$$\mathbf{y}_{M,L^2} = \mathbf{x}_M := \sum_{k=0}^{M-1} a_k \phi_k, \quad a_k = \langle \mathbf{x}, \phi_k \rangle, \tag{9}$$

a truncation of the exact expansion of $\mathbf{x}$ in Eq. (4). In terms of Eq. (6),

$$c_k = a_k, \quad 0 \le k \le M - 1 \quad \text{and} \quad c_k = 0, \quad M \le k \le N - 1. \tag{10}$$

As is also well known,

$$\mathbf{y}_{M,L^2} = \arg \min_{z \in A_m} \|x - z\|_2, \tag{11}$$

the unique element in A_M that that lies closest to $\mathbf{x} \in \mathbb{R}^N$.

In [3], the best SSIM-based approximation $\mathbf{y}_{SSIM} \in A_M$ to $\mathbf{x}$, using the SSIM function $S(\mathbf{x}, \mathbf{y}) = S_1(\mathbf{x}, \mathbf{y}) S_{2'}(\mathbf{x}, \mathbf{y})$, was found to be

$$\mathbf{y}_{M,SSIM} = \arg \max_{\mathbf{z} \in A_M} S(\mathbf{x}, \mathbf{z}) = \sum_{k=0}^{M-1} c_k \phi_k, \tag{12}$$

where $c_0 = a_0$ and

$$c_k = \alpha a_k, \quad 1 \le k \le M - 1. \tag{13}$$

The scaling coefficient α is given by

$$\alpha = \frac{-\epsilon_2 + \sqrt{\epsilon_2^2 + \left(\frac{4}{N-1} \sum_{k=1}^{M-1} a_k^2\right)(s_\mathbf{x}^2 + \epsilon_2)}}{\frac{2}{N-1} \sum_{k=1}^{M-1} a_k^2}. \tag{14}$$

In the special case $\epsilon_2 = 0$,

$$\alpha = \left[\sum_{k=1}^{N-1} a_k^2\right]^{1/2} \left[\sum_{k=1}^{M-1} a_k^2\right]^{-1/2}. \tag{15}$$

When $M < N$, the scaling coefficient $\alpha > 1$, which implies that the $\mathbf{y}_{M,SSIM}$ is a *contrast enhanced* version of $\mathbf{y}_{M,L^2}$.

3   Best S_3/Correlation-Based Approximations

Here we consider the following problem: Given an $\mathbf{x} \in \mathbb{R}^N$, find, if possible, the best S_3-based approximation to $\mathbf{x}$ in A_M, i.e.,

$$\mathbf{y}_{M,S_3} = \arg\max_{\mathbf{z} \in A_M} S_3(\mathbf{x}, \mathbf{z}). \tag{16}$$

As mentioned in Section 1, in the case $\epsilon_3 = 0$, $S_3(\mathbf{x}, \mathbf{y}) = C(\mathbf{x}, \mathbf{y})$, the correlation between $\mathbf{x}$ and $\mathbf{y}$. It is necessary to express the function $S_3(\mathbf{x}, \mathbf{y})$ in terms of the unknown coefficients c_k of the expansion for $\mathbf{y}(\mathbf{c})$. The following results, which are obtained after some simple algebra, are useful:

$$s_{\mathbf{x}}^2 = \frac{1}{N-1} \sum_{k=1}^{N-1} a_k^2, \quad s_{\mathbf{xy}} = \frac{1}{N-1} \sum_{k=1}^{M-1} a_k c_k, \quad s_{\mathbf{y}}^2 = \frac{1}{N-1} \sum_{k=1}^{M-1} c_k^2. \tag{17}$$

We then have that

$$S_3(\mathbf{x}, \mathbf{y}(\mathbf{c})) = \frac{\frac{1}{N-1} \sum_{k=1}^{M-1} a_k c_k + \epsilon_3}{\frac{1}{N-1} \left[\sum_{k=1}^{N-1} a_k^2\right]^{1/2} \left[\sum_{k=1}^{M-1} c_k^2\right]^{1/2} + \epsilon_3}. \tag{18}$$

Note that the right side is a function of the coefficients $c_1, c_1, \cdots c_{M-1}$, but *not* of c_0. This is already an indication that the maximizer of S_3 may not be unique.

We now look for stationary points that will be candidates for maximum points of $S_3(\mathbf{x}, \mathbf{y}(\mathbf{c}))$. Imposition of the stationarity conditions $\partial S_3/\partial c_p = 0$ for $1 \le p \le M-1$ leads to the following set of equations,

$$\frac{1}{s_{\mathbf{xy}} + \epsilon_3} a_p - \frac{1}{s_{\mathbf{x}} s_{\mathbf{y}} + \epsilon_3} \frac{s_{\mathbf{x}}}{s_{\mathbf{y}}} c_p = 0, \quad 1 \le p \le M-1. \tag{19}$$

If $a_p = 0$ for any $1 \le p \le M-1$, then $c_p = 0$. Otherwise, we may rewrite the above relations as

$$\frac{c_p}{a_p} = \frac{s_{\mathbf{x}} s_{\mathbf{y}} + \epsilon_3}{s_{\mathbf{xy}} + \epsilon_3} \frac{s_{\mathbf{y}}}{s_x}, \quad 1 \le p \le M-1. \tag{20}$$

The RHS of each equation is independent of p, implying that

$$c_p = \alpha a_p, \quad 1 \le p \le M-1, \tag{21}$$

Such a proportionality between the c_p and a_p was also found in [3] for the case of best SSIM-based approximations. We now attempt to determine α by rewriting Eq. (20) and using Eq. (21) to obtain the relation

$$\alpha s_{\mathbf{x}}(s_{\mathbf{xy}} + \epsilon_3) = s_{\mathbf{y}}(s_{\mathbf{x}}s_{\mathbf{y}} + \epsilon_3) . \tag{22}$$

Substition of the expansions in (17) followed by simplification yields

$$\alpha^2 \epsilon_3^2 \sum_{k=1}^{N-1} a_k^2 = \alpha^2 \epsilon_3^2 \sum_{k=1}^{M-1} a_k^2 . \tag{23}$$

In the special case that $M = N$, Eq. (23) is an identity that is satisfied by any $\alpha \in \mathbb{R}$, independent of the value of ϵ_3. This is due to the following result, the proof of which is very straightforward and therefore omitted.

Theorem 1: Let $\mathbf{x} \in \mathbb{R}$ and $\mathbf{y} = a\mathbf{x} + b\mathbf{1}$, where $a, b \in \mathbb{R}$, $a \neq 0$ and $\mathbf{1} = (1, 1, \cdots, 1) \in \mathbb{R}$. Then

$$C(\mathbf{x}, \mathbf{y}) = \frac{s_{\mathbf{xy}}}{s_{\mathbf{x}} s_{\mathbf{y}}} = \operatorname{sgn}(a) = \begin{cases} 1, & a > 0, \\ -1, & a < 0. \end{cases} \tag{24}$$

When $2 \leq M < N$, we must consider two cases in Eq. (23):

1. $\epsilon_3 = 0$: Eq. (23) is satisfied for all $\alpha \in \mathbb{R}$. This is again a consequence of Theorem 1 and can be confirmed by substituting Eq. (21) into Eq. (18).
2. $\epsilon_3 \neq 0$: In order that Eq. (23) be satisfied for any sequence of Fourier coefficients $\{a_k\}_{k=1}^{N-1}$, it is necessary that $\alpha = 0$, which implies that $\mathbf{y}_{M,S_3} = c_0\phi_0 \in A_1$, i.e., the constant approximation, with c_0 as yet undetermined.

The conclusion is that S_3-based best approximation is possible only in the case $\epsilon_3 = 0$. But even in this case, the result is not unique since α is arbitrary (but positive). What makes matters worse is that the leading coefficient c_0 of the approximation $\mathbf{y}(\mathbf{c})$ also remains undetermined! It appears that two additional conditions are required in order to obtain unique values of c_0 and α.

Eqs. (5) and (7) imply that a unique value of c_0 can be obtained by imposing a relation between the means $\bar{\mathbf{x}}$ and $\bar{\mathbf{y}}$. It would seem natural to impose the following "equal means" condition,

$$\bar{\mathbf{x}} = \bar{\mathbf{y}} , \tag{25}$$

which, as is well known, maximizes the component function $S_1(\mathbf{x}, \mathbf{y})$ in Eq. (1). In this case, $c_0 = a_0$, as was found in [3].

Using this result, we must still determine a unique value of the proportionality coefficient α in Eq. (21). If we impose a condition of "equal norms," i.e.,

$$\|\mathbf{x}\|_2 = \|\mathbf{y}_{M,S_3}\|_2 , \tag{26}$$

then squaring both sides and substituting the respective expansions along with the property in Eq. (21) and the condition $c_0 = a_0$ yields

$$a_0^2 + \sum_{k=1}^{N-1} a_k^2 = c_0^2 + \sum_{k=1}^{M-1} c_k^2 = a_0^2 + \alpha^2 \sum_{k=1}^{M-1} a_k^2 . \tag{27}$$

This result leads to the (positive) value of α in Eq. (15).

Here it is important to mention that if the "equal means" condition of (25) is replaced by another relationship between c_0 and a_0, then the "equal norms" condition of (26) yields a scaling coefficient α different from that in Eq. (15).

The results in this section lead to the following important conclusions:

1. Using only the component function $S_3(\mathbf{x}, \mathbf{y})$ is insufficient to determine a best SSIM-based approximation $y_{M,S_3} \in A_M$ to $\mathbf{x}$.
2. Using the components $S_1(\mathbf{x}, \mathbf{y})$ and $S_3(\mathbf{x}, \mathbf{y})$ is also insufficient to find a best approximation. In the special case, $\epsilon_3 = 0$, however, a unique solution may be obtained by imposing two additional conditions, e.g., equality of means, Eq. (25), and equality of norms, Eq. (26).

4   Best S_2/Contrast-Based Approximations

We now consider the following problem: Given an $\mathbf{x} \in \mathbb{R}^N$, find, if possible, the best S_2-based approximation to $\mathbf{x}$ in A_M, i.e.,

$$\mathbf{y}_{M,S_2} = \arg \max_{\mathbf{z} \in A_M} S_2(\mathbf{x}, \mathbf{z}) , \tag{28}$$

where $S_2(\mathbf{x}, \mathbf{y})$ is defined in Eq. (1). From the equations in (17) we may express $S_2(\mathbf{x}, \mathbf{y})$ in terms of the expansion coefficients c_k. It is not absolutely necessary to present this expansion here, but only to note that, as in the case of the $S_3(\mathbf{x}, \mathbf{y})$ function examined in the previous section, $S_2(\mathbf{x}, \mathbf{y})$ is a function of the $M - 1$ coefficients $c_1, c_1, \cdots c_{M-1}$ and independent of the coefficient c_0.

Imposition of the stationarity conditions $\partial S_2 / \partial c_p = 0$, for $1 \leq p \leq M - 1$ leads to the following set of equations,

$$\left[\frac{s_{\mathbf{x}}}{s_{\mathbf{y}}} (s_{\mathbf{x}}^2 + s_{\mathbf{y}}^2 + \epsilon_2) - (2s_{\mathbf{x}}s_{\mathbf{y}} + \epsilon_2) \right] c_p = 0, \quad 1 \leq p \leq M - 1 . \tag{29}$$

The most noteworthy feature of these equations is the absence of of a direct relation between c_p and a_p as was seen in Eq. (19) for the S_3 case. As such, the existence of a proportionality result of the form in Eq. (21) cannot be proved. Since all of the coefficients c_p cannot, in general, be zero, it follows that the term in the square brackets must vanish. We now examine two cases:

1. $\epsilon_2 = 0$: The vanishing of the term in the square brackets of Eq. (29) reduces to the result

$$s_{\mathbf{x}}^2 = s_{\mathbf{y}}^2 \implies \sum_{k=1}^{N-1} a_k^2 = \sum_{k=1}^{M-1} c_k^2 . \tag{30}$$

If we now *assume* a proportionality between the c_p and a_p as in Eq. (21), we arrive at the result for α in Eq. (15). Note that we must still impose the equal-means condition of Eq. (25) to obtain a unique approximation $y_{M,S_2} \in A_M$ in this case.

2. $\epsilon_2 \neq 0$: Assuming that $s_\mathbf{y} \neq 0$, the vanishing of the term in square brackets implies that

$$s_\mathbf{x}^3 - s_\mathbf{x} s_\mathbf{y}^2 + \epsilon_2 s_\mathbf{x} - \epsilon_2 s_\mathbf{y} = 0. \tag{31}$$

If we once again *assume* a proportionality between the c_p and the a_p as in Eq. (21), a quadratic equation in α is obtained. It is convenient to rewrite it as an equation in a scaled variable β as follows,

$$s_\mathbf{x}\beta^2 + \epsilon_2\beta - s_\mathbf{x}^3 - \epsilon_2 s_\mathbf{x} = 0, \text{ where } \beta = \frac{\alpha}{\sqrt{N-1}}\left[\sum_{k=1}^{M-1} a_k^2\right]^{1/2} = s_{\mathbf{x}_M}\alpha. \tag{32}$$

The definition of $s_{\mathbf{x}_M}$ follows from Eqs. (9) and (17). The value of α which results from the positive solution of this quadratic equation is

$$\alpha = \frac{-\epsilon_2 + \sqrt{\epsilon_2^2 + 4s_\mathbf{x}^2(s_\mathbf{x}^2 + \epsilon_2)}}{2s_\mathbf{x} s_{\mathbf{x}_M}}. \tag{33}$$

In the case $\epsilon_2 \to 0$, the result in Eq. (15) is obtained. For $\epsilon_2 \neq 0$, however, a comparision between this equation and Eq. (14) shows that the results are *almost* the same. They do differ, however, except in the case $M = N$. The reason for this difference is the appearance of the term $s_\mathbf{xy}$ in the numerator of the SSIM function $S_{2'}(\mathbf{x}, \mathbf{y})$, cf. Eq. (3), as opposed to $s_\mathbf{x} s_\mathbf{y}$ in the SSIM function $S_2(\mathbf{x}, \mathbf{y})$, cf. Eq. (1).

In summary, the S_2-based best approximation method of this section is possible with a scaling condition of the form Eq. (21). As with the S_3-based case, however, the coefficient c_0 is undetermined. If the equal-means condition of Eq. (25) is employed then we obtain, as before, $c_0 = a_0$.

In this section, we have arrived at the following important conclusions:

1. Using only the component function $S_2(\mathbf{x}, \mathbf{y})$ is insufficient to determine a best SSIM-based approximation $y_{M,S_2} \in A_M$ to $\mathbf{x}$.
2. Using components $S_1(\mathbf{x}, \mathbf{y})$ and $S_2(\mathbf{x}, \mathbf{y})$ is sufficient to find a unique, best SSIM-based approximation y_{M,S_2} for both zero and nonzero values of the stability constant ϵ_2. For all $M < N$, however, this approximation is different from the best SSIM-based counterpart of Eq. (12), obtained by using the entire SSIM function $S(\mathbf{x}, \mathbf{y})$ in Eq. (1).

5   A Family of Higher-Order Rational SSIM Functions

In this section, we show how a rationalization procedure that can be used to construct the SSIM functions $S_1(\mathbf{x}, \mathbf{y})$ in Eq. (1) and $S_{2'}(\mathbf{x}, \mathbf{y})$ in Eq. (3) may be used to construct higher order SSIM-like rational functions. We then consider the use of these functions for best SSIM-based approximations and present some preliminary results. In the discussion that follows, as before, $\mathbf{x}, \mathbf{y} \in \mathbb{R}^N$.

With reference to the function $S_1(\mathbf{x}, \mathbf{y})$, note that $\mathbf{x} = \mathbf{y}$ implies $\bar{\mathbf{x}} = \bar{\mathbf{y}}$ and $S_1(\mathbf{x}, \mathbf{y}) = 1$. But $\bar{\mathbf{x}} = \bar{\mathbf{y}}$ also implies $(\bar{\mathbf{x}} - \bar{\mathbf{y}})^2 = 0$, so that

$$\bar{\mathbf{x}}^2 + \bar{\mathbf{y}}^2 = 2\bar{\mathbf{x}}\bar{\mathbf{y}}. \tag{34}$$

Now add a "stability constant" $\epsilon_1 > 0$ to each side and divide to obtain

$$S_1(\mathbf{x}, \mathbf{y}) = \frac{2\bar{\mathbf{x}}\bar{\mathbf{y}} + \epsilon_1}{\bar{\mathbf{x}}^2 + \bar{\mathbf{y}}^2 + \epsilon_1} = 1. \tag{35}$$

Now define

$$\mathbf{x}_0 = \mathbf{x} - \bar{\mathbf{x}}\mathbf{1}, \qquad \mathbf{y}_0 = \mathbf{y} - \bar{\mathbf{y}}\mathbf{1}, \tag{36}$$

where $\mathbf{1} = (1, 1, \cdots, 1) \in \mathbb{R}^N$. By construction, $\mathbf{x}_0$ and $\mathbf{y}_0$ have zero-mean. Clearly, $\mathbf{x} = \mathbf{y}$ implies that $\mathbf{x}_0 = \mathbf{y}_0$ which, in turn, implies that

$$\|\mathbf{x}_0 - \mathbf{y}_0\|_n^n = 0, \quad n = 2, 3, 4, \cdots. \tag{37}$$

We consider only the case that n is even, so that Eq. (37) becomes

$$\sum_{k=1}^N [(x_k - \bar{\mathbf{x}}) - (y_k - \bar{\mathbf{y}})]^n = 0, \quad n = 2, 4, 6, \cdots. \tag{38}$$

Now use the binomial theorem and then rearrange to produce the result,

$$\sum_{l=0}^n (-1)^l B_{nl} \sum_{k=1}^N (x_k - \bar{\mathbf{x}})^{n-l}(y_k - \bar{\mathbf{y}})^l = 0, \quad \text{where } B_{nl} = \binom{n}{l}. \tag{39}$$

Dividing by $N - 1$, this relation becomes

$$\sum_{l=0}^n (-1)^l B_{nl} s_{n-l,l} = 0, \tag{40}$$

where we have defined

$$s_{p,q} = \frac{1}{N-1} \sum_{k=1}^N (x_k - \bar{\mathbf{x}})^p (y_k - \bar{\mathbf{y}})^q, \quad p, q \geq 0. \tag{41}$$

Now rewrite Eq. (40) as follows,

$$\sum_{l \text{ even}} B_{nl} s_{n-l,l} = \sum_{l \text{ odd}} B_{nl} s_{n-l,l}. \tag{42}$$

Once again we add a "stability constant" $\epsilon_n \geq 0$ to both sides and divide by the left-hand term to obtain the result,

$$\Sigma_n(\mathbf{x}, \mathbf{y}) := \frac{\sum_{l \text{ odd}} B_{nl} s_{n-l,l} + \epsilon_n}{\sum_{l \text{ even}} B_{nl} s_{n-l,l} + \epsilon_n} = 1. \tag{43}$$

The rational functions $\Sigma_n(\mathbf{x}, \mathbf{y})$, $n \in \{2, 4, 6, \cdots\}$ define a set of *generalized SSIM functions* between vectors $\mathbf{x}$ and $\mathbf{y}$. When $n = 2$, $\Sigma_2(\mathbf{x}, \mathbf{y}) = S_{2'}(\mathbf{x}, \mathbf{y})$, the SSIM function of Eq. (3). For $n = 4$, we have the function

$$\Sigma_4(\mathbf{x}, \mathbf{y}) = \frac{4s_{\mathbf{xxxy}} + 4s_{\mathbf{xyyy}} + \epsilon_4}{s_{\mathbf{xxxx}} + 6s_{\mathbf{xxyy}} + s_{\mathbf{yyyy}} + \epsilon_4}. \tag{44}$$

At this point it is helpful to recall that the construction of the function $\Sigma_n(\mathbf{x}, \mathbf{y})$ is based on the L^n norm in Eq. (37). The closeness of $\Sigma_n(\mathbf{x}, \mathbf{y})$ to 1 is related to the closeness of $\|\mathbf{x}_0 - \mathbf{y}_0\|_n^n$ to 0.

We now define the following family of associated distance functions,

$$\begin{aligned} T_n(\mathbf{x}, \mathbf{y}) &:= 1 - \Sigma_n(\mathbf{x}, \mathbf{y}) \\ &= \frac{\sum_{l \text{ even }} B_{nl} s_{n-l,l} - \sum_{l \text{ odd }} B_{nl} s_{n-l,l}}{\sum_{l \text{ even }} B_{nl} s_{n-l,l} + \epsilon_n}. \end{aligned} \tag{45}$$

From (37) and (40),

$$T_n(\mathbf{x}, \mathbf{y}) = \frac{\|\mathbf{x}_0 - \mathbf{y}_0\|_n^n}{\sum_{l \text{ even }} B_{nl} s_{n-l,l} + \epsilon_n}. \tag{46}$$

If $\mathbf{x} = \mathbf{y}$, then $T_n(\mathbf{x}, \mathbf{y}) = 0$. The $T_n(\mathbf{x}, \mathbf{y})$ functions are weighted L^n distances – to the nth power – between $\mathbf{x}_0$ and $\mathbf{y}_0$. The case $n = 2$ in Eq. (46) has been examined in the past [3, 4]:

$$T_2(\mathbf{x}, \mathbf{y}) = 1 - S_{2'}(\mathbf{x}, \mathbf{y}) = \frac{\|\mathbf{x}_0 - \mathbf{y}_0\|_2^2}{s_{\mathbf{xx}} + s_{\mathbf{yy}} + C_2} = \frac{\|\mathbf{x}_0 - \mathbf{y}_0\|_2^2}{\|\mathbf{x}_0\|_2^2 + \|\mathbf{y}_0\|_2^2 + C_2}. \tag{47}$$

It is an example of a *normalized metric* [1, 2].

One may now wish to consider the problem of finding best approximations, using these rational SSIM-like functions as the objective functions: Given an $\mathbf{x} \in \mathbb{R}^N$, an $M < N$ and and $n \geq 1$, find, if possible,

$$\mathbf{y}_{M, \Sigma_{2n}} = \arg \max_{\mathbf{z} \in A_M} \Sigma_{2n}(\mathbf{x}, \mathbf{z}) = \arg \min_{\mathbf{z} \in A_M} T_{2n}(\mathbf{x}, \mathbf{z}). \tag{48}$$

The case $n = 1$, which corresponds to the function $S_{2'}(\mathbf{x}, \mathbf{y})$, along with the equal-means condition coming from the function $S_1(\mathbf{x}, \mathbf{y})$, was analyzed in [2].

The cases $n \geq 2$ present a major challenge, however, since we may no longer exploit the orthogonality properties of the ϕ_k basis in the computation of the functions $s_{p,q}$ in Eq. (41). At this time, only a little progress has been made on this problem. For example, in the case $n = 2$, the generalized SSIM function Σ_4 is a complicated rational function of the unknown expansion coefficients c_k:

$$\Sigma_4(\mathbf{c}) = \frac{\sum_{n,m,p,q} [4a_n a_m a_p c_q + 4a_n c_m c_p c_q] P_{nmpq}}{\sum_{n,m,p,q} [a_n a_m a_p a_q + 6a_n a_m c_p c_q + c_n c_m c_p c_q] P_{nmpq}}, \tag{49}$$

where the summation limits are $1 \le m, n \le N - 1$ and $1 \le p, q \le M - 1$ and

$$P_{nmpq} = \sum_{k=1}^{N} \phi_{nk} \phi_{mk} \phi_{pk} \phi_{qk} . \qquad (50)$$

These coefficients are clearly basis-dependent. Moreover, $P_{nmpq} = P_{\mathcal{P}[nmpq]}$, where $\mathcal{P}$ denotes any permutation. Numerical experiments indicate that many of these coefficients are zero.

The stationarity conditions $\partial \Sigma_4 / \partial c_p = 0$, $1 \le p \le M - 1$, yield an enormously complicated set of coupled nonlinear equations in the c_p. In the special case that $M = N$, the solution of this system is $c_p = a_p$, as expected. When $M < N$, there exist solutions of the form $c_p = \alpha a_p$, as was found in in Eq. (21). The scaling coefficient α, however, satisfies a cubic equation in α^2. The coefficients of this equation are complicated functions of the Fourier coefficients a_k and the P_{nmpq}.

The fact that solutions of the form $c_p = \alpha a_p$ exist is interesting. They will, however, probably turn out to be of little use since they have the same basic form as those obtained from the S_2 and S_3 SSIM functions (along with S_1), which represents nothing more than another adjustment in the contrast.

In summary, we have introduced, and hopefully motivated, the idea of constructing higher-order rational SSIM-like functions. The method outlined above is the most straightforward one. It may well be useful to consider other methods which are based on higher-order statistics of images.

Acknowledgments. We gratefully acknowledge that this research has been supported in part by a Natural Sciences and Engineering Research Council of Canada (NSERC) Discovery Grant (ERV).

References

1. Brunet, D.: A Study of the Structural Similarity Image Quality Measure with Applications to Image Processing, Ph.D. Thesis, University of Waterloo (2010)
2. Brunet, D., Vrscay, E.R., Wang, Z.: On the mathematical properties of the structural similarity index. IEEE Trans. Image Proc. **21**(4), 1488–1499 (2012)
3. Brunet, D., Vrscay, E.R., Wang, Z.: Structural similarity-based approximation of signals and images using orthogonal bases. In: Campilho, A., Kamel, M. (eds.) ICIAR 2010. LNCS, vol. 6111, pp. 11–22. Springer, Heidelberg (2010)
4. Richter, T., Kim, K.J.: A MS-SSIM optimal JPEG 2000 encoder. In: Data Compression Conference, Snowbird, Utah, pp. 401–410 (March 2009)
5. Wainwright, M.J., Schwartz, O., Simoncelli, E.P.: Natural image statistics and divisive normalization: Modeling nonlinearity and adaptation in cortical neurons. In: Rao, R., Olshausen, B., Lewicki, M. (eds.) Probabilistic Models of the Brain: Perception and Neural Function, pp. 203–222. MIT Press (2002)
6. Wang, Z., Bovik, A.C.: Mean squared error: Love it or leave it? A new look at signal fidelity measures. IEEE Signal Proc. Mag. **26**(1), 98–117 (2009)
7. Wang, Z., Bovik, A.C., Sheikh, H.R., Simoncelli, E.P.: Image quality assessment: From error visibility to structural similarity. IEEE Trans. Image Proc. **13**(4), 600–612 (2004)
8. Wandell, B.A.: Foundations of Vision. Sinauer Publishers, Sunderland (1995)

2D Thinning Algorithms with Revised Endpixel Preservation

Gábor Németh[✉], Péter Kardos, and Kálmán Palágyi

Institute of Informatics, University of Szeged, Szeged, Hungary
{gnemeth,pkardos,palagyi}@inf.u-szeged.hu

Abstract. Skeletons are shape descriptors that summarize the general forms of objects. Thinning is a frequently applied technique for digital binary pictures to extract skeleton-like shape features. Most of the existing thinning algorithms preserve endpixels that provide relevant geometrical information relative to the shape of the objects. The drawback of this approach is that it may produce numerous unwanted side branches. In this paper we propose a novel strategy to overcome this problem. We present a thinning strategy, where some endpixels can be deleted.

Keywords: Shape represantation · Thinning · Endpixel revision

1 Introduction

Skeletons are region-based shape descriptors that summarize the general forms of objects. Skeletonization techniques are widely applied for shape representation, geometric and topological analysis, pattern recognition, and computer vision [10,11]. Thinning as an iterative object reduction is capable of producing both 2D skeleton-like shape features (i.e., topological kernels and centerlines) in a topology preserving way [3,10,11].

In each iteration step of a thinning process, some certain boundary pixels which do not hold relevant geometric information are deleted, and it is repeated until stability is reached. Some thinning algorithms aim to preserve the shape of objects by retaining so-called endpixels that provide relevant geometric information. Unfortunately, some extremities that appear in the current object boundary are endpixels and their preservation may lead to producing of numerous unwanted side branches. As a solution Németh et al. proposed a thinning strategy with iteration-level smoothing [6,7]. Furthermore, Bertrand and Aktouf [2] also proposed some new geometric constraints called *isthmus*es that yield less unwanted side branches.

In this work we propose a novel approach for revising endpixels. Moreover, we will show that this concept can be applied in any conventional thinning algorithms as well.

A. Campilho and M. Kamel (Eds.): ICIAR 2014, Part I, LNCS 8814, pp. 65–72, 2014.
DOI: 10.1007/978-3-319-11758-4_8

2   Basic Notions and Related Results

In this section we use the fundamental concepts of digital topology as reviewed by Kong and Rosenfeld [5].

We consider (8,4) *binary pictures* [5], where black pixels form 8-connected *objects*, and 4-connectivity is used for white pixels. It is assumed that the pictures to be thinned contain finitely many black pixels, hence we can store these pictures in finite arrays.

A black pixel is called a *border pixel* if it is 4-adjacent to at least one white pixel. A black pixel is said to be an *interior pixel* if it is not a border pixel.

A reduction can delete some black pixels (i.e., changes some black pixels to white ones). Parallel reductions may delete a set of pixels at a time. A reduction in 2D is not *topology preserving* if it disconnects or completely eliminates any black component, creates or merges white components [5]. A black pixel is a *simple pixel* if its deletion is a topology preserving reduction. From various characterizations of simple pixels, we recall the following one:

Theorem 1. [5] *Black pixel p is simple in an $(8, 4)$ picture, if p is a border pixel, and the black pixels that are 8-adjacent to p form exactly one 8-component.*

The simplicity of a pixel in $(8, 4)$ pictures is a local property, therefore it can be decided by investigating its 3×3 neighborhood. Although deletion of an individual simple pixel is a topology preserving reduction, simultaneous deletion of a set of simple pixels may alter the topology. Various sufficient conditions have been proposed for topology preserving parallel reductions [4,6,9]. In this paper we use the following one:

Theorem 2. [4] *A parallel reduction operation is topology preserving for $(8, 4)$ pictures if all of the following conditions hold:*

1. *Only simple pixels are deleted.*
2. *For any two 4-adjacent pixels p and q that are deleted, p is simple after q is deleted, or q is simple after the deletion of p.*
3. *No object contained in a 2×2 square is deleted completely.*

3   Thinning Algorithms with Revised Endpixels

Parallel thinning algorithms are composed of successive parallel reductions [3, 11]. *Endpixels* are simple pixels that hold some relevant geometrical information respect to the shape of objects [3]. The considered type of endpixels are preserved during the entire thinning process. Let us consider a phase of a thinning process (i.e., a parallel reduction) with deletion rule $\mathcal{R}$, see Alg. 1. We assume that deletion rule $\mathcal{R}$ fulfills all conditions of Theorem 2 (i.e., the reduction associated with $\mathcal{R}$ is topology preserving).

Now we introduce the *revised reduction* strategy. According to this concept the endpixel preservation is not determined at the moment of its detection.

Algorithm 1. CONVENTIONAL PARALLEL REDUCTION

1: INPUT: A // the array that stores the picture to be thinned
       $\mathcal{R}$ // deletion rule
       ε // the considered type of endpixels
2: OUTPUT: B // the array that stores the resulted picture
3: $B \leftarrow A$;
4: **for each** pixel (x, y) **do**
5:     **if** $A[x, y]$ is deletable by $\mathcal{R}$ and it is not an endpixel of type ε **then**
6:         $B[x, y] \leftarrow$ WHITE;

Endpixel deletion and further restoration (i.e., turning back a white pixel to black one) are also allowed. The general scheme of the revised reduction is sketched in Alg. 2, where a topology preserving deletion rule $\mathcal{R}$ is applied. Note that in this case we use labeled image arrays, where cells marked as BLACK, ENDPIXEL, DELEND1, DELEND2, RESTORED, and WHITE, respectively, means object pixels, endpixels, endpixels deleted in Step 1, endpixels deleted in Step 2, restored pixels, and white pixels. Pixels marked BLACK, ENDPIXEL, and RESTORED are black pixels, while the others are white.

Here we explain the three-step process of revised reduction:

Step 1 – Endpixel deletion: Those border pixels that fulfill the endpixel characterization of type ε are labeled as ENDPIXEL. All endpixels of type ε that satisfy the deletion rule $\mathcal{R}$ are deleted simultaneously. Deleted endpixels are labeled as DELEND1, and preserved endpixels ε are labeled as ENDPIXEL.

Step 2 – Shrinking: Border pixels that fulfill the endpixel characterization of type ε are labeled as ENDPIXEL. We apply a parallel reduction with deletion rule $\mathcal{R}$ again. Those pixels that are deleted in this step and have a label of ENDPIXEL are labeled as DELEND2.

Step 3 – Restoration: Let E be the set of pixels that are black or deleted endpixels and Y be the set of black pixels in the current picture. Any pixel p deleted in Step 2 is *restorable* if it is non-simple and non-isolated in $(N_8(p) \cap (Y \cup E)) \cup \{p\}$, where $N_8(p)$ denotes the set of pixels that are 8-adjacent to p. Each restorable endpixel changes to black pixel again and marked as a restored pixel. It is composed of the following steps:

a) Each restorable endpixel deleted in Step 2 is restored. Each restorable pixel p marked as DELEND2 is labeled as RESTORED.

b) Each restorable endpixel deleted in Step 1 is restored. Each restorable pixel p marked as DELEND1 is labeled as RESTORED.

For the efficient implementation of the algorithm, we propose to store labeled pixels in a linked list rather than in a temporary array T (see Alg. 2), similarly as described in [8]. In order to avoid repeated scannings of the picture array, we can use two linked lists: first we collect the border pixels to a linked list, and this list is updated during Steps 1 and 2. The second list is a LIFO data structure which is used for the deleted endpixels. It is necessary, since in Step 3 we try to restore

---

Algorithm 2. REVISED PARALLEL REDUCTION

1: INPUT: A // the array that stores a labeled picture
            $\mathcal{R}$ // deletion rule
            ε // the considered type of endpixels
2: OUTPUT: B // the array that stores the resulted picture
3: // —   Step 1: Endpixel reduction   —
4: $T \leftarrow A$;   // T is a temporary array
5: **for each** pixel $p = (x, y)$ **do**
6:     **if** $(A[x, y] = \text{BLACK})$ and $(p$ is an endpixel of type $\varepsilon)$ **then**
7:         $T[x, y] \leftarrow \text{ENDPIXEL}$;   // p is marked as an endpixel
8:         **if** p is deletable by $\mathcal{R}$ in picture stored in A **then**
9:             $T[x, y] \leftarrow \text{DELEND1}$;   // p is marked as a deleted endpixel
10: $B \leftarrow T$;
11: // —   Step 2: Shrinking   —
12: **for each** pixel $p = (x, y)$ **do**
13:     **if** $(B[x, y] = \text{BLACK or } B[x, y] = \text{ENDPIXEL})$ and $(p$ is deletable by $\mathcal{R})$ in
        picture stored in B **then**
14:         **if** p is an endpixel of type ε **then**
15:             $T[x, y] \leftarrow \text{DELEND2}$;   // p is marked as a deleted endpixel
16:         **else**
17:             $T[x, y] \leftarrow \text{WHITE}$;   // p is deleted
18: $B \leftarrow T$;
19: // —   Step 3(a): Restoration   —
20: **for each** pixel $p = (x, y)$ **do**
21:     **if** $(B[x, y] = \text{DELEND2})$ and $(p$ is a *restorable pixel*) **then**
22:         $T[x, y] \leftarrow \text{RESTORED}$;   // p is restored
23: // —   Step 3(b): Restoration   —
24: **for each** pixel $p = (x, y)$ **do**
25:     **if** $(B[x, y] = \text{DELEND1})$ and $(p$ is a *restorable pixel*) **then**
26:         $T[x, y] \leftarrow \text{RESTORED}$;   // p is restored
27: $B \leftarrow T$;
28: **return** B;

---

endpixels deleted in Step 2, then we continue the restoration with endpixels deleted in Step 1. The deletable pixel configurations and endpixel configurations can be stored in two precalculated look-up tables making the repeatable checking more efficient. Labels in arrays also increase the efficiency.

Let us see how the revised reduction works in an example depicted in Fig. 1. Here we present the same deletion rule and endpixel characterization with and without the revised endpixel strategy. Revised reduction works with any type of endpixels, but in this example we use the following characterization: a black pixel is an endpixel if it is 8-adjacent to at most two black pixels that are 4-adjacent to each other. Here we assume a deletion rule $\mathcal{R}$ that satisfies all conditons of Theorem 2.

Now we will show that revised reduction strategy is topology preserving.

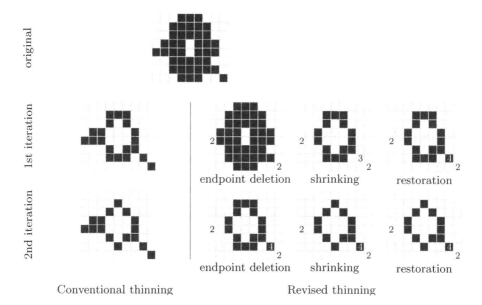

Fig. 1. Example of conventional fully parallel thinning (left) and revised fully parallel thinning (right). Labels "2","3", and "4" indicate deleted endpixels in Step 1 (i.e., DELEND1), deleted endpixels in Step 2 (i.e., DELEND2), and restored endpixels (i.e., RESTORED), respectively. Note that label "1" (i.e., ENDPIXEL) does not appear in this example, since each detected endpixel is deletable by the considered deletion rule $\mathcal{R}$ and their labels are changes to "2" in Step 1. Here an endpixel is considered as a black pixel being 8-adjacent to at most two 4-adjacent black pixels. The deletion rule $\mathcal{R}$ fulfills each condition of Therorem 2.

Theorem 3. *If the reduction with deletion rule $\mathcal{R}$ (see Alg. 1) is topology preserving, and endpixels of type ε are simple, then Alg. 2 also specifies a topology preserving reduction.*

Proof. We will show that three steps of revised reduction strategy (i.e., endpixel deletion, shrinking, and restoration) is topology preserving.

1. *Endpixel deletion:* Let us consider a set of endpixels that satisfy the conditions of deletion rule $\mathcal{R}$. Since deletion rule $\mathcal{R}$ fulfills the conditions of Theorem 2, deletion of any set of endpixels is topology preserving.
2. *Shrinking:* This phase is topology preserving, since $\mathcal{R}$ is assumed as a topology preserving reduction.
3. *Restoration:* We restore a set of deleted endpixels within two steps. The proof of topological correctness is similar in both cases. Each deleted endpixel p is deleted by a topology preserving deletion rule $\mathcal{R}$, hence any deleted pixel fulfills the conditions of Theorem 2. Let E be the set of detected endpixels and Y be the set of black pixels in the current picure. A pixel p is restored if it is non-simple and non-isolated in $(N_8(p) \cap (Y \cup E)) \cup \{p\}$ in the current

picture. According to this condition the restored pixel p does not form any new black component, since it can not be an isolated black pixel in $(N_8(p) \cap Y) \cup \{p\}$. On the other hand, each restored pixel was simple and border pixel at the moment of its deletion, hence restoration of any pixel does not merge black components, does not fill any cavity, or split any white component. Consequently, restoration of any restored pixel is a topology preserving addition.

Further advantageous property of the novel strategy is that the remaining skeletal branches are important indeed, since the environment of the restored endpixels contains some other detected endpixels (but they are already deleted and not restored). These properties are illustrated in Figs. 1-4.

Here we give a general scheme to convert any parallel thinning algorithm to its revised alternative. In some thinning algorithms, the considered type of endpixel is given explicitly [6], but usually only the deletion conditions are given and endpixel conditions stay hidden. If the cosidered type of endpixels ε is preserved by the given reduction as in Alg. 1, then Step 1 and Step 2 can be performed with no changes. However, if only the deletion condition are given, then we can express the endpixel conditions from non-deletable ones. Here we suppose that all endpixels are simple pixels. Those pixels that are simple but non-deletable by deletion rule $\mathcal{R}$ are considered as endpixels.

4 Results

Due to the lack of space here we present only three examples for applying the revised reduction strategy, but in a website[1] more results for various algorithms are presented. We implemented the often referred topology preserving parallel thinning algorithm proposed by Bernard and Manzanera (denoted by BM99) [1] and its revised alternatives (denoted by R-BM99). This algorithm does not define any endpixel characterization directly, hence the rules described at the end of the previous section are used for conversion. Results are depicted in Figs. 2-4.

Fig. 2. Centerlines produced by BM99 (left) and R-BM99 (right) superimposed on the 400×305 picture of an elephant

---

[1] http://www.inf.u-szeged.hu/~gnemeth/kutatas/revisedthinning2d/

Fig. 3. Centerlines produced by BM99 (left) and R-BM99 (right) superimposed on the 470 × 448 picture of a horse

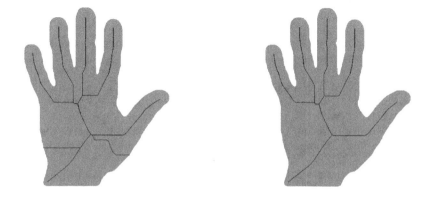

Fig. 4. Centerlines produced by BM99 (left) and R-BM99 (right) superimposed on the 500 × 560 picture of a hand

5   Conclusions

In this paper we propose a new strategy for thinning algorithms. Conventional thinning algorithms are composed of iterative object reductions where a set of pixels from the object boundary is deleted in each reduction phase. Some algorithms apply endpixel preservation as a geometric constraint. Since they may not delete the detected endpixels, some unwanted side branches can be produced. The new thinning strategy allows us to delete endpixels. Restored endpixels hold significant geometrical information respect to the shape, since some other endpixels are also detected in their neighborhood (but some of them are not restored). Furthermore, we gave a general scheme to apply revised reduction strategy in any conventional thinning algorithm. Thanks to the proposed strategy, thinning algorithms become less sensitive to boundary noise.

Acknowledgments. This work was supported by European Union and the State of Hungary, co-financed by the European Social Fund in the framework of TÁMOP 4.2.4. A/2-11-1-2012-0001 'National Excellence Program'.

References

1. Bernard, T., Manzanera, A.: Improved low complexity fully parallel thinning algorithm. In: 10th International Conference on Image Analysis and Processing (ICIP 1999), pp. 215–220 (1999)
2. Bertrand, G., Aktouf, Z.: A three-dimensional thinning algorithm using subfields. In: Vision Geometry III, vol. 2356, pp. 113–124. SPIE (1994)
3. Hall, R.: Parallel connectivity-preserving thinning algorithms. In: Kong, T.Y., Rosenfeld, A. (eds.) Topological Algorithms for Digital Image Processing, pp. 145–179. Elsevier Science B. V. (1996)
4. Kong, T.Y.: On topology preservation in 2-d and 3-d thinning. Int. Journal of Pattern Recognition and Artificial Intelligence **9**, 813–844 (1995)
5. Kong, T.Y., Rosenfeld, A.: Digital topology: Introduction and survey. Computer Vision, Graphics, and Image Processing **48**, 357–393 (1989)
6. Németh, G., Kardos, P., Palágyi, K.: 2D parallel thinning and shrinking based on sufficient conditions for topology preservation. Acta Cybernetica **20**, 125–144 (2011)
7. Németh, G., Kardos, P., Palágyi, K.: Thinning combined with iteration-by-iteration smoothing for 3D binary images. Graphical Models **73**, 335–345 (2011)
8. Palágyi, K., Németh, G., Kardos, P.: Topology preserving parallel 3D thinning algorithms. In: Brimkov, V.E., Barneva, R.P. (eds.) Digital Geometry Algorithms. Lecture Notes in Computational Vision and Biomechanics, vol. 2, ch. 6, pp. 165–188. Springer (2012)
9. Ronse, C.: Minimal test patterns for connectivity preservation in parallel thinning algorithms for binary digital images. Discrete Applied Mathematics **21**, 67–79 (1988)
10. Siddiqi, K., Pizer, S.M. (eds.): Medial Representations - Mathematics, Algorithms, and Applications. Series in Computational Imaging. Springer (2008)
11. Suen, C.Y., Wang, P.S.P. (eds.): Thinning Methodologies for Pattern Recognition. Series in Machine Perception and Artificial Intelligence, vol. 8. World Scientific (1994)

Sparse Representation

A New Landmark-Independent Tool for Quantifying and Characterizing Morphologic Variation

S.M. Rolfe[1]([⊠]), L.L. Cox[3,4], L.G. Shapiro[1,2], and T.C. Cox[3,4,5]

[1] Departments of Electrical Engineering, University of Washington, Seattle, USA
sara.rolfe@seattlechildrens.org
[2] Departments of Computer Science, University of Washington, Seattle, USA
[3] Departments of Pediatrics, University of Washington, Seattle, USA
[4] Seattle Children's Research Institute, Seattle, USA
[5] Department of Anatomy and Developmental Biology,
Monash University, Clayton, Australia

Abstract. This paper develops a landmark-independent, deformable-registration-based framework that can utilize 3D surface images generated by any multidimensional imaging modality. The framework provides compact representations of image differences that are used to assess and compare potentially biologically relevant changes in 3D shape. The utility and sensitivity of the tools developed in this work are demonstrated using similarity retrieval of shape changes in a normal developmental time series of chick embryos. The results motivate future use of these tools for defining trajectories of normal growth, aiding research into conditions causing disruptions to normal growth.

Keywords: Biomedical imaging · Feature extraction · Mathematical morphology · Image representation and models

1 Introduction

Quantitative assessment of morphologic variation is complicated by the difficulty of analyzing three-dimensional shape change. Traditional shape analysis methods generally rely on the use of landmarks manually placed on an image by an expert. These landmarks are chosen at locations that are easy to identify across specimens, such that the relative difference in position of the landmarks can be compared across individuals. However, the use of landmarks to analyze shape change has several drawbacks. Placement of landmark points is tedious and subject to variability. In addition, no shape information is provided about regions between landmark points, which may be scientifically interesting. For some biological structures, such as embryos, reliable identification of landmarks

© Springer International Publishing Switzerland 2014
A. Campilho and M. Kamel (Eds.): ICIAR 2014, Part I, LNCS 8814, pp. 75–83, 2014.
DOI: 10.1007/978-3-319-11758-4_9

can be challenging because of ill-defined boundaries between tissues and the rapid morphological changes that occur during development.

This paper develops a landmark-independent deformable-registration-based framework for quantifying morphologic change over a normal developmental time series of embryonic facial development. The development of these tools will help define and efficiently describe trajectories of normal growth and assist in understanding the pathogenetic mechanisms of conditions causing disruptions to normal growth. This tool is suited to the analysis of 3D images generated by any multidimensional imaging modality.

2   Related Work

In previous work of ours, deformable registration was used to produce a dense vector field describing the point correspondences between two images, from which features were extracted to find regions of organized differences that were biologically relevant. These methods were validated by detecting regions of difference on chick embryo images that were warped with known small magnitude deformations in regions critical to midfacial development [9] and used to quantify and characterize asymmetry in bilaterally paired structures [8].

Ashburner *et al.* [1] introduced the term deformation-based morphology to describe a method for analyzing group differences in brain shape using deformation vector fields, which arose as a spin-off from the problem of brain registration. Deformation morphology has also been applied to more standard morphometric measurement applications. Olafsdottir *et al.* presented a computational mouse atlas in [7] that represented the average of a group of normal, wild-type mice. Principal Component Analysis (PCA), Independent Component Analysis (ICA) and Sparse Principal Component Analysis (SPCA) were all applied to reduce the data dimensionality and find the modes of the deformation that could discriminate between groups.

3   Data and Preprocessing

The data set used for the experiments in this paper contains 16 optical projection tomography (OPT) images of normal chick embryos from 5 developmental stage groups. A representative image from each developmental stage is shown in figure 1. This is a complex data set due to natural variation within and subtlety of facial changes between normal developmental stage groups. A method based on geodesic active contours is used to extract a smooth, closed contour from each image for shape analysis [9].

4   Methodology

The goal of the method presented in this work is to assess pairwise morphological differences in normal chicken embryo faces over different developmental

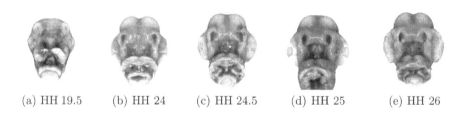

(a) HH 19.5   (b) HH 24   (c) HH 24.5   (d) HH 25   (e) HH 26

Fig. 1. Examples of midface development for each developmental (Hamburger and Hamilton [4]; HH) stage in the dataset

ages and provide a compact description of the shape change that can be used to quantify the similarity between two growth trajectories. A deformable registration is applied to assess local differences at every point between two aligned images. The deformable registration determines the spatial transform mapping points from a source to homologous points on an object in a target image. The output is a dense deformation vector field in which the vector at each point describes the spatial transformation between the source and target images at that point. For this application, a B-spline deformable transform using a mutual information metric was chosen, since it is widely applicable and computationally efficient [3].

To interpret the deformation vectors in a meaningful way, low-level features are extracted from the vector field and mid-level feature organization is calculated. For the experiments in this work two low-level features were selected as relevant: 1) *magnitude*, the deformation vector magnitude and 2) *normal angle*, the cosine distance between the deformation vector and the surface normal vector. One mid-level feature, *average neighborhood difference*, is also used in this application. This feature is defined as the difference between a vector field property at a point and its average value within a radius r.

4.1   Spatiogram Framework for Representing Image Differences

Once the features are extracted, we use a spatiogram-based framework to represent the feature values and their spatial distributions. This framework provides compact descriptions of the image differences described by the dense transformation vector field. Birchfield and Rangarajan [2] introduced the concept of a spatiogram as a histogram modified to include spatial information. Spatial information about the distribution of points assigned to each bin is retained by modeling it as a Gaussian distribution. Lyons [5] extends this by allowing multiple Gaussians per bin and defines the Mixture of Gaussian (MoG) spatiogram $h(b)$ as:

$$h(b) = < n_b, m_b = ((\alpha_{b1}, \mu_{b1}, \Sigma_{b1}), ..., (\alpha_{bm}, \mu_{bm}, \sigma_{bm})) >, \tag{1}$$

where n_b is the number of pixels with values assigned to the b, m_b is the number of mixtures in bin b, α_{bi} is the weight of the ith mixture and μ_{bi} and Σ_{bi} are the ith mixture parameters.

The distance between two MoG spatiograms is then defined as:

$$\rho^{mm}(h, h') = \sum_{b=1}^{|B|} \Psi_b^{mm} \sqrt{n_b n_b'}, \tag{2}$$

where the normalized spatial weighting term for bins with m mixtures is:

$$\Psi_b^{mm} = \sum_{i=1}^{m} \alpha_{bi} \sum_{j=1}^{m} \alpha_{bj} \eta_{bij} N(\mu_{bj}; \mu_{bi}', 2(\Sigma_{bi} + \Sigma_{bj}')) \tag{3}$$

and

$$\eta_{bij} = 2(2\pi)^{0.5} |\Sigma_{bj} \Sigma_{bi}'|^{0.25}. \tag{4}$$

In this formulation, the number of Gaussians, m, is required to be fixed for the bins being compared. Spatiograms have been primarily used for tracking color patches in video images, and for these applications a single or fixed number of Gaussians is sufficient [5]. In our application, where the goal is a description of more complex regions, this approach could overgeneralize the feature descriptions. To allow the number of Gaussians in a bin to be assigned based on information about the spatial distribution of the contents of that bin, a connected components algorithm was used to estimate the number of spatially separate distributions in a bin and initialize the number of distributions. A new variable Mixture of Gaussians metric is now introduced that accommodates this flexibility in the number of Gaussians per bin. The one-directional distance between two MoG spatiograms h and h' is defined as:

$$d^{mn}(h, h') = \sum_{b=1}^{|B|} \Psi_b^{mn} \sqrt{n_b n_b'}, \tag{5}$$

where

$$\Psi_b^{mn} = \sum_{i=1}^{m} \alpha_{bi} \max_{j \in [n]} (\eta_{bij} N(\mu_{bj}; \mu_{bi}', 2(\Sigma_{bi} + \Sigma_{bj}'))), \tag{6}$$

m and n are the respective numbers of distributions, $[n] = [1, ..., n]$, and

$$\eta_{bij} = 2(2\pi)^{0.5} |\Sigma_{bi} \Sigma_{bj}'|^{0.25}. \tag{7}$$

To achieve a symmetric distance measure, the total distance between h and h' is defined as:

$$\rho^{mn}(h, h') = \frac{(d^{mn}(h, h') + d^{mn}(h', h))}{2}. \tag{8}$$

This distance metric is symmetric, normalized over the mixture components, and has a maximum value of $\rho(h, h') = 1$ when $h' = h$.

MoG spatiograms are used in the experiments in this paper to represent each low-level and mid-level feature type describing the difference between two images. High-level features of the MoG spatiogram will quantify characteristics of the image difference and the MoG spatiogram metric will define the similarity between two shape change trajectories.

The MoG spatiogram distance metric allows for efficient combination of multiple feature types. Since the spatiogram distances for each feature are normalized, they can be combined using the weighted mean:

$$\hat{\rho}^{mn}(h, h') = \sum_{i=1}^{f} w_i \rho_i^{mn}(h, h'), \tag{9}$$

where

$$\sum_{i=1}^{f} w_i = 1, \tag{10}$$

f is the number of feature types, and $\rho_i^{mn}(h, h')$ is the MoG spatiogram distance for feature type i. The weights allow for optional inclusion of prior knowledge about the relative importance of the feature types for a specific application. Without prior knowledge, w_i is set to $1/f$ and the weighted mean reduces to:

$$\hat{\rho}^{mn}(h, h') = \frac{1}{f} \sum_{i=1}^{f} \rho_i^{mn}(h, h'). \tag{11}$$

5   Experiments

The goal of these tools is to provide quantitative information about shape differences which are not currently known, such as differences between normal and abnormal growth, or differences within a developmental stage. In this paper, these tools are demonstrated on known differences due to embryonic developmental age to motivate their future use to accomplish this goal.

5.1   Retrieval of Similar Normal Growth Trajectories

Using the MoG spatiogram representation of shape difference features and new spatiogram distance measure, similarity between two difference images can be expressed using a single distance value. These distance values can be used to perform similarity-based retrieval of difference images. Results are retrieved from the database by ranking them in order of the spatiogram distance from the query.

In this experiment, difference images representing the trajectory of normal growth between two developmental stages were used as queries to find similar growth trajectories. It is expected that a query representing a growth trajectory between two stages would return other growth trajectories between the same two stages. In this experiment a representative template image was selected for a developmental stage and the MoG spatiograms describing the pairwise difference between the template image and each embryo in the data set were obtained. The normal angle and magnitude features from the midface region were used for retrieval and were weighted equally. An example of the feature heat maps for one such query and the top ranking results is shown in figure 2, where the features from the top ranked results are visually similar to the query image features, and represents a transition between the same stages as the query.

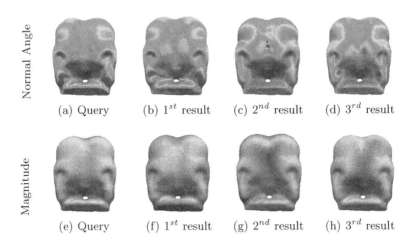

(a) Query   (b) 1st result   (c) 2nd result   (d) 3rd result

(e) Query   (f) 1st result   (g) 2nd result   (h) 3rd result

Fig. 2. Normal angle and magnitude heat maps for a sample query and the 3 top ranked results. The sample query and all 3 results represent growth trajectories between HH 24 and HH 26. Only the midface region is shown.

Each of the resulting difference images was used as a separate query, and the success of each query was scored using the average normalized rank of the relevant difference images [6]. In this case, the relevant difference images are those representing a trajectory of growth between the same two stages as the query. The evaluation score for a query q is defined as:

$$score(q) = \frac{1}{N \cdot N_{rel}} \left(\sum_{i=1}^{N_{rel}} R_i - \frac{N_{rel}(N_{rel}+1)}{2} \right) \tag{12}$$

where N is the number of objects in the database, N_{rel} is the number of database objects that are relevant to the query object q, and R_i is the rank assigned to the ith relevant object. The evaluation score ranges from 0 to 1, where 0 is the best score.

The overall average evaluation score for all the queries in this experiment was 0.049. This is very close to the ideal score of 0, validating the methods used.

5.2 Retrieval of Normal Average Growth Trajectories

To summarize the differences between developmental stages, an average growth trajectory was defined as the average transformation of all embryos from one developmental stage to a representative template image from a second stage.

Representative templates were chosen over the use of average images to eliminate concerns about the biological relevance of average images in this application where the variation within groups is not well documented. These average growth trajectories are helpful in providing a visual representation of the average feature values that can be quickly and easily interpreted by researchers. In addition, statistics about the group, such as the standard deviation of the features, can be plotted on the image surface so any within-group variation can be visualized. An example of the average growth trajectory feature maps and their standard deviation maps is shown in figure 3. The average growth trajectories in figure 3 are between HH 24 and HH 26 and can be compared to individual growth trajectories between these two stages shown in figure 2.

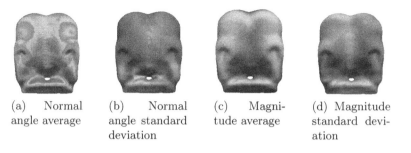

(a)   Normal angle average

(b)   Normal angle standard deviation

(c)   Magnitude average

(d) Magnitude standard deviation

Fig. 3. Average and standard deviation of growth trajectory features between HH 24 and HH 26

In addition to providing a useful visual representation, the average growth trajectories can be used for retrieval. The second retrieval experiment demonstrates that individual growth trajectories between two stages are more similar to the average growth trajectory between the same two stages than to any other average growth trajectory. To show this, an average growth trajectory was generated for every possible transition between two developmental stages in the data set. Hold-out averages excluding the query were generated where relevant. Transitions between the largest group, stage 26, and all other groups were chosen for the queries, since the average growth trajectories have the most statistical significance for larger groups. The retrievals were then scored using the evaluation score defined in equation 12. In this experiment, the relevant retrieval was the correct average growth trajectory. The overall average evaluation score for the retrievals in this experiment was 0.041, which is very close to the ideal value of 0 for a perfect retrieval.

6   Conclusion

The results from the retrieval experiments summarized in table 1 motivate the use of the method developed in this paper for compactly describing and comparing image differences. In the future they will be applied to image differences that are not well known such as those within developmental stages and those due to abnormal growth. For example, figure 4 shows magnitude heat maps describing the difference between 1) a normal chick embryo and a perfectly symmetric embryo of the same age in figure 4(a) and 2) a chick embryo affected by a unilateral facial defect and a perfectly symmetric chick embryo of the same age in figure 4(b). The affected chick embryo has higher magnitude values that are localized to the left side of the face, where the defect impacts normal development. In future work, this framework will be demonstrated for the classification of affected specimens, description of differences from normal growth, and retrieval of specimens with similar defects.

Table 1. Summary of Experimental Results

Retrieval Type	Average Retrieval Score
Similar growth trajectories	0.049
Relevant average growth trajectory	0.041

(a) Difference between control and symmetric images

(b) Difference between affected and symmetric images

Fig. 4. Magnitude heat maps for a control and a chick embryo displaying a facial cleft, each warped to a perfectly symmetric image

Acknowledgments. We thank Tina Fu for optical projection tomography. This research was supported by NIH/NIDCR grants 1U01DE020050 (PI: L Shapiro) and DE022561 (PI: T Cox), and the Laurel Foundation (PI: T Cox).

References

1. Ashburner, J., Hutton, C., Frackowiak, R., Johnsrude, I., Price, C., Friston, K.: Identifying global anatomical differences: deformation-based morphometry. Human Brain Mapping **6**(5-6), 348–357 (1998)
2. Birchfield, S.T., Rangarajan, S.: Spatiograms versus histograms for region-based tracking. In: IEEE Computer Society Conference on Computer Vision and Pattern Recognition, CVPR 2005, vol. 2, pp. 1158–1163. IEEE (2005)
3. Crum, W.R., Hartkens, T., Hill, D.L.G.: Non-rigid image registration: theory and practice. British Journal of Radiology **77**(Special Issue 2), S140 (2004)

4. Hamburger, V., Hamilton, H.L.: A series of normal stages in the development of the chick embryo. Journal of Morphology **88**(1), 49–92 (1951)
5. Lyons, D.M.: Sharing landmark information using mixture of gaussian terrain spatiograms. In: Proceedings of the 2009 IEEE/RSJ International Conference on Intelligent Robots and Systems, pp. 5603–5608. IEEE Press (2009)
6. Müller, H., Marchand-Maillet, S., Pun, T.: The truth about corel - evaluation in image retrieval. In: Lew, M., Sebe, N., Eakins, J.P. (eds.) CIVR 2002. LNCS, vol. 2383, pp. 38–49. Springer, Heidelberg (2002)
7. Ólafsdóttir, H., Darvann, T.A., Hermann, N.V., Oubel, E., Ersboll, B.K., Frangi, A.F., Larsen, P., Perlyn, C.A., Morriss-Kay, G.M., Kreiborg, S.: Computational mouse atlases and their application to automatic assessment of craniofacial dysmorphology caused by the crouzon mutation fgfr2c342y. Journal of Anatomy **211**(1), 37–52 (2007)
8. Rolfe, S.M., Camci, E.D., Mercan, E., Shapiro, L.G., Cox, T.C.: A new tool for quantifying and characterizing asymmetry in bilaterally paired structures. In: 2013 35th Annual International Conference of the IEEE Engineering in Medicine and Biology Society (EMBC), pp. 2364–2367. IEEE (2013)
9. Rolfe, S.M., Shapiro, L.G., Cox, T.C., Maga, A.M., Cox, L.L.: A landmark-free framework for the detection and description of shape differences in embryos. In: 2011 Annual International Conference of the IEEE Engineering in Medicine and Biology Society, EMBC, pp. 5153–5156. IEEE (2011)

Low Light Image Enhancement via Sparse Representations

Konstantina Fotiadou$^{(\boxtimes)}$, Grigorios Tsagkatakis, and Panagiotis Tsakalides

Institute of Computer Science, Foundation for Research and Technology - Hellas
(FORTH-ICS), Department of Computer Science, University of Crete,
Heraklion, Crete, Greece
{kfot,greg,tsakalid}@ics.forth.gr

Abstract. Enhancing the quality of low light images is a critical processing function both from an aesthetics and an information extraction point of view. This work proposes a novel approach for enhancing images captured under low illumination conditions based on the mathematical framework of Sparse Representations. In our model, we utilize the sparse representation of low light image patches in an appropriate dictionary to approximate the corresponding day-time images. We consider two dictionaries; a *night dictionary* for low light conditions and a *day dictionary* for well illuminated conditions. To approximate the generation of low and high illumination image pairs, we generated the day dictionary from patches taken from well exposed images, while the night dictionary is created by extracting appropriate features from under exposed image patches. Experimental results suggest that the proposed scheme is able to accurately estimate a well illuminated image given a low-illumination version. The effectiveness of our system is evaluated by comparisons against ground truth images while compared to other methods for image night context enhancement, our system achieves better results both quantitatively as well as qualitatively.

Keywords: De-nighting · Contrast enhancement · Sparse representations

1 Introduction

Recently, the demand for the enhancement of low light images has grown tremendously. Images captured during day-time exhibit higher dynamic range, better quality and can be useful for extracting contextual information. Night-time images on the other hand, are characterized by low intensities and usually suffer from the existence of severe noise due to the very small signal power. The aim

This work was funded by the IAPP CS-ORION (PIAP-GA-2009-251605) grant within 7th Framework Program of the European Community.

© Springer International Publishing Switzerland 2014
A. Campilho and M. Kamel (Eds.): ICIAR 2014, Part I, LNCS 8814, pp. 84–93, 2014.
DOI: 10.1007/978-3-319-11758-4_10

of *image de-nighting* techniques is to increase the contrast and the sharpness of an image, in order to improve its visual appearance and support the extraction of valuable information, that can be used for analysis, detection and segmentation purposes. As a result, image de-nighting operators have attracted broad interests recently, partially due to the numerous applications that require night image enhancement including surveillance, astronomical and medical imaging.

Early approaches in the problem relied on Histogram Equalization (HE) techniques [2],[3]. HE is a relatively simplistic strategy which usually introduces multiple artifacts and leads to significant loss of image details. Authors in [4] demonstrated a Colour Estimation Model (CEM) based on a parameter that controls the range of the image colors on the RGB-scale. Dong *et al.* [5] proposed an algorithm for the enhancement of low-light videos, that inverts the dark input frames and then performs a de-hazing algorithm to improve the quality of the low light images. Another night content enhancement technique, was proposed in [6], where an image is separated into the reflectance and the illuminant component, according to the *retinex theory*, and the enhanced image is generated from the reconstruction of the reflectance component. Due to the challenges associated with the separation of the two components, errors that occur during this process lead to the introduction of artifacts in the reconstructed image. Recently, in [8] a gradient domain technique was proposed, where the authors estimate the mixed gradient field of the intensities from multiple night-time, along with their correspondent day-time images.

Unlike other approaches, our method relies on a single image for the estimation of the enhanced image, using a sparse signal representation technique. Particularly, sparsity suggests that a high-frequency signal can be accurately recovered from its corresponding low-frequency representation. Many ill-posed and inverse problems such as image super-resolution and image denoising [1, 14] introduce the sparsity assumption in the form of a prior, that is able to distinguish the ground truth image content from the degradation effects. Motivated by these approaches, this paper focuses on the problem of recovering the illuminated and enhanced version of a given low-light image, using the sparsity constraint as prior knowledge. We work on image patch pairs sampled from images captured under different exposure times, which are used as proxies to day and night time images. Furthermore, we consider two dictionaries (night and day) for our representation. The dark, under-exposed image patches are used for the creation of the night dictionary $\mathbf{D}_n$, while the corresponding better exposed image patches (day patches) are used for the creation of the day dictionary, $\mathbf{D}_d$. The main purpose of this work, is to extract the sparse representation of a night image patch subject to $\mathbf{D}_n$ and directly use it for the reconstruction of corresponding day image patch in terms of $\mathbf{D}_d$. Our method can be applied for the enhancement of generic images that were captured under poor-illumination conditions. The evaluation of our results are accomplished using both quantitative metrics and visual quality.

The rest of the paper is organized as follows. Section 2, provides an overview of the Sparse Representations (SR) framework and then extensively presents our proposed method. Section 3, presents the results on performance of our and state-of-the-art methods, while our conclusions are given in Section 4.

2   Image De-nighting Using Sparsity

2.1   Sparse Representations Framework

This paper focuses on the problem of recovering the well illuminated version of a given low-intensity image. Our approach is patch-based and we assume that image patches can be represented as linear combinations of elements from an over-complete dictionary. Formally, given a signal $\mathbf{y} \in \mathbb{R}^M$ extracted from an image patch and a dictionary $\mathbf{D}$, the challenge is to find a vector $\mathbf{x} \in \mathbb{R}^N$ satisfying the relationship: $\mathbf{y} = \mathbf{D}\mathbf{x}$. When the dictionary is overcomplete, *i.e.* $M \ll N$, this problem admits infinite solutions. Motivated by the SR framework, we search for a vector $\mathbf{x}$ that optimizes a certain sparsity measure. An initial approach to this problem is the minimization of the general l_p-norm. In this case the minimization problem becomes:

$$\hat{\mathbf{x}} = \arg \min_{\mathbf{x}} ||\mathbf{x}||_p \quad \text{subject to} \quad ||\mathbf{D}\mathbf{x} - \mathbf{y}||_2 \leq \epsilon \tag{1}$$

where $||\mathbf{x}||_p = (\sum_i |\mathbf{x}_i|^p)^{1/p}$ and ϵ is a threshold on the approximation error. When $p = 0$, the sparsity of the coefficient vector $\mathbf{x}$, is measured by the non-zero counting pseudo-norm, l_0. Although, the l_0-norm is the optimal choice for the recovery of the sparse vector $\mathbf{x}$, it leads to an NP-hard problem. Fortunately, the theory of SR suggests that one can replace the l_0-norm with the l_1-norm, leading to following optimization problem:

$$\min ||\mathbf{x}||_1 \quad \text{subject to} \quad ||\mathbf{D}\mathbf{x} - \mathbf{y}||_2 \leq \epsilon, \tag{2}$$

where $||x||_1 = \sum_i |x_i|$ is the l_1-norm. This linear regression of the l_1-norm is denoted as the LASSO problem [12]. Furthermore, one can add the non-negative constraint $x \geq 0$ in order to account for the additive nature of the features we utilize in our representations.

2.2   Dictionary Model

A crucial aspect of the above reconstruction is the proper selection of the dictionary $\mathbf{D}$, where we seek a dictionary which can sparsify the input data. In general, dictionaries can be analytic or trained [13]. Analytic dictionaries arise from an existing family of transforms, such as histograms, DCT, curvelets, contourlets, wavelets and so on. On the other hand, trained dictionaries are learned from a collection of training data. Although this approach can offer various benefits due to the selection of the most representative examples, it is very computationally expensive. A variant of the later relies on the creation of the dictionary by randomly selecting patches extracted from images that exhibit the same statistical nature (training images). In our setting, we follow the latter approach, working with two coupled dictionaries, $\mathbf{D}_n$ corresponding to the night-time image patches and $\mathbf{D}_d$, for the day-time image patches. At the training phase, we utilized multiple registered pairs of day-time and their corresponding night-time images for patch extraction. As a consequence, corresponding elements of the two dictionaries encode the same part of the scheme but at different illumination conditions and can thus serve for the estimation of the high intensity image from the low intensity one.

Feature Selection. The features computed from the night-time image patches, have to ensure that the sparse coefficients will have an accurate representation in the appropriate dictionary. State-of-the-art methods use different features for the representation of the degraded components. For instance, Raskar *et al.* [8] reconstructed the final image by integrating first order gradients of the input images, by creating a mixed gradient field. Yang *et al.* [1] used first and second order gradients to represent the low-resolution images. In our representation, for each night-time image patch, we extract the Cumulative Histograms(CH), as features, due to their representation capabilities of varying illuminations conditions. The intensity histogram of a low-illumination patch y_n expresses a discrete representation of the probability density function for the pixel intensities, and may be expressed as:

$$P_{y_n(x,y)}(v) = P(y_n(x,y) = v) = \frac{n_v}{N} \tag{3}$$

where, where $0 \le v \le 255$ and N is the total number of pixels in the image patch. Then, the CH of each night-time patch, is measured by summing up the histogram values from gray level 0 to V:

$$CH_{y_n(x,y))} = \sum_{i=0}^{V} P_{y_n(x,y)}(i) \tag{4}$$

For the day-time dictionary $\mathbf{D}_d$, we utilized normalized pixel intensities for the reconstruction since they offer a natural approach in modeling the day-time images.

2.3   Image Reconstruction

Given a low-light version of the scene $\mathbf{Y}$, our task is to generate the corresponding illuminated image $\mathbf{X}$. According to theory of SR the enhanced image patch $\mathbf{x}$ can be sparsely represented in an over-complete dictionary $\mathbf{D}_d$ created from day-time patches according to:

$$\mathbf{x} = \mathbf{D}_d\mathbf{w}, \ \mathbf{w} \in \mathbb{R}^K \tag{5}$$

The key insight of our methods is that the sparse representations vector $\mathbf{w}$ can be accurately estimated from low-illumination patches extracted from the input image $\mathbf{Y}$, by utilizing the night-time dictionary $\mathbf{D}_n$. By jointly constructing the two dictionaries $\mathbf{D}_d$ and $\mathbf{D}_n$, we expect to observe the same sparse representations for each patch pair of night-time and day-time images. For each low-illumination image patch, we find a sparse representation with respect to $\mathbf{D}_n$. Then, in order to extract the illuminated image patch $\mathbf{x}$ we utilize the sparse coefficients with the day-time dictionary $\mathbf{D}_d$. Since the dictionary $\mathbf{D}_n$ is overcomplete, the equation is under-determined for the unknown coefficients $\mathbf{w}$. The equivalent l_1-minimization problem is thus given by:

$$\min ||\mathbf{w}||_1 \quad \text{s.t} \quad ||\mathbf{D}_n\mathbf{w} - \mathbf{y}||_2 \leq \epsilon \quad \text{and} \quad \mathbf{w} \geq 0 \tag{6}$$

Given the optimal sparse coefficients $\mathbf{w}^*$, the reconstructed illuminated image patch becomes:

$$\mathbf{x} = \mathbf{D}_d\mathbf{w}^* \tag{7}$$

In order to enforce the compatibility between adjacent patches, we process the input image's patches starting from the upper-left corner with a small overlapping factor in each direction. Due to this fact, the reconstructed image appears with a slight blurring effect. In order to overcome this issue, we perform a back-projection technique, motivated by Yang *et al.* [1]. The main idea is to project the day-time image $\mathbf{X}_0$ at the solution space $\mathbf{Y} = a\mathbf{HX}$, where $\mathbf{Y}$ is a dark and blurred version of the day-time image $\mathbf{X}$, $\mathbf{H}$ is an operator matrix that represents the blurring effect, a low pass Gaussian filter in our case, and a is a small parameter that uniformly changes the illumination of the target day-time image $\mathbf{X}$. The value of a was set manually after cross validation in order to achieve the best possible result. This operation can be formulated as:

$$\mathbf{X}^* = \arg \min_{\mathbf{X}} ||a H\mathbf{X} - \mathbf{Y}||_2 + c||\mathbf{X} - \mathbf{X}_0||_2, \tag{8}$$

which can be solved using by gradient descent technique.

3   Experimental Results

3.1   Algorithmic Details

To validate the proposed approach, a series of experiments was conducted using data from a High Dynamic Range (HDR) image dataset [9]. We selected HDR registered images in our experiments motivated by the approximation of a low intensity night image by an image captured with a very short exposure time and a daytime image by a well exposed one. The number of atoms for both the day-time, $\mathbf{D}_d$ and night-time, $\mathbf{D}_n$ dictionaries was set to 550. For the creation of the day-time dictionary, the best performance is achieved using 3x3 patch size, with 1 overlapping factor between adjacent patches.

Our method can be applied on both gray-scale and color images. When color images are processed, instead of processing each color channel separately, we transform the image into the HSV color space and apply our night context enhancement technique to the V channel only. As a pre-processing step, we normalize the dark image by dividing with the mean value of the three components (HSV). In order to evaluate the results of the proposed scheme, we use both quality measures and visual perception. The reconstruction quality is measured via the Structural Similarity Image Quality Index (SSIM)[15], between the illuminated ground-truth image and the reconstructed image.

3.2   Evaluation of the Results

Fig. 1 serves as a motivation of our work, depicting a low light (left) and the reconstructed well illuminated (right) image pair along with the corresponding histograms where we observe that the histogram of the reconstructed image is a shifted and distributed version of the original image's histogram.

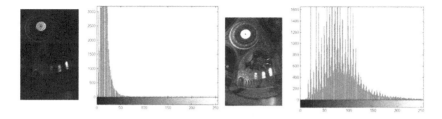

Fig. 1. Memorial dataset:(left) Input dark image along with its histogram, (right) Reconstructed illuminated image with its histogram

We proceed by showing results from experimental scenes to validate our approach. The proposed algorithm is compared against state-of-the-art image de-nighting methods including the Histogram Equalization method (HE) [2], serving as a baseline processing module,[3], the method proposed by Dong *et al.* [5] for enhancement of low-light video frames, and Color Estimation Model (CEM) [4]. Unlike our method, the other methods under consideration, do not include a dictionary training phase. In order to achieve a fair comparison, we perform the same pre-processing step to all methods, even it is not part of their algorithms. Figs. 2-7, depict the reconstruction achieved by our algorithm when applied to natural scenes and compared to the previously described methods.

In Fig. 2 one can visualize the performance of the above described methods on the Memorial dataset. We observe that all methods enhance and illuminate the dark test image, but our algorithm produces results closer to the ground truth image. In terms of SSIM [15], our reconstruction achieves better similarity index compared to the other approaches. Figs. 3 and 4, demonstrate the ability of our algorithm to enhance the office and the office very dark datasets, without adding noise or introducing saturation effects, compared to the other methods, which introduce significant noise to the reconstructed image. Furthermore, in Fig. 5,

Fig. 2. Memorial dataset:(Top left) Original Image, (Top middle) Reference Image, (Top right) Dong's method, (Bottom left) HE, (Bottom middle) CEM, (Bottom right) Proposed method

Fig. 3. Office dataset: (Top left) Original Image, (Top middle) Reference Image, (Top right) Dong's method, (Bottom left) HE, (Bottom middle) CEM, (Bottom right) Proposed method

one can notice the visible distortions caused by all three comparable state-of-the-art methods while the proposed method enhances the UWMech image and reveals sufficient information on the dark parts, without amplifying the noise.

Another example of our reconstruction is presented in Fig. 6. Dong's enhancement approach leads to significant loss of details (especially on the image's background and on the baby's face), due to the saturation of the image pixels. HE enhancement, also leads to the introduction of artifacts, artificial colours (especially on the image's background) and to the amplification of noise. CEM model has provided a noticeable improvement at the image's contrast, but the resulted

Fig. 4. Office very dark dataset: (Top left) Original Image, (Top middle) Reference Image, (Top right) Dong's method, (Bottom left) HE, (Bottom middle) CEM, (Bottom right) Proposed method

Fig. 5. UWMechDept dataset: (Top left) Original Image, (Top middle) Reference Image, (Top right) Dong's method, (Bottom left) HE, (Bottom middle) CEM, (Bottom right) Proposed method

Fig. 6. Baby on grass dataset:(Top left) Original Image, (Top middle) Reference Image, (Top right) Dong's method, (Bottom left) HE, (Bottom middle) CEM, (Bottom right) Proposed method

Fig. 7. Piano man dataset: (Top left) Original Image, (Top middle) Reference Image, (Top right) Dong's method, (Bottom left) HE, (Bottom middle) CEM, (Bottom right) Proposed method

image is not close to the ground truth ones. We observe that the proposed scheme, reveals sufficient information in the dark parts, without illuminating the already sufficiently illuminated parts.

Finally, Fig. 7 depicts the results of the proposed reconstruction against the compared methods, to the Piano-man dataset. We observe that both HE and Dong's method introduce significant saturation effects on the resulting image. CEM's reconstruction in this case is good and the method does not enhance any artifacts or noise. Our method is able to reconstruct the details present in the dark regions of the image and produces an artifact-free result, very close to the ground truth image.

The quantitative results are presented in Table 1. We are able to confirm that our method achieves better results in the terms of the SSIM [15] and visual perception compared to other three state-of-the-art methods.

Table 1. Quality (SSIM [15]) measurements of the enhancement methods

Test image	Memorial	Office	Office very dark	UWMech	Baby	Piano
Dong's [5]	0.5354	0.4116	0.6518	0.2922	0.2973	0.3821
HE [2]	0.5830	0.5654	0.4140	0.2182	0.3014	0.5451
CEM [4]	0.7497	0.7676	0.7314	0.4156	0.5461	0.8011
Proposed	**0.8579**	**0.9498**	**0.8666**	**0.6212**	**0.6504**	**0.8520**

4   Discussion and Future Work

This paper introduced a novel approach for the enhancement of low illumination images. We considered a sparse signal representation approach based on the joint creation of the low and high illumination dictionaries, sampled for appropriate image pairs. The proposed scheme, successfully extracts the necessary information from an image, by illuminating the dark regions, without causing artifacts or saturation effects. Future work includes the investigation of alternative feature operators that could further increase the reconstruction quality.

References

1. Yang, J., Wright, J., Huang, T., Ma, Y.: Image Super-Resolution Via Sparse Representations. IEEE Trans. on Image Processing **19**(11), 2861–2873 (2010)
2. Kim, Y.T.: Contrast Enhancement Using Brightness Preserving Bi-Histogram Equalization. IEEE Trans. Consumer Electronics **43**(1), 1–8 (1997)
3. Kaur, M., Kaur, J., Kaur, J.: Survey of Contrast Enhancement Techniques based on Histogram Equalization. Int. Journal of Advanced Computer Science and Applications (IJACSA) **2**(7) (2011)
4. Fu, H., Ma, H., Wu, S.: Night Removal by Color Estimation and Sparse Representations. In: 21st Int. Conference on Pattern Recognition, ICPR 2012, Tsukuba, Japan, pp. 3656–3659 (2012)
5. Dong, X., Pang, Y., Wen, J., Wang, G., Li, W., Gao, Y., Yang, S.: A fast efficient algorithm for enhancement of low lighting video. Journal of Information and Computational Science **7**(10), 2021–2030 (2010)
6. Yamasaki, A., Takauji, H., Kaneko, S., Kanade, T., Ohki, H.: Denighting: Enhancement of Nighttime Images for a Surveillance Camera. In: 19th Int. Conference on Pattern Recognition (ICPR 2008) (2008)
7. Loza, A., Bull, D., Hill, P., Achim, A.: Automatic contrast enhancement of low-light images based on local statistics of wavelet coefficients. Digital Signal Processing **23**(6), 1856–1866 (2013)
8. Raskar, R., Ilie, A., Yu, J.: Image fusion for context enhancement and video surrealism. In: 3rd Int. Symposium on Non-photorealistic Animation and Rendering, New York, pp. 85–152 (2004)
9. Sen, P., Khademi Kalantari, N., Yaesoubi, M., Darabi, S., Goldman, D., Shechtman, E.: Robust Patch-Based HDR Reconstruction of Dynamic Scenes. ACM Trans. on Graphics (TOG). SIGGRAPH Asian. **31**(6), Art. 203 (2012) (Technical paper)
10. Shan, Q., Jia, J., Brown, M.: Globally Optimized Linear Windowed Tone-Mapping. IEEE Trans. on Visualization and Computer Graphics **16** (2010)
11. Elad, M.: Sparse and Redundant Representations: From Theory to Applications in Signal and Image Processing. Springer (2010)
12. Tibshirani, R.: Regression Shrinkage and Selection via the Lasso. Journal of the Royal Statistical Society **58**(1), 267–288 (1996)
13. Aharon, M., Elad, M., Bruckstein, A., Katz, Y.: K-SVD: An Algorithm for Designing of Overcomplete Dictionaries for Sparse Representations. IEEE Trans. on Signal Processing **54**(11), 4311–4322 (2006)
14. Elad, M., Aharon, M.: Image denoising via sparse and redundant representations over learned dictionaries. IEEE Trans. Image Processing **15**(12), 3736–3745 (2006)
15. Wang, Z., Bovik, A., Sheikh, H., Simoncelli, E.: Image Quality Assessment: From Error Visibility to Structural Similarity. IEEE Trans. on Image Processing **13**(4), 600–612 (2004)

Incremental and Multi-feature Tensor Subspace Learning Applied for Background Modeling and Subtraction

Andrews Sobral[1]([✉]), Christopher G. Baker[3],
Thierry Bouwmans[2], and El-hadi Zahzah[1]

[1] Laboratoire L3I, Université de La Rochelle, 17000 La Rochelle, France
andrewssobral@gmail.com
[2] Laboratoire MIA, Université de La Rochelle, 17000 La Rochelle, France
[3] Computer Sciences Corporation, Falls Church, USA

Abstract. Background subtraction (BS) is the art of separating moving objects from their background. The Background Modeling (BM) is one of the main steps of the BS process. Several subspace learning (SL) algorithms based on matrix and tensor tools have been used to perform the BM of the scenes. However, several SL algorithms work on a batch process increasing memory consumption when data size is very large. Moreover, these algorithms are not suitable for streaming data when the full size of the data is unknown. In this work, we propose an incremental tensor subspace learning that uses only a small part of the entire data and updates the low-rank model incrementally when new data arrive. In addition, the multi-feature model allows us to build a robust low-rank background model of the scene. Experimental results shows that the proposed method achieves interesting results for background subtraction task.

1 Introduction

The detection of moving objects is the basic low-level operations in video analysis. This basic operation (also called "background subtraction" or BS) consists of separating the moving objects called "foreground" from the static information called "background". The background subtraction is a key step in many fields of computer vision applications such as video surveillance to detect persons, vehicles, animals, etc., human-computer interface, motion detection and multimedia applications. Many BS methods have been developed over the last few years [3, 4, 24, 25] and the main resources can be found at the Background Subtraction Web Site[1]. Typically the BS process includes the following steps: a) background model initialization, b) background model maintenance and c) foreground detection. The Figure 1 shows the block diagram of the background subtraction process described here.

---

[1] https://sites.google.com/site/backgroundsubtraction/Home

© Springer International Publishing Switzerland 2014
A. Campilho and M. Kamel (Eds.): ICIAR 2014, Part I, LNCS 8814, pp. 94–103, 2014.
DOI: 10.1007/978-3-319-11758-4_11

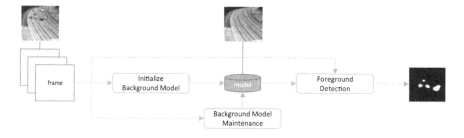

Fig. 1. Block diagram of the background subtraction process

In this paper, we show how to initialize and maintain the background model by an incremental and multi-feature subspace learning approach, as well our foreground detection method. First, we start with the notation conventions and related works. The remainder of the paper is organized as follows: Section 2 describes our incremental and multi-feature tensor subspace learning algorithm. Section 3 present our foreground detection method. Finally, in Sections 4 and 5, the experimental results are shown as well as conclusions.

1.1 Basic Notations

This paper follows the notation conventions in multilinear and tensor algebra as in [10,14]. Scalars are denoted by lowercase letters, e.g., x; vectors are denoted by lowercase boldface letters, e.g., $\mathbf{x}$; matrices by uppercase boldface, e.g., $\mathbf{X}$; and tensors by calligraphic letters, e.g., $\mathcal{X}$. In this paper, only real-valued data are considered.

1.2 Related Works

In 1999, Oliver et al. [22] are the first authors to model the background by Principal Component Analysis (PCA). Foreground detection is then achieved by thresholding the difference between the generated background image and the current image. PCA provides a robust model of the probability distribution function of the background, but not of the moving objects while they do not have a significant contribution to the model. Recent research on robust PCA [8,9] can be used to alleviate these limitations. For example, Candes et al. [8] proposed a convex optimization to address the robust PCA problem. The observation matrix is assumed represented as: $\mathbf{M} = \mathbf{L} + \mathbf{S}$ where $\mathbf{L}$ is a low-rank matrix and $\mathbf{S}$ is a matrix that can be sparse or not. This decomposition can be obtained by named as Principal Component Pursuit (PCP), $\min_{\mathbf{L},\mathbf{S}} ||\mathbf{L}||_* + \lambda ||\mathbf{S}||_1$, s.t. $\mathbf{M} = \mathbf{L} + \mathbf{S}$, where λ the weighting parameter (trade-off between rank and sparsity), $||\mathbf{L}||_*$ denotes the nuclear norm of $\mathbf{L}$ (i.e. the sum of singular values of $\mathbf{L}$) and $||\mathbf{S}||_1$ the ℓ_1 norm of the matrix $\mathbf{S}$ (i.e. sum of matrix elements magnitude). The background sequence is then modeled by a low-rank subspace that can gradually change over time, while the moving foreground objects constitute the correlated sparse outliers.

The different previous subspace learning methods consider the image as a vector. So, the local spatial information is almost lost. Some authors use tensor representation to solve this problem. Wang and Ahuja [28] propose a rank-R tensor approximation which can capture spatiotemporal redundancies in the tensor entries. He et al. [12] present a tensor subspace analysis algorithm called TSA (Tensor Subspace Analysis), which detects the intrinsic local geometrical structure of the tensor space by learning a lower dimensional tensor subspace. Wang et al. [29] give a convergent solution for general tensor-based subspace learning. Recently, online tensor subspace learning approaches have been introduced. Sun et al. [26] propose three tensor subspace learning methods: DTA (Dynamic Tensor Analysis), STA (Streaming Tensor Analysis) and WTA (Window-based Tensor Analysis). However, Li et al. [13] explains the above tensor analysis algorithms cannot be applied to background modeling and object tracking directly. To solve this problem, Li et al. [13,17,18] proposes a high-order tensor learning algorithm called incremental rank-(R1,R2,R3) tensor based subspace learning. This online algorithm builds a low-order tensor eigenspace model in which the mean and the eigenbasis are updated adaptively. The authors model the background appearance images as a 3-order tensor. Next, the tensor is subdivided into sub-tensors. Then, the proposed incremental tensor subspace learning algorithm is applied to effectively mine statistical properties of each sub-tensor. The experimental result shows that the proposed approach is robust to appearance changes in background modeling and object tracking. The method described above only uses the gray-scale and color information. In some situations, only the pixels intensities may be insufficient to perform a robust foreground detection. To deal with this situation, an incremental and multi-feature tensor subspace learning algorithm is presented in this paper.

2 Incremental and Multi-feature Tensor Subspace Learning

First, basic concepts of tensor algebra are introduced. Then, the proposed method is described.

2.1 Tensor Introduction

A *tensor* can be considered as a multidimensional or N-way array. As in [10, 14, 20], an Nth-order tensor is denoted as: $\mathcal{X} \in \mathbb{R}^{I_1 \times I_2 \times \dots \times I_N}$, where $I_n(n = 1, \dots, N)$. Each element in this tensor is addressed by $x_{(i_1, \dots, i_n)}$, where $1 \leq i_n \leq I_N$. The *order* of a tensor is the number of dimensions, also know as ways or modes [14]. By unfolding a tensor along a mode, a tensor's unfolding matrix corresponding to this mode is obtained. This operation is also known as mode-n matricization[2]. For a Nth-order tensor $\mathcal{X}$, its unfolding matrices are denoted by

---

[2] Can be regarded as a generalization of the mathematical concept of vectorization.

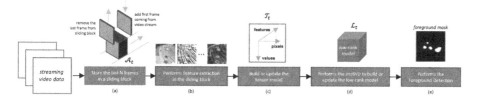

Fig. 2. Block diagram of the proposed approach. In the step (a), the last N frames from a streaming video are stored in a sliding block or tensor $\mathcal{A}_t$. Next, a feature extraction process is done at step (b) and the tensor $\mathcal{A}_t$ is transformed in another tensor $\mathcal{T}_t$ (step (c)). In (d), an incremental higher-order singular value decomposition (iHoSVD) is applied in the tensor $\mathcal{T}_t$ resulting in a low-rank tensor $\mathcal{L}_t$. Finally, in the step (e) a foreground detection method is applied for each new frame to segment the moving objects.

$\mathcal{X}^{(1)}, \mathcal{X}^{(2)}, \ldots, \mathcal{X}^{(N)}$. A more general review of tensor operations can be found in Kolda and Bader [14].

2.2 Building Tensor Model

Differently from previous related works where tensor model is built directly from the video data, i.e., each frontal slice of the tensor is a gray-scale image, in this work our tensor model is built from the feature extraction process. First, the last N frames from a streaming video data are stored in a tensor $\mathcal{A}_t \in \mathbb{R}^{A_1 \times A_2 \times A_3}$, where t represents the tensor $\mathcal{A}$ at time t. A_1 and A_2 is the frame width and frame height respectively, and A_3 is the number of stored frames (i.e. $A_3 = 25$ in the experiments). Subsequently the tensor $\mathcal{A}_t$ is transformed into a tensor $\mathcal{T}_t \in \mathbb{R}^{T_1 \times T_2 \times T_3}$ after a feature extraction process, where T_1 is the number of pixels (i.e. $A_1 \times A_2$), T_2 the feature values' for each frame (i.e. A_3) and T_3 the number of features. In this work, 8 features are extracted: 1) red channel, 2) green channel, 3) blue channel, 4) gray-scale, 5) local binary patterns (LBP), 6) spatial gradients in horizontal direction, 7) spatial gradients in vertical direction, and 8) spatial gradients magnitude. All frames' resolution are resized to 160x120 (19200 pixels), so the dimension of our tensor model is $\mathcal{T}_t \in \mathbb{R}^{19200 \times 25 \times 8}$. The steps described here are shown in Figure 2 (a), (b) and (c). The steps (d) and (e) will be described in the next sections.

2.3 Incremental Higher-Order Singular Value Decomposition

Tensor decompositions have been widely studied and applied to many real-world problems [10, 14, 20]. CANDECOMP/PARAFAC(CP)-decomposition[3] and Tucker decomposition are two widely-used low rank decompositions of

---

[3] The CP model is a special case of the Tucker model, where the core tensor is super-diagonal and the number of components in the factor matrices is the same [14].

tensors[4]. Today, the Tucker model is better known as the Higher-order SVD (HoSVD) from the work of Lathauwer et al. [15]. The HoSVD is a generalization of the matrix SVD. The HoSVD of a tensor $\mathcal{X}$ involves the matrix SVDs of its unfolding matrices. Let $\mathbf{A} \in \mathbb{R}^{m \times n}$ a matrix of full rank $r = \min(m, n)$, then its singular value decomposition can be expressed as a sum of r rank one matrices: $\mathbf{A} = \mathbf{U}\mathbf{\Sigma}\mathbf{V}^T$, where $\mathbf{U} \in \mathbb{R}^{m \times m}$ and $\mathbf{V} \in \mathbb{R}^{n \times n}$ are orthonormal matrices containing the eigenvectors of $\mathbf{A}\mathbf{A}^T$ and $\mathbf{A}^T\mathbf{A}$, respectively (i.e. right and left singular vectors of $\mathbf{A}$), and $\mathbf{\Sigma} = diag(\sigma_1, \ldots, \sigma_r)$ is a diagonal matrix with the eigenvalues of $\mathbf{A}$ in descending order. However, the matrix factorization step in SVD is computationally very expensive, especially for large matrices. Moreover, the entire data may be not available for decomposition (i.e. streaming data when the full size of the data is unknown). Businger (1970) [7], and Bunch and Nielsen (1978) [6] are the first authors who have proposed to update SVD sequentially with the arrival of more samples, i.e. appending/removing a row/column. Subsequently various approaches [2,5,16,21,23] have been proposed to update the SVD more efficiently and supporting new operations. Recently Baker et al. [1] has provided a generic approach to performs a low-rank incremental SVD. The algorithm is freely available in the IncPACK MATLAB package[5].

In this work, we have used a modified version of the previous algorithm. The original version supports only the *updating* operation. As described in Section 2.2 the tensor model $\mathcal{T}_t$ is updated dynamically. The last feature values are appended (i.e. *updating* operation) and the old feature values are removed (i.e. *downdating* operation) for each new frame. A simpler change would be to modify the algorithm so that, instead of using a hard window, we have inserted an exponential forgetting factor $\lambda < 1$ ($\lambda = 1$ no forgetting occurs), weighting new columns preferentially over earlier columns. The forgetting factor is explained in the work of Ross et al. [23].

The proposed iHoSVD is shown in Algorithm 1. It creates a low-rank tensor model $\mathcal{L}_t$ with the dominant singular subspaces of the tensor model $\mathcal{T}_t$. As previous described in Section 2.1, $\mathcal{T}_t^{(n)}$ denotes the mode-n unfolding matrix of the tensor $\mathcal{T}$ at time t. $r^{(n)}$ and $t^{(n)}$ are the desired rank r and its thresholding value of the mode-n unfolding matrix (i.e. $r^{(1)} = 1$, $r^{(2)} = 8$, $r^{(3)} = 2$, and $t^{(1)} = t^{(2)} = t^{(3)} = 0.01$ in the experiments). $\mathbf{U}_{t-1}^{(n)}$, $\mathbf{\Sigma}_{t-1}^{(n)}$, and $\mathbf{V}_{t-1}^{(n)}$ denotes the previous SVD of the mode-n unfolding matrix of the tensor $\mathcal{T}$ at time $t - 1$.

3   Foreground Detection

The foreground detection consists in segmenting all foreground pixels of the image to obtain the foreground components for each frame. As explained in the previous sections, a low-rank model $\mathcal{L}_t$ is built from the tensor model $\mathcal{L}_t$ incrementally. Then, for each new frame a weighted combination of similarity

---

[4] Please refer to Grasedyck et al. [10] for a complete review of low-rank tensor approximation techniques.

[5] http://www.math.fsu.edu/~cbaker/IncPACK/

Algorithm 1. Proposed iHoSVD algorithm

---

function INCREMENTALHOSVD($\mathcal{T}_t$, $r^{(n)}$, $t^{(n)}$)

    $\mathcal{S}_t \leftarrow \mathcal{T}_t$

    if $t = 0$ **then** $\triangleright$ Performs the standard rank-r SVD

        for $i = 1$ to n **do**

            $[\mathbf{U}_t^{(n)}, \mathbf{\Sigma}_t^{(n)}, \mathbf{V}_t^{(n)}] \leftarrow \text{SVD}(\mathcal{T}_t^{(n)}, r^{(n)}, t^{(n)})$

        end for

    else $\triangleright$ Performs the incremental rank-r SVD

        for $i = 1$ to n **do**

            $[\mathbf{U}_t^{(n)}, \mathbf{\Sigma}_t^{(n)}, \mathbf{V}_t^{(n)}] \leftarrow \text{iSVD}(\mathcal{T}_t^{(n)}, r^{(n)}, t^{(n)}, \mathbf{U}_{t-1}^{(n)}, \mathbf{\Sigma}_{t-1}^{(n)}, \mathbf{V}_{t-1}^{(n)})$

        end for

    end if

    $\mathcal{S}_t \leftarrow \mathcal{T}_t \times_1 (\mathbf{U}_t^{(1)})^T \ldots \times_n (\mathbf{U}_t^{(n)})^T$ $\triangleright \times_n$ denotes the n-mode tensor times matrix

    return $\mathcal{S}_t$, $\mathbf{U}_t^{(1)}$, ..., $\mathbf{U}_t^{(n)}$

end function

---

measures is performed. This process has two stages: first a similarity function is calculated, then a weighted combination is performed. Let $\mathbf{F}_n$ the feature's set extracted from the input frame and $\mathbf{F}'_n$ the set of low-rank features reconstructed from the low-rank model $\mathcal{L}_t$, the similarity function $\mathbf{S}$ for each feature n at the pixel (i, j) is computed as follows:

$$\mathbf{S}_n(i,j) = \begin{cases} \frac{\mathbf{F}_n(i,j)}{\mathbf{F}'_n(i,j)} & \text{if } \mathbf{F}_n(i,j) < \mathbf{F}'_n(i,j) \\ 1 & \text{if } \mathbf{F}_n(i,j) = \mathbf{F}'_n(i,j) \\ \frac{\mathbf{F}'_n(i,j)}{\mathbf{F}_n(i,j)} & \text{if } \mathbf{F}_n(i,j) > \mathbf{F}'_n(i,j) \end{cases}$$

where $\mathbf{F}_n(i,j)$ and $\mathbf{F}'_n(i,j)$ are respectively the feature value of pixel (i, j) for the feature n. Note that $\mathbf{S}_n(i,j)$ is between 0 and 1. Furthermore, $\mathbf{S}_n(i,j)$ is close to one if $\mathbf{F}_n(i,j)$ and $\mathbf{F}'_n(i,j)$ are very similar. Next, a weighted combination of similarity measures is computed as follows:

$$\mathbf{W}(i,j) = \sum_{n=1}^{K} w_n \mathbf{S}_n(i,j)$$

where K is the total number of features and w_n the set of weights for each feature n ($w_1 = w_2 = w_3 = w_6 = w_7 = w_8 = 0.125, w_4 = 0.225, w_5 = 0.025$ in the experiments). The weights are chosen empirically to maximize the true pixels and minimize the false pixels in the foreground detection. The foreground mask is obtained by applying the following threshold function:

$$\mathbf{F}(i,j) = f(\mathbf{W}(i,j)) = \begin{cases} 1 & \text{if } \mathbf{W}(i,j) < t \\ 0 & \text{otherwise} \end{cases}$$

where t is the threshold value ($t = 0.5$ in the experiments). In the next section we shows the experimental results of the proposed method.

Table 1. Visual comparison with real videos of the BMC data set

Sequence Video "Wandering student"(frame #651)

Sequence Video "Traffic during windy day"(frame #140)

4   Experimental Results

In order to evaluate the performance of the proposed method for background modeling and subtraction, the BMC data set proposed by Vacavant et al. [27] is selected. We have compared our method with GRASTA algorithm proposed by He et al. [11] and BLWS algorithm proposed by Lin and Wei [19]. Tables 1 and 2 show the quantitative and the visual results (input image, ground-truth and foreground detection, respectively) with synthetic and real video sequences of the BMC data set. The quantitative results in Table 2 show that the proposed method outperforms the previous methods, with the highest F-measure average and best scores over all video sequences except in 212, 312, 412 and 512. The visual results in Table 2 show the foreground detection for the frame #300 (Street) and frame #645 (Rotary), respectively. All experiments are performed on a computer running Intel Core i7-3740qm 2.7GHz processor with 16Gb of RAM. However, the proposed system requires aprox. 2min per frame for background subtraction, which > 95% of time is used for low-rank decomposition. Further research consists to improve the speed of the incremental low-rank decomposition for real-time applications. Matlab codes and experimental results can be found in the iHoSVD homepage[6].

5   Conclusion

In this paper, an incremental and multi-feature tensor subspace learning algorithm is presented. The multi-feature tensor model allows us to build a robust low-rank model of the background scene. Experimental results shows that the proposed method achieves interesting results for background subtraction task. However, additional features can be added, enabling a more robust model of the background scene. In addition, the proposed foreground detection approach can be changed to automatically selects the best features allowing an accurate foreground detection. Further research consists to improve the speed of the incremental low-rank decomposition for real-time applications. Additional supports for dynamic backgrounds might be interesting for real and complex scenes.

---

[6] https://sites.google.com/site/ihosvd/

Table 2. Quantitative and visual results with synthetic videos of the BMC data set

Scenes	Method	Recall	Precision	F-measure	Visual Results
Street					
	IHOSVD	**0.725**	0.945	**0.818**	
112	GRASTA [11]	0.700	0.980	0.817	
	BLWS [19]	0.700	**0.981**	0.817	
	IHOSVD	0.692	0.845	0.761	
212	GRASTA [11]	**0.787**	**0.847**	**0.816**	
	BLWS [19]	0.786	**0.847**	**0.816**	
	IHOSVD	0.566	0.831	0.673	
312	GRASTA [11]	0.695	0.965	0.807	
	BLWS [19]	0.697	0.971	**0.812**	
	IHOSVD	0.637	0.838	0.723	
412	GRASTA [11]	**0.787**	0.843	0.814	
	BLWS [19]	0.785	**0.848**	**0.815**	
	IHOSVD	0.652	0.893	0.753	
512	GRASTA [11]	**0.669**	0.960	**0.789**	
	BLWS [19]	0.664	**0.966**	0.787	
Rotary					
	IHOSVD	**0.748**	**0.956**	**0.839**	
122	GRASTA [11]	0.680	0.902	0.776	
	BLWS [19]	0.663	0.921	0.771	
	IHOSVD	**0.649**	**0.913**	**0.759**	
222	GRASTA [11]	0.637	0.548	0.589	
	BLWS [19]	0.633	0.560	0.594	
	IHOSVD	0.555	**0.927**	**0.694**	
322	GRASTA [11]	**0.619**	0.530	0.571	
	BLWS [19]	0.603	0.538	0.569	
	IHOSVD	0.548	**0.942**	**0.693**	
422	GRASTA [11]	**0.623**	0.778	0.692	
	BLWS [19]	0.620	0.775	0.689	
	IHOSVD	0.677	**0.932**	**0.784**	
522	GRASTA [11]	0.791	0.714	0.751	
	BLWS [19]	**0.793**	0.711	0.750	
Average					
	IHOSVD	-	-	**0.749**	
	GRASTA [11]	-	-	0.618	
	BLWS [19]	-	-	0.742	

Acknowledgments. The authors gratefully acknowledge the financial support of CAPES (Brazil) through Brazilian Science Without Borders program (CsF) for granting a scholarship to the first author.

References

1. Baker, C.G., Gallivan, K.A., Van Dooren, P.: Low-rank incremental methods for computing dominant singular subspaces. Linear Algebra and its Applications **436**(8), 2866–2888 (2012). Special Issue dedicated to Danny Sorensen's 65th birthday
2. Balzano, L., Wright, S.J.: On GROUSE and incremental SVD. CoRR, abs/1307.5494 (2013)
3. Bouwmans, T.: Traditional and recent approaches in background modeling for foreground detection: An overview. Computer Science Review (2014)
4. Bouwmans, T., Zahzah, E.: Robust PCA via Principal Component Pursuit: A review for a comparative evaluation in video surveillance. Special Isssue on Background Models Challenge, Computer Vision and Image Understanding, CVIU, vol. 122, pp. 22–34 (May 2014)
5. Brand, M.: Fast low-rank modifications of the thin singular value decomposition. Linear Algebra and Its Applications **415**(1), 20–30 (2006)
6. Bunch, J.R., Nielsen, C.P.: Updating the singular value decomposition. Numerische Mathematik **31**(2), 111–129 (1978)
7. Businger, P.A.: Updating a singular value decomposition. Nordisk Tidskr, 10 (1970)
8. Candes, E., Li, X., Ma, Y., Wright, J.: Robust principal component analysis? Int. Journal of ACM **58**(3), 117–142 (2011)
9. De La Torre, F., Black, M.: A framework for robust subspace learning. Int. Journal on Computer Vision, 117–142 (2003)
10. Grasedyck, L., Kressner, D., Tobler, C.: A literature survey of low-rank tensor approximation techniques (2013)
11. He, J., Balzano, L., Lui, J.C.S.: Online robust subspace tracking from partial information. CoRR, abs/1109.3827 (2011)
12. He, X., Cai, D., Niyogi, P.: Tensor subspace analysis. In: Advances in Neural Information Processing Systems 18 (2005)
13. Hu, W., Li, X., Zhang, X., Shi, X., Maybank, S., Zhang, Z.: Incremental tensor subspace learning and its applications to foreground segmentation and tracking. Int. Journal of Computer Vision **91**(3), 303–327 (2011)
14. Kolda, T.G., Bader, B.W.: Tensor decompositions and applications. SIAM Review (2008)
15. Lathauwer, L.D., Moor, B.D., Vandewalle, J.: A multilinear singular value decomposition. SIAM J. Matrix Anal. Appl. **21**(4), 1253–1278 (2000)
16. Levy, A., Lindenbaum, M.: Sequential karhunen-loeve basis extraction and its application to images. IEEE Trans. on Image Processing **9**(8), 1371–1374 (2000)
17. Li, X., Hu, W., Zhang, Z., Zhang, X.: Robust foreground segmentation based on two effective background models. In: Proceedings of the 1st ACM Int. Conf. on Multimedia Information Retrieval, MIR 2008, pp. 223–228. ACM, New York (2008)
18. Li, X., Hu, W., Zhang, Z., Zhang, X., Luo, G.: Robust visual tracking based on incremental tensor subspace learning. In: IEEE 11th Int. Conf. on Computer Vision (ICCV), pp. 1–8 (October 2007)
19. Lin, Z., Wei, S.: A block lanczos with warm start technique for accelerating nuclear norm minimization algorithms. CoRR, abs/1012.0365 (2010)

20. Lu, H., Plataniotis, K.N., Venetsanopoulos, A.N.: A survey of multilinear subspace learning for tensor data. Pattern Recogn. **44**(7), 1540–1551 (2011)
21. Melenchón, J., Martínez, E.: Efficiently downdating, composing and splitting singular value decompositions preserving the mean information. In: Martí, J., Benedí, J.M., Mendonça, A.M., Serrat, J. (eds.) IbPRIA 2007. LNCS, vol. 4478, pp. 436–443. Springer, Heidelberg (2007)
22. Oliver, N.M., Rosario, B., Pentland, A.P.: A bayesian computer vision system for modeling human interactions. IEEE Trans. on Pattern Analysis and Machine Intelligence **22**(8), 831–843 (2000)
23. Ross, D.A., Lim, J., Lin, R., Yang, M.: Incremental learning for robust visual tracking. Int. J. Comput. Vision **77**(1–3), 125–141 (2008)
24. Shah, M., Deng, J., Woodford, B.: Video background modeling: Recent approaches, issues and our solutions. In: Machine Vision and Applications, Special Issue on Background Modeling for Foreground Detection in Real-World Dynamic Scenes (December 2013)
25. Shimada, A., Nonaka, Y., Nagahara, H., Taniguchi, R.: Case-based background modeling: associative background database towards low-cost and high-performance change detection. In: Machine Vision and Applications, Special Issue on Background Modeling for Foreground Detection in Real-World Dynamic Scenes (December 2013)
26. Sun, J., Tao, D., Papadimitriou, S., Yu, P.S., Faloutsos, C.: Incremental Tensor Analysis: Theory and applications. ACM Trans. Knowl. Discov. Data **2**(3), 11:1–11:37 (2008)
27. Vacavant, A., Chateau, T., Wilhelm, A., Lequièvre, L.: A benchmark dataset for outdoor foreground/background extraction. In: Park, J.-I., Kim, J. (eds.) ACCV Workshops 2012, Part I. LNCS, vol. 7728, pp. 291–300. Springer, Heidelberg (2013)
28. Wang, H., Ahuja, N.: Rank-r approximation of tensors using image-as-matrix representation. In: IEEE Computer Society Conf. on Computer Vision and Pattern Recognition (CVPR), vol. 2, pp. 346–353 (June 2005)
29. Wang, H., Yan, S., Huang, T., Tang, X.: A convergent solution to tensor subspace learning. In: Proceedings of the 20th Int. Joint Conf. on Artifical Intelligence, IJCAI 2007, pp. 629–634. Morgan Kaufmann Publishers Inc., San Francisco (2007)

Face Image Super-Resolution Based on Topology ICA and Sparse Representation

Yongtao Liu[✉], Hua Yan, Xiushan Nie, and Zhen Liu

School of Computer Science and Technology,
Shandong University of Finance and Economics, Jinan, China
liuyt8705@163.com

Abstract. In this paper, a new learning-based face super-resolution (SR) algorithm is proposed considering the similarity of topology structure between low-resolution (LR) image and high-resolution (HR) image and the sparseness of cells' response in visual cortex. Firstly, we obtain coupling dictionary which are corresponding to LR and HR image patch pairs by applying topology ICA. Then, the sparse coefficients of input LR image according to LR dictionary can be got based on sparse representation theory. Furthermore, primary HR face image is reconstructed using HR dictionary. Finally, finer HR face image can be got by back-projection step. Experiments demonstrate the proposed approach can get good SR results in subjective perception and objective evaluation.

Keywords: Face image · Super-resolution · Topology ICA · Sparse representation

1 Introduction

Image super-resolution (SR) is a technique that recovers a high-resolution (HR) image from a single or a series of input low-resolution (LR) images. With the development of face detection, recognition, and facial expression analysis, face image super-resolution becomes more and more important.

At present, the methods of SR can be broadly classified into three families: interpolation-based, reconstruction-based and learning-based methods. Interpolation-based methods only use the information of input LR image, and tend to generate overly smooth images with serious blurring. Reconstruction-based methods utilize the complementary information from the multiple input LR images of the same scene. The performance of these algorithms degrades rapidly when the magnification factor becomes large. To overcome these drawbacks, a learning-based SR method was proposed [1]. Learning-based SR methods use the certain characteristics of training images as a prior knowledge to constrain the SR reconstruction and recover the missing information of LR images. Thus, better high-frequency detail can still be produced without increasing the number of input image samples. It is commonly referred to face hallucination when applying learning-based SR technique to face image.

Face hallucination was addressed in the pioneering work of Baker et al. [2]. They used Gaussian and Laplacian pyramid models to reconstruct SR face images. Chang

© Springer International Publishing Switzerland 2014
A. Campilho and M. Kamel (Eds.): ICIAR 2014, Part I, LNCS 8814, pp. 104–111, 2014.
DOI: 10.1007/978-3-319-11758-4_12

[3] proposed a neighbor embedding-based SR algorithm, which used the Locally Linear Embedding (LLE) manifold learning to realize SR reconstruction. Wang et al. [4] proposed a face SR method based on eigentransformation, and this method used PCA to reconstruct SR image. Zhang et al. [5] proposed a face hallucination method in DCT domain. Yang et al. [6] [7] presented a kind of approach based on sparse representation which got good SR performance.

Given the advantages of learning-based SR methods, we propose a new learning-based face SR approach. Considering the similarity of the topology structure between LR and HR image, we firstly obtain a pair of dictionaries of LR and HR image patches by applying topology ICA. Secondly, the coefficients of LR image according to LR dictionary can be got by using sparse representation. Then we use HR dictionary to reconstruct primary HR face image. Finally, final HR face image can be got by back-projection step. Experimental results show that our approach can get good super-resolution performance in subjective perception and in objective evaluation.

2   Theoretical Basis

2.1   Image Super-Resolution Theory

Generally, LR image can be obtained by blurring and down-sampling to original HR image, followed by addition of noise. This can be expressed in matrix form:

$$y = DHx + n = Lx + n \qquad (1)$$

Here, x and y are HR and LR image, respectively. D and H represent the blurring and down-sampling matrices, respectively. n is the noise. Combining D and H, degeneracy operator L can be defined. When n is small, (1) can be transformed into the following form:

$$y \approx Lx \qquad (2)$$

Given a LR image y, the task of SR can be regarded as finding the HR image x. SR is an extremely ill-posed problem because of the information insufficiency. We can regularize them via some constraint conditions and then estimate the optimal solution.

2.2   Topology Independent Component Analysis

Topology independent component analysis (TICA) [8] is the extended model of independent component analysis (ICA). TICA is a statistical model where the observed data is expressed as a linear transformation of latent variables that are topography independent. The model of TICA can be expressed as:

$$X = AS \qquad (3)$$

Here, $X = (x_1, x_2, ..., x_l)$, and $x_i (i = 1, 2, ..., l)$ is the column vector of observed random variables. $A = (a_1, a_2, ..., a_k)$, and $a_j (j = 1, 2, ..., k)$ is denoted as topography independent component. S is the mixing matrix. x_i can be expressed as following :

$$x_i = As_i = \sum_j a_j s_{ji} \qquad (4)$$

TICA model defines a neighborhood function to express the correlation among different components. In this model, the adjacent components are higher-order correlative, in contrast, components that are not close to each other in the topography are independent. Here, the latent variable a_j is defined as:

$$a_j = \phi(\sum_k h(j,k)u_k)z_j \qquad (5)$$

Here, $h(j,k)$ is a neighborhood function, which expresses the correlation between j-th and k-th component. u_k and z_j are mutually independent random variables. $\phi(t)$ is a scalar function which is usually defined as $\phi(t) = t^{-1/2}$.

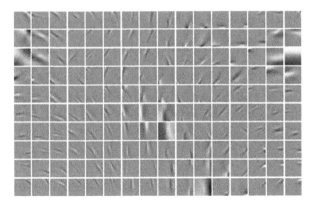

Fig. 1. Topographic independent component of natural image data

The obtained basis vectors of nature image, i.e. columns of matrix A, are shown in Fig 1. Here, the neighborhood size is 3*3. We can see that the basis vectors have a clear topographic organization. Basis vectors that are similar in location and orientation are close to each other. According to visual perception theory, the feature of basis vectors is consistent with the distribution characteristics of complex cells in mammalian primary visual cortex (V1 region). In fact, TICA is widely applied in modeling V1 region. Vinje [9] found that the response of complex cells to stimulation meet the sparse distribution. For instance, when we see an image, the response of most neurons is weak, only few neurons have strong response. This means that when image is represented by basis vectors extracted by TICA, most of the coefficients are small and only few coefficients are larger, that is to say, the distribution of coefficients is sparse.

3   Face Super-Resolution Based on TICA and Sparse Representation Theory

Given that the coefficients are sparse when the basis vectors extracted by TICA are used to represent image, this paper plans to combine TICA and the sparse representation theory to learning-based face SR. The following section includes dictionary training and SR reconstruction steps.

3.1   Dictionary Training

The approach is patch-based, so the training step is fit for image patches. Firstly, all training face image are normalized to zero-mean and unit variance. Then we randomly choose $m*m$ image patches from LR training face images and $dm * dm$ image patches from the corresponding HR training face images as training samples. Here, d denotes the magnification factor. Stretch these two patches to m^2-dimension column vector y_i^p and $(dm)^2$-dimension column vector x_i^p respectively by the way of column-priority. The mean gray value of each column is subtracted. X represents the union training samples, which is shown as follows:

$$X = \begin{bmatrix} Y_p \\ X_p \end{bmatrix} = \begin{bmatrix} y_1^p, y_2^p, ..., y_l^p \\ x_1^p, x_2^p, ..., x_l^p \end{bmatrix} \tag{6}$$

Here, Y_p represents LR training samples and X_p represents HR training samples.

Use TICA approach to extract the topology independent components of training set X and construct TICA dictionary A. The training basis vector, i.e. the atom of the dictionary, is marked as a_j. Each atom a_j can be divided into two parts a_j^{LR} and a_j^{HR} according to the dimensions of y_i^p and x_i^p. A can be shown as follows:

$$A = \begin{bmatrix} A_{LR} \\ A_{HR} \end{bmatrix} \tag{7}$$

Here, A_{LR} and A_{HR} represent the LR dictionary and HR dictionary, respectively.

3.2   Face Super-Resolution Reconstruction

Firstly, the input LR face image y is preprocessed. y is normalized to zero-mean and unit variance. Successively obtain the overlapping image patch whose size is $m * m$ from the upper-left corner of the image and then transform them to column vector y_i^p by the way of column-priority. The mean gray value of each image patch is subtracted, only leaving the texture feature. Finally, arrange all the column vectors together to form the input data $Y_p = [y_1^p, y_2^p, ..., y_N^p]$.

For each input LR image patch, calculating the coefficient according to the LR dictionary and get the HR image patch by replacing the LR dictionary with HR dictionary while the coefficient is invariant. As is known in section 2, when the image is represented by TICA basis, the coefficient matrix is sparse, so the calculating process of coefficient S can be represented as follows:

$$S^* = \arg\min_s \left\| A_{LR}S - Y_p \right\|_2^2 + \lambda \|S\|_0 \tag{8}$$

According to the sparse representation theory, the solving problem of norm L_0 in (8) can be converted to the convex optimization problem of norm L_1 under the premise of sparse [10]. As a result, (8) can be converted to the following form:

$$S^* = \arg\min_s \left\| A_{LR}S - Y_p \right\|_2^2 + \lambda \|S\|_1 \tag{9}$$

In this paper, orthogonal matching pursuit (OMP) is used to solve the optimization problem in (9), and the sparse coefficient matrix S^* about Y_p is obtained according to LR dictionary A_{LR}. Then we calculate $X_p^* = A_{HR}S^*$ where $X_p^* = [x_1^p, x_2^p, ..., x_N^p]$. The HR patch vectors $x_i^p (i=1,2,...,N)$ are transformed to image patches and primary HR image x_0 can be reconstructed by combining the image patches. Calculate the mean of the overlapping area of different patches when synthesizing the patches.

Patch-based algorithm does not consider the global model, so the patch-combined image often generates some unnatural phenomenon, such as ringing and jagged artifacts. The global model can be applied to remove unnatural problem caused by the patch-based step. This can be realized by simulating the degradation process of images. The process can be solved as an optimization problem as follows:

$$x^* = \arg\min_x \|Lx - y\|_2^2 \tag{10}$$

In this paper, IBP is used as the global constraint to optimize x:

$$x_{t+1} = x_t + ((y - Lx_t) \uparrow d) * P \tag{11}$$

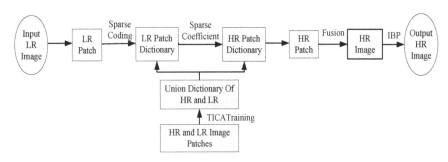

Fig. 2. The flow chart of our algorithm

In (11), x_{t+1} represents the estimated images after $t+1$-th iteration. The obtained HR image x_0 is used as the initial estimation in the iteration. $\uparrow d$ represents interpolation magnification with the factor of d. P represents back-projection filter, and Gaussian filter is often chosen.

The flow chart of our algorithm is shown in Fig. 2.

4   Experimental Results and Analysis

In this paper, we use ORL face database. ORL database contains 40 persons. Each person has 10 face images. We choose the first face of each person as testing images and the others as training images. We define the size of LR image patch is 4, that means $m=4$. Each image patch has 2 pixels overlap. The sparsity is set to 10 in OMP algorithm. The iteration of back-projection is set to 10. The size of neighborhood is set to be 3*3 during the step of TICA basis vectors training. Fig. 3 shows the TICA basis extracted by ORL database. From Fig. 3, we can observe the topology structure of the basis vectors is the same as TICA basis extracted by natural images in Fig. 1.

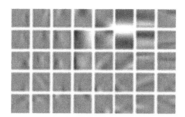

Fig. 3. The topology ICA basis images extracted by ORL face images

We compare our method with several other methods, including bicubic interpolation, hallucinating face by eigentransformation [4], and super-resolution based on sparse representation [6]. The SR results of different algorithms with magnification factor 2 and 4 are shown in Fig. 4 and Fig. 5 (from left to right columns: (a) Bicubic interpolation; (b) Hallucinating face by eigentransformation; (c) SR based on sparse representation; (d) Our algorithm; (e) The original HR face image), respectively.

From Fig. 4 and Fig. 5, we can see that the SR results of our algorithm have more clearly edge detail and the visual effect is more real and natural than others. With the increase of magnification factor, the SR results of our algorithm have more advantages in intuitive visual.

We use normalized mean square error (NMSE), peak signal to noise ratio (PSNR) and mean structural similarity (MSSIM) as objective evaluation criteria in this paper.

The means of evaluation criteria of all testing images with magnification factor 2 and 4 are listed in Table 1. As can be seen from Table 1, the mean of NMSE is reduced, while the means of PSNR and MSSIM are increased in our algorithm comparing with others. Meanwhile, with the increase of magnification factor, the evaluation criteria means of our algorithm have greater advantages than others. This fully proves the effectiveness and good performance of our algorithm.

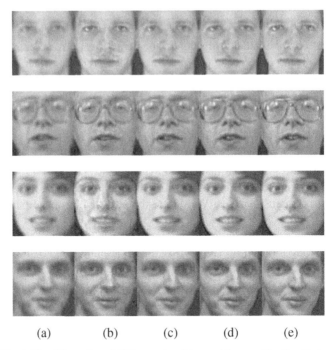

(a)   (b)   (c)   (d)   (e)

Fig. 4. The SR results of different algorithms with magnification factor 2

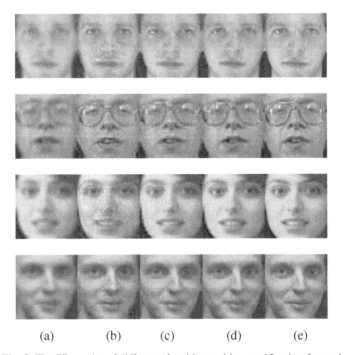

(a)   (b)   (c)   (d)   (e)

Fig. 5. The SR results of different algorithms with magnification factor 4

Table 1. The mean of NMSE, PSNR and MSSIM of SR results of different algorithms

Magnification Factor	Criteria	Bicubic	eigentransformation	Sparse Representation	Our Algorithm
	NMSE	0.0033	0.0030	0.0012	0.008
Factor 2	PSNR	28.167	28.889	32.476	33.159
	MSSIM	0.8819	0.8666	0.9420	0.9563
	NMSE	0.0050	0.0059	0.0030	0.0021
Factor 4	PSNR	26.132	26.615	28.973	30.371
	MSSIM	0.8157	0.7876	0.8796	0.9018

5   Conclusion

Learning-based SR algorithms are restricted by the dependence on training dictionary. In this paper, TICA and sparse representation theory are applied for face hallucination. Considering the similarity of the topology structure between LR and HR image, TICA is used as a tool to obtain the coupling dictionary of LR and HR image patches. Then, the theory of sparse representation is applied to hallucinate the primary high-resolution face. Finally, the back-projection step is applied to get the finer high resolution face. Experimental results show that our approach can obtain good SR results in subjective perception and objective evaluation.

References

1. Baker, S., Kanade, T.: Limits on super-resolution and how to break them. IEEE Computer Vision and Pattern Recognition 9(2), 372–379 (2000)
2. Baker, S., Kanade, T.: Hallucinating faces. In: IEEE International Conference on Automatic Face and Gesture Recognition, pp. 83–88 (2000)
3. Chang, H., Yeung, D.Y.: Super-resolution through neighbor embedding. In: IEEE Computer Society Conference on Computer Vision and Pattern Recognition, pp. 275–282 (2004)
4. Wang, X.G., Tang, X.O.: Hallucinating face by eigentransformation. IEEE Trans. on Systems 35(3), 425–435 (2005)
5. Zhang, W., Cham, W.K.: Hallucinating face in the dct domain. IEEE Trans. on Image Processing 20(10), 2769–2779 (2011)
6. Yang, J.C., Wright, J., Huang, T.: Image super-resolution via sparse representation. IEEE Trans. on Image Processing 19(11), 2861–2873 (2010)
7. Yang, J.C., Wang, Z., Lin, Z., et al.: Coupled dictionary training for image super-resolution. IEEE Trans. on Image Processing 21(8), 3467–3478 (2012)
8. Hyvärinen, A., Hoyer, P.O., Inki, M.: Topographic independent component analysis. Neural Computation 13(7), 1527–1558 (2001)
9. Vinje, W.E., Gallant, J.L.: Sparse coding and decorrelation in primary visual cortex during natural vision. Science 287, 1273–1276 (2000)
10. Gribonval, R., Nielsen, M.: Sparse representations in unions of bases. IEEE Trans. on Information Theory 49(12), 3320–3325 (2003)

Iterative Sparse Coding
for Colorization Based Compression

Suk-Ho Lee[1], Paul Oh[2], and Moon Gi Kang[2][(✉)]

[1] Department of Software Engineering, Dongseo University, 47 Jurye-ro, Busan,
Sasang-Gu 617-716, Korea
[2] Department of Electrical and Electronic Engineering, Yonsei University, 134,
Shinchon-Dong, Seoul, Seodaemun-Gu 120-749, Korea
mkang@yonsei.ac.kr

Abstract. Colorization based coding is a technique which compresses a color image using the colorization method. The main issue in colorization based coding is to extract a good RP(representative pixel) set from the original color image from which the colored image can be reconstructed in the decoder to a sufficient level. In this paper, we propose an iterative sparse coding method for the extraction of the RP set. Observations show that the proposed method computes simultaneously the locally optimal RP set and the locally optimal Levin's colorization matrix. Furthermore, experimental results show that the proposed method provides better color image reconstruction and compression rate than conventional colorization based coding methods.

Keywords: Colorization · Compression · Optimization · Sparse coding · Color image

1 Introduction

Colorization is a technique which automatically colorizes a grey image with only few color information [1][2]. Colorization based coding refers to the color compression technique which utilizes the fact that the required number of pixels for colorization is small [3]-[6]. The encoder chooses a set of pixels called RP(representative pixels) set and sends only the position information and color values for this RP set to the decoder. In the decoder, the color information for all the remaining pixels are restored using colorization methods. The main issue in colorization based coding is how to extract the RP set such that the compression rate and the quality of the restored image become good.

In [7], we proposed for the first time an optimization based RP set extraction method for colorization based coding. The method formulates the problem of RP extraction into a sparse coding problem, and obtains the RP set via a minimization with L_0 constraint. The RP set obtained by this method is optimal with respect to a specific colorization matrix constructed by the meanshift segmentation method.

© Springer International Publishing Switzerland 2014
A. Campilho and M. Kamel (Eds.): ICIAR 2014, Part I, LNCS 8814, pp. 112–120, 2014.
DOI: 10.1007/978-3-319-11758-4_13

In this paper, we propose a colorization based coding method which computes the locally optimal RP set with respect to the locally optimal Levin's colorization matrix. We use the term 'local', since the global optimality of the proposed method is not proved. An iterative sparse coding algorithm is proposed to compute the RP set. Experimental results show that the reconstructed color images with the proposed method are good in terms of both quantitative measure and visual perception quality.

2   Related Works

In this section, we give a brief review on the Levin's colorization and the optimization based colorization based coding.

2.1   Levin's Colorization

In [1], Levin *et al* proposed a colorization method based on optimization. The colorization process is performed by minimizing the following cost function with respect to $\mathbf{u}$:

$$J(\mathbf{u}) = \|\mathbf{x} - A\mathbf{u}\|^2. \tag{1}$$

Here, $\mathbf{u}$ is the solution vector, i.e., the color component vector (Cb or Cr component vector), and $\mathbf{x}$ is the vector which contains the color values only at the positions of the RP, and zeros at the other positions. The vectors $\mathbf{u}$ and $\mathbf{x}$ are all in raster-scan order. Furthermore, $A = I - W$, where I is an $n \times n$ identity matrix, n is the number of pixels in $\mathbf{u}$, and W is an $n \times n$ matrix containing the w'_{rs} weighting components. The w'_{rs} weighting components are

$$w'_{rs} = \begin{cases} 0 & \text{if } r \in \Omega \\ w_{rs} & \text{otherwise,} \end{cases}$$

where

$$w_{rs} \propto e^{(y(r)-y(s))^2/2\sigma_r^2}. \tag{2}$$

Here, Ω denotes the set of the positions of the RP, σ_r^2 is a small positive value, and w_{rs} is the weighting component between the pixels at the r's and the s's positions, where $s \in N(r)$, and $N(r)$ is the 8-neighborhood of the r's pixel. Furthermore, $y(r)$ and $y(s)$ are the luminance values at the r's and the s's positions in the luminance channel, respectively. The minimizer of (1) can be explicitly computed as

$$\mathbf{u} = A^{-1}\mathbf{x}. \tag{3}$$

The obtained vector $\mathbf{u}$ used together with the luminance channel produces the colorized image.

2.2   Colorization Based Compression Framework

Colorization based compression makes use of the fact that there exists correlation between the luminance channel and the chrominance channels in the color image. Only the luminance channel is compressed by conventional compression standards such as the JPEG standard. Figure 1 shows the general framework of the colorization based decoding for the case of using the Levins colorization [1] as the colorization method. For the encoding of the chrominance channels, first, the RP are extracted using the information of the luminance channel. These are then encoded and sent to the decoder. In the decoder, the luminance channel is reconstructed from the DCT coefficients, and the colorization matrix A^{-1} is constructed from the reconstructed luminance channel. The colorization matrix operates on the RP set ($\mathbf{x}$) sent from the encoder to obtain the chrominance channels ($\mathbf{u}$). Thus, the color image is reconstructed.

Conventionally, the initial RP set is set as a random set, and then, redundant RP have to be eliminated, and required RP have to be additionally extracted by additional RP elimination/extraction methods. In [3] and [4], new pixels are added to the initial set of RP by iterative selection based on machine learning, while in [5], the RP is selected iteratively constrained to a set of color line segments. In [6], redundant RP are reduced and required RP are extracted iteratively based on the characteristics of the colorization basis.

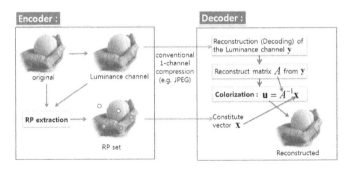

Fig. 1. General framework of colorization based coding using the Levin's colorization matrix

2.3   Optimization Based Colorization Coding

In [7], we proposed an optimization based colorization coding scheme, which computes the RP set by a minimization problem:

$$\operatorname*{argmin}_{\mathbf{x}} \|\mathbf{u}_0 - C\mathbf{x}\|^2, \ s.t. \ |\mathbf{x}|_0 \leq L. \tag{4}$$

Here, C is the colorization matrix, $\mathbf{u}_0$ is the original color component vector, $\mathbf{x}$ is the solution vector sought, i.e., the vector containing the RP set, and L is a positive integer that controls the number of nonzero components in $\mathbf{x}$. The minimization of (4) finds the RP set ($\mathbf{x}$) which minimizes the error between the reconstructed and the original color images, while constraining the number of nonzero components in $\mathbf{x}$ to be less than L. The problem (4) can be solved by well-known solvers such as the BP or the OMP solver.

3   Proposed Method

The motivation problem of the proposed method is to solve the following minimization problem with respect to both the RP set $\mathbf{x}$ and the colorization matrix C:

$$\operatorname*{argmin}_{\mathbf{x},C} \|\mathbf{u}_0 - C\mathbf{x}\|^2, \ s.t. \ |\mathbf{x}|_0 \leq L, \tag{5}$$

This is different from the optimization problem in [7], where the colorization

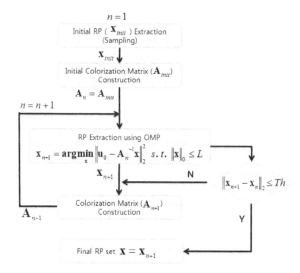

Fig. 2. Flowchart of the proposed method

matrix C is obtained by a segmentation method. The aim is to find the optimal RP set $\mathbf{x}$ with respect to the optimal colorization matrix. However, problem (5) cannot be solved as such, since it is a two variable problem. A second try would be an iterative two-step minimization algorithm, where (5) is solved iteratively for $\mathbf{x}$ and C by iteratively fixing one of them. However, still the problem of solving (5) for C is an ill-posed problem and needs extra constraints to be solved.

The constraint we introduce in our problem is the constraint used in the colorization problem in [1], i.e., the constraint that the colorization matrix should minimize the difference between the color at a certain pixel and the colors of the weighted average of the colors at neighboring pixels, while letting the colors of the RP intact. In fact, the colorization matrix that satisfies this constraint can be uniquely determined, and becomes the Levin's colorization matrix. However, it should be taken into account the fact that the Levin's colorization matrix depends on the RP set, and therefore, can be thought of as a variable depending on the RP set.

Taken the above mentioned facts into account, we propose to iteratively solve the following two steps:

1. Construct the colorization matrix A^{-1} from the RP set $\mathbf{x}$.
2. Compute the RP set $\mathbf{x}$ by solving the following sparse coding problem:

$$\underset{\mathbf{x}}{\operatorname{argmin}} \|\mathbf{u}_0 - A^{-1}\mathbf{x}\|^2, \ s.t. \ |\mathbf{x}|_0 \leq L \tag{6}$$

3. Iterate step 1 and 2 until a convergent RP set $\mathbf{x}$ is obtained.

Figure 2 shows the flowchart of the proposed method. At first, a random initial RP set is chosen. In our experiments, we used a regularly distributed RP set as the initial set. Using the initial RP set, the Levin's colorization matrix is constructed. Then, using this colorization matrix, we solve (6) to obtain the optimal RP set for the current Levin's colorization matrix. Again, the Levin's colorization matrix is constructed for the current optimal RP set, and thus, step 1 and 2 are iterated. The iteration terminates if the L_2 difference between the current RP set and the previous RP set is less than a pre-defined threshold value. The RP set converges to two oscillatory states, which we believe to be locally optimal. This is due to the fact that the proposed algorithm is a two step algorithm. This is verified by experimental results. However, we could not prove the optimality in this paper and leave the problem as an open problem.

After the first iteration, the RPs concentrate at some regions as can be seen in the top left image of Fig. 5. This is due to the fact that the column vectors in the Levin's colorization matrix A^{-1} at the first iteration have only a small non-zero support domain, since the initial RP set is regularly distributed.

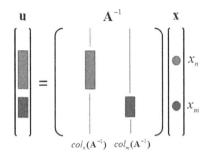

Fig. 3. The RP x_n corresponding to the colorization vector $col_n(A^{-1})$ with large non-zero domain has a large effect on the color component vector $\mathbf{u}$ while the RP x_m corresponding to $col_m(A^{-1})$ with small non-zero domain has a small effect

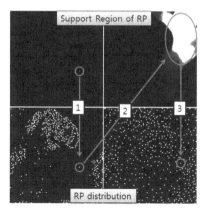

Fig. 4. 1. The initial small support domain results in a sparse RP distribution in the non-red region of the 'Pepper' image. 2. The sparse RP distribution results in colorization vector with large support domain. 3. The colorization vector with large support domain results in a denser RP distribution in this region.

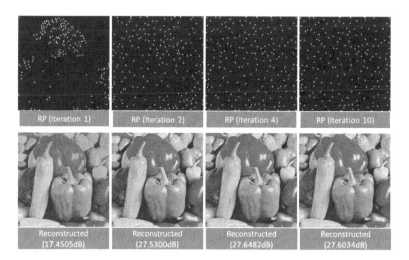

Fig. 5. Showing the RP sets and the colorized results along the even-number iteration of the 'Pepper' image

When the colorization matrix A^{-1} is constructed using this RP distribution, the column vectors in A^{-1} have non-zero values only for a small region in the image. Therefore, each RP can have an effect only on a small region of the reconstructed color image. Figure 3 illustrates the fact that an RP corresponding to a colorization vector with large non-zero support region has a large effect on the reconstructed color component, while an RP corresponding to a colorization vector with small non-zero support region has a small effect. At this condition, the RP which are selected to minimize the L_2 energy in (6) have a tendency to concentrate in the red and/or yellow colored regions, since the red and/or yellow colors have relatively large Cr and Cb values, and therefore, contribute much to the L_2 energy. This fact is shown in Fig. 4. However, the concentration of the RP in the red or yellow regions result in the construction of the corresponding colorization vectors with small support regions, while the RP in sparse regions result in the construction of the corresponding colorization vectors with large support regions. The bottom images in Fig. 4 show the colorization vectors in two dimensional form corresponding to the RP in dense region and the RP in sparse region, respectively. As can be seen, the non-zero values in the colorization vector corresponding to the RP in the sparse region cover a large region. This is also true for the neighboring colorization vectors. This means that the effect of the RPs (in the sparse region) become large in the next minimization step of (6). Therefore, at the next step, more RP are extracted from this region and the final RP set has a less concentrated distribution as can be seen from the bottom right image in Fig. 4.

4   Experiments

We compared the proposed scheme with the method of Cheng *et al.*[3], the method of Ono *et al.* [6], and the JPEG standard. We used the original Y component in each experiment. The number of RP obtained with the proposed scheme is 200, and the size of the test image is 256×256. Therefore, the file size for the color components becomes 0.78125KB (4×200 bytes = 0.7812KB) where we used 2 bytes for the color components, and 2 bytes for the spatial coordinates. For the methods of Cheng *et al.* and Ono *et al.*, the number of RP varies depending on the initial setting. Therefore, the comparison of the compression performance is made in the file size.

Figure 5 shows the RP sets and the reconstructed color images after different iterations. It can be seen that the reconstructed color image improves according to the iteration. Figure 6 compares the reconstructed color images for different methods and Table 1 summarizes the PSNR and SSIM values, where all the RGB channels are taken into account in the computation of the PSNR values, while the SSIM values are computed for the Cb and Cr channels independently. Compared with other colorization coding methods, the proposed scheme shows less color permeation, and therefore, has higher SSIM and PSNR values. The proposed method shows better compression rate for the color components than the JPEG standard, while showing visually comparable results.

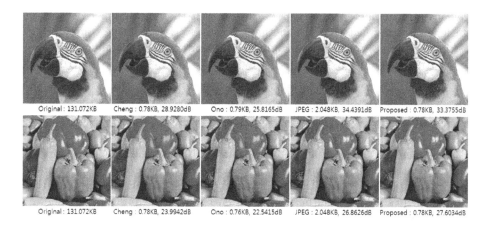

Fig. 6. Reconstructed color image of different compression methods

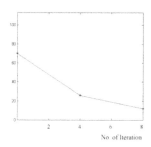

No. of Iteration

Fig. 7. Number of RP different from the previous even numbered iteration regarding Fig. 5

Table 1. Summarization of the comparison of the file size (KB), PSNR, SSIM values between the different compression methods

Image	Method	File Size	PSNR	SSIM(Cb)	SSIM(Cr)
Pepper	Proposed	0.78(KB)	27.603	0.952	0.958
	Ono *et al*	0.76(KB)	22.541	0.781	0.757
	Cheng *et al*	0.78(KB)	23.994	0.872	0.796
	JPEG	2.048(KB)	26.863	0.954	0.870
Parrot	Proposed	0.78(KB)	33.376	0.969	0.964
	Ono *et al*	0.79(KB)	25.817	0.696	0.696
	Cheng *et al*	0.78 (KB)	28.928	0.885	0.867
	JPEG	2.048(KB)	34.439	0.974	0.975

Figure 7 shows the number of RP which are different from those at the previous odd numbered iteration. It can be seen that the number decreases, which implies the fact that the method converges. However, the computation cost for the proposed scheme is high due to the iteration. The computation time for iterating 10 times was about 7.2 sec with a 3.4 GHz Intel processor running on Windows7.

5   Conclusion

In this paper, we proposed an iterative sparse coding method for the colorization colorization based compression application. The proposed scheme automatically computes the optimal RP (representative pixel) set with respect to the optimal Levin's colorization matrix in the encoder. It is experimentally shown that the reconstruction result and the compression rate is better than those of conventional colorization based compression methods and the JPEG standard. However, the convergence of the proposed method is theoretically not proven in this paper and left as an open problem.

Acknowledgments. This work was supported by the Mid-career Researcher Program (No. 2012R1A2A4A01003732) and the Basic Science Research Program (2013R1A1A4A01007868) through the National Research Foundation of Korea (NRF) funded by the Ministry of Education, Science and Technology.

References

1. Levin, A., Lischinski, D., Weiss, Y.: Colorization using Optimization. ACM Transactions on Graphics **23**, 689–694 (2004)
2. Yatziv, L., Sapiro, G.: Fast image and video colorization using chrominance blending. IEEE Trans. Image Processing **15**(5), 1120–1129 (2006)
3. Cheng, L., Vishwanathan, S.V.N.: Learning to Compress Images and Videos. In: Proc. ICML, vol. 227, pp. 161–168 (2007)
4. He, X., Ji, M., Bao, H.: A Unified Active and Semi-supervised Learning Framework for Image Compression. In: Proc. IEEE CVPR 2009, pp. 65–72. IEEE Press, Miami (2009)
5. Miyata, T., Komiyama, Y., Inazumi, Y., Sakai, Y.: Novel Inverse Colorization for Image Compression. In: Proc. Picture Coding Symposium, Chicago, pp. 1–7 (2009)
6. Ono, S., Miyata, T., Sakai, Y.: Colorization-based Coding by focusing on Characteristics of Colorization Bases. In: Proc. Picture Coding Symposium, Nagoya, pp. 11–17 (2010)
7. Lee, S., Park, S., Oh, P., Kang, M.: Colorization based Compression using Optimization. IEEE Trans. Image Process. **22**(7), 2627–2636 (2013)

Noise Modelling in Parallel Magnetic Resonance Imaging: A Variational Approach

Adrián Martín[1,2]($\boxtimes$) and Emanuele Schiavi[1]

[1] Applied Mathematics Department, Universidad Rey Juan Carlos, 28933 Móstoles, Madrid, Spain

[2] Magnetic Resonance Imaging Group, RLE-EECS, Massachusetts Institute of Technology, Cambridge, MA, USA
{adrian.martin,emanuele.schiavi}@urjc.es

Abstract. We proposed a new variational model for parallel Magnetic Resonance Imaging (MRI) processing including denoising, deblurring and super-resolution. In the context of *Maximum A Posteriori* (MAP) estimation it takes into account the non-central χ (nc-χ) distribution of the noise in parallel magnitude magnetic resonance (MR) images. This leads to the resolution of an energy minimization problem. In this Bayesian modelling framework the Total Generalized Variation (TGV) is proposed as the regularization term. A primal-dual algorithm is then implemented to solve numerically the presented model. The effectiveness of our approach is shown through a successful comparison of its performance to previous TGV methods for MRI denoising based on Gaussian noise.

1 Introduction

It is well known that noise is the main limitation for image processing, subsequent analysis and quantitative measurements derived from Magnetic Resonance Images. The noise modelling exercise has evolved in the last decade because of the consolidation of parallel MRI as the standard acquisition technique in clinical practice. Parallel imaging protocols consists of an established yet still developing family of procedures which aim to accelerate the data acquisition process so reducing scanning times in MRI. This technology based in the NMR phased array developed in the late 1980s [1] became predominant more recently with the development of well known techniques such as SiMultaneous Acquisition of Spatial Harmonics (SMASH) [2], SENSitivity Encoding for fast MRI (SENSE) [3] and GeneRalized Autocalibrated Partially Parallel Aquisitions (GRAPPA) [4] and a large list of methods proposed in the last years based in these three different approaches (see [5] for a discussion about SMASH, SENSE and GRAPPA).

How to model the noise for the different reconstruction algorithms has been the subject of intense research in the last years [6–8] concluding that there is no noise model generally applicable to all the reconstructed data. Nevertheless when

© Springer International Publishing Switzerland 2014
A. Campilho and M. Kamel (Eds.): ICIAR 2014, Part I, LNCS 8814, pp. 121–128, 2014.
DOI: 10.1007/978-3-319-11758-4_14

the global image is reconstructed in the frequency domain before Fourier transformation as in GRAPPA, the noncentral-χ (nc-χ) distribution function emerges
as a feasible likelihood function [9], even when the data are obtained from a correlated multiple-coil system [10]. In the case of SENSE and related algorithms
that calculate the final image in the image domain, the magnitude signal may be
considered Rician distributed but the value of the statistical parameters becomes
spatially dependent[7]. In a very recent work [11], a new method for the estimation of the noise for both GRAPPA and SENSE reconstructed images has been
presented.

Some recent works in MRI denoising take into account this nc-χ distribution
of the noisy MR data using LMMSE techniques [12] and non-local methods [13],
but to the best of our knowledge no variational image processing model exists
for these images. This introduce the principal aim of our work which is to show
how a variational approach can deal with these advanced statistical models. We
present a general framework where the nc-χ distribution of the noise is considered
for different image processing problems including pure denoising, deblurring and
super-resolution. The generality of this approach allows the implementation of
different image priors based in sparse representations such as the well known
Total Variation operator and more advanced operators as the Total Generalized
Variation (TGV) recently proposed in [14].

As a proof of concept we demonstrate the effectiveness of this approach in
the case of pure denoising of GRAPPA images using the TGV prior. This operator selects discontinuous (piecewise) smooth solutions which has been recently
shown to be a feasible MRI model outperforming Total Variation (TV) based
preprocessing methods [15–17].

This paper is organized as follows: the model equations are proposed in
section 2 while the numerical implementation is detailed in section 3. Finally
some preliminary results obtained with phantom and real brain images are presented and discussed in section 4.

2   Model Equations

We briefly sketch the derivation of the proposed model. In a bayesian framework
let $f \in L^\infty(\Omega)$ be the known noisy image and u the underlying clean image. The
MAP estimate of u is given by:

$$\hat{u} = \max_u p(u|f) \Leftrightarrow \min_u \{-\log p(u) - \log p(f|u)\} \tag{1}$$

The probability $p(u)$ is called the prior of u and acts as a regularization on what
u is likely to be. The second term $p(f|u)$ describes the degradation process that
produces f from u. Magnitude MRI obtained from a multiple-coil acquisition
follows a nc-χ distribution given by:

$$p(f|u) = \frac{f}{\sigma^2} \left(\frac{f}{u}\right)^{n-1} \exp\left(-\frac{f^2 + u^2}{2\sigma^2}\right) I_{n-1}\left(\frac{uf}{\sigma^2}\right) \tag{2}$$

with σ being the noise standard deviation of the Gaussian noise present in the complex acquisition channels, n the number of channels used for the acquisition and I_{n-1} being the $(n-1)$th order modified Bessel function of the first kind. Introducing the noise distribution in a variational formulation results:

$$G(Au) = -\int_\Omega \log \mathrm{p}(f|(Au)) =$$

$$= \int_\Omega \left[-\log((Au)^{1-n}) + \frac{(Au)^2}{2\sigma^2} - \log I_{n-1}\left(\frac{(Au)f}{\sigma^2}\right) \right] dx \qquad (3)$$

where A is a linear operator. Notice that some constant terms have been dropped because they do not affect to the minimization result. In the case of pure denoising A is the identity. In the cases of image deblurring and image super-resolution A describes the blurring kernel and the downsampling procedure respectively, being the downsampling procedure often assumed to be a blurring kernel followed by a subsampling operator. Denoting the prior term $F(u) = -\int_\Omega \log \mathrm{p}(u)$ the optimal u is given by the solution of the following variational problem

$$\min_u F(u) + G(Au)$$

An introduction to this kind of general framework for image processing can be found in the books [18,19]. The second order Total Generalized Variation $\mathrm{TGV}^2_\alpha(u)$ is considered here as the regularization term, defined for (α_0, α_1) as:

$$\mathrm{TGV}^2_\alpha(u) = \sup \left\{ \int_\Omega u \, \mathrm{div}^2 v \, dx \mid v \in \mathcal{C}^2_c(\bar{\Omega}, S^{d\times d}), \|v\|_\infty \le \alpha_0, \|\mathrm{div}\, v\|_\infty \le \alpha_1 \right\}$$
$$(4)$$

with $\mathcal{C}^2_c(\bar{\Omega}, S^{d\times d})$ denoting the space of the twice continuously differentiable symmetric matricial functions with compact support. Following [14], $\mathrm{TGV}^2_\alpha(u)$ can also be formulated as:

$$\mathrm{TGV}^2_\alpha(u) = \min_{u\in\mathrm{BGV}^2_\alpha(\Omega), v\in\mathrm{BD}(\Omega)} \alpha_1 \int_\Omega |\nabla u - v| + \alpha_0 \int_\Omega |\mathcal{E}(v)| \qquad (5)$$

where $\mathcal{E}(v) = \frac{1}{2}(\nabla v + \nabla v^\mathsf{T})$, BGV^2_α is the space of functions of bounded generalized variation and $\mathrm{BD}(\Omega)$ is the space of vector fields of Bounded Deformation. Defining $F(u) = \frac{1}{\lambda}\mathrm{TGV}^2_\alpha(u)$ with λ a trade-off parameter between the regularization and the data fidelity, the variational problem is described by:

$$\min_{u\in\mathrm{BGV}^2_\alpha(\Omega)} \mathrm{TGV}^2_\alpha(u) + \lambda \int_\Omega \left[-\log((Au)^{1-n}) + \frac{(Au)^2}{2\sigma^2} - \log I_{n-1}\left(\frac{(Au)f}{\sigma^2}\right) \right] dx$$
$$(6)$$

Such minimization is outlined in the next section.

3 Numerical Implementation

Given $U = \mathbb{R}^{MN}$, $V = \mathbb{R}^{2MN}$, we define the discrete minimization problem associated with (6) :

$$\min_{u\in U, v\in V} \lambda G(Au) + \alpha_1 \|\nabla u - v\|_1 + \alpha_0 \|\mathcal{E}v\|_1 \qquad (7)$$

Details of the discretization of the continuous elements including the differential operators can be found in [14]. Following [20], this problem can be reformulated using duality arguments as the saddle-point problem:

$$\min_{u \in U, v \in V} \max_{p \in V, q \in W} \lambda G(Au) + \langle \nabla u - v, p \rangle - I_P(p) +$$

$$+ \langle \mathcal{E}v, q \rangle - I_Q(q) \tag{8}$$

where $W = \mathbb{R}^{3MN}$, p, q are the dual variables and the convex sets associated with these variables are given by $P = \{p \in V \mid \|p\|_\infty \leq \alpha_1\}$, $Q = \{q \in W \mid \|q\|_\infty \leq \alpha_0\}$. Finally the functions $I_P(p)$, $I_Q(q)$ denote the indicator functions of the sets P and Q respectively. The primal-dual algorithm for the denoising reads as follows:

Algorithm 1. TGV$^2_\alpha$ nc-χ image processing

1: Set $p^0 = 0, q^0 = 0, u^0 = f, v^0 = f$

2: **repeat**

3: $\quad p^{k+1} = \dfrac{p^k + \tau_d(\nabla u^k - v^k)}{\max\left(1, \dfrac{\|p^k + \tau_d(\nabla u^k - v^k)\|_\infty}{\alpha_1}\right)}$

4: $\quad q^{k+1} = \dfrac{q^k + \tau_d \mathcal{E} v^k}{\max\left(1, \dfrac{\|q^k + \tau_d \mathcal{E} v^k\|_\infty}{\alpha_0}\right)}$

5: $\quad u^{k+1} = u^k + \tau_p(\mathrm{div}p^k - \lambda \partial_u G(Au^k))$

6: $\quad v^{k+1} = v^k + \tau_p\left(p - \mathcal{E}^{*h}q\right)$

7: **until** convergence of u

---

with $-\mathrm{div} = (\nabla)^*$, $\mathcal{E}^{*h} = (\mathcal{E})^*$ and

$$\partial_u G(Au^k) = A^* \left(\frac{Au^k}{\sigma^2} - \left[I_n \left(\frac{(Au^k)f}{\sigma^2} \right) / I_{n-1} \left(\frac{u^k f}{\sigma^2} \right) \right] \frac{f}{\sigma^2} \right)$$

where I_n is the nth order modified Bessel function of the first kind.

4   Results and Discussion

In order to demonstrate the effectiveness of the proposed approach to deal with the nc-χ distribution of the noise of the data we consider the implementation of the pure denoising case. This allow a direct analysis of the performance of the model not perturbed by other artifacts (blurring, low resolution, etc.).

4.1   Material and Methods

For the model validation we used a Matlab toolbox (avaliable online in http://www.mathworks.com/matlab/central/fileexchange/36893-parallel-mri-/noisy-phantom-simulator) to generate a GRAPPA noisy phantom from 2, 4 and 8 coils for noise of $\sigma = 5, 7, 10$. The proposed model is compared with the original TGV denoising method described in [15] where the noise is assumed to be gaussian. Two different choices for the pair of weights $(\alpha_0, \alpha_1) = (2, 1)$ and $(\alpha_0, \alpha_1) = (0.5, 1)$ where used in the experiments while the parameter λ was optimized for the two methods in order to obtain the best Peak-Signal-to-Noise-Ratio (PSNR) with the original phantom. In both denoising models the best results were always obtained for the pair $(\alpha_0, \alpha_1) = (0.5, 1)$. We also use a real dataset of Diffusion Weighted Images (DWI) obtained from a 32-coil Verio B173T MR Scanner Siemens with GRAPPA factor of 2 kindly provided by the Neurinfo platform of the University of Rennes I and Inria Visages team. The acquisition parameters were: $T_E/T_R = 99ms/11s$, matrix 128×128, 60 slices, resolution $2 \times 2 \times 2mm/s^2$, space between slice $2mm$. The DWI data consists on a volume obtained with b=0/mm^2 and 30 volumes with b=1000s/mm^2. For the noise estimation (σ parameter) we applied the Brummer-Aja's method proposed in [8] and we used the values $(\alpha_0, \alpha_1) = (0.5, 1)$ and $\lambda = 0.5$ for the DWI denoising. The Diffusion Tensor Image (DTI) was reconstructed from the original and the denoised DWI dataset with the FSL software (http://fsl.fmrib.ox.ac.uk/fsl).

4.2   Results Analysis

The best PSNR results obtained with the two algorithms are shown in Figure 1 for a different number of coils and noise levels. The image quality is always higher for the nc-χ denoising and the difference between the methods grows when the number of coils rises, suggesting the importance of modelling the nc-χ distribution of the noise when the complexity of the multichannel system is increased. The visual aspects of the denoising performance can be seen in

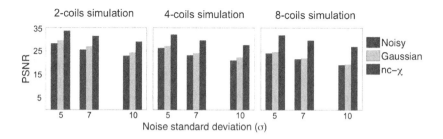

Fig. 1. Best PSNR values obtained by Gaussian (in green) and nc-χ denoising (in red) of the artificially contaminated phantom reconstructed from 2, 4 and 8 coils and contaminated with values of $\sigma = 5, 7, 10$. In blue the PSNR of the noisy image.

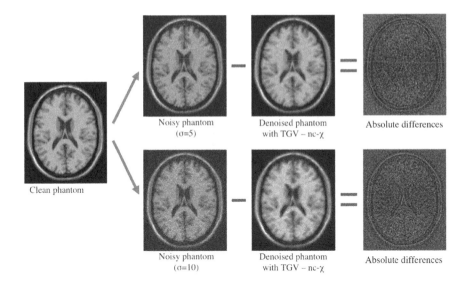

Fig. 2. Central slice of the phantom generated with 8 coils and contaminated with noise with parameter $\sigma = 5$ and 10. The noisy images are denoised with the proposed method and the noise removed is shown as the absolute difference between the noisy and the denoised images.

Figure 2. Observing the absolute difference between the noisy and the denoised images it is clear that the noise has been removed with a minimum loss of structure details. For the test with real brain images, the DWI dataset was denoised with the proposed method. The DTI was then reconstructed from the original and the denoised images and scalar measurements of the tensor as the Fractional Anisotropy (FA) were calculated. In Figure 3 the visual results of this preliminary study can be observed. In the example of a pre- and post-denoised DWI we can see that the method remove the inhomogeneities produced by noise. How this denoising affect to the subsequent DTI reconstruction is clearly visible in the FA examples, where in the image obtained from a denoised dataset the structures and details are enhanced and the noise have been removed.

These results validate the proposed variational model for noisy MR images obtained from parallel acquisition systems. As a conclusion we observe that to consider the non-central χ distribution of the data is crucial for accurate noise treatment. This preliminary study also shows the feasibility of using the proposed framework to deal with more complex image processing task such as the deblurring or the super-resolution of parallel MR images. Further parametric study in undoubtedly necessary for the application in clinical routine. The consideration of non-stationary distributions of the noise can also be explored and introduced in the suggested variational model.

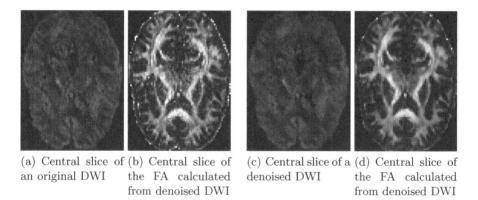

(a) Central slice of an original DWI (b) Central slice of the FA calculated from denoised DWI (c) Central slice of a denoised DWI (d) Central slice of the FA calculated from denoised DWI

Fig. 3. Examples of the original and denoised DWI sets and the FA calculated from these two data sets

Acknowledgments. This work was supported by project TEC2012-39095-C03-02 of the Spanish Ministry of Economy and Competitiveness. We also want to thank PhD J.F. Garamendi and the Neurinfo platform of the University of Rennes I and Inria Visages team for their kindly contribution with the set of Diffusion Weighted Images.

References

1. Roemer, P.B., Edelstein, W.A., Hayes, C.E., Souza, S.P., Mueller, O.M.: The NMR phased array. Magnetic Resonance in Medicine **16**(2), 192–225 (1990)
2. Sodickson, D.K., Manning, W.J.: Simultaneous acquisition of spatial harmonics (SMASH): Fast imaging with radiofrequency coil arrays. Magnetic Resonance in Medicine **38**(4), 591–603 (1997)
3. Pruessmann, K.P., Weiger, M., Scheidegger, M.B., Boesiger, P.: SENSE: sensitivity encoding for fast MRI. Magnetic Resonance in Medicine **42**(5), 952–952 (1999)
4. Griswold, M.A., Jakob, P.M., Heidemann, R.M., Nittka, M., Jellus, V., Wang, J., Kiefer, B., Haase, A.: Generalized autocalibrating partially parallel acquisitions (GRAPPA). Magnetic Resonance in Medicine **47**(6), 1202–1210 (2002)
5. Blaimer, M., Breuer, F., Mueller, M., Heidemann, R.M., Griswold, M.A., Jakob, P.M.: Smash, sense, pils, grappa. Topics in Magnetic Resonance Imaging **15**(4), 223–236 (2004)
6. Constantinides, C.D., Atalar, E.: Signal-to-Noise Measurements in Magnitude Images from NMR Phased Arrays. Magnetic Resonance in Medicine **38**(5), 852–857 (2008)
7. Dietrich, O., Raya, J.G., Reeder, S.B., Ingrisch, M., Reiser, M.F., Schoenberg, S.O.: Influence of multichannel combination, parallel imaging and other reconstruction techniques on MRI noise characteristics. Magnetic Resonance Imaging **26**(6), 754–762 (2008)
8. Aja-Fernández, S., Tristán-Vega, A., Alberola-López, C.: Noise estimation in single- and multiple-coil magnetic resonance data based on statistical models. Magnetic Resonance Imaging **27**(10), 1397–1409 (2009)

9. Aja-Fernández, S., Tristán-Vega, A., Hoge, W.S.: Statistical noise analysis in GRAPPA using a parametrized noncentral Chi approximation model. Magnetic Resonance in Medicine **65**(4), 1195–1206 (2011)
10. Aja-Fernández, S., Brion, V., Tristán-Vega, A.: Effective noise estimation and filtering from correlated multiple-coil MR data. Magnetic Resonance Imaging (October 2012)
11. Aja-Fernández, S., Vegas-Sánchez-Ferrero, G., Tristán-Vega, A.: Noise estimation in parallel MRI: GRAPPA and SENSE. Magnetic Resonance Imaging **32**(3), 281–290 (2014)
12. Brion, V., Poupon, C., Riff, O., Aja-Fernández, S., Tristán-Vega, A., Mangin, J.-F., Le Bihan, D., Poupon, F.: Parallel MRI noise correction: an extension of the LMMSE to non central χ distributions. In: Fichtinger, G., Martel, A., Peters, T. (eds.) MICCAI 2011, Part II. LNCS, vol. 6892, pp. 226–233. Springer, Heidelberg (2011)
13. Rajan, J., Veraart, J., Van Audekerke, J., Verhoye, M., Sijbers, J.: Nonlocal maximum likelihood estimation method for denoising multiple-coil magnetic resonance images. Magnetic Resonance Imaging (July 2012)
14. Bredies, K., Kunisch, K., Pock, T.: Total Generalized Variation. SIAM Journal on Imaging Sciences **3**(3), 492–526 (2010)
15. Knoll, F., Bredies, K., Stollberger, R., Pock, T.: Second Order Total Generalized Variation (TGV) for MRI. Magnetic Resonance in Medicine **65**(2), 480–491 (2011)
16. Valkonen, T., Bredies, K., Knoll, F.: Total Generalized Variation in Diffusion Tensor Imaging. SIAM Journal on Imaging Sciences **6**(1), 487–525 (2013)
17. Martín, A., Schiavi, E.: Automatic Total Generalized Variation-Based DTI Rician Denoising. In: Kamel, M., Campilho, A. (eds.) ICIAR 2013. LNCS, vol. 7950, pp. 581–588. Springer, Heidelberg (2013)
18. Chan, T.F., Shen, J.: Image Processing and Analysis: variational, PDE, wavelet, and stochastic methods. Society for Industrial and Applied Mathematics (2005)
19. Scherzer, O., Grasmair, M., Grossauer, H., Haltmeier, M., Lenzen, F.: Variational Methods in Imaging. Springer (2009)
20. Chambolle, A., Pock, T.: A first-order primal-dual algorithm for convex problems with applications to imaging. Journal of Mathematical Imaging and Vision **40**(1), 120–145 (2011)

Image Restoration and Enhancement

An Examination of Several Methods of Hyperspectral Image Denoising: Over Channels, Spectral Functions and Both Domains

Daniel Otero[1]([✉]), Oleg V. Michailovich[2], and Edward R. Vrscay[1]

[1] Department of Applied Mathematics, Faculty of Mathematics,
University of Waterloo, Waterloo, ON N2L 3G1, Canada
[2] Department of Electrical and Computer Engineering, Faculty of Engineering,
University of Waterloo, Waterloo, ON N2L 3G1, Canada
{dotero,olegm,ervrscay}@uwaterloo.ca

Abstract. The corruption of hyperspectral images by noise can compromise tasks such as classification, target detection and material mapping. For this reason, many methods have been proposed to recover, as best as possible, the uncorrupted hyperspectral data from a given noisy observation. In this paper, we propose and compare the results of four denoising methods which differ in the way the hyperspectral data is treated: (i) as 3D data sets, (ii) as collections of frequency bands and (iii) as collections of spectral functions. In the case of additive noise, these methods can be easily adapted to accommodate different degradation models. Our methods and results help to address the question of how hyperspectral data sets should be processed in order to obtain useful denoising results.

1 Introduction

In this paper we consider the problem of denoising digital hyperspectral (HS) images obtained from remote sensing of the earth's surface. In this case, the HS image associated with a given surface region R is comprised of a set of reflectance values – ratios of reflected energy vs. incident energy – of electromagnetic radiation at a number of frequencies (or, equivalently, wavelengths) at each pixel location in R. The number of frequencies depends upon the spectral resolution of the sensor of the hyperspectral camera and may range from tens to hundreds. For example, the well-known AVIRIS (Airborne Visible/Infrared Imaging Spectrometer) satellite images [1] typically contain 224 frequencies.

Suppose that a region R of the earth's surface is represented by an $M \times N$ pixel array and that associated with each pixel in the array there are P reflectance values. The first, and most obvious, way of viewing this HS data set is as a $M \times N \times P$ "data cube." The correlations between neighbouring entries of this cube give rise to two additional and complementary ways of viewing this 3D data set: (ii) as a collection of P images of region R at different frequencies – often referred to as *spectral channels* or *frequency/wavelength bands* – and

© Springer International Publishing Switzerland 2014
A. Campilho and M. Kamel (Eds.): ICIAR 2014, Part I, LNCS 8814, pp. 131–140, 2014.
DOI: 10.1007/978-3-319-11758-4_15

(iii) as a collection of $M \times N$ P-vectors, each of which corresponds to a given pixel location (i, j) of R – often referred to as the *spectral function* or, simply, *spectrum* at (i, j). These three views of the HS image will play a central theme in this paper.

Let us very briefly recall the importance of spectral functions. Since different materials, e.g., minerals, water, vegetation, exhibit different reflectance spectra, the latter serve as "spectral fingerprints". The spectrum at a pixel (i, j) makes it possible to determine the composition/nature of material situated at that location. This makes the study of HS images useful in a variety of applications, including agriculture, mineralogy, geography and surveillance, the latter involving hyperspectral imaging tasks such as target detection and classification [23]. In light of the acquisition process, HS images are, as in the case of many other images, prone to contamination by noise which can compromise the performance of such tasks. As a result, it is desirable to develop reconstruction techniques that recover good approximations of noise-free HS images.

Indeed, many different methods for denoising HS data have been proposed. For example, in [18], diffusion-based filtering is adapted to HS images. The proposed method consists of two diffusion processes, one confined to each band of the HS image, and the another restricted to the spectral domain. The overall anisotropic diffusion is basically a combination of these two processes, which are carried out in a controlled fashion. In [19], a rather novel wavelet-based denoising approach is proposed. This method transforms the HS data set into a spectral-derivative domain, in which the irregularity of noise is more easily detected. The transformed HS image is denoised using wavelet shrinkage (WS) independently in both the spatial and spectral domains. A reconstruction is then obtained by first computing the corresponding inverse wavelet transforms of the denoised data followed by an integration in the spectral direction. Another method that carries out denoising employing WS is presented in [9]. Here, principal component analysis (PCA) is used to decorrelate the most relevant HS data from the noise, most of which is assumed to be contained in the lowest energy components of the transformed data. The noise is removed from these components using WS in both spatial and spectral domains. The denoised HS data set is then retrieved by means of the inverse PCA transform. Variational approaches are proposed in [8,26]. In [26], a total variation (TV) model that considers the changes of noise intensity present across the bands and pixels of an HS image is proposed. In [8], a method that employs a TV model along with sparse representations of each band is also introduced. More approaches can also be found in [20,21].

In this study, we wish to examine the roles of both spatial (pixel) and spectral domains in the denoising of HS images. For example, is it preferable to focus the denoising in one domain at the expense of the other, or should both domains be considered? In order to shed some light on this and related questions, we compare four different denoising approaches. The main difference between these approaches lies in the way that the HS image is treated, using the three views mentioned earlier, i.e., as a (i) 3D data "cube", (ii) a set of frequency bands or (iii) a set of spectral functions.

In our first approach, the denoising process is performed in the spectral domain, corresponding to (iii) above. In particular, we apply ℓ_1-norm regularization [2,17,24] to the spectral functions. In the second approach, the denoising process is performed in the spatial domain, corresponding to (ii) above. As expected, any denoising technique applicable to 2D signals/images can be employed – here, we focus our attention on the TV approach [6,22]. Our third approach employs a formulation of vectorial TV to denoise the entire HS image at once [5,14], corresponding to (i) above. Finally, in our fourth approach, an HS image is viewed as a collection of both spectra and frequency bands. Our method involves a combination of the first two approaches so that denoising is carried out by regularization in both the spatial and spectral domains. To solve this inverse problem we employ the Alternating Direction Method of Multipliers (ADMM) [4]. Experimental results are then presented so that the performance of these methods can be compared.

2 Denoising

In practice, the strengths of the denoising process across spatial and spectral domains of an HS image should be different. Even within the spatial domain, different features such as edges and flat regions should not be denoised with the same intensity. In addition, it is quite common that the power of noise across bands is not constant [3,26]. Some methods that address these possible scenarios can be found in the literature, e.g., [19,26]. Nevertheless, in this study, for the sake of simplicity we assume that the power of the noise is constant over the entire HS data set, i.e., it is independent of the location and band of a given voxel. As such, we consider the following simple degradation model,

$$f = u + n, \tag{1}$$

where f is the noisy observation, u is the noiseless HS data we wish to recover, and n is additive white Gaussian noise (AWGN). In this case, f, n and u are considered as $M \times N \times P$ HS data cubes. Moreover, for the remainder of the paper, this interpretation of HS images as 3D discrete data sets is the one that we will consider, unless otherwise stated.

Despite that Eq. (1) may not always be a proper model for noise in HS images, it will be seen that some of the methods presented below can be easily adapted for different scenarios in which the noise characteristics change over space and wavelength.

2.1 Denoising of Hyperspectral Images as a Collection of Spectra

Here we view f as a collection of P spectra. The problem is therefore split into $M \times N$ subproblems, with the denoising being carried out in the spectral direction on each of the P spectral functions.

Each spectral function may be denoised with any of the available denoising techniques that can be applied to 1D signals, e.g., wavelet shrinkage, linear filtering, 1D total variation denoising, etc.. Here, however, we investigate the effectiveness of ℓ_1-norm regularization, primarily because of the good performance of methods that exploit sparse representations of signals [2,17,24].

In this approach, we solve the following sparse approximation problem independently at each pixel (i, j),

$$\min_{c_{ij}} \left\{ \frac{1}{2} \|Dc_{ij} - s_{ij}\|_2^2 + \lambda \|c_{ij}\|_1 \right\}, \tag{2}$$

where s_{ij} denotes the noisy spectrum, D is an appropriate transformation matrix (e.g., frame, random matrix, etc.), and c_{ij} is the set of coefficients that is to be recovered at the pixel location (i, j).

In the literature, many algorithms for solving (2) can be found [2,17,24], however, we focus our attention on the special case in which the matrix D is an orthogonal transformation (e.g., DCT, wavelet transform, Fourier matrix, etc.). In this particular case, problem (2) can be solved by means of the soft thresholding (ST) operator [4,24].

It is worth pointing out that this approach allows us to change the strength of the denoising process across the spatial domain, i.e., different regularization parameters can be used at different pixels or in different regions of the HS image.

2.2   Denoising of Hyperspectral Images as a Collection of Bands

In this approach, the denoising process takes place in the spatial domain. Each frequency/wavelength band is treated independently and the denoising problem is split into P independent subproblems. Here, we consider each k-th band u_k as a scalar function $u_k : \Omega \to \mathbb{R}$, where $\Omega \subset \mathbb{R}^2$ and $1 \leq k \leq P$.

As expected, any denoising method for 2D images can be employed here, e.g., linear filtering, non-local means denoising, total variation, non-linear filtering, etc.. Nevertheless, in this study, we employed a TV denoising approach for which a number of fast algorithms exist, e.g., [6,15,22]. As well, some TV-based denoising methods for HS images have yielded promising results [8,26].

Our approach, a channel-by-channel TV method in the spatial domain where each band u_k is treated independently, translates to the following approximation problem,

$$\min_{u_k} \left\{ \frac{1}{2\mu} \|u_k - f_k\|_2^2 + \|u_k\|_{TV} \right\}, \tag{3}$$

where $\| \cdot \|_{TV}$ is the total variation norm and f_k is the k-th noisy band or channel. To solve this problem numerically, we employ the method introduced by Chambolle in [6], which has received special attention because of its excellent performance. Here, the following definition of the isotropic TV norm is employed,

$$\|u_k\|_{TV} = \int_\Omega \|Du_k\|_2 dxdy = \sup_{\xi_k \in \Xi_k} \left\{ \int_\Omega u_k \nabla \cdot \xi_k \, dxdy \right\}, \tag{4}$$

where $\Xi_k = \{\xi_k : \xi_k \in C_c^1(\Omega, \mathbb{R}^2), \|\xi_k(x)\|_2 \le 1 \; \forall x \in \Omega\}$, and $\nabla \cdot$ is the divergence operator. If $u_k \in C_c^1(\Omega, \mathbb{R})$, $Du_k = \nabla u_k$ in the distributional sense. This approach is convenient since only the integrability, and not the differentiability, of u_k is required.

By using (4), Chambolle shows that the optimal solution $u_k^\star$ of (3) is given by $u_k^\star = f_k - \Pi_{\mu\Gamma_k}(f_k)$, where $\Pi_{\mu\Gamma_k}(f_k)$ is the non-linear projection of f_k onto the convex set $\mu\Gamma_k$, and Γ_k is the closure of the set $\{\nabla \cdot \xi_k : \xi_k \in C_c^1(\Omega, \mathbb{R}^2), \|\xi_k(x)\|_2 \le 1 \; \forall x \in \Omega\}$. Such projection is obtained by solving the following minimization problem:

$$\min_{\|\xi_k(x)\|_2 \le 1} \{\mu\nabla \cdot \xi_k - f_k\}. \tag{5}$$

Thus, we have that for each band the optimal reconstruction is given by $u_k^\star = f_k - \mu\nabla \cdot \xi_k^\star$.

This approach may easily be modified to accommodate the case in which the power of the noise is not constant throughout the bands. In this case, one can specify the degree of regularization to be applied to each channel independently by means of the parameter μ.

2.3   Denoising of Hyperspectral Images as a Whole

In this case, we view a HS image as a vector-valued function $u : \Omega \to \mathbb{R}^P$, where $\Omega \subset \mathbb{R}^2$. To denoise it, we follow a variational approach, employing a definition of the Vectorial TV seminorm (VTV).

Given the effectiveness of TV for denoising images – along with its applicability to other image processing tasks such as inpainting, zooming, etc. – many extensions for vector-valued functions have been proposed [5,14]. Indeed, a practical application already exists for colour images, which are essentially low-dimensional HS images. This approach can easily be extended to HS images, with no required changes to the definitions presented in the literature. In particular, we use Bresson and Chan's approach [5], which is a generalization of Chambolle's algorithm for vector-valued functions. Here, the authors extend the Rudin-Osher-Fatemi model [22] as follows,

$$\min_u \left\{ \frac{1}{2\mu}\|u - f\|_{L_2(\Omega;\mathbb{R}^P)}^2 + \|u\|_{VTV} \right\}, \tag{6}$$

where f is the noisy observation. The VTV seminorm is defined as

$$\|u\|_{VTV} = \int_\Omega \|Du\|d\mathbf{x} = \sup_{\xi \in \Xi} \left\{ \int_\Omega \langle u, \nabla \cdot \xi \rangle d\mathbf{x} \right\}; \tag{7}$$

where $\Xi = \{\xi : \xi \in C_c^1(\Omega, \mathbb{R}^{2 \times P}), \|\xi(\mathbf{x})\|_2 \le 1 \; \forall \mathbf{x} \in \Omega\}$; $\langle \cdot, \cdot \rangle$ is the standard Euclidean scalar product in $\mathbb{R}^P$; and $\|Du\|^2 = \sum_{k=1}^P \|\nabla u_k\|_2^2$ if $u \in C_c^1(\Omega, \mathbb{R}^P)$, that is, the ℓ_2 norm of the TV norm of all the bands u_k of the HS image u.

Substitution of (7) into (6) yields to the following minimization problem:

$$\min_{\|\xi(\mathbf{x})\|_2 \leq 1} \left\{ \left\| \nabla \cdot \xi - \frac{f}{\mu} \right\|^2_{L_2(\Omega;\mathbb{R}^P)} \right\}, \tag{8}$$

whose solution $\xi^\star$ is computed using a semi-implicit gradient descent scheme. The solution $u^\star$ of the original problem in (6) is obtained using $u^\star = f - \mu \nabla \cdot \xi^\star$. In our case, f is the noisy HS image.

2.4 Denoising of Hyperspectral Images a Collection of Both Bands and Spectra

In this fourth approach, we perform regularization in both the spectral and spatial domains. This can be done in various ways, but we focus our attention on the methods employed previously, that is, TV- and ℓ_1-norm regularization.

As expected, denoising in the spectral domain is carried out by solving an optimization problem in which the ℓ_1 norm of a set of coefficients is used as a regularizing term. Denoising in the spatial domain is performed using a variational approach. In other words, we consider a good reconstruction of the original HS data u from the noisy observation f to be one with bounded variation across bands and with spectral functions that possess sparse representations in a certain domain. In order to find such a reconstruction, we solve the following optimization problem,

$$\min_c \left\{ \frac{1}{2} \|S(c) - f\|^2_2 + \mu \|S(c)\|_{VTV} + \lambda \|c\|_1 \right\}, \tag{9}$$

where $S(\cdot)$ is a synthesis operator that reconstructs the HS image from the set of coefficients c. More specifically, at each pixel (i, j), the operator $S(\cdot)$ recovers the spectrum located at that pixel location by computing Dc_{ij}, where c_{ij} is the set of coefficients associated to such spectrum.

For solving problem (9) we employ ADMM, which is a method well suited for convex optimization and large scale problems [4]. We first need to express (9) in ADMM form:

$$\min_{c,u} \left\{ \frac{1}{2} \|u - f\|^2_2 + \mu \|u\|_{VTV} + \lambda \|c\|_1 \right\} \tag{10}$$

$$\text{subject to } S(c) - u = 0.$$

It is well known [4] that this new problem can be solved by forming the augmented Lagrangian and minimizing with respect to the variables c and u in an alternate fashion. Given this, we propose the following ADMM iterations for solving (9):

$$c^{n+1} := \min_c \left\{ \frac{1}{2} \left\| S(c) - \frac{f + \delta(u^n - p^n)}{\delta + 1} \right\|^2_2 + \frac{\lambda}{\delta + 1} \|c\|_1 \right\} \tag{11}$$

$$u^{n+1} := \min_u \left\{ \frac{\delta}{2\mu} \|u - (S(c^{n+1}) + p^n)\|^2_2 + \|u\|_{VTV} \right\} \tag{12}$$

$$p^{n+1} := p^n + S(c^{n+1}) - u^{n+1}, \tag{13}$$

where p is the dual variable associated to the augmented Lagrangian, (13) its update, and δ is a penalty parameter. Problem (11) can be solved by any algorithm capable of carrying out sparse reconstruction using the ℓ_1 norm as a regularizing term. Problem (12) can be addressed using any method employing the vectorial TV norm. In particular, we have used ST to solve (11) at each pixel and Bresson and Chan's algorithm for problem (12).

It is important to mention that different regularization terms can be used in problem (11) since it is solved at each pixel independently. Moreover, problem (12) can be solved using our second approach in Section 2.2, that is, denoising each band independently, in which case the regularization can be changed from band to band. In other words, our fourth approach may be adapted for denoising with different intensities across both spatial as well as spectral domains.

3   Experiments

In order to compare the performance of the four methods described above, they were applied to noisy versions of the Indian Pines and Salinas-A HS images. The latter is a subset of the Salinas HS image – both of them can be downloaded from [16]. The sizes of the 3D Indian Pines and Salinas-A data sets are $145 \times 145 \times 220$ and $83 \times 86 \times 224$, respectively. White additive Gaussian noise was added to these HS data (assumed to be noiseless). In all experiments, the Peak Signal-to-Noise Ratio (PSNR) before denoising was 30.103 dB.

In the approaches where a set of optimal coefficients was to be determined, the transformation matrix D employed was the Karhunen-Loève Transform (KLT), which was computed for each HS image. The KLT was chosen since it gives a very sparse representation of the HS data (as compared to DCT, wavelet and other transforms), as well as being optimal in the ℓ_2 sense. When the KLT is used, the mean of the HS data must be subtracted prior to processing.

As for measures of performance, we employed the Mean Square Error (MSE), PSNR, and the Structural Similarity Index Measure (SSIM) [25]. For the latter, we computed the SSIM between the original and recovered HS images in both the spatial and spectral domains. For the spatial case, the SSIM is computed between bands; whereas in the spectral case, the SSIM is computed between spectra. An overall SSIM is obtained by simply averaging all the computed SSIMs for both the spatial and the spectral cases. Observe that the greater the similarity between two images, the closer their SSIM is to 1. In Table 1, a summary of these quantitative results is shown.

According to these results, the fourth approach (ADMM) outperforms all the other methods respect to any of the metrics of performance that were considered. Only in the denoising results for Indian Pines, the spectral-oriented method described in section 2.1 is as good as ADMM in the "spectral-SSIM sense". The latter suggests that methods that carry out regularization in both the spectral and spatial domains may perform better than methods in which the denoising process is not carried out in this fashion. We believe this to be the case because the fourth approach captures best the "nature" of HS data, that is, data that is correlated in both the spatial and spectral domains.

For visual comparison, some results are presented in Figures 1 and 2. Figure 1 demonstrates how the methods achieve the denoising in the spatial domain. The SSIM maps, shown in the top row of Figure 1, illustrate the similarity between the reconstructions (denoised) and the original (noiseless) HS data for a particular band. The brightness of these maps is an indication of the magnitude of the local SSIM, i.e., the brighter a given location the greater the similarity between the retrieved and the original bands at that point [25]. Figure 2 shows the denoising yielded by different methods in the spectral domain.

Table 1. Numerical results for the different approaches. Numbers in bold identify the best results with respect to each of the four measures of performance considered. In all cases, the PSNR prior to denoising was 30.103 dB.

SALINAS-A				
	ST	TV	VTV	ADMM
MSE	4860.8284	4944.6999	4853.3592	**4218.4193**
PSNR (dB)	41.5905	41.5162	41.5972	**42.2061**
SPATIAL SSIM	0.9812	0.9575	0.9658	**0.9855**
SPECTRAL SSIM	0.9977	0.9977	0.9979	**0.9980**
INDIAN PINES				
MSE	13803.4370	15516.8153	18415.5653	**13268.2362**
PSNR (dB)	38.2492	37.7410	36.9972	**38.3046**
SPATIAL SSIM	0.9533	0.9338	0.9132	**0.9556**
SPECTRAL SSIM	**0.9972**	0.9970	0.9963	**0.9972**

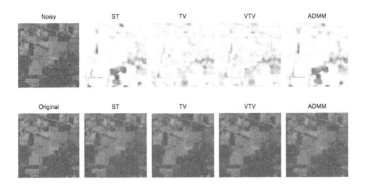

Fig. 1. Visual results for Band No. 23 of the Indian Pines HS image. Beside the original (noiseless) image in the lower row are shown the various reconstruction results. Beside the noisy image in the upper row are shown the corresponding SSIM maps between the reconstructed (denoised) images and the original image.

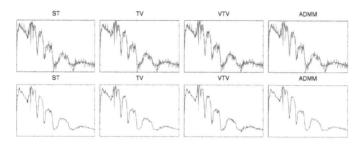

Fig. 2. Denoising results for a particular spectral function of the Indian Pines HS image. Plots in green, blue and red correspond to the original, recovered and noisy spectra, respectively.

Acknowledgments. We gratefully acknowledge that this research was supported in part by the Natural Sciences and Engineering Research Council (NSERC).

References

1. AVIRIS website: http://aviris.jpl.nasa.gov/index.html
2. Amir Beck, A., Teboulle, M.: A fast iterative shrinkage-thresholding algorithm for linear inverse problems. SIAM Journal on Imaging Sciences Archive **2**(1), 183–202 (2009)
3. Bioucas-Dias, J.M., Nascimento, J.M.P.: Hyperspectral Subspace Identification. IEEE Trans. Geoscience and Remote Sensing **46**, 2435–2445 (2008)
4. Boyd, S.P., Parikh, N., Chu, E., Peleato, B., Eckstein, J.: Distributed Optimization and Statistical Learning via the Alternating Direction Method of Multipliers. Foundations and Trends in Machine Learning **3**, 1–122 (2011)
5. Bresson, X., Chan, T.: Fast Dual Minimization of the Vectorial Total Variation Norm and Applications to Color Image Processing. Inverse Problems and Imaging **2**(4), 455–484 (2008)
6. Chambolle, A.: An algorithm for total variation minimization and applications. Journal of Mathematical Imaging and Vision **20**(1–2), 89–97 (2004)
7. Chan, T., Shen, J.: Image Processing and Analysis. Society for Industrial and Applied Mathematics, Philadelphia (2005)
8. Chang, Y., Yan, L., Fang, H., Liu, H.: Simultaneous Destriping and Denoising for Remote Sensing Images With Unidirectional Total Variation and Sparse Representation. IEEE Geoscience and Remote Sensing Letters **11**(6), 1051–1055 (2014)
9. Chen, G., Qian, S.E.: Denoising of Hyperspectral Imagery Using Principal Component Analysis and Wavelet Shrinkage. IEEE Trans. Geoscience and Remote Sensing **49**, 973–980 (2011)
10. Donoho, D.: Denoising by Soft-Thresholding. IEEE Trans. Information Theory **41**(3), 613–627 (1995)
11. Donoho, D., Johnstone, I.M.: Adapting to Unknown Smoothness Via Wavelet Shrinkage. J. of the Amer. Stat. Assoc. **90**(432), 1220–1224 (1995)
12. Donoho, D., Johnstone, I.M., Kerkyacharian, G., Picard, D.: Wavelet shrinkage: asymptopia. Journal of the Royal Statistical Society, Ser. B, 371–394 (1995)
13. Elad, M., Aharon, M.: Image denoising via sparse and redundant representations over learned dictionaries. IEEE Trans. Image Proc. **15**(12), 3736–3745 (2006)

14. Goldlücke, B., Strekalovskiy, E., Cremers, D.: The Natural Vectorial Total Variation Which Arises from Geometric Measure Theory. SIAM J. Imaging Sciences **5**, 537–563 (2012)
15. Goldstein, T., Osher, S.: The Split Bregman Method for ℓ_1-Regularized Problems. SIAM J. Imaging Sciences **2**, 323–343 (2009)
16. http://www.ehu.es/ccwintco/index.php/Hyperspectral_Remote_Sensing_Scenes
17. Mairal, J., Bach, F., Jenatton, R., Obozinski, G.: Convex Optimization with Sparsity-Inducing Norms. Optimization for Machine Learning. MIT Press (2011)
18. Martín-Herrero, J.: Anisotropic Diffusion in the Hypercube. IEEE Trans. Geoscience and Remote Sensing **45**, 1386–1398 (2007)
19. Othman, H., Qian, S.E.: Noise Reduction of Hyperspectral Imagery Using Hybrid Spatial-Spectral Derivative-Domain Wavelet Shrinkage. IEEE Trans. Geoscience and Remote Sensing **44**, 397–408 (2006)
20. Renard, N., Bourennane, S., Blanc-Talon, J.: Denoising and Dimensionality Reduction Using Multilinear Tools for Hyperspectral Images. IEEE Geoscience and Remote Sensing Letters **5**(2), 138–142 (2008)
21. Rasti, B., Sveinsson, J.R., Ulfarsson, M.O., Benediktsson, J.A.: Hyperspectral image denoising using 3D wavelets. In: 2012 IEEE International Geoscience and Remote Sensing Symposium (IGARSS), pp. 1349–1352 (2012)
22. Rudin, L., Osher, S., Fatemi, E.: Nonlinear total variation based noise removal algorithms. Physica D: Nonlinear Phenomena **60**(1–4), 259–268 (1992)
23. Shippert, P.: Why use Hyperspectral imaging? Photogrammetric Engineering and Remote Sensing, 377–380 (2004)
24. Turlach, B.A.: On algorithms for solving least squares problems under an ℓ_1 penalty or an ℓ_1 constraint. In: Proceedings of the American Statistical Association, Statistical Computing Section, pp. 2572–2577 (2005)
25. Wang, Z., Bovik, A.C., Sheikh, H.R., Simoncelli, E.P.: Image Quality Assessment: from Error Visibility to Structural Similarity. IEEE Trans. Image Processing **13**, 600–612 (2004)
26. Yuan, Q., Zhang, L., Shen, H.: Hyperspectral Image Denoising Employing a Spectral-Spatial Adaptive Total Variation Model. IEEE Trans. Geoscience and Remote Sensing **50**, 3660–3677 (2012)

Towards a Comprehensive Evaluation of Ultrasound Speckle Reduction

Fernando C. Monteiro[1]([✉]), José Rufino[1,2], and Vasco Cadavez[1,3]

[1] Polytechnic Institute of Bragança, 5301-857 Bragança, Portugal
monteiro@ipb.pt
[2] Laboratório de Instrumentação e Física Experimental de Partículas,
Campus de Gualtar, 4710-057 Braga, Portugal
[3] Mountain Research Center (CIMO), Bragança, Portugal

Abstract. Over the last three decades, several despeckling filters have been developed to reduce the speckle noise inherently present in ultrasound images without losing the diagnostic information. In this paper, a new intensity and feature preservation evaluation metric for full speckle reduction evaluation is proposed based contrast and feature similarities. A comparison of the despeckling methods is done, using quality metrics and visual interpretation of images profiles to evaluate their performance and show the benefits each one can contribute to noise reduction and feature preservation. To test the methods, noise-free images and simulated B-mode ultrasound images are used. This way, the despeckling techniques can be compared using numeric metrics, taking the noise-free image as a reference. In this study, a total of seventeen different speckle reduction algorithms have been documented based on adaptive filtering, diffusion filtering and wavelet filtering, with sixteen qualitative metrics estimation.

1 Introduction

Medical ultrasound imaging is a technique that has become more widespread than other medical imaging techniques since this technique is more accessible, less expensive, non-invasive and non-ionizing, simpler to use and produces images in real-time. However, B-mode ultrasound images are usually corrupted by the speckle artifact, which introduces fictitious structures that can not be removed by the imaging system [11,14]. Speckle noise is defined as multiplicative noise with a granular pattern formed due to coherent processing of backscattered signals from multiple distributed targets. Speckle degrades the quality of ultrasound images, and thus affects diagnosis. Thus, speckle reduction has become an important task in many applications with ultrasound imaging [13].

Removing noise from the original image is still a challenging research in image processing and many studies have been conducted to develop specific methods dedicated to despeckling ultrasound images [4,13,14]. With the rapid proliferation of despeckling filters, denoise evaluation has been becoming an important

© Springer International Publishing Switzerland 2014
A. Campilho and M. Kamel (Eds.): ICIAR 2014, Part I, LNCS 8814, pp. 141–149, 2014.
DOI: 10.1007/978-3-319-11758-4_16

issue. A great deal of effort has been made in recent years to develop objective image quality metrics that correlate with perceived quality measurement [16,17]. Test data for evaluation includes clinical and phantom images, as well as simulated ultrasound which allow evaluation of filtering relative to an ideal speckle free reference. However, objective evaluation of noise reduction on ultrasound images is a challenging task due to the relatively low image quality.

In this study, filtered images were evaluated using several quality evaluation metrics such as average difference (AD), coefficient of correlation (CoC), gradient similarity measure (GSM), Laplacian mean square error (LMSE), maximum difference (MD), mean structural similarity index (MSSIM), the multiscale extension of MSSIM (M3SIM), normalized absolute error (NAE), normalized cross-correlation (NK), peak signal to noise ratio (PSNR), quality index based on local variance (QILV), root mean square error (RMSE), signal to noise ratio (SNR), structural content (SC) and universal quality index (UQI). All these metrics are self explanatory and hence a separate explanation for each metrics is not included due to page limitation. We also propose a new evaluation metric, the Speckle Reduction Evaluation Measure (SREM), presented in Sect 3.

The remainder of this paper is organized as follows: Sect. 2, describes the used despeckling filters. The proposed evaluation metric is explained in Sect. 3. In Sect. 4, we present the results and the discussion of the findings. Finally, conclusions are drawn in Sect. 5.

2   Speckle Filtering Techniques

Speckle noise reduction has been extensively studied and many denoising algorithms have been proposed. They are classified into three groups: (i) techniques that are applied directly in the original image, (ii) techniques based on anisotropic diffusion and (iii) techniques that are applied in the wavelet domain.

Adaptive filters take a moving filter window and estimate the statistical characteristics of the image inside the filter region, such as the local mean and the local variance. Spatial adaptive filters like median, Lee [10], Frost [5] and Kuan [9] filters assume that the speckle noise is essentially a multiplicative noise. Wiener filter [7] performs smoothing of the image based on the computation of local image variance. Ideal Fourier and Butterworth filtering performs image enhancement by applying the filter function and inverse FFT on the image [11]. Bilateral filtering technique is a combination of a spatial and range filter, where each output pixel value is a Gaussian weighted average of its neighbours in both space and intensity range. This nonlinear combination of nearby pixel values, gives the well-known good performance of this filter in smoothing while preserving edges. Coup et al. [2] proposed the nonlocal means (NL-means) filter which is based on estimating each pixel intensity from the information provided from the entire image and hence it exploits the redundancy caused due to the presence of similar patterns and features in the image.

Diffusion filters remove noise from an image by modifying the image via solving a partial differential equation. Speckle reducing filters based on anisotropic diffusion algorithms were introduced by Perona and Malik [15] (PM-AD). Unlike conventional spatial filtering techniques, anisotropic diffusion techniques can simultaneously reduce noise and preserve image details [15]. Due to this attractive feature, many researchers have used anisotropic diffusion techniques in speckle noise reduction. Weickert [18] introduced the coherence enhancing diffusion (CED), that allows the level of smoothing to vary directionally by a tensor diffusion function. The edge enhanced anisotropic diffusion (EEAD) method is also proposed, which includes anisotropic diffusion and edge enhancement. Yu and Acton [19] first introduced partial differential equation by integrating the Lee adaptive filter and the Perona-Malik diffusion, which they called Speckle Reducing Anisotropic Diffusion (SRAD). SRAD provides significant improvement in speckle suppression and edge preservation when compared to traditional methods like Lee, Frost and Kuan filters.

Wavelet transform, unlike Fourier transform, shows localization in both time and frequency and it has proved itself to be an efficient tool for noise removal [8]. One widespread method exploited for speckle reduction is wavelet shrinkage, including VisuShrink, SureShrink [3] and BayeShrink [1]. A wavelet-based multiscale linear minimum mean square-error estimation (LMMSE) is proposed in [20], where an interscale model, the wavelet coefficients with the same spatial location across adjacent scales, was combined as a vector, to which the LMMSE in then applied.

3   Speckle Reduction Evaluation Metric

The speckle reduction and the preservation of edges are in general divergent. A trade-off between noise reduction and the preservation of the actual image features and contrast has to be made in order to enhance the relevant image content for diagnostic purposes. Best contrast is meant in the sense of decreasing the variance in a homogeneous region while distinct regions are well defined.

We propose a new speckle reduction evaluation metric, the SREM, that is based on the contrast and gradient similarity maps between two images. The computation of SREM index consists of two stages. In the first stage, the contrast similarity map is computed, and then in the second stage, we combine it with the gradient similarity map (GSM) to encode feature information.

Consider $f(i, j)$ as the original (noise free) image and $g(i, j)$ as the filtered image. The contrast similarity map (CSM) is defined as follow:

$$CSM(f, g) = \frac{4\mu_f \mu_g \cdot \sigma_{f,g}}{\left(\mu_f^2 + \mu_g^2 + c_1\right) \cdot \left(\sigma_f^2 + \sigma_g^2 + c_2\right)} \tag{1}$$

where μ and σ are the mean intensity and the standard deviation of each image, $\sigma_{f,g}$ is the covariance between them, C_1 and C_2 are two constants to avoid instability when $\mu_f^2 + \mu_g^2$ is very close to zero.

The gradient computation step is crucial in image processing and segmentation. Several approaches have been proposed in literature that start by convolving the image with a bank of linear filters tuned to various orientation and spatial frequencies [12]. These approaches were inspired by models of processing in the early stages of the primate visual system providing a simple but biologically plausible model.

In our approach, the image is first convolved with Gaussian oriented filter pairs to extract the magnitude of orientation energy (OE) of edge responses as used by Malik et al. in [12]. The filters are tuned to detect edges of different shapes, parametrized by $\rho = \{\rho_o, \rho_s, \rho_e\}$, where ρ_o, ρ_s and ρ_e refer to orientation, scale and elongation respectively. Given image I, the orientation energy approach can be used to detect and localize the composite edges, and it is defined as:

$$OE\left(\rho\right) = \left(I * F_e(\rho)\right)^2 + \left(I * F_o(\rho)\right)^2 \tag{2}$$

where $F_e(\rho)$ and $F_o(\rho)$ represent a quadrature pair of even and odd-symmetric filters which differ in their spatial phases. The even-phase filters are the second-order derivative and the corresponding odd-symmetric filters are their Hilbert transforms which correspond to the first-order derivative, both smoothed with Gaussian functions specified by ρ.

At each pixel i, we can define the dominant orientation energy $(OE_i\left(\rho\right)^*)$ and the parameter (ρ_i^*) as the maximum energy across scale, orientation and elongation:

$$OE_i\left(\rho\right)^* = \max OE\left(\rho\right) \qquad \rho_i^* = \arg\max OE\left(\rho\right) \tag{3}$$

Gradient orientation energy $OE\left(\rho\right)$ has a maximum response for contours of shape ρ, whereas the zero-crossing of filter $F_e(\rho)$ locate the positions of the edges. The value OE^* is kept at the location of i only if it is greater than or equal to the neighbouring values. Otherwise it is replaced with a value of zero.

The gradient similarity map (GSM) between images $f\left(i, j\right)$ and $g\left(i, j\right)$ is defined as follow:

$$GSM = \frac{2OE_f \cdot OE_g + T_1}{OE_f + OE_g + T_1} \tag{4}$$

where T_1 is a positive constant depending on the dynamic range of GSM values.

Having obtained the contrast similarity CSM and the gradient orientation similarity at each location, the overall similarity between images $f\left(i, j\right)$ and $g\left(i, j\right)$ can be calculated:

$$SREM = \frac{\sum CSM\left(i, j\right) \cdot GSM\left(i, j\right)}{\sum GSM\left(i, j\right)} \tag{5}$$

4   Experimental Results

The performance of the proposed SREM will be evaluated and compared with representative state-of-the-art noise reduction evaluation metrics. In this action, the evaluation metrics are tested on seventeen despeckling filters, with simulated ultrasound images.

4.1   Field II Speckle Noise Images

To evaluate the denoising filters it is necessary to have reference images (without noise or with low level of noise) used to measure the improvement in image quality. Ideally both noisy and reference images must be obtained with the same ecograph and under the same conditions. However, due to the highly operator dependence of the ultrasound exams and the random variation of scattering it is useful to use synthetic images obtained, e.g., by means of computer simulations.

We used the Field II [6] to simulate the ultrasound images. This program assumes that the pressure field has linear propagation and is able to calculate the pulsed and continuous pressure field for different transducers. Depending on the number of points and transducer frequency, each image simulation can take several hours when executed sequentially. In order to decrease the simulation times, we have decided to parallelize its execution.

It was concluded from the code that the image lines were processed without any data dependencies; moreover, the code was already prepared to support the processing of the same image by several application instances, by skipping a line if its specific result file was detected in the file system; the code was then modified in order to accept the necessary parameters to process a line interval, instead of the full set of lines. In this way, different line intervals could be assigned to different CPU cores; this assignment was conducted by a set of wrapper scripts, developed in BASH, that generated jobs submitted to the job manager of a Linux HPC cluster; a separate queue was created for the simulations, with 5 nodes, each one with an Intel Core i7 4770 quad-core CPU, for a total of 20 cores.

The simulated images were generated using three levels of point scatterers randomly distributed within the field, 5×10^5, 1×10^6 and 2×10^6 points, and transducer frequencies of 3, 5 and 7 MHz. These parameters produce different levels of speckle noise as shown in Fig. 1.

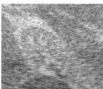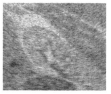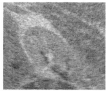

Fig. 1. Speckle simulations with Field II. (a) Reference image. (b) Speckle with 5×10^5 points and 3 MHz. (c) Speckle with 10^6 points and 5 MHz. (d) Speckle with 2×10^6 points and 7 MHz.

4.2   Example to Demonstrate the Effectiveness of SREM

Figure 2 shows an example to demonstrate the effectiveness of SREM in evaluating the perceptible speckle reduction. Figure 2(a) is the simulated noisy image, with 10^6 points and transducer frequency of 7 MHz. Figures 2(b)-(d) show three filtered images with different despeckled levels.

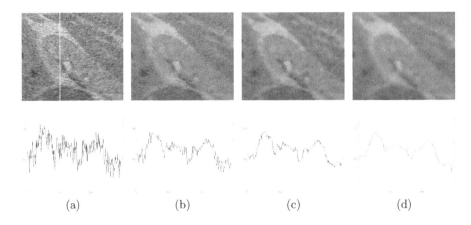

(a)   (b)   (c)   (d)

Fig. 2. Profile extracted from the white column before and after denoising. (a) Noisy image. (b) Kuan Filter. (c) Bilateral filter. (d) PM-AD filter.

The speckle evaluation of Fig. 2, with reference image from Fig. 1(a), are summarized in Table 1, where a higher score mean higher image quality.

Table 1. Quality evaluation of images in Fig.2

Metric	Fig. 2(a)	Fig. 2(b)	Fig. 2(c)	Fig. 2(d)
SREM	0.129	0.456	0.679	0.760
SNR	6.938	7.257	7.277	7.386
UQI	0.025	0.046	0.068	0.090
CoC	0.458	0.587	0.623	0.644
GSM	0.928	0.964	0.972	0.972
MSSIM	0.124	0.338	0.449	0.520

From the profiles of Fig.2 and from the scores in Table 1, we can conclude that the quality scores computed by SREM correlate with the other evaluation metric. Even more, the SREM produces a higher variation over the different results, only followed by UQI and MSSIM.

4.3   Overall Performance Comparison

We apply despeckling filters over the simulated images and evaluate the results with the evaluation metrics. The average of the results obtained with each metric is presented in Table 2. The arrow under each metric indicates the expected measure tendency for the best despeckling filters. The Pearson linear correlation coefficient (PCC) is also presented on the table.

From the analysis of PCC we can see that most of the metrics have a low variation in their evaluations. The exception are the LMSE, MMSIM, UQI, QILV and SREM. However, as LMSE quantifies only the average distortion in edge pixel locations between each filtered image it does not evaluate the speckle reduction inside the regions.

Table 2. Ranking of despeckling filters according to their performance computed by SREM and state-of-the-art evaluation metrics

Filters	RMSE ↓	MD ↓	AD ↓	NAE ↓	SC ↓	SNR ↑	PSNR ↑	LMSE ↑	UQI ↑	NK ↑	CoC ↑	MSSIM ↑	M3SIM ↑	QILV ↑	GSM ↑	SREM ↑
PM-AD	69.19	141.78	62.22	0.96	0.34	6.84	11.37	1.06	0.06	1.56	0.59	0.49	0.23	0.01	0.97	0.72
NL-means	72.61	152.00	65.88	1.01	0.32	6.59	10.94	1.25	0.06	1.60	0.58	0.46	0.23	0.02	0.97	0.69
Frost	70.03	148.33	62.85	0.97	0.34	6.77	11.26	1.10	0.06	1.57	0.57	0.45	0.22	0.02	0.97	0.69
Median	71.08	151.22	63.86	0.99	0.33	6.70	11.13	1.86	0.06	1.58	0.56	0.45	0.22	0.03	0.97	0.67
EEAD	69.08	162.00	61.19	0.95	0.34	6.83	11.38	20.46	0.06	1.55	0.54	0.46	0.23	0.04	0.97	0.67
Bayes	70.30	158.11	62.90	0.97	0.34	6.75	11.23	1.07	0.05	1.57	0.56	0.44	0.22	0.04	0.97	0.66
Sure	70.30	158.11	62.90	0.97	0.34	6.75	11.23	1.07	0.05	1.57	0.56	0.44	0.22	0.04	0.97	0.66
Wiener	70.05	163.78	62.54	0.97	0.34	6.76	11.26	5.54	0.05	1.57	0.55	0.42	0.21	0.06	0.97	0.62
Bilateral	70.69	151.67	63.55	0.98	0.33	6.72	11.18	3.47	0.05	1.58	0.57	0.41	0.22	0.05	0.97	0.62
Fourier	70.58	174.22	62.69	0.97	0.34	6.71	11.19	1.15	0.05	1.57	0.53	0.41	0.20	0.05	0.97	0.60
LMMSE	70.68	162.11	62.91	0.97	0.34	6.71	11.18	1.16	0.05	1.57	0.54	0.38	0.20	0.07	0.97	0.57
Butter	70.86	179.22	62.09	0.96	0.32	6.78	11.15	1.83	0.05	1.62	0.59	0.37	0.24	0.12	0.97	0.54
CED	70.55	155.78	62.92	0.97	0.34	6.72	11.20	3.28	0.04	1.57	0.54	0.32	0.19	0.06	0.96	0.44
Lee	70.35	156.44	62.75	0.97	0.34	6.73	11.22	5.44	0.04	1.57	0.54	0.33	0.20	0.09	0.96	0.44
Visu	70.74	167.00	62.93	0.98	0.34	6.70	11.17	4.30	0.04	1.57	0.53	0.30	0.19	0.08	0.96	0.41
Kuan	70.47	157.56	62.78	0.97	0.34	6.72	11.21	6.11	0.04	1.57	0.54	0.31	0.19	0.09	0.96	0.41
SRAD	74.30	176.11	66.31	1.03	0.32	6.45	10.74	15.79	0.04	1.61	0.51	0.29	0.18	0.08	0.95	0.37
Noisy	73.60	189.33	62.91	0.99	0.33	6.44	10.82	59.55	0.02	1.57	0.42	0.11	0.14	0.02	0.92	0.12
PCC	1.91	7.44	1.93	1.76	2.09	1.62	1.49	186.46	23.24	1.11	6.91	23.94	11.21	56.60	1.18	28.41

To test the effectiveness of detail preservation of the despeckling filters, we compared the despeckled images and the profile extracted from an image column before and after denoising, as shown in Fig. 3, for a transducer frequency of 5 MHz. From the profiles analysis, we find that almost every methods reduced the speckle noise in homogeneous regions. The intensity variation caused by speckle is still obvious in the images filtered by Kuan, CED and VisuShrink filters. The visual analysis indicates that the best despeckling filters are PM-AD, NL-means and Frost. The SRAD, Kuan and VisuShrink filters exhibit poor performance results. This analysis correlates well with the SREM evaluation results.

5   Conclusion

In this paper, a new evaluation metric, namely SREM, is proposed based on contrast similarity map and edge preservation which correlates well with other evaluation metrics. The underlying principle of SREM is that humans distinguish an image mainly based on its salient low-level features. The SREM uses contrast and gradient maps to represent complementary aspects of the image visual quality. In this study, a total of eighteen different speckle reduction algorithms have been documented based on spatial filtering, diffusion filtering and wavelet filtering, with seventeen quantitative metrics estimation.

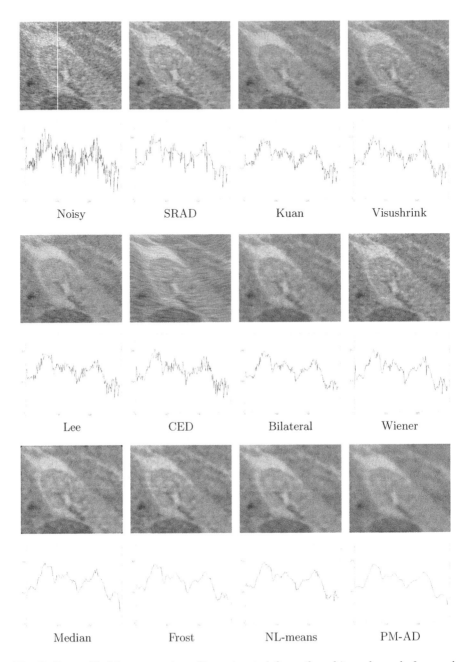

Fig. 3. Despeckled images and profiles extracted from the white column before and after denoising in simulated images with 10^6 points and 5 MHz transducer

References

1. Chang, S., Yu, B., Vetterli, M.: Adaptive wavelet thresholding for image denoising and compression. IEEE Trans. Image Processing **9**(9), 1532–1546 (2000)
2. Coupé, P., Hellier, P., Kervrann, C., Barillot, C.: Nonlocal means-based speckle filtering for ultrasound images. IEEE Transactions on Image Processing **18**(10), 2221–2229 (2009)
3. Donoho, D.L., Johnstone, I.M.: Adapting to unknown smoothness via wavelet shrinkage. Journal of American Statistical Association **90**(432), 1200–1224 (1995)
4. Finn, S., Glavin, M., Jones, E.: Echocardiographic speckle reduction comparison. IEEE Trans. Ultrasonics, Ferroelectrics Freq. Control **58**(1), 82–101 (2011)
5. Frost, V., Stiles, J., Shanmugan, K., Holtzman, J.: A model for radar images and its application to adaptive digital filtering of multiplicative noise. IEEE Transactions on Pattern Analysis and Machine Intelligence **4**(2), 157–166 (1982)
6. Jensen, J.: Simulation of advanced ultrasound systems using field ii. In: International Symposium on Biomedical Imaging: Nano to Macro, pp. 636–639 (2004)
7. Jin, F., Fieguth, P., Winger, L., Jernigan, E.: Adaptive wiener filtering of noisy images and image sequences. In: Proceedings of International Conference on Image Processing, vol. 3, p. III-349 (2003)
8. Khare, A., Khare, M., Jeong, Y., Kim, H., Jeon, M.: Despeckling of medical ultrasound images using daubechies complex wavelet transform. Signal Processing **90**(2), 428–439 (2010)
9. Kuan, D., Sawchuk, A., Strand, T., Chavel, P.: Adaptive noise smoothing filter for images with signal-dependent noise. IEEE Transactions on Pattern Analysis and Machine Intelligence **7**(2), 165–177 (1985)
10. Lee, J.-S.: Digital image enhancement and noise filtering by use of local statistics. IEEE Trans. on Pattern Analysis and Machine Intelligence **2**(2), 165–168 (1980)
11. Loizou, C., Pattichis, C.: Despeckle filtering algorithms and software for ultrasound imaging. Synthesis Lect. Algorithms Soft. Engineering **1**(1), 1–166 (2008)
12. Malik, J., Belongie, S., Leung, T., Shi, J.: Contour and texture analysis for image segmentation. International Journal of Computer Vision **43**(1), 7–27 (2001)
13. Mateo, J.L., Fernández-Caballero, A.: Finding out general tendencies in speckle noise reduction in ultrasound images. Expert Systems with Applications **36**(4), 7786–7797 (2009)
14. Ortiz, S., Chiu, T., Fox, M.D.: Ultrasound image enhancement: A review. Biomedical Signal Processing and Control **7**(5), 419–428 (2012)
15. Perona, P., Malik, J.: Scale-space and edge detection using anisotropic diffusion. IEEE Trans. on Pattern Analysis and Machine Intelligence **12**(7), 629–639 (1990)
16. Rosa, R., Monteiro, F.C.: Speckle ultrasound image filtering: Performance analysis and comparison. In: Computational Vision and Medical Image Processing: VIPIMAGE 2013, pp. 65–70 (2013)
17. Wang, Z., Li, Q.: Information content weighting for perceptual image quality assessment. IEEE Transactions on Image Processing **20**(5), 1185–1198 (2011)
18. Weickert, J.: Coherence-enhancing diffusion filtering. International Journal of Computer Vision **31**(2–3), 111–127 (1999)
19. Yu, Y., Acton, S.T.: Speckle reducing anisotropic diffusion. IEEE Transactions on Image Processing **11**(11), 1260–1270 (2002)
20. Zhang, D., Bao, P., Wu, X.: Multiscale lmmse-based image denoising with optimal wavelet selection. IEEE Transactions on Circuits and Systems for Video Technology **15**(4), 469–481 (2005)

An Evaluation of Potential Functions
for Regularized Image Deblurring

Buda Bajić[1]([✉]), Joakim Lindblad[1], and Nataša Sladoje[1,2]

[1] Faculty of Technical Sciences, University of Novi Sad, Novi Sad, Serbia
[2] Centre for Image Analysis, Uppsala University, Uppsala, Sweden
buda.bajic@uns.ac.rs, joakim@cb.uu.se, sladoje@uns.ac.rs

Abstract. We explore utilization of seven different potential functions in restoration of images degraded by both noise and blur. Spectral Projected Gradient method confirms its excellent performance in terms of speed and flexibility for optimization of complex energy functions. Results obtained on images affected by different levels of Gaussian noise and different sizes of the Point Spread Functions, are presented. The Huber potential function demonstrates outstanding performance.

1 Introduction

Images are generally degraded in various ways in the acquisition process: by camera motion, imperfect optics, presence of noise, atmospheric turbulence, etc. Degradation is often modelled as linear and shift invariant; it is assumed that the original image is convolved by a spatially invariant Point Spread Function (PSF) and corrupted by noise. If the original image is denoted u and the acquired image v, the degradation can be expressed as

$$v = h * u + \eta, \tag{1}$$

where h is the PSF, η represents noise and $*$ denotes convolution.

Image restoration methods aim at recovering the original image u from the degraded image v. However, this inverse problem is severely ill-posed and the solution is highly sensitive to noise in the observed image. Ringing effects and blurred edges are undesired consequences often appearing in restored images. A good balance between frequency recovery and noise suppression is essential for satisfactory deconvolution. A common approach is to apply some regularization, utilizing a priori knowledge when performing deconvolution. Regularization should provide numerical stabilization and impose desired properties to the solution. Total variation (TV) regularization [15] is among most popular approaches, due to its generally good performance.

Our previous studies on image denoising confirm that improved performance of TV based regularization can be achieved if potential functions are utilized. Potentials are designed to enhance/preserve particular image features during the processing; preservation of sharp edges is typically targeted. Potential functions,

A. Campilho and M. Kamel (Eds.): ICIAR 2014, Part I, LNCS 8814, pp. 150–158, 2014.
DOI: 10.1007/978-3-319-11758-4_17

in general being non-convex, introduce additional complexity to the optimization problem. We have previously experienced excellent performance of the Spectral Gradient type of optimization methods on similar tasks. These flexible methods allow a wide class of potentials to be used in the energy function, while exhibiting fast convergence.

In this paper we present an empirical evaluation of seven potential functions (listed in Table 1) when used for image deblurring/deconvolution based on regularized energy minimization utilizing the Spectral Projected Gradient (SPG) method. Image degradation includes different levels of blur (Gaussian PSF) and additive Gaussian white noise. Tests include classic TV regularization, and by that an implicit comparison with the large number of methods based on the TV model. We conclude that an appropriately chosen potential function can significantly increase the method performance at essentially no additional cost.

2   Background and Previous Work

2.1   TV Regularization and Potential Functions

Total Variation regularization is commonly used to address inverse problems in image processing, such as image denoising, deblurring, inpainting, etc. The approach involves minimization of an energy function which incorporates a gradient based regularization term, well balanced with a data fidelity term. Ideally, minimization of the energy function provides suppression of noise while retaining true image information. One approach for improving performance of TV regularization involves the utilization of potential functions.

Typically the energy functional of regularized deblurring is of the form

$$E(u) = \frac{1}{2} \iint |h(x,y) * u(x,y) - v(x,y)|^2 \, dx\, dy + \alpha \iint \phi(|\nabla u(x,y)|) \, dx\, dy,$$

$$(2)$$

where ∇ stands for gradient and $|\cdot|$ denotes ℓ_2 norm. The energy functional consists of a data fidelity term, which drives the solution towards the observed data (degraded image v), and a regularization term which utilizes the image gradient to provide noise suppression. The balancing parameter α controls the trade-off between the terms, i.e., the level of smoothing vs. faithful recovery of the (possibly noisy) image detail.

The function ϕ is referred to as *potential function*. By using a potential equal to the identity function, the regularization term reduces to classic TV regularization. In most cases the potential function is designed s.t. small intensity changes (assumed to be noise) are penalized, while large changes (assumed to be edges) are preserved. A number of potentials are studied and used in image restoration problems [3,4,8–12,16,17]. In [3] theoretical conditions for edge preserving potentials are given. In [11] examples using the Huber potential for deblurring are presented, however no explicit performance evaluation of potentials is presented. A study of effectiveness of different potentials in image denoising is given in [9], where it is concluded that the Huber potential (ϕ_5 in Table 1) works best overall, and that the Geman & McClure potential (ϕ_2) shows best performance in low noise settings.

2.2   Optimization

An important issue in energy based image restoration is efficient optimization of the energy function. A variety of approaches and algorithms to minimize TV regularized energy function are presented in the literature; a number of references on the topic are given in [14] and some later ones can be found in [5] and [7].

Non-convexity of potentials may lead to non-convexity of the objective function (2), which makes optimization additionally challenging and excludes a number of methods specifically designed for convex minimization. Our studies presented in [9] indicated that Spectral Gradient based optimization can be successfully applied in denoising for a wide range of potential functions. Thus, we herein utilize an optimization method from the same family. SPG is an efficient tool for solving a constrained optimization problem $\min_{x \in \Omega} f(x)$, where Ω is a closed convex set in $\mathbb{R}^n$ and f is a function which has continuous partial derivatives on an open set that contains Ω. Weak requirements on the objective function, as well as efficiency in solving large scale problems [1], make this optimization tool attractive for our purpose. The method is briefly outlined in Algorithm 1. We define the projection P_Ω of a vector $x \in \mathbb{R}^n$ to the feasible set $\Omega = [0, 1]^n$ as: $[P_\Omega(x)]_i = \min\{1, \max\{0, x_i\}\}$, for all $i = 1, 2, \ldots, n$.

A scaled version of SPG is used for image deblurring in [2]. However, data fidelity term is considered without regularization, and robustness of the solution is achieved by early stopping. The efficiency of the SPG method in regularized restoration of images degraded by both blur and noise is confirmed by this study.

3   Image Deconvolution by SPG Minimization of a Regularized Energy Functional with Potentials

In the observed model (1) we assume that the spatially invariant PSF is known, or can be estimated by point spread estimation techniques; the deblurring that we perform here belongs to the group of linear non-blind methods. We assume that acquired images are corrupted by additive Gaussian noise with a standard deviation σ_n. We consider grey scale images and represent them as vectors with intensity values from $[0, 1]$. Let the vector $u = [u_1, \ldots, u_n]^T$ of length $n = r \times c$ represent an image u of size $r \times c$, where image rows are sequentially concatenated. Minimization of (2) can be seen as a constrained optimization problem:

$$\min_u E(u) \quad \text{s.t. } 0 \leq u_i \leq 1, \quad i = 1, 2, \ldots, n. \tag{3}$$

A discrete formulation of the objective function (2) is:

$$E(u) = \frac{1}{2} \sum_{i=1}^n \left((Hu - v)_i\right)^2 + \alpha \sum_{i=1}^n \phi\left(|\nabla(u_i)|\right), \tag{4}$$

Table 1. Potential functions

Potential	Convex
TV [15] $\phi_1(s) = s$	yes
Geman&McClure [4] $\phi_2(s) = \dfrac{\omega s^2}{1 + \omega s^2}$	no
Hebert&Leahy [8] $\phi_3(s) = \ln(1 + \omega s^2)$	no
Perona&Malik [12] $\phi_4(s) = 1 - e^{\omega s^2}$	no
Huber [17] $\phi_5(s) = \begin{cases} s^2, & s \le \omega \\ 2\omega s - \omega^2, & s > \omega \end{cases}$	yes
Tikhonov [16] $\phi_6(s) = s^2$	yes
Nikolova&Chan [10] $\phi_7(s) = \begin{cases} \sin(\omega s^2), & s \le \sqrt{\dfrac{\omega}{2\pi}} \\ 1, & s > \sqrt{\dfrac{\omega}{2\pi}} \end{cases}$	no

Table 2. Algorithm 1

Spectral Projected Gradient

Choose values for parameters:
$\theta_{min}, \theta_{max}, \gamma, \sigma_1, \sigma_2, tol$ s.t. $0 < \theta_{min} < \theta_{max}$, $\gamma \in (0,1)$, $0 < \sigma_1 < \sigma_2 < 1$, $tol > 0$.

Choose initial guess $x_0 \in \Omega$ and $\theta_0 = 1$.
Compute x_{k+1} and θ_{k+1} as follows:
$\quad d_k = P_\Omega(x_k - \theta_k \nabla f(x_k)) - x_k$
$\quad x_{k+1} = x_k + d_k; \quad \delta = \nabla f(x_k)^T d_k$
$\quad \lambda_k = 1$
while $f(x_{k+1}) > f(x_k) + \gamma \lambda_k \delta$
$\quad \lambda_{temp} = -\frac{1}{2}\lambda_k^2 \delta / (f(x_{k+1}) - f(x_k) - \lambda_k \delta)$
$\quad$**if** $(\lambda_{temp} \ge \sigma_1 \wedge \lambda_{temp} \le \sigma_2 \lambda_k)$
$\quad\quad$**then** $\lambda_k = \lambda_{temp}$ **else** $\lambda_k = \lambda_k / 2$
$\quad x_{k+1} = x_k + \lambda_k d_k$
end while
$\quad s_k = x_{k+1} - x_k$
$\quad y_k = \nabla f(x_{k+1}) - \nabla f(x_k); \quad \beta_k = s_k^T y_k$
if $\beta_k \le 0$ **then** $\theta_{k+1} = \theta_{max}$
else
$\quad \theta_{k+1} = \min\left\{\theta_{max}, \max\{\theta_{min}, \frac{s_k^t s_k}{\beta_k}\}\right\}$
Repeat until: $\|x_{k+1} - x_k\|_\infty \le tol$.

where vector v is an observed image and $H_{n \times n}$ is a block circulant matrix s.t. Hu is equal to convolution $h * u$. $\nabla(u_i)$ is the discrete image gradient at point u_i, computed as $\nabla(u_i) = (u_r - u_i, u_b - u_i)$, where r and b denote indexes of the edge neighbours to the right and below the pixel u_i, respectively. The gradient of (4) is given by $\nabla E(u) = [\nabla E(u)_i]_{i=1}^n$ and

$$\nabla E(u)_i = (H^T(Hu - v))_i + \alpha\phi'(|\nabla(u_i)|)\frac{2u_i - u_r - u_b}{|\nabla(u_i)|}$$
$$+ \alpha\phi'(|\nabla(u_l)|)\frac{u_i - u_l}{|\nabla(u_l)|} + \alpha\phi'(|\nabla(u_a)|)\frac{u_i - u_a}{|\nabla(u_a)|}, \tag{5}$$

where u_a and u_l denote edge neighbours above and left of the pixel u_i, respectively. Edges are handled using periodic boundary condition.

The gradient defined by (5) is non-differentiable at points where $|\nabla u_i| = 0$. To meet requirements of SPG, we consider a smoothed version of (4), where $|\nabla u_i|$ is replaced with $\sqrt{|\nabla(u_i)|^2 + \varepsilon^2}$ and where ε is a small positive number (we used $\varepsilon = 10^{-5}$ throughout). The use of a relaxed gradient could possibly lead to a less accurate solution. It was observed in [9] that differences are negligible.

Fig. 1. Used test images, all 256×256. Intensities in $[0, 255]$ are mapped to $[0, 1]$.

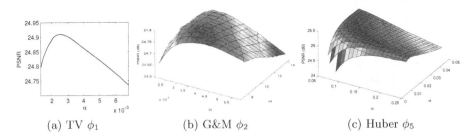

(a) TV ϕ_1 (b) G&M ϕ_2 (c) Huber ϕ_5

Fig. 2. Examples of average deblurring performance plotted for different parameter settings. Graphs for ϕ_1, ϕ_2, ϕ_5, $\sigma_p = 2$, and $\sigma_n^2 = 0.001$ are shown. Graphs for other potentials, PSFs, and noise levels exhibit similar characteristics.

4   Evaluation

To evaluate the performance of different potentials, we utilize ten standard images shown in Fig. 1. For every original image u^* we construct noisy and blurred image v by convolving it with PSF h and adding white Gaussian noise, $v = h * u^* + \eta$. We consider Gaussian PSFs, closely resembling real PSFs in many imaging systems. We evaluate PSFs with standard deviation $\sigma_p \in \{1, 2, 3\}$ and observe noise with variance $\sigma_n^2 \in \{0, 0.0001, 0.001, 0.01\}$. For each PSF and noise level, we obtain one degraded image v from which we reconstruct u^* using the seven considered potentials. Quality of reconstruction is measured with Peak Signal-to-Noise Ratio $PSNR = 10 \log_{10} \left(\dfrac{(\max(u_i^*))^2}{MSE} \right)$, where $MSE = \dfrac{1}{n} \sum_{i=1}^{n} (u_i^* - \bar{u}_i)^2$ and $\bar{u}$ is reconstructed image.

A number of approaches for selection of regularization parameter(s) (in our case α and ω) exist [6, 13]. To ensure optimal selection of parameters we exhaustively explore the parameter space and selected the best performing separately for each PSF size σ_p and each noise level σ_n^2 (i.e., $3 \times 4 \times 7$ sets of parameters). This leads to a positive bias on our results, since we perform evaluation on the training data.

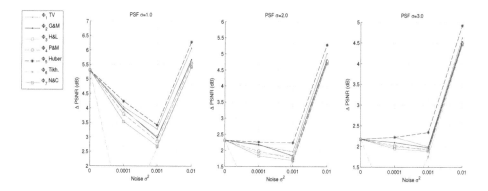

Fig. 3. Average improvement of PSNR over ten test images for different PSFs and different noise levels considering all seven evaluated potentials

This bias does not favour any of the potentials. Partial evaluation on separated test and training sets, show that: (i) the bias is very limited, (ii) results are not overly sensitive to parameter tuning. Examples of typical deblurring performance (PSNR) for varying parameter settings are shown in Fig. 2.

Optimization is performed using SPG with settings recommended in [1]: $\theta_{min} = 10^{-3}$, $\theta_{max} = 10^{3}$, $\gamma = 10^{-4}$, $\sigma_1 = 0.1$, $\sigma_2 = 0.9$. Algorithm is terminated when the max-norm between two consecutive images is less than $tol = 10^{-3}$.

5   Results

The improvement in PSNR between before and after performed deblurring, $\Delta\text{PSNR} = \text{PSNR}_{\text{out}} - \text{PSNR}_{\text{in}}$, for each of the seven potentials, and each of the 3×4 blur and noise levels, is presented in Fig. 3. Table 3 shows ΔPSNR, as well as number of iterations, averaged over all images and all types of degradations. CPU time in seconds is approx. the number of iterations divided by 50 (Matlab, 3GHz Intel Core i7). A very clear result is that the Huber potential, ϕ_5, shows superior performance in all of the evaluated settings. As a second runner-up comes TV based deblurring (ϕ_1), clearly behind in most situations, but providing a similar performance in the case $\sigma_p = 3, \sigma_n^2 = 0.0001$. On a third place comes the non-convex Geman & McClure potential (ϕ_2) which also showed to perform well in denoising [9]. The G&M potential performs slightly better than TV regularization for the case $\sigma_p = 2, \sigma_n^2 = 0.0001$. As opposed to the denoising study however, at no place does it outshine the Huber potential.

Table 3. Average ΔPSNR and number of iterations for the studied potentials

Potential	ϕ_1	ϕ_2	ϕ_3	ϕ_4	ϕ_5	ϕ_6	ϕ_7
ΔPSNR [dB]	3.43	3.32	3.28	3.24	**3.58**	2.55	3.17
No. iterations	30	65	26	52	40	11	30

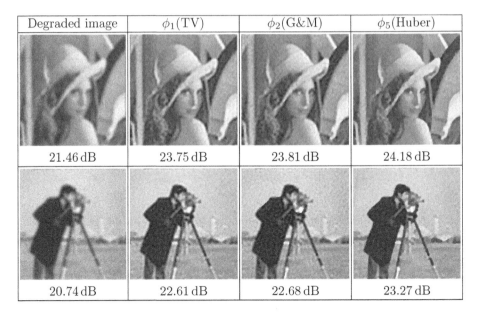

Degraded image	ϕ_1(TV)	ϕ_2(G&M)	ϕ_5(Huber)
21.46 dB	23.75 dB	23.81 dB	24.18 dB
20.74 dB	22.61 dB	22.68 dB	23.27 dB

Fig. 4. First column: images degraded with PSF $\sigma_p = 3$ and noise with variance $\sigma_n^2 = 0.001$. Columns 2–4: recovered images using best performing potentials ϕ_1, ϕ_2, and ϕ_5, respectively. PSNR is stated below each image.

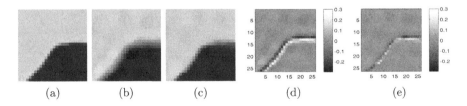

(a)   (b)   (c)   (d)   (e)

Fig. 5. Illustration of improved edge preservation by Huber potential, ϕ_5. (a) Original image, part of Cameraman's shoulder. (b) Deblurred image using ϕ_1 (TV). (c) Deblurred image using ϕ_5. (d) Residual for ϕ_1. (e) Residual for ϕ_5.

Visual examples of deblurring performance of TV, G&M, and Huber potentials are presented in Fig. 4. In Fig. 5 we show a zoomed-in view on the shoulder of the Cameraman, to highlight the edge preservation performance of the Huber potential over the commonly used TV regularization. It is apparent that the Huber potential does a much better job in preserving the sharp edges in the image (as also can be confirmed by looking at the residual errors in Fig. 5(d,e)).

6   Conclusions

Performed tests confirm that utilization of potential functions in regularized image denoising and deblurring provides a straightforward way to increase quality of the restored images. We have tested seven potential functions suggested in the literature, utilizing optimal parameter values for each of them, empirically found in our study. Optimization of both convex and non-convex energy functions is performed by a flexible and efficient SPG method. Our conclusion is that the Huber potential performs outstandingly best, providing best PSNR and improved edge preservation, compared to all the observed potentials.

Acknowledgments. Bajić, Lindblad and Sladoje are supported by the Ministry of Science of the Republic of Serbia through Projects ON174008 and III44006 of MISANU. Sladoje is supported by the Swedish Governmental Agency for Innovation Systems.

References

1. Birgin, E., Martinez, J., Raydan, M.: Algorithm: 813: SPG - software for convex-constrained optimization. ACM. Trans. Mathematical Software **27**, 340–349 (2001)
2. Bonettini, S., Zanella, R., Zanni, L.: A scaled gradient projection method for constrained image deblurring. Inverse Problems **25**, 015002 (2009)
3. Charbonnier, P., Blanc-Féraud, L., Aubert, G., Barlaud, M.: Deterministic edge-preserving regularization in computed imaging. IEEE Trans. Image Process. **6**(2), 298–311 (1997)
4. Geman, S., McClure, D.: Bayesian image analysis: an application to single photon emission tomography. In: Proc. Statistical Computation Section, pp. 12–18. Am. Statistical Assoc., Washington, DC (1985)
5. Getreuer, P.: Total variation deconvolution using Split Bregman. Image Processing On Line **2**, 158–174 (2012)
6. Hansen, P.C., Kilmer, M.E., Kjeldsen, R.H.: Exploiting residual information in the parameter choice for discrete ill-posed problems. BIT Numerical Mathematics **46**(1), 41–59 (2006)
7. He, C., Hu, C., Zhang, W., Shi, B., Hu, X.: Fast total variation image deconvolution with adaptive parameter estimation via Split Bregman method. Mathematical Problems in Engineering **2014**, Article ID 617026 (2014)
8. Hebert, T., Leahy, R.: A generalized EM algorithm for 3D Bayesian reconstruction from Poisson data using Gibbs priors. IEEE Trans. Med. Imaging **8**, 194–202 (1989)
9. Lukić, T., Lindblad, J., Sladoje, N.: Regularized image denoising based on spectral gradient optimization. Inverse Problems **27**, 085010 (2011)
10. Nikolova, M., Chan, R.: The equivalence of half-quadratic minimization and the gradient linearization iteration. IEEE Trans. Image Process. **16**, 1623–1627 (2007)
11. Nikolova, M., Ng, M.: Analysis of half-quadratic minimization methods for signal and image recovery. SIAM J. Sci. Comput. **27**, 937–966 (2005)
12. Perona, P., Malik, J.: Scale-space and edge detection using anisotropic diffusion. IEEE Trans. Pattern Anal. Mach. Intell. **12**, 345–362 (1990)
13. Ramani, S., Blu, T., Unser, M.: Monte-Carlo SURE: A black-box optimization of regularization parameters for general denoising algorithms. IEEE Trans. Image Processing **17**(9), 1540–1554 (2008)

14. Rodriguez, P., Wohlberg, B.: Efficient minimization method for generalized total variation functional. IEEE Trans. Image Processing **18**(2), 322–332 (2009)
15. Rudin, L.I., Osher, S., Fatemi, E.: Nonlinear total variation based noise removal algorithms. Physica D **60**(1–4), 259–268 (1992)
16. Tikhonov, A., Arsenin, V.: Solutions of ill-posed problems. Winston and Wiley, Washington, DC (1977)
17. Schultz, R., Stevenson, R.: Stochastic modeling and estimation of multispectral image data. IEEE Trans. Image Process. **4**, 1109–1119 (1995)

Drawing Parrots with Charcoal

A. Alsam[(✉)] and H.J. Rivertz

Sør-Trøndelag University College, Trondheim, Norway
ali.alsam@gmail.com

Abstract. We present an algorithm to convert color images to gray scale that ensures the separation between iso-luminance color regions and improves the contrast in the resulting image. The algorithm calculates a local vector in the neighborhood of a pixel with the property of being able to separate the different colors locally. This vector is then added to the global luminance vector resulting in a direction that includes both global and local changes. In a region with a flat uniform color the algorithm returns the global luminance. The more color variations there are locally the more the luminance vector will be shifted to achieve the increased separation and contrast.

Keywords: Color to gray · Contrast enhancing

1 Introduction

Converting color images to gray-scale is a challenging problem that has attracted the interest of many researchers in the image processing community.

Given an image with a single uniform color, the problem of finding a gray value that represents the amount of luminance reflected off the image surface is well defined and can be estimated by the sensitivity of the human eye in the different parts on the visible spectrum. From vision studies, it is known that the cones are concentrated in the green part of the visible spectrum followed by less concentration in the red and blue. Thus, given a three dimensional color value we can estimate the corresponding gray luminance as a linear sum of the intensities of each color channel with green having a greater weight than red and blue.

The problem arises, when two different neighboring colors are converted to gray-scale using the same weights. In this case, the averaging process can lead to identical gray values for two noticeably different colors. Different colors that have the property of resulting in an identical gray value are known as iso-luminance and can be typically seen in nature in the feathers of parrots. Such colors have also attracted many artists who aim to paint colorful scenes with uniform luminance.

A different problem which arises in color to gray scale conversion, is that it is an averaging process by definition: A process in which the luminance is estimated by averaging the intensities of the color channels. Like all averaging processes the conversion of color images to gray-scale leads to a reduction in contrast.

© Springer International Publishing Switzerland 2014
A. Campilho and M. Kamel (Eds.): ICIAR 2014, Part I, LNCS 8814, pp. 159–166, 2014.
DOI: 10.1007/978-3-319-11758-4_18

Based on the above mentioned problems, we can divide the algorithms that we have reviewed into two categories: In the first, we have algorithms that aim to remedy the problem of neighboring iso-luminance colors or generally assign different gray values to different colors and in the second we have methods that aim to increase contrast.

In the recent algorithms of the first category, the idea is to calculate a three dimensional gradient based on the original image, as a second step estimate a one dimensional representation and finally, integrate the gradient to result in a gray-scale representation.

Representing the three dimensional gradient in a one dimensional space is one of the important questions in these algorithms. However, here we would like to point out a problem that is shared with algorithms that aim to increase contrast-specifically that these algorithms alter the luminance value of the color based on its spacial location which might result in a dark gray tone as a representation of a bright yellow. In other words, there is no control of the similarity of the resulting gray value with the original luminance; and when such similarity is imposed the results are less satisfying.

In this paper, we present an algorithm that combines the global luminance transformation, i.e. representing the gray values of the image as an average sum of the color channels, with a spatial transformation based on the level of local variation.

We summarize the basic idea as follows: As a first step, we assume that the global luminance vector is the best vector to project the color values onto. As a second step, we calculate a vector that captures the local changes. The local vector is defined as the difference between an image pixel and the average of its neighborhood. Finally, we add the local vector to the global luminance direction and project the color value onto the resultant vector.

If there are no local changes in color then the resultant vector will be identical to the luminance. The more the color changes locally, the more the luminance vector is going to be shifted in the direction that captures the local changes.

After implementing algorithm, we found that applying a power function to the elements of the local vector greatly improves the separation between the color regions and also the local contrast. This experimental finding might be attributed to the fact that color differences are not linear in the camera RGB space.

The title of this paper was chosen after many years of experimenting with photos of parrots and thinking of how an artist drawing with charcoal might make the decision of darkening or lightening colors with the same luminance in order to show the separation. In the results section, we include such an image and compare the separation achieved with a number of algorithms including the one proposed in this article.

2   Background

It is possible to divide the solution domain of color to gray transformation into two groups. In the first we have global projection based methods. In the second we have spatial methods.

Global methods can further be divided into image independent and image dependent algorithms. Image independent algorithm, such as the calculation of luminance, assume that the transformation from color to gray is related to the cone sensitives of the human eye. Based on that, the luminance approach is defined as a weighted sum of the red, green and blue values of the image without any measure of the image content. The weights assigned to the red, green and blue channels are derived from vision studies where it is known that the eye is more sensitive to green than red and blue.

The luminance transformation is known to reduce the contrast between color regions [1,2]. A classical example that is used to demonstrate this property is averaging two black and white checkerboard patterns with grey values reversed. In this case, the features of both channels are completely obliterated.

To improve upon the performance of the image-independent averaging methods, we can incorporate statistical information about the image's color, or multi-spectral, information. Principal component analysis (PCA) achieves this by considering the color information as vectors in an n-dimensional space. The covariance matrix of all the color values in the image, is analyzed using PCA and the principal vector with the largest principal value is used to project the image data onto the vector's, one dimensional, space [3]. It has, however, been shown that PCA shares a common problem with the global averaging techniques [2]: Unless there is only one channel the contrast between adjacent pixels in an image is always less than the original. This problem becomes more noticeable when the number of channels increases [2].

Spatial methods are based on the assumption that the transformation from color to gray-scale needs to be defined such that differences between pixels are preserved. Bala and Eschbach [1], introduced a two step algorithm. In the first step the luminance image is calculated based on a global projection. In the second, the chrominance edges that are not present in the luminance are added to the luminance. Similarly, Grundland and Dodgson [4], introduced an algorithm that starts by transforming the image to YIQ colour space. The Y-channel is assumed to be the luminance of the image and treated separately from the the chrominance IQ plane. Based on the chrominance information in the IQ plane, they calculate a single vector: The predominant chromatic change vector[4]. The final gray-scale image is defined as a weighted sum of the luminance Y and the projection of the 2-dimensional IQ onto the predominant vector.

Gooch et al, proposed an iterative optimization to map colors to gray maintaining chromatic plus luminance difference as well as possible. The proposed optimization is unconstrained, involves multiple local minima and, for the best results, requires user input. With similar reasoning Socolinsky and Wolff [2,5], proposed that the best gray-scale image is defined as an image which, when differentiated, returns gradients that are, in a least square sense, as close as possible to the color image. A similar approach was used by Alsam and Drew where they defined used the maximum value of the gradient in any color channel as an estimation of the gray-scale gradient [6].

Alsam and Rivertz [7], presented a method to increase the local contrast of the resultant gray-scale image by calculating local weights based on the variations in color. This method, however, changes the original luminance even in uniform color regions and results in a dark yellow representation.

3   Method Description

The luminance channel of a color image is defined as a weighted sum of the color channels.

$$L = \nu_R R + \nu_G G + \nu_B B.$$

Here, the weights are normalized by their sum. Typical values of the weights are $\nu_R = 0.29$, $\nu_G = 0.59$ and $\nu_B = 0.11$ where we notice that the weight given to the green channel is greater than that assigned to the red and blue channels respectively.

By applying a Gauss filter to each of the color channels, we calculate a weighted local average value at each image pixel. The differences $R - \tilde{R}$, $G - \tilde{G}$ and $B - \tilde{B}$ measures the amount of red green and blue in a pixel compared to the average values in the surrounding neighborhood. This three dimensional difference is what we refer to as the local luminance direction.

We then add the local luminance to the global vector:

$$\mu_R = \mid R - \tilde{R} + \nu_R \mid$$
$$\mu_G = \mid G - \tilde{G} + \nu_G \mid$$
$$\mu_B = \mid B - \tilde{B} + \nu_B \mid$$

Here, we note that in regions of uniform color, i.e. with no variations, the differences $R - \tilde{R}$, $G - \tilde{G}$ and $B - \tilde{B}$ are zero and the luminance vector remains unchanged.

Based on the local vectors, we propose a spatial varying color to luminance mapping defined as:

$$g = \left(\frac{R^\gamma \mu_R^\alpha + G^\gamma \mu_G^\alpha + B^\gamma \mu_B^\alpha}{\mu_R^\beta + \mu_G^\beta + \mu_B^\beta} \right)^{1/\gamma},$$

where γ, α and β are power functions. If the powers γ, α and β are set to one the the method becomes a linear transformation of the color values to gray-scale, however, we have experimentally found that the values $\gamma = 2$, $\alpha = 3$ and $\beta = 2$ result in the best enhancement of separation and local contrast. This aspect of the algorithm is highlighted in the results section where we present results with differen powers.

4   Results

We start this section, by presenting a parrot image that highlights the problems with color to gray-scale conversion. In figure 1, we notice that the colorful wing of

(a) The original color image of two parrots. Notice the colorful wing feathers of the bird to the right.

(b) The luminance conversion of the image where the discrimination between the colors is lost.

Fig. 1. The original image of two parrots and its gray-scale conversion using the luminance transformation

(a) The original color image of two parrots. Notice the colorful wing feathers of the bird to the right.

(b) The gray-scale conversion obtained from the Grundland and Dodgson algorithm.

(c) The gray-scale conversion obtained by the new method of a filter size of a 100×100.

(d) The gray-scale conversion obtained by the new method of a filter size of a 200×200.

Fig. 2. In the first row: The original image of two parrots and its gray-scale conversion using the Grundland and Dodgson algorithm. In the second row: The conversion using the proposed algorithm with filter sizes of 100×100 and 200×200.

the bird to the right has three distinct colors with very similar luminance. When the image is converted to gray-scale, using the traditional luminance conversion we find that the color regions are not longer distinguishable. In figure 2, we present the conversion obtained by the Grundland and Dodgson algorithm for the same parrot image. Here, we notice that while red is distinguishable from blue and green the latter colors are merged into a single gray tone. We also notice that the yellow region on the chest of the bird to the left is darker in luminance than what we perceive making the distinction between the chest and the wing less visible.

In the second row of figure 2, we present the results achieved when using the proposed algorithm using a filter size of 100×100 and 200×200 respectively. Here, we notice that the distinction between the color regions as well as the local

(a) The original color portrait of a woman.

(b) The gray-scale conversion obtained from the luminance conversion.

(c) The gray-scale conversion obtained by the new method of a filter size of a 10×10.

(d) The gray-scale conversion obtained by the new method of a filter size of a 100×100.

Fig. 3. In the first row: The original color portrait of a woman and its gray-scale conversion using the luminance channel. In the second row: The conversion using the proposed algorithm with filter sizes of 10×10 and 100×100.

contrast are improved. We also notice that the yellow region has good contrast while maintaining the luminosity at a level that is similar to the tradition gray-scale conversion. In figure 3, we present a portrait of a women. In the first row, we present the luminance conversion of the image. In the second row, we present the conversion obtained by the propose algorithm with filter sizes of 10×10 and 100×100. We notice that the small filter size results in an increased contrast at the level of fine edges while the larger filter achieves a more global increase in contrast. We also notice that the method results in no visible artifacts and that the conversion appears natural and smooth.

Finally, in figure 4, we present the conversion results obtained with the new algorithm using different values for the powers. We notice that values of $\gamma = 2$, $\alpha = 2$ and $\beta = 2$ result in no visible increase of contrast while the values $\gamma = 2$, $\alpha = 3$ and $\beta = 2$ achieve a clear improvement in contrast and $\gamma = 2$, $\alpha = 4$ and $\beta = 2$ results in too much increase and subsequently visible halo artifacts.

(a) The original color image of two women.

(b) The gray-scale conversion obtained from the proposed algorithm with values $\gamma = 2$, $\alpha = 2$ and $\beta = 2$.

(c) The gray-scale conversion obtained from the proposed algorithm with values $\gamma = 2$, $\alpha = 2$ and $\beta = 2$.

(d) The gray-scale conversion obtained from the proposed algorithm with values $\gamma = 2$, $\alpha = 4$ and $\beta = 2$.

Fig. 4. The original color of two women and its conversion to gray scale using the proposed algorithm with variable values of the powers γ, α and β. For all the images the filter size is fixed at 100×100.

5 Conclusion

A spatial method for converting color image to gray-scale that increases local contrast an improves the separation between adjacent iso-luminance regions is presented. The method is based on adding a vector that separates colors locally to the global luminance direction. If the local region is uniform the resultant vector is identical to the luminance while large local variations result in noticeable modifications of the original luminance.

References

1. Bala, R., Eschbach, R.: Spatial color-to-grayscale transform preserving chrominance edge information. In: 14th Color Imaging Conference: Color, Science, Systems and Applications, pp. 82–86 (2004)
2. Socolinsky, D.A., Wolff, L.B.: Multispectral image visualization through first-order fusion. IEEE Trans. Im. Proc. **11**, 923–931 (2002)
3. Lillesand, T.M., Kiefer, R.W.: Remote Sensing and Image Interpretation, 2nd edn. Wiley, New York (1994)
4. Grundland, M., Dodgson, N.A.: Decolorize: Fast, contrast enhancing, color to grayscale conversion. Pattern Recognition **40**(11), 2891–2896 (2007)
5. Socolinsky, D.A., Wolff, L.B.: A new visualization paradigm for multispectral imagery and data fusion. In: CVPR, pp. I:319–I:324 (1999)
6. Alsam, A., Drew, M.: Fast multispectral2gray. Journal of Imaging Science and Technology **53**(6), 60401-1 (2009)
7. Alsam, A., Rivertz, H.J.: Algebraic color to grayscale. In: Proceedings of the 14th IASTED International Conference on Signal and Image Processing, pp. 198–203 (2012)

Unconstrained Structural Similarity-Based Optimization

Daniel Otero$^{(\boxtimes)}$ and Edward R. Vrscay

Department of Applied Mathematics, Faculty of Mathematics,
University of Waterloo, Waterloo, ON N2L3G1, Canada
{dotero,ervrscay}@uwaterloo.ca

Abstract. We establish a general framework, along with a set of algorithms, for the incorporation of the Structural Similarity (SSIM) quality index measure as the fidelity, or "data fitting," term in objective functions for optimization problems in image processing. The motivation for this approach is to replace the widely used Euclidean distance, known as a poor measure of visual quality, by the SSIM, which has been recognized as one of the best measures of visual closeness. Some experimental results are also presented.

1 Introduction

Many image processing tasks, e.g., denoising, inpainting, deblurring, are usually carried out by solving an appropriate optimization problem. In most cases, the objective function associated with such a problem is expressed as the sum of a fidelity term (or terms) $f(x)$ and a regularization term (or terms) $h(x)$. The optimization problem then assumes the form

$$\min_{x} \{f(x) + \lambda h(x)\}, \qquad (1)$$

where the constant λ is a regularization parameter.

The role of the fidelity term $f(x)$ is to keep the solution to (1) close to the observed data. A typical choice is $f(x) = \frac{1}{2}\|x - y\|_2^2$, where y is the (corrupted) observation, e.g., a noisy image. The regularization term $h(x)$ has a twofold purpose: (i) It prevents over-fitting to the observed data and (ii) it imposes constraints on the solution based upon prior information or assumptions. For instance, if the optimal solution is assumed to be sparse, a typical regularization term is $h(x) = \|x\|_1$ [5,11,16].

Using the squared Euclidean distance as a measure of closeness is convenient since it is convex, differentiable, and usually mathematically tractable, not to mention easily computed. Furthermore, widely used metrics of visual quality such as Mean Squared Error (MSE) and Peak to Signal Noise Ratio (PSNR) are based on this definition of closeness. Nevertheless, it has been shown that such distortion measures are not the best choice when it comes to quantify visual

© Springer International Publishing Switzerland 2014
A. Campilho and M. Kamel (Eds.): ICIAR 2014, Part I, LNCS 8814, pp. 167–176, 2014.
DOI: 10.1007/978-3-319-11758-4_19

quality [17,18]. For this reason, many measures of visual quality have been proposed in an attempt to model the Human Visual System (HVS). The Structural Similarity (SSIM) image quality measure, originally proposed by Wang *et al.* [18], was based upon the assumption that the HVS evolved to perceive visual errors as changes in structural information. On the basis of subjective quality assessments involving large databases, SSIM has been generally accepted to be one of the best measures of visual quality/closeness.

With these comments in mind, it would seem natural to consider the SSIM as a replacement for the widely-used squared Euclidean distance in the fidelity term $f(x)$ of Eq. (1), given the limitations of the latter to measure visual closeness. Indeed, from a practical point of view, it is easy to make such a replacement since the mathematical expression for the SSIM between x and the observed data y is rather straightforward. One may then be tempted to simply start computing. There is a problem, however, in that the actual mathematical framework behind such an SSIM-based optimization, which would be important for the establishment of existence and uniqueness of solutions, is more complicated due to the fact that the SSIM is not a convex function.

Notwithstanding these obstacles, optimization problems that employ the SSIM as a fitting term have already been addressed. For instance, in [3] the authors find the best approximation coefficients in the SSIM sense when an orthogonal transformation is used (e.g., Discrete Cosine Transform (DCT), Fourier, etc.). Very briefly, a contrast-enhanced version of the best ℓ_2-based approximation is obtained. Based on this result, Rehman *et al.* [13] address the SSIM version of the image restoration problem proposed by Elad *et al.* in [10], where the denoising of images is performed using sparse and redundant representations over learned dictionaries. Furthermore, in [13] the authors also introduce a super-resolution algorithm – also based on the SSIM – to recover from a given low resolution image its high resolution version.

Another interesting application for reconstruction and denoising was proposed in [7]. Here, the authors define the statistical SSIM index (statSSIM), an extension of the SSIM for wide-sense stationary random processes. By optimizing the statSSIM, an optimal filter in the SSIM sense is found. The non-convex nature of the statSSIM is overcome by reformulating its maximization as a quasi-convex optimization problem, which is solved using the bisection method [6,7]. Nevertheless, it is not mentioned that the SSIM – under certain conditions – is a quasi-convex function (see [4]). As a result, it can be minimized using quasi-convex programming techniques, which permits the consideration of a much broader spectrum of SSIM-based optimization problems.

More imaging techniques based on the SSIM can also be found in [14,19]. In these works, optimization of rate distortion, video coding and image classification are explored using the SSIM as a measure of performance.

Note that maximizing $\mathrm{SSIM}(x, y)$ is equivalent to mimizing the function,

$$T(x, y) = 1 - \mathrm{SSIM}(x, y), \tag{2}$$

which may be viewed as a kind of distance function or *dissimilarity* between x and y, i.e., $T(x, y) = 0$ if and only if $x = y$. Many SSIM-based imaging tasks, including all of the applications mentioned above, may now be expressed in terms of the following optimization problem,

$$\min_{x} \{T(\Phi(x), y) + \lambda h(x)\}, \tag{3}$$

where Φ is usually a linear transformation. As such, we consider Eq. (3) to define a general set of problems involving *unconstrained SSIM-based optimization*.

In this paper, we introduce a set of algorithms to solve the general problem in (3), in the effort of providing a unified framework as opposed to developing specific methods that address particular applications, which has been the tendency of research literature to date. In particular, we focus our attention on the case in which $h(x)$ is convex. Mathematical and experimental comparisons between ℓ_2 and SSIM approaches are also provided.

Finally, in a future paper we shall address the general complementary problem of *constrained SSIM-based optimization*.

2   The Structural Similarity Index Measure (SSIM)

Structural similarity (SSIM) [18] provides a measure of visual closeness of two images (or local image patches) by quantifying similarities in three fundamental characteristics: luminance, contrast and structure. Luminances are compared in terms of a relative change in means. Contrasts are compared in terms of relative variance. Finally, structures are compared in terms of the correlation coefficient between the two images. The SSIM value is computed by simply taking the product of these changes.

In what follows, we let $x, y \in \mathbb{R}^n$ denote two n-dimensional signal/image blocks. The SSIM between x and y is defined as [18],

$$\text{SSIM}(x, y) = \left(\frac{2\mu_x \mu_y + C_1}{\mu_x^2 + \mu_y^2 + C_1} \right) \left(\frac{2\sigma_x \sigma_y + C_2}{\sigma_x^2 + \sigma_y^2 + C_2} \right) \left(\frac{\sigma_{xy} + C_3}{\sigma_x \sigma_y + C_3} \right). \tag{4}$$

Here, μ_x and μ_y denote the mean values of x and y, respectively, and σ_{xy} denotes the cross correlation between x and y, from which all other definitions follow. The small positive constants, C_1, C_2, C_3 provide numerical stability and can be adjusted to accommodate the HVS. Note that $-1 \leq \text{SSIM}(x, y) \leq 1$. Furthermore, $\text{SSIM}(x, y) = 1$ if and only if $x = y$. As such, x and y are considered to be more similar the closer $\text{SSIM}(x, y)$ is to 1.

Setting $C_3 = C_2/2$ leads to the following definition of the SSIM index found in [18] and used in [3] and elsewhere,

$$\text{SSIM}(x, y) = \left(\frac{2\mu_x \mu_y + C_1}{\mu_x^2 + \mu_y^2 + C_1} \right) \left(\frac{2\sigma_{xy} + C_2}{\sigma_x^2 + \sigma_y^2 + C_2} \right). \tag{5}$$

Since the statistics of images vary greatly spatially, the $\text{SSIM}(x, y)$ is computed using a sliding window of 8×8 pixels. The final result, i.e., the so-called *SSIM index*, is basically an average of the individual SSIM measures.

Definition as a Normalized Metric

In the special case that x and y have equal means, i.e., $\mu_x = \mu_y$, the luminance component of Eq. (5) is unity so that the SSIM becomes

$$\text{SSIM}(x, y) = \frac{2\sigma_{xy} + C_2}{\sigma_x^2 + \sigma_y^2 + C_2}. \tag{6}$$

A further simplification results when x and y have zero mean, i.e., $\mu_x = \mu_y = 0$. In this special case,

$$\sigma_{xy} = \frac{1}{n-1} \sum_{i=1}^{n} x_i y_i \quad \text{and} \quad \sigma_x^2 = \frac{1}{n-1} \sum_{i=1}^{n} x_i^2. \tag{7}$$

Substitution of these equations into Eq. (6) yields the following simplified formula for the SSIM,

$$\text{SSIM}(x, y) = \frac{2x^T y + C}{\|x\|_2^2 + \|y\|_2^2 + C}, \tag{8}$$

where $C = (n-1)C_2$. For the remainder of this paper, we shall be working with zero mean vectors, so that Eq. (8) will employed in all computations of the SSIM. In this case, the corresponding distance/dissimilarity function $T(x, y)$ in Eq. (2) becomes

$$T(x, y) = 1 - \text{SSIM}(x, y) = \frac{\|x - y\|_2^2}{\|x\|_2^2 + \|y\|_2^2 + C}. \tag{9}$$

Note that $0 \leq T(x, y) \leq 2$. Furthermore, $T(x, y) = 0$ if and only if $x = y$.

As mentioned earlier, since $\text{SSIM}(x, y)$ is a measure of similarity, $T(x, y)$ can be considered as a measure of dissimilarity between x and y. Eq. (9) is, in fact, an example of a (squared) normalized metric, which has been discussed in [2,4].

3   Unconstrained SSIM-Based Optimization

In [2,4], it was shown that the function $\text{SSIM}(x, y)$ is not convex, but locally quasiconvex. This implies that the unconstrained SSIM-based optimization problem defined in Eq. (3) is, in general, not convex. This, in turn, implies that the existence of a global optimal point cannot be guaranteed. Nevertheless, algorithms that converge to either a local or global minimum can be developed. The algorithm to be used for solving (3) depends on whether the regularizing term $h(x)$ is differentiable or not. We consider these two cases separately below.

3.1   Differentiable $h(x)$

When the regularizing term is differentiable, root-finding algorithms can be employed to find a local zero-mean solution x^* to (3). For example, if Tikhonov regularization is used, we have the following SSIM-based optimization problem,

$$\min_{x} \{T(Dx, y) + \lambda \|Ax\|_2^2\}, \tag{10}$$

where D is an $m \times n$ matrix. By computing the gradient of (10), we find that the solution x^* must satisfy

$$[(\text{SSIM}(Dx^*, y)D^T D + \lambda(\|Dx^*\|_2^2 + \|y\|_2^2 + C)A^T A]x^* = D^T y. \quad (11)$$

If we define the following function,

$$f(x) = [(\text{SSIM}(Dx, y)D^T D + \lambda(\|Dx\|_2^2 + \|y\|_2^2 + C)A^T A]x - D^T y, \quad (12)$$

then x^* is a (zero-mean) vector in $\mathbb{R}^n$ such that $f(x^*) = 0$.

We may use the Generalized Newton Method [12] to find x^*. From Kantorovich's Theorem, it is known that convergence in any open subset X of Ω, where $\Omega \subset \mathbb{R}^n$, is guaranteed if the initial guess x_0 satisfies the following condition,

$$K\|J_f(x_0)^{-1}\|\|J_f(x_0)^{-1}J_f(x_0)\| \leq \frac{1}{2}. \quad (13)$$

Here, $J_f(\cdot)$ is the Jacobian of $f(\cdot)$, $J_f(\cdot)^{-1}$ denotes its inverse, and $K > 0$ is a constant less or equal than the Lipschitz constant of $J_f(\cdot)$. In fact, it can be proved that for any open subset $X \subset \Omega$, $J_f(\cdot)$ is Lipschitz continuous, that is, there exists a constant $L > 0$ such that for any $x, z \in X$,

$$\|J_f(x) - J_f(z)\|_F \leq L\|x - z\|_2. \quad (14)$$

Here $\|\cdot\|_F$ denotes the Frobenius norm and

$$L = K_1\|D^T D\|_F + \lambda K_2\|A^T A\|_F, \quad K_1, K_2 > 0. \quad (15)$$

From this discussion, and the notation $\mathbf{1} = [1, 1, \cdots, 1]^T \in \mathbb{R}^n$, we propose the following algorithm for solving the problem in Eq. (10).

Algorithm I: Generalized Newton's Method for unconstrained SSIM-based optimization with Tikhonov regularization

initialize Choose $x = x_0$ according to (13);
data preprocessing $\bar{y} = \frac{1}{n}\mathbf{1}^T y$, $y = y - \bar{y}\mathbf{1}^T$;
repeat
    $x = x - J_f(x)^{-1}f(x)$;
until stopping criterion is met (e.g., $\|x^{(new)} - x^{(old)}\|_\infty < \epsilon$);
return x, $y = y + \bar{y}\mathbf{1}^T$.

Furthermore, this algorithm can be used for any unconstrained SSIM-based optimization problem by defining $f(\cdot)$ and $J_f(\cdot)$ accordingly.

It is worthwhile to mention that it is not always possible to recover the mean of the non-zero-mean optimal solution x^*. This is because the luminance component of the SSIM is not taken into account. Nevertheless, in some circumstances (e.g., denoising of a signal corrupted by zero-mean additive white

Gaussian noise), the mean of y and $\Phi(x^\star)$ coincide. In this case, we have that $x^\star = x^* + \hat{x}$, where x^* is the zero-mean optimal solution and $\hat{x}$ is a vector such that $D\hat{x} = \bar{y}\mathbf{1}$. If $\Phi(\cdot)$ is any $m \times n$ matrix D, it can be seen that $\hat{x}$ is given by:

$$\hat{x} = \bar{y}(D^T D)^{-1} D^T \mathbf{1}, \tag{16}$$

provided that the inverse of $D^T D$ exists.

3.2   Non-differentiable $h(x)$

In this case, a different approach must be taken. Let us consider the particulary important example $h(x) = \|x\|_1$, i.e., we minimize the following functional

$$\min_{x} \{T(Dx, y) + \lambda \|x\|_1\}, \tag{17}$$

In this case, the optimal x^* satisfies

$$D^T D x^* \in \frac{D^T y}{\text{SSIM}(Dx^*, y)} - \lambda \left(\frac{\|Dx^*\|_2^2 + \|y\|_2^2 + C}{2\text{SSIM}(Dx^*, y)} \right) \partial(\|x^*\|_1), \tag{18}$$

where $\partial(\cdot)$ is the sub-gradient operator [11].

To find x^* we employ a coordinate descent approach [15], that is, we minimize (17) along each component of x while the other components are fixed. From (18), for the i-th entry of $x \in \mathbb{R}^n$, the optimal coordinate x_i is given by

$$x_i \in \frac{D_i^T y}{\text{SSIM}(Dx, y)\|D_i^T\|_2^2} - D_i^T Dx_{-i} - \lambda \left(\frac{\|Dx\|_2^2 + \|y\|_2^2 + C}{2\text{SSIM}(Dx, y)\|D_i^T\|_2^2} \right) \partial(|x_i|), \tag{19}$$

where D_i^T is the i-th row of the transpose of D, and x_{-i} is the vector x whose i-th component is set to zero.

The value of x_i can be found by examining the different cases that arise in (19). To begin with, we define

$$\tau_i(x_i) = \lambda \left(\frac{\|Dx\|_2^2 + \|y\|_2^2 + C}{2\text{SSIM}(Dx, y)\|D_i^T\|_2^2} \right) \tag{20}$$

and

$$a_i(x_i) = \frac{D_i^T y}{\text{SSIM}(Dx, y)\|D_i^T\|_2^2} - D_i^T Dx_{-i}. \tag{21}$$

Then, $x_i = 0$ if

$$a_i(0) \in \tau_i(0)[-1, 1]. \tag{22}$$

As expected, $x_i > 0$ if $a_i(0) > \tau_i(0)$, so that

$$x_i = a_i(x_i) - \tau_i(x_i). \tag{23}$$

Similarly, we obtain $x_i < 0$ if $a_i(0) < -\tau_i(0)$, in which case x_i is given by

$$x_i = a_i(x_i) + \tau_i(x_i). \tag{24}$$

Notice that when $x_i \neq 0$, we have a result of the form $x_i = g(x_i)$, a non-linear equation that may be solved using either a fixed-point iteration scheme – provided that $g_{\pm}(x_i) = a_i(x_i) \mp \tau_i(x_i)$ is a contraction – or a root-finding algorithm by defining $f_{\pm}(x) = x_i - g_{\pm}(x_i)$. In particular, we follow a fixed-point approach. Moreover, equations (22), (23) and (24) can be combined into the following single operator:

$$\Phi_{\tau_i(0)}(a_i(0)) = \begin{cases} \text{Solve } x_i = a_i(x_i) - \tau_i(x_i), & \text{if } a_i(0) > \tau_i(0), \\ \text{Solve } x_i = a_i(x_i) + \tau_i(x_i), & \text{if } a_i(0) < -\tau_i(0), \\ x_i = 0, & \text{if } |a_i(0)| \leq \tau_i(0). \end{cases} \quad (25)$$

Eq. (25) is an important result since it may be considered an extension of the widely used soft-thresholding (ST) operator [8,16] for the purpose of solving the unconstrained SSIM-based optimization problem (17).

With regard to initial conditions, experimental results show that the optimal ℓ_2 solution of the unconstrained problem $\|Dx - y\|_2^2$ is a good initial guess, i.e., $x_0 = (D^T D)^{-1} D^T y$.

From the above discussion, we introduce the following algorithm to determine the optimal x^* for problem (17).

Algorithm II: Coordinate Descent algorithm for unconstrained SSIM-based optimization with ℓ_1 norm regularization

initialize $x = (D^T D)^{-1} D^T y$;
data preprocessing $\bar{y} = \frac{1}{n} 1^T y$, $y = y - \bar{y} 1^T$;
repeat
    for $i = 1$ **to** n **do**
        $x_i = \Phi_{\tau_i(0)}(a_i(0))$;
    end
until stopping criteria is met (e.g., $\|x^{(new)} - x^{(old)}\|_\infty < \epsilon$);
return x, $y = y + \bar{y} 1^T$.

As expected, equation (16) can be used to recover the non-zero mean optimal solution x^*, provided that the means of y and Dx^* are equal.

4 Experiments

Algorithms I and II can be used for many different SSIM-based applications. In the results presented below, however, we have focussed our attention on the performance of Algorithm II for solving problem (17) when D is an orthogonal transformation. To measure its efficacy, we compare the solutions obtained by the proposed method with the set of solutions of the ℓ_2 version of problem (17), namely,

$$\min_x \left\{ \frac{1}{2} \|Dx - y\|_2^2 + \lambda \|x\|_1 \right\}, \quad (26)$$

which can be solved by means of the ST operator [11,16] if D is an orthogonal matrix.

The experiments reported below were concerned with the recovery of Discrete Cosine Transform (DCT) coefficients. All images were divided into non-overlapping 8×8 pixel blocks, the means of which were subtracted prior to processing. After a block has been processed, its mean is added. Although this procedure is not required for ℓ_2 approaches, it has been performed for the sake of a fair comparison between the two methods.

In Figure 1, the first two plots from left to right corresponds to the average SSIM of all the reconstructions versus the ℓ_0 norm of the recovered coefficients for the test images *Lena* and *Mandrill*. The average SSIM was computed by combining and averaging all the computed SSIMs from all 4096 non-overlapping blocks for both *Lena* and *Mandrill* (both test images have 512×512 pixels). It can be clearly seen that the proposed algorithm outperforms the ℓ_2-based method (ST). This is because minimization of the dissimilarity measure $T(x, y)$ in Eq. (2) is equivalent to maximization of $SSIM(Dx, y)$, which produces an enhancement in contrast [3]. This effect is demonstrated in the nature of the recovered coefficients. Firstly, the degree of shrinking and thresholding of DCT coefficients by our proposed method is not at strong as ST. Secondly, in some cases, there are DCT coefficients which are thresholded (i.e., set to zero) by the ℓ_2 approach, but kept non-zero by the SSIM-based method for the sake of contrast. These effects are demonstrated in the third and fourth plots in Figure 1. In these two plots, the same block from the image *Lena* was processed, but subjected to two different amounts of regularization.

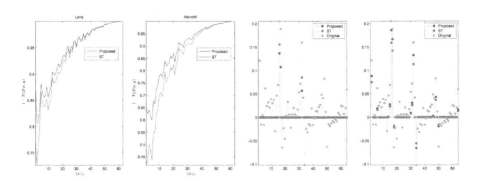

Fig. 1. The first two plots from left to right correspond to the average SSIM versus the ℓ_0 norm of the recovered coefficients for the test images *Lena* and *Mandrill*. In the last two plots, a visual comparison between the original and recovered coefficients from a particular block of the *Lena* image can be appreciated. Regularization is carried out so that the two methods being compared induce the same sparseness in their recoveries. In the two shown examples, the same block was processed but subjected to different amounts of regularization. In particular, the ℓ_0 norm of the set of DCT coefficients that were recovered by both the proposed method and ST is 3 for the first example (third plot), and 15 for the second (fourth plot).

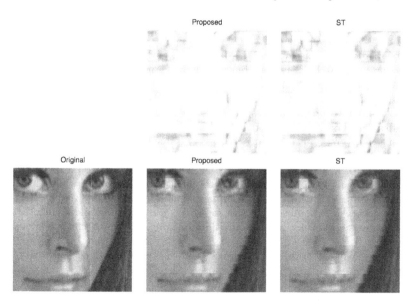

Fig. 2. Visual results for a patch from the test image *Lena*. In all cases, the ℓ_0 norm of the recovered DCT coefficients for each non-overlapping block is 13. In the upper row, the SSIM maps between the reconstructions and the original patch are shown. Reconstructed and original patches can be seen in the lower row. The average $T(Dx, y)$ of all non overlapping blocks for the proposed method is 0.8864, whereas for ST is 0.8609.

In addition, some visual results are shown in Figure 2. In this case, a sub-image from the test image *Lena* was used. The original and recovered images are presented in the bottom row. Regularization was carried out so that the sparsity induced by each method is the same; that is, the ℓ_0 norm of the set of recovered coefficients is 13 in all cases. In the top row of the Figure are shown the SSIM maps that illustrate the similarity between the reconstructions and the original image. The brightness of these maps indicates the degree of similarity between corresponding image blocks – the brighter a given point the greater the magnitude of the SSIM between the retrieved and the original image blocks at that location [18]. It can be seen that the performance of the proposed method and the ℓ_2 approach is very similar. However, the proposed algorithm does perform better than ST in terms of SSIM . This can be seen at some locations in the SSIM maps. For instance, note that the upper left corner of the SSIM map of the proposed method is slightly brighter than the corresponding regions of the other two SSIM maps. This is also evident at other locations. Moreover, the enhancement of contrast is clearly seen when the pupils of the left eyes are compared. With regard to numerical results, the average $T(Dx, y)$ for the ℓ_2 approach is 0.8609, whereas for the proposed method is 0.8864, which is moderately better.

Acknowledgments. This research was supported in part by the Natural Sciences and Engineering Research Council (NSERC).

References

1. Albuquerque, G., Eisemann, M., Magnor, M.A.: Perception-based visual quality measures. In: 2011 IEEE Conference on Visual Analytics Science and Technology (VAST), pp. 13–20 (2011)
2. Brunet, D.: A Study of the Structural Similarity Image Quality Measure with Applications to Image Processing. Ph.D. Thesis, Department of Applied Mathematics, University of Waterloo (2012)
3. Brunet, D., Vrscay, E.R., Wang, Z.: Structural similarity-based approximation of signals and images using orthogonal bases. In: Campilho, A., Kamel, M. (eds.) ICIAR 2010. LNCS, vol. 6111, pp. 11–22. Springer, Heidelberg (2010)
4. Brunet, D., Vrscay, E.R., Wang, Z.: On the mathematical properties of the structural similarity index. Proc. IEEE Trans. Image Processing **21**(4), 1488–1499 (2012)
5. Amir Beck, A., Teboulle, M.: A fast iterative shrinkage-thresholding algorithm for linear inverse problems. SIAM Journal on Imaging Sciences Archive **2**(1), 183–202 (2009)
6. Boyd, S., Vandenberghe, L.: Convex Optimization. Cambridge University Press (2004)
7. Channappayya, S.S., Bovik, A.C., Caramanis, C., Heath Jr, R.W.: Design of linear equalizers optimized for the structural similarity index. IEEE Transactions on Image Processing **17**(6), 857–872 (2008)
8. Donoho, D.: Denoising by Soft-Thresholding. IEEE Transactions on Information Theory **41**(3), 613–627 (1995)
9. Efron, B., Hastie, T., Johnstone, I., Tibshirani, R.: Least Angle Regression. The Annals of Statistics **32**, 407–451 (2004)
10. Elad, M., Aharon, M.: Image denoising via sparse and redundant representations over learned dictionaries. IEEE Transactions on Image Processing **15**(12), 3736–3745 (2006)
11. Mairal, J., Bach, F., Jenatton, R., Obozinski, G.: Convex Optimization with Sparsity-Inducing Norms. Optimization for Machine Learning. MIT Press (2011)
12. Ortega, J.M.: The Newton-Kantorovich Theorem. The American Mathematical Monthly **75**(6), 658–660 (1968)
13. Rehman, A., Rostami, M., Wang, Z., Brunet, D., Vrscay, E.R.: SSIM-inspired image restoration using sparse representation. EURASIP J. Adv. Sig. Proc. (2012). doi:10.1186/1687-6180-2012-16
14. Rehman, A., Gao, Y., Wang, J., Wang, Z.: Image classification based on complex wavelet structural similarity. Sig. Proc. Image Comm. **28**(8), 984–992 (2013)
15. Tseng, P., Yun, S.: A Coordinate Gradient Descent Method for Non-smooth Separable Minimization. Journal of Mathematical Programming **117**(1–2), 387–423 (2009)
16. Turlach, B.A.: On algorithms for solving least squares problems under an ℓ_1 penalty or an ℓ_1 constraint. In: Proceedings of the American Statistical Association, Statistical Computing Section, pp. 2572–2577 (2005)
17. Wang, Z., Bovik, A.C.: A universal image quality index. IEEE Signal Processing Letters **9**(3), 81–84 (2002)
18. Wang, Z., Bovik, A.C., Sheikh, H.-R., Simoncelli, E.S.: Image quality assessment: From error visibility to structural similarity. IEEE Trans. Image Processing **13**(4), 600–612 (2004)
19. Wang, S., Rehman, A., Wang, Z., Ma, S., Gao, W.: SSIM-motivated rate-distortion optimization for video coding. IEEE Trans. Circuits Syst. Video Techn. **22**(4), 516–529 (2012)

Feature Detection
and Image Segmentation

Reflectance-Based Segmentation Using Photometric and Illumination Invariants

Jose-Antonio Pérez-Carrasco[1]($\boxtimes$), Begoña Acha-Piñero[1],
Carmen Serrano-Gotarredona[1], and Theo Gevers[2]

[1] Signal and Communications Department, University of Seville,
Camino de los Descubrimientos, s/n., 41092 Sevilla, Spain
{jperez2,cserrano,bacha}@us.es
[2] Faculty of Science, Amsterdam University Informatics Institute, Science Park 904,
1098 XH Amsterdam, The Netherlands
th.gevers@uva.nl

Abstract. In this paper we propose a three-stage algorithm to implement effective segmentation of an object's counterparts when illumination variance is present. A color constancy algorithm and color-based invariant parameters insensitive to a large set of different illumination conditions are used. Then reflectance images are considered after discarding the shadowing information present in the images. A color-based segmentation algorithm using Graph Cuts is applied to the reflectance images. Improvements in the segmentation are obtained after using these illumination invariants.

Keywords: Color-invariants · Graph cuts · Reflectance · Intrinsic images

1 Introduction

Humans are able to distinguish the counterparts of an object even when there are differences in illuminations and presence of shadows in the scene. Differences in illumination cause measurements of object colors to be biased toward the color of the light source. Shadows make it difficult for state-of-art algorithms to implement an efficient segmentation. However, Humans have the ability to solve these two separate problems. They are able to distinguish between reflectance and shadowing information and they implement color constancy: They perceive the same color of an object despite large differences in illumination.

Segmentation is a very important prior step to implement before object recognition or categorization and color provides powerful information in these tasks [1]. However, color-based camera-obtained images are sensitive to many factors, such us changes in the illumination, changes in the viewing directions, etc.

State-of-art segmentation techniques apply the segmentation to the image under analysis and have to face problems due to changes in illuminants, shadowing and shadows, etc. Few works have been reported applying segmentation

© Springer International Publishing Switzerland 2014
A. Campilho and M. Kamel (Eds.): ICIAR 2014, Part I, LNCS 8814, pp. 179–186, 2014.
DOI: 10.1007/978-3-319-11758-4_20

to the reflectance images, which are free of all the problems that illumination involves.

In this work we propose a three-stages strategy to implement efficient segmentation using reflectance images. First, a color constancy algorithm is applied to the images. Secondly, intrinsic images (Reflectance and Shadowing) images are obtained using invariant ratios and a color-retinex based algorithm. Finally, a segmentation algorithm based on Kmeans and Graph-Cuts is applied to the reflectance image. A ground-truth database is used to measure the accuracy and improvement of our algorithm.

2   Implementation

2.1   Color Constancy Algorithm

Regarding to the color constancy problem, many computational algorithms have been proposed. However, no algorithm can be considered as universal and with the large variety of available methods is difficult to select the method that performs best for a specific image. Gijsenij and Gevers [2] gets very good results when compared to state-of-art color constancy algorithms. In their work they use natural image statistics based on a Weibull parameterization to identify the most important characteristics of color images. Then, based on these image characteristics, the proper color constancy algorithm (or best combination of algorithms) is selected for a specific image. This selection is implemented by a MoG-classifier. The output of the classifier is the selection of the best performing color constancy method for a certain image. In our work we have used this algorithm because of its color constancy performance improvement up to 20 percent when compared to the best-performing single algorithms.

2.2   Color Illumination Invariant Ratios

In the work by Gevers and Smeulders [1], a set of color constant color ratios independent to viewing direction, surface orientation, illumination direction and intensity, illumination color and interreflection is proposed. These parameters $m1_x$, $m2_x$ and $m3_x$, where x denotes derivating accross the x direction, can be computed as:

$$m1_x = \frac{R_xG - G_xR}{RG}; m2_x = \frac{G_xB - B_xG}{GB}; \tag{1}$$

$m3_x$ is not considered as it can be obtained using $m1_x$ and $m2_x$. The same computations are implemented for the y direction. These three parameters at each point allow us to compute the two different gradient invariant images $M1$ and $M2$ as

$$M_i = \sqrt{mi_x^2 + mi_y^2}, i = 1, ..., 2 \tag{2}$$

In [3] J. van de Weijer et al. propose a set of photometric variants and quasi-invariants. To this end, the derivative of an image f_x is projected on three directions. By removing the variance from the derivative of the image, they construct a complementary set of derivatives which they call quasi-invariants. Among these invariants we have used the shadow-shading-specular quasi-invariant which is obtained by projecting the derivative of the image on the hue direction

$$H_x = (f_x \cdot \hat{b})\hat{b}; H_x^c = f_x - H_x; \tag{3}$$

where $\hat{b}$ is used for the hue direction. Superscript c is used to indicate what remains after subtraction of the variant H_x. H_x^c does not contain specular or shadow-shading edges. As the parameters described above provide shading invariance, the edges in the invariant images M_i and H_x^c will correspond mainly to reflectance information, thus allowing us to create three different reflectance edge maps.

2.3   Intrinsic Images Recovery

As in the work by R. Grosse et al. [4], we consider that our images contain only a single direct light source and the shading at each pixel can be represented as a scalar S(x, y). Therefore, the image decomposes as a product of shading and reflectance:

$$I(x,y) = S(x,y)R(x,y) \tag{4}$$

It is commonly assumed that it is unlikely that significant shading boundaries and reflectance edges occur at the same point. We can then recover the reflectance intrinsic image from its derivatives with the same method used by Weiss in [5] to find the pseudoinverse of the overconstrained system of derivatives. One nice property of this technique is that the computation can be done using the efficiently FFT. Thus, our aim is to compute a reflectance mask to be applied to the derivatives of the image. The resulting image will be the reflectance edge $R(x,y)$ image that can serve us in the above algorithm to recover an image free of shadowing information. Then, using Eq. 4 and the input image we can compute the shadowing image $S(x,y)$.

To compute the reflectance mask there are many algorithms. To assess the efficiency of some of the state-of-art methods, R. Grosse et al. [4] performed an evaluation using a ground-truth dataset for intrinsic images. The dataset is composed by the decompositions in the corresponding intrinsic images (shading and reflectance) of real objects. In the study, the combination of the *Weiss's multi-image algorithm* with the *color-retinex* algorithm outperforms all the described implementations. In the color Retinex algorithm (COL-RET), two separate thresholds are used, one for brightness changes and one for color changes. In the Weiss's multi-image algorithm, multiple photographs of the same scene with different lighting conditions are required, thus making it easier to factor out the shading. A drawback of the Weiss algorithm is that multiple photographs of the same scene are not usually available (strongly required by the Weiss method). Therefore, we have not consider the implementations using Weiss's multi-image algorithm but just the color-retinex algorithm, which was still better than the other ones.

We have used the invariant ratios M_i and H_x^c described through Eqs. 2 and 3 to create the reflectance edge maps. As the parameters described provide shading invariance, the edges in the invariant images obtained will correspond mainly to reflectance information. Appliying independent thresholds to these ratios, values lower than the threshold are set to '0', and values higher than the threshold are set to '1'. This way a reflectance edge map is computed using the invariant features. As some edges can be unconnected, morphogical operations are employed such us bridging previously unconnected pixels, binary closure opening, and the use of a morphological structuring element. The color Retinex algorithm (*COL-RET*) described above was also use to create an alternative reflectance edge map and for comparison purposes.

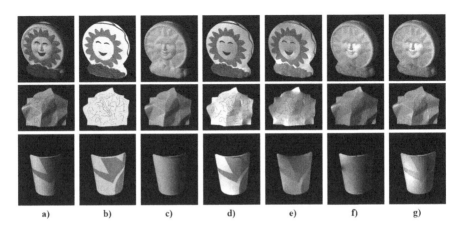

a)   b)   c)   d)   e)   f)   g)

Fig. 1. Intrinsic images obtained after applying the color retinex algorithm and our fusion between the color-retinex and the invariant edge maps. Column *a)*, *b)* and *c)* correspond to the original, ground-truth reflectance and ground-truth shadowing images respectively. Columns *d)* and *f)* shows the reflectance and shadowing images obtained using our fusioned algorithm. Columns *e)* and *g)* are used to show the reflectance and shadowing images obtained using only the color-retinex algorithm.

2.4   Reflectance-Based Segmentation

For the segmentation stage to the reflectance obtained images we have implemented a segmentation strategy based on kmeans and min-cut max-flow optimization methods for graph-cuts [6]. In graph-cuts, the pixels of the image are defined as the vertices of the graph. All neighboring pairs of pixels of the image are assumed to be connected to each other with a link and these links are called the edges. The goal in these algorithms is to find a cut or a set of edges that separates the regions in a way that the cut has the minimum cost. To perform the minimization process the cost or energy function is defined. We have implemented the segmentation algorithm using the Matlab wrapper for graph cuts implemented by Bagon [7]. More specifically, the segmentation consists of two stages. First, k distinct clusters where identified using a kmeans algorithm and the image is pre-segmented according to these regions. Then each pixel is assigned to its cluster and the GraphCut poses smoothness constraint on this labelling. The Matlab wrapper executes the energy minimization software [6][8] based on the fast min-cut/max-flow algorithm developed by Boykov and Kolmogorov [9].

3   Experimental Results

In the approach here presented we have used 12 images belonging to the database created by R. Grosse et al. [4] to assess the performance of our intrinsic images extraction and segmentation algorithm. Some images belonging to the Amsterdam Library of Object Images (ALOI) data set [10], composed by more than 48,000 images of 1,000 objects under various illumination conditions (including changes in the illumination color temperature) were also considered.

The Color-Retinex algorithm and the thresholded invariant image parameters $M1$, $M2$ and H_x^c described in Eq. 2 and Eq. 3 generate four different edge maps corresponding to reflectance information. The optimum thresholds to compute reflectance edge maps for the $M1$, $M2$ and H_x^c invariant parameters were obtained with the *simulated annealing algorithm* [11]. The *simulated annealing algorithm* minimizes a cost function, while providing lower and upper bounds for the parameters. For the cost function we used the local mean squared error metric ($LMSE$) as computed by Grosse [4] to assess the similarity between the obtained reflectance and shadowing images with the ground-truth respective ones.

We have compared this error using three different experiments. First, using only the provided by the COL-RET algorithm edge map. Secondly, using an edge map obtained using an OR operation between the masks obtained by $M1$, $M2$ and H_x^c. The mask obtained this way was called *invariant mask*. Finally we combined (again with an OR operation) the *invariant mask* and the COL-RET edge map. The errors obtained which each of the implementations are shown in Table 1.

Table 1. Results obtained using the edge map using the three different implementations

METHOD	INVAR	COL-RET	INVAR+COL-RET
ERROR	0.026	0.023	0.019

Note from Table 1 that the combination of methods reduces the error around 17.3% when compared to the score obtained using separately the COL-RET and the $INVARIANTS$ algorithmn. Fig. 1 shows some of the images obtained by our method and the *COL-RET* implementation. Note how our implementation clearly outperformed visually the *COL-RET* implementation even when the images in the figure provided similar score results.

Once the reflectance images have been obtained using the *COL-RET* + *INVARIANTS* parameters combination, the segmentation stage as described in Subsection 2.4 was implemented. To assess the accuracy of the segmentation achieved we used the following computation

$$S = \sum_{k \in K} \frac{Np_{Rest}^k}{Np_{Rgt}^k} \qquad (5)$$

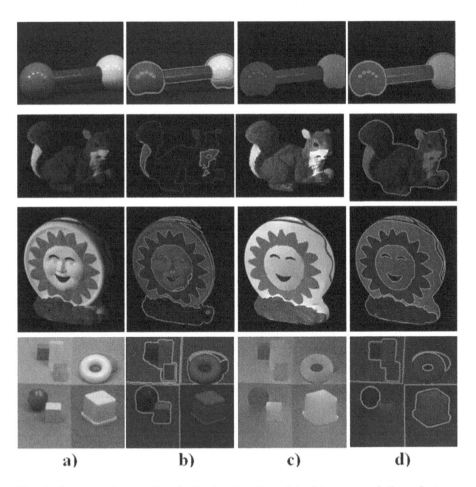

a)   b)   c)   d)

Fig. 2. Segmentation results obtained using the original images and the reflectance images. Column *a)* corresponds to the original images. Column *b)* shows the regions segmented using the original images. Column *d)* shows the segmentation obtained using the reflectance images appearing in column *c)*.

Where, K is the number of categories considered during segmentation, Np^k_{Rgt} is the number of pixels with label k in the segmented ground-truth reflectance image and Np^k_{Rest} is the number of pixels in Np^k_{Rgt} also appearing with label k in an under-assessment segmented image (original or estimated reflectance image). Note that we are using the ground-truth reflectance segmented images as ground-truth for segmentation to assess our algorithm, as segmentation results on these images were on concordance with manual segmentations. With Eq. 5 we assessed the segmentation obtained with the original images (composed of reflectance and shadowing components) and with the reflectance estimated images. We obtained an averaged performance value of 89.8% for the original images and 96.7% for the estimated reflectance images. Note that the accuracy of the segmentation have been increased by 7%. In Fig. 2 some results are shown. Note how our implementation (right column) is able to isolate the objects and counterparts of the objects more accurately.

4   Conclusions

In this paper an algorithm for implementing object segmentation using reflectance information has been described. The first stage is to adequate the images using a color constancy algorithm to remove illuminant dependences. The second stage involves the computation of several invariant parameters in order to retrieve the reflectance information in the images avoiding the undesirable effects of shadowing and orientation variations in illumination. With these parameters the reflectance and shadowing intrinsic images can be obtained using reintegration algorithms. Invariant parameters combined with the color-retinex algorithm improve state-of-art results. Once the reflectance images are available, a graph-cut color-based segmentation algorithm is applied. Using a ground-truth database it has been clearly shown that applying segmentation to the reflectance components improves the segmentation results. In future implementations categorization of objects using the intrinsic images obtained together with the segmentation results will be implemented considering different viewing conditions, different databases and the presence of more objects in the same scene.

Acknowledgments. This research has been supported by P11-TIC-7727.

References

1. Gevers, T., Smeulders, A.: Color based object recognition. Pattern Recognition **32**, 453–464 (1997)
2. Gijsenij, A., Gevers, T.: Color constancy using natural image statistics and scene semantics. IEEE Transactions on Pattern Analysis and Machine Intelligence **33**(4), 687–698 (2011)
3. van de Weijer, J., Gevers, T., Geusebroek, J.M.: Edge and corner detection by photometric quasi-invariants. IEEE Transactions on Pattern Analysis and Machine Intelligence **27**(4), 625–630 (2005)

4. Grosse, R., Johnson, M.K., et al.: Ground truth dataset and baseline evaluations for intrinsic image algorithms. In: IEEE International Conference on Computer Vision, pp. 2335–2342 (2009)
5. Weiss, Y.: Deriving intrinsic images from image sequences. In: IEEE International Conference on Computer Vision, vol. 2(1), p. 68 (2001)
6. Boykov, Y., et al.: Efficient approximate energy minimization via graph cuts. IEEE Transactions on Pattern Analysis and Machine Intelligence **20**(12), 1222–1239 (2001)
7. Bagon, S: Matlab wrapper for graph cut (December 2006)
8. Kolmogorov, V., Zabih, R.: What energy functions can be minimized via graph cuts? IEEE Transactions on Pattern Analysis and Machine Intelligence **26**(2), 147–159 (2004)
9. Boykov, Y., Kolmogorov, V.: An experimental comparison of min-cut/max-flow algorithms for energy minimization in vision. IEEE Transactions on Pattern Analysis and Machine Intelligence **26**(9), 1124–1137 (2004)
10. Mark Geusebroek, J., et al.: The amsterdam library of object images. Int. J. Comput. Vision **61**, 103–112 (2005)
11. Kirkpatrick, S., et al.: Optimization by simulated annealing. Science **220**, 671–680 (1983)

Meta-learning for Adaptive Image Segmentation

Aymen Sellaouti[1,2], Yasmina Jaâfra[1(✉)], and Atef Hamouda[1]

[1] Faculté des Sciences de Tunis, LIPAH, Université de Tunis El Manar,
2092 Tunis, Tunisia
[2] LSIIT, Pôle API, Université de Strasbourg, Bd Sbastien Brant,
67412 Illkirch, France
{aymen.sellaouti,yasmina.jaafra}@gmail.com, atef_hammouda@yahoo.fr

Abstract. Most image segmentations require control parameters setting that depends on the variability of processed images characteristics. This paper introduces a meta-learning system using stacked generalization to adjust segmentation parameters within an object-based analysis of very high resolution urban satellite images. The starting point of our system is the construction of the knowledge database from the concatenation of images characterization and their correct segmentation parameters. Meta-knowledge database is then built from the integration of base-learners performance evaluated by cross-validation. It will allow knowledge transfer to second-level learning and the generation of the meta-classifier that will predict new image segmentation parameters. An experimental study on a satellite image covering the urban area of Strasbourg region enabled us to evaluate the effectiveness of the adopted approach.

Keywords: Object-based analysis · Segmentation · Very high resolution satellite image · Meta-learning · Stacked generalization

1 Introduction

The object-based image analysis (OBIA) [1] has grown in importance with the advent of the very high resolution (VHR) satellite imagery as pixels considered individually no longer capture the characteristics of classified targets. The initial step in OBIA approaches is segmentation which defines thematic image objects by clustering adjacent pixels with similar characteristics. Inserting a segmentation step prior to classification has demonstrated its effectiveness in the case of VHR remote sensing images [2]. Despite the various developed segmentation techniques, no general methods have been stated to process efficiently the wide diversity of images in real world applications. Most of these techniques require control parameters setting that depends on the variability of processed images characteristics. This variability is caused by weather and lighting conditions, imaging devices, clouds, etc [3]. However, segmentation parameters selection is problematic because the user is forced to adopt an exhausting trial-and-error procedure to achieve an acceptable quality of segmentation. Indeed, default

© Springer International Publishing Switzerland 2014
A. Campilho and M. Kamel (Eds.): ICIAR 2014, Part I, LNCS 8814, pp. 187–197, 2014.
DOI: 10.1007/978-3-319-11758-4_21

parameters settings identified by algorithms designers lose effectiveness when the conditions under which they have been designed are changed. Furthermore, the impact and interaction of parameters are complex and can't be modeled in a rule-based framework [4].

Various machine learning techniques have been proposed for the adjustment of segmentation parameters. Derivaux et al. [5] apply a genetic algorithm to generate the elevation map of the Watershed transform and tune segmentation parameters. Bhanu et al. [3] propose connectionist reinforcement learning techniques to adjust the four most critical parameters of Phoenix segmentation algorithm. The selection of the most appropriate learning method to solve a specific problem is not an easy task. In fact, according to " No Free Lunch " theorems there is no algorithm better than all others on all tasks [6]. The solution specifying the optimal learning model in a given context has been defined within the discipline of machine learning as meta-learning. It refers to the ability of a learning system to increase its effectiveness and ability to learn how to learn through experience. It is differentiated from conventional base-learning by the extent of its adaptation level. While the latter has a fixed bias a priori, meta-learning selects dynamically its bias according to the context of study [7].

Although numerous learning models have been applied to the setting of segmentation parameters, no meta-learning approach was proposed to solve this problem. In this paper, our main goal is to provide the segmentation process with the ability to adapt to image characteristics variations. A meta-learning strategy using stacked generalization is assigned to adjust Watershed segmentation parameters according to combined predictions provided by a set of learning algorithms. Our approach aims at achieving a better performance of image interpretation than the one obtained with conventional learning. Although several studies have been conducted in the field of image analysis with machine learning, to our knowledge, no one of them has implemented a stacking approach in setting segmentation parameters.

In the remainder of this paper, we present in Section 2 the details of used segmentation algorithm and related parameters. Section 3 describes the stacking approach implementation. Section 4 exposes experimental results. The last section is dedicated to findings and conclusions discussion.

2   Watershed Segmentation Parameters

Watershed segmentation presented in [8] belongs to the family of edge-based algorithms and is considered as the main method of mathematical morphology segmentation. The Watershed transform is a well-known segmentation method that has been widely used and tested. It considers the image as a topographic surface where the gradient function is used to attribute a gray level corresponding to the height of each pixel. An immersion procedure is applied to this surface that is flooded from its minima generating different growing catchment basins. Watershed lines are built to avoid merging water from two different basins.

The Watershed algorithm is characterized by its tendency to generate over-segmented images where each object of interest is represented by several regions.

Different solutions were proposed in the literature to reduce over-segmentation. In our study, it consists in integrating three parameters in Watershed algorithm that will define thresholding controls for segments construction [9]:

- Gradient threshold: Once the topographic surface is created, any pixel p with a gradient value $G(p)$ below a certain threshold h_{min} is set to zero. Thus, small variations belonging to homogeneous areas, which correspond to low values of the gradient, are removed.

$$G_{h_{min}}(p) = \begin{cases} G(p) & if \ G(p) > h_{min} \\ 0 & otherwise \end{cases} \tag{1}$$

- Basin dynamic: A catchment basin r_i will be separated from another by a watershed line if its dynamic d_i is greater than a given threshold d_{min}. Indeed, small dynamic basins are filled during immersion stage.

$$keep(r_i) = \begin{cases} True & if \ d_i > d_{min} \\ False & otherwise \end{cases} \tag{2}$$

- Regions merging: This technique is based on the idea that similar related areas should be merged. If the Euclidian distance between the spectral averages of each band b for two neighboring regions r_i and r_j is below a threshold m_{min}, these two regions are merged.

$$neighbor(r_i, r_j) = \begin{cases} True & if \ p_i \in r_i, p_j \in r_j | \ p_i \ and \ p_j \ are \ adjacent \\ False & otherwise \end{cases} \tag{3}$$

$$dissimilarity(r_i, r_j) = \sqrt{\sum_{b=1}^{B}(avg(r_i, b) - avg(r_j, b))^2} \tag{4}$$

$$merge(r_i, r_j) = \begin{cases} True & if \ neighbor(r_i, r_j) = true \ and \\ & dissimilarity(r_i, r_j) < m_{min} \\ False & otherwise \end{cases} \tag{5}$$

Dealing with the over-segmentation effects of Watershed segmentation requires the adjustment of parameters h_{min}, d_{min} and m_{min}. We propose a stacked generalization approach to solve this problem. As part of our experiment, we will define 3 classes P_1, P_2 and P_3 representing different combinations of parameters h_{min}, d_{min} and m_{min}. Each image from our test database is segmented using these combinations. The best parameterization assigned to the processed image is determined according to the evaluation of the corresponding classification.

3   Stacking for Watershed Parameters Selection

We aim at establishing a meta-learning strategy using stacked generalization to adjust Watershed segmentation parameters. This adaptation is performed according to the variability of processed satellite images features caused mainly by environmental conditions. Our adaptive Watershed segmentation approach set in the stacking framework is structured around the following main phases, illustrated in Figure 1:

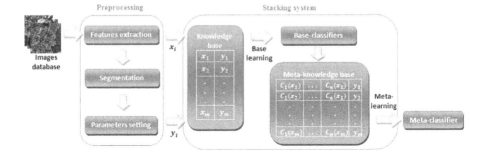

Fig. 1. Stacking approach for adaptive image segmentation

- Preprocessing: The objective of this step is to construct knowledge database where each instance is the concatenation of image characteristics and its correct segmentation parameters class.
- First level or base-learning: Base learners are applied to knowledge database in order to infer base-classifiers. Meta-knowledge database is generated from the integration of base-classifiers predictions into the representation of instances original features.
- Second level or meta-learning: This step consists in applying a meta-learner to the new meta-knowledge database to induce prediction rules of the appropriate segmentation class for new received cases.

3.1 Preprocessing

This phase leads to the realization of knowledge database D which is the starting point of our stacking approach. First, images are characterized in order to identify the group of images that need the same processing parameters achieving the best segmentation results. Attig et al. [10] study the impact of four different image descriptions on the determination of appropriate segmentation parameters and confirm the relevance of texture characteristics. We determine for each image a vector x_i of four texture characteristics that are contrast, energy, homogeneity, and sum variance. These criteria have been selected among those defined by Haralick [11] using a descriptive discriminant analysis.

We assign thereafter to each image its correct parameters class y_i. We set the range of testing parameters to three combinations P_1, P_2 and P_3 of variables h_{min}, d_{min} and m_{min} estimated through a manual trial-and-error procedure operated on a sample of images selected from different areas of the original image. Identifying a good measure for segmentation quality is a known complex problem since the criteria of a good segmentation are generally hard to explicitly define. Nevertheless, segmentation algorithm is used as a preprocessing step within an OBIA, therefore it is natural to use the overall performance of image interpretation to evaluate the segmentation quality. In our approach, the evaluation of the segmentation performed with the three sets of parameters for each image consists in estimating the accuracy of the classification applied to these segmentations [5]. The OBIA used in this study is the hierarchical classification based on a region growing approach introduced by Sellaouti et al. [12] that establishes a collaborative interaction between object segmentation and classification.

Every image is attributed the best segmentation parameters setting among P_1, P_2 or P_3. The classification is evaluated through quantitative comparisons between classification result and image benchmarks using a confusion matrix. The evaluation criteria are precision, recall and F-measure computed from this matrix [13]. Three benchmarks of classes (road, building and vegetation) are constructed for every image on the basis of its corresponding ground-truth. The set of used ground-truths are extracted from a digital map of Strasbourg city[1]. Figure 2 presents an example of a classified image and its related benchmarks.

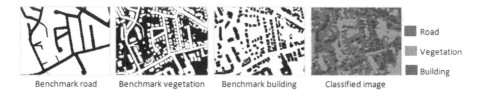

Benchmark road   Benchmark vegetation   Benchmark building   Classified image

■ Road

■ Vegetation

■ Building

Fig. 2. Classified image and related benchmarks

The construction of the knowledge database D is completed by assigning the appropriate correct segmentation parameters y_i among P_1, P_2 and P_3 to test images that were characterized previously with their textural properties vector x_i. It will serve as an entry point to the meta-learning system.

3.2 Stacking System

Meta-learning main focus is to learn about the learning task itself. It employs a meta-classifier that takes as input the space of results from base-level classifiers and generalizes over them. The main meta-learning tasks that have been considered within literature are learning to select the best learner, to dynamically select an appropriate bias, and to combine predictions of base-level classifiers [7]. Stacked generalization [14] is a meta-leaning scheme that aims at learning a meta-level classifier to combine the predictions of multiple base-level classifiers. It differs from the conventional meta-learning strategy of selecting the best classifier by exploiting the diversity in the predictions of base-level classifiers and therefore predicting with higher accuracy at meta-level [15].

---

[1] http://www.carto.strasbourg.eu/

The proposed stacking method is a two-layer structure. At the first level, learning algorithms take as input the initial training data to generate the base-level classifiers. The second layer takes as input the predictions of the previous one and a meta-learner combines them to provide the final meta-classifier. One of the advantages to use stacking is that the transfer of knowledge between levels allows the meta-classifier to learn the base-classifiers errors.

More precisely, the input to the stacking system consists of the knowledge database D. In the base level of learning, a set of classifiers $C_1, ..., C_n$ is generated by using different learning algorithms $L_1, ..., L_n$ on dataset D where $C_i = L_i(D)$ and D consists of examples $e_i = (x_i, y_i)$, i.e., pairs of feature vectors x_i and their parameters classes y_i. To generate meta-knowledge database, a J-fold cross-validation procedure is applied. D is randomly split into disjoint and equal parts $D^1, ..., D^J$. At each jth-fold, $j = 1..J$, the $L_1, ..., L_n$ learning algorithms are applied to the training dataset part $D - D^j$ inducing classifiers $C_1, ..., C_n$ which are then applied to the test part D^j. The predictions of the base-classifiers on each feature vector x_i in D^j are concatenated with the original segmentation parameters class to generate a new set MD^j of meta-feature vectors.

By the end of the entire cross-validation procedure, the meta-knowledge database is constituted from the union $MD = \bigcup MD^j$, $j = 1..J$ and used for applying a learning algorithm L_M and inferring the meta-classifier C_M. Finally, the base-learning algorithms are applied to the entire knowledge database D inducing the final base-classifiers $C_1, ..., C_n$ to be used at the execution of the stacking approach. In order to determine the appropriate segmentation parameters of a new image, the latter is first attributed the base-classifiers predictions vector, then assigned the appropriate parameters class by the meta-classifier C_M. Algorithm 1 presents an algorithmic description of the stacking framework dedicated to adaptive image segmentation approach.

4   Experiment and Results

The empirical evaluation of our approach is conducted on 50 VHR Quickbird images covering the urban area of Strasbourg. A sample from used images dataset is presented in Figure 3:

Fig. 3. A sample of test images

The choice of learners is not restricted and considered as " black art " issue in stacked generalization systems in the sense that there are no specific recommendations in this regard [14]. We built our choice on the findings of Seewald [16] which affirms that stacked generalization works better with a small number of diversified base-learners and those of Skalak [17] who confirms the effectiveness of decision tree as meta-learner. Learning algorithms selected for our experiment are support vector machine (SVM) and discriminant analysis used as base learners while decision tree fills the role of both base and meta-learner [18].

Algorithm 1: Stacking for adaptive image segmentation

Input: Knowledge database D, base-learners $L_1, ..., L_n$, meta-learner L_M, J, new image I

Output: Final prediction of segmentation parameters

1 **Begin**
2 | $MD = \emptyset$
3 | **for** $j = 1$ *to* J **do**
4 | | $MD^j = \emptyset$
5 | | **for** $i = 1$ *to* n **do**
6 | | | $C_i = L_i(D - D^j)$
7 | | | $Pred_i(j) = C_i(D^j)$ // prediction of base-classifier i
8 | | | $MD^j = MD^j \bigcup Pred_i(j)$
9 | | **endfor**
10 | | $MD = MD \bigcup MD^j$
11 | **endfor**
12 | // end of cross-validation procedure
13 | $C_M = L_M(MD)$ // training of meta-classifier
14 | **for** $i = 1$ *to* n **do**
15 | | $C_i = L_i(D)$ /* training of base-classifier i to entire knowledge database D */
16 | **endfor**
17 | // new image execution
18 | $x_I = extract - features(I)$ // construct new image features vector
19 | **for** $i = 1$ *to* n **do**
20 | | $Pred_i(I) = C_i(x_I)$ // prediction of base-classifier i
21 | | $VPred = VPred \bigcup Pred_i(I)$ /* construct new image meta-features vector */
22 | **endfor**
23 | $y_I = C_M(VPred)$ // final prediction of segmentation parameters
24 **End**

Base-classifiers are inferred by running 25-fold cross-validation resulting in the attribution of three predictions of parameters to each image. Despite cross-validation may be computationally expensive for large J, it is generally considered reliable [19]. This database transformation by integrating information on base-classifiers predictions allows us to switch to the second level of learning. The meta-learner L_M is trained on the meta-knowledge database in order to induce the meta-classifier C_M that will be used in predicting the appropriate segmentation parameters for new images. Figure 4 illustrates the impact of learned Watershed segmentation parameters on image interpretation result.

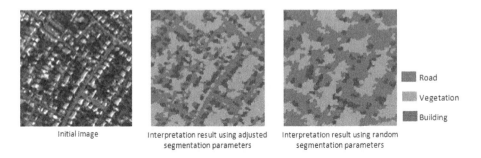

| Initial image | Interpretation result using adjusted segmentation parameters | Interpretation result using random segmentation parameters |

Fig. 4. Impact of Watershed parameters adjustment on image interpretation

Stacking approach global performance is evaluated using a cross-validation technique in order to increase training data for the applied meta-learner and lead therefore to more accurate predictions [15]. We use a " leave-one-out " cross-validation where each instance is a fold itself to maximize meta-learner training data. Table 1 presents segmentation parameters predictions produced by base-classifiers and stacking system for a sample of images. The contribution of our system is brought out when the base-classifiers predictions diverge (cases 2 and 6) or when they are all incorrect (case 7), however the stacking system is able to predict the correct parameterization class.

Table 1. A comparison between stacking system and base-classifiers predictions

	Decision Tree	SVM	Discriminant Analysis	Stacking	Correct Class
Case 1	1	1	1	1	1
Case 2	2	3	1	3	3
Case 3	2	2	2	2	2
Case 4	3	1	1	1	1
Case 5	2	2	1	2	2
Case 6	1	2	3	1	1
Case 7	1	2	2	3	3
Case 8	1	3	3	1	1
Case 9	3	1	1	1	2
Case 10	2	1	1	2	3

The overall performance of our meta-learning approach is measured by the percentage of correct predictions commonly used in learning problems and also called success rate ratio [20]:

$$SRR = \frac{Number\ of\ correct\ predictions}{Number\ of\ total\ predictions} \times 100$$

We need to ensure that the stacking system is more efficient than base-learning in predicting the best segmentation parameters and therefore achieves a more efficient image analysis. In the assessment of their stacking approaches, Fan et al. [15] compared the performance of meta-learning system to the base-learners one applied individually. We present in Figure 5 a comparison of stacking SRR to those of base-learners applied separately. The stacked generalization, with a SRR of 64%, exceeds significantly the performance of decision tree, SVM and discriminant analysis algorithms whose SRR reached respectively 52%, 50% and 42%.

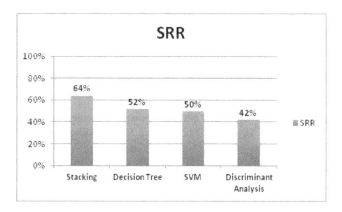

Fig. 5. Comparison between stacking system and base-classifiers performances

The results of the experiment described above confirms the hypothesis that meta-learning increases the efficiency of a learning task (OBIA in our case) through knowledge transfer from the first to the second learning level.

5   Conclusions and Future Work

In this paper we have presented a meta-learning system using stacked generalization to adjust Watershed segmentation parameters. The empirical evaluation of our approach is conducted on VHR satellite images covering the urban area of Strasbourg. The results show that the performance of stacked generalization system exceeds significantly base-learners applied individually. These findings confirm the assumption that meta-learning increases the efficiency of OBIA task.

In future work, we plan to use base-learners that produce class probabilities instead of class predictions. Indeed, some studies state that this type of learners enhances the performance of stacked generalization approach [21].

References

1. Blaschke, T.: Object based image analysis for remote sensing. ISPRS Journal of Photogrammetry and Remote Sensing **65**(1), 2–16 (2010)
2. Cleve, C., Kelly, M., Kearns, F., Moritz, M.: Classification of the wildland urban interface: A comparison of pixel and object-based classifications using high-resolution aerial photography. Computers, Environment and Urban Systems **32**(4), 317–326 (2008)
3. Bhanu, B., Peng, J.: Adaptive integrated image segmentation and object recognition. IEEE Transactions on Systems Man and Cybernetics **30**, 427–441 (2000)
4. Bhanu, B., Lee, M., Ming, J.: Adaptive image segmentation using a genetic algorithm. IEEE Transactions on Systems, Man, and Cybernetics **25**(12), 1543–1567 (1995)
5. Derivaux, S., Lefevre, S., Wemmert, C., Korczak, J.: On machine learning in watershed segmentation. In: IEEE International Workshop on Machine Learning in Signal Processing (MLSP), pp. 187–192 (2007)
6. Wolpert, D.H., Macready, W.G.: No free lunch theorems for optimization. IEEE Transactions on Evolutionary Computation **1**(1), 67–82 (1997)
7. Vilalta, R., Drissi, Y.: A perspective view and survey of meta-learning. Artificial Intelligence Review **18**(2), 77–95 (2002)
8. Vincent, L., Soille, P.: Watersheds in digital spaces: An efficient algorithm based on immersion simulations. IEEE Pattern Recognition and Machine Intelligence **13**(6), 583–598 (1991)
9. Derivaux, S., Lefevre, S., Wemmert, C., Korczak, J.: Watershed Segmentation of Remotely Sensed Images Based on a Supervised Fuzzy Pixel Classification. In: Proceedings of the IEEE International Geosciences And Remote Sensing Symposium (IGARSS), pp. 3712–3715 (2006)
10. Attig, A., Perner, P.: A study on the case image description for learning the model of the watershed segmentation. Transactions on Case-Based Reasoning **2**(1), 41–53 (2009)
11. Haralick, R.: Statistical and structural approaches to texture. Proceedings of the IEEE **67**(5), 786–804 (1979)
12. Sellaouti, A., Hamouda, A., Deruyver, A., Wemmert, C.: Hierarchical classification-based region growing (HCBRG): a collaborative approach for object segmentation and classification. In: Campilho, A., Kamel, M. (eds.) ICIAR 2012, Part I. LNCS, vol. 7324, pp. 51–60. Springer, Heidelberg (2012)
13. Kurtz, C., Passat, N., Ganarski, P., Puissant, A.: Extraction of complex patterns from multiresolution remote sensing images: A hierarchical top-down methodology. Pattern Recognition **45**(2), 685–706 (2012)
14. Wolpert, D.H.: Stacked generalization. Neural Networks **5**(2), 241–259 (1992)
15. Fan, D., Chan, P., Stolfo, S.: A comparative evaluation of combiner and stacked generalization. In: Proceedings of AAAI 1996 Workshop on Integrating Multiple Learned Models, pp. 40–46 (1996)
16. Seewald, A.: Towards Understanding Stacking: Studies of a General Ensemble Learning Scheme. The Vienna University of Technology (2003)
17. Skalak, D.: Prototype Selection for Composite Nearest Neighbor Classifiers. PhD thesis (1997)
18. Alpaydin, E.: Introduction to Machine Learning, 2nd edn. The MIT Press (2010)

19. Perlich, C., Swirszcz, G.: On cross-validation and stacking: building seemingly predictive models on random data. SIGKDD Explorations **12**, 11–15 (2010)
20. Brazdil, P., Soares, C., Costa, J.D.: Ranking learning algorithms: Using ibl and meta-learning on accuracy and time results. Machine Learning **50**(3), 251–277 (2003)
21. Ting, K., Witten, I.: Issues in stacked generalization. Journal of Artificial Intelligence Research **10**, 271–289 (1999)

Dynamic Multiple View Geometry
with Affine Cameras

Cheng Wan[1]([✉]), Yiquan Wu[1], and Jun Sato[2]

[1] College of Electronic and Information Engineering,
Nanjing University of Aeronautics and Astronautics, Nanjing 210016, China
wanch@nuaa.edu.cn
[2] Department of Electrical and Computer Engineering,
Nagoya Institute of Technology, Nagoya 466-8555, Japan

Abstract. A new multiple view geometry is addressed in this paper, which is obtained in a dynamic environment with a dynamic scene and moving cameras. Multiple affine cameras are considered which move along degree-n Bezier curves. The new multiple view geometry can represent the multiple view geometry in different dimensions. In the experiments, we show two applications of the new multiple view geometry: view transfer and 3D reconstruction.

Keywords: Multiple view geometry · Affine camera · Bezier curve · Multifocal tensor · Dynamic scene

1 Introduction

Multiple view geometry is known for the functions such as extracting the 3D shape of the scenes and describing the relationship between images taken from multiple cameras [1,2,5,6]. In the traditional multiple view geometry, the projection from the 3D space to 2D images has been assumed [2], which is limited to represent the case where enough corresponding points are visible from a static configuration of multiple cameras.

Some works for extending the multiple view geometry for more general point-camera configurations have been made [4,7,12,13] in these years. From stationary configurations [2,3,7] to dynamic configurations [8,10,11,13], the multiple view geometry has been extensively developed. However, previous multiple view geometry involving dynamic scenes are constrained from the motion of the cameras or points moving independently along some low-order trajectories. [11] introduced multiple view geometry with projective cameras moving alone Bezier curves.

Supported by the Fundamental Research Funds for the Central Universities (56XAA14043); China Postdoctor Foundation (2011M501231); Priority Academic Program Development of Jiangsu Higher Education Institutions.

© Springer International Publishing Switzerland 2014
A. Campilho and M. Kamel (Eds.): ICIAR 2014, Part I, LNCS 8814, pp. 198–206, 2014.
DOI: 10.1007/978-3-319-11758-4_22

In this paper we investigate the multiple view geometry with multiple affine cameras whose trajectories are degree-n Bezier curves. Affine camera model is an ideal camera model. Multiple view geometry with affine cameras has simpler properties and less requirements on corresponding points than the case of projective cameras. Meanwhile, affine cameras can be approximated with projective cameras under some conditions [9]. The newly proposed multiple view geometry can describe the traditional multiple view geometry in a static environment, multiple view geometry in space-time, as well as the multiple view geometry in N-Dimension.

In this research, points in 3D undergo arbitrary non-rigid motion and the affine cameras move along Degree-n Bezier curve. We find that the affine projections of non-rigid 3D motion to Degree-n Bezier curve can be represented by a projection from $(n+3)$D to 2D space. We analyze the affine projection from $(n+3)$D to 2D and deduce the degree of freedom of the extended affine camera. $(n+3)$-Dimension multiple view geometry involving several such extended cameras and a dynamic scene is also addressed. Multilinear relationships and the maximal linear relationship in the $(n+3)$D space are derived from the multifocal point relations. The counting arguments are also executed. From the geometric degree of freedom of extended affine cameras and the degree of freedom of the points in $(n+3)$D and all the images, the minimum number of points required for computing the multifocal tensors are available.

We next take $n = 2, 3$ as instances to introduce the dynamic multiple view geometry in the cases of non-rigid arbitrary motion viewed from quadratic and cubic Bezier curve motion cameras. We use affine camera model to describe the multilinear relationship under the projection from 5D to 2D and 6D to 2D. As mentioned above, multilinear relationship among affine cameras brings us simpler results. For example, we just need 6 and 7 points respectively to compute multifocal tensors when $n = 2, 3$, which are much less than in the case of projective cameras [11]. We show the multifocal tensors can be computed from non-rigid object motion viewed from multiple cameras with unknown curvilinear motion. We also show that the multilinear relationships are very useful to generate arbitrary view images with arbitrary curvilinear motion and reconstruct the motion in 3D space. The method was tested in real images.

2   Dynamic Multiple View Geometry

2.1   Camera Trajectory Modeled by Degree-n Bezier Curve

We in this section consider the multiple view geometry in a dynamic environment, in which the point motion in 3D space is non-rigid and the camera trajectory is modeled by the degree-n Bezier curve.

A Bezier curve is a parametric curve frequently used in computer graphics and related fields. In vector graphics, Bezier curves are used to model smooth curves. Bezier curves are also used in animation as a tool to control motion.

Degree-n Bezier curve is defined as follows:

$$\mathbf{B} = \sum_{i=0}^{n} \mathbf{b}_{i,n}(t)\mathbf{G}_i, \qquad t \in [0,1] \tag{1}$$

where $\mathbf{G}_i$ is the ith control point and the polynomials $\mathbf{b}_{i,n}(t)$ known as Bernstein basis polynomials of degree n is written as:

$$\mathbf{b}_{i,n}(t) = \binom{n}{i} t^i (1-t)^{n-i} = \binom{n}{i} t^i \sum_{j=0}^{n-i} \binom{n-i}{n-i-j} (-t)^{n-i-j}$$

$$= \sum_{j=0}^{n-i} \binom{n}{i} \binom{n-i}{j} (-1)^{n-i-j} t^{n-j} = \sum_{j=0}^{n-i} C(n,i,j) t^{n-j}$$

Here, $\binom{n}{i} = \frac{n!}{i!(n-i)!}$, and $C(n,i,j) = \binom{n}{i}\binom{n-i}{j}(-1)^{n-i-j}$. Suppose T denotes time, a nonnegative integer and T_a represents the total time of the camera motion, a positive integer. Then, the relationship among parameter t, time T and total time T_a can be described as: $t = \frac{T}{T_a}$. Then, Bezier curve $\mathbf{B}$ which we utilize to model the trajectory of camera motion can be rewritten as follows:

$$\mathbf{B} = \sum_{i=0}^{n} \mathbf{b}_{i,n}(t)\mathbf{G}_i = \sum_{i=0}^{n} \mathbf{G}_i \sum_{j=0}^{n-i} C(n,i,j) t^{n-j}$$

$$= \begin{bmatrix} \mathbf{G}_0 \ \mathbf{G}_1 \ \cdots \ \mathbf{G}_n \end{bmatrix} \mathbf{A} \begin{bmatrix} t^n \\ t^{n-1} \\ \vdots \\ 1 \end{bmatrix} = \mathbf{GAE} \begin{bmatrix} T^n \\ T^{n-1} \\ \vdots \\ 1 \end{bmatrix} \tag{2}$$

where,

$$\mathbf{G} = \begin{bmatrix} \mathbf{G}_0 \ \mathbf{G}_1 \ \cdots \ \mathbf{G}_n \end{bmatrix},$$

$$\mathbf{A} = \begin{bmatrix} A_{00} & A_{01} & A_{02} & \cdots & A_{0n-1} & A_{0n} \\ A_{10} & A_{11} & A_{12} & \cdots & A_{1n-1} & 0 \\ A_{20} & A_{21} & A_{22} & \cdots & 0 & 0 \\ \vdots & & & & & \vdots \\ A_{n0} & 0 & 0 & \cdots & 0 & 0 \end{bmatrix},$$

$$A_{ij} = C(n,i,j), \quad (i = 0, \cdots, n, \quad j = 0, \cdots, n-i),$$

$$\mathbf{E} = diag[\frac{1}{T_a^n}, \frac{1}{T_a^{n-1}}, \cdots, 1].$$

Consider a usual affine camera which projects points in 3D to 2D images. The motions of a point in the 3D space can be represented by homogeneous coordinates, $\mathbf{W}(T) = [X(T), Y(T), Z(T), 1]^{\mathsf{T}}$. The motions are projected to images, and can be observed as a set of points, $\mathbf{w}(T) = [x(T), y(T), 1]^\top$. Thus, point motions are projected to the Bezier curve motion affine camera as follows:

$$\mathbf{w}(T) = \mathbf{P_w}(\mathbf{W}(T) - \mathbf{B}) \tag{3}$$

where $\mathbf{P_w}$ denotes a 3×4 affine camera matrix, whose third row is $[0,0,0,1]$. By substituting (2) into (3), we have the following equations:

$$\mathbf{w}(T) = \mathbf{P_w}(\mathbf{W}(T) - \mathbf{GAE} \begin{bmatrix} T^n \\ T^{n-1} \\ \vdots \\ 1 \end{bmatrix}) = \mathbf{P_w}[\mathbf{I}, -\mathbf{GAE}] \begin{bmatrix} \mathbf{W}(T) \\ T^n \\ T^{n-1} \\ \vdots \\ 1 \end{bmatrix}$$

$$= \mathbf{P}_a \begin{bmatrix} \mathbf{W}(T) \\ T^n \\ T^{n-1} \\ \vdots \\ 1 \end{bmatrix} = \mathbf{P}_a \begin{bmatrix} X(T) \\ Y(T) \\ Z(T) \\ 1 \\ T^n \\ T^{n-1} \\ \vdots \\ 1 \end{bmatrix} = \mathbf{P}_b \begin{bmatrix} X(T) \\ Y(T) \\ Z(T) \\ T^n \\ T^{n-1} \\ \vdots \\ 1 \end{bmatrix} \tag{4}$$

where $\mathbf{P}_a = \mathbf{P}[\mathbf{I}, -\mathbf{GAE}]$ represents a $3 \times (n+5)$ matrix and $\mathbf{P}_b$ denotes a $3 \times (n+4)$ matrix. The $(n+4)$th column of $\mathbf{P}_b$ is derived by merging the 4th column and the $(n+5)$th column of $\mathbf{P}_a$. $\mathbf{P}_b$ describes the projection from $[X(T), Y(T), Z(T), T^n, T^{n-1}, \cdots, T, 1]^\top$ to $[x(T), y(T), 1]^\top$, so $\mathbf{P}_b$ is also a projection from $(n+3)$D to 2D, and its third row is $[0, 0, 0, \cdots, 1]$. When we have multiple affine cameras which move along Bezier curves, we find that, from (4), the projections of 3D point motions can be described by the multilinear relationship under the projection from $(n+3)$D to 2D. In the next section, the geometry of such projections will be analyzed in more detail.

2.2   Affine Projection from $(n+3)$D to 2D

We first consider a projection from $(n+3)$D space to 2D space. Let $\mathbf{X} = [X, Y, Z, T^n, T^{n-1}, \cdots, 1]^\top$ be the homogeneous coordinates of a $(n+3)$D space point projected to a point in the 2D space, whose homogeneous coordinates are represented by $\mathbf{x} = [x^1, x^2, x^3]^\top$. Then, the extended affine projection from $\mathbf{X}$ to $\mathbf{x}$ can be described as follows:

$$\lambda\mathbf{x} = \mathbf{P}\mathbf{X} \tag{5}$$

where λ denotes equality up to a scale, and $\mathbf{P}$ denotes the following $3 \times (n+4)$ matrix:

$$\mathbf{P} = \begin{bmatrix} p_{11} & p_{12} & \cdots & p_{1(n+4)} \\ p_{21} & p_{22} & \cdots & p_{2(n+4)} \\ 0 & 0 & \cdots & 1 \end{bmatrix} \tag{6}$$

From (6), we find that the extended affine camera, $\mathbf{P}$, has $2 \times (n+4) = 2n+8$ DOF. In the next section, we consider the new multiple view geometry of the extended affine cameras.

2.3 $(n+3)$-Dimension Multiple View Geometry

Multilinear Relationships. From (5), we have the following equation for K extended affine cameras:

$$
\begin{bmatrix}
\mathbf{P} & \mathbf{x} & 0 & 0 & \cdots & 0 \\
\mathbf{P}' & 0 & \mathbf{x}' & 0 & \cdots & 0 \\
\mathbf{P}'' & 0 & 0 & \mathbf{x}'' & \cdots & 0 \\
\vdots & & & & \vdots
\end{bmatrix}
\begin{bmatrix}
\mathbf{X} \\
\lambda \\
\lambda' \\
\lambda'' \\
\vdots
\end{bmatrix}
=
\begin{bmatrix}
0 \\
0 \\
0 \\
\vdots
\end{bmatrix}
\tag{7}
$$

where, $\mathbf{x}, \mathbf{x}', \mathbf{x}'', \cdots$, the projections of $\mathbf{X}$ in K views, are called one set of corresponding points, and the leftmost $3K \times (K+n+4)$ matrix in (7) is defined as $\mathbf{H}$. If (7) has a non-zero solution, the vector $[\mathbf{X}^\top, \lambda, \lambda', \lambda'', \cdots]^\top$, the rank of $\mathbf{H}$ must be at most $K+n+3$. Hence any $(K+n+4) \times (K+n+4)$ minors $\mathbf{Q}$ of $\mathbf{H}$ has zero determinant, that arises the constitute multilinear relationships under the extended projection as: $\det \mathbf{Q} = 0$. We can choose any $K+n+4$ rows from $\mathbf{H}$ to constitute $\mathbf{Q}$, but we have to take at least 2 rows from each camera for deriving meaningful K view relationships (note, each camera has 3 rows in $\mathbf{H}$). Thus, the following inequality must hold for defining multilinear relationships for K view geometry in the $(n+3)$D space: $K+n+4 \geq 2K$. Thus, we find that, the multilinear relationship for $n+4$ views is the maximal linear relationship in the $(n+3)$D space.

Counting Arguments. We next consider the minimum number of points required for computing the multifocal tensors. The geometric DOF S of K extended affine cameras is as: $S = (2n+8)K - (n+4)*(n+3)$, since each extended affine camera has $(2n+8)$ DOF and these K cameras are in a single $(n+3)$D affine space whose DOF is $(n+4)*(n+3)$, the DOF of a $(n+3)$D affine transformation. Meanwhile, if we are given M points in the $(n+3)$D space, and let them be projected to K cameras defined in (5). Then, we derive $2MK$ measurements from images, while we have to compute $(n+3)M + S$ components for fixing all the geometry in the $(n+3)$D space. Thus, the following condition must hold for computing the multifocal tensors from images: $2MK \geq (n+3)M + S$. Then, we have the following inequality: $M \geq \frac{S}{2K-n-3}$. Thus, we find that minimum of $\frac{S}{2K-n-3} = n+4$ points are required to compute multifocal tensors in new multiple view geometry.

2.4 Dynamic Configurations for Multiple View Geometry in Dynamic Environment

In our dynamic multiple view geometry theory, it has different dynamic configurations in different dimension space. We list several typical and basic examples of dynamic configurations to demonstrate this property. By substituting degree $n = 0, 1, 2, 3$ into (1) respectively, we find that the camera motions can be represented as follows:

$$\mathbf{B}_0 = \sum_{i=0}^{0} \mathbf{b}_{i,0}(t)\mathbf{G}_i = \mathbf{b}_{0,0}(t)\mathbf{G}_0 = \mathbf{G}_0 \tag{8}$$

$$\mathbf{B}_1 = \sum_{i=0}^{1} \mathbf{b}_{i,1}(t)\mathbf{G}_i = (1-t)\mathbf{G}_0 + t\mathbf{G}_1 \tag{9}$$

$$\mathbf{B}_2 = (1-t)^2\mathbf{G}_0 + 2(1-t)t\mathbf{G}_1 + t^2\mathbf{G}_2 \tag{10}$$

$$\mathbf{B}_3 = (1-t)^3\mathbf{G}_0 + 3(1-t)^2 t\mathbf{G}_1 + 3(1-t)t^2\mathbf{G}_2 + t^3\mathbf{G}_3 \tag{11}$$

In the case of (8), the camera is not moving but static, that is a special case and just coincides with the traditional multiple view geometry [2]. Therefore, our dynamic multiple view geometry theory can also be used to describe the case of the traditional multiple view geometry. The trajectory of camera is a line which goes through $\mathbf{G}_0$ and $\mathbf{G}_1$, that means the cameras are translational. The dynamic multiple view geometry defined here can represents the relationship among several translational motion cameras [8]. As shown in (10), the camera motion is a quadratic curve. The geometry among such curvilinear motion cameras can also be described by the dynamic multiple view geometry. The camera motion follows a cubic curve as shown in (11). Furthermore, even if the cameras undergo more complex curvilinear motions, the dynamic multiple view geometry is still competent. We will study multiple view geometry in 5D and 6D extensively in the following sections.

3   Dynamic Multiple View Geometry in 5D Space

The dynamic multiple view geometry of multiple cameras with arbitrary Degree-2 Bezier curve motions enables us to define multilinear relationship among image points derived from non-rigid object motions viewed from multiple cameras with arbitrary quadratic Bezier curve motions. From Section 2, we can see: (1) the extended camera matrix is 3×6 who has 12 DOF. (2) the multilinear relationship for 6 views is the maximal linear relationship in the 5D space; (3) the geometric DOF S of K extended affine cameras is $6(2K - 5)$; (4) the minimum of 6 points are required to compute multifocal tensors in 3, 4, 5, 6 views.

For three views, the sub square matrix $\mathbf{Q}$ is 9×9. From $\det \mathbf{Q} = 0$, we have the following trilinear relationship under extended camera projections:

$$x^i x'^j x''^k \mathcal{T}_{ijk} = 0 \tag{12}$$

where $\mathcal{T}_{ijk}$ is the trifocal tensor for the extended cameras and has the following form:

$$\mathcal{T}_{ijk} = \epsilon_{ipq}\epsilon_{jrs}\epsilon_{ktu} \det \left[\mathbf{a}^p, \mathbf{a}^q, \mathbf{b}^r, \mathbf{b}^s, \mathbf{c}^t, \mathbf{c}^u \right]^\top \tag{13}$$

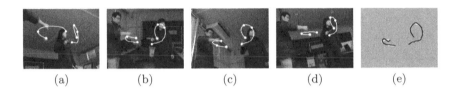

(a)   (b)   (c)   (d)   (e)

Fig. 1. Multiple point motion experiment

where ϵ_{ipq} (or its contravariant counterpart, ϵ^{ipq}) denotes a tensor, which represents a sign based on permutation from $\{i,p,q\}$ to $\{1,2,3\}$. $\mathbf{a}^w$, $\mathbf{b}^w$ and $\mathbf{c}^w$ denote the wth row of three camera matrices respectively. The trifocal tensor $\mathcal{T}_{ijk}$ is $3 \times 3 \times 3$ and has 27 entries. Since all the third rows of the extended affine camera matrices are $[0,0,0,0,0,1]$, many zero entries arise in $\mathcal{T}_{ijk}$. As a result, $\mathcal{T}_{133}, \mathcal{T}_{233}, \mathcal{T}_{313}, \mathcal{T}_{323}, \mathcal{T}_{331}, \mathcal{T}_{332}, \mathcal{T}_{333}$ are non-zero entries and thus we have only 6 free parameters in $\mathcal{T}_{ijk}$ except a scale ambiguity. On the other hand, (12) provides us one linear equation on $\mathcal{T}_{ijk}$. Thus, at least 6 corresponding points are required to compute $\mathcal{T}_{ijk}$ from images linearly.

4   Dynamic Multiple View Geometry in 6D Space

We in this Section address the dynamic multiple view geometry of multiple cameras with arbitrary cubic Bezier curvilinear motions ($n = 3$). From (4), we know the extended affine camera matrix in 6D Space is 3×7 and has 14 DOF. From Section 2, we also can see: (1) the multilinear relationship for 7 views is the maximal linear relationship in the 6D space; (2) the geometric DOF S of K extended affine cameras is $7(2K - 6)$; (3) the minimum of 7 points are required to compute multifocal tensors in 4, 5, 6, 7 views. However, in the case of dynamic multiple view geometry with projective cameras, we at least need 16, 13, 12, 12 points to compute tensors [11]. For four views, the sub square matrix $\mathbf{Q}$ is 11×11. From $\det \mathbf{Q} = 0$, we have this quadrilinear relationship: $x^i x'^j x''^k x'''^h \epsilon_{hvd} \mathcal{Q}_{ijk}^v = 0_d$. The quadrifocal tensor $\mathcal{Q}_{ijk}^v$ has 81 entries and 15 non-zero entries. Then at least 7 corresponding points are required to compute $\mathcal{Q}_{ijk}^v$ from images.

5   Applications

Here we introduce two applications for dynamic multiple view geometry: view transfer and 3D reconstruction.

5.1   View Transfer

If the constraints between corresponding points and multifocal tensors are derived, multifocal tensors can be computed by 7 corresponding points in 4

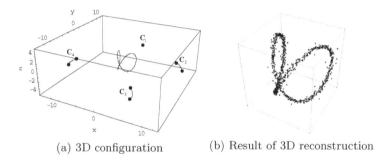

(a) 3D configuration   (b) Result of 3D reconstruction

Fig. 2. 3D reconstruction

to 7 views in 6D. Thus, when we have the image motions in $N - 1$ images, the image motion in the remaining image can be calculated from N view tensor. It realizes the view transfer from $N - 1$ views to the left one. Here, four cameras (Sony DFW-VL500) are used, one of which is static (Camera 4) and three of which (Camera 1-3) are controlled by 3-axis robots (Originalmind 3-Axis Robot) respectively to undergo different cubic Bezier curve motions. We computed quadrifocal tensor among these four cameras by using two moving points in the 3D space. Experiment is shown in Figure 1. (a), (b), (c) and (d), whose size are 320×240, show image motions of two points viewed from 4 camera. The white curves represent two different image motions. The 7 white points on the two curves in each image are corresponding points used for computing the quadrifocal tensor. The black curves in (e) show image motions computed from the extended quadrifocal tensor in camera 3. As we can see, the quadrifocal tensor defined under extended projection can be derived from arbitrary multiple point motions viewed from the 4 cameras with arbitrary curvilinear motions, and they are practical for generating images of multiple point motions viewed from curvilinear motion camera. The average error of the recovered image motion is 6.3 pixels.

5.2   3D Reconstruction

If image points are given, actually the extended camera matrices can be derived. Then from (5), the coordinates of points in 3D can be obtained. We next show the results of 3D reconstruction with dynamic multiple view geometry in 6D whose 3D configurations shown in Figure 2(a). We assumed that camera $\mathbf{C}_1$ is a static camera in this experiment and other cameras u undergo cubic Bezier curvilinear motions. The non-rigid 3D motion is projected to four cameras. The corresponding points with Gaussian noise of standard deviation of 1 pixel in the four images were used to figure out the coordinates of each point in the 3D space. The reconstructed result is shown in Figure 2(b). We can see the shape of the 3D motion is recovered properly. The ratio of the average reconstruction error to the range of the 3D motion is 0.074.

6   Conclusion

In this paper, we presented the multiple view geometry which unifies the traditional multiple view geometry and the high-dimension multiple view geometry. We modeled the camera trajectory by Degree-n Bezier curves and made points in 3D undergo non-rigid motions. We found that the affine projection from non-rigid 3D motion to view image with Degree-n Bezier curve motion can be represented by a projection from $(n + 3)$D to 2D. Therefore, the multilinear relationship under the projection from $(n + 3)$D to 2D can be derived when 3D point motions are tracked by multiple arbitrary Degree-n Bezier curve motion cameras. We also introduced the multiple view geometry of multiple cameras with arbitrary degree-2 and degree-3 Bezier curve motions and verified that the multifocal tensors are very useful to realize view transfer and 3D reconstruction.

References

1. Faugeras, O., Mourrain, B.: On the geometry and algebra of the point and line correspondences beterrn n images. In: Proc. 5th International Conference on Computer Vision, pp. 951–956 (1995)
2. Hartley, R., Zisserman, A.: Multiple View Geometry in Computer Vision. Cambridge University Press (2000)
3. Hartley, R.I., Schaffalitzky, F.: Reconstruction from projections using grassmann tensors. Int. J. Comput. Vision **83**(3), 274–293 (2009)
4. Hayakawa, K., Sato, J.: Multiple view geometry in the space-time. In: Proc. 7th Asian Conference on Computer Vision, pp. 437–446 (2006)
5. Heyden, A.: Tensorial properties of multiple view constraints. Mathematical Methods in the Applied Sciences **23**, 169–202 (2000)
6. Shashua, A., Wolf, L.: Homography tensors: on algebraic entities that represent three views of static or moving planar points. In: Vernon, D. (ed.) ECCV 2000. LNCS, vol. 1842, pp. 507–521. Springer, Heidelberg (2000)
7. Sturm, P.: Multi-view geometry for general camera models. In: Proc. Conference on Computer Vision and Pattern Recognition, pp. 206–212 (2005)
8. Wan, C., Sato, J.: Multiple view geometry under projective projection in space-time. IEICE Transactions **91–D**(9), 2353–2359 (2008)
9. Wan, C., Sato, J.: Multiple view geometry for curvilinear motion cameras. IEICE Transactions **94–D**(7), 1479–1487 (2011)
10. Wan, C., Sato, J.: Multiple view geometry for non-rigid motions viewed from curvilinear motion projective cameras. In: Proc. 20th International Conference on Pattern Recognition, pp. 181–184 (2010)
11. Wan, C., Wu, Y., Sato, J.: Multiple view geometry in dynamic environment. In: Proc. 2nd Asian Conference on Pattern Recognition, pp. 532–536 (2013)
12. Wexler, Y., Shashua, A.: On the synthesis of dynamic scenes from reference views. In: Proc. Conference on Computer Vision and Pattern Recognition, pp. 576–581 (2000)
13. Wolf, L., Shashua, A.: On projection matrices $p^k \rightarrow p^2$, $k = 3, \cdots, 6$, and their applications in computer vision. In: Proc. 8th International Conference on Computer Vision, vol. 1, pp. 412–419 (2001)

Energy Minimization by α-Erosion for Supervised Texture Segmentation

Karl Skretting$^{(\boxtimes)}$ and Kjersti Engan

Department of Electrical Engineering and Computer Science,
University of Stavanger, Stavanger, Norway
`karl.skretting@uis.no`

Abstract. In this paper we improve image segmentation based on texture properties. The already good results achieved using learned dictionaries and Gaussian smoothing are improved by minimizing an energy function that has the form of a Potts model. The proposed α-erosion method is a greedy method that essentially relabels the pixels one by one and is computationally very fast. It can be used in addition to, or instead of, Gaussian smoothing to regularize the label images in supervised texture segmentation problems. The proposed α-erosion method achieves excellent results on a much used set of test images: on average we get 2.9 % wrongly classified pixels. Gaussian smoothing gives 10 % and the best results reported earlier give 4.5 %.

1 Introduction

Image segmentation has many important applications in the image processing field, mainly since it is a common step in scene interpretation, and it is used in areas such as medical diagnostics, geophysical interpretation, industrial automation and image indexing. For image segmentation, edges and colors are often more important features than texture. Nevertheless, the texture property is relevant in many image processing applications [11]. An important benchmark application to test how well a system can utilize texture information that may be present in an image, is to segment the image based on texture properties alone. This is what we do here.

Texture segmentation finds a boundary map between different texture regions of an image. This map may be given by a labeling L which assigns a label $L_p \in \{1, 2, \ldots, C\}$ to every pixel $p \in \mathcal{P}$ of the observed image, and C is the number of candidate texture classes. A common way to label the image is to associate a *feature vector* x_p to every pixel in the image and then do common *vector classification*. This approach, however, ignores the fact that texture regions should be piecewise constant in the labeling. Gaussian smoothing of the features before classification will give larger segments and has been much used [13].

An alternative to Gaussian smoothing is Energy Minimization (EM) [1–3]. For each pixel (feature vector) an associated *cost vector* y_p is calculated, element c gives the cost (energy) for assigning class c to this pixel. The cost may be the

© Springer International Publishing Switzerland 2014
A. Campilho and M. Kamel (Eds.): ICIAR 2014, Part I, LNCS 8814, pp. 207–214, 2014.
DOI: 10.1007/978-3-319-11758-4_23

estimated negative log probability for pixel p belonging to class c. The set of energy images $R = \{R^{(c)}\}_{c=1}^{C}$, where pixel p in energy image c is $R_p^{(c)} = y_p(c)$, can now be used to calculate the data cost for a given labeling L. In addition to the data term $E_d(\cdot)$ a smoothing term $E_s(\cdot)$ is added to the energy function, thus the problem of finding the "best" labeling can be formulated as an energy minimization problem using

$$E(L, R) = E_d(L, R) + E_s(L). \qquad (1)$$

When piecewise constant labeling is desired the *Potts model* is a popular choice for the smoothing term. It can be formulated as equation (18) in [3]:

$$E(L, R) = \sum_{p \in \mathcal{P}} R_p^{(L_p)} + \sum_{p,q \in \mathcal{N}} u_{p,q} \cdot (L_p \neq L_q). \qquad (2)$$

$R_p^{(L_p)}$ is the cost (energy) associated with assigning label L_p to pixel p. $\mathcal{N}$ is the set of all neighboring pixel pairs and $(L_p \neq L_q)$ is a logical expression evaluating to 1 if the two labels are different. The factor $u_{p,q}$ is independent of the labeling but may depend on the pair (p, q) [3].

To minimize an energy function of the form as in Eq. 1 or Eq. 2 is in general an NP-hard problem [3] except for some simple cases; the two label-problem can be minimized via graph cuts [7]. One method to approximately minimize the energy function for the several-label problem is to start with an initial labeling and then do a sequence of *moves*; each move may change the labeling of some of the pixels under consideration. Two popular moves are the α-β-swap-move where the optimal division between the two labels in a two label region is found, and the α-expansion-move where "not-α-pixels" may be relabeled as α [3]. The optimal solution for each of these two moves can be found by graph-cuts-algorithms.

A crucial point for the success of EM is that the energy function Eq. 1 reflects the texture segmentation. For many test images this is often only an approximation where the ground truth labeling L^{gt} gives a higher value for the energy function than the value obtained by EM using expand-moves L^{ex} or swap-moves L^{sw}, as seen in Fig. 3. In these cases further improvement in the segmentation can be achieved by: 1) Better observations and better features which gives better cost vectors and energy images. This is important, but in this work we do not investigate this part any more but simply accept a method to make feature vectors that have worked well previously [16]. 2) Better and more sophisticated energy function, more advanced forms are proposed in [4,6], may improve segmentation. Both how to define a better form, and then how to minimize the energy function, are difficult tasks which we here leave to future work. 3) Inferior method for energy minimization, i.e. even if the method gives higher energy than another method it may be better when it comes to segmentation. This latter approach is used in this work. We propose a method that usually does not find the minimum of the energy function, even though all the moves it makes reduce it. The algorithm is designed such that each move tries to reduce the number of segments in the labeled image, and in this way follows

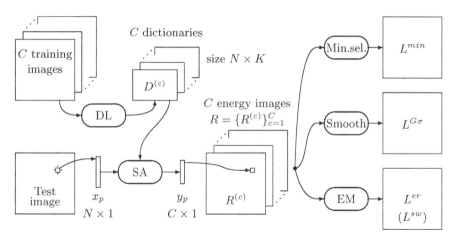

Fig. 1. The Frame Texture Classification Method (FTCM). Dictionary Learning (DL) learn one dictionary with K atoms for each candidate texture. The feature vector x_p is made from a neighborhood of pixel p. Sparse Approximation (SA) uses the candidate dictionaries and gives the energy vector y_p where element c is pixel p in error image $R^{(c)}$. Different labelings are made by the minimum selector, the Gaussian smoothing, and the energy minimization (EM) methods.

a path that is intuitive in image segmentation (few segments). In addition the proposed method is fast, up to 100 times faster than the graph-cuts-methods.

2 Frame Texture Classification Method (FTCM)

The Frame Texture Classification Method (FTCM) [14,16] is used to generate the data term in the energy function of Eq. 1, an overview is shown in Fig. 1. It is based on sparse representation and dictionary learning, for details on these parts see [5,15].

FTCM generates a simple feature vector x_p for each pixel p in a test image using pixel values from its neighborhood directly. Sparse approximations of x_p are made using dictionaries learned for each of the candidate textures. An energy vector y_p is then calculated from the approximation errors,

$$y_p(c) = R_p^{(c)} = \|x_p - D^{(c)}w_p^{(c)}\|_2. \tag{3}$$

where $w_p^{(c)}$ is the $K \times 1$ sparse coefficient vector used when vector x_p is approximated by dictionary $D^{(c)}$. A simple segmentation scheme can be to assign class labels for each pixel, according to the minimum selector method

$$L_p^{min} = c \quad \text{if} \quad R_p^{(c)} \le R_p^{(k)} \quad \forall \quad k. \tag{4}$$

Segmentation can however be substantially improved by smoothing the C energy images $\{R^{(c)}\}_{c=1}^{C}$ prior to the final labeling. A common smoothing approach has

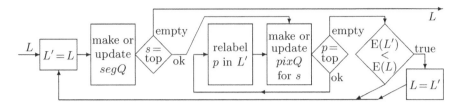

Fig. 2. The main flow for the erode algorithm. The input labeling L is processed segment by segment, the unprocessed segments are kept in a queue, $segQ$. The smallest segment, s from the top of the queue, is processed by relabeling the pixels one by one in L' and if this improves energy the labeling L is updated (bottom right box in figure).

been to use the Gaussian low-pass filter $G_\sigma(\cdot)$ where the parameter σ gives the width of the filter. The smoothed labeling can be denoted:

$$L_p^{G\sigma} = c \quad \text{if} \quad G_\sigma(R^{(c)})_p \le G_\sigma(R^{(k)})_p \quad \forall \quad k.$$

3   Erode Algorithm for Energy Minimization

The energy function used here is a variant of the Potts model Eq. 2, restricted to 4-neighborhood $\mathcal{N}_4$ and 8-neighborhood $\mathcal{N}_8$ systems:

$$E(L, R) = \sum_{p \in \mathcal{P}} R_p^{(L_p)} + \frac{\lambda}{k_4} \left(\sum_{p,q \in \mathcal{N}_4} (L_p \ne L_q) + b \sum_{p,q \in (\mathcal{N}_8 \setminus \mathcal{N}_4)} (L_p \ne L_q) \right). \quad (5)$$

where λ gives the weight of the smoothing term and $k_4 = |\mathcal{N}_4| = \sum_{p,q \in \mathcal{N}_4} 1$. The factor $b \in [0, 1]$ gives the relative weight for corner connected pixels pairs to side connected pixels pairs. For the data term the set of the C energy images $R = \{R^{(c)}\}_{c=1}^C$ is scaled such that $E_d(L^{min}, R) = 0$ and $E_d(L^{max}, R) = 1$. The labeling L^{min} is defined in Eq. 4 and L^{max} is defined as $L_p^{max} = c$ if $R_p^{(c)} \ge R_p^{(k)} \forall k$.

The proposed energy minimization algorithm is a greedy algorithm that reduces the value of the objective function in each move, an overview is shown in Fig. 2. The main idea behind the algorithm is quite simple, it is based on the assumption that removing a small segment is more likely to reduce the value of the objective function than to remove a larger segment. A segment is defined as a 4-neighborhood *connected component* of the current labeling L. The α-erosion method starts with the current labeling and do a sequence of α-erode-moves, as described below. The labeling after all the α-erode-moves is denoted L^{er}, and an example can be seen in Fig. 3d. The second idea is that the border between two segments should be smooth, here we found that using an extra erode-move (or swap-moves) on the border region worked well, doing these moves the labeling is denoted as L^{er+}, an example can be seen in Fig. 3e.

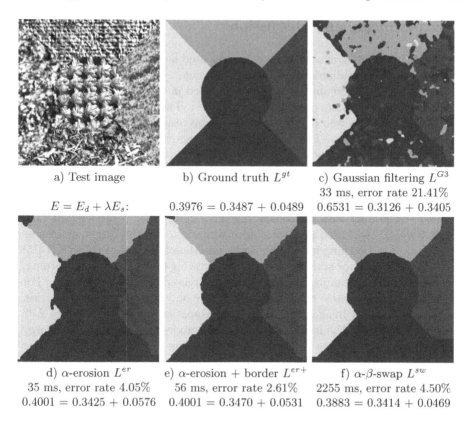

a) Test image   b) Ground truth L^{gt} c) Gaussian filtering L^{G3}
33 ms, error rate 21.41%

$E = E_d + \lambda E_s$: $0.3976 = 0.3487 + 0.0489$ $0.6531 = 0.3126 + 0.3405$

d) α-erosion L^{er} e) α-erosion + border L^{er+} f) α-β-swap L^{sw}
35 ms, error rate 4.05%   56 ms, error rate 2.61%   2255 ms, error rate 4.50%
$0.4001 = 0.3425 + 0.0576$ $0.4001 = 0.3470 + 0.0531$ $0.3883 = 0.3414 + 0.0469$

Fig. 3. Test image number 4 and different labeling results. The second line below each image shows the execution time (in ms) and the error rate, the third line shows the value of the objective function, $E = E_d + \lambda E_s$, here $\lambda = 3$ (and $b = 0.7$ in Eq. 5). The label images are hopefully shown in color but a grayscale image will also show the different segments even though the center segment and the bottom segment then look quite similar to each other. The problem with corners is because the smoothing term favors short, rather than straight, border lines.

Each erode-move considers all pixel within one label segment, s in Fig. 2. A queue of the pixels $pixQ$ is made, it is ordered by the effect relabeling this pixel will have on the objective function. The pixels are now relabeled and removed from the top of the queue, and the remaining queue is updated. In this way it is like the surrounding segments "eat" the pixels of the segment s one pixel at a time, we may also say that the segment is eroded. If the objective function value actually does decrease after the whole segment is "eaten" the "meal" is accepted, i.e. the segment is relabeled. If not the labeling is kept as it was. After a segment is relabeled the segment queue $segQ$ is ordered by size again, i.e. updated. The α-erode-move is tried on all segments smaller than a given limit in the label image.

4   Experiments and Discussion

The training and test grayscale texture images used here are from the *Outex test suites* [10] and are available from Outex web page[1]. The test set Contrib_SS_-00000 consists of 12 test images. It has been used in several papers on texture segmentation; some results are collected in Table 1. The test images are shown in [8,13] and on the UiS web page[2] where also more results and some Matlab files used in this paper can be found. The UiS web page also gives more details on how the parameters, like dictionary size $N \times K$, sparseness factor s, and factors λ and b in Eq. 5 were selected, many are simply used as in earlier papers [15,16] and some are set empirically.

The results for the fourth test image are presented in Fig. 3. The data term was made by FTCM with dictionary size 17×200. Order recursive matching pursuit (ORMP) was used for sparse approximation, and the target sparseness factor was $s = 3$. Learning was done using a mini-batch variant of RLS-DLA [15] using a forgetting factor starting at 0.996 and growing towards 1 during learning, processing 4 million training vectors (many are reused) for each dictionary. For each test image the sparse representations, using only the relevant dictionaries, give the set of energy images R. In Fig. 3 the Gaussian smoothing labeling L^{G3} is shown as this is used as initial labeling for the erode- and swap-moves. Energy minimization is done using α-erosion as described in Sec. 3, both the labeling L^{er} and L^{er+} are shown in Fig. 3. Also the labeling using only α-β-swap-moves until convergence L^{sw} is shown. The labeling for α-expansion-moves L^{ex} were similar to L^{sw} and is not shown.

The results of the proposed method are compared to those reported by other works in Table 1. Randen used filtering methods, Ojala Local Binary Pattern (LBP) and Mäenpää Multi-Predicate (MP) LBP. Skretting used FTCM with reconstructive dictionaries and Gaussian smoothing. Mairal used learned discriminative dictionaries and EM by α-expansion-moves (D-EMex). The last line of Table 1 shows the results for the proposed method, i.e. the α-erosion method followed by erode-moves to straighten the border lines.

Table 2 also shows results for Gaussian smoothing, α-β-swap and α-expansion, and erode with and without extra border region erode-moves. The results for Gaussian smoothing are only marginally better than results of [14], average for the test images 1 to 9 is 12.95% errors, in [14] it was 13.2%, Table 1. The small improvement is because the 17×200 sized dictionaries used here are marginally better than the ones used ten years ago, sized 25×100. The major improvement here is due to the energy minimization (EM) used for regularization. All EM methods do significantly better than Gaussian smoothing. The results for the α-β-swap L^{sw} and α-expansion L^{ex}, both using $\lambda = 1.5$, are comparable to what Mairal reported for discriminative dictionaries in [9]. The proposed methods L^{er} and L^{er+}, here using $\lambda = 2.0$, are both fast and effective, as seen in Table 2. Especially, using extra erode-moves on border regions L^{er+} achieves

---

[1] Outex web page: http://www.outex.oulu.fi/
[2] UiS web page: http://www.ux.uis.no/~karlsk/tct/

Table 1. Reported average error rates for texture classification on the set of test images. The second column is average for images 1 to 9, and the last column is average for all 12 test images.

Paper and method	Avg. 1-9	Avg. 1-12
Randen 1999 (best) [13]	24.1	18.4
Mäenpää 2000 MP-LBP [8]	13.8	10.9
Skretting 2001 FTCM [14]	13.2	-
Ojala 2001 LBP [12]	15.2	12.4
Mairal 2008, D-EMex [9]	5.84	4.50
This paper, FTCM-EMer	3.63	2.87

Table 2. Percentage of wrongly classified pixels for the 12 test images and execution time for different methods. Note that L^{er+} use extra erode-moves on border regions, as in Fig. 3e.

image	Gaussian filter		Energy minimization				Execution time [s]			
no.	L^{G3}	L^{G12}	L^{sw}	L^{ex}	L^{er}	L^{er+}	L^{G3}	L^{sw}	L^{er}	L^{er+}
1	6.08	8.15	3.31	3.38	4.34	2.00	0.038	1.037	0.026	0.072
2	15.42	10.85	2.85	2.75	3.88	3.24	0.037	2.123	0.032	0.068
3	25.33	11.41	2.56	2.56	3.47	4.01	0.038	2.961	0.033	0.063
4	21.41	9.31	4.34	4.34	5.08	2.55	0.040	1.304	0.031	0.064
5	18.20	6.57	2.47	2.47	3.86	1.26	0.040	2.000	0.028	0.058
6	33.69	21.25	10.56	10.74	7.98	6.72	0.369	26.1	0.241	0.334
7	37.09	19.99	3.80	8.49	4.20	4.14	0.355	25.7	0.238	0.317
8	34.94	16.03	12.77	12.68	6.23	4.80	0.153	11.9	0.106	0.151
9	38.57	13.02	2.07	2.02	5.61	3.90	0.155	11.5	0.107	0.160
10	2.27	0.34	0.57	0.57	0.66	0.42	0.038	0.172	0.032	0.064
11	2.44	2.04	1.09	1.09	1.50	0.61	0.034	0.278	0.031	0.060
12	12.00	1.91	3.79	3.79	5.55	0.70	0.033	0.737	0.043	0.080
Average	20.62	10.07	4.18	4.57	4.36	2.87				

impressing segmentation. Using extra swap-moves on border regions, this case is not included in Table 2, also worked very well. The execution times were 10-50 percent of L^{sw}, and for one case ($\lambda = 3$) the achieved average error rate was impressing 2.74%.

5   Conclusions

The proposed α-erosion method is a greedy method that tries to minimize an objective function based on the Potts model and can be used to regularize a label image. It is shown that the α-erosion method achieves results close to those achieved by methods based on the graph-cut algorithm, i.e. the α-β-swap and α-expansion methods, but *is much faster*.

For a common set of test images the average segmentation error rate is even better for the α-erosion method than for the graph cut based methods, even though the achieved values for the objective function are not. The best average error rate achieved here (2.74%) is better than all earlier reported results.

References

1. Besag, J.: On the statistical analysis of dirty pictures. Journal of the Royal Statistical Society. Series B (Methodological) **48**(3), 259–302 (1986)
2. Boykov, Y., Kolmogorov, V.: An experimental comparison of min-cut/max-flow algorithms for energy minimization in vision. IEEE Trans. Pattern Anal. Machine Intell. **26**(9), 1124–1137 (2004)
3. Boykov, Y., Veksler, O., Zabih, R.: Fast approximate energy minimization via graph cuts. IEEE Trans. Pattern Anal. Machine Intell. **23**(11), 1222–1239 (2001)
4. Delong, A., Gorelick, L., Veksler, O., Boykov, Y.: Minimizing energies with hierarchical costs. Int. J. Comput. Vision **100**(1), 38–58 (2012)
5. Elad, M.: Sparse and Redundant Representations, from Theory to Applications in Signal and Image Processing. Springer, New York (2010)
6. Kohli, P., Ladický, L., Torr, P.H.S.: Robust higher order potentials for enforcing label consistency. Int. J. Comput. Vision **82**(3), 302–324 (2009)
7. Kolmogorov, V., Zabih, R.: What energy functions can be minimized via graph cuts. IEEE Trans. Pattern Anal. Machine Intell. **26**, 147–159 (2004)
8. Mäenpää, T., Pietikäinen, M., Ojala, T.: Texture classification by multi-predicate local binary pattern operators. In: Proc. ICPR (2000)
9. Mairal, J., Bach, F., Ponce, J., Sapiro, G., Zisserman, A.: Discriminative learned dictionaries for local image analysis. In: 2008 IEEE Computer Society Conference on Computer Vision and Pattern Recognition (June 2008)
10. Ojala, T., Mäenpää, T., Pietikäinen, M., Viertola, J., Kyllönen, J., Huovinen, S.: Outex - new framework for empirical evaluation of texture analysis algorithms. In: Proc. 16th Int. Conf. Pattern Recognition (2002)
11. Ojala, T., Pietikäinen, M., Mäenpää, T.: Multiresolution gray-scale and rotation invariant texture classification with local binary patterns. IEEE Trans. Pattern Anal. Machine Intell. **24**(7), 971–987 (2002)
12. Ojala, T., Valkealahti, K., Oja, E., Pietikäinen, M.: Texture discrimination with multidimensional distributions of signed gray-level differences. Pattern Recognition **34**(3), 727–739 (2001)
13. Randen, T., Husøy, J.H.: Filtering for texture classification: A comparative study. IEEE Trans. Pattern Anal. Machine Intell. **21**(4), 291–310 (1999)
14. Skretting, K.: Sparse Signal Representation using Overlapping Frames. PhD thesis, NTNU Trondheim and Høgskolen i Stavanger (October 2002), http://www.ux.uis.no/~karlsk/
15. Skretting, K., Engan, K.: Recursive least squares dictionary learning algorithm. IEEE Trans. Signal Processing **58**, 2121–2130 (2010)
16. Skretting, K., Husøy, J.H.: Texture classification using sparse frame based representations. EURASIP Journal on Applied Signal Processing **2006**, Article ID 52561 (2006)

ALOE: Augmented Local Operator for Edge Detection

Maria De Marsico[1], Michele Nappi[2], and Daniel Riccio[3(✉)]

[1] Sapienza Università di Roma, Roma, Italia
demarsico@di.uniroma1.it
[2] Università di Salerno, Salerno, Italy
mnappi@unisa.it
[3] Università di Napoli, Federico II, Napoli, Italy
daniel.riccio@unina.it

Abstract. We present here a novel approach to edge detection exploiting a local operator. One of the advantages of such operator is that its results are augmented with the edge direction without any further processing.

Keywords: Edge detection · Local operator · Divided difference method

1 Introduction

Being a basic task, edge detection underlies many more complex procedures in image processing and computer vision, such as shape detection and description [13], object recognition, image compression [9], or recognition of biometric traits [15]. Many dedicated operators have been devised [4], whose performance is characterized by their robustness to distortions like contrast and illumination variations. The results can often be enhanced by tuning some parameters to specific situations. However, no edge filter fully and automatically adapts to the image at hand. We propose a new local operator to detect contour points. It exploits a fourth degree polynomial function to evaluate the neighborhood of a pixel and to assign it a score, so to highlight the points on a contour and discard those of an homogeneous region. We also discuss aspects of computational cost/time, which are addressed by ALOE (Augmented Local Operator for Edge Detection) to dramatically reduce the required processing time.

2 Related Work

Literature about edge detection is hardly summarized. Detectors can be first distinguished in first and second order derivative edge detectors. The operators in the first class use the convolution of the image with a kernel to generate a gradient image, to which a threshold is applied to extract contours. The operators in the second locate zero-crossing points, corresponding to points of minimum/maximum in the image. Available techniques can be further divided in: search based, and zero-crossing based. The former compute the intensity of a possible contour in a point-wise manner and select the local maxima. The latter rely on differentiation, smoothing, and labelling.

© Springer International Publishing Switzerland 2014
A. Campilho and M. Kamel (Eds.): ICIAR 2014, Part I, LNCS 8814, pp. 215–223, 2014.
DOI: 10.1007/978-3-319-11758-4_24

The differentiation step exploits a discrete approximation of differential operators. Among the many operators in literature under this category, Sobel is surely one of the most popular ones. One of its limits is related to the way it computes the gradient according to horizontal and vertical components, which are often not sufficient [12]. Some similar operators achieve better results by an extended support element (up to 7×7) to consider more rotations. As a common limit, these methods return quite thick edges, possibly not suited to applications requiring one-pixel wide contours.

Marr and Hildreth [10] proposed the Laplacian of Gaussian (LOG) operator, which solves that problem. It relies on the consideration that the variation of image intensity occurs at different levels. The limit of LOG is the use of zero-crossing, which is only reliable in locating well separated edges in images with a high signal-to-noise ratio (SNR). Another problem is the detection of false edges, while also missing true ones.

Canny filter [2] aims to provide a solution to the edge displacement which is often caused by noise pre-filtering. It relies on the three criteria of good detection, good localization, and one response. For a 1D step edge the optimal filter can be approximated by the first derivative of a Gaussian function, while in 2D the property of separability of the 2D Gaussian function allows to decompose it into two 1D filters (derivatives along the horizontal and vertical directions). The proposal further includes a scheme for combining the outputs from different scales. The final algorithm is more sensitive to weak edges, but also less robust to spurious boundaries.

Gaussian filtering is also the basis for multi-resolution methods, exploiting edge detection at different scales of the Gaussian filter. An example is the so called edge focusing by Bergholm [1]. All these methods share two main issues: the choice of the scale range to process and the fusion of the results. Many of the problems normally encountered with multi-resolution are overcome by wavelet-based approaches [14]. One of the main limits of such approaches is that wavelets are able to detect point-singularities, therefore originating, in many cases, discontinuous edges.

A different solution is provided by morphology based edge detectors [8], which however suffer for the strong dependency on the adopted Structuring Element (SE).

Among the most recent approaches, we can mention statistical and contextual methods. An example of the former is proposed by Konishi et al. in [7], while an example of methods based on context analysis is presented by Yu and Chang [16]. Both kinds of approaches may need a different learning phase for different kinds of images.

3   Edge Characterization

In Section 2 we underlined that one of the limits of existing operators is the use of the gradient computed on the base of horizontal and vertical components. ALOE (Augmented Local Operator for Edge detection) exploits the information in the full neighborhood of a pixel, in order to better evaluate the strength of a potential edge.

Given a point $P(x_P, y_P)$ in an image I, ALOE considers a set of n concentric circumferences C_k centered in P and with increasing radius $\rho_k \in R$, with $k = 1, 2, ..., n$. For each such circumference, ALOE performs a polar clockwise visit of the pixels in I lying on it. The coordinates of a visited point $Q(x_Q, y_Q)$ can be expressed in polar form, with respect to C_k as $Q(\rho_k, \theta_Q)$, with $\theta_Q = atan((y_Q - y_P)/(x_Q - x_P))$ in $[0, 2\pi]$. In practice, we do not adopt a regular angular sampling, but rather visit all points. Therefore, the number of pixels N_k visited on each circumference depends on the length of C_k, or, equivalently, on radius ρ_k. We indicate with superscript j the order in which points $Q(x_Q, y_Q)$ are visited along the circumference C_k, and we insert the pixels $z_j = I(x_Q, y_Q)$ in a vector $v_k = \{z_j | j = 1, \ldots, N_k\}$. The values z_j in the vector v_k are grey levels in the range $[0, 255]$ and can be interpreted as the discrete values sampled by a function $z = f(\theta_j)$.

Once computed the function interpolating the values of the points z_j, the core idea of ALOE is to investigate the shape such function would assume for each C_k; for instance, if all points had a practically constant value, making up an homogeneous region, we would obtain a polynomial of degree 0, and vice versa. Therefore, we want to characterize the shape and the degree of the polynomial function which approximates the case when point P is on a step edge, as shown in Fig. 1. We can preliminarily observe that, when P is on an edge, the approximating polynomial has a degree higher than 1 (straight line). In order to reduce the distribution of samples z_j to a typical condition, we identify the position $\theta_{min} = argmin_j(f(\theta_j))$ of the absolute minimum and perform a left shift of vector v_k by θ_{min} positions, which is equivalent to consider the function $z_{SHIFT} = f(\theta_j - \theta_{min})$. As we can observe from the bottom graphic in Fig. 1, the shape of the function is well approximated by a polynomial of degree 4, which assumes a typical "M" shape. By exploiting this feature, a possible criterion to characterize edges might be to evaluate the error of approximating the distribution of samples with that polynomial; the lower the error, the higher the probability that the pixel lies on an edge. This gives a kind of weight for the pixel, which is computed for all the n different circumferences C_k to obtain a final "edge-ity" score. This operation must be repeated for each pixel in the image; this means to solve n polynomial approximation problems for each pixel, with the corresponding error evaluation, making the method extremely inefficient.

Actually, it is possible to reduce the computational cost of the method, while maintaining good accuracy of the result. When the distribution of points z_j can be well approximated also by a polynomial of degree less than 4, the coefficient a_4 associated with term θ^4 tends to zero. Therefore, it would be sufficient to evaluate only the coefficient a_4 to assign a partial score to the pixel P pertaining to a certain circumference. A high value of this coefficient corresponds to a high probability for the pixel P to lie on an edge; otherwise, it would be considered as part of a homogeneous zone. Furthermore, the shift to the left of the samples z_j in the vector v_k, allows to possibly obtain the typical shape shown in Fig. 1, with three minima, interleaved by two maxima. In addition, these minima and maxima tend to be arranged in stable positions: a) two minima at the extremes 0 and 2π, and one at the center (π), b) two maxima at $\pi/2$ and $3/2\pi$.

Relying on the above observation, it is possible to select only a subset of five samples $S = \{z_h = f(\theta_h), \theta_h = h \cdot \pi/2 \text{ e } h = 0, \ldots, 4\}$ and use them to compute the approximant polynomial. This can reduce the complexity of the problem, as it is no longer necessary to solve a regression problem, but it is sufficient to use a standard interpolation

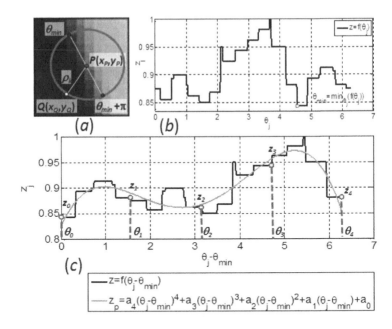

Fig. 1. A point P on a step edge, with circumference C_k with radius ρ_k centered on it. The graphic on its right shows the gray levels z_j of pixels $Q_j(\rho_k,\theta_Q)$ on the circumference and the position θ_{min} of the absolute minimum. In the lower graphic the same values have been shifted on the left by θ_{min} positions and the approximating polynomial of fourth degree is shown.

method. However, many methods such as the Lagrange one, build the interpolating polynomial iteratively, making the computation of coefficients still inefficient, given the high number of times in which this problem must be solved. A solution which is effective and efficient at the same time is provided by the divided difference method of Newton. Unlike others, this method calculates the coefficients individually, by creating what is called the table of divided differences. On the base of Newton method, we derive the following closed form for the coefficient a_4:

$$a_4 = \frac{1}{\displaystyle\prod_{\substack{i=1\\h=i+1}}^{4}(\theta_i-\theta_h)}\left(\frac{(z_0-z_1)\displaystyle\prod_{\substack{i=2\\h=i+1}}^{4}(\theta_i-\theta_h)}{\theta_0-\theta_1}-\frac{(z_0-z_2)\displaystyle\prod_{\substack{i=1,i\neq2\\h=i+1,h\neq2}}^{4}(\theta_i-\theta_h)}{\theta_0-\theta_2}+\frac{(z_0-z_3)\displaystyle\prod_{\substack{i=1,i\neq3\\h=i+1,h\neq3}}^{4}(\theta_i-\theta_j)}{\theta_0-\theta_3}-\frac{(z_0-z_4)\displaystyle\prod_{\substack{i=1\\h=i+1}}^{3}(\theta_i-\theta_h)}{\theta_0-\theta_4}\right). \tag{1}$$

A high value of a_4 makes ALOE assign a high probability to the pixel in P to be on an edge. The score assigned to the pixel P from the processing performed on the circumference C_k is then given by $s_k = |a_4|$. As previously mentioned, ALOE performs this processing for n different circumferences centered in P and with growing radius $\rho_k \in R$, with $k=1, 2, \ldots, n$. It follows, that n partial scores are assigned to the point P, one for each circumference. The total score for P is computed as:

$$S_{all} = \sum_{h=1}^{n} \sum_{k=h+1}^{n} (s_k \cdot s_h) \qquad (2)$$

This privileges points achieving a high partial score on more adjacent circumferences. Finally, the range of values for the result s_{all} is compressed by an exponential function, which produces the final score s which is assigned to P:

$$s = e^{-\frac{1}{\gamma \cdot s_{all}}} \qquad (3)$$

The value of γ in (3) is a control parameter, allowing to decide the intensity of detected contours.

4   Angular Direction

One of the basic steps in the elaboration carried out by ALOE for the calculation of the edge is determining the point θ_{min} on the circumference C_k, corresponding to the pixel with the minimum gray level value, in order to shift to the left the values z_j in the vector v_k. This side information is such that ALOE is not only a technique for the contour extraction, but also a local directional operator. In this way, ALOE is able, in a single step, to detect both the contours and the angular directions in an image, producing a map of the directions that can be used as a set of features in an image for classification purposes, in a way similar to what happens for many other operators developed specifically for this purpose, as for instance Local Binary Patterns (LBP) [11] or Local Directional Patterns (LDP) [5]. The additional advantage offered by ALOE in this sense is the high precision with which it is able to calculate this information. In fact, it examines a set of N_k points on the circumference C_k, so that the greater the number of such points, the better the accuracy of the detection of the angular direction. Similarly to what happens for the detection of the intensity of the contour points, the angular direction for each point P is associated with n estimates α_k ($k=1, \ldots, n$) of the direction. The angular direction α associated with the point P is given by the mean value of the α_k. Fig. 2 shows an example of the result produced by ALOE on the popular image Lena.

5   Experiments

A standard form to compare detector performance, which is quite natural to assume, is obtained by transforming the original image, according to the detector results, into a binary one, where a 1 denotes that the corresponding point was identified as an edge point and a 0 means the contrary.

The specific characteristics of edge detection schemes, that should be taken into consideration for comparative purposes, include both performance issues (such as possible bias of orientation of detected edges, ability to detect edges in the presence of noise, range in scale of edge detectability, ability to detect blurred edges, ability to detect curved edges, and ability to extract an edge in the presence of other edges), as well as more computation-related issues such as computational effort.

Despite its importance, quantitative performance evaluation is often neglected in most of the available literature on contour detection. As a matter of fact, while quantitative evaluation is quite readily accomplished using artificial pictures as a test-bed, the most faithful test of an edge detector requires to measure its performance with real pictures. This means that an obvious ground-truth, trivially related to the way the image has been synthetized, is missing. The alternative to the above is to use ground truth (GT) data, which is widely considered as a good compromise between completely objective and completely subjective quantitative performance evaluation.

Fig. 2. Example of the detection of angular direction of contours by ALOE on image Lena: black represents a $\pi/2$ angle, while white is a π angle

ALOE is compared with Canny, Sobel and a fuzzy edge detector provided in MATLAB library [17]. In order to evaluate ALOE performance, we propose both a qualitative and a quantitative evaluation. The former is left to the reader (see Fig. 3), by presenting some examples of results from the different systems. For sake of space, we were only able to show two of the most classical ones.

Afterwards, the same edge detectors have been tested on a synthetic dataset, which was built *ad hoc* in order to have an objective GT. The dataset is composed of 20 images with resolution 334×426 pixels, with geometrical figures (rectangles, circles, triangles) with contours of different width (1, 2, 3 and 4 pixels). Examples of images and of results are in Figure 4. The parameters used for ALOE are $n=3$, $\rho_k=\{0.334, 0.667, 1.00\}$, $\gamma=0.001$. The average time for ALOE (C implementation) to process such images is about 235ms on a Genuine Intel(R) U7300 1.30 GHz with 4Gb RAM and 64 bit operating system.

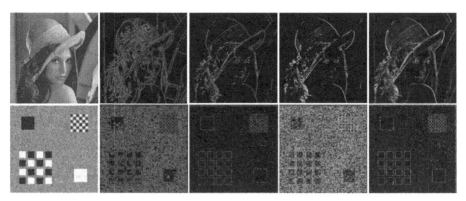

Fig. 3. An example of the results produced by the different edge detectors. In the order: the original image, Canny, Sobel, Fuzzy and ALOE.

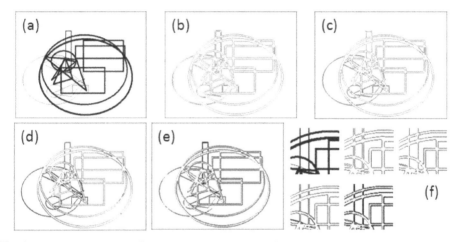

Fig. 4. An example of synthetic image (a) and results produced by the detectors considered; in the order: (b) Canny, (c) Sobel, (d) Fuzzy, (e) ALOE. A detail of the image with the same order in given in (f).

Quantitative performance have been measured using PRATT Figure of Merit (FoM), which measures the disagreement between the Detected Contour (DC) and Ground Truth (GT) and is defined as follows:

$$PRATT = \frac{1}{\max\left(card\{DC\}, card\{GT\}\right)} \sum_{x \in DC} \frac{1}{1 + \lambda \cdot d_{GT}(x)^2} \tag{4}$$

where d_{GT} is the distance transform of GT and λ is a scale parameter. PRATT ranges in (0,1], being equal to 1 iff DC coincides with GT, and is non-symmetric with respect to DC and GT. The parameter λ controls the sensitivity to differences between

GT and DC: for small values, PRATT is close to 1 only if DC is very similar to GT, while for large values larger differences between GT and DC can be tolerated. In practice, PRATT provides an overall evaluation of the quality of a given contour map, by taking into account false positives (i.e. undesired responses in the contour map), false negatives (i.e. missing contours), and shifting or deformation of a correctly detected contour from its position in GT. For our experiments we set $\lambda=0.5$. The average values obtained for the different detectors are summarized in Table 1.

Table 1. Average values of PRATT FoM computed over a set of 20 synthetic images for which a GT was derived

Canny	Sobel	Fuzzy	ALOE
0.7110	0.7691	0.8330	0.8510

As highlighted by Table 1, ALOE outperforms classical methods, and achieves better performances even with respect to state of the art recent techniques, such as the Fuzzy edge detector introduced in [17]. From the detail in Fig.4 (f), it is possible to observe that Canny, and also Sobel and Fuzzy in lower measure, tend to round the contours of squared figures or corresponding to cross lines, while ALOE better returns the original shape of the objects, even when they overlap.

6   Conclusions

We presented a novel approach to edge detection exploiting a local operator. ALOE results are augmented with the edge direction without any further processing. We use an approximating polynomial to estimate the belonging of a pixel to a contour. However, in order to reduce the computational cost of the method, while maintaining good accuracy of the result, we also propose some turnarounds based on the characteristic shape of relevant polynomials and the divided difference method of Newton. The method has been compared with both classical ones (Canny and Sobel) and with a recent fuzzy technique. The obtained results are very satisfying from both a subjective and objective point of view.

References

1. Bergholm, F.: Edge focusing. IEEE Transactions on Pattern Analysis and Machine Intelligence **9**, 726–741 (1987)
2. Canny, J.: A Computational Approach to Edge Detection. IEEE Transactions on Pattern Analysis and Machine Intelligence **8**(6), 679–698 (1986)
3. Gao, W., Zhan, X., Yang, L., Liu, H.: An improved Sobel edge detection. In: 3rd IEEE International Conference on Computer Science and Information Technology (ICCSIT), vol. 5, pp. 67–71 (2010)
4. Gonzalez, R.C., Woods, R.E.: Digital image processing. Prentice Hall, Upper Saddle River (2008)

5. Jabid, T., Kabir, M.H., Chae, O.: Local directional pattern (LDP)–A robust image descriptor for object recognition. In: Seventh IEEE International Conference on Advanced Video and Signal Based Surveillance (AVSS), pp. 482–487 (2010)
6. Kirsch, R.: Computer determination of the constituent structure of biological images. Computers and Biomedical Research **4**, 315–328 (1971)
7. Konishi, S., Yuille, A.L., Coughlan, J.M., Zhu, S.C.: Statistical Edge Detection: Learning and Evaluating Edge Cues. IEEE Transactions on Pattern Analysis and Machine Intelligence **25**(1), 57–74 (2003)
8. Lee, J., Haralick, R.M., Shapiro, L.G.: Morphologic edge detection. IEEE Journal of Robotics and Automation **3**(2), 142–156 (1987)
9. Mainberger, M., Weickert, J.: Edge-based image compression with homogeneous diffusion. In: Jiang, X., Petkov, N. (eds.) CAIP 2009. LNCS, vol. 5702, pp. 476–483. Springer, Heidelberg (2009)
10. Marr, D., Hildreth, E.: Theory of edge detection. Proc. Royal Society of London, B **207**, 187–217 (1980)
11. Ojala, T., Pietikainen, M., Maenpaa, T.: Multiresolution gray-scale and rotation invariant texture classification with local binary patterns. IEEE Transactions on Pattern Analysis and Machine Intelligence **24**(7), 971–987 (2002)
12. Pinho, A.J., Almeida, L.B.: A review on edge detection based on filtering and differentiation. Revista DO DETUA **2**(1), 113–126 (1997)
13. Schindler, K., Suter, D.: Object Detection by Global Contour Shape. Pattern Recognition **41**(12), 3736–3748 (2008)
14. Shih, M.Y., Tseng, D.C.: A wavelet-based multiresolution edge detection. Image and Vision Computing **23**, 441–451 (2005)
15. Yongsheng, G., Leung, M.K.H.: Face recognition using line edge map. IEEE Transactions on Pattern Analysis and Machine Intelligence **24**(6), 764–779 (2002)
16. Yu, Y., Chang, C.: A new edge detection approach based on image context analysis. Image and Vision Computing **24**, 1090–1102 (2006)
17. http://www.mathworks.it/it/help/fuzzy/examples/fuzzy-logic-image-processing.html?prodcode=FL&language=en

Multiple Object Detection with Occlusion Using Active Contour Model and Fuzzy C-Mean

Sara Memar$^{(\boxtimes)}$, Riadh Ksantini, and Boubakeur Boufama

School of Computer Science, University of Windsor, Windsor, ON, Canada
memark@uwindsor.ca
http://www.cs.uwindsor.ca

Abstract. This paper presents a novel two-stage unsupervised method using Active Contour Model (ACM) and Fuzzy C-mean (FCM) for image segmentation and object detection. In the first stage, ACM is applied to identify the regions of interest, making it possible to subtract the background. Then, an FCM-based algorithm is used to detect the objects in a given image. Unlike existing techniques where the number of clusters is typically set manually, the proposed method is able to automatically estimate the cluster number. Moreover, the proposed method can effectively handle the multi-object case, even in the presence of occlusions where, images may contain an arbitrary number of unknown objects. Experimental results on several images have shown the success and effectiveness of our method in detecting the salient objects.

Keywords: Active contour · Fuzzy c-mean · Microsoft Kinect · Depth clue · Object detection

1 Introduction

Object detection is a challenging vision task that is an important step in numerous applications, such as, scene understanding, video surveillance, image search and medical applications. Most object detection techniques have been designed for a specific class of objects like, pedestrians, cars and faces [7,11,15]. For example, several approaches have been proposed for detecting moving objects in video shots [5,12]. However, detecting different unknown objects in static images is still an open challenge due to the complexity of images and object classes. In this study, we explore the problem of detecting multiple salient unknown objects in a given static image.

Image segmentation, a prerequisite for many computer vision applications, can be used to help with object detection. Image segmentation can be defined as the process of dividing an image into homogenous and meaningful regions [13]. Although classical segmentation methods typically used grey-level images only, more and more newer methods have used color images [1,4]. Generally, segmentation techniques were categorized into five groups, namely threshold-based

© Springer International Publishing Switzerland 2014
A. Campilho and M. Kamel (Eds.): ICIAR 2014, Part I, LNCS 8814, pp. 224–233, 2014.
DOI: 10.1007/978-3-319-11758-4_25

techniques, edge-based methods, region-based methods, clustering techniques, and matching [13]. In particular, ACM, an edge-based segmentation technique and FCM, a clustering technique, are our main focus in this study that aim at segmenting and detecting objects in still images. Note that both ACM and FCM have been used in a variety of applications [10,18,19].

FCM algorithm has shown promising results in segmentation by improving the compactness of the regions. It is a pixel clustering technique where, similar pixels should be in the same group while, the dissimilar ones are assigned to different clusters. Although FCM algorithm benefits from simplicity of its implementation, it has two major drawbacks. First, cluster centers should be initialized randomly when using FCM. This issue may have negative effects on the outcome of the segmentation quality. To overcome this problem, some researchers proposed a number of efficient initialization algorithms [3,4]. For example, the Fuzzy Maximum Likelihood Estimation (FMLE) was used as a clustering technique for classifying data points in [3] where, FCM algorithm was applied as an initialization first step for the FMLE algorithm. In [4], a centroid initialization method, called ordering split, was proposed, where all n-dimensional samples are converted to 1-dimension by getting the mean over the feature space. Then, all samples are uniformly split into C groups and C subsets of indices that are iteratively built. Finally, cluster centers are calculated. More details about this method can be found in [4]. The second main issue about FCM is the number of clusters, the C value, which should be known in advance. Several validity indices have been proposed to determine the best number of clusters [2,3]. However, various validity indices have yielded different cluster numbers that depend on the genre of the specific data. The reason is that most of these proposed methods are based on statistical information, and they are typically sensitive to noisy data, like real images, which might consist of texture and illumination.

To address the above problems, this paper proposes a new unsupervised method for segmentation and object detection, in the challenging case of occluded multi-object scenes. Our method makes use of the color images as well as the depth clue, obtained using the Microsoft Kinect sensor. Because salient objects in an image scene might be surrounded by irrelevant information, an Active Contour Model (ACM) algorithm is first applied, as a pre-processing step, on RGB image. The output of this step consists of a set of contours containing the salient regions of the image. The area outside the obtained contours is the image background, which is removed by setting its color to white. Then, the histogram of depth information for each contour is constructed and analyzed. The number of peaks (non-zero bins) in depth histogram indicates the C-value (i.e. cluster number or the number of objects in the contour). Then, our FCM-based method is employed on image blocks for each contour to identify the different salient and occluded objects. Once there are no more contours, the results of the FCM-based method for all contours are integrated. The total number of C-value for all contours, excluding the background, indicates the number of objects in the image.

Section 2 describes the two-stage unsupervised proposed method for multi-object detection and Section 3 presents the experimental results and discussions. A conclusion is given at the end.

2   The Proposed Two-Stage Unsupervised Method for Multiple Object Detection

2.1   Background Subtraction Using Active Contour Model

Active Contour Model (ACM), an edge-based segmentation technique, has been widely employed for extracting an object outline, and it is implemented via a level set function by means of an energy minimization. Generally, the energy of ACM includes an external term and an internal term. Such energy functions aim at controlling the shape and size of the curve and make the zero-level set function move towards objects boundaries. Traditional level-set methods go through the expensive and complicated process of re-initialization in order to keep the level-set function close to its main pose during the curve evolution. More recently, variational re-initialization free level set methods have been proposed [10,20]. In this paper, we follow the ACM-based method given in [10] which is re-initialization free and performs effectively in the presence of intensity inhomogeneity. The energy function used in this paper is based on the following one.

$$\varepsilon(\phi) = \mu R_p(\phi) + \varepsilon_{g,\lambda,v} \tag{1}$$

where $R_p(\phi)$ is the internal energy function and the constant $\mu \succ 0$ is considered as the distance regularization term, for controlling the deviation of the level set function from the signed distance function. For more details about Equation 1, the reader may consult [10]. However, in the external energy function of above equation only gradient was used as an edge indicator. This will allow the detection of objects with well defined gradient-based edges only. Furthermore, because the gradient is sensitive to textured and/or noisy regions, the curve will likely stop before reaching the object boundaries. In some cases, it may even pass through the edges, if the gradient has small local maxima on the object edges. To overcome this problem, image polarity was applied in the external energy function as a stopping term in [1,8,9]. It was shown in particular that polarity is better at detecting the object boundaries in the presence of texture. Polarity is a local image feature that measures the extent to which gradient vectors are oriented in some dominant direction, around a specific pixel. However, the use of polarity has its own weakness as well. In particular, it is outperformed by gradient in the absence of texture.

In addition to these two features, depth information can be a good clue for detecting salient objects as the pixels of the depth image correspond to a depth or a distance. Disparity map, obtained from two images, can be used as a depth clue and is a good alternative feature in an ACM stopping term [14]. There are also newly available and affordable depth sensors that can be used to obtain depth clue. However, even with such 3D sensors, it is still difficult to clearly detect and/or differentiate objects with no depth, and also when they are located at similar depths. To overcome the above problems, we propose a new method to automatically select the best candidate features, to be used in the ACM, and combine them using a semi-supervised classification method, based on

Support Vector Machine (SVM). First, given an input image, the three features, namely gradient (F_g), polarity (F_p) and depth (F_D), are computed. Second, unlike previous known methods, we automatically select either the gradient or the polarity, based on our texture/noise indicator calculated over the mean of the gradient values in the target area. Then, the histogram of depth on the initial contour is extracted and analyzed. If the number of peaks (non-zero bin) is greater than 1, it means that depth information is available and can be combined with another feature (i.e. either gradient or polarity) to be used as a stopping function in the ACM. If more than one feature is selected as a stopping term, they should be combined using SVM. The gradient (F_g), polarity (F_p) and depth (F_D) values are between 0 and 1, and such values are very close to 0 on edge and 1 on non-edge areas.

Every pixel should be classified either to 0 (edge) or 1 (Non-edge) classes. Since SVM is a supervised method, some training samples (i.e. pixels are samples in our case) should be provided to train it. However, in practice, class labels for pixels of real images are not available. To overcome this, we have used the target image itself as our training samples. The two ideal vectors, namely truly edge with values being 0 (i.e. [0,..,0]) and truly non-edge with values being 1 (i.e. [1,..,1]) are defined. The size of these two vectors depends on the subset of features used. For example, the size is set to 2 if only F_g and F_D are used. First, for every pixel the Euclidean distances between its feature vector and the ideal vectors are calculated. Then, these scores of distances are sorted, and only N pixels, the closest ones to the ideal vectors, are kept as training sets, to represent edges and non-edge. Note that the training samples for both classes are equal to N, which can be determined through experiments. Once the training samples are obtained, the classifier can be trained and applied on the testing set. The output of applying our ACM-based method is a set of final contours containing regions of interest in the image. This allows us to remove the background and any irrelevant information. Hence, the process of salient object detection can be accomplished in a more effective manner.

2.2 Salient Object Identification Using FCM

This section describes the process of salient object detection, and how the number of salient objects, or clusters, in a given image is calculated.

Determining Cluster Number. In the previous section, ACM as a preprocessing stage, yielded a set of final contours. However, when objects are occluded by each other, a single contour may contain more than one object. Because objects might have similar colors and could be difficult to separate using classical methods [6,17,19], we have used depth information to explore the content of each final contour, and to help obtain the number of clusters. Both the color and depth images were obtained with the affordable Microsoft Kinect sensor. Note that such depth, even if it is not very accurate, it is beneficial for the clustering method, as it provides approximate distances between

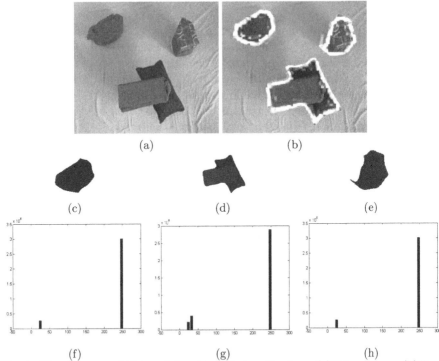

(a)   (b)

(c)   (d)   (e)

(f)   (g)   (h)

Fig. 1. The Process of Determining the Cluster Number. (a)Color image (b)Final Contours of ACM (c)Depth of Contour 1 (d)Depth of Contour 2 (e)Depth of Contour 3 (f)Histogram of Contour 1 (g)Histogram of Contour 2 (h)Histogram of Contour 3.

objects and the sensor. In particular, depth histograms, well-known graphical tools for frequency distribution, were successfully experimented in [16] for the detection of the hand contour. In this paper, we have used depth histograms to determine the number of potential objects within the given contour. Figure 1 depicts how the number of objects (clusters) in each contour is extracted from the three final contours of the ACM's result. Each contour is given a label while the background (the area out of the final contours) is removed by setting its color to white. Then, the histogram of depth information for each contour, including the background is constructed. The analysis of each histogram, i.e., the number of peaks or non-zero bins, gives us a good indication of the number of available objects in that contour. The number of peaks in a histogram is also considered the number of clusters or C-value in the Fuzzy C-mean. So, a C-value is always greater or equal to two when there is at least one object in the scene. In the minimum case, one peak belongs to the background and the other peak corresponds to the contour of a single object. For example, as Figure 1 shows, the number of peaks for the middle contour is three, suggesting that two objects are available inside this contour. Note that the highest peak corresponds to the background (white color) in the histogram of each contour.

Object Detection. Once the cluster number for each contour is found, FCM can be used to explore the possible occlusions. Color (we have used the CIE-L*a*b* color space), texture and depth are the three features used in our FCM. Energy and homogeneity are two texture features computed from the co-occurrence matrix. Co-occurrence matrix determines the frequency of a pixel with grey value i occurs adjacent to a pixel with grey value j in a specific orientation. We compute the co-occurrence matrix for four orientations $\theta \in \{0, 45, 90, 135\}$ and one distance value $D \in \{1\}$. Then the average of energy and homogeneity are calculated over the number of orientations and distances. The other feature we can use is the depth obtained from Microsoft Kinect. So, the feature space is six-dimensional, including color (L, a, b), texture (Energy, Homogeneity) and depth. Because pixel clustering is computationally costly, especially for today high resolution images, we have followed the approach in [18], where block-wise clustering was used. In particular, the image is divided into several blocks, where the block size should cover approximately 17% of the maximum number of pixels in the height and width of the image. Then the average of all features values for each block is calculated. Finally, FCM is applied to cluster the blocks instead of pixels. The occluded objects are hence identified by their corresponding contours. This process is done for all contours, and the different FCM results are combined to identify the number of objects in the whole image.

3   Experimental Results

The proposed method has been tested on five real images with a 640×480 resolution. Microsoft Kinect was used to obtain both RGB and depth images. However, since the depth image is not registered to its corresponding RGB image, a function from OpenNI was applied to approximately register the depth image with its corresponding RGB image. In the first stage, our ACM-based method was applied on the images with the goal of subtracting the background. Some parameters like λ, μ, v, and Δt (*time step*) should be set for implementing the ACM. These parameters were set to $\lambda = 5$, $\mu = 0.04$ and $\Delta t = 5$, and they were kept constant throughout all our experiments. The initial contour is set globally, and it goes through the 430 iterations during the curve evolution. We set the threshold in this stage, and the final contours with the number of pixels less than this threshold are ignored. In the second stage, our FCM-based algorithm was employed on each contour to identify the objects and handle occlusions. To improve the efficiency, images were divided into blocks, and FCM is applied on blocks rather than pixels. The block size was set to 8, considering the resolution of our images. Figure 2 indicates the effectiveness and success of our proposed method in detecting the multiple salient objects in the image. The first column in Fig 2 depicts the RGB images while the middle and third columns are the results of our ACM-based and FCM-based algorithms, respectively. As Fig 2 suggests, our ACM-based algorithm is able to effectively extract the regions of interests from the images. However, it was not able to handle occlusions correctly. Hence, our FCM-based algorithm was applied on each contour to remedy this situation.

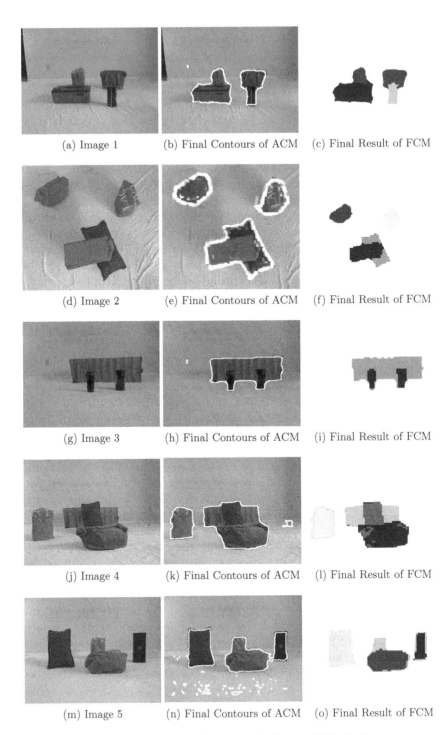

Fig. 2. Results of Applying the Proposed Method

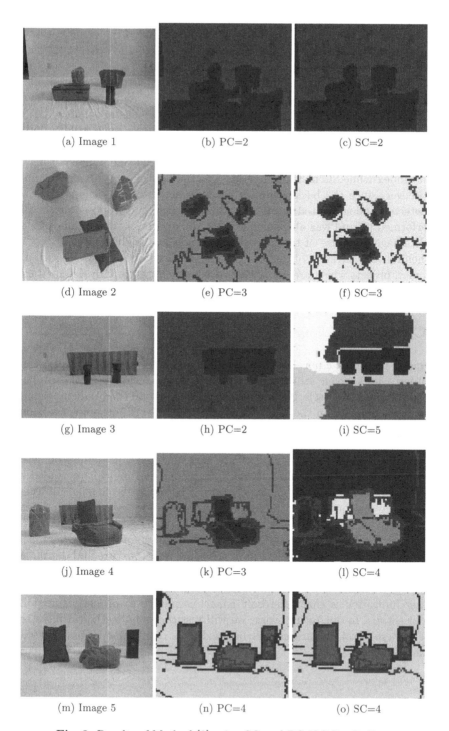

Fig. 3. Results of Method [3] using SC and PC Validity Indices

As discussed earlier, the depth histogram of each contour is taken into account to determine the C-value for the FCM algorithm. Finally, the results after this second stage, for all contours, are combined to detect and extract all salient objects in a given still image.

We have also tested the method in [3] and compared it to our proposed method. Two validity indices, namely SC (compactness and separation) [3] and PC (Partition Coefficient) [2], are used to validate the cluster number, i.e., the number of objects in the image. However, as Fig 3 shows, such validity indices may get different values for the same image due to texture and outliers. For example, Image 3 in Fig 3 shows that 2 is the best cluster number using PC validity index while SC method suggests 5 as the best cluster number for image 3. Moreover, since the background is not subtracted, objects cannot be properly detected and separated from each other. Overall, our proposed method has outperformed [3] and was able to effectively and accurately detect all objects in a given image. The use of the depth information in the clustering process was very helpful to accurately obtain the cluster number for the FCM algorithm. In particular, objects which are occluded by each other are properly detected using our method.

4   Conclusion

This paper presented a novel method that can accurately detect multiple occluding objects in a given still image. Unlike existing techniques, the proposed method automatically selects the best feature(s), among the gradient, polarity, and depth depending on the input image, to be used in the stopping function in the ACM-based algorithm. In addition to the RGB image, the proposed method takes advantage of depth information to estimate the C-value to be used with an FCM algorithm. We have successfully experimented our method on several images, captured with Microsoft Kinect, where we had multiple occluded and non-occluded objects. In all our experiments, the numbers of salient objects in the images were correctly estimated and properly detected. Our experimental results clearly show that our method outperforms some existing techniques that used validity indices for specifying the best cluster number. However, in the extremely rare case where objects have the same color, texture and depth, they may not be discriminated from each other. In this situation, spatial information and pixel continuity could be taken into account to overcome this problem. Another limitation is that Microsoft Kinect is unable to properly function in outdoor setups. In our future work, we will test the same method using stereo-images where pixel disparities will be used as a depth clue instead of sensor calculated depth.

References

1. Allili, M.S., Ziou, D.: Globally adaptive region information for automatic colortexture image segmentation. Pattern Recognition Letters **28**(15) (November 2007)
2. Bezdek, J.C., Pal, M.R., Keller, J., Krisnapuram, R.: Fuzzy Models and Algorithms for Pattern Recognition and Image Processing. Kluwer Academic Publishers, Norwell (1999)
3. Bouguessa, M., Wang, S., Sun, H.: An objective approach to cluster validation. Pattern Recognition Letters **27**(13), 1419–1430 (2006)
4. Capitaine, H.L., Frlicot, C.: A fast fuzzy c-means algorithm for color image segmentation. In: Proceedings of European Society for Fuzzy Logic and Technology (EUSFLAT 2011), pp. 1074–1081 (2011)
5. Cheng, F.H., Chen, Y.L.: Real time multiple objects tracking and identification based on discrete wavelet transform. Pattern Recognition **39**(6) (2006)
6. Huang, Z.K., Xie, Y.M., Liu, D.H., Hou, L.Y.: Using fuzzy c-means cluster for histogram-based color image segmentation. In: ITCS 2009, vol. 1, pp. 597–600 (2009)
7. Jun, B., Kim, D.: Robust face detection using local gradient patterns and evidence accumulation. Pattern Recognition **45**(9), 3304–3316 (2012)
8. Ksantini, R., Shariat, F., Boufama, B.: An efficient and fast active contour model for salient object detection. In: Canadian Conference on Computer and Robot Vision, CRV 2009, pp. 124–131. IEEE (May 2009)
9. Ksantini, R., Boufama, B., Memar, S.: A new efficient active contour model without local initializations for salient object detection. EURASIP Journal on Image and Video Processing **2013**(1), 1–13 (2013)
10. Li, C., Xu, C., Gui, C., Fox, M.D.: Distance regularized level set evolution and its application to image segmentation. Trans. Img. Proc. **19**(12), 3243–3254 (2010)
11. Li, L.J., Socher, R., Fei-Fei, L.: Towards total scene understanding: Classification, annotation and segmentation in an automatic framework. In: CVPR 2009, pp. 2036–2043. IEEE (June 2009)
12. Liu, C., Yuen, P.C., Qiu, G.: Object motion detection using information theoretic spatio-temporal saliency. Pattern Recognition **42**(11), 2897–2906 (2009)
13. Lucchese, L., Mitra, S.K., Barbara, S.: Color image segmentation: A state-of-the-art survey. Citeseer **67**(2), 207–221 (2001)
14. Memar, S., Jin, K., Boufama, B.: Object detection using active contour model with depth clue. In: Kamel, M., Campilho, A. (eds.) ICIAR 2013. LNCS, vol. 7950, pp. 640–647. Springer, Heidelberg (2013)
15. Negri, P., Goussies, N., Lotito, P.: Detecting pedestrians on a movement feature space. Pattern Recognition **47**(1), 56–71 (2014)
16. Park, M., Hasan, M.M., Kim, J., Chae, O.: Hand detection and tracking using depth and color information. Las Vegas Nevada, USA (2012)
17. Qiu, G., Feng, X., Fang, J.: Compressing histogram representations for automatic colour photo categorization. Pattern Recognition **37**(11), 2177–2193 (2004)
18. Rafiee, G., Dlay, S., Woo, W.: Region-of-interest extraction in low depth of field images using ensemble clustering and difference of gaussian approaches. Pattern Recognition **46**(10), 2685–2699 (2013)
19. Siang Tan, K., Mat Isa, N.A.: Color image segmentation using histogram thresholding fuzzy c-means hybrid approach. Pattern Recognition **44**(1), 1–15 (2011)
20. Zhang, K., Zhang, L., Song, H., Zhou, W.: Active contours with selective local or global segmentation: A new formulation and level set method. Image Vision Comput. **28**(4), 668–676 (2010)

Classification and Learning Methods

Conversational Interaction Recognition Based on Bodily and Facial Movement

Jingjing Deng, Xianghua Xie$^{(\boxtimes)}$, and Shangming Zhou

Department of Computer Science, Swansea University, Swansea, UK
x.xie@swansea.ac.uk
http://csvision.swan.ac.uk

Abstract. We examine whether 3D pose and face features can be used to both learn and recognize different conversational interactions. We believe this to be among the first work devoted to this subject and show that this task is indeed possible with a promising degree of accuracy using both features derived from pose and face. To extract 3D pose we use the Kinect Sensor, and we use a combined local and global model to extract face features from normal RGB cameras. We show that whilst both of these features are contaminated with noises. They can still be used to effectively train classifiers. The differences in interaction among different scenarios in our data set are extremely subtle. Both generative and discriminative methods are investigated, and a subject specific supervised learning approach is employed to classify the testing sequences to seven different conversational scenarios.

Keywords: Human interaction modeling · Conversantional interaction analysis · 3D human pose · Face analysis · Randomized decision trees · HMM · SVM

1 Introduction

There has been some success in using features extracted from high-level information such as body pose, e.g. automatically learning sign language to perform classificaiton task [5]. However, assumptions about the subjects in the scenes, such as body orientation, are routinely made to constrain the solution. A further problem with studying social interaction is that there are often occlusion since usually participants would face one another, meaning observations are often incomplete. For this reason, often the interactions examined are less intimate and can be viewed at a coarser resolution. For example Zhang et al. [21] studied group interactions in a work meeting between multiple people, detecting events such as presenting to the group, conducting a group discussion or note taking etc. This is achieved by first estimating the state of each participant and then using this information to infer the group action. Decomposing the group interaction

© Springer International Publishing Switzerland 2014
A. Campilho and M. Kamel (Eds.): ICIAR 2014, Part I, LNCS 8814, pp. 237–245, 2014.
DOI: 10.1007/978-3-319-11758-4_26

into a two level process of firstly inferring what each person is doing, and then from this deducing the group action is a common approach [1,19,21]. Probabilistic models such as Hidden Markov Models (HMM) can be employed to overcome noisy observations, both at the image level and on the person dependent action classification level. However, for this approach to be effective there needs to be an understanding of which motions, poses or gestures that an individual performs is likely to be an important building block. Often this is dependent on the granularity of the actions being observed.

In order to understand the high-level semantic human activity, accurate pose estimation is generally required. To perform such as task using RGB cameras, e.g. [8,9], remains an open challenge. In [10,11], we proposed to leverage recent advances in technology in extracting 3D pose using a consumer sensor (Microsoft Kinect) to examine the feasibility of recognizing human interactions between two people using the body pose only. Rather than recognizing just key social events, we attempt to analyze and classify different conversational interactions. In this work, we investigate both bodily and facial pose features for recognizing the type of conversation they are conducting. We do not examine strongly differentiable interactions, such as high-tempered arguments or disputes, as in previous research efforts studying interaction. Neither do we employ the use of actors. Different from affect recognition, where a single observation can typically be used to identify the affective state (e.g. smile implies happiness), there is not a direct connection between a single observation and the type of the conversation being performed; rather it is the sequence of observations as an interaction is in progress and is of importance. We acknowledge that bodily and facial movements are not necessarily generalizable across subjects. Here, we aim to find out whether it is possible to generalize subject specific motion cues which can be used to identify the topic of a conversation.

2   Data Acquisition

Data was collected using a multi-camera set-up. Each person was recorded using a Kinect Sensor, which captured pose at 30fps. The face images were captured using two high definition cameras operating at 25fps. The first task was to discuss an area of current work that the participant was undertaking. The second task was to prepare an interesting story to tell their partner, such as a holiday experience. The third task was to jointly find the answer to a problem. The fourth task was a debate, where the participants were asked to prepare arguments for a particular point of view on an issue we gave to them. In the fifth task they were asked to discuss between them the issues surrounding a statement and come to agreement whether they believe the statement is true or not. The sixth task was to answer a subjective question, and the seventh task was to tell jokes in turn. In total, there are about 8 hours long Kinect sequences and equal length of face sequences. The dataset is available for download from http://csvision.swan.ac. uk/converse.html.

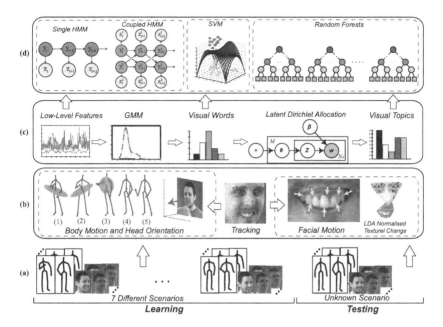

Fig. 1. Flowchart of the proposed method

3 Methodology

The proposed method first extract motion features from Kinect output and local-ize facial fiducial points in RGB face images using a two level shape model. The head orientation is then computed based on face localization and is treated as part of the pose feature. The localization of face fiducial points also provides two sets of features: shape and appearance. The shape features are derived from the coefficients of a global shape model that is used for face localization. The appear-ance features are obtained from the textural coefficients of two local face models after Linear Discriminant Analysis. Hidden Markov Models (HMMs) are then used to model the conversational interactions based on these low level features at individual time instances. Interactions between pair of subjects are captured using coupled HMM. A temporal generalization of both pose and face features are also carried out to encapsulate temporal dynamics, which first produces a visual vocabulary features and then further generalizes them to visual topics through Latent Dirichlet Allocation analysis. Discriminative classifiers, Support Vector Machine (SVM) and Random Forests (RF), are applied to classify inter-actions into seven different scenarios. Moreover, we apply modulator functions to those mid level features so that we can learn the importance of those individual features, which is then used in the SVM classification. Fig. 1 illustrates the steps from low level feature extraction, to unsupervised feature generalization, and to supervised modeling and classification.

3.1   Pose Feature Extraction

Motivated by recent work, such as [2,16,17], we extract three types of low level features to depict the pose and motion of the upper body. These geometry features extracted from a kinematic chain are simple but powerful for representing human gesture and motion over time. The first set of feature measures the distance between two joints at different time intervals. The second set of feature measures the distance between a joint and a reference plane defined using different parts of the body. The third set of feature measures the velocity of individual joints. These are depicted in row (b) in Fig. 1.

In this study, we use three reference planes, (1) (2) and (3) showed in row (b) in Fig. 1. The first two reference planes, (1) and (2) are used to measure the distance and velocity of joints on the lower arms, i.e. hands, wrists and elbows. Both planes are located at the same spine point. One of the two planes is defined by the vector connecting the spine and left shoulder (Fig. 1, row (b), (1)), and the other is defined by the vector connecting the spine and right shoulder (Fig. 1, row (b), (2)). The former is used to measure the lower arm joints on the left side and the latter is for right side. The two vectors connecting hip center from two shoulders define the third reference plan (Fig. 1, row (b), (3)), which is used to measure movements of lower arm joints from both arms. The overlapping in measurement is to make sure that the 3D motion of those joints are captured among those 2D measurement combinations.

3.2   Face Feature Extraction

The face images acquired have varied poses and sometimes contain occlusions (e.g. glasses and hand movement). Consequently, holistic models, such as active appearance models, [6], have been found not robust enough to track the faces beyond a few dozens of frames. We thus integrate the local component shape models with a global shape model [12]. We use the point distribution model [6] to build two local shape models, which are trained using feature points from upper and lower faces, respectively, with overlapping nostril fiducial points. The two models hence are focusing on local deformations at eyes and mouth regions that are important to model interactions. The overlap provides a weak constraint between two local models. The result from local models provides a good initialization for the second level global shape model. Each of the fitness function is composed of a texture cost and a shape cost. Response scores based on Haar-like rectangular features [20] and the GentleBoost algorithm [13] are used to evaluate the texture fitness. We follow [7] to formulate a generic shape cost function, which is applied to both local and global models. The two level fitness functions are then optimized using the simplex algorithm.

Based on the localization results, two types of features are extracted to capture facial dynamics: shape and appearance. For each face image there are 35 fiducial points, many of which are for localization purposes, and are not contributing to deformations. We hence project those localized points to the global shape model space learned at the localization stage and retain 90% eigenvalue, which results in

9-dimensional shape features. This dimensionality reduction is also desirable for training classifiers. For appearance feature, we similarly project the facial texture to a PCA texture model that is learned from the training samples used for localization. Since there are significant differences between the upper part and lower part of the face, two separate PCA models are built. Again, 90% eigenvalue is retained, which results in 14-dimensional features for both upper part and lower part. However, for appearance feature we also perform a Linear Discriminant Analysis [3] to minimize the individual textural characteristics in derived appearance features. We re-project the coefficients back into the texture subspace and calculate the residue, which is used as the final appearance feature. Thus, a total of 37-dimensional features are learned for capturing facial dynamics.

3.3 Head Orientation Estimation

Currently the Kinect sensor has the ability of facial tracking and head pose estimation. However, the performance and accuracy are greatly affected by the data acquisition environment and experiment set-up, especially the imaging distance and the participant's pose. Hence, we perform head orientation estimation by extending the results from face tracking. As part of facial feature extraction, we obtain a set of five fiducial points for each face image: two external eye corners, two mouth corners, and nose tip. We follow the work by Gee and Cipolla [14] to estimate the head orientation from a single image using these fiducial points.

3.4 Temporal Feature Descriptors

To determine which conversational scenario directly based on short-term, primitive actions is unlikely going to be successful. Instead, the temporal dynamics of those short-term motions and primitive actions are useful in revealing the topic of conversation. To capture such dynamics, we employ Hidden Markov Model (HMM) which is well suited to model temporal sequential data. However, we also attempt to generalize those face and pose features to a middle level to summarize the distributions of those primitive motions in a reasonable time span, 5 seconds in our case. The common approach of appending feature vectors will result in prohibitively long feature vectors for discriminative classifiers to train. We thus adopt the bag of words approach to derive middle level features that are suitable for classification of conversational interactions, each of which may contain various amount of primitive motions.

The Latent Dirichlet Allocation (LDA) model [4] has been widely used to discover abstract "topics" from a collection of words or low level features, e.g. [18]. In this work, we use unsupervised clustering to generate visual words across the whole sequence and across all subjects to create a visual vocabulary. A further generalization to visual topics is then performed based on the distribution of visual words in an extended time span that is often larger than typical primitive actions.

We first construct a visual vocabulary by fitting Gaussian Mixture Model to each dimension of the low-level feature space. We consider each Gaussian component as a visual word. Then, we further assume that those visual words are generated by a mixture of visual topics. To learn those visual topics, we split the sequences into 20 seconds sections, each of which is considered as a visual document that contains multiple visual topics. The LDA model is learned by using Gibbs sampling inference method, [15], and applied to extract interaction categories from low level temporal visual words. The distribution of both visual words and visual topics are used as temporal feature descriptors for conversational interaction modeling and classification.

3.5   Modeling Using Coupled HMM

In order to explicitly model the dependence between the two subjects we use separate HMM to represent each person and then adding an edge between the subjects across time to build a Coupled HMM (CHMM), e.g. [19]. Row (d) in Fig. 1 depicts the CHMM used in this work. To perform classification, CHMMs are learned for each of the seven classes, $\{A_1, .., A_7\}$. Given a set of T observations $Z_T = \{z_T, z_{T-1}, .., z_1\}$ from an unknown class we classify it to the model that maximizes $p(A_n | Z_T)$, where n denotes class ID. This is calculated in two stages. Firstly the forward-backward algorithm is used to calculate $p(Z_T | A_n)$ by recursively computing $p(y_t = j | z_{t-1}, .., z_1, A_n) = \sum_{i=1}^{m} \mathbf{A}_{ij} p(z_{t-1} | y_{t-1} = i) p(y_{t-1} = i | z_{t-2}, .., z_1, A_n)$, where $\mathbf{A}$ denotes the transition matrix, and then summing the probabilities over all states in the final time instance, i.e. $p(Z_T | A_n) = \sum_{i=1}^{m} p(z_T | y_T = i) p(y_T = i | z_{T-1}, .., z_1, A_n)$, following which, $p(A_n | Z_T)$ can be calculated using Bayes' rule assuming a flat prior across all classes.

3.6   Classification Using Discriminative Classifiers

Whilst generative models, such as HMM, is important in explaining the data, discriminative ones tend to be more effective in classification tasks. In this work, we also employ SVM and Random Forests to study the discriminative power of the features, and only the middle level features are used since a concatenation of low level features will result in a too large dimensional feature space.

3.7   Classification Using SVM Ranked Features

In order to automatically identify the influential features from high dimensional space, we conduct feature ranking via a scheme that applies the entropy regularization and particle swarm optimization (PSO) techniques to the construction of an optimal SVM model [22]. The novelty of this scheme lies in that the model selection, feature identification and dimensionality reduction are performed simultaneously in an integrated manner. During learning process the importance of less influential attributes automatically approaches to zero, whilst the importance of the most important attributes turns to be one. As a result, only the most influential features remain in the final SVM model.

Specifically, given a data set $\{x_l, y_l\}_{l=1}^{N_p}$ used for performing model selection by the PSO, where $y_l \in \{-1, 1\}$ denotes the label of data x_l and N_p denotes the number of classes, the following fitness function is used to identify optimal hyper-parameters for SVM: $f = \frac{1}{N_p} \sum_{k=1}^{N_p} (\bar{y}_k - y_k)^2 + \lambda_1 \left(- \sum_{i=1}^{n} \theta_i \log(\theta_i)\right) + \lambda_2 \left(\sum_{i=1}^{n} \theta_i\right)$, where $\theta_i \in (0, 1)$ indicates the importance of the input variable to the classification task, λ_i (> 0) are called regularization coefficients, $\bar{y}_k$ are the labels predicted by the SVM model. The second term, an entropy penalty, is used to remove redundant features. Because the entropy distribution of importance ranks would become zero (minimum) if importance values of features reach {0, 1}, during the training process the importance ranking values associated with redundant features would be forced to approach to zero and the importance ranks associated with influential features would move towards one. The third term encourages feature sets that are as compact as possible.

4   Results and Discussions

All 7 tasks were completed by 8 different pairs of people in a total of 482 mins, producing a total of 869,142 pose frames and 724,285 RGB face images. Together with estimated head orientation, 35 low level pose features were extracted. 37 low level face features were derived from face localization. To extract the visual words, for each feature, a Gaussian Mixture Model with 10 components was fitted to the low level features across different pairs. In order to extract the visual topic from the visual word, the sequences were chopped into 20-second sections, each of which was considered as a visual document. We learned LDA models with 25 visual topics for pose and face separately, and each visual word was inferred and assigned with a potential visual topic. Finally, at the scenario classification stage, each recorded sequence is split into 5-second sections. For the discriminative classifiers, the histogram of visual words or topics is computed, and used as a feature vector for each section. For the CHMM, the feature vector of every 10 frames, for the sake of computational feasibility, in the section corresponds to an observation node expanded across time. To carry out the classification, 10-fold cross validation is adopted. Note, neighboring segments are not distributed across different folders.

The results of using CHMM are summarized as following. Using face and pose features alone achieved 53.2% and 55.9% respectively, compared to a random

Table 1. Classification results using visual words (%)

	Face&Pose			
	KNN	RF	SVM	SVM-R
Describing Work	81.2	90.6	88.4	100.0
Story Telling	59.7	51.0	70.6	80.2
Problem Solving	41.4	12.8	35.1	80.7
Debate	55.3	51.6	67.7	91.8
Discussion	50.0	62.7	69.5	61.1
Subjective Question	30.8	5.2	35.8	91.7
Jokes	36.3	14.2	47.7	80.0
Average	50.7	41.2	59.3	89.1

Table 2. Classification results using visual topics (%)

	Face&Pose			
	KNN	RF	SVM	SVM-R
Describing Work	63.5	91.7	76.4	100.0
Story Telling	35.1	73.2	68.3	80.2
Problem Solving	37.1	73.6	74.3	80.7
Debate	48.6	73.6	67.1	81.97
Discussion	38.4	78.7	63.5	61.11
Subjective Question	22.5	63.3	63.5	91.74
Jokes	27.5	70.3	66.3	80.0
Average	38.9	74.9	68.5	87.3

chance of around 14%. The combination of face and pose feature achieved an average of 59.6%. When using visual words and visual topics, the performance decreased significantly. With visual words, overall accuracy of 32.0%, 33.6% and 36.4% were produced using face, pose, face and pose, respectively. After further generalization to visual topic, its performance reduced further to 28.3%, 30.8% and 30.7%. This was generally expected, since the feature generalization causes an enhancement of commonality among different scenarios, which caused HMMs modeling slightly more common features and hence reduced their discriminative power.

Next, we tested the mid level features with discriminative classifiers, i.e. SVM and RF, see Tables 1 and 2. The classification results are considerably better. For example, the overall accuracy using standard SVM with face and pose visual words achieved 59.3%, compared with a mere 36.4% achieved by CHMM. With visual topics, the difference is even more evident: 68.5% vs. 30.7%. The combination of pose and face features showed markable improvements over using face or pose features alone. We also present the results using KNN. With visual words, RF was inferior to others and SVM is clearly performed better. With further generalized features, there are clear improvements for both RF and SVM, but not for KNN, and RF slightly out-performed SVM.

However, using our SVM ranked features, there were substantial improvements for all features and raised the performance close to 90%. It is evidently clear that feature selection is important in differentiating different conversation scenarios.

Whilst the Kinect sensor permits direct estimation of 3D pose that is currently more robust and accurate than RGB camera methods, the accuracy of the data collected still contains some noise, as does the face features used in this work. However, despite this we have shown that good recognition of conversational interactions can still be achieved. The suggests that it is possible to recognize the conversational topics based on gesture and facial dynamics.

References

1. Aggarwal, J.K., Ryoo, M.S.: Human activity analysis: A review. ACM Computing Survey **43**(16), 1–43 (2011)

2. Yao, A., Gall, J., Fanelli, G., Gool, L.V.: Does human action recognition benefit from pose estimation? In: BMVC (2011)
3. Belhumeur, P., Hespanha, J., Kriegman, D.: Eigenfaces vs fisherfaces: recognition using class specific linear projection. IEEE T-PAMI **19**(7), 711–720 (1997)
4. Blei, D., Ng, A., Jordan, M.: Latent dirichlet allocation. J. of Machine Learning Research **3**, 993–1022 (2003)
5. Buehler, P., Everingham, M., Zisserman, A.: Learning sign language by watching TV (using weakly aligned subtitles). In: CVPR (2009)
6. Cootes, T., Edward, G., Taylor, C.: Active appearance models. IEEE T-PAMI **23**(6), 681–685 (2001)
7. Cristinacce, D., Cootes, T.: Automatic feature localisation with constrained local models. PR **41**, 3054–3067 (2008)
8. Daubney, B., Xie, X.: Entropy driven hierarchical search for 3d human pose estimation. In: BMVC, pp. 1–11 (2011)
9. Daubney, B., Xie, X.: Tracking 3d human pose with large root node uncertainty. In: 2011 IEEE Conference on Computer Vision and Pattern Recognition (CVPR), pp. 1321–1328 (June 2011)
10. Deng, J., Xie, X., Daubney, B.: A bag of words approach to subject specific 3d human pose interaction classification with random decision forests. Graphical Models **76**(3), 162–171 (2014)
11. Deng, J., Xie, X., Daubney, B., Fang, H., Grant, P.W.: Recognizing conversational interaction based on 3D human pose. In: Blanc-Talon, J., Kasinski, A., Philips, W., Popescu, D., Scheunders, P. (eds.) ACIVS 2013. LNCS, vol. 8192, pp. 138–149. Springer, Heidelberg (2013)
12. Fang, H., Deng, J., Xie, X., Grant, P.: From clamped local shape models to global shape model. In: IEEE ICIP, pp. 3513–3517 (September 2013)
13. Friedman, J., Hastie, T., Tibshirani, R.: Addictive logistic regression: a statistical view of boosting. Annals of Statistics **28**, 337–407 (2000)
14. Gee, A.H., Cipolla, R.: Determining the gaze of faces in images. IVC **12**, 639–647 (1994)
15. Griffiths, T.L., Steyvers, M.: Finding scientific topics. Proceedings of the National Academy of Sciences of the United States of America **101**, 5228–5235 (2004)
16. Kovar, L., Gleicher, M.: Automated extraction and parameterization of motions in large data sets. ACM ToG **23**(3), 559–568 (2004)
17. Müller, M., Röder, T., Clausen, M.: Efficient content-based retrieval of motion capture data. ACM ToG **24**(3), 677–685 (2005)
18. Niebles, J., Wang, H., Fei-Fei, L.: Unsupervised learning of human action categories using spatial-temporal words. IJCV **79**(3), 299–318 (2008)
19. Oliver, N., Rosario, B., Pentland, A.: A bayesian computer vision system for modeling human interactions. IEEE T-PAMI **22**(8), 831–843 (2000)
20. Viola, P., Jones, M.: Robust real-time face detection. IJCV **57**(2), 137–154 (2004)
21. Zhang, D., Gatica-Perez, D., Bengio, S., McCowan, I.: Modeling individual and group actions in meetings with layered hmms. IEEE Multimedia **8**(3), 509–520 (2006)
22. Zhou, S.M., Lyons, R.A., Bodger, O., Demmler, J.C., Atkinson, M.A.: Svm with entropy regularization and particle swarm optimization for identifying childrens health and socioeconomic determinants of education attainments using linked datasets. In: IEEE Inter. Conf. Neural Networks, pp. 3867–3874 (2010)

Handwritten Digit Recognition Using SVM Binary Classifiers and Unbalanced Decision Trees

Adriano Mendes Gil[1], Cícero Ferreira Fernandes Costa Filho[2(✉)], and Marly Guimarães Fernandes Costa[2]

[1] Instituto Nokia de Tecnologia, Manaus, Brazil
adrianomendes.gil@gmail.com
[2] Universidade Federal do Amazonas/Centro de Pesquisa e Desenvolvimento em Tecnologia Eletrônica e da Informação , UFAM/CETELI, Manaus, Brazil
{ccosta,mcosta}@ufam.edu.br

Abstract. In this work, we use SVM binary classifiers coupled with a binary classifier architecture, an unbalanced decision tree, for handwritten digit recognition. According to input variables, two classifiers were trained and tested. One using digit characteristics and the other using the whole image as input variables. Developed recently, the unbalanced decision tree architecture provides a simple structure for a multiclass classifier using binary classifiers. In this work, using the whole image as input, 100% handwritten digit recognition accuracy was obtained in the MNIST database. These are the best results published in the literature for the MNIST database.

Keywords: Handwritten digit recognition · MNIST database · Support vector machine · Unbalanced decision tree · Binary classifiers

1 Introduction

In recent decades, character recognition technology has been driven by the increasing demand of converting an enormous amount of printed or handwritten information to a digital format [1]. This conversion from paper to computer in the past required human operators who processed billions of checks, mail correspondence, etc. This process was time consuming and error prone, motivating the development of optical character recognition (OCR), a technique for reading data and recognizing one character after another. OCR is an important pattern recognition technique. There are vast amounts of historical, technical and economic documents only in a printed form. An OCR system drastically reduces cost of digitalizing them. There are some successful techniques for OCR implementation applied in digitalization of handwritten and mechanical printed texts, and musical scores.

Character recognition is a very difficult problem, due to the great variability in writing styles, in other words, wide interclass variability: the same character can be written in different sizes and orientation angles.

As shown if Fig. 1, an OCR system is comprised of certain steps: image acquisition – a color, gray level or binary image is acquired; pre-processing – image processing

© Springer International Publishing Switzerland 2014
A. Campilho and M. Kamel (Eds.): ICIAR 2014, Part I, LNCS 8814, pp. 246–255, 2014.
DOI: 10.1007/978-3-319-11758-4_27

techniques are applied to improve image quality; layout analysis – the text structure is understood to facilitate text interpretation; word segmentation in characters; classification – pattern recognition is employed for character recognition and post-processing – gather the recognized characters to obtain the original words (opposite for word segmentation).

In this work we focused attention only on the classification step of digit recognition. Table 1 provides details about some digit recognition studies published in the literature. The columns of this table include: database, input data, classifier used and results.

Concerning input characteristics, the studies can be divided into two main groups: the first group consists of studies using digit extracted characteristics as input data [5,6,9,10,11] and the second one consists of studies using the whole image as input data [2,3,4,7,8].

Concerning the databases used, the studies shown in Table 1 can be divided into four groups: MNIST database, proprietary databases, CENPARMI database and NIST-SD19 database.

For performance comparison between different studies it is necessary that a common database be used for all them. In this work the MNIST handwritten digits database is adopted as the common database [12]. This database is suited for training and testing digit recognition algorithms and consists of 60,000 training patterns and 10,000 testing patterns. The patterns were obtained from 250 different authors. One digit is centralized in a gray level figure with 20x20 pixel size. This database presents two advantages: the digits need not be pre-processed and it is extensively used in the literature, enabling a performance comparison between different algorithms.

Consulting the web site of MNIST database, it can be verified that a total of 68 classifiers have been used for digit recognition [12]. The most used are: SVM, MLP and neural networks using convolutional algorithms.

In general, neural classifiers perform better than other classifiers. Convolutional algorithms have the best classifier performance. The best results for the accuracy in the classification step using convolutional algorithms, 99.73%, were obtained by Ciseran et al. [4]. In this study, the authors expanded the training and testing database, including elastic distortions. Deng [13] concluded that the use of distortion to expand the database is necessary to obtain high accuracy in digit classification. Studies that do not use distortion obtained low accuracy rates, varying between 99.47% and 99.65%.

Concerning the MNIST database and Table 1, it should also be noted that classifiers that use a whole image as input characteristics perform better than those that use digit characteristics as input.

Although impressive results for digit recognition using the MNIST database have been reported in the literature, this work focuses on improving state-of-the-art digit recognition, investigating the use of SVM.

In the literature, using SVM, the best results for digit recognition in the MNIST database, an accuracy of 99.44%, was obtained by Decoste and Scholkpf [2]. The authors employed a multiclass SVM classifier associated with the support virtual-vectors technique.

In this work, we intend to use SVM binary classifiers associated with a multiclass binary architecture, the unbalanced decision tree. According to input variables, two classifiers were trained and tested. One of them used digit characteristics and the other used the whole image as input variables.

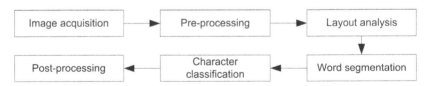

Fig. 1. Block diagram of an optical character recognition system

Table 1. A brief review of digit recognition

Reference	Database	Input data	Classifier	Results (accuracy)
[2]	MNIST Database	Whole image	SVM	99.44%
[3]	MNIST Database	Whole image	Combination of Convolutional Neural Networks	99.73%
[4]	MNIST Database	Whole image	Combination of Convolutional Neural Networks	99.77%
[5]	Proprietary Database	Fourier Descriptors + Border Transition Technique	MLP	96%
[6]	Proprietary Database	Fourier Descriptors	MLP + Models Previously Defined	90%
[7]	MNIST Database	Whole image	Perceptron	99.37%
[8]	Proprietary Database	Whole image	MLP	90%
[9]	Not cited	Hough Transform	MLP + Dempster-Shafer Theory	Not cited
[10]	NIST-SD19 Database	Kirsch Masks and Elliptic Fourier Descriptors	Combination of SVM Classifiers	98.55%
[11]	CENPARMI Database	Directional Distances	Modular Neural Networks	97.30%

2   Methods

2.1   Multiclass Binary Architectures

In both items 2.2 and 2.3, which address, respectively, the use SVM classifiers for digit recognition using digit characteristics and the whole image as input data, unbalanced decision trees, a type of multiclass binary architecture, is employed for digit recognition. So, in this item, we briefly review the different architectures of binary classifiers and, particularly, unbalanced decision trees.

According to Hassan and Demper [14], there are four different multiclass architectures using binary classifiers: one-against-rest, one-against-one, acyclic direct graph - ADG and unbalanced decision tree - UDT. Fig. 2 shows these architectures for a special case of four classes. In each one of these architectures, the output is the selection of only one class.

To distinguish between m classes, the architecture one-against-rest requires the training of m classifiers. Each classifier C_i is trained for recognizing class i. C_i returns a 1 if a given sample belongs to class i and 0 if a given samples does not belong to class i. It is only necessary to train m classifiers. When the training set is highly unbalanced, the performance of this architecture can be seriously affected. For a sample classification, m classifiers are used.

The one-against-one architecture uses the major voting rule. One sample is defined as belonging to class i if there are more votes for this class than for the others. A total of $m(m-1)/2$ binary classifiers are constructed, one for each different class pair. These classifiers are evaluated in parallel. Each classifier C_{ij} is trained using only samples of classes i and j. If a sample x is recognized by classifier C_{ij} as belonging to class i, a vote is assigned to class i. Otherwise, if it is recognized as belonging to class j, a vote is assigned to class j. After the sample is classified by all classifiers, the class that received more votes is considered the one to which the sample belongs. For a sample classification, $m(m-1)/2$ classifiers are used.

A set of binary classifiers can also be structured as an ADG. For this architecture, $m(m-1)/2$ binary classifiers are also necessary. In the architecture shown in Fig. 2, it can be observed that if the output of a classifier C_{ij} is class i, in the following node the class j is no longer considered a possible output class. This is why only $m-1$ classifiers are used for a pattern classification. Differing from the one-against-one architecture, only m-1 classifiers are evaluated to obtain a sample classification.

UDT was proposed by Ramanan et al. [15]. In each node, a decision is made regarding the type one-against-rest. Comparing with the architecture one-against-rest previously presented, this architecture uses only *m-1* classifiers. A sample classification begins in the node located on the top of the tree, using the classifier C_i. If the sample does not belong to class i, the decision process follows with the next right classifier of the tree. The classification process finishes when the sample is recognized as belonging to class n, by classifier C_n. As noted in Fig. 2, the lowest node of the tree decides only between two classes. According to Hassan & Damper [14], UDT follows a knockout strategy that, in the worst case, for a sample classification, requires $m-1$ classifiers. For a sample classification, on average, $(m-1)/2$ classifiers are used. Table 2 summarizes the main information of the four multiclass binary architectures. As shown, the UDT classifiers require a smaller number of classifiers both for training and classification. This is why in this paper we used SVM binary classifiers with a UDT multiclass architecture for digit recognition.

2.2 Digit Recognition Using Multiclass Binary Architecture with SVM Binary Classifiers and Digit Characteristics as Input Data

The block diagram of Fig. 3 shows a block diagram of the pattern recognition system used for digit recognition, using digit characteristics as inputs.

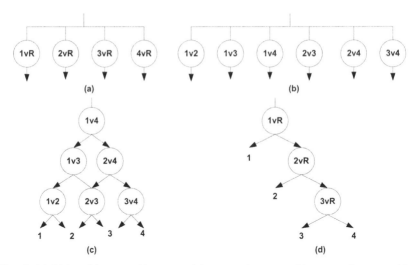

Fig. 2. Multiclass binary architectures: (a) one against rest; (b) one against one, (c) acyclic direct graph, (d) unbalanced decision tree

Table 2. Summary binary classifier architectures

Architecture	Number of classifiers	Classifiers used for a sample classification
one-versus-rest	m	m
one-versus-one	$(m*(m-1))/2$	$(m*(m-1))/2$
acyclic direct graph	$(m*(m-1))/2$	$m-1$
unbalanced decision tree	$m-1$	$(m-1)/2$ *

* Average value

Fig. 3. Block diagram of a digit recognition system using multiclass binary architecture with SVM binary classifiers and digit characteristics as input data

Digit Characteristic Extraction. A set of 28 characteristics was used: twenty parameters corresponding to Fourier descriptors and eight parameters associated with border transition technique.

The twenty Fourier descriptors selected were the low frequency ones. The higher frequencies coefficients were discarded because they have insignificant values.

The border transition technique divides the digit image into four quadrants. For each quadrant, it calculates the transitions of pixel values from 0 to 1. In other words, a summation of the first order gradient in vertical and horizontal directions is done, totaling 8 parameters. In this work this complementary technique was used associated with Fourier descriptors, because the latter is invariant with rotation and displacement, impairing the distinction between ´6´and ´9´.

Characteristic Selection. Not all the 20 Fourier descriptors were used for classification. To select the best Fourier descriptors the scalar characteristic selection was used [16]. This is an "ad-hoc" technique that incorporates correlation information combined with criteria tailored for scalar characteristics. The procedure is divided into three parts. The first part is devoted to selecting only the first characteristic. The second part is devoted to selecting the second characteristic and the third part is used to select the other characteristics. In the first part, a class separability measure is selected and its value is computed for all the available characteristics. These values are ranked in descending order and the characteristic with higher value is chosen. In this paper, for this first part, a Fisher´s Discriminant Ratio (FDR) was used.

According to Theodoridis and Koutroumbas [16], FDR is sometimes used to quantify the separability capabilities of individual characteristics in a two-class problem, as is the case in this paper (pixels belong to bacillus or to background). FDR is defined as:

$$FDR = \frac{(\mu_1 - \mu_2)}{\sigma_1^2 + \sigma_2^2}$$
(1)

Where μ_1 and σ_{12} represent the mean value and standard deviation, respectively, of a characteristic in class ω_1; μ_2 and σ_{22} represent the mean value and standard deviation, respectively, of the same characteristic in class ω_2.

In the second and third parts, two other separability class measures are used: the divergence separability measure and the cross-correlation coefficient. The divergence measure between two classes ω_i and ω_j, for a given characteristic with mean value and standard deviation μ_i and σ_{i2} and μ_j and σ_{j2}, respectively, is defined as:

$$d_{ij} = \frac{1}{2}\left(\frac{\sigma_j^2}{\sigma_i^2} + \frac{\sigma_i^2}{\sigma_j^2} - 2\right) + \frac{1}{2}(\mu_i - \mu_j)^2\left(\frac{1}{\sigma_i^2} + \frac{1}{\sigma_j^2}\right)$$
(2)

To define the cross-correlation coefficient between two characteristics, let x_{nk}, $n = 1, 2, \ldots N$ and $k = 1, 2, \ldots m$, be the kth characteristic of the nth pattern. The cross-correlation coefficient between any two characteristics is defined as [11]:

$$\rho_{ij} = \frac{\sum_{n=1}^{N} x_{ni} x_{nj}}{\sqrt{\sum_{n=1}^{N} x_{ni}^2 \sum_{n=1}^{N} x_{nj}^2}}$$
(3)

The second part selects x_{i_2} which

$$i_2 = \arg \max_j \{\alpha_1 \min_{i,j} d_{ij} - \alpha_2 \mid \rho_{i_1 j} \mid\}, \text{ for all } j \neq i$$
(4)

where α_1 and α_2 are weighting factors that determine the relative importance given to the two terms inside the brackets.

The third part selects x_{i_k}, k=3,...l, which

$$i_k = \arg\max_j \left\{ \alpha_1 \min_{i,j} d_{ij} - \frac{\alpha_2}{k-1} \sum_{r=1}^{k-1} |\rho_{i_r j}| \right\} \tag{5}$$

With this technique, sets with the best 18, 17, 16, 15, 14, 13, 12 ,11, 10 and 9 Fourier descriptors were selected.

SVM Classifiers. Support vector machines (SVM) can be defined as binary learning machines used to separate data belonging to two classes using a hyperplane that maximizes the separation margin [17].

According to Theodoridis and Koutroumbas [16], for separable classes, the parameters of the hyperplane that maximize the margin are calculated through the determination of weight vector w and polarization w0, such that expression (6) is minimized and the Karush-Kuhn-Tucker (KKT) conditions are satisfied.

$$J(\mathbf{w}) \equiv \frac{1}{2} \| \mathbf{w} \|^2 \tag{6}$$

For nonseparable classes, the same parameters can be calculated minimizing expression (7), where new variables ξi, known as slack variables, are introduced. The goal now is to make the margin as large as possible but at the same time to keep the number of points with ξ > 0 as small as possible [16].

$$J(\mathbf{w}, w_0, \xi) = \frac{1}{2} \| \mathbf{w} \|^2 + C \sum_{i=1}^{N} \xi_i \tag{7}$$

Parameter C in expression (7) is a constant positive that controls the tradeoff between the slack variable penalty and the margin. The value of the C parameter used in this work was 0.5.

SVMs use kernels to map the characteristic vector into a high dimensional space to exploit the nonlinear power of this tool. In this work, radial base function kernels were used, as shown in expression (8).

$$\exp(-\gamma \| \mathbf{x} - \mathbf{z} \|^2)^d, \gamma > 0 \tag{8}$$

3   Results

For SVM binary classifiers with an UDT architecture and digit characteristics as input data, the best results were obtained using the set of the best nine Fourier descriptors selected with the scalar selection technique, with the eight parameters obtained with a border transition technique, totaling 16 input variables for the SVM classifier. The nine best Fourier descriptors were the ones corresponding to the nine lower frequencies. For pattern classification, nine SVM binary classifiers were used with a UDT architecture, as shown in Fig. 4. Fig. 5 shows the confusion matrix obtained with the ORL test set. With the ORL training set, the accuracy was 85.27%. Table 3 shows the accuracy obtained for the ten digit classification.

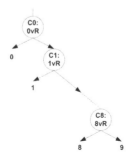

Fig. 4. UDT architecture used with SVM classifiers $C_0, C_1 ... C_8$

```
>>    ConfusionMatrix

ConfusionMatrix =

739     0     7     1     8     0    21     8    14     2
  2   747    15     0     6     2     9     3     8     8
  8     0   685    18    17     4    44     8     7     9
  5     0    75   665     2     7    11    10    17     8
 12     5    19     0   692     3    10     6    10    43
  3     2    27    11     8   669    34     7    22    17
 12    12    18     5    11    20   694     4    16     8
  4     7    29    10    12     2     8   698    13    17
 31    10    28    20    17     8    36     8   585    57
  4    11    18    10    44     7     4    22    42   638
```

Fig. 5. Confusion matrix for multiclass binary architecture with SVM binary classifiers and digit characteristics as input data

For digit recognition using multiclass binary architecture with SVM binary classifiers and the whole image as input data, the number of inputs of each SVM classifier used in the UDT architecture (shown if Fig. 4) was 400, which corresponds to the pixels of an image with 20x20 pixels. Fig. 6 shows the confusion matrix obtained with the ORL test set. As shown in Fig. 6 no classification error occurred. So the obtained accuracy with the ORL test set was 100%. With the ORL training set, the accuracy was also 100%.

For SVM binary classifiers with an UDT architecture and digit characteristics as input data, the training time was 25h, while the answer time is about 1s. For SVM binary classifiers with an UDT architecture and the whole image as input data, the training time was 6h, while the answer time is less than 1s.

Table 3. Accuracy obtained for digit recognition using multiclass binary architecture with SVM binary classifiers and digit characteristics as input data

Digit	Accuracy	
	Training	Test
0	97.43%	93.50%
1	98.62%	96.56%
2	90.31%	85.31%
3	90.25%	91.44%
4	93.97%	90.50%
5	96.59%	93.87%
6	93.63%	91.63%
7	96.49%	92.94%
8	89.75%	89.56%
9	94.42%	90,28%
Mean Value	93.85%	91.56%

```
>>> modular_classifier.getConfusionMatrix(mnist_experiments.MnistData.TestingData)
array([[ 980,    0,    0,    0,    0,    0,    0,    0,    0,    0],
       [   0, 1135,    0,    0,    0,    0,    0,    0,    0,    0],
       [   0,    0, 1032,    0,    0,    0,    0,    0,    0,    0],
       [   0,    0,    0, 1010,    0,    0,    0,    0,    0,    0],
       [   0,    0,    0,    0,  982,    0,    0,    0,    0,    0],
       [   0,    0,    0,    0,    0,  892,    0,    0,    0,    0],
       [   0,    0,    0,    0,    0,    0,  958,    0,    0,    0],
       [   0,    0,    0,    0,    0,    0,    0, 1028,    0,    0],
       [   0,    0,    0,    0,    0,    0,    0,    0,  974,    0],
       [   0,    0,    0,    0,    0,    0,    0,    0,    0, 1009]])
```

Fig. 6. Confusion matrix for multiclass binary architecture with SVM binary classifiers and the whole image as input data (400 pixel values as input data)

4   Conclusion

Developed recently, UDT architecture provides a simple structure for a multiclass classifier using binary classifiers. In this work, the association of SVM binary classifiers with a UDT architecture, using the whole image as input, makes it possible to obtain an accuracy of 100% with handwritten digit recognition, using the MNIST database. This is the best recognition rate found in the literature for the MNIST database. As stated earlier, before this work, the best results for the accuracy in MNIST database was obtained by Ciseran et al. [4], 99.73%, using neural networks with convolutional algorithms.

The large number of support vectors used is a drawback of this approach. These vectors must be available at classification time, requiring nearly 1GB of memory.

The UDT architecture can be explored using any type of binary classifier, such as MLP and neural networks using convolutional algorithms, etc.

Acknowledgments. We thank AcademicEnglishSolutions.com for revising the English.

References

1. Cheriet, M., Kharma, N., Liu, C.L., Suen, C.: Character Recognition Systems. Wiley, New Jersey (2007)
2. Decoste, D., Schölkopf, B.: Training Invariant Support Vector Machines. Kluwer Academic Publishers, The Netherlands (2002)
3. Ciresan, D.C., Meier, U., Gambardella, L.M., Schmidhuber, J.: Convolutional Neural Network Committees for Handwritten Character Classification. In: International Conference on Document Analysis and Recognition (ICDAR), pp. 1135–1139 (2011)
4. Ciresan, D., Meier, U., Schmidhuber, J.: Multi-column Deep Neural Networks for Image Classification. Dalle Molle Institute for Artificial Intelligence. IDSIA/USI-SUPSI, Manno, Switzerland (2012)
5. Chung, Y.Y., Wong, M.T.: Handwritten character recognition by Fourier descriptors and neural network. In: IEEE Region 10 Annual Conference on Speech and Image Technologies for Computing and Telecommunications, vol. 1, pp. 391–394 (2007)
6. Poon, J.C., Man, G.M.: An enhanced approach to character recognition by Fourier descriptor. In: ICCS/ISITA 1992, vol. 2, pp. 558–562 (1992)
7. Kussul, E., Baidyk, T.: Improved method of handwritten digit recognition tested on MNIST database. In: 15th International Conference on Vision Interface, vol. 22, pp. 971–981 (2004)
8. Masmoudi, M., Samet, M., Taktak, F., Alimi, A.M.: A hardware implementation of neural network for the recognition of printed numerals. In: The Eleventh International Conference on Microelectronics, pp. 113–116 (1999)
9. Mandalia, A.D., Pandya, A.S., Sudhakar, R.: A hybrid approach to recognize handwritten alphanumeric characters. In: International Conference on System, Man and Cybernetics, vol. 1, pp. 723–726 (1992)
10. Travieso, C.M., Alonso, J., Ferrer, M.A.: Combining different off-line handwritten character recognizers. In: 15th International Conference on Intelligent Engineering Systems, Propad, pp. 315–318 (2011)
11. Oh, I.-S., Suen, C.Y.: A class-modular feedforward neural network for handwriting recognition. Pattern Recognition 35(1), 229–244 (2002)
12. LeCun, Y., Cortes, C., Burges, C.J.: The MNIST database of Handwritten Digits, http://yann.lecun.com/exdb/mnist/ (accessed in January 02, 2014)
13. Deng, L.: The MNIST Database of Handwritten Digit Images for Machine Learning Research. IEEE Signal Processing Magazine, 141–142 (2012)
14. Hassan, A., Damper, R.I.: Classification of emotional speech using 3DEC hierarchical classifier. Speech Communication 54, 903–916 (2012)
15. Ramanan, A., Suppharangsan, S., Niranjan, M.: Unbalanced Decision Trees for Multiclass Classification. In: International Conference on Industrial and Information Systems, Sri Lanka, pp. 291–294 (2007)
16. Theodoridis, S., Koutroumbas, K.: Pattern Recognition. Elsevier Academic Press, San Diego (2006)

A Visual-Based Driver Distraction Recognition and Detection Using Random Forest

Amira Ragab[✉], Celine Craye, Mohamed S. Kamel, and Fakhri Karray

Center for Pattern Analysis and Machine Intelligence Electrical and Computer
Engineering Department, University of Waterloo, 200 University Avenue,
Waterloo, ON N2L 3G1, Canada
{amira.ragab,ccraye,mkamel,karray}@uwaterloo.ca

Abstract. Driver distraction and fatigue are considered the main cause
of most car accidents today. This paper compares the performance of
Random Forest and a number of other well-known classifiers for driver
distraction detection and recognition problems. A non-intrusive system,
which consists of hardware components for capturing the driver's driving
sessions on a car simulator, using infrared and Kinect cameras, combined
with a software component for monitoring some visual behaviors that
reflect a driver's level of distraction, was used in this work.

In this system, five visual cues were calculated: arm position, eye
closure, eye gaze, facial expressions, and orientation. These cues were
then fed into a classifier, such as AdaBoost, Hidden Markov Models,
Random Forest, Support Vector Machine, Conditional Random Field, or
Neural Network, in order to detect and recognize the type of distraction.
The use of various cues resulted in a more robust and accurate detection
and classification of distraction, than using only one. The system was
tested with various sequences recorded from different users. Experimental
results were very promising, and show the superiority of the Random
Forest classifier compared to the other classifiers.

1 Introduction

Many efforts have been made recently to ensure the driver safety and to decrease
car accidents. According to [12], around 80% to 90% of accidents involving fatali-
ties or injuries are mainly related to the driver's absence of alertness. Specifically,
the driver's alertness is affected by distraction and fatigue. In order to detect
whether the driver is distracted or fatigued, many car manufacturing companies
have started to embed audio-visual sensors in intelligent vehicle systems. These
sensors are either intrusive or non-intrusive, and the non-intrusive systems are
much more appealing to drivers for their naturalness.

This paper studies the classification performance of various well-known classifiers in a non-intrusive computer vision system for monitoring drivers distraction.
This system started by capturing the driver sessions while driving a car simulator, followed by a feature extraction module, which consisted of five sub-modules:

© Springer International Publishing Switzerland 2014
A. Campilho and M. Kamel (Eds.): ICIAR 2014, Part I, LNCS 8814, pp. 256–265, 2014.
DOI: 10.1007/978-3-319-11758-4_28

analyzing eye gaze and closure, arm position, facial expressions, and facial orientation. Finally, the extracted features were merged together and classified using a number of well-known classifiers, such as AdaBoost, Hidden Markov Models, Random Forest, Support Vector Machine, Conditional Random Field, and Neural Network. Experimental results from six subjects were promising for both detection and recognition problems (82.9% accuracy for the type of distraction and 90% for distraction detection).

The rest of the paper is organized as follows: Section 2 discusses related work, then the system used is described in Section 3. Section 4 depicts the experiments and results. Conclusions and future work are presented in Section 5.

2   Related Work

Typically, the main causes of driver inattention are distraction and fatigue. However, according to the study in [7], the main contributor for 10% to 25% of vehicle accidents is distraction, which is our main focus in this work. According to [1], distraction can be classified into three main categories:

- Visual: The driver takes his eyes off the road for some reason, such as reading or watching a video.
- Manual: The driver takes his hands off the wheel for some reason, such as text messaging, eating, using a navigation system, or adjusting the radio.
- Cognitive: The driver's mind is taken away from driving. This can happen when talking on the phone, text messaging, or simply thinking.

Generally, systems for detecting driver distraction are non-intrusive (i.e., do not require attaching cumbersome devices to the driver). These systems detect distraction based on driver's behavior using camera(s), driving or car behavior using sensors that measure steering, braking, lane keeping, etc. or both.

A wide range of sensors and classifiers have been utilized in the literature for capturing and detecting driver distraction. In [6], Neural Network, with a back propagation algorithm and 80 nodes in the hidden layer, was used to detect distraction using eye closure only. Murphy-Chutorian et al. [9] used Support Vector Machine with Localized Gradient Orientation histograms to estimate the orientation of the driver's head. Earlier in [11], driver visual attention was modeled with three independent Finite State Machines, in order to monitor both eye and head movements.

Recently, Butakov et al. [4] suggested using a Gaussian Mixture Model to analyze the driver or vehicle response in the vehicle following case to create a normal behavior model, which can then be used to detect distraction if the driving behavior deviates from the saved model. In [13], two subsets of features were extracted. The first one included accelerator pedal position and steering wheel position, while the second subset included both of these elements, as well as the Collision Avoidance Systems (CAS) sensors (lane boundaries and upcoming road curvatures). This data was then classified using Random forest (with 75 trees). The results revealed that adding the CAS sensors features increased the accuracy considerably. However, depending only on driving behavior can be misleading, as it can be affected by external factors such as driver experience, road type, weather, and outdoor lighting.

A more promising way for modeling driver distraction is to combine information from both the driver and driving behaviors. Liang et al. [8] extracted the driver's eye movements as well as driving performance data, such as lane position, steering wheel angle, and steering error calculated from steering wheel angle, to capture distraction. This data was then classified using Support Vector Machine. A distraction detection system which infers visual driver information about head position, head pose, and eye pose, as well as car information using a lane-keeping module, was presented in [10]. No training was included in this system, however.

Almost none of the works in the literature have aimed to detect the type of distraction created by the driver, and have instead focused only on recognizing whether the driver is distracted or not. Determining the type of driver distraction provides higher level information which can be used for a number of applications related to intelligent transportation systems. The applications can be implemented in smart cars to provide statistics on the driver's behavior, which could increase the help the vehicle can provide to keep the driver safe.

3   Methodology

The non-intrusive system used in this study consisted mainly of three phases: (1) the data acquisition phase, during which the driving sessions were recorded, (2) the feature extraction phase, during which certain features that reflect distraction were extracted, and (3) the classification phase, during which a classification model was learned using the extracted features.

3.1   Data Acquisition

In this phase, the driving sessions from six drivers of different ethnic backgrounds, genders, ages, and with or without glasses, were recorded. Driving sessions were captured using infrared (IR) and Kinect cameras mounted in front of the driver while he or she drove a car simulator. Each driver was first introduced to the car driving simulator, during which time they were asked to drive for a few minutes in order to familiarize themselves with the simulator. Then, during the driving sessions, instructions for each of the different actions were displayed on the screen. Four driving sessions were recorded for each subject. Each session lasted for around ten minutes. The actions involved in the experiments were a phone call, a text message, drinking, object distraction, and normal driving. For each driver, normal driving represented around 40% to 50% of each sequence, while the remaining were distraction actions. Each of the distraction actions represented between 10% to 20% of the each sequence. An image of the driving simulator is shown in Fig.1.

Fig. 1. Driving simulator used in the experiments

3.2   Feature Extraction

The feature extraction module consisted of five main sub-modules:

- **Arm Position.** After segmenting the body from the background by combining the output from the Kinect segmentation with the output from the background removal, the arm position was represented using the segmented depth map acquired using Kinect. Since Kinect records drivers with a frontal view, their right arm is therefore on the right side of their body. Based on this, the features were extracted based on foreground contours. First, the marching squares algorithm was applied to the binary foreground image, which outputs an ordered list of contour pixels. Then, the left section of the contour was removed (since the right arm was the one used for the distraction actions). The remaining "half" contour was then divided into twenty successive segments. Using the depth map, each pixel of the contour was associated with a 3D point, such that each segment of the contour corresponded with a 3D point cloud. For each point cloud, a principal component analysis was applied, and the eigenvector of the main principal component was kept.
  However, using only the right contour from the frontal view was not enough, as some actions, such as texting, cannot be detected from the frontal view. In order to overcome this problem, the aforementioned approach was applied to the profile view as well, resulting in a 120 feature vector. This vector was then fed into a 1-vs-all AdaBoost to create a model which was used to classify the rest of the data. The output of the classifier was a feature vector of size 4, which represented the estimated position among four possible states: arm up, arm down, arm right, and arm forward, as depicted in Fig.2.
- **Facial Orientation.** First, the face was extracted using the face tracking algorithm provided by Kinect SDK [2]. Then, based on the coordinates of the face 3D vertices, the face tracking provided a feature vector of size 3, which represented the head orientation angles, namely the pitch, roll, and yaw angles, whose values were between -180 and 180 degrees.

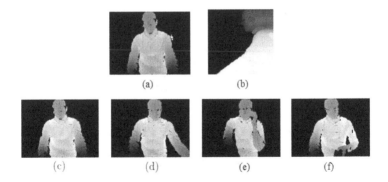

Fig. 2. An example of (a) frontal view and its (b) associated profile view, as well as their forward, right, up and down arm positions and associated features in (c)-(f) respectively. In (c)-(f) the red dots represent projections of a point clouds' local orientations from the frontal view, while blue dots are from the profile view.

- **Facial Expressions.** The face tracking algorithm provided by Kinect SDK was also used to provide four animation units (AUs). AUs were expressed as coefficients, and represented how strongly distorted features of the face were. The four AUs extracted were the ones related to the mouth only, such as upper lip raiser (AU10), jaw lowerer (AU26/27), lip stretcher (AU20), and lip corner depressor (AU13/15).
- **Eye Gaze.** First, the eye position was extracted using the SDK face tracking algorithm. Then, an efficient iris detection method based on cost function maximization and spatio-temporal considerations was applied. The cost function was the result of two main filters: circular Hough transform and circular Gabor filter. The cost function was also inspired by the filter introduced by [8], and depends on the high intensity difference between the iris and its neighborhood. Finally, the iris center was estimated as the summation of the three normalized filter responses. Then, an approximate gaze estimation was carried out by calculating the position of the iris relative to the eyes' corners. The output of this module was a feature vector of size 4.
- **Eye Closure.** In order to determine whether the eye was opened or closed, a database of opened and closed eyes was constructed. In turn, this database constructed an SVM model with Radial Basis Function (RBF) kernel, which was used afterward to classify the data. The output of this module was the decision for each eye: open(1), closed(0), or something else(-1).

3.3   Classification

Both sequential and non-sequential classifiers were deployed in this work. The non-sequential classifiers used were the Support Vector Machine (SVM), the Random Forest (RF) and the AdaBoost (Adaptive Boosting). The strength of the SVM mainly depends on the selection of the kernel, as well as its parameters.

In this work, the best value for C was selected by searching with the exponentially growing sequences of C, e.g., $C\epsilon\{10^{-2}, 5^{-1}, ..., 5^3, 10^2\}$. A C-SVM was deployed for its efficiency, and after experiments with the different kernels, the Radial Basis Function kernel was chosen for producing the best results. Random Forest is an ensemble of many decision trees, and its strength relies on combining diverse classifiers. In this work, several values for the number of trees were experimented and the size 75 was chosen. Whereas the number of features used to train each tree was set to $\sqrt{M}$ (where M is the total number of features), as proposed by Breiman [3]. For the Adaboost, a simple real 1-vs-all AdaBoost initialized with a decision tree of depth four and 300 iterations, was used.

Sequential classifiers which predict sequences of labels for sequences of input samples, such as Hidden Markov Model (HMM), Conditional Random Field (CRF) and Neural Networks (NNs) were also experimented with. For the HMM, a different Markov model was trained for each class, and the Viterbi algorithm was used to decide which state each sample belongs to. The best value for the number of hidden states is chosen experimentally. For the CRF, the CRF++ library [1] was utilized in this work. Since this library does not handle continuous features, the features were quantized using a simple quantization method. Finally, the nonlinear property of the NNs allows them to solve some complex problems more accurately than linear methods. Recurrent NNs, with Levenberg-Marquardt training function and hidden layer of size 10 neurons, were chosen in this work, since they have proved their superiority to feedforward networks in modeling time series data with lower errors [5]. However, Recurrent NNs are not suitable for large datasets, so we had to randomly sample the dataset to reduce its size.

4   Experiments and Results

As explained earlier, data was collected from sessions recorded for six subjects. The features from the five different aforementioned sub-modules were combined to form a feature vector of length 17 (i.e. 4 + 3 + 4 + 4 +2). Then, a median filter with a sliding window of size 100 was used to temporarily smooth this feature vector. Also, the standard deviation within the hundred-sample window was computed. The resulting feature vector of length 34 is then classified.

Due to the randomness of the RF and the random sampling used in the NN, the experiments involving the RF and NN were repeated for 5 runs. Then the accuracy average of the runs, as well as the standard deviation, were calculated. Both classification recognition (five classes) and detection (two classes) were computed. The performance measures used to evaluate the system and compare between the different classifiers were accuracy, specificity, precision, recall, f-measure, g-means, and prediction time/sample in msec.

---

[1] The used library is available at http://crfpp.googlecode.com/svn/trunk/doc/index.html

4.1 Driver Distraction Recognition

Driver distraction was recognized using AdaBoost, RF, CRF, HMM and Recurrent NN classifiers. The evaluation protocol was leave-one-subject-out, wherein each classifier was trained using all sessions except that of the driver to be evaluated, and tested using all sessions involving this driver. A comparison between the performance of the different classifiers for the distraction recognition problem per subject is shown in Table 1. The first six rows show the accuracy for each of the six subjects, while the next rows show the overall performance.

Table 1. A per subject comparison between the different classifiers for the distraction recognition problem

	CRF	HMM	AdaBoost	RF	NN
1	68.53	75.98	90.38	88.36±1.59	48.23±14.59
2	73.07	89.29	89.16	89.23±0.13	73.61±2.96
3	66.08	86.6	82.21	81.17±1.03	68.57±3.77
4	70.68	81.41	82.75	76.09±1.55	72.94±8.78
5	73.49	81.78	79.67	81.92±0.94	74.69±2.36
6	53.55	62.01	73.64	78.81±0.87	72.26±2.32
Accuracy	67.57	79.5	**82.97**	**82.78±0.07**	68.38±3.02
Specificity	71.97	84.62	87.26	86.81±0.16	71.61±2.49
Precision	37.47	37.47	43.54	42.26±0.43	19.38±4.62
Recall	59.13	68.34	72.81	71.59±1.25	50.49±11.68
F_measure	32.21	48.4	54.49	53.15±0.65	28±6.54
G-means	65.22	76.04	79.71	78.83±0.67	59.85±7.57
Prediction Time	0.6	0.03	0.6	0.05	0.03

The classifiers' performance for each subject varied significantly. However, the RF was very close to the AdaBoost in producing the highest overall accuracy, besides being computationally efficient. On the other hand, the CRF and NN proved to be inappropriate for this task, producing the worst performance.

Another test was performed to provide more insight into how well each class was recognized. Table 2 provides a few classification metrics for each class, based on the average of the driver's performance. It is clear from the results that actions such as *phone call* and *normal driving* were successfully recognized. The low results for *drinking* were produced due to two main reasons. First, the action was sometimes very fast (the driver held the cup for few moments before putting it away). Second, there was a large variance between the different subjects, in performing this action. The worst performance was for *object distraction*, probably because this action required neither huge visual nor cognitive attention. It was often misclassified as *normal driving* or *text messaging*, which made it harder to be recognized. Fortunately, *object distraction* and *drinking* were the least dangerous among the distraction actions, making the misclassification in these cases less critical.

Fig.3 displays a frame-by-frame classification for a given sequence. The blue lines represent the ground truth, while the red lines represent the estimated classes. In this example, *phone call* and *text message* were almost accurately detected, *drinking* produced some false positives, and *object distraction* was often considered *text message*.

Table 2. A per class comparison between the different classifiers for the distraction recognition problem

Action		CRF	HMM	AdaBoost	RF	NN
Phone Call	precision	63.96	81.04	90.98	81.44±1.88	70.52±6.95
	recall	64.02	68.34	72.81	72.22±1.19	50.49±11.68
	f-measure	63.99	74.15	80.89	76.53±0.64	58.52±9.8
Text Message	precision	61.55	79.08	79.52	75.94±0.76	40.16±6.61
	recall	40.94	74.96	76.05	79.31±1.4	39.64±7.46
	f-measure	49.17	76.96	77.74	77.58±1.01	39.81±6.75
Drinking	precision	4.39	47.21	68.21	67.94±1.58	21.94±4.39
	recall	1.6	91.89	68.67	79±1.84	40.1±5.95
	f-measure	2.35	62.37	68.44	73.04±1.22	28.25±4.89
Object Distraction	precision	17.94	54.42	58.24	53.34±4.06	23.23±5.05
	recall	6.6	21.89	27.4	27.86±2.11	27.72±5.41
	f-measure	9.65	31.22	37.27	36.56±2.4	25.22±5.08
Normal Driving	precision	90.12	90.62	88.32	90.32±0.25	94.01±0.82
	recall	88.4	92.76	97.54	95.41±0.5	84±3.49
	f-measure	89.25	91.67	92.7	92.79±0.33	88.69±1.73

4.2 Driver Distraction Detection

The distraction detection was also classified using the aforementioned classifiers, in addition to the SVM. The evaluation protocol is leave-one-subject-out also. In this case, all the distraction classes were merged into a single class and compared to the normal driving class. A comparison between the performance of the different classifiers for the distraction detection problem per subject is depicted in Table 3. The first six rows show the accuracy for each of the six subjects, while the next rows show the overall performance. The results show the superiority of the RF to the other classifiers in producing the best overall accuracy in a reasonable time. It can also be deduced that decreasing the number of classes enhances the performance of classifiers such as CRF and NN significantly, as for this task, they produce results much closer to the other classifiers.

5 Conclusions and Future Work

A comparison between the performance of Random Forest and other well-known classifiers was investigated for evaluating a visual-based distraction detection and recognition system. The system was based on five modules for extracting

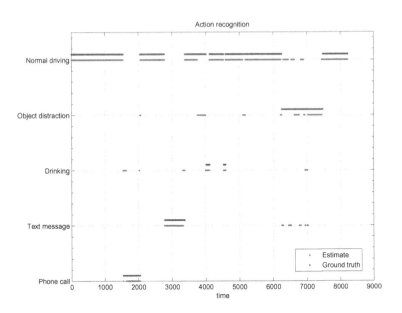

Fig. 3. Results of action recognition for a given sequence using RF. Ground truth (red) and estimated actions (blue) are displayed for each frame (x-axis).

Table 3. A per subject comparison between the different classifiers for the distraction detection problem

	CRF	HMM	AdaBoost	RF	SVM	NN
1	84.46	82.32	89.81	89.69±0.16	87.47	86.07±1.58
2	82.48	93.46	92.22	92.39±0.72	90.1	87.6±1.22
3	84.24	93.72	93.39	92.25±0.2	89.15	88.49±1.37
4	72.97	88	87.8	90.08±0.85	91.63	87.25±2.93
5	82.53	89.13	87.37	87.3±0.43	89.85	90.66±0.73
6	80.99	82.26	82.84	88.35±3.46	83.09	89.84±5.9
Average	82.55	88.15	88.9	**90.47±0.28**	88.54	88.32±1.65
Specificity	86.95	87.38	94.28	94±0.38	93.51	94.07±1.22
Precision	74.95	79.59	88.39	88.7±0.64	86.39	87.38±2.34
Recall	74.18	93.53	82.66	85.12±0.27	78.28	77.83±1.31
F_measure	74.56	86	85.43	86.87±0.21	82.14	82.32±1.55
G-means	80.31	90.4	88.28	89.58±0.1	85.56	85.56±1.08
Prediction Time	0.63	0.04	0.13	0.08	0.01	0.014

data: arm position, face orientation, facial expression, eye gaze, and eye closure. A real dataset was collected from six subjects using IR and Kinect cameras, while the subjects drove a simulator and performed different distraction actions. The classifiers employed included AdaBoost, HMM, RF, SVM, CRF, and NN, and the results for detecting and recognizing the drivers distraction show the superiority of the RF for the two tasks in real-time.

This work can be extended by increasing the dataset, adding more subjects to create a more generalized system and more reliable results. Another extension would be increasing the number of sensors, such as ones that measure the pressure on the steering wheel.

References

1. Distracted driving, http://www.cdc.gov/Motorvehiclesafety/Distracted_Driving/index.html
2. Microsoft kinect face tracking, http://msdn.microsoft.com/en-us/library/jj130970.aspx
3. Breiman, L.: Random forests. Machine Learning **45**(1), 5–32 (2001)
4. Butakov, V., Ioannou, P., Tippelhofer, M., Camhi, J.: Driver/vehicle response diagnostic system for vehicle following based on gaussian mixture model. In: 2012 IEEE 51st Annual Conference on Decision and Control (CDC), pp. 5649–5654. IEEE (2012)
5. Connor, J.T., Martin, R.D., Atlas, L.E.: Recurrent neural networks and robust time series prediction. IEEE Transactions on Neural Networks **5**(2), 240–254 (1994)
6. D'Orazio, T., Leo, M., Guaragnella, C., Distante, A.: A visual approach for driver inattention detection. Pattern Recognition **40**(8), 2341–2355 (2007)
7. Holahan, C.J.: Relationship between roadside signs and traffic accidents: A field investigation, Research Report 54. Council for Advanced Transportation Studies, Austin, TX (1977)
8. Liang, Y., Reyes, M.L., Lee, J.D.: Real-time detection of driver cognitive distraction using support vector machines. IEEE Transactions on Intelligent Transportation Systems **8**(2), 340–350 (2007)
9. Murphy-Chutorian, E., Doshi, A., Trivedi, M.M.: Head pose estimation for driver assistance systems: A robust algorithm and experimental evaluation. In: IEEE Intelligent Transportation Systems Conference, ITSC 2007, pp. 709–714. IEEE (2007)
10. Pohl, J., Birk, W., Westervall, L.: A driver-distraction-based lane-keeping assistance system. Proceedings of the Institution of Mechanical Engineers, Part I: Journal of Systems and Control Engineering **221**(4), 541–552 (2007)
11. Smith, P., Shah, M., da Vitoria Lobo, N.: Determining driver visual attention with one camera. IEEE Transactions on Intelligent Transportation Systems **4**(4), 205–218 (2003)
12. Stanton, N.A., Salmon, P.M.: Human error taxonomies applied to driving: A generic driver error taxonomy and its implications for intelligent transport systems. Safety Science **47**(2), 227–237 (2009)
13. Torkkola, K., Massey, N., Wood, C.: Driver inattention detection through intelligent analysis of readily available sensors. In: Proceedings of the The 7th International IEEE Conference on Intelligent Transportation Systems, pp. 326–331. IEEE (2004)

Improving Representation of the Positive Class in Imbalanced Multiple-Instance Learning

Carlos Mera[1]([⊠]), Mauricio Orozco-Alzate[2], and John Branch[1]

[1] Universidad Nacional de Colombia, Sede Medellín, Medellín, Colombia
[2] Universidad Nacional de Colombia, Sede Manizales, Manizales, Colombia
{camerab,morozcoa,jwbranch}@unal.edu.co

Abstract. In standard supervised learning, the problem of learning from imbalanced data has been addressed to improve the performance of learning algorithms in the presence of underrepresented data. However, in Multiple-Instance Learning (MIL), where the imbalance problem is more complex, there is little discussion about it. Motivated by the need of further studies, we discuss the multiple-instance imbalance problem and propose a method to improve the representation of the positive class. Our approach looks for the target concept in positive bags and tries to strength it using an oversampling technique while removes the borderline (ambiguous) instances in positive and negative bags. We evaluate our method on several standard MIL benchmarking data sets in order to show its ability to get an enhanced representation of the positive class.

Keywords: Multiple-instance learning · Class imbalance learning · Oversampling · Undersampling

1 Introduction

Multiple-instance learning (MIL) is a relatively new learning paradigm that was firstly introduced by Dietterich et al. [1]. In MIL, a single example (a bag) is represented by multiple feature vectors (instances) which very often correspond to the characterization of segments in images; e.g. multiple objects in the same scene such as trees, a mountain, the sky, sand and the sea [2]. Each bag in the training set has an associated class label, but labels of individual instances are unknown. By the standard multiple-instance assumption, a bag is labeled positive if at least one of its instances is positive; otherwise, the bag is labeled negative. It means that not all instances in a positive bag are necessarily relevant and, consequently, it may contain negative instances causing ambiguity inside the bag. Some of the existing MIL frameworks, which are briefly summarized in the subsequent paragraph, require that all positive instances are grouped in a compact cluster in the feature space.

The early work in MIL is axis-parallel concept [1], whose basic idea is to find an Axis-Parallel Rectangle (APR) in the feature space to represent the target

© Springer International Publishing Switzerland 2014
A. Campilho and M. Kamel (Eds.): ICIAR 2014, Part I, LNCS 8814, pp. 266–273, 2014.
DOI: 10.1007/978-3-319-11758-4_29

concept. In [3], a MIL framework, named Diversity Density (DD), was proposed. It aims to find the most positive point in the input space with the maximum diversity density. A few years later, Zhang & Goldman proposed the EM-DD algorithm [4], which combined the Expectation Maximization (EM) approach with the DD algorithm to speed up the optimization process of the later. In [5], Wang & Zuker put forward the Citation-kNN algorithm which adapts the k-NN algorithm for MIL problems. Andrews et al. [6] proposed two methods based on Support Vector Machines (SVM): mi-SVM for instance-level classification and MI-SVM for bag-level classification. A different approach is followed by Gärtner et al. in [7] where the statistics of the bags are used to construct a MIL kernel and, then, a standard SVM is applied. Another approach is followed by MILES [8] and MILIS [9] which embed each bag into a feature space, based on a representative set of instances selected from the training bags and, afterwards, learn a classifier in this feature space. Some boosting approaches for MIL have been developed, like MIL-Boost proposed [10] which uses the gradient boosting framework to train a boosting MIL classifier.

Several methods have been proposed to tackle the problem of class imbalance learning in single-instance data [11]. However, in MIL, most of the existing methods do not directly consider the problem of imbalanced data sets, which decreases the performance typically achievable by most MIL algorithms. Based on it, we discuss the multiple-instance imbalance problem and propose a method to improve the prediction of the positive class. Our method uses density estimation of the negative population to find the most positive and the most negative instances on positive bags. They are used to oversample positive instances in positive bags and undersample negative instances in the borderline of both, positive and negative bags. The method, therefore, makes sense particularly for cases when there are few positive examples as well as a number of ambiguous negative ones.

The structure of this paper is as follows: Section 2 presents and discusses the problem of multiple-instance imbalanced data sets and its related work on MIL. In Section 3, the proposed method is described. Section 4 reports and discusses the experiments. Finally, Section 5 presents the conclusion and future work.

2   The Class Imbalance Problem in MIL

In standard supervised learning, a data set that exhibits significant and unequal distributions between its classes is considered imbalanced [11]. However, in MIL, the problem of imbalanced data sets is more complex because the imbalance can occur at both levels: instances and bags [12,13], see Fig. 1.

Amores [2] has pointed out that there are three different paradigms for MIL. The first one, named Instance-Space (IS) paradigm, in which the discriminative learning process occurs at the instance-level; the second one, the Bag-Space (BS) paradigm, where each bag is treated has a whole entity, and the learning process discriminates between entire bags; and finally, the Embedded-Space (ES) paradigm, where each bag is mapped to a single feature vector that summarizes

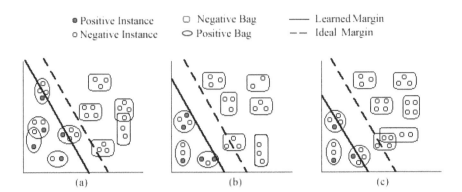

Fig. 1. The imbalance multiple-instance problem at: (a) instance-level, (b) bag-level and (c) both, instance- and bag-level [13]

the relevant information about the whole bag, so a classifier is learned in the new embedded space.

When a MIL data set is imbalanced either at instance-level or at bag-level, the learned margin would be biased by the majority class (typically, the negative one). In the IS paradigm, since a discriminative instance-level classifier is trained to separate instances in positive bags from those in negative ones, the bias in the learned margin can be explained in the same way like in the imbalance problem for single-instance classifiers [11] because the true positive instances (responsible for the positive label of a positive a bag) are underrepresented in the training set. In BS and ES paradigms, where the discriminative process occurs at bag-level, decision boundaries could be biased too, due the poor representation of the true positive instances. Both types of imbalance in multiple-instance data sets may generate a decision boundary that weakly describes positive bags in comparison with the negative ones, because the true positive instances are often underrepresented, as shown in Fig. 1.

The problem of class imbalance has been widely addressed for single-instance data, tackling it with methods at data and algorithm levels. Data-level methods include a variety of re-sampling techniques in order to provide a balanced distribution of the data sets, SMOTE [14] is an example. Algorithm-level methods address class imbalance by modifying their training mechanism with the goal of getting a better accuracy on the minority class, like one-class learning [15] and cost-sensitive learning [16]. In addition, ensemble learning approaches, such as SMOTE-Boost [17], have become another alternative to handle imbalanced data.

On the contrary, in MIL there is little discussion about the imbalance problem. Wang et al. consider it in [13] and [12] and propose two approaches at bag- and instance-level. In the former, they introduce cost items into the weight updating strategy of AdaBoost; for the latter they use an oversampling technique based on SMOTE over instances and bags of the minority class. Indirectly, other MIL approaches have considered the imbalance problem at instance-level trying to identify the target concept in the positive bags and then represent the positive bag based on it; these approaches indirectly perform an informative undersampling on positive bags, MILES [8] is a well-known example of them. It embeds each bag into a feature space based on a representative set of instances (undersampling) selected from the training bags, similar to MILIS [9].

In contrast to the above-mentioned approaches, we try to find the true positive instances on positive bags. Based on kernel density estimation, we oversample them to reinforce the target concept, meanwhile we perform an undersampling in the borderline instances in order to reduce their ambiguity.

Now we introduce some of the notations used in the subsequent section. Let $B = \{(B_1^+, y_1), \ldots, (B_P^+, y_P), (B_{P+1}^-, y_{P+1}), \ldots, (B_{P+Q}^-, y_{P+Q})\}$ denotes the training set consisting of P positive and Q negative bags, $y_i \in \{-1, +1\}$ is the label for the bag and $B_i = \{x_{i1}, \ldots, x_{in_i}\}$ is a collection of n_i instances, where each instance $x_{ij} \in \mathbb{R}^d$. Different bags may have different cardinalities, hence n_i may vary for different i's. For the sake of convenience, we line up all the instances in every negative bag together, and re-index them as $B^- = \{x_i \mid i = 1, 2, \ldots, r^-\}$; where $r^- = \sum_{i=1}^{Q} |B_i^-|$ is the total number of instances within negative training bags.

3   Improving Representation of the Positive Class

If we exploit the MIL assumption, we can effectively model the distribution of the negative population, by using Kernel Density Estimation (KDE) [18], and use it to find the true positive instances and the borderline instances in order to oversample the former and undersample the latter. If instances $\{x_i\} \in B^-$ are i.i.d. data drawn from an unknown density $p(x|B^-)$, it can be estimated by KDE according to:

$$\hat{p}\left(x|B^-\right) = \frac{1}{r^- h^d} \sum_{i=1}^{r^-} k\left(\frac{x - x_i}{h}\right) \tag{1}$$

where h is a tunable smoothing parameter, and $k(\cdot)$ is the kernel of the estimator. We adopt the typical choice of using a Gaussian kernel.

The density estimation $\hat{p}(x|B^-)$ obtained from the training set gives us a quantitative measure of the degree of negativity for each instance; the farther x is away from B^-, the higher is the probability that x is positive given B^-. Accordingly, we can define the target concept of a positive bag as the most positive instance in the bag, that is, the instance that is farthest from the negative instance model. Similarly, we determine that the most negative instances in positive bags are likely to be borderline instances. Once they are identified, we can oversample the most positive instances and undersample the borderline ones. Figure 2 summarizes our method.

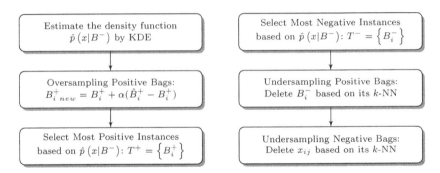

Fig. 2. Block diagram for the proposed method. Left-hand column: oversampling phase; right-hand: undersampling phase.

3.1 Oversampling Instances in Positive Bags

Since the responsible for the positive label in a positive bag is the true positive instance, we can use Eq. (1) to find it. We define a true positive instance set as $T^+ = \{B_i^+\}$, where every instance B_i^+ is the most likely one to be positive in the positive bag B_i for $i = 1, 2, \ldots, P$. Thus, B_i^+ can be defined as:

$$B_i^+ = \arg\min_{j=1,\ldots,n_i} \hat{p}(x_{ij}|B^-) \qquad (2)$$

Now, we can use SMOTE [14] to oversample the positive bags based on T^+. With SMOTE we create synthetic instances; specifically, consider the k-nearest neighbors for each instance B_i^+ in T^+ and, then, randomly select one of them denoted hereafter as $\hat{B}_i^+$. SMOTE generates a new synthetic instance along the line between B_i^+ and $\hat{B}_i^+$ according to: $B_i^+{}_{new} = B_i^+ + \alpha(\hat{B}_i^+ - B_i^+)$ with $\alpha \in [0, 1]$ at random. Finally, every synthetic instance should be added to its corresponding bag.

Different positive bags may have different (and unknown) numbers of true positive instances. The first application of Eq. (2) finds the most positive instance in the bag. By removing that instance and applying Eq. (2) again, the second most positive instance is found, and so on. For our experiments we empirically noticed that two positive instances from each positive bag is enough for enhancing the representation of the target concept for most MIL-based tasks.

3.2 Undersampling Instances in Positive Bags

MIL algorithms are prone to be affected by the negative instances in the positive bags due to the ambiguity that these instances produce. An approach to reduce this ambiguity is undersampling false positive instances, which are very likely those with the highest values of $\hat{p}(x|B^-)$. The set of false positive candidates is created according to the most negative instances in positive bags: $T^- = \{B_i^-\}$, where B_i^- is the most negative instance in the positive bag B_i with $i = 1, \ldots, P$ and

$$B_i^- = \arg\max_{j=1,\dots,n_i} \hat{p}(x_{ij}|B^-) \tag{3}$$

After that, for every B_i^- in T^- its k-nearest neighbors from the whole training set are found. If m_1 is the number of k-nearest neighbors for the instance B_i^- that belong to negative bags, m_2 is the number of k-nearest neighbors that belong to positive bags and $m_1 \geq m_2$, then we decide to remove B_i^- due to consider it as a false positive instance.

3.3 Undersampling Instances in Negative Bags

Finally, borderline instances in negative bags are removed. An instance is considered a borderline instance in a negative bag if it is surrounded by instances from the positive bags. Therefore, an instance $x_i \in B^-$ is removed from its negative bag if $m_1 \leq m_2$, where m_1 and m_2 have the same meaning as above.

4   Experiments

We use five standard MIL benchmark data sets to evaluate our method. Table 1 shows their details.

Table 1. Details of standard MIL benchmark data sets

Dataset	Size	Attributes	Positive Bags	Negative Bags	Positive Instances	Negative Instances
Elephant	1391	230	100	100	762	629
Fox	1320	230	100	100	647	673
Tiger	1120	230	100	100	544	676
Musk1	476	166	47	45	207	269
Musk2	6598	166	39	63	1017	5581
Mutagenesis1	10486	7	125	63	7790	2696
Mutagenesis2	2132	7	13	29	660	1472
Bird (Brown Creeper)	10232	38	197	351	4759	5473
Bird (Winter Wren)	10232	38	109	439	1824	8408

As suggested in [11], we chose the F-measure $F = \frac{(1+\beta^2)\cdot Recall\cdot Precision}{\beta^2\cdot Recall+Precision}$ and the AUC (Area Under ROC Curve) to evaluate the performance. In the first one, we used the customary option of setting β to 1. For both measures, the larger the better.

Tables 2 and 3 present the experimental results of the MIL algorithms over the data sets described above. For each MIL algorithm there are two columns, the first one corresponds to the performance obtained for the MIL algorithm in the original (Org) data set and the second one corresponds to the performance obtained for the algorithm in the balanced (Blc) data set with the proposed method. We repeated the experimental process 5 times with different randomly selected training and test sets using 10-fold cross-validation.

Table 2. Results for AUC. Best results are highlighted in boldface.

Dataset/Algorithm	APR		MIL-Boost		Citation-kNN		mi-SVM		MILES	
	Org	Blc	Org	Blc	Org	Blc	Org	Blc	Org	Blc
Elephant	0,75	0,83	0,89	0,96	0,90	0,95	0,91	**0,98**	0,90	0,94
Fox	0,57	0,64	0,62	0,82	0,64	0,75	0,68	**0,84**	0,72	0,82
Tiger	0,56	0,66	0,87	0,93	0,83	0,88	0,88	**0,97**	0,87	0,95
Musk1	0,77	0,79	0,64	0,75	0,93	0,93	0,94	**0,98**	0,94	0,98
Musk2	0,80	0,82	0,71	0,71	0,86	0,90	0,92	0,96	0,95	**0,98**
Mutagenesis1	0,50	0,50	**0,86**	0,85	0,84	0,82	0,66	0,74	0,84	0,84
Mutagenesis2	0,47	0,47	0,65	0,69	0,63	0,63	0,70	**0,80**	0,47	0,64
Bird(Brown Creeper)	0,54	0,57	0,95	**0,99**	0,76	0,81	0,87	**0,99**	0,89	0,98
Bird (Winter Wren)	0,60	0,61	0,99	**1,00**	0,94	0,98	0,92	0,97	0,86	0,90

Table 3. Results for F-Measure. Best results are highlighted in boldface.

Dataset/Algorithm	APR		MIL-Boost		Citation-kNN		mi-SVM		MILES	
	Org	Blc	Org	Blc	Org	Blc	Org	Blc	Org	Blc
Elephant	0,68	0,78	0,80	0,90	0,76	0,83	0,53	0,61	0,83	**0,94**
Fox	0,44	0,55	0,50	0,64	0,53	0,62	0,43	0,40	0,60	**0,75**
Tiger	0,44	0,57	0,77	0,83	0,76	0,81	0,58	0,61	0,82	**0,94**
Musk1	0,63	0,68	0,41	0,44	0,72	0,68	0,78	0,84	0,86	**0,94**
Musk2	0,68	0,72	0,65	0,68	0,71	0,72	0,62	0,62	0,88	**0,91**
Mutagenesis1	0,01	0,00	0,19	0,24	0,74	0,72	0,00	0,00	**0,79**	0,78
Mutagenesis2	0,02	0,02	0,22	0,16	0,30	0,30	0,45	0,51	0,05	**0,43**
Bird (Brown Creeper)	0,16	0,22	0,87	0,93	0,66	0,71	0,29	0,42	0,85	**1,00**
Bird (Winter Wren)	0,21	0,23	0,95	0,98	0,86	**0,99**	0,73	0,66	0,88	0,95

Notice that our approach outperforms the state-of-the-art MIL algorithms in most cases. The improvement is due to our method gives a possible solution to the problem in how removing the borderline instances and how detecting the true positive instances in positive bags in order to reinforce them.

5   Conclusion and Future Research

Despite the class imbalance problem is inherent in many MIL problems, there is very little related discussion about it. Most of the existing methods do not directly consider the problem of multiple-instance imbalanced data sets, which decreases the performance achieved by most algorithms. We proposed a method for MIL which considers the problem of multiple-instance imbalance at instance-level. Our method exploits the information in negative bags to identify the true positive instances and the borderline ones. Based on true positive instances, an oversampling is applied trying to reinforce the target concept in positive bags, while the borderline instances are undersampled in order to reduce the ambiguity between positive and negative bags. Experiments showed that the classification performance of our method is at least comparable with the state-of-the-art MIL methods in diverse applications. Moreover, our method can be used for either instance- or bag-level classification.

Continuations of this work could take several directions. First, other over/undersampling methods, aimed at improving the performance, must be evaluated and compared with our proposal. Second, in this work we only tackled the problem of imbalance at instance-level; however, solutions for the imbalance at bag-level are required. Lastly, the influence of free parameters such as the density kernel and the number of nearest neighbors must be studied.

References

1. Dietterich, T., Lathrop, R., Lozano-Pérez, T.: Solving the multiple instance problem with axis-parallel rectangles. Artif. Intell. **89**(1–2), 31–71 (1997)
2. Amores, J.: Multiple instance classification: Review, taxonomy and comparative study. Artif. Intell. **201**, 81–105 (2013)
3. Maron, O., Lozano-Pérez, T.: A framework for multiple-instance learning. In: Adv. Neural Inf. Process. Syst., pp. 570–576. MIT Press (1998)
4. Zhang, Q., Goldman, S.: EM-DD: An improved multiple-instance learning technique. In: Adv. Neural Inf. Process. Syst., pp. 1073–1080. MIT Press (2001)
5. Wang, J., Zucker, J.D.: Solving the multiple-instance problem: A lazy learning approach. In: Proc. of the Int. Conf. on Machine Learning, pp. 1119–1126 (2000)
6. Andrews, S., Tsochantaridis, I., Hofmann, T.: Support vector machines for multiple-instance learning. In: Adv. Neural Inf. Process. Syst., pp. 561–568 (2003)
7. Gärtner, T., Flach, P., Kowalczyk, A., Smola, A.: Multi-Instance kernels. In: Proc. of the Int. Conf. on Machine Learning, pp. 179–186 (2002)
8. Chen, Y., Bi, J., Wang, J.: MILES: Multiple-instance learning via embedded instance selection. IEEE Trans. Pattern Anal. Machine Intell. **28**(12), 1931–1947 (2006)
9. Fu, Z., Robles-Kelly, A., Zhou, J.: MILIS: Multiple instance learning with instance selection. IEEE Trans. Pattern Anal. Machine Intell. **33**(5), 958–977 (2011)
10. Viola, P., Platt, J., Zhang, C.: Multiple instance boosting for object detection. In: Adv. Neural Inf. Process. Syst., pp. 1417–1426 (2005)
11. He, H., Garcia, E.: Learning from imbalanced data. IEEE Trans. on Knowl. and Data Eng. **21**(9), 1263–1284 (2009)
12. Wang, X., Liu, X., Japkowicz, N., Matwin, S.: Resampling and cost-sensitive methods for imbalanced multi-instance learning. In: IEEE ICDMW, pp. 808–816 (2013)
13. Wang, X., Matwin, S., Japkowicz, N., Liu, X.: Cost-Sensitive Boosting Algorithms for Imbalanced Multi-instance Datasets. In: Zaïane, O.R., Zilles, S. (eds.) Canadian AI 2013. LNCS, vol. 7884, pp. 174–186. Springer, Heidelberg (2013)
14. Chawla, N., Bowyer, K., Hall, L., Kegelmeyer, W.: SMOTE: synthetic minority over-sampling technique. J. Artif. Intell. Res. **16**(1), 321–357 (2002)
15. Tax, D., Duin, R.: Support vector data description. Mach. Learn. **54**(1), 45–66 (2004)
16. Cao, P., Zhao, D., Zaiane, O.: An optimized cost-sensitive SVM for imbalanced data learning. In: Pei, J., Tseng, V.S., Cao, L., Motoda, H., Xu, G. (eds.) PAKDD 2013, Part II. LNCS, vol. 7819, pp. 280–292. Springer, Heidelberg (2013)
17. Chawla, N.V., Lazarevic, A., Hall, L.O., Bowyer, K.W.: SMOTEBoost: improving prediction of the minority class in boosting. In: Lavrač, N., Gamberger, D., Todorovski, L., Blockeel, H. (eds.) PKDD 2003. LNCS (LNAI), vol. 2838, pp. 107–119. Springer, Heidelberg (2003)
18. Parzen, E.: On estimation of a probability density function and mode. The Annals of Mathematical Statistics **33**(3), 1065–1076 (1962)

Restricted Boltzmann Machines for Gender Classification

Jordi Mansanet[1], Alberto Albiol[1(✉)], Roberto Paredes[2],
Mauricio Villegas[2], and Antonio Albiol[1]

[1] iTEAM - Instituto de Telecomunicaciones y Aplicaciones Multimedia, Universitat
Politècnica de València, Valencia, Spain
alalbiol@iteam.upv.es
[2] PRHLT Research Centre, Universitat Politècnica de València, Valencia, Spain

Abstract. This paper deals with automatic feature learning using a
generative model called Restricted Boltzmann Machine (RBM) for the
problem of gender recognition in face images. The RBM is presented
together with some practical learning tricks to improve the learning
capabilities and speedup the training process. The performance of the
features obtained is compared against several linear methods using the
same dataset and the same evaluation protocol. The results show a classification accuracy improvement compared with classical linear projection methods. Moreover, in order to increase even more the classification
accuracy, we have run some experiments where an SVM is fed with the
non-linear mapping obtained by the RBM in a tandem configuration.

Keywords: Representation learning · RBM · Gender classification

1 Introduction

Gender recognition of face images is an important task in computer vision as
many applications depend on the correct gender assessment. Examples of applications of gender recognition include visual surveillance, marketing, intelligent
user interfaces, demographic studies, etc.

There exist many approaches in the literature that deal with the problem of
gender recognition [18]. In most cases, the first stage of gender recognition is to
extract a set of handcrafted features, such as Haar [13], LBP [16], IDP [17], that
are fed into a suitable classifier. The problem of this paradigm is that it is based
on the expertise of the researcher to find the best feature set for a given problem.
For this reason, representation learning emerged as a promising research field.
The main goal of representation learning is to automatically convert data into
a form that makes it easier to extract useful information when building classifiers [1]. The success of representation learning will be the key to board complex
problems in the future.

© Springer International Publishing Switzerland 2014
A. Campilho and M. Kamel (Eds.): ICIAR 2014, Part I, LNCS 8814, pp. 274–281, 2014.
DOI: 10.1007/978-3-319-11758-4_30

Classical methods for representation learning are usually focused on dimensionality reduction techniques that preserve the representation capability (principal component analysis (PCA), independent component analysis (ICA), etc). When class information is available, these techniques focuses on obtaining discriminative features (discriminant analysis) as well as a reduction of dimensionality. All these methods have been widely used because of their simplicity and effectiveness [3].

In this paper, we propose the use of a powerful generative graphical model called Restricted Boltzmann Machine (RBM) for feature learning. Recently, RBMs have become very popular for its success in an impressive variety of applications [7] [15] [5]. RBMs model non-linear statistical dependencies of observed variables by introducing binary latent variables. Although the idea of extracting independent features is common to other algorithms (such as PCA), the main contribution of RBMs is that their non linear nature is able to find more complex relations between input variables. Also, another important difference is that the number of learned features will be much greater than in the case of PCA or LDA.

To our knowledge, this is the first paper that analyzes the performance of RBMs applied to gender recognition. Moreover, we will discuss some practical issues that illustrate how to train the RBM model in a practical application.

The remainder of the paper is organized as follows. Section 2 describes the RBM model and the main notation used throughout the paper. In section 3 and 4 we describe the dataset used and the set of experiments carried out. The final section draws the conclusions and directions for future research.

2   Restricted Boltzmann Machine

2.1   Generative Models

A Restricted Boltzmann Machine (RBM) is a stochastic generative model that can learn probability distributions over its inputs. This generative model can be implemented as a neural network with two layers ("visible" and "hidden"). Every RBM is characterized by an energy model function that assigns low energy values to high probability samples. The standard type of RBM uses binary visible and hidden units. The problem of using binary visible units is that they are not appropriate for real-valued data, such as pixel intensities in images. To deal with this situation, a new model called Gaussian RBM (GRBM) [12] is defined. The energy function of this model is defined by:

$$E_{GRBM}(\mathbf{v}, \mathbf{h}) = \sum_{i \in vis} \frac{(v_i - a_i)^2}{2\sigma_i^2} - \sum_{j \in hid} b_j h_j - \sum_{i,j} \frac{v_i}{\sigma_i} h_j w_{ij} \qquad (1)$$

where v_i denotes the real-valued activity of visible unit i, σ_i is its corresponding standard deviation and h_j is the binary state of the hidden unit j. The parameters of the model are the biases a_i, b_j and the weights w_{ij} that connect visible and hidden units.

A nice property of the GRBMs model is that the hidden units are mutually independent given the visible units and vice versa. Therefore, the conditional distribution over the hidden units can be factorized given the visible units:

$$p(h_j = 1|\mathbf{v}) = \frac{1}{1 + exp(-\sum_i w_{ij}\frac{v_i}{\sigma_i} - b_j)} \qquad (2)$$

Likewise, the conditional distribution over the visible units given the hidden units also factorizes:

$$p(v_i|\mathbf{h}) = \mathcal{N}(v_i|\mu_i, \sigma_i^2) \qquad (3)$$

where $\mu_i = a_i + \sigma_i^2 \sum_j w_{ij}h_j$. The previous equation is important because it shows explicitly the Gaussian nature of the visible units.

During the training process, the parameters of the model are adjusted, so that the log-likelihood of the training data is maximized using stochastic gradient descent. It is important to note that the log-likelihood definition does not depend on the labels of samples, so the training process is completely unsupervised.

The derivative of the log probability with respect to the weights leads to a very simple weight update rule:

$$\Delta w_{ij} = \epsilon \left(\langle v_i h_j \rangle_{data} - \langle v_i h_j \rangle_{model} \right) \qquad (4)$$

where ϵ is a learning rate and the angle brackets are used to denote expectations under the distribution specified by the subscript that follows. A simplified version of the same learning rule is used for the biases. It is important to mention that to accelerate the learning process it is essential to approximate the unbiased samples of $\langle v_i h_j \rangle_{model}$ using the Contrastive Divergence algorithm (CD) [10].

Although the GRBM is a powerful model, it is possible to improve its performance and speed up the learning procedure [11]. One common trick to increase the speed of learning is to use the momentum method that takes into account the update rule from the previous state, i.e. $\Delta w_{ij}^{(t-1)}$. Weight-decay is another trick that usually improves generalization to new data by reducing the overfitting to the training set. The simplest form of weight-decay, called L_2, adds an extra term to the standard gradient cost that penalizes large weights. Finally, encouraging sparse hidden activities it is important to easily interpret the function of each hidden unit. Also, discriminative performance is sometimes improved by using features that are only rarely active [14]. This trick can be achieved by adding a penalty term that fixes a "sparsity target", which is the desirable probability of being active. In the results section, we will show the effect of these tricks on the classification performance.

3   Dataset

Although there are several works on gender recognition of human face images [3] [8], there is no standard database or protocol for experimentation in this task. Labeled Faces in the Wild (LFW) [6] was compiled to aid the study of unconstrained face recognition. The dataset contains faces that show a large range of

original

PCA (64 comp)

RBM (100 hid)

RBM (2000 hid)

Fig. 1. Original images and reconstructions for different models

variation typically encountered in everyday life, exhibiting natural variability in factors such as pose, lighting, race, accessories, occlusions, and background. The problem of LFW is that number of males is much higher than the number of females, with some individuals appearing more than once.

In many datasets, the images are not annotated with gender information. Therefore researchers had to manually label the ground truth using visual inspection, either by themselves or with the help of others. Also, it is very important to take special care that any person does not appear in both training and test sets, to prevent the classifier to learn the identity instead of the gender.

As a conclusion, no large, publicly available dataset specifically designed for the problem of face gender recognition has been established. For our experiments we have taken a set of 1892 images (946 males and 946 females) from many public face databases (FERET, BANCA, FRGC, AR ...) using the first frontal view from each subject only. The images were converted to gray-scale, cropped to a size of 32 × 40 and histogram equalized. For aditional details about the composition of the dataset the reader is encourage to check [18].

4 Experiments

We have carried out three different sets of experiments. First we have run experiments in order to assess the gender classification performance of GRBM w.r.t. the number of hidden units and the application of sparsity and regularization terms. Second, we have compared these results with those from [18], where different linear methods are applied to the same dataset and the same evaluation protocol. Finally, in order to increase even more the classification accuracy we have ran some experiments where an SVM is fed with the non-linear mapping obtained by the GRBM in a *tandem* configuration.

In general, in all the experiments the GRBMs were trained using the $CD-1$ algorithm for 100 epochs using the training set, without the class-labels information. The weights of the GRBMs were initialized with small random values

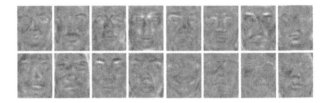

Fig. 2. Examples of features learned by the GRBM model using 2000 hidden units

sampled from a normal distribution with zero mean and standard deviation of 0.05. The learning rate value was set to 0.001 for both weights and biases. Optionally, in some experiments, we have applied a sparsity target in the binary hidden units and a weight decay term on the weights, as it is explained in 2. The sparsity target was fixed to 0.01 and the L_2 regularization was used as a weight decay term.

4.1   Gaussian RBM

In order to evaluate the behaviour of the GRBM we have run experiments varying the number of hidden units from 100 to 2000. Note that the GRBM can be seen as an unsupervised technique that leads to a non-linear mapping of the original representation space. Figure 2 shows a few examples of the type of features learned by the GRBM model using 2000 hidden units. These features correspond to the weight vectors ($\mathbf{w_j}$) associated with the hidden units. Note that these features might not be orthogonal as in the case of PCA. Moreover a sigmoid function is applied to the result of the projection $\mathbf{v} \cdot \mathbf{w_j}$ obtaining a non-linear mapping of $\mathbf{v}$. Another important difference w.r.t. PCA projection is that the GRBM features are more spatially localized so that each feature explains a part of the input sample.

To visually asses the quality of the non-linear mapping obtained by the GRBM, Figure 1 shows a few examples and the corresponding reconstructions using PCA and GRBM with different number of hidden units. It can be seen that the quality of the reconstruction using PCA is very good using only 64 principal components. In the case of GRBMs each hidden unit carries exactly one bit of information due to the saturation produced by the sigmoid function, for this reason the number of hidden units required to capture the input information must be much higher than in the case of PCA. Another interesting result is that the information about the gender (and identity) is lost in some cases for low number of hidden units. This fact explains the poor results obtained for the GRBM when the number of hidden units is too low.

A quantitative assessment of the performance of the GRBM for gender classification is carried out by means of adding a discriminative layer (a linear classifier) after the output of the GRBM. This is a standard procedure using GRBM for classification. This discriminative layer is trained using supervised data.

Table 1. Face gender recognition results varying the number of hidden units in the GRBM

	Error rate (%)			
Regularization	Number of hidden units			
	100	500	1000	2000
None	14.3 ± 2.3	11.3 ± 1.2	10.6 ±1.4	**10.1 ± 1.1**
sparsity $+L_2$ reg	14.2 ± 2.7	11.1 ± 2.1	10.2 ± 1.4	10.3 ± 1.0

However it is important to note that the non-linear projection is learned from unsupervised data, normally easier to obtain and leading to very large training sets, while for the discriminative layer we can use smaller datasets, even different. Table 1 shows the gender classification results of the GRBM w.r.t the number of hidden units and the application of sparsity and regularization. Normally this sparsity and regularization are used to improve the results but for the 2000 hidden units the best results is obtained without sparsity and regularization.

4.2   GRBM as a Non-linear Projection Technique

In this section, we aim at comparing the classification performance of the GRBM model versus other projection methods. For the other projection methods, a k-NN classifier was used in order to provide a classification. In each case, the corresponding algorithm parameters were properly adjusted, and only the best result obtained is shown for each algorithm.

We propose to compare the GRBM's performance with the following well-known linear mappings: Supervised Locality Preserving Projections (SLPP) [9], Locality Sensitive Discriminant Analysis (LSDA) [4] and Non-parametric Discriminant Analysis (NDA) [2].

Essentially, we want to test whether the non-linear mapping of the GRBM model, together with a plain (linear) discriminative layer, provides any benefit in front of a linear projection mapping and a non-linear classifier (k-NN). Table 2 shows the results of GRBM using 2000 hidden units. In general the linear techniques tend to work bad handling the original high dimensional space (except PCA), making these techniques inadequate for high-dimensional problems. Note that in [18] these linear techniques worked better using a previous PCA. However the GRBM, despite of being a non-linear mapping, is able to manage adequately the original high dimensionality representation and to obtain an adequate mapping, from the discriminative point of view.

4.3   Tandem Classification: GRBM + SVM

In this section we aim at increasing the classification performance of the GRBM-based representation and compare with the state-of-the-art results in the same dataset with the same evaluation protocol. After the unsupervised pre-train, we

Table 2. Face gender recognition results for different projection techniques

Technique	PCA	LSDA	SLPP	NDA	GRBM
Error rate(%)	17.7 ± 2.0	35.7 ± 2.6	34.0 ± 2.9	29.6 ± 2.3	**10.1 ± 1.1**

get a new representation of each sample in the data set, given by its hidden unit outputs after the sigmoid function. This new feature vector (and its label) is used as an input to feed an SVM with a Radial Basis Function (RBF) kernel. To set the best parameters of the SVM a grid search over the parameters was performed using a five-fold cross validation set in each subset.

Table 3 shows a comparison where different number of hidden units has been tested and the GRBM results are compared with the LDPP algorithm [18], and with the tandem PCA+SVM as well.

Table 3. Face gender recognition results using SVM

Technique	Error rate(%)
LDPP	8.5 ± 1.3
PCA+SVM	10.4 ± 1.6
GRBM+SVM	
100 units	11.6 ± 1.9
100 units + L_2 + sparse	11.5 ± 1.9
500 units	8.6 ± 1.5
500 units + L_2 + sparse	8.9 ± 1.4
1000 units	8.4 ± 1.6
1000 units + L_2 + sparse	7.9 ± 1.6
2000 units	8.2 ± 1.9
2000 units + L_2 + sparse	**7.8 ± 1.7**

The best results are obtained using a GRBM with 2000 hidden units, better than the LDPP algorithm. Note that in this case, the SVM classification accuracy is higher when the GRBM is trained using sparsity and regularization. Moreover it is important to note the good performance of PCA+SVM, but still worse that the LDPP algorithm.

5   Conclusions

This paper presents a new scheme to perform gender classification using a Gaussian Restricted Boltzmann Machine as a non-linear feature extractor method. First of all we have carried out a comparison of the GRBM classification performance varying some parameters of the model: number of hidden units, using a sparsity criterion on hidden units and using weight decay with L_2 regularization. We have evaluated the performance of the GRBM as a non-linear projection method jointly with a linear classifier. The results show an important improvement compared with a classical linear projection mapping methods (PCA, LSDA, SLPP, NDA) followed by a non-linear classifier (k-NN). Finally, in order to increase even more the classification accuracy, we have run some experiments where an SVM is fed with the non-linear mapping obtained by the GRBM in a tandem configuration. This model outperforms the best gender classification performance published with this database.

Future research will be focused on the use of deep architectures based on stacking RBMs as a pre-train for the entire network. Usually these deep models are able to yield more abstract (and useful) representations.

References

1. Bengio, Y., Courville, A., Vincent, P.: Representation learning: A review and new perspectives. IEEE Trans. on PAMI **35**(8), 1798–1828 (2013)
2. Bressan, M., Vitrià, J.: Nonparametric discriminant analysis and nearest neighbor classification. Pattern Recognition Letters **24**(15), 2743–2749 (2003)
3. Buchala, S., et al.: Dimensionality reduction of face images for gender classification. In: Proceedings of the Intelligent Systems, vol. 1, pp. 88–93 (2004)
4. Cai, D., He, X., Hu, Y., Han, J., Huang, T.: Learning a spatially smooth subspace for face recognition. In: CVPR, pp. 1–7 (2007)
5. Courville, A., Bergstra, J., Bengio, Y.: Unsupervised models of images by spike-and-slab rbms. In: ICML, pp. 1145–1152 (2011)
6. Huang, G.B., et al.: Labeled faces in the wild: A database for studying face recognition in unconstrained environments. Technical Report 07–49, Univ. of Massachusetts (October 2007)
7. Schmah, T., et al.: Generative versus discriminative training of rbms for classification of fmri images. In: NIPS, pp. 1409–1416 (2008)
8. Graf, A.B.A., Wichmann, F.A.: Gender classification of human faces. In: Bülthoff, H.H., Lee, S.-W., Poggio, T.A., Wallraven, C. (eds.) BMCV 2002. LNCS, vol. 2525, pp. 491–500. Springer, Heidelberg (2002)
9. He, X., Niyogi, P.: Locality preserving projections. In: NIPS (2004)
10. Hinton, G.E.: Training products of experts by minimizing contrastive divergence. Neural Comput. **14**(8), 1771–1800 (2002)
11. Hinton, G.E.: A practical guide to training restricted boltzmann machines. Technical report, University of Toronto (2010)
12. Hinton, G.E., Salakhutdinov, R.: Reducing the dimensionality of data with neural networks. Science **313**(5786), 504–507 (2006)
13. Moghaddam, B., Yang, M.-H.: Learning gender with support faces. IEEE Trans. on PAMI **24**(5), 707–711 (2002)
14. Nair, V., Hinton, G.E.: 3d object recognition with deep belief nets. In: NIPS, pp. 1339–1347 (2009)
15. Salakhutdinov, R., Mnih, A., Hinton, G.: Restricted boltzmann machines for collaborative filtering. In: ICML, pp. 791–798 (2007)
16. Shan, C.: Learning local binary patterns for gender classification on real-world face images. Pattern Recognition Letters **33**(4), 431–437 (2012)
17. Shobeirinejad, A., Gao, Y.: Gender classification using interlaced derivative patterns. In: ICPR, pp. 1509–1512 (2010)
18. Villegas, M., Paredes, R.: Dimensionality reduction by minimizing nearest-neighbor classification error. Pattern Recognition Letters **32**(4), 633–639 (2011)

DropAll: Generalization of Two Convolutional Neural Network Regularization Methods

Xavier Frazão[1] and Luís A. Alexandre[1,2](✉)

[1] Department of Informatics, Univ. Beira Interior, Covilhã, Portugal
[2] Department of Informatics, Instituto de Telecomunicações, Covilhã, Portugal
xavierfrazao@gmail.com, lfbaa@ubi.pt
http://www.ubi.pt

Abstract. We introduce DropAll, a generalization of DropOut [1] and DropConnect [2], for regularization of fully-connected layers within convolutional neural networks. Applying these methods amounts to subsampling a neural network by dropping units. Training with DropOut, a randomly selected subset of activations are dropped, when training with DropConnect we drop a randomly subsets of weights. With DropAll we can perform both methods. We show the validity of our proposal by improving the classification error of networks trained with DropOut and DropConnect, on a common image classification dataset. To improve the classification, we also used a new method for combining networks, which was proposed in [3].

1 Introduction

Convolutional neural networks (CNNs) are hierarchical neural networks whose convolutional layers alternate with subsampling layers, reminiscent of simple and complex cells in the primary visual cortex [4]. Although these networks are efficient when performing classification, they have the disadvantage of being computationally heavy, which makes their training slow and cumbersome.

With the emergence of parallel programming and taking advantage of the processing power of Graphics Processing Units (GPUs), training these networks takes significantly less time, making it possible to train large networks [5,6] and also making it possible to train multiple networks for the same problem and combine their results [1,2], an approach that can significantly increase the classification accuracy.

Besides the training time, the major problem of these networks is the overfitting. Overfitting still remains a challenge to overcome when it comes to training extremely large neural networks or working in domains which offer very small amounts of data. Many regularization methods have been proposed to prevent

We acknowledge the support given by Instituto de Telecomunicações through project PEst-OE/EEI/LA0008/2013

A. Campilho and M. Kamel (Eds.): ICIAR 2014, Part I, LNCS 8814, pp. 282–289, 2014.
DOI: 10.1007/978-3-319-11758-4_31

this problem. These methods combined with large datasets have made it possible to apply large neural networks for solving machine learning problems in several domains. Two new approachs have been recently proposed: DropOut [1] and DropConnect [2], which is a generalization of the previous. When training with DropOut, a randomly selected subset of activations is droped. With Drop-Connect, we randomly drop the weights. Both techniques are only possible for fully connected layers.

In this paper, we propose a generalization of both methods named DropAll. With this approach we were able to train a network with DropOut, DropConnect or both and taking advantage of each method.

2   Convolutional Neural Networks

A classical convolutional network is composed of alternating layers of convolution and pooling. The purpose of the first convolutional layer is to extract patterns found within local regions of the input images. This is done by convolving filters over the input image, computing the inner product of the filter at every location in the image and outputting the result as feature maps c. A non-linear function $f()$ is then applied to each feature map $c : a = f(c)$. The resulting activations a are passed to the pooling/subsampling layers. These layers aggregate the information within a set of small local regions, $\{R_j\}_{j=1}^n$, producing a pooled feature map s of smaller size as output.

Representing the aggregation function as $pool()$, then for each feature map c, we have: $s_j = pool(f(c_i)) \ \forall_i \in R_j$.

The two common choices to perform $pool()$ are average and max-pooling. The first takes the arithmetic mean of the elements in each pooling region, while max-pooling selects the largest element of the pooling region.

A range of functions $f()$ can be used as a non-linearity – $tanh$, $logistic$, $softmax$ and $relu$ are the most common choices.

In a convolutional network model, the convolutional layers, which take the pooled maps as input, can thus extract features that are increasingly invariant to local transformations of the input image.

The last layer is always a fully connected layer with one output unit per class in the recognition task. The activation function $softmax$, is the most common choice for the last layer such that each neuron output can be interpreted as the probability of a particular input image belonging to that class.

3   Related Work

3.1   Ensembles of CNNs

Model combination improves the performance of machine learning models. Averaging the predictions of several models is most helpful when the individual models are different from each other, in other words, to make them different they must have different hyperparameters or be trained on different data.

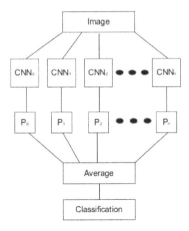

Fig. 1. The output probabilities are averaged to make the final prediction

The standard model architecture to combine networks can be seen in figure 1. Given some input pattern, the output probabilities from all CNN are averaged before making a prediction. For output i, the average output S_i is given by:

$$S_i = \frac{1}{n} \sum_{j=1}^{n} r_j(i) \tag{1}$$

where $r_j(i)$ is the output i of network j for a given input patern.

We recently proposed a new approach to combining neural networks called Weighted Convolutional Neural Network Ensemble (WCNNE)[3] that presented better results than doing just the simple average of the predictions. This method consists in applying a different weight for each network. Networks that had a lower classification error in the validation set, will have a larger weight when combining the results. The model architecture can be seen in figure 2. Given some input pattern, the output probabilities from all CNNs are multiplied by a weight before the prediction:

$$S_i = \sum_{j=1}^{n} W_j r_j(i) \tag{2}$$

The weights W_k is choosen by rank and are based on the order of accuracy in the validation set. This means that the weights are fixed, independently on the value of the error:

$$W_k = \frac{R(A_k)}{\sum_{i=1}^{n} R(A_i)} \tag{3}$$

where $R()$ is a function that gives the position of the network based on the validation accuracy sorted in increasing order. For example, the network with

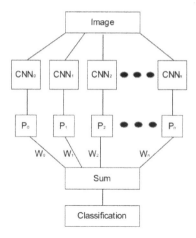

Fig. 2. The output probabilities are weighted based on the accuracy of the network evalueted on the validation set

largest accuracy will have an $R()$ value of n, the network with the second largest accuracy an $R()$ value of $n-1$ and so on until the network with lowest accuracy gets an $R() = 1$.

This method has the particularity of not looking only at the value of the validation error, but also for the network positions in terms of the ranked error list. Even though the difference in error between the two networks might be minimal, the weight value remains fixed, attributing a significantly greater importance to the network that achieved better results in the validation set.

3.2   Regularization

Two approachs for regularizing CNNs have been recently proposed, DropOut [1] and DropConnect [2]. Applying DropOut and DropConnect amounts to subsampling a neural network by dropping units. Since each of these processes acts differently as a way to control overfitting, the combination of several of these networks can bring gains, as will be shown below.

DropOut is applied to the outputs of a fully connected layer where each element of an output layer is kept with probability p, otherwise being set to 0 with probability $(1-p)$. If we further assume a neural activation function with $a(0) = 0$, such as $tanh$ and $relu$, the output of a layer can be written as:

$$r = m * a(Wv) \tag{4}$$

where m is a binary mask vector of size d with each element j coming independently from a Bernoulli distribution $m_j \sim Bernoulli(p)$, W is a matrix with weights of a fully-connected layer and v are the fully-connected layer inputs [2].

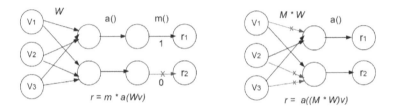

Fig. 3. The left figure is an example of DropOut. Right figure is an example of Drop-Connect

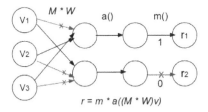

Fig. 4. Example of DropAll model

DropConnect is similar to DropOut, but applied to the weights W. The connections are choosen randomly during the training. For a DropConnect layer, the output is given as:

$$r = a((M * W)v) \qquad (5)$$

where M is weight binary mask, and $M_{ij} \sim Bernoulli(p)$. Each element of the mask M is drawn independently for each example during training [2]. Figure 3 illustrates the differences between the two methods.

4   DropAll

DropAll is a generalization of DropOut [1] and DropConnect [2], for regularizing fully-connected layers within neural deep networks. In the previous section we saw that DropOut is described by equation 4 and DropConnect is described by equation 5. For a DropAll layer, the output is given as:

$$r = m * a((M * W)v) \qquad (6)$$

The DropAll model is presented graphically in figure 4. This approach has the particularity of being easily adaptable to one of the previous methods. In these two methods, we had only one variable where we choose the percentage of drops, with DropAll we have 2 variables. One variable controls the drop rate of the activation while the other variable controls the drop rate of the weight. If we

Table 1. CIFAR-10 average classification error in percentage and standard deviation using 4 types of networks and 2 types of combiners, using 64 feature maps

Model	DropAll	DropConnect	DropOut	NoDrop
5 networks	11.20 ± 0.10	11.18 ± 0.15	11.28 ± 0.17	10.92 ± 0.15
WCNNE	10.01	9.81	10.31	10.03
Simple Average	10.03	9.84	10.48	10.06

set one of these variables to one, the drop rate value will be zero and we obtain either DropOut or DropConnect.

In both methods the value of the drop rate used is usually 0.5, however if we train with DropAll with 0.5 in both rates, network discards a lot of information, which is reflected in the results. To solve this problem, the drop rate must be smaller for both variables. When testing the network with different drop rates, we concluded that 0.25 is a good compromise.

In the following section we compare DropAll with DropConnect, DropAll and NoDrop (trained network without dropping units). All of these methods used in conjunction, provide a greater randomness when tested and combining the results from different networks trained by these techniques significantly improves the classification rates.

5 Experiments

Our experiments use a fast GPU based convolutional network library called Cuda-convnet [7] in conjunction with Li's code [2] that allows training networks with DropOut, Dropconnet and DropAll. We use a NVIDIA TESLA C2075 GPU to run the experiments. For each dataset we train five networks with DropAll, DropConnect, DropOut and NoDrop (five of each).

Once the networks are trained we save the mean and standard deviation of the classification errors produced individually by each network and the classification error produced by these networks when combined with our proposed method [3] and simple average. These results are shown in Tables 1-3. We used the CIFAR-10 dataset [8] to evaluate our approach.

5.1 CIFAR-10

The CIFAR-10 dataset [8] consists of 32 x 32 color images drawn from 10 classes split into 50 000 train and 10 000 test images.

Before feeding these images to our network, we subtract the per-pixel mean computed over the training set from each image as was done in [2]. The images are cropped to 24x24 with horizontal flips.

We use two feature extractors to perform the experiment. The first, consists in 2 convolutional layers, with 64 feature maps in each layer, 2 maxpooling layers, 2 locally connected layers, a fully connected layer which has 128 *relu*

Table 2. CIFAR-10 average classification error in percentage and standard deviation using 4 types of networks and 2 types of combiners, using, using 128 feature maps

Model	DropAll	DropConnect	DropOut	NoDrop
5 networks	10.67 ± 0.11	10.53 ± 0.14	10.53 ± 0.13	10.53 ± 0.17
WCNNE	9.57	9.68	9.55	9.61
Simple Average	9.62	9.81	9.71	9.64

Table 3. CIFAR-10 average classification error combining our 12 best networks using 2 types of combiners, using 128 feature maps. Previous state-of-the-art using the same architecture is 9.32% [2]. Current state-of-the art of CIFAR-10 is 8.81% [9].

Model	WCNNE	Simple Average
12 networks	9.09	9.22

units on which NoDrop, DropOut, DropConnect or DropAll are applied and a output layer with *softmax* units. We train for three stages of epochs, 500-100-100 with an initial learning rate of 0.001, that its reduced by factor 10 between each stage. We chose this fixed number of epochs because it is when the validation error stops improving. Training a network takes around 4 hours. The second feature extractor is similar but with 128 feature maps in each layer and the number of epochs is smaller, 350-100-50. Training a network with 128 maps takes around 20 hours. In these experiments we compared the results using our approach (WCNNE) [3] for combining networks and simple average, both described in this paper.

The first experiment used a feature extractor with 64 feature maps (summarized in Table 1) and combined networks that were trained with DropAll, Drop-Connect, DropOut and NoDrop. NoDrop individually obtained better results and networks with DropOut were the ones with the worst individual results. By combining the nets, DropConnect achieved better results.

The second experiment used a feature extractor with 128 feature maps (summarized in Table 2), we also combine networks that were trained with DropAll, DropConnect, DropOut and NoDrop. DropOut individually achieved better results, and networks trained with DropAll were the ones with worst result. By combining the nets, DropOut achieved better results.

In addition we join all models and combine our 12 best networks with lowest validation error, and the results were significantly better (see Table 3). All of these methods used in conjunction provide a greater randomness and significantly improve the classification rate. If we combine our 12 best networks without DropAll networks the error is slightly worse, 9.12%.

6   Conclusions

In this paper, we propose a new method named DropAll that is a generalization of two well-known methods for regularization of convolutional neural networks, used to avoid overfitting. These problem still remains a challenge to overcome when it comes to training extremely large neural networks or working in domains which offer very small amounts of data.

DropAll by itself, did not increase performance when we evaluate a network, however, the flexibility of this method makes it possible to train a network using the potential of DropOut and DropConnect. In general, networks trained with these forms of regularization benefit from an increase randomness, which is a plus when we wish to combine the results of multiple networks. As shown, the combination of all methods significantly improves the classification rate of the problem used in the experiments section to validate our proposal.

References

1. Hinton, G.E., Srivastava, N., Krizhevsky, A., Sutskever, I., Salakhutdinov, R.: Improving neural networks by preventing co-adaptation of feature detectors, CoRR, abs/1207.0580 (2012)
2. Wan, L., Zeiler, M., Zhang, S., Cun, Y.L., Fergus, R.: Regularization of neural networks using dropconnect. In: Dasgupta, S., Mcallester, D. (eds.) Proceedings of the 30th International Conference on Machine Learning (ICML 2013). JMLR Workshop and Conference Proceedings, vol. 28, pp. 1058–1066 (May 2013)
3. Frazao, X., Alexandre, L.A.: Weighted convolutional neural network ensemble (in submitted, 2014)
4. Fukushima, K.: A neural network model for selective attention in visual pattern recognition. Biol. Cybern. **55**(1), 5–16 (1986)
5. Jarrett, K., Kavukcuoglu, K., Ranzato, M., LeCun, Y.: What is the best multi-stage architecture for object recognition? In: 2009 IEEE 12th International Conference on Computer Vision, pp. 2146–2153 (September 2009)
6. Chellapilla, K., Puri, S., Simard, P.: High Performance Convolutional Neural Networks for Document Processing. In: Lorette, G. (eds.) Tenth International Workshop on Frontiers in Handwriting Recognition, La Baule (France). Suvisoft, Université de Rennes 1 (October 2006), http://www.suvisoft.com
7. Krizhevsky, A.: Cuda-convnet (2012), http://code.google.com/p/cuda-convnet/
8. Krizhevsky, A.: Learning multiple layers of features from tiny images, Tech. Rep. (2009)
9. Lin, M., Chen, Q., Yan, S.: Network in network, CoRR, abs/1312.4400 (2013)

Transfer Learning Using Rotated Image Data to Improve Deep Neural Network Performance

Telmo Amaral[1](✉), Luís M. Silva[1,2], Luís A. Alexandre[3],
Chetak Kandaswamy[1], Joaquim Marques de Sá[1,4], and Jorge M. Santos[1,5]

[1] Instituto de Engenharia Biomédica (INEB), Universidade do Porto, Porto, Portugal
Telmo.Amaral@newcastle.ac.uk
[2] Departamento de Matemática, Universidade de Aveiro, Aveiro, Portugal
lmas@ua.pt
[3] Instituto de Telecomunicações, Universidade da Beira Interior, Covilhã, Portugal
[4] Dep. de Eng. Electrotécnica e de Computadores, Fac. de Eng. da Univ. do Porto,
Porto, Portugal
[5] Dep. de Matemática, Instituto Superior de Engenharia do Instituto Politécnico do
Porto, Porto, Portugal

Abstract. In this work we explore the idea that, in the presence of a small training set of images, it could be beneficial to use that set itself to obtain a transformed training set (by performing a random rotation on each sample), train a source network using the transformed data, then retrain the source network using the original data. Applying this transfer learning technique to three different types of character data, we achieve average relative improvements between 6 % and 16 % in the classification test error. Furthermore, we show that it is possible to achieve relative improvements between 8 % and 42 % in cases where the amount of original training samples is very limited (30 samples per class), by introducing not just one rotation but several random rotations per sample.

Keywords: Transfer learning · Deep learning · Stacked auto-encoders

1 Introduction

Deep architectures, such as neural networks with two or more hidden layers, are a class of networks that comprise several levels of non-linear operations, each expressed in terms of parameters that can be learned [1]. Until 2006, attempts to train deep architectures generally resulted in poorer performance but a breakthrough took place with the introduction by Hinton et al. [7] of the deep belief network, whose hidden layers are initially treated as restricted Boltzmann machines (RBMs) and pre-trained, one at a time, in an unsupervised greedy approach. This pre-training procedure was soon generalised to rely on machines easier to train than RBMs, such as auto-encoders [8].

© Springer International Publishing Switzerland 2014
A. Campilho and M. Kamel (Eds.): ICIAR 2014, Part I, LNCS 8814, pp. 290–300, 2014.
DOI: 10.1007/978-3-319-11758-4_32

The goal of transfer learning (TL) is to reuse knowledge associated with a source problem to improve the learning required by a target problem [9]. The source and target problems may be, for example, classification tasks that differ as to the data distributions, or that involve different sets of classes. A common approach to TL is that of transferring representations that were learned from one problem to another problem.

In this paper we investigate if, in the presence of a small training set, it is possible to use that set itself to obtain a transformed training set (by performing for example a random rotation on each sample), train a source network using the transformed data, then retrain that network using the original data, to achieve lower classification errors than would be possible by using only the original data. We explore this idea using three types of character image data. We achieved significant improvements in the classification error by fully training a source network using slightly rotated versions of the original training samples, then fine-tuning that network again using the original samples. For very small amounts of training data, it was possible to further improve performance by introducing more than one rotation per sample.

Deep architectures have been used recently in TL settings, as discussed in reviews by Bengio et al. [2, Sec. 2.4] and Deng and Yu [5, Ch. 11]. For example, Glorot et al. [6] pre-trained stacked denoising auto-encoders using unlabelled data from multiple domains, thus learning a generic representation that could be used to train SVMs for sentiment classification on a specific domain. This differs from our work, as the target network was not obtained by fully retraining a source network and no data transformations (in fact no image data) were involved. In the field of character recognition, Ciresan et al. [4] trained convolutional neural networks (CNNs) on either digits or Chinese characters and retrained them to recognise uppercase Latin letters. Again, no data transformations were involved.

Affine and elastic transformations have been used extensively to increase the amount data available to train neural networks, as in the work of Ciresan et al. [3] with very large (but shallow) multi-layer perceptrons trained through parallelisation. Simard et al. [10] suggest the use of distorted data as good practice in the supervised training of CNNs. These two works did not involve networks pre-trained without supervision, or transfer learning. More generally, existing work with deep architectures does not address the use of transformed image data as a means to obtain an artificial problem from which knowledge can be gathered and transferred to the original problem, to improve performance.

2   Stacked Auto-Encoders

The auto-encoder (AE) is a simple network that tries to produce at its output what is presented at the input. The basic AE is in fact a simple neural network with one hidden layer and one output layer, subject to two restrictions: the number of output neurons is equal to the number of inputs; and the weight matrix of the output layer is the transposed of the weight matrix of the hidden layer (that is, the weights are clamped). The values of the hidden layer neurons are called the *encoding*, whereas the values of the output neurons are called the *decoding*. Unsupervised learning of the weights and biases of AEs can be achieved by gradient descent, based on a training set of input vectors.

Consider a network designed for classification, with a layer of inputs, two or more hidden layers, and a softmax output layer with as many units as classes. The hidden layers of such a network can be *pre-trained* one at a time in an unsupervised way. Each hidden layer is "unfolded" to form an AE. Once that AE has learned to reconstruct its own input, its output layer is no longer needed and its hidden layer becomes the input to the next hidden layer of the network. The next hidden layer is in turn pre-trained as an individual AE and the process is repeated until there are no more hidden layers. A deep network pre-trained in this fashion is termed a stacked auto-encoder (SAE).

The goal of unsupervised pre-training is to bring the network's hidden weights and biases to a region of the parameter space that constitutes a better starting point than random initialisation, for a subsequent supervised training stage. In this context, the supervised training stage is usually called *fine-tuning* and can be achieved by conventional gradient descent, based on a training set of input vectors paired with class labels. The output layer weights are randomly initialised and learned only in the fine-tuning stage.

3   Transfer Learning Based Approach

We used a TL approach where the involved problems differed only in terms of the data distribution. Let $X_{ds.ori}$ be an original design set containing $n_{ds.ori}$ data samples. We assume that each data sample contains not only an input vector (representing for example an image) but also the corresponding class label, and the design set contains both training and validation data. Let $X_{ds.tra}$ be a design set containing $n_{ds.ori}$ transformed data samples, obtained by doing a transformation (such as a random rotation, in the case of image data) on each data sample from $X_{ds.ori}$. Let $X_{ts.ori}$ be a test set containing $n_{ts.ori}$ original data samples.

Given $X_{ds.tra}$, $X_{ds.ori}$ and $X_{ts.ori}$, we can use TL to design and test a classifier, by applying Algorithm 1. Specifically, in steps 2 and 3 the initialised network is trained (first without supervision, then with supervision) to classify transformed data and, in step 4, the resulting network is retrained (with supervision) to classify original data. The idea is to transfer knowledge from an artificially created source problem to the original target problem. Algorithm 1 can be trivially modified by omitting step 3, so that the source network is only pre-trained, instead pre-trained and fine-tuned.

We compared the performance of classifiers obtained via the TL approach described above with the performance of classifiers obtained via the baseline (BL) method defined in Algorithm 2. In this BL approach, a classifier is pre-trained and fine-tuned in a conventional way, using data from a single distribution, then tested on original data. When design set X_{ds} is the original design set $X_{ds.ori}$, the last two steps of the BL approach perform the same operations as the last two

Algorithm 1. Transfer Learning approach

Given design sets $X_{ds.tra}$ and $X_{ds.ori}$, and test set $X_{ts.ori}$,

1. Randomly initialise a classifier network;
2. Pre-train the network using $X_{ds.tra}$ (ignoring labels);
3. Fine-tune the network using $X_{ds.tra}$;
4. Fine-tune the network using $X_{ds.ori}$;
5. Test the network using $X_{ts.ori}$, obtaining classification error ε.

Algorithm 2. Baseline approach

Given design set X_{ds} and test set $X_{ts.ori}$,

1. Randomly initialise a classifier network;
2. Pre-train the network using X_{ds} (ignoring labels);
3. Fine-tune the network using X_{ds};
4. Test the network using $X_{ts.ori}$, obtaining classification error ε.

steps of the TL approach: fine-tuning and testing using only original data. This yields a test error that can be directly compared with the test error obtained with TL. Alternatively, when X_{ds} is a transformed design set $X_{ds.tra}$, the BL approach is equivalent to TL without step 4: pre-training and fine-tuning using transformed data and testing *directly* on original data, without retraining on original data. As seen later in Section 5, this helped us to determine whether TL was really beneficial, or if simply transforming design data was enough to improve performance on original test data.

4   Data and Hyper-Parameters

The data used in this work consisted of grey-level images of handwritten digits, typewritten (synthesised) digits, and lowercase letters, all containing $28{\times}28{=}784$ pixels. For each data type, we prepared a test set $X_{ts.ori}$ containing $n_{ts.ori}$ original samples and a design set $X_{ds.ori.full}$ containing $n_{ds.ori.full}$ original samples. We use the subscript $full$ because, in practice, only randomly picked subsets of $X_{ds.ori.full}$ were used in the experiments. Table 1 shows the numbers of samples available from each data type, as well as the number of classes involved, c. All data originated from the MNIST-basic set prepared by the LISA lab[1] and the Chars74K set prepared by Microsoft Research India[2].

All the deep networks we used had an architecture with two hidden layers composed of 100 units each and an output layer appropriate to the number of classes being considered. Using an additional hidden layer did not have a significant effect on the observed validation errors.

---

[1] See http://www.iro.umontreal.ca/~lisa/twiki/bin/view.cgi/Public/ MnistVariations.

[2] See http://www.ee.surrey.ac.uk/CVSSP/demos/chars74k/.

Table 1. Numbers of design and test samples available from each data type

Data type	c	$n_{ds.ori.full}$	$n_{ts.ori}$
Handwritten digits	10	3000	50000
Typewritten digits	10	3000	7160
Typewritten letters	26	7800	18616

Algorithm 3. Experimental procedure

Given $X_{ds.ori.full}$, $X_{ds.tra}$ and an integer $k \geq 1$,

For each data type (handwritten digits, typewritten digits, and typewritten letters),

1. For each $n_{ds.ori}$ such that $\frac{n_{ds.ori}}{c} \in [30, 60, 90, 120, 150]$,
   (a) Obtain $X_{ds.ori}$ by randomly picking $n_{ds.ori}$ samples from $X_{ds.ori.full}$;
   (b) Obtain $X_{ds.tra}$ by creating k random rotations of each sample from $X_{ds.ori}$;
   (c) Run baseline approach using $X_{ds.ori}$ and $X_{ts.ori}$;
   (d) Run baseline approach using $X_{ds.tra}$ and $X_{ts.ori}$;
   (e) Run transfer learning approach using $X_{ds.tra}$, $X_{ds.ori}$ and $X_{ts.ori}$.

Hidden layers were pre-trained via online gradient descent, the cross-entropy cost function and a learning rate of 0.001, for a minimum of 15 epochs and then until the relative improvement in the validation error fell below 1%. Whole networks were fine-tuned via online gradient descent, the cross-entropy cost function and a learning rate of 0.1, until the validation error did not decrease for 50 epochs. These hyper-parameter values did not result from a thorough selection procedure, but we believe they yielded validation errors that were sufficiently low to enable the comparisons done in this work.

Our code was based on an implementation of SAEs originally developed by Hugo Larochelle[3]. All experiments ran on an Intel Core i7-950 and enough physical memory to prevent swapping. A pool of five parallel processes was used.

5   Experiments and Results

We followed the procedure shown in Algorithm 3. In step 1a, two thirds of the randomly picked $n_{ds.ori}$ design samples are assigned to training and one third is assigned to validation. The transformed $X_{ds.tra}$ obtained in step 1b contains $k \times n_{ds.ori}$ samples, since it is generated by creating k distinct randomly rotated versions of each sample from the original design set. In practice, actually two variants of $X_{ds.tra}$ were obtained in this step: $X_{ds.tra.030}$, by doing random rotations in the interval $[-30°, 30°]$; and $X_{ds.tra.180}$, by using the interval $[-180°, 180°]$ instead. In addition, in step 1e two variants of TL are tried: one using $X_{ds.tra}$ only for pre-training (this is later denoted as PT); the other using $X_{ds.tra}$ for both pre-training and fine-tuning (denoted as PT+FT).

---

[3] See http://www.dmi.usherb.ca/~laroheh/mlpython/.

5.1 Using a Single Rotation (k=1)

In a first series of experiments we set k to 1 in Algorithm 3. The experimental procedure was repeated 20 times. At each repetition, a new random number generator seed was used to pick $n_{ds.ori}$ design samples in step 1a, to rotate samples in step 1b, and to initialise the networks trained in steps 1c, 1d and 1e.

Table 2 shows the average classification error $\bar{\varepsilon}$ obtained using $X_{ts.ori}$, for the three data types and for different numbers $n_{ds.ori}/c$ of design samples per class. For each data type and value of $n_{ds.ori}/c$, the lowest mean error is underlined. The p-value for the Student's t-test is also reported in square brackets, to help assess if the errors obtained in that experiment were significantly lower than those obtained with the BL approach using $X_{ds.ori}$.

Table 2. Percent average classification test error $\bar{\varepsilon}$ (standard deviation) [p-value] obtained for different data types, approaches, design sets, and numbers $n_{ds.ori}/c$ of design samples per class

Data	Approach and design sets	$n_{ds.ori}/c$ 30	60	90	120	150
Handwritten digits	BL $X_{ds.ori}$	27.2 (02.4)	16.3 (01.6)	12.8 (01.0)	11.1 (00.7)	10.3 (00.6)
	BL $X_{ds.tra.030}$	33.5 (02.5) [<0.01]	18.3 (01.3) [<0.01]	13.9 (00.6) [<0.01]	12.4 (00.5) [<0.01]	11.2 (00.5) [<0.01]
	BL $X_{ds.tra.180}$	66.0 (04.7) [<0.01]	57.5 (03.3) [<0.01]	45.9 (03.6) [<0.01]	39.3 (02.4) [<0.01]	36.0 (02.2) [<0.01]
	TL $X_{ds.ori}$ after $X_{ds.tra.030}$ PT	31.5 (03.4) [<0.01]	16.4 (01.4) [0.40]	12.5 (00.7) [0.15]	11.1 (00.5) [0.47]	10.2 (00.5) [0.33]
	TL $X_{ds.ori}$ after $X_{ds.tra.180}$ PT	32.8 (03.8) [<0.01]	19.2 (01.4) [<0.01]	12.8 (00.7) [0.45]	11.0 (00.4) [0.45]	10.4 (00.6) [0.34]
	TL $X_{ds.ori}$ after $X_{ds.tra.030}$ PT+FT	22.7 (02.0) [<0.01]	13.5 (00.9) [<0.01]	10.8 (00.5) [<0.01]	9.9 (00.5) [<0.01]	9.1 (00.4) [<0.01]
	TL $X_{ds.ori}$ after $X_{ds.tra.180}$ PT+FT	27.9 (02.4) [0.20]	17.2 (01.2) [0.02]	12.6 (00.6) [0.19]	11.0 (00.4) [0.33]	10.1 (00.5) [0.11]
Typewritten digits	BL $X_{ds.ori}$	12.4 (01.5)	8.6 (00.7)	7.1 (00.4)	6.1 (00.3)	5.5 (00.4)
	BL $X_{ds.tra.030}$	18.4 (02.9) [<0.01]	9.9 (00.8) [<0.01]	7.8 (00.6) [<0.01]	7.0 (00.4) [<0.01]	6.4 (00.4) [<0.01]
	BL $X_{ds.tra.180}$	55.7 (06.0) [<0.01]	36.3 (07.1) [<0.01]	27.6 (03.6) [<0.01]	23.5 (02.9) [<0.01]	21.3 (02.5) [<0.01]
	TL $X_{ds.ori}$ after $X_{ds.tra.030}$ PT	14.1 (01.4) [<0.01]	8.8 (00.7) [0.17]	7.1 (00.4) [0.47]	6.1 (00.4) [0.44]	5.3 (00.4) [0.04]
	TL $X_{ds.ori}$ after $X_{ds.tra.180}$ PT	15.8 (01.7) [<0.01]	9.2 (00.9) [0.02]	6.9 (00.4) [0.13]	6.1 (00.5) [0.47]	5.6 (00.5) [0.37]
	TL $X_{ds.ori}$ after $X_{ds.tra.030}$ PT+FT	11.0 (01.0) [<0.01]	7.4 (00.4) [<0.01]	5.9 (00.6) [<0.01]	5.3 (00.4) [<0.01]	4.8 (00.3) [<0.01]
	TL $X_{ds.ori}$ after $X_{ds.tra.180}$ PT+FT	14.8 (01.4) [<0.01]	9.2 (00.7) [0.01]	7.1 (00.4) [0.48]	6.2 (00.4) [0.08]	5.6 (00.4) [0.32]
Typewritten letters	BL $X_{ds.ori}$	21.6 (00.7)	16.4 (00.7)	14.6 (00.4)	13.4 (00.3)	12.8 (00.3)
	BL $X_{ds.tra.030}$	26.4 (01.4) [<0.01]	19.7 (00.6) [<0.01]	17.6 (00.4) [<0.01]	16.2 (00.4) [<0.01]	15.7 (00.4) [<0.01]
	BL $X_{ds.tra.180}$	63.7 (04.1) [<0.01]	50.5 (03.2) [<0.01]	46.6 (02.1) [<0.01]	43.2 (02.1) [<0.01]	41.1 (01.9) [<0.01]
	TL $X_{ds.ori}$ after $X_{ds.tra.030}$ PT	22.2 (01.4) [0.03]	16.2 (00.7) [0.19]	14.2 (00.4) [<0.01]	13.1 (00.4) [<0.01]	12.3 (00.3) [<0.01]
	TL $X_{ds.ori}$ after $X_{ds.tra.180}$ PT	20.9 (00.9) [0.01]	15.7 (00.6) [<0.01]	13.8 (00.3) [<0.01]	12.7 (00.3) [<0.01]	12.1 (00.4) [<0.01]
	TL $X_{ds.ori}$ after $X_{ds.tra.030}$ PT+FT	19.4 (01.1) [<0.01]	15.3 (00.6) [<0.01]	13.6 (00.5) [<0.01]	12.5 (00.3) [<0.01]	11.9 (00.4) [<0.01]
	TL $X_{ds.ori}$ after $X_{ds.tra.180}$ PT+FT	21.4 (01.9) [0.36]	16.0 (00.5) [0.01]	14.1 (00.3) [<0.01]	13.1 (00.2) [<0.01]	12.5 (00.3) [<0.01]

As shown, for each data type, the BL approach was tried not only with $X_{ds.ori}$, but also with $X_{ds.tra.030}$ and $X_{ds.tra.180}$. The obtained results show that training a model with transformed data and directly testing it on original data invariably led to worse results than training and testing with original data.

For all data types, the results obtained with TL when transformed design data were used for both pre-training and fine-tuning (PT+FT) were generally better than the results obtained when transformed data were used only for pre-training (PT).

The average test error $\bar{\varepsilon}$ obtained with the BL approach and with TL when using transformed data for PT+FT is plotted in Fig. 1, for handwritten digits and typewritten letters. Training times were found to increase linearly with the amount of design data. Partial and total average training times are reported in

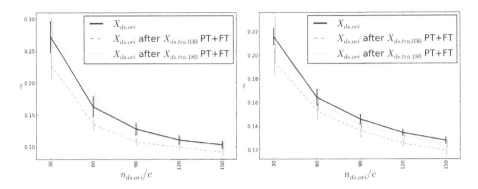

Fig. 1. Average classification test error $\bar{\varepsilon}$ obtained with the BL and TL approaches, for each data type, for different numbers $n_{ds.ori}/c$ of original design samples per class. Left: handwritten digits; right: typewritten letters.

Table 3, for the case of $n_{ds.ori}/c=150$ samples per class. Times are shown for the BL approach and for TL, when slightly rotated data ($X_{ds.tra.030}$) were used both to pre-train and to fine-tune (PT+FT). The table rows corresponding to $k=5$ and $k=10$ will be addressed later.

Table 3. Average time in seconds (standard deviation) needed to pre-train and fine-tune source and target models, for different data types, approaches, and values of k

Data type	Approach an design sets	k	Source		Target		Total	
			PT	FT	PT	FT		
Handwritten	BL $X_{ds.ori}$				97 (15)	53 (14)	150 (19)	
digits	TL $X_{ds.ori}$ after $X_{ds.tra.030}$ PT+FT	1	83 (10)	64 (12)		102 (32)	248 (38)	
	TL $X_{ds.ori}$ after $X_{ds.tra.030}$ PT+FT	5	302 (48)	438 (172)		84 (20)	824 (170)	
	TL $X_{ds.ori}$ after $X_{ds.tra.030}$ PT+FT	10	514 (58)	770 (473)		98 (18)	1382 (491)	
Typewritten	BL $X_{ds.ori}$				112 (12)	63 (26)	175 (28)	
digits	TL $X_{ds.ori}$ after $X_{ds.tra.030}$ PT+FT	1	88 (13)	67 (25)		97 (15)	252 (36)	
	TL $X_{ds.ori}$ after $X_{ds.tra.030}$ PT+FT	5	334 (51)	420 (229)		101 (22)	855 (245)	
	TL $X_{ds.ori}$ after $X_{ds.tra.030}$ PT+FT	10	581 (64)	662 (356)		124 (45)	1367 (369)	
Typewritten	BL $X_{ds.ori}$				260 (29)	197 (68)	457 (79)	
letters	TL $X_{ds.ori}$ after $X_{ds.tra.030}$ PT+FT	1	212 (24)	217 (84)		402 (165)	832 (193)	
	TL $X_{ds.ori}$ after $X_{ds.tra.030}$ PT+FT	5	786 (57)	1664 (520)		352 (146)	2801 (507)	
	TL $X_{ds.ori}$ after $X_{ds.tra.030}$ PT+FT	10	1359 (94)	3558 (1288)		327 (123)	5243 (1274)	

The results show that, for all data types and for all numbers of design samples per class, TL based on variant $X_{ds.tra.030}$ of the transformed data led to significantly lower errors than the BL approach. This improved accuracy had a price in terms of time needed to design the classifiers: total training times needed by TL were 50% to 100% longer than those needed by the BL approach. This was not surprising, as TL involves unsupervised and supervised training stages that yield a first classifier (steps 2 and 3 in Algorithm 1) followed by a supervised training stage that yields a second classifier (step 4), whereas the BL approach involves the unsupervised and supervised training of a single classifier (steps 2 and 3 in Algorithm 2).

For all data types and for all amounts of design samples per class, variant $X_{ds.tra.030}$ of the transformed data used for PT+FT always led to better results than variant $X_{ds.tra.180}$, as illustrated in Fig. 1. This indicates that it was better to restrict the random rotation of original images to a small range than to allow it to assume any value.

Fig. 2 (left) shows the average relative improvement in the test error $(\overline{\Delta\varepsilon_r})$ obtained over 20 repetitions when TL was applied instead of the BL approach, in experiments that used slightly rotated design data to pre-train and fine-tune the source classifier. The relative improvement was computed as $\Delta\varepsilon_r=(\varepsilon_{BL}-\varepsilon_{TL})/\varepsilon_{BL}$, where ε_{BL} and ε_{TL} are the test errors yielded by the BL approach and TL, respectively. For all data types, the observed improvements in the average error were roughly constant across the different numbers of original design samples per class.

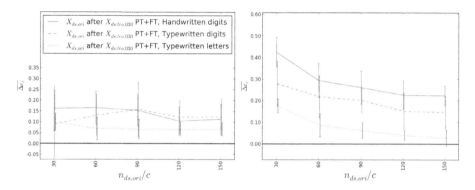

Fig. 2. Average relative improvement in the classification test error $\overline{\Delta\varepsilon_r}$ yielded by TL (using slightly rotated design data for pre-training and fine-tuning), for different data types, for different amounts $n_{ds.ori}/c$ of original design samples per class. Left: for $k{=}1$. Right: for $k{=}5$.

5.2   Using Several Rotations ($k > 1$)

In a second series of experiments, we used transformed design data obtained by creating several rotated versions of each original design sample, by using first $k{=}5$ and then $k{=}10$ in Algorithm 3. Steps 1c and 1d were skipped, because now we were not concerned with comparing the TL and BL approaches. Rather we wanted to compare TL results obtained using $k > 1$ with the TL results previously obtained using $k{=}1$. In addition, when applying TL, we considered only cases where the transformed design data were obtained via small rotations ($X_{ds.tra.030}$) and used both to pre-train and to fine-tune the source model (PT+FT).

The experimental procedure was repeated 20 times for each value of k. The obtained results are shown in Table 4, together with results for $k{=}1$ reproduced from Table 2. For each data type and value of $n_{ds.ori}/c$, the two p-values shown for $k=5$ and $k=10$ were computed in relation to the results obtained with $k=1$. Some of the results shown in Table 4 are also plotted in Fig. 3.

Table 4. Percent average classification test error $\bar{\varepsilon}$ (standard deviation) [p-value] obtained for different data types, approaches, design sets, and numbers $n_{ds.ori}/c$ of design samples per class

Data	Approach and design sets	k	$n_{ds.ori}/c$ 30	60	90	120	150
H. digits	TL $X_{ds.ori}$ after $X_{ds.tra.030}$ PT+FT	1	22.7 (02.0)	13.5 (00.9)	10.8 (00.5)	9.9 (00.5)	9.1 (00.4)
	TL $X_{ds.ori}$ after $X_{ds.tra.030}$ PT+FT	5	15.6 (01.4) [<0.01]	11.4 (00.8) [<0.01]	9.4 (00.6) [<0.01]	8.5 (00.5) [<0.01]	8.0 (00.4) [<0.01]
	TL $X_{ds.ori}$ after $X_{ds.tra.030}$ PT+FT	10	15.2 (02.0) [<0.01]	10.9 (00.5) [<0.01]	9.2 (00.5) [<0.01]	8.6 (00.5) [<0.01]	8.0 (00.4) [<0.01]
T. digits	TL $X_{ds.ori}$ after $X_{ds.tra.030}$ PT+FT	1	11.0 (01.0)	7.4 (00.4)	5.9 (00.6)	5.3 (00.4)	4.8 (00.3)
	TL $X_{ds.ori}$ after $X_{ds.tra.030}$ PT+FT	5	8.8 (00.7) [<0.01]	6.7 (00.6) [<0.01]	5.7 (00.5) [0.07]	5.1 (00.5) [0.12]	4.7 (00.2) [0.08]
	TL $X_{ds.ori}$ after $X_{ds.tra.030}$ PT+FT	10	8.9 (00.7) [<0.01]	6.8 (00.5) [<0.01]	6.0 (00.7) [0.43]	5.3 (00.5) [0.49]	4.8 (00.4) [0.45]
T. letters	TL $X_{ds.ori}$ after $X_{ds.tra.030}$ PT+FT	1	19.4 (01.1)	15.3 (00.6)	13.6 (00.5)	12.5 (00.3)	11.9 (00.4)
	TL $X_{ds.ori}$ after $X_{ds.tra.030}$ PT+FT	5	17.8 (00.7) [<0.01]	15.0 (00.5) [0.06]	13.7 (00.4) [0.33]	12.9 (00.2) [<0.01]	12.4 (00.3) [<0.01]
	TL $X_{ds.ori}$ after $X_{ds.tra.030}$ PT+FT	10	18.0 (00.7) [<0.01]	15.1 (00.5) [0.22]	14.0 (00.4) [0.01]	13.6 (00.4) [<0.01]	13.1 (00.3) [<0.01]

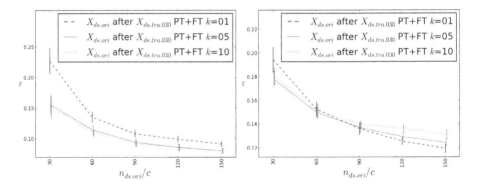

Fig. 3. Average classification test error $\bar{\varepsilon}$ obtained with TL, for different values of k, for each data type, for different numbers $n_{ds.ori}/c$ of original design samples per class. Left: handwritten digits; right: typewritten letters.

For all data types, when only 30 original design samples per class were used, the errors yielded by TL were significantly lower when the transformed design set was formed by several rotations of each original sample ($k=5$ or $k=10$) than when the transformed set was obtained via a single rotation ($k=1$). In the case of typewritten digits, this benefit persisted for 60 samples per class and, in the case of handwritten digits, it was visible for any number of samples per class.

For handwritten and typewritten digit data, regardless of the amount of design data per class, the performances obtained with $k=10$ and $k=5$ were not distinguishable. With typewritten letters, for more than 90 samples per class, the errors obtained with $k=10$ were actually higher than those obtained with $k=5$.

The effects discussed above can also be observed in Fig. 2 (right), which plots the improvements that the average TL errors shown in Table 4 for k=5 achieved in relation to the average BL errors shown in Table 2.

Average training times observed for $n_{ds.ori}/c$=150 are included in Table 3. The benefits obtained by using k=5 rotations per original design sample had a clear cost in terms of total training times, which were about three times longer than the times observed when k=1.

6   Conclusions and Future Directions

In this work we explored the idea that, in the presence of a small design set of image data, it could be beneficial to use that same set to obtain a transformed design set (by performing a random rotation on each original sample), train a source network using the transformed data, then retrain that network using the original data. For the three data types involved in our experiments, networks designed via this TL approach yielded significantly lower errors than networks trained using only original (non-rotated) data. Relative improvements between 6% and 16% were observed in the average errors, at the expense of training times 50% to 100% longer.

In general, pre-training and fine-tuning a source network led to better results than just pre-training it. Restricting the rotations performed on the original design samples to a small range led to better results than freely rotating the samples. It would be interesting to study in finer detail the relationship between performance and the range of allowed rotation, and also try transformations other than rotation.

For small amounts of original design data, it was possible to further improve performance by including in the transformed data more than one randomly rotated version of each original sample. With k=5 rotations per original sample, relative improvements between 8% and 42% were observed in the average test error. This implied training times about three times longer than those associated with a single rotation.

References

1. Bengio, Y.: Learning deep architectures for AI. Foundations and Trends in Machine Learning **2**(1), 1–127 (2009)
2. Bengio, Y., Courville, A., Vincent, P.: Representation learning: A review and new perspectives. IEEE Transactions on Pattern Analysis and Machine Intelligence **35**(8), 1798–1828 (2013)
3. Ciresan, D., Meier, U., Gambardella, L., Schmidhuber, J.: Deep, big, simple neural nets for handwritten digit recognition. Neural Computation **22**(12), 3207–3220 (2010)
4. Ciresan, D., Meier, U., Schmidhuber, J.: Transfer learning for Latin and Chinese characters with deep neural networks. In: International Joint Conference on Neural Networks (IJCNN), pp. 1–6 (2012)

5. Deng, L., Yu, D.: Deep learning for signal and information processing. Microsoft Research Monograph (2013)
6. Glorot, X., Bordes, A., Bengio, Y.: Domain adaptation for large-scale sentiment classification: a deep learning approach. In: International Conference on Machine Learning (ICML), pp. 513–520 (2011)
7. Hinton, G., Osindero, S., Teh, Y.-W.: A fast learning algorithm for deep belief nets. Neural Computation **18**(7), 1527–1554 (2006)
8. Larochelle, H., Erhan, D., Courville, A., Bergstra, J., Bengio, Y.: An empirical evaluation of deep architectures on problems with many factors of variation. In: International Conference on Machine Learning (ICML), pp. 473–480 (2007)
9. Pan, S., Yang, Q.: A survey on transfer learning. IEEE Transactions on Knowledge and Data Engineering **22**(10), 1345–1359 (2010)
10. Simard, P., Steinkraus, D., Platt, J.C.: Best practices for convolutional neural networks applied to visual document analysis. In: International Conference on Document Analysis and Recognition (ICDAR), vol. 3, pp. 958–962 (2003)

Catalogue-Based Traffic Sign Asset Management: Towards User's Effort Minimisation

Kelwin Fernandes[1]([⊠]), Pedro F.B. Silva[1],
Lucian Ciobanu[1], and Paulo Fonseca[2]

[1] INESC TEC, Porto, Portugal
[2] MonteAdriano, Grupo Elevo, Porto, Portugal
{kafc,pedro.f.silva,lucian.ciobanu}@inesctec.pt

Abstract. Automatic traffic sign recognition is a difficult task, as it is necessary to distinguish between a very high number of classes with low inter-class variability. The state-of-the-art methods report very high accuracy rates but just a few classes are covered and several training samples are required. For the sake of the development of an asset management system, these approaches are out of reach. Furthermore, in this context, minimizing user's effort is more important than achieving maximal classification accuracy. In this paper, we propose a catalogue-based traffic sign classifier which doesn't require real training samples for model building and promotes minimal user's workload involving the catalogue's semantic structure in the error propagation. Experimental results reveal that user's workload was reduced by 20 % while accuracy was improved by 2 %.

Keywords: Traffic sign recognition · Discriminative local regions · Distance transform · Traffic sign asset management · User centered machine learning

1 Introduction

Automatic traffic sign recognition using image processing has been an active topic of research since the earliest steps of Computer Vision, given the high industrial interest on the development of driver's assistance technologies and the need to diminish road maintenance costs.

In this context, several different image processing algorithms have been proposed for both traffic sign detection and recognition, which, although reporting good accuracy rates, are confined to a relatively small number of classes and demand fair amounts of training data for model building.

A road asset management system is basically a program allowing the construction of an inventory of traffic signs along a given itinerary. Several aspects

© Springer International Publishing Switzerland 2014
A. Campilho and M. Kamel (Eds.): ICIAR 2014, Part I, LNCS 8814, pp. 301–308, 2014.
DOI: 10.1007/978-3-319-11758-4_33

hinder the success of developing automatic approaches to solve this task, namely, the huge number of different existent signs and the difficulty to obtain representative training data.

Given these constraints, human operators remain the most reliable and most used source when it comes to traffic sign asset management, having to frequently revise or validate the results of automatic systems and indicate multiple, interacting labels. Ensuring a minimal classification rate is, therefore, less important than minimising the user's workload. That is, uniquely identifying a given sign is less important than minimising the user's effort to fix possible incorrect results.

In this paper, we propose a semi-automatic traffic sign recognition system for road asset management focusing on user's effort minimisation.

2   Related Work

Different methods have been proposed in the literature to automatically detect and recognise traffic signs [1–5]. Commonly, the detection and recognition steps are sequentially integrated but rather independent from each other.

Considering the detection task, both colour-based [2] and shape-based [4,6] algorithms have been developed. Colour-based algorithms are more straightforward and take advantage of the fact that colour is the most salient feature of traffic signs.

Some authors argue, however, that colour segmentation is not reliable given its sensitivity to several factors (target distance, illumination, etc.) and prefer to detect traffic signs by their well-defined shape (squares, triangles, circles) [1].

Addressing the recognition task, both pixel-based and feature-based methods have been reported [1,3,5]. Pixel-based algorithms use variations of template matching and feature-based techniques use machine learning algorithms over different features (colour, shape, motion information and statistical properties).

Most available studies consider simplified settings: limited subsets of traffic signs or impose rather simple restrictions on the experimental setting by considering just a single semantic category or signs from structurally different categories [1].

State of the art methods on traffic sign classification are mainly based on machine learning techniques which although providing high accuracy, as much as 99.15%, are dependent on a high number of training examples [5]. These are out of reach for catalogue-based traffic sign asset management, as it is not possible to gather a representative training dataset for the different traffic signs. To overcome this difficulty, we adapted the approach proposed by Ruta et. al. [1] using a Distance Transform algorithm for sign classification using template images.

3   System Outline

Generally, a traffic sign recognition system involves the following steps: 1) traffic sign detection; 2) discretisation of the identified regions of interest; 3) classification of the instances obtained in 2).

In this paper, we are interested in proposing a new classification method (step 3) and we assume, therefore, that traffic sign detection has been done exactly (manual segmentation) in order to avoid the propagation of segmentation errors to misclassification.

3.1   Colour Initialisation

Using the full colour spectrum to recognise traffic signs is both inefficient and unnecessary as traffic signs contain just up to four distinctive colours per category [1]. Thus, obtaining a discrete image representation is advantageous.

Prior to processing, input RGB images are converted into indexed images using a clustering algorithm (K-means) in a two stage cascade over the (H, S) channel space. This colour space was chosen, as it is generally understood as robust against illumination changes and as it reproduces human visual experience.

3.2   Template Matching

Consider two indexed, size normalized images, I and J, divided into small, regularly spaced, non-overlapping $m \times m$ blocks, r_k. Comparing images I and J means comparing their subregions r_k using a distance transform $\psi(I, J)$ [1]. The dissimilarity between I and J in region r_k is $d_{r_k} = m^{-2} \sum_{t=1}^{m^2} \psi(I, J)$.

For each discrete colour, the weighted dissimilarity between I and J is given by

$$\hat{d}_{S,W}(I, J) = \frac{\sum_{k=1}^{|S|} w_k d_{r_k}(I, J)}{\sum_{k=1}^{|S|} w_k},$$

where S is the set of regions r_k considered and W is a weight vector codifying the importance of each region r_k.

Ruta et al. argue that using all regions r_k uniformly is inadequate for traffic sign recognition and they proposed a discriminative region selection procedure using template images (cf. Algorithm 1).

Algorithm 1. Discriminative Region Selection

```
1   Input: Sign category C = {Tⱼ : j = 1,...,N}, target template index i,
2   region pool R = {rₖ|k = 1,...,M}, dissimilarity threshold t_D

3   initialise an array of region weights W = {wₖ|wₖ = 0, k = 1,...,M}
4   for each template Tⱼ ∈ C, j ≠ i do
5       sort R by decreasing dissimilarity d_{rⱼ}(Tᵢ, Tⱼ)
6       S_{i,j} = [], W_{i,j} = [], D_{i,j} = 0

7       for ( l = 1; l < M and D_{i,j} < t_D; l = l+1 ) do
8           set weight of the new region to: wˡ_j = drⱼ⁽ˡ⁾(Tᵢ, Tⱼ)²
9           add region rⱼ⁽ˡ⁾ to S_{i,j} and weight wⱼ⁽ˡ⁾ to W_{i,j}
10          update D_{i,j}: D_{i,j} = D_{i,j} + drⱼ⁽ˡ⁾(Tᵢ, Tⱼ)

11      for each region rₖ ∈ S_{i,j} do
12          update region weight: wₖ = wₖ + wⱼ⁽ᵗ⁾
13  Output: ordered sets Sᵢ = {rₖ|wₖ > 0} and Wᵢ = {wₖ|wₖ > 0}
```

Algorithm 1 depends on the definition of an appropriate threshold t_D to limit admissible dissimilarities $D_{i,j}$. As the number of categories increases, both the value of t_D and the number of regions r_k used become larger.

The best model is found by maximising the following objective function $O(\theta_i) = \sum_{j \neq i} \hat{d}_{S_i}(T_i, T_j)$, where $\theta_i = (S, W)_i$.

3.3   User's Effort Minimisation

Some efforts have been made within the active learning framework to reduce user's effort by means of sorting the classification output. Cullota et al. proposed a framework to reduce the user's effort in labelling tasks within structured prediction problems, where it is necessary to identify multiple, sometimes interacting labels for data [7].

Catalogue-based traffic sign asset management is a structured prediction task as it is not only necessary to identify the different signs but also their category, type and subgroup according to varying national regulations (cf. Figs. 1 and 2).

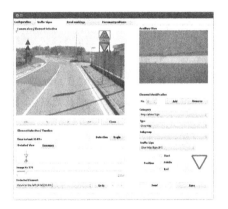 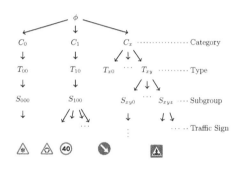

Fig. 1. GUI integrating the proposed algorithm

Fig. 2. Traffic sign catalogue tree derived from the GUI

In this context, we developed a novel approach based on Ruta's work that embodies user's effort in the training process, trying to increase the discriminability of those pairs of classes that require higher amount of user intervention. In real life problems, these classes are semantically different.

This can be achieved in general learning tasks by considering different error propagation according to user's effort when correcting possible mistakes. In our case, we adapted the weight region definition (line 12, Alg. 1) to $w_k = w_k + 2^{uid(j,i)} \cdot w_j^{(t)}$, measuring user's effort by means of the following function:

$$uid(a,b) = \begin{cases} 0 & ,a = b \\ 1 + \dfrac{\mid a.\text{index} - b.\text{index} \mid}{\mid a.\text{siblings} \mid} & ,a.\text{parent} = b.\text{parent} \\ uid(a.\text{parent}, b.\text{parent}) & ,\mid b.\text{siblings} \mid = 1 \\ 1 + uid(a.\text{parent}, \ b.\text{parent}) & ,\text{otherwise} \end{cases}$$

The proposed user interface distance measures the user's effort to correct a wrongly labelled prediction a to its real label b by considering two different types of actions on the graphic user interface (cf. Fig. 1), namely clicks and partial scrolling, and the cost of changing states in the catalogue-driven action-tree (cf. Fig. 2).

If the classification algorithm's output is correct, the user workload is 0. Otherwise, if the output is not correct but semantically approximate, i.e., both the candidate and the real traffic signs have the same category, type and subgroup (same parent in the action-tree), the user's effort consists in one click and a partial scrolling. Furthermore, in the particular case when b has no siblings, the workload is defined in terms of its parent in the action-tree (cf. Fig. 2) . In all other cases, the user effort consists in iteratively summing up the costs of each necessary correction.

In this case, uid's contribution to the region weight definition was set as exponential but it could be changed to perceive finest characteristics of the underlying workload function.

3.4   Classification

Let $C = \{T_i | i = 1, \ldots, N\}$ be the set of traffic signs. Given a new image I, classifying it means identifying the template T_i which maximises the posterior probability

$$p(T_i | I, \theta_i) = \frac{p(I | T_i, \theta_i) \ p(T_i)}{\sum_{k=1}^{N} p(I | T_k, \theta_k) \ p(T_k)}$$

4   Experimental Study

Two different datasets have been used in the development of the present system. For model building, a dataset of traffic sign pictograms (artificial images) directly extracted from the Portuguese catalogue was considered [8].

Models were generated considering a total of 394 different traffic signs organized in 5 categories, 14 types and 2 subgroups according to official portuguese catalogue specifications [8].

For model testing, a dataset of 633 real images of a total of 30 different traffic signs was considered. This dataset is consistent with the catalogue previously referred and it was built in the scope of the project SARA (cf. acknowledgements). Traffic sign images were collected using a frontal camera in a moving vehicle at varying distances and angles and with different illumination conditions. Images are from urban scenarios and highways.

Figure 3 illustrates template and real images of some of the traffic signs present in the considered datasets.

Fig. 3. Dataset overview: template and real images

Original traffic sign images were compared with catalogue images (templates) after image normalization using the 1-versus-all scheme [1]. In order to avoid the propagation of segmentation errors to the classification accuracy, these images have been manually segmented.

To evaluate the results of the proposed system against the base model of Ruta et. al., we have used the following indicators: accuracy, workload and average workload. Accuracy was calculated considering the mean average error. Workload was defined as the sum of the user interface distance values of all classification results. Finally, average workload was defined as the sum of the user interface distance when wrong classification results were obtained. The results of the experimental study carried out are presented in Table 1 and in Fig. 4.

Table 1. Method Evaluation: Summary

Region Size	Method	Accuracy	Workload	Gain (%)	Average Workload	Gain (%)
1 × 1	Base	82.62	209.29	–	1.90	–
	Proposed	**84.67**	**167.09**	20.16	**1.72**	9.47
2 × 2	Base	81.99	211.71	–	1.85	–
	Proposed	**84.04**	**173.21**	18.18	**1.71**	7.65
4 × 4	Base	82.14	207.42	–	1.83	–
	Proposed	**83.41**	**177.34**	14.50	**1.68**	7.98
8 × 8	Base	82.30	189.05	–	1.68	–
	Proposed	**82.93**	**178.73**	5.46	**1.65**	1.95
16 × 16	Base	**79.62**	229.77	–	1.78	–
	Proposed	**79.62**	**217.49**	5.34	**1.68**	5.34
32 × 32	Base	**78.83**	264.72	–	1.97	–
	Proposed	**78.83**	**259.61**	1.93	**1.93**	2.03

The proposed method successfully reduced user's workload for all region sizes considered. Additionally, classification results were improved for smaller region sizes and maintained for bigger region sizes.

The average workload was consistently improved in all variations of the region size used. The most significant performance gains were observed for smaller region sizes (higher number of regions). This result was expected given the fact that, as region size increases, a smaller number of regions is used by the classification algorithm which necessarily leads to decreasing discriminative power.

On the other hand, our empirical observation suggests that considering the finest possible resolution (1×1) does not qualitatively improve results.

Fig. 4 shows the minimum workload needed to correct all misclassifications when the user has access to the K highest probable results determined by the classifier, considering 2×2 region size.

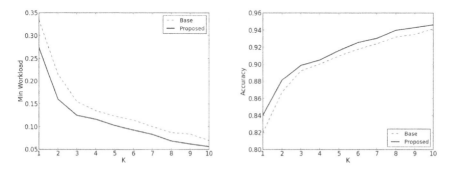

Fig. 4. Workload (left) and accuracy (right) as function of the number of proposed candidates (K)

The proposed model scored better than the base model in terms of both minimum necessary workload and accuracy. Furthermore, the best candidates tend to be among the first suggested classes, given that the accuracy increment is higher for lower values of K. Also, these candidates are easier to correct in case of misclassification (cf. Fig. 4).

5   Conclusions

The proposed system successfully decreased user's workload in all variations of the experimental setting, achieving better or equivalent accuracy rates as the base model. In the best case, the classification accuracy was improved by 2% and the user's workload was reduced by 20%. The reported improvement was achieved thanks to an effective reduction of user's workload rather than a better classification accuracy as pointed out by the average workload when mistaken (cf. Table 1).

Our work can be thought of an extension of that of Ruta et al., as a far greater number of different traffic signs was considered. Ruta et al. highlight as an important advantage of their method, the fact that the algorithm can classify several traffic signs using just a small number of regions. This holds for the number of different signs used by them in the training procedure (below 50). In our work, we considered around 400 classes and, in practice, it was not possible to keep the threshold to the number of regions (cf. line 7, Alg. 1), as more regions are needed for discrimination.

The improvement to the base model was found to be less significant as the region size increases (lower number of regions used), as classification aspects become dominant.

In the future, we would like to extend this work by improving the *uid* function within the active learning framework considering user's feedback to set differentiate action-tree costs.

Acknowledgments. This work is financed by the ERDF - European Regional Development Fund through the COMPETE Programme (operational programme for competitiveness) and by National Funds through the FCT - Fundação para a Ciência e a Tecnologia (Portuguese Foundation for Science and Technology) within project « FCOMP-01-0124-FEDER-037281 » and within post-doctoral grant SFRH/BPD/ 85225/2012.

References

1. Ruta, A., Li, Y., Liu, X.: Real-time traffic sign recognition from video by class-specific discriminative features. Pattern Recogn. **43**(1), 416–430 (2010)
2. Broggi, A., Cerri, P., Medici, P., Porta, P., Ghisio, G.: Real time road signs recognition. In: 2007 IEEE Intelligent Vehicles Symposium, pp. 981–986 (June 2007)
3. Bahlmann, C., Zhu, Y., Ramesh, V., Pellkofer, M., Koehler, T.: A system for traffic sign detection, tracking, and recognition using color, shape, and motion information. In: Proceedings of the Intelligent Vehicles Symposium, pp. 255–260. IEEE (June 2005)
4. Moutarde, F., Bargeton, A., Herbin, A., Chanussot, L.: Modular traffic sign recognition applied to on-vehicle real-time visual detection of american and european speed limit signs. CoRR (2009)
5. Ciresan, D., Meier, U., Masci, J., Schmidhuber, J.: A committee of neural networks for traffic sign classification. In: The 2011 International Joint Conference on Neural Networks (IJCNN), pp. 1918–1921. IEEE (2011)
6. Moutarde, F., Bargeton, A., Herbin, A., Chanussot, L.: Robust on-vehicle real-time visual detection of american and european speed limit signs, with a modular traffic signs recognition system. In: 2007 IEEE Intelligent Vehicles Symposium, pp. 1122–1126 (June 2007)
7. Culotta, A., McCallum, A.: Reducing labeling effort for structured prediction tasks. In: Veloso, M.M., Kambhampati, S. (eds.), pp. 746–751. AAAI Press/The MIT Press (2005)
8. Diário da Républica:
   http://aiweb.techfak.uni-bielefeld.de/content/bworld-robot-control-software/
   I Série B N° 227 (October 1, 1998)

Scalable Prototype Learning Using GPUs

Tonghua Su[1(✉)], Songze Li[1], Peijun Ma[1], Shengchun Deng[1], and Guangsheng Liang[2]

[1] School of Software, Harbin Institute of Technology, Harbin, People's Republic of China
thsu@hit.edu.cn
[2] The Second Artillery Force of the PLA, People's Republic of China
{ma,dsc}@hit.edu.cn

Abstract. Prototype learning is widely used in character recognition field. Unfortunately, current learning algorithms require intensive computation burden for large category applications, such as Japanese/Chinese character recognition. To resolve this challenge, a principled parallel method is proposed on GPUs instead of CPUs. We have implemented the method in mini-batch manner as well as stochastic gradient descent (SGD) manner. Our evaluations on a Chinese character database show that our method posses a high scalability while preserving its performance precision. Up to 194X speedup can be achieved in the case of mini-batch. Even to the more difficult SGD occasion, a more than 30-fold speedup is observed.

Keywords: Prototype learning · Learning vector quantization · Chinese character recognition · Parallel reduction · GPU computing · CUDA

1 Introduction

Learning vector quantization (LVQ) is an elegant prototype learning algorithm for large category classification in both its small storage requirement and high throughput recognition. Previous studies show that prototype learning can yield a state-of-the-art performance both on digit recognition and Japanese/Chinese recognition when a discriminative learning criteria is used [1]. LVQ is also extremely useful to pick up a limited candidate classes for further process. For example, a LVQ classifier is employed to reduce the high training demanding of PL-MQDF [2]. Perhaps most significantly, with the emergence of mobile applications, LVQ models are especially well-suited to character input demand [3] in embedded devices, such as smartphones, tablets.

To discriminatively learn a robust LVQ model, there is a daunting computing complexity. It may take several days using conventional implementation on a single CPU core. As for discriminative learning, it is extremely true that more data win. Some works attempt to collect more training samples or synthesize artificial ones. Using orders of magnitude more training samples, steady improvements are reported in recent studies [4, 5]. Therefore, there is a great need to scale up those learning algorithms.

Recent works had shown that GPUs were outstanding accelerators for many pattern recognition tasks. Raina et al [6] studied sparse coding on GPUs. Their

© Springer International Publishing Switzerland 2014
A. Campilho and M. Kamel (Eds.): ICIAR 2014, Part I, LNCS 8814, pp. 309–319, 2014.
DOI: 10.1007/978-3-319-11758-4_34

implementation of sparse coding led to 5~15-fold speedup. There was couple of groups studying big multilayer neural networks using GPUs. Ciresan et al made it possible to train a deep MLP of best performance with the help of GPUs [7]. More recently, Zhou et al [5] proposed a GPU-based discriminative training method for Chinese character recognition. Their mini-batch implementation yielded a speedup of 15 times.

This paper presents a GPU-intensive parallel method which can scale prototype learning up remarkably. Unlike to previous works, our method schedules almost all computation workloads onto the GPU device, requiring little CPU coordination. Our method is benchmarked on Chinese character recognition and a high scalability is obtained.

The remainder of the paper is organized as follows. The next section provides some preliminaries relating to LVQ. Then Sect. 3 presents the principled parallel framework which gives GPUs the main role in workload computation. Implementation of the framework is unfolded further in Sect. 4. Each step of the method is refined and we focus on the tiling and reduction strategy. To benchmark the method, we conduct experiments on the Chinese character recognition task in Sect. 5. Finally, the last section summarizes the paper.

2   Preliminaries

Assuming a C-class classification task, prototype learning is to generate a set of prototype vectors $\Theta = \{ \mathbf{m}_i, i=1, 2,...,C \}$. Here we just allocate single prototype to each class for simplicity and extending to multiple prototypes is straightforward.

For learning the prototypes, a collection of training samples is used as teachers. Let's denote the training samples as $\{ (\mathbf{x}_n, y_n), n=1,2,...,N \}$, where y_n is the class label of $\mathbf{x}_n$. In practice, the objective is to minimize the empirical loss on training set:

$$\hat{\Theta} = \arg\min_{\Theta} \frac{1}{N} \sum_{n=1}^{N} \phi(f(\mathbf{x}_n, \Theta)) \quad , \tag{1}$$

where $\phi(.)$ is the loss function on a scoring $f(\mathbf{x}, \Theta)$.

We take generalized learning vector quantization (GLVQ) [8] to illustrate the underlying discriminative thinking. Firstly, we define an error measure for $\mathbf{x}$:

$$f(\mathbf{x}) = \frac{d_c - d_r}{d_c + d_r} \quad , \tag{2}$$

where d_c and d_r are the distances of $\mathbf{x}$ from genuine class ω_c and rival class ω_r, respectively. Then the loss function can be approximated by the sigmoid function:

$$\phi(f(\mathbf{x})) = \frac{1}{1 + e^{-\xi f(\mathbf{x})}} \quad , \tag{3}$$

where ξ is used to tune the smoothness of the sigmoid function.

If a squared Euclidean distance is used, we can obtain the following learning rule for ω_c and ω_r depending on $\mathbf{x}$:

$$
\begin{cases}
\mathbf{m}_c \leftarrow \mathbf{m}_c + \eta f(\mathbf{x})\left(1 - f(\mathbf{x})\right)\dfrac{d_r}{\left(d_c + d_r\right)^2}\left(\mathbf{x} - \mathbf{m}_c\right) \\[2ex]
\mathbf{m}_r \leftarrow \mathbf{m}_r - \eta f(\mathbf{x})\left(1 - f(\mathbf{x})\right)\dfrac{d_c}{\left(d_c + d_r\right)^2}\left(\mathbf{x} - \mathbf{m}_r\right)
\end{cases}
\tag{4}
$$

We thus arrive at GLVQ learning algorithm in Algorithm I.

Algorithm I. GLVQ Learing Algorithm (Sequencial Version)

Input: training set $\{\mathbf{x}_n, y_n\}_{n=1,\ldots,N}$, initial prototypes $\{\mathbf{m}_i\}_{i=1,\ldots,C}$
Output: $\{\mathbf{m}_i\}_{i=1,\ldots,C}$

1:	**while** not convergent **do**
2:	**for each** $\{\mathbf{x}_n, y_n\}$
3:	find out $(\mathbf{m}_c, \mathbf{d}_c)$ and $(\mathbf{m}_r, \mathbf{d}_r)$ through compute-then-compare distances
4:	compute error measure $f(\mathbf{x})$ using Equation (2)
5:	derive loss function $\phi(\mathbf{x})$ using Equation (3)
6:	update $\mathbf{m}_c, \mathbf{m}_r$ using Equation (4)
7:	**end for**
8:	**end while**
9:	**return** $\{\mathbf{m}_i\}_{i=1,\ldots,C}$

3   Principle

Algorithm I repeatedly executes the following workloads: pick one sample, compute the distances from the sample to all prototypes, find out the genuine pair and rival pair, compute loss function and gradient, and finally update the prototype vectors. Inherently, it is a sequential process. To port it to parallel architectures, we extend SGD as a mini-batch (size of mb) gradient descent and rearrange the process as in Algorithm II. Each main step can be parallelized.

Algorithm II. GLVQ Learing Algorithm (Parallel Framework)

Input: training set $\{\mathbf{x}_n, y_n\}_{n=1,\ldots,N}$, initial prototypes $\{\mathbf{m}_i\}_{i=1,\ldots,C}$
Output: $\{\mathbf{m}_i\}_{i=1,\ldots,C}$

1:	**while** not convergent **do**
2:	**for each** mini-batch $T_i = \{(\mathbf{x}_{i_1}, y_{i_1}), \ldots, (\mathbf{x}_{i_M}, y_{i_M})\}$
3:	compute all distances as a matrix **in parallel**
4:	find out genuine/rival pair **in parallel**
5:	derive loss function **in parallel**
6:	update prototypes **in parallel**
7:	**end for**
8:	**end while**
9:	**return** $\{\mathbf{m}_i\}_{i=1,\ldots,C}$

To successfully exploit GPUs, we need to match two best practices. Firstly, memory transfers between CPU and the GPU's global memory need to be minimized. For pattern recognition applications, we can achieve this by storing all prototypes permanently in GPU global memory during learning. Training samples usually cannot all be stored in global memory, but they should be transferred only occasionally into global memory in as large chunks as possible. With both parameters and training data in GPU global memory, the updates can be computed without any memory transfer operations.

A second practice is that the learning should be implemented to fit the two level hierarchies of blocks and threads, in such a way that shared memory can be used where possible, and global memory accesses can be coalesced. Often, blocks can exploit data parallelism, while threads can exploit more fine-grained parallelism because they have access to very fast shared memory and can be synchronized. Further, the graphics hardware can hide memory latencies for blocks waiting on global memory accesses by scheduling a ready-to-run block in that time. To fully use such latency hiding, it is beneficial to use a large number of independently executing blocks.

In light of above GPU programming practices, we develop an intense GPU solution as shown in Fig. 1. Seen from the figure, the prototype vectors only transfer to and from GPU global memory once at the beginning and ending of the whole process, respectively. If there is too big training set to accommodate at global memory, the selected mini-batch samples should be transferred to GPU at the start of that sweep. Otherwise, we can just copy all of them to the global memory, without multiple transfer requests. Overall, there is few workload that done by CPU, except controlling execution flow.

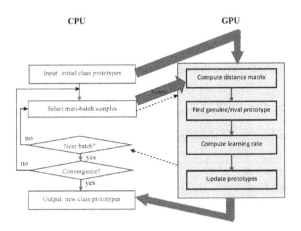

Fig. 1. Heterogeneous computing model for prototype learning

4   Implementation

We implemented the principled method on CUDA programming architecture. We invoke three CUDA kernel functions during one sweep of training. Lines 3~6 in

Algorithm II are executed as separate kernel functions except that line 4 and 5 are combined into a single kernel. Among those kernels, the first two are most time consuming. We investigate two different algorithms to distance computing in subsection 4.1 and 4.2 respectively. Similarly, in subsection 4.3 and 4.4, we present parallel reduction and compare-and-exchange strategy to compute the minimum distance and associated prototype index. In the last subsection, we provide our implementation solution to parallel parameter updating. For brevity, we just assign one prototype to each class. However, more prototypes can be implemented with ease.

4.1   Distance Computing: Parallel Reduction

Reduction delivers a $O(1)$ result over $O(K)$ input elements. It can be used to execute a binary associative operation $\oplus$ in parallel. The standard reduction algorithm can be found in [9]. Herein we apply it to compute the squared Euclidean distance between two vectors. During distance computing, operator $\oplus$ can be defined as:

$$a_i \oplus b_i \equiv (a_i - b_i)^2$$

Fig. 2 shows a reduction structure using 16 threads (one element per thread). In the first round, the upper half elements operate $\oplus$ onto the lower half elements with 8 operations. The second round requires 4 operations. Assuming K is power of 2, the squared distance of two K-dimension vectors can be derived in $\log_2(K)+1$ rounds.

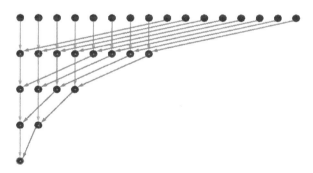

Fig. 2. Reduction of 16 elements

Initially, we let each block compute one squared distance, loading one sample vector and one prototype vector from global memory. Thus we need (C, mb) thread blocks to compute a distance matrix of $mb*C$ distances. Some of the practical issues should be considered carefully.

On the one hand, the feature dimensionality of samples (we denote it as dim, say 160) may be different than power of 2. We can set the block size as the largest power of 2 that below its dimensionality and contribution from any threads above that power of 2 is accumulated through one round of $\oplus$ operation before continuing on log-step reduction. On the other hand, we shall maximize data reuse via shared memory. Instead of computing one distance, each block is in charge of *TILE_LEN* distances from one sample to *TILE_LEN* prototypes.

4.2   Distance Computing: Tiling Sum

Unlike to subsection 4.1, we can let each thread compute a distance independently. Under this thinking, each thread first fetches $2*dim$ values from global memory and then performs a serial reduction. There is inefficient global memory traffic. A tiling idea is presented to matrix-matrix multiplication in [10] to reduce the heavy traffic of the global memory. Such idea is also adapted to solve our computation of squared distance.

Since our target is to compute $mb*C$ distances, we use a $TILE\_LEN*TILE\_LEN$ tile to cover this distance matrix. The tile dimensions equal those of the block and can be accommodated in shared memory. Then we divide the prototype matrix and sample matrix into tiles. The squared distance calculations performed by each thread are now divided into $(dim+TILE\_LEN$ -1$)/TILE\_LEN$ phases. The partial distances are iteratively accumulated to arrive at the final distance. Some of the key process is illustrated in Fig. 3. The global memory traffic can be reduced to $1/TILE\_LEN$ in this way.

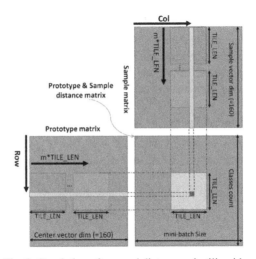

Fig. 3. Caculation of squared distances via tiling idea

4.3   Minima Searching: Parallel Reduction

Given C distances from sample $(\mathbf{x}_n, y_n)$, our task is to retrieve the genuine (d_c, ω_c) and rival (d_r, ω_r). These pairs are needed to derive a new m_c and m_r. We develop a parallel reduction to search the minimal distance and the associated class index. Since d_r is the minimal distance other than d_c, we use a trick to avoid conditional code: first retrieve the d_c through y_n, and then write back a very large value to that position. If using multiple prototypes per class instead, we can execute another pass of reduction to retrieve the closest prototype from genuine class in advance.

We invoke a kernel of mb blocks each of which is of 1024 (or 512) threads. All threads in a block collaborate to perform a minima reduction in shared memory. Again, the value of C may be not a power of 2 and similar trick is used as in subsection 4.4.1. Moreover, C may be much larger than block size. This issue can be solved by iteratively considering those elements block-size away before continuing log-step minima reduction.

4.4   Minima Searching: Compare-and-Exchange

We can also simply invoke mb threads for minima searching. If mb is large than the theoretical limitation of block dimension, more blocks can be automatically dispatched. Each thread computes the needed (d_c, ω_c) and (d_r, ω_r) pairs via iterative compare-and-exchange operation.

It is a most straightforward way to port serial searching algorithms. It will take a thread $O(C)$ steps to arrive at the output. Therefore, this is a thread-intensive strategy. Once mb is relatively small, it may certainly underutilize GPU resources.

4.5   Parameter Updating

In SGD updating mode ($mb=1$), two prototype vectors are involved in the updating process. We invoke dim threads and within each thread, one element of the vector evolves following Equation (4). When $mb>1$, each thread will run mb times iteratively; contribution from one sample is considered within each iteration.

5   Experiments

Experiments are conducted on the Chinese character recognition task to evaluate the proposed method. We firstly describe the database used for our benchmarks. Then we show the correctness of our implementation in subsection 5.2. Timing of key kernel executions is presented and compared in subsection 5.3. In the last subsection, we evaluate the overall scalability of our method.

The CPU implementation is run on a Xeon X3440 sever with a 2.53 GHZ clock rate, while the GPU we used is GTX 680 which is a consumer-level card. During the benchmarks, we consider both single prototype per class and eight prototypes per class. The parameter *TILE-LEN* is set to 16 empirically.

5.1   Database Description

A large handwritten Chinese character database is used to verify the efficacy of our method. We select the most popular two subsets similar to [2], those are CASIA-HWDB1.0 (DB1.0) and CASIA-HWDB1.1 (DB1.1) [11]. There are 3,755 classes (GB1 character set) and each class has about 570 training instances. We have 2,144,749 training samples and 533,675 test samples. The Chinese characters of each set are preprinted in six different orders to balance the writing quality variation of each writer through the writing process.

Each character sample is mapped to a 512 gradient feature space initially. Then LDA is employed to reduce the feature dimensionality from 512 to 160. Thus, the variable *dim* is set to 160 in this paper.

5.2 Performance Evaluation

We run the CPU implementation and the proposed GPU implementation back to back. Both of them sweep over the training set 40 times. At each sweep, we collect their recognition error rate on training set (fitting error) and that on test set (test error). We also use different mini-batch size. Their learning process and corresponding performance are depicted in Fig. 4(a) and (b), respectively. Seen from these figures, there are invisible performance differences between the CPU implementation and the GPU implementation.

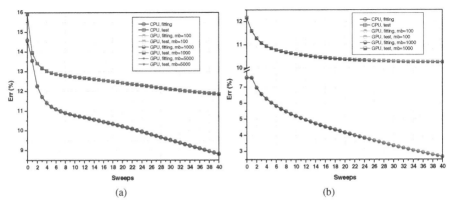

(a)   (b)

Fig. 4. Learning process comparison between CPU and GPU: (a) single prototype/class; (b) eight prototypes/class

5.3 Algorithmic Evaluation

Distance computation and minima searching tasks are two most compute-intensive workloads in Algorithm I. We first evaluate the efficiency of distance computation. Both parallel reduction and tiling sum can be used. We consider different mini-batch size *mb* in $\{2^0, 2^1, ..., 2^{13}\}$. The results are plotted in Fig. 5(a) and (b) with one pass of learning on training data. It shows that parallel reduction has a consistent execution time while tiling sum has high throughput when *mb* is larger or equal than *TILE-LEN*.

Then we inspect the efficiency of minima searching task. Similarly, we evaluate both parallel reduction and compare-and-exchange solutions and their results with one sweep of learning are shown in Fig. 6(a) and Fig. 6(b). From the figures, parallel reduction demonstrates a remarkable scalability in any mini-batch scales. Seen from the subfigures, even when *mb* is large, the compare-and-exchange strategy is running slower greatly. Moreover, more prototypes per class are used, slower the compare-and-exchange strategy is. It also reveals that small overhead will result from too large *mb*.

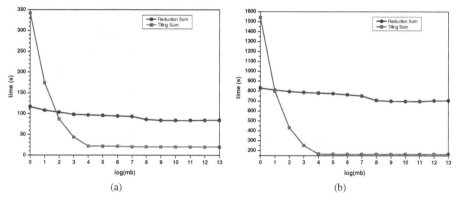

(a)   (b)

Fig. 5. Distance computation comparison between parallel reduction and tiling sum: (a) single prototype/class; (b) eight prototypes/class

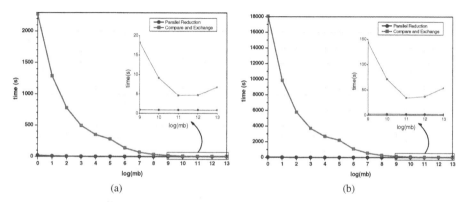

(a)   (b)

Fig. 6. Minima searching comparison between parallel reduction and compare-and-exchange: (a) single prototype/class; (b) eight prototypes/class

5.4   Speedup Benchmarks

Combining all together, we can develop an intensive-GPU implementation that can adaptively invoke kernels depending on their problem scale. As for one sweep of learning on single CPU core, it consumes 4,332 seconds (with single prototype/class) or 32,843 seconds (with eight prototypes/class). Thus to derive a robust LVQ model using 40 sweeps of learning, it takes days to weeks.   When ported to GTX 680 using our proposed method, we can achieve up to 184-fold (with single prototype/class) or 194-fold (with eight prototypes/class) acceleration than CPU implementation as shown in Fig. 7.

As we known, SGD ($mb = 2^0$) is more difficult to accelerate since it presents limited workloads. Our scheme adopts parallel reduction algorithms in both distance computation and minima searching when SGD is used. Thus, we can greatly exploit the fine-grained parallelism. As a result, our method successfully accelerates the SGD more than 30 times.

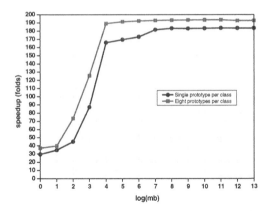

Fig. 7. Prototype learning speedup (with both single prototype/class and eight prototypes/class)

6   Conclusions

In this paper, we motivate to resolve the intensive learning challenges inherently in prototype learning using GPUs and a GPU programming architecture. We present an intensive-GPU parallel method after rearranging current prototype learning algorithm. Our method schedules almost all computation workloads onto the GPU device, requiring little CPU coordination. To maximize the utilization of the GPU resources, our implementation adaptively exploits tiling pattern and parallel reduction algorithm. Benchmarks are conducted on Chinese character recognition. Experimental results show that our method has a high scalability. Up to 194-fold acceleration is observed in mini-batch mode. Even to stochastic gradient descent, there are 30X+ speedups.

Acknowledgements. This work was supported by "National Natural Science Foundation of China" (Grant No. 61203260), "Postdoctoral Science-Research Developmental Foundation of Heilongjiang Province" (Grant No. LBH-Q13066), and "the Fundamental Research Funds for the Central Universities" (Grant No. HIT.NSRIF. 2015083). The work was also supported by NVIDIA CUDA Teaching Center program.

References

1. Liu, C., Nakagawa, M.: Evaluation of prototype learning algorithms for nearest-neighbor classifier in application to handwritten character recognition. Pattern Recognition **34**, 601–615 (2001)
2. Su, T., Liu, C., Zhang, X.: Perceptron learning of modified quadratic discriminant function. In: ICDAR (2011)
3. Lv, Y., Huang, L., et al.: Learning-Based Candidate Segmentation Scoring for Real-Time Recognition of Online Overlaid Chinese Handwriting. In: ICDAR (2013)
4. Su, T., Ma, P., et al.: Exploring MPE/MWE Training for Chinese Handwriting Recognition. In: ICDAR (2013)

5. Zhou, M., Yin, F., Liu, C.: GPU-Based Fast Training of Discriminative Learning Quadratic Discriminant Function for Handwritten Chinese Character Recognition. In: ICDAR (2013)
6. Raina, R., Madhavan, A., Ng, A.Y.: Large-scale deep unsupervised learning using graphics processors. In: ICML (2009)
7. Ciresan, D.C., Meier, U., et al.: Deep, big, simple neural nets for handwritten digit recognition. Neural Computation 22, 3207–3220 (2010)
8. Sato, A., Yamada, K.: Generalized learning vector quantization. In: NIPS (1996)
9. Wilt, N.: The CUDA Handbook: A Comprehensive Guide to GPU Programming. Addison-Wesley (2013)
10. Kirk, D.B., Wen-mei, W.H.: Programming massively parallel processors: a hands-on approach. Morgan Kaufmann (2010)
11. Liu, C., Yin, F., et al.: CASIA Online and Offline Chinese Handwriting Databases. In: ICDAR (2011)

Fuzzy Integral Combination of One-Class Classifiers Designed for Multi-class Classification

Bilal Hadjadji, Youcef Chibani$^{(\boxtimes)}$, and Hassiba Nemmour

Speech Communication and Signal Processing Laboratory,
Faculty of Electronics and Computer Science
University of Science and Technology Houari Boumediene (USTHB),
32, El Alia, Bab Ezzouar, 16111, Algiers, Algeria,
{bhadjadji,ychibani,hnemmour}@usthb.dz

Abstract. One-Class Classifier (OCC) has been widely used for its ability to learn without counterexamples. Its main advantage for multi-class is offering an open system and therefore allows easily extending new classes without retraining OCCs. Generally, pattern recognition systems designed by a single source of information suffer from limitations such as the lack of uniqueness and non-universality. Thus, combining information from multiple sources becomes a mode for designing pattern recognition systems. Usually, fixed rules such as average, product, minimum and maximum are the standard used combiners for OCC ensembles. However, fixed combiners cannot be useful to treat some difficult cases. Hence, we propose in this paper a combination scheme of OCCs based on the use of fuzzy integral (FI) operators. Experimental results conducted on different types of OCC and two different handwritten datasets prove the superiority of FI against fixed combiners for an open multi-class classification based on OCC ensemble.

1 Introduction

One Class classifiers (OCCs) are classifiers with spatial assumptions, which allow them to learn restricted domains in a multi-dimensional pattern space, using only a set of the target class [1]. Hence, the OCC has been successfully employed in many applications such as image retrieval [2], automated document retrieval and classification [3] and combining different biometric traits [4].

Nowadays, extended multi-class implementation to new classes is strongly required for instance, in biometric identification. However, that needs to retrain the system again on all classes. Recently, OCC has been successfully used to achieve extensible multi-class implementations [5], [6], [7]. Indeed, extending the classifier to new classes does not require retraining the used OCCs for a second time. Besides, the OCC offers less computational cost in terms.

Generally, pattern recognition systems designed by a single source of information suffer from limitations such as the lack of uniqueness and non-universality to the problem at hand. Thus, Multiple Classifiers System (MCS) combine information from multiple sources by taking advantage of individual classifiers and avoiding their

© Springer International Publishing Switzerland 2014
A. Campilho and M. Kamel (Eds.): ICIAR 2014, Part I, LNCS 8814, pp. 320–328, 2014.
DOI: 10.1007/978-3-319-11758-4_35

weakness, resulting in the improvement of classification accuracy. Indeed, the benefits of multiple classifiers based on different information sources for the same problem have been judged in various fields of pattern recognition, including handwritten recognition [8], speech verification [9], and other [10].

Recently, it has been demonstrated that combining classifier can also be effective for OCCs. Therefore, OCC ensemble has been explored to deal with a variety of applications such as image retrieval [11] and other recognition applications. Consequently, we can distinguish between OCC ensemble for solving one class problems [11], multi-class implementation [5], [6], [7], [12] and ensemble of multi-class implementations [13], [14], [15], which represents our interest.

Furthermore, fixed rules such as average, product, minimum and maximum are the standard used combiners for OCC ensembles [6], [13], [14]. However, fixed combiners cannot be useful to treat some difficult cases. Fixed rules are optimal for special cases for which the combined systems are similar in terms of performance and competence.

However, classifiers designed by different information sources are different from each other, because the members of the ensemble are built on diverse feature spaces [16]. Therefore, trained combiners are more suitable since the behavior of the ensemble members is learned during the training phase. Thus, the final decision is made by taking into account the competence of each member. Indeed, Abbas et al. (2013) [15] used the Dezert-Smarandache Theory (DSmT) to achieve one class support vector machine (OC-SVM) ensemble trained on different feature sets of handwritten digit recognition. The DSmT shows its superiority in term of performance versus the sum rule. However, the proposed scheme violence the best advantage of using OCCs as multi-class system which is the extension to new classes and therefore, achieves closed system. Indeed, adding new classes require updating all parameters and retrain the combination model.

Fuzzy Integral (FI) and the associated fuzzy measures [16] initially introduced by Sugeno are reported to give excellent results for classifier aggregating. The ability of the fuzzy integral to enhance the results produced by multiple information sources has been researched in various application areas of pattern recognition [8], [9].

In order to achieve an open and powerful MCS we propose a combination scheme based on the use of fuzzy integral operators for combining OCCs. Hence, we study in this paper the ability of fuzzy integral operators against fixed rules for achieving MCS that is dedicated to solve the multi-class classification problem. Results are carried out on different types of OCC and two different handwritten datasets, leading to have a larger view on the usefulness of FI to the addressed problem.

The remaining of this paper is organized as follows. Section 2 reports an overview of fuzzy measure and fuzzy integral operators. Section 3 describes the formalization of the proposed MCS based on OCC ensemble. Section 4 presents experimental results conducted on various types of OCC and two different handwritten datasets in order to prove the effective use of the proposed combination scheme. Finally, the conclusion and future work are provided in the last section.

2   Overview of Fuzzy Integral Combiners

Fuzzy integrals are non-linear combiners defined with respect to fuzzy measures. Therefore, the main advantage of FI is its ability to combine the objective evidences denoted by $h(z_i)$ issued from a set of information sources $Z = \{z_1, ..., z_L\}$ by taking into account subjective evaluation of their competence expressed by the λ-fuzzy measure. In table 1, we briefly present the definition of the fuzzy measures and fuzzy integral operators including Sugeno, Choquet and Weighted Averaging (OWA) operators [17], [18].

Table 1. Definition of fuzzy measure and fuzzy integral operators

Function	Definition
Fuzzy mesure	$g(A_1) = g(\{z_1\}) = g^1,$ $g(A_i) = g(A_{i-1}) + g^{i-1} + \lambda g(A_{i-1})g^{i-1}, 2 \leq i \leq L$
Sugeno	$I_S = max_{i=1}^{L}\left[min\left(h(z_i), g(A_i)\right)\right]$
Choquet	$I_C = \sum_{i=1}^{L}\{h(z_i) - h(z_{i-1})\}\, g(A_i), h(z_0) = 0.$
OWA-AND	$\widehat{h(z_l)} = \dfrac{(1-\alpha)}{l} \sum_{i=1}^{l} h(z_i) + \alpha\, min_{z_l \in Z}\{h(z_l)\}$
OWA-OR	$I_{OR} = \dfrac{1-\beta}{2^L} \sum_{i=1}^{L} min\left(\widehat{h(z_l)}, g(A_i)\right) + \beta\, max_{i=1}^{L}\left[min\left(\widehat{h(z_l)}, g(A_i)\right)\right]$

For the OWA-AND new evidences $\widehat{h(z_l)}$ are used by Sugeno integral termed I_{S-AND}. In addition, we propose in this paper to calculate by these new evidences the Choquet integral termed I_{C-AND} via applying its defined equation. On the other hand, OWA-OR is applied via using new decision function as it is defined in Table 1. Moreover, both operators need parameters α and β to be tuned in the unit interval, which may lead to achieve better results than the Sugeno and Choquet operators [18]. Thus, we define five different operators for FI aggregating: Sugeno I_S, Choquet I_C, S-OWA-AND I_{S-AND}, C-OWA-AND I_{C-AND} and OWA-OR I_{OR}

3   Fuzzy Integral Combiners for MCS Based on OCC Ensemble

The MCS as it is depicted in figure 1 is composed of m classes and L different information sources. Therefore, each class is represented by a single OCC ensemble which is composed of L OCCs trained on different information sources, their normalized outputs are aggregated through a FI operator. Finally, the class label of the test pattern is assigned to the single OCC ensemble that achieves the maximum prediction.

Let $\{D_i, i = 1, .. m\}$ as the set of m single OCC ensembles and denoting d_j^i the output value of the OCC_j^i which is trained on the ith information source of the jth class.

$$D = \begin{pmatrix} D_1 \\ D_2 \\ \cdot \\ \cdot \\ \cdot \\ D_m \end{pmatrix} = \begin{pmatrix} d_1^1 & d_1^2 & \cdots & d_1^L \\ d_2^1 & d_2^2 & \cdots & d_2^L \\ \cdot & \cdot & \cdots & \cdot \\ \cdot & \cdot & \cdots & \cdot \\ \cdot & \cdot & \cdots & \cdot \\ d_m^1 & d_m^2 & \cdots & d_m^L \end{pmatrix} \qquad (1)$$

The combination of OCCs requires the normalization of outputs for each classifier for performing correctly the combination. In this way, a straightforward approach consists to transform the classifier outputs into posteriori probabilities.

Thus, we propose to use the softmax normalization method [20] for its simplicity and effectiveness to map the outputs in the range [0, 1]. For each test pattern x, the softmax function assigns a posteriori probability $P_i(c_j/x)$ for each output d_j^i as follows:

$$P_i(c_j/x) = \frac{1 + exp\left(d_j^i(x) \right)}{\sum_{j=1}^{m} 1 + exp\left(d_j^i(x) \right)} \qquad (2)$$

Such that, $0 \le P_i(c_j/x) \le 1$ and $\sum_{j=1}^{m} P_i(c_j/x) = 1$.

It has been noticed that the successful key of the FI is the density measures, which represent the importance of each information source. Generally, a density measure represents the competence of the ensemble member measured by its achieved performance. However, this value must be normalized in order to obey the same proprieties of the posteriori probability. Denoting by p_j^i the performance of the OCC_j^i achieved in the training step, the density measure g_j^i is determined as follows:

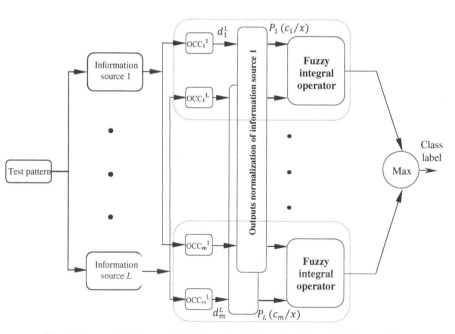

Fig. 1. Proposed scheme of MCS based on FI combination of OCC ensemble

$$g_j^i = \frac{p_j^i}{\sum_{j=1}^{m} p_j^i} \qquad (3)$$

Such that, $0 \leq g_j^i \leq 1$ and $\sum_{j=1}^{m} g_j^i = 1$

After getting the densities, we calculate the fuzzy measures $g_j(A_i)$, for $1 \leq i \leq L$ and $1 \leq j \leq m$ through applying equations its defined equation in table 1.

Denoting by $y(x)$ the class label of a test pattern x and one of the defined FI operators (I_S, I_C, I_{S-AND}, I_{C-AND} or I_{OR}), the aggregation of posteriori probabilities of the different information sources and their corresponding fuzzy measures to be combined is defined as:

$$y(x) = \underset{j=1}{\overset{m}{argmax}} \left(FIOP_j \left(P_i\left(c_j/x \right), g_j(A_i) \right) \right), 1 \leq i \leq L \qquad (4)$$

$FIOP$ is one of the defined FI operator.

4   Experimental Results

4.1   Datasets Description and Feature Generation

In order to validate the proposed architecture, two handwritten datasets are used, which are Arabic handwritten words and handwritten digits, respectively. Both datasets and their feature generations are presented in the following section.

4.1.1   Arabic Handwritten Word

For an effective evaluation of the MCS, the well known IFN/ENIT database [21] is used. It contains more than 26400 images of Tunisian town names. Words are written by 411 scripts using different writing tools. In our experiment, we collect 30 classes of interest grouping names with the largest appearance frequencies. We select randomly for each class 25 samples for training the classifier and we let the remaining samples for the evaluation step.

For a suitable feature generation, the Curvelet transform [22] is used, since, it offers enhanced directional capacity to characterize edges and singularities along curves that compose handwritten Arabic word.

Recently, the curvelet transform has been successfully used for offline handwritten signature retrieval, where the feature vector is generated using the energy and the standard deviation of the curvelet coefficient [23]. In our case, we explore the energy of the curvelet coefficient computed from the handwritten word image. In order to maintain the local information, we apply the curvelet transform on different section of the word image grid. Finally, the feature vector is achieved through the concatenation of all computed wedge energies for the defined image sections.

In order to perform the combination, different information sources should be created [24]. For this reason, we use two different ways for decomposing an image into variety of sections (before applying the curvelet transform), which are equal space and equal masse grids with same size 2×8, respectively.

4.1.2   Handwritten Digit

Experiments are conducted on the well-known US Postal Service (USPS) [25] hand-writing recognition task. This dataset contains normalized grey-level handwritten digit images of 10 numeral classes, extracted from US postal envelopes. Feature extraction methods are the same as Arabic handwritten word with grid size of 2×2 for both equal space and mass, respectively. Both datasets are summarized in Table 2.

Table 2. Datasets Used for Evaluating the Proposed MCS

Dataset	# Classes	# Features	# Training samples	# Testing samples
Word	30	736	750	1929
Digit	10	192	7287	2007

4.2   MCS Design and Evaluation

The aim of this work is to show the superiority of fuzzy integral operators against fixed combiners for achieving the MCS. Hence, both of which will be examined under the same experimental protocol and therefore, we shall not be overly concerned with the absolute value of the accuracy.

In order to make a larger view on the usefulness of the proposed architecture, results are carried out on different types of OCC (One Class Support Vector Machine (OC-SVM) [26], K-means, Principal Component Analysis (PCA), one Nearest Neighbor (1-NN), K-center [1]). Therefore, different systems are built according to the used type of OCC.

The MCS is composed of two OCCs for each class, which differs from feature extraction method. Hence, they are trained separately on specific information source for each. However, each classifier has its own parameters which must be carefully tuned. Hence, the classifiers are trained with different parameter values and then the optimal values are selected when the best performance of the training dataset is achieved.

After having trained the classifiers, the combination model is performed by means of the FI operators, however, it requires parameters to be fixed. According to equation 3 the density of each class is calculated via the classifier performance. Hence, the leave-one out and two-fold cross validations are performed separately on each class using training dataset for generating the performances and therefore, the densities for Arabic word and digit, respectively. When using the OR and AND operators two parameters (α and β) should be fixed. In this paper, we propose a dynamic find of the optimal parameters. More precisely, we compute for each test sample the class label using different parameter values ranging between 0 and 1 with step of 0.1. Finally, the last decision is obtained by majority voting of the generated labels.

4.3   Results and Discussion

Results for the individual classifiers and their combination with different aggregating rules conducted on both Arabic word and digit datasets are reported in Tables 3 and 4, respectively. Firstly, when comparing the individual classifiers, we can note that OC-SVM and PCA are the most suitable for both applications. For instance, the OC-

SVM provides the highest results for digit dataset regarding both information sources. Secondly, we can also note that combining information sources allows improving the recognition rates than the single source for all classifiers and both datasets. Besides, when observing carefully the obtained results, we can note that the FI combiners offer an improved recognition rate whatever the selected application and the type of classifier. Therefore, FI combiners are more suitable than fixed ones for OCCs combination.

Table 3. Classification accuracy (%) of individual classifiers and MCS with different combination rules for Arabic word recognition

	SVM	PCA	K-means	K-center	1NN
Source 1	80.82	87.14	77.44	66.87	73.82
Source 2	72.99	82.68	74.85	59.82	73.61
Average	82.06	87.81	83.92	73.56	84.08
Prod	85.07	87.97	84.03	73.35	84.34
Min	81.80	86.93	79.00	67.85	80.16
Max	80.87	83.46	76.77	68.74	80.41
FI-Sugeno	81.80	82.68	79.00	67.70	80.66
FI-Choquet	**88.08**	89.42	80.97	69.72	81.02
FI-OR	82.32	86.00	**84.65**	**74.75**	**84.96**
FI-AND-S	84.50	87.30	83.72	72.31	82.58
FI-AND-C	83.67	**89.78**	84.08	73.56	84.29

Table 4. Classification accuracy (%) of individual classifiers and MCS with different combination rules for digit recognition

	SVM	PCA	K-means	K-center	1NN
Source 1	93.32	92.02	89.08	81.96	89.20
Source 2	91.38	89.08	85.15	68.01	85.71
Average	94.57	93.67	90.58	82.16	89.33
Prod	94.57	93.77	90.18	81.81	89.33
Min	93.47	93.12	88.44	79.32	89.18
Max	93.67	93.22	90.08	80.11	89.38
FI-Sugeno	93.22	93.72	88.44	77.72	92.97
FI-Choquet	94.22	93.47	89.13	80.71	89.28
FI-OR	**94.67**	93.77	90.28	82.16	**93.62**
FI-AND-S	94.62	93.72	89.78	81.06	**93.62**
FI-AND-C	94.57	**93.92**	**90.68**	**82.41**	89.28

5   Conclusion and Future Work

We studied in this paper the potential of FI operators, for combining ensemble of OCCs designed by different information sources for an open multi-class pattern classification.

Experimental results carried out on different types of OCC and two different handwritten datasets, prove the superiority of FI against fixed combiners, whatever the selected type of classifier or application. Besides, OWA operators appeared to be the most suitable and powerful from FI aggregators. Thus, this study suggests keeping fuzzy integral operators high on the list of options when achieving OCC ensembles.

It is clearly that, developing combination schemes for OCC ensemble still await a proper attention. Hence, the extension of this work consists of developing robust combination schemes for multiple OCC ensembles.

References

1. Tax, D.M.J.: One-class classification, PhD Thesis, Delft University of Technology (2001), ISBN: 90-75691-05-x
2. Kwang-Kyu, S.: An application of one-class support vector machines in content-based image retrieval. Expert System with Applications **33**(2), 491–498 (2007)
3. Manevitz, L., Yousef, M.: One-class document classification via Neural Networks. Neurocomputing **70**, 1466–1481 (2007)
4. Bergani, C., Oliveira, L.S., Koreich, A.L., Sabourin, R.: Combining different biometric traits with one-class classification. Signal Processing **89**, 2117–2127 (2009)
5. Sun, B.-Y., Huang, D.-S.: Support vector clustering for multi-class classification problems. In: The Congress on Evolutionary Computation, Canberra, Australia, pp. 1480–1485
6. Yeh, C.Y., Lee, Z.Y., Lee, S.J.: Boosting one-class support vector machines for multi-class classification. Applied Artificial Intelligence **23**(4), 297–315 (2009)
7. Boehm, O., Hardoon, D.R., Manevitz, L.M.: Classifying cognitive states of brain activity via one-class neural networks with feature selection by genetic algorithms. International Journal of Machine Learning & Cyber **2**, 125–134 (2011)
8. Chiang, J.H., Gaber, P.D.: Hybrid fuzzy-neural systems in handwritten word recognition. IEEE Trans. Fuzzy Syst. **5**, 497–510 (1997)
9. Pham, T., Wagner, M.: Similarity normalization for speaker verification by fuzzy fusion. Pattern Recognit. **33**, 309–315 (2000)
10. Chiang, J.H.: Choquet fuzzy integral-based hierarchical networks for decision analysis. IEEE Trans. Fuzzy Syst. **7**, 63–71 (1999)
11. Cabrera, J.B.D., Gutiérrez, C., Mehra, R.K.: Ensemble methods for anomaly detection and distributed intrusion detection in Mobile Ad-Hoc Networks. Information Fusion **9**, 96–119 (2008)
12. Wilk, T., Wozniak, M.: Soft computing methods applied to combination of one-class classifiers. Neurocomputing **75**, 185–193 (2012)
13. Juszczak, P., Duin, R.P.: Combining One-Class Classifiers to Classify Missing Data. In: Roli, F., Kittler, J., Windeatt, T. (eds.) MCS 2004. LNCS, vol. 3077, pp. 92–101. Springer, Heidelberg (2004)
14. Muñoz-Marí, J., Camps-Valls G., Gómez-Chova, L., Calpe-Maravilla, J.: Combination of one class remote sensing image classifiers. In: IGARSS, pp. 1509–1512 (2007)
15. Abbas, N., Chibani, Y., Belhadi, Z., Hedir, M.: A DSmT Based Combination Scheme for MultiClass Classification. In: 16th International Conference on Information FUSION: ICIF 2013, Instanbul, Turkey, July 9–12 (2013)
16. Kuncheva, L.: Combining Pattern Classifiers: Methods and Algorithms. Wiley-Interscience Publication, New Jersey (2004)

17. Cho, S.-B., Kim, J.H.: Combining multiple neural networks by fuzzy integrals for robust classification. IEEE Trans. Syst. Man Cybern. **25**(2), 380–384 (1995)
18. Cho, S.-B.: Fuzzy aggregation of modular neural networks with ordered weighted averaging operators. International Journal of Approximate Reasoning **13**(4), 359–375 (1995)
19. Cho, S.-B.: Fusion of neural networks with fuzzy logic and genetic algorithm. Integrated Computer-Aided Engineering **9**(4), 363–372 (2002)
20. Duda, R.O., Hart, P.E., Stork, D.G.: Pattern classification, 2nd edn. John Wiley & Sons, NY (2001)
21. www.ifnenit.com
22. Candès, E., Donoho, D.L.: New tight frames of curvelets and optimal representations of objects with piecewise singularities. Comm. Pure Appl. Math **57**, 219–266 (2004)
23. Shirdhonkar, M.S., Kokare, M.: Off-Line Handwritten Signature Retrieval using Curvelet Transforms. International Journal of Computer and Engineering **3**(4), 1658–1665 (2011)
24. Duin, R.P.W.: The combining classifier: to train or not to train?. In: Proc. 16th International Conference on Pattern Recognition, ICPR 2002, Canada, pp. 765–770 (2002)
25. http://www.gaussianprocess.org/gpml/data/
26. Schölkopf, B., Platt, J., Shawe-Taylor, J., Smola, A., Williamson, R.: Estimating the support of a high dimensional distribution. Neural Computation **13**(7), 1443–1472 (2001)

Automatic Classification of Human Body Postures Based on Curvelet Transform

N. Zerrouki[(✉)] and A. Houacine

LCPTS, Faculty of Electronics and Computer Science,
University of Sciences and Technology Houari Boumédienne (USTHB)
Algiers, Algeria
{nzerrouki,ahouacine}@usthb.dz

Abstract. This paper presents the design and implementation of a posture classification method. A new feature extraction strategy according to curvelet transform is provided for identifying the posture in images. First of all, human body is segmented. For this purpose, a background subtraction technique is applied. Then, a curvelet transform is used for extracting features from the posture image. To address the rotation invariance problem, five ratios are evaluated from the human body and they are also included in the set of features. Finally the human body postures are classified through support vector machines (SVM). Experimental results are obtained on the "Fall Detection" dataset. For evaluation, different state of the art statistical measures have been considered such as overall accuracy, the kappa coefficient, the F-measure coefficient, and the area under ROC curve (AUC) value. All of these evaluation measures demonstrate that the proposed approach provides a significant recognition rate.

Keywords: Human body postures · Classification · Support vector machines · Curvelet transform · Statistical performance · Evaluation measures

1 Introduction

With the rapid development of image processing technology, the posture identification is gaining interest for a wide range of applications, such as in the field of video monitoring, human-computer interaction, etc. Recently, the human gesture interpretation technology has made large progress. There exist many applications in the literature; one can cite for example human gesture identification [1], sign language recognition [2], and human motion interpretation and classification [3]. However, in practice there are a series of problems which influence the accuracy of classification, like complicated backgrounds, illumination conditions, changes of the posture, and presence of shadows, etc. This paper focuses on classification of four main body postures, including standing, bending, sitting, and lying postures. Several studies on this topic have been proposed in the literature [1-4]. Li et al. [4] used a multiscale morphological method to recognize human postures. Wang et al. [5] proposed an algorithm based on an unsupervised clustering approach for posture recognition. Sullivan et al. [6] used exemplar frames to achieve human action tracking. This latter method was based

© Springer International Publishing Switzerland 2014
A. Campilho and M. Kamel (Eds.): ICIAR 2014, Part I, LNCS 8814, pp. 329–337, 2014.
DOI: 10.1007/978-3-319-11758-4_36

on a learning strategy that was not very effective because the recognition rate is strongly depended on the degree of similarity between exemplar frames and classified frames. A method for the tracking and recognition of moving postures using neural networks and active contours is proposed in [7]. Truncated singular value decomposition coefficients and height-width ratio of human body are used as posture features in [8]. However height-width ratio is not discriminant in several cases, especially between sitting and bending postures, due to the degree of similarity between the two postures for different positions. Vertical and horizontal projection histograms (VHPHs) are also involved to describe the body postures [9]. On the other hand, VHPH shifting and calibration phases are required to avoid a distortion of the extracted histograms [7]. Other body posture features can be extracted from VHPHs [10]. Juang and Chang [7] applied discrete Fourier transform (DFT) on VHPHs of human body. Chenet.al. used Radon transform as feature for gait recognition [3]. However, the features used in most of these studies are strongly dependent on the body silhouette size and position. The silhouette size changes as the distance from people to camera varies. A scaling operation using the distance factor is needed, requiring an a priori camera calibration [10].

In this work we apply a recently introduced transform for feature extraction that is the curvelet transform. This transform is known to be translation, scaling and rotation invariant. However, the rotation invariance is rather a drawback for posture recognition. In order to overcome this inconvenient, other features are extracted from the human body and added to the feature vector to account for angular information. These complementary features are obtained by considering five partial occupancy areas of the body obtained by a partitioning centered on the gravity center, as illustrated by Fig.2. These features are then defined as the five ratios of partial occupancy areas over the whole body area. An SVM classifier is trained on the extracted feature vectors, and used to recognize the human body postures.

Furthermore, we have investigated several evaluation measures based on different values of the classifier parameter. Considered measures are the overall accuracy, the Kappa coefficient, the F-measure coefficients and the ROC curve area.

The remaining of this paper is organized as follows. Section II deals the image processing steps that include segmentation and image quality enhancement. Section III describes in detail the curvelet transform for feature extraction phase. Section IV presents the classification approach. Section V presents the evaluation measures. Section VI covers the experimental results (dataset, experiments, obtained results and interpretation). And finally, a conclusion and future work discussion are given.

2   Human Body Segmentation Method

The segmentation consists in extracting the body silhouette from image sequence. This latter is a very essential initial step for many vision-based applications. And it remains a challenging task to achieve automatic and robust action recognition in cases where no prior information is available on background, lighting changes, environment constraints, .etc. Many methods [11] assume that the background does not vary and hence can be captured prior to any other processing. In this paper, we use background subtraction technique based on sequential kernel density approximation SKDA [12], because it operates efficiently even in cases of multiple component models.

An example of the background subtraction technique is shown in Fig.1. The background and the input images correspond to the first and the second column respectively, while third and last columns illustrate the background subtraction result by SKDA method, respectively before and after morphological processing.

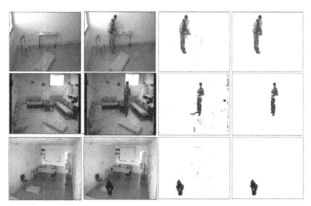

Fig. 1. Results of background subtraction algorithm

The morphological processing is applied to eliminate remaining small area noise components. The considered operator performs erosion and dilation with a 3 by 3 structuring element.

3   Human Body Feature Extraction

Feature extraction is a crucial task for the classification of human postures. The extracted features have a direct impact on the recognition performances. In this section, we give more details on how one could extract feature vectors in order to better characterize the human postures.

The curvelet transforms are multi-resolution transforms, introduced by Candes and Donoho [13] in 1999. These can detect boundaries better than wavelet transform, and permit extraction of useful features that are generally missed with other transforms. Directionality and anisotropy are the important characteristics of curvelet transforms. Directionality is tied to the associated basis functions, as defined for many directions, while there are only three directions considered in wavelet transform. Another motivation for using curvelet transforms is related to the fact that singularities are often joined by edges or contours in images. Curvelet transforms capture structural information of an image based on multiple radial directions in the frequency domain. Curvelets are proven to be particularly effective for detecting image activity along curves instead of radial directions, what is appropriate for human images [13].

As already mentioned, curvelet transforms are rotation invariant. This invariance leads to confusion between certain postures such as sitting and standing. To overcome this rotation issue, we propose adding a complementary feature set, which is based on a simple human body partitioning. These features should be discriminative enough to obtain interesting classification rates, and not too complex in order to permit a fast processing.

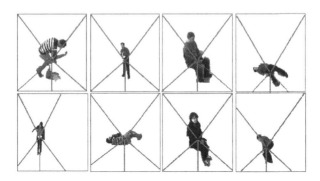

Fig. 2. Human body area partitioning

The foreground silhouette is divided into five areas using a partitioning centered at the body gravity center as shown in Fig.2. These areas should generally correspond to the head, arms and legs in the standing posture. Given the whole body area A, and the partial areas $\{Ai, i=1...5\}$, the ratios of partial areas to the total area are defined, as:

$$R_i = \frac{A_i}{A} \tag{1}$$

These ratios are added to curvelet features to constitute the whole feature vector to be used in the classification process.

4   Posture Classification Using SVM

The classification process consists of two steps: (i) training the system using image posture samples, and (ii) classify a given image posture in the feature space via the trained classifier model. Several types of classifiers have been deployed by the human posture and gesture interpretation community [2, 3]. In this work, we have selected an SVM classifier due to its high generalization performance. It is well known that SVM classifier can be adapted to behave as a nonlinear classifier through the use of nonlinear kernels. The SVM were initially designed to solve binary classification. Their training consists of finding the optimal separating hyperplane between two classes. Specifically, let $(P_n, y_n) \in R^M \times \{\pm 1\}$ be a set of training patterns so that M is data dimension, $\{n=1,..N_c\}$, N_c is the number of samples in the class C. The training process selects the function $f{:}R^M{\rightarrow}\{\pm 1\}$ which maximizes the margin between the two classes. Then, data are classified according to the signal of the decision function so that:

$$f(P) = sign \ [\textstyle\sum_{i=1}^{SV} y_i \alpha_i k(P_i, P) + b] \tag{2}$$

The optimal hyperplane corresponds to $f(x) = 0$ while b is a bias. SV is the number of support vectors, and $\{\alpha_i\}$ are Lagrange multipliers. The kernel $k(.,.)$ is any mathematical function, respecting Mercer's conditions [14]. Commonly, the Radial Basis Function (RBF) kernel provides the best performances for pattern recognition applications. For two samples P_l and P, this kernel is expressed as:

$$k(P_i, P) = exp\left[-\frac{1}{2\sigma^2} d(P_1, P)\right] \tag{3}$$

$$d(P_1, P) = \|P_1 - P\|^2 \tag{4}$$

Where, σ is user-defined.

For solving multi-class problems, two multi-class implementations of SVM are widely used. The One-Against-All (OAA) approach, which is the earliest one, performs N binary SVMs to solve a problem with N classes. The second approach that can be used is the One-Against-One (OAO) which employs $N\times(N-1)/2$ SVMs each of which is designed to separate two classes.

In this study, we have implemented the SVM based on the OAA approach based on the RBF kernel. To estimate the optimal SVM classifier, we used different kernel parameters γ and cost parameters C: $\gamma = [\ 2^4, 2^3, 2^2, ..., 2^{-10}\ ]$ and C= $[2^{12}, 2^{11}, 2^{10}, ..., 2^{-2}]$. The pair of (C, γ) that achieves the best results is selected. SVM classification output represents the decision values of each posture for each class. The LIBSVM package [15] is used.

5   Evaluation Measures

5.1   Overall Accuracy

This measure is computed from the confusion matrix represented by the mean of the diagonal cells. The confusion matrix is derived from a comparison of reference postures with the classified postures [16]. It is expressed as:

$$accuracy = \frac{tp + tn}{tp + fp + fn + tn} \tag{5}$$

where tp is for true positives, tn for true negatives, fp for false positive, and fn accounts for false negatives. To obtain an unbiased global accuracy, we have conducted a 3-fold cross-validation procedure.

5.2   Kappa Coefficient

Another measure which can be extracted from a confusion matrix is the Kappa coefficient. It is a statistical measure of inter-raters agreement [16]. This measure is more robust than the accuracy measure since it subtracts the agreement occurring by chance. This coefficient is expressed as:

$$Kappa = \frac{P(a) - P(e)}{1 - P(e)} \tag{6}$$

where P(a) is the probability of relative observed agreement among raters, and P (e) is the probability of by chance agreement. The range of the kappa coefficient is [-1, 1].

5.3   F-Measure

The F-measure coefficient is another performance index that is derived in the field of information retrieval. The F-measure combines the two ratios known as recall and precision [16]. It is expressed as follows:

$$F = (1 + \beta^2) \times \frac{p \times r}{(\beta^2 \times p) + r} \tag{8}$$

Where

$$p = \frac{tp}{tp + fp} \tag{9}$$

$$r = \frac{tp}{tp + fn} \tag{10}$$

The precision, recall, and F-measure vary from 0 to 1. The F-measure reaches its best value at 1 whenever p and r are simultaneously equal to 1. The parameter β is positive and represents the weight assigned to the two different types of errors. In our evaluation, the value of β is set to 1.

5.4   ROC Curve

ROC curve plots the true positives (sensitivity) versus false positives (1–specificity) for a classifier system when the discrimination threshold is modified. In ROC coordinate system, X axis is marked by false positives (1–specificity), and Y axis is marked by true positives (sensitivity) [16].The area under curve (AUC) associated to the ROC evaluation method is proportional to the objective model performance. Since, a random method depicts the first bisector; it has an AUC value equal to 0.5. Efficient classifier's areas should have an AUC value larger than 0.5. It is well known that the higher is the AUC value, the more efficient is the classifier.

6   Experimental Results

6.1   Dataset and Experiments

Our experimental data are extracted from "fall detection dataset" [10]. This dataset contains 191 Video sequences. The frame rate is 25 frames/s and the resolution is 320 × 240 pixels. The videos are recorded from different environments and contain variable illumination as well as shadows and reflections that can be detected as moving objects [15]. We manually denoted the ground truth of data samples for 4 classes. To evaluate the proposed method, we have selected 4000 images. The selected images should contain one of the four postures previously defined. These images were then split into training and testing sets for a 3-fold cross-validation procedure.

Furthermore, we have iteratively tested different SVM parameter settings (The parameters for RBF kernel: "Cost" C and "Sigma" σ). The pair that has produced a higher accuracy has been selected.

We have also presented a comparative task between two posture classifications. In the first one, only curvelet transforms have been used as posture features, and in the second classification the five ratios have been also included in the feature vector.

6.2   Results and Interpretation

For the proposed classification method, a confusion matrix is computed (see Table I), along with the overall accuracy, F-measure and the Kappa coefficient. The overall accuracy, the Kappa coefficient, and the F-measure achieved by posture classification are 92.97%, 0908 and 0.9091, respectively. It is clear from these results that the proposed classification enables robust recognition in very challenging situations.

Table 1. Human body posture classification results

		Reference data			
		Standing	Lying	Bending	Sitting
Classified data	Standing	**96.17**	0	1.24	2.82
	Lying	0	**100**	0.86	0
	Bending	2.89	0	**89.79**	3.98
	Sitting	0.92	0	8.11	**93.13**
	Overall Accuracy = 94.77% ; Kappa Coefficient = 0.908 ; F-measure=0.9091				

It is also apparent (from Table I) that the bending class remains a challenge for the proposed approaches where it is characterized by the lowest classification accuracy (89.79%). In fact, the bending class is slightly confused with the sitting class as often as 8.11% of cases. This confusion is due to: (i) the degree of similarity between the two classes, and (ii) segmentation errors generally induced by the presence of shadows; and partial occlusions or confusion of human body parts with environment objects. In fact, it is well-established that the segmentation task conducted in many different areas is always error prone.

On the contrary, the standing class is correctly classified in the most of cases, and the Lying class is perfectly accurate with 100% of its reference images; this result is explained by the incorporation of the curvelet features in the classification process.

The ROC curves corresponding to the posture classification using only curvelet transforms as features, and posture classification when the five ratios are added in the set of posture features are illustrated in Fig. 3; their AUC values are equal to 0.895 and 0.9109, respectively. One can clearly notice that the posture classification using the additional five area ratios is more accurate.

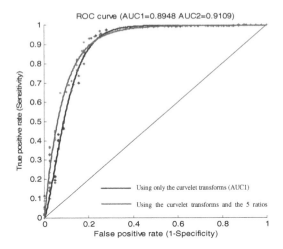

Fig. 3. The ROC obtained for proposed method

7   Conclusion

We have presented an automatic classification of human body postures based on curvelet transform and body area ratios, and using the SVM as classifier. This classification is evaluated using various complementary statistical measures. The experiments conducted via these metrics have on the one hand revealed the advantage of the use of curvelet transforms as body features, due to their scale and translation invariance, and on the other hand, it has been shown that adding five area ratios solves the rotation invariance problem.

We believe that the proposed work provides a tool for researchers and practitioners that perform human posture classification. Possible improvements of the classification approach through combining classifiers are under evaluation.

References

1. Meng, H., Pears, N., Bailey, C.: A human action recognition system for embedded computer vision application. In: Proc. CVPR (2007)
2. Hsuan Yang, M., Ahuja, N., Tabb, M.: Extraction of 2D Motion Trajectories and Its Application to Hand Gesture Recognition. IEEE Trans. PAMI **24**(8) (2002)
3. Chen, Y., Wu, Q., He, X.: Human Action Recognition by Radon Transform. In: Proc. IEEE International Conference on Data Mining Workshops, pp. 862–868 (2008)
4. Li, Y., Ma, S., Lu, H.: A multiscale morphological method for human posture recognition. In: Proc. IEEE Int. Conf. Autom. Face and Gesture Recog., pp. 56–61 (1998)
5. Wang, C.: An Algorithm of Unsupervised Posture Clustering and Modeling Based on GMM and EM Estimation. Journal of Software **6**(7) (2011)
6. Sullivan, J., Carlsson, S.: Recognizing and Tracking Human Action. In: Heyden, A., Sparr, G., Nielsen, M., Johansen, P. (eds.) ECCV 2002, Part I. LNCS, vol. 2350, pp. 629–644. Springer, Heidelberg (2002)

7. Juang, C., Chang, C.: Human Body Posture Classification by a Neural Fuzzy Network and Home Care System Application. IEEE Trans. Syst. Man & Cyb. **37**(6) (2007)
8. Zerrouki, N., Houacine, A.: Automatic Classification of Human Body Postures Based on the Truncated SVD. Jour. of Advances in Comp. Networks **2**(1), 58–62 (2014)
9. Haritaoglu, I., Harwood, D., Davis, L.S.: *W4* real-time surveillance of people and their activities. IEEE Trans. Pattern Anal. Mach. Intell. **22**(8), 809–830 (2000)
10. Cucchiara, R., Grana, C., Prati, A., Vezzani, R.: Probabilities posture classification for human-behavior analysis. IEEE Trans. Syst. Man & Cyb. **35**(1) (2005)
11. Chan, A., Vasconcelos, N.: Modeling, clustering, and segmenting video with mixtures of dynamic textures. IEEE Trans. PAMI **30**(5), 909–926 (2008)
12. Han, B., Comaniciu, D., Davis, L.: Sequential kernel density approximation through mode propagation: applications to background modeling. In: Asian Conf. on Comp. Vision (2004)
13. Starck, J.L., Emmanuel, J.: The Curvelet transform for image denoising. IEEE Trans. Image Process. **11**, 670–684 (2002)
14. Vapnik, V.: The Nature of Statistical Learning Theory. Springer (1995)
15. Chang, C.C., Lin, C.J.: LIBSVM: a library for support vector machines. ACM Transactions on Intelligent Systems and Technology **2**(3), 1–27 (2011)
16. Hand, D.J.: Assessing the performance of classification methods. International Statistical Review **80**, 400–414 (2012)

QR Code Localization Using Boosted Cascade of Weak Classifiers

Péter Bodnár$^{(\boxtimes)}$ and László G. Nyúl

Department of Image Processing and Computer Graphics, University of Szeged,
Szeged, Hungary
{bodnaar,nyul}@inf.u-szeged.hu

Abstract. Usage of computer-readable visual codes became common in
our everyday life at industrial environments and private use. The reading process of visual codes consists of two steps: localization and data
decoding. Unsupervised localization is desirable at industrial setups and
for visually impaired people. This paper examines localization efficiency
of cascade classifiers using Haar-like features, Local Binary Patterns and
Histograms of Oriented Gradients, trained for the finder patterns of QR
codes and for the whole code region as well, and proposes improvements
in post-processing.

Keywords: QR code · Object detection · Cascade classifier · HAAR ·
LBP · HOG

1 Introduction

QR code is a common type of visual code format that is used at various industrial
setups and private projects as well. Its structure is well-defined and makes automatic reading available by computers and embedded systems. In the last couple
of years, image acquisition techniques and computer hardware have improved
significantly, that made automatic reading of QR codes available. State of the
art algorithms do not require human assistance and assumptions on code orientation, position and coverage rate in the image [1] any longer. However, image
quality and acquisition techniques vary considerably and each application has
its own requirements for speed and accuracy, making the task more complex.

The recognition process consists of two steps: localization and decoding. The
literature already has a wide selection of papers proposing algorithms for efficient
QR code localization [2–4], however, each has its own strengths and weaknesses.
For example, while those methods are proven to be accurate, morphological
operations, convolutions, corner detection can be a bottleneck for processing
performance.

Belussi et al. [4] built an algorithm around the Viola-Jones framework [5],
which proved that, even though the framework was originally designed for face
detection, it is also suitable for QR code localization, even on low resolutions.

© Springer International Publishing Switzerland 2014
A. Campilho and M. Kamel (Eds.): ICIAR 2014, Part I, LNCS 8814, pp. 338–345, 2014.
DOI: 10.1007/978-3-319-11758-4_37

The authors used a cascade of weak classifiers, trained on the finder patterns (FIP) of the QR code. In the next section, their original idea is extended and examined, and results are discussed. We propose alternatives of both choosing the feature type of classifiers and their training target.

2 Localization Using Cascade Classifier Training

Using boosted cascade of weak classifiers is a common approach in general classification problems. A single classifier can be trained quickly, however, it will have low classification power, and thus it is considered weak. To overcome this issue, weak classifiers are chained, so the first classifier gets the original input, and each consecutive one has its input from the output of the preceeding one. If all classifiers have a high hit rate (typically from $0.990 - 0.999$) and a moderate false positive rate (around 0.5), the overall hit rate of the cascade is the product of the hit rates of all weak classifiers, and false positive rate is calculated in a similar manner. Using this approach, it is possible to train classifiers with high overall classification power, but without the need of complex features.

2.1 Features for Object Recognition

In image processing, Viola and Jones [5] introduced the use of Haar-like features as the core of these weak classifiers. There are three sets of features, edge-type, line-type and center-type, and each set has its 45-degree rotated extension, proposed by Lienhart et al. [6].

Each classifier has one or more features, defined by shape, scale and orientation within the image region of interest. The classification process is the evaluation of these weak classifiers assembled in a cascade way, using a sliding window. The process is repeated on more than one scales, so a trained cascade can be used to detect objects of equal and larger size than they were present in the training database. Recurrences of a detected object are often filtered by grouping the overlapping results of different scales. Furthermore, we used Gentle AdaBoost in order to increase accuracy.

Instead of Haar-like features, Local Binary Patterns (LBP) and Histograms of Oriented Gradients (HOG) can also be used for the feature evaluation. A paper on bar code localization [7] proposes partitioning of the image, and reading each block in a circular pattern. A 1D feature vector is formed this way, which makes a feature of bar code presence within the block. This concept is analogous to LBP [8], with the main difference of not using the center point for making the feature.

HOG descriptors were first introduced in pedestrian detection [9], however, it is often used in areas of computer vision where LBP, SIFT or shape context is applicable. There are some special cases [10] where LBP and HOG can be used together with improved overall accuracy, too.

2.2   Localization Based on FIPs and Whole Object

A classifier based on a Haar-like feature set is already discussed in the literature
[4], and will serve as a reference method to our further experiments. The basic
idea of QR code localization is the quick localization of possible FIPs in the image
with high hit rate, then aggregation of the FIP candidates to FIP triplets of a
possible QR code. FIP candidate localization is based on the cascade of boosted
weak classifiers using Haar-like features, while the decision on a FIP candidate
to be kept or dropped is decided by a geometrical constraint on distances and
angles with respect to other probable FIPs.

While Haar-like feature based classifiers are the state of the art in face detection, the training process is more difficult on FIPs. A face has more, empirically
observable, strong features. In order to increase the strong features of the object
intended to detect, we propose training of a classifier for the whole code area.
Even though QR codes have high variability on the data region, they contain
data density patterns, a fourth, smaller FIP that can be perfectly covered with
the center-type Haar-feature, furthermore, they contain the three discussed FIPs
at the corners of the ROI (Fig. 1(b)).

LBP and HOG based classifiers also can be trained both to FIPs and whole
code areas, and since they are also considered fast and accurate general purpose
object detectors, evaluation of their performance on code localization is highly
motivated. Furthermore, LBP can be more suitable than Haar classifiers, since
it is not restricted to a pre-selected set of patterns, while HOG can also be
efficient due to the strict visual structure and limited number of distinct gradient
directions of the QR code.

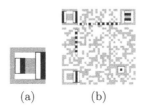

(a)   (b)

Fig. 1. (a): FIP with two instances of a Haar-like feature. The feature fits for both
the inner and outer black regions in all directions, however, this is the only feature
that perfectly fits to the FIP. (b): Examples of Haar-like features fitting on a QR code,
using FIPs and data density pattern.

2.3   Classifier Training

The default weak classifier parameter values for true positive rate (TPR, recall)
and false positive rate (FPR) are 0.995 and 0.5, respectively, which means 99.5 %
of the positive samples are classified correctly at each stage. We have set the
number of stages to 10, according to the experiments of [4]. For the first four

stages, using only one feature was sufficient to reach the TPR and FNR defined above, while in later stages, more features were required, from 9 up to 15. The training did not contain a priori information about which features to prefer, they were chosen empirically as it is implemented in the OpenCV library. We trained a total number of six classifiers, based on Haar-like features, LBP and HOG, both for FIPs and full code objects. For the FIPs, feature symmetry is also recommended to speed up the training process, while usage of the rotated features of Lienhart et al. is not very useful, since these classifiers are not flexible enough to detect QR codes of any orientation. However, this issue can be solved by training two classifiers, for codes with orientation of 0° and 45°, respectively. We used a 32 × 32 sample size, which is larger than the one of the reference method, since training to the whole code object requires finer sample resolution. We decided on the cascade topology for the classifier instead of a tree, since it showed higher overall hit rate in [4], and left required hit rate and false positive rate at the default values for each stage, with a total number of 10 stages. We trained our classifiers on a synthetic database consisting of 10 000 images. Images of the database are artificially generated QR codes, each containing a permutation of all lower– and uppercase letters and numerals, rendered with perspective distortion on to images not having QR codes. During the selection of the applied transformation matrices, we used such that shift the FIP not more than one FIP width, which property is needed for the assumption of maximum expected distortion at the postprocessing step of the FIP-based classification. However, this limit is large enough to render FIP-based classifiers unreliable. After that, Gaussian smoothing and noise have been gradually added to the images. The σ of the smoothing Gaussian kernel fell into the [0,3] range. For adding noise, a random image (I_n) was generated with intensities ranging from [-127, 127] following normal distribution. This image was added gradually to the original 8-bit image (I_o) as $I = \alpha I_n + (1 - \alpha)I_o$, with α ranging [0,0.5]. The noise was added to the image using saturation arithmetic, i.e. values falling beyond the [0,255] range were clamped to the appropriate extreme intensities.

2.4   Postprocessing

For the classifiers trained to FIPs, post-processing is needed to reduce the amount of false detections. Belussi et al. proposes searching through the set of FIP candidates for triplets that can form QR code, using geometrical constraints. Since real-life images of QR codes also suffer perspective distortion, it is obligatory to give tolerance values for positive triplet response. We had to make assumptions on the geometry of the expected codes with respect to the distance of FIPs and the angle they enclose. In our case, 62 bytes of information are embedded into each QR code, which results in 33:7 as Code:FIP width ratio (Fig. 2(a)).

To the synthetic image set, we added perspective distortions that were capable of shifting the FIPs of the QR code by one FIP width at most. Let a be the FIP width and b the distance of the outer edges of two FIPs. For a code with no distortion, $a + b$ is the distance of the two other FIPs to the upper

left FIP of the code, and their enclosed angle is 90° looking from the upper left
(Fig. 2(a)). A QR code having a distortion that warps the FIP center inward
by a (Fig. 2(b)), can be detected by letting $T_d = c/(a + b)$ tolerance to FIP
distance, where $c = \sqrt{a^2 + b^2}$. Calculating with $(a + b) : a = 33 : 7$, the formula
gives 0.7788 for T_d, which shows that letting 22.12 % of tolerance to the expected
code size can detect codes up to the discussed distortion. The expected enclosing
angle is $90 \pm 20.22°$, calculated by $T_a = \tan^{-1}(a/b)/90$, which is a 22.47 % of
tolerance. The other case of distortion (Fig. 2(c)) can be calculated in a similar
manner, and results in $T_d = 0.7707$ and $T_a = 0.1331$. According to these results,
the post-processing step of triplet formation has to have a tolerance set to 23 %
for FIP candidate distance and also for enclosing angle in order to not to lose
any successfully localized QR codes during that step. Since detected FIPs are
of different sizes, it would be possible to add a new constraint to the triplet
formation defined as a tolerance factor for FIP size differences among triplets.
However, due to the perspective distortions, it is not possible to narrow down
results by FIP size variability, it only causes decreased hit rate. Furthermore,
even with those relatively small degrees of distortion, necessary tolerances for
distance and angle are high enough to compromise the filtering power of the
triplet formation rule.

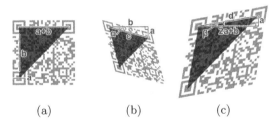

(a)   (b)   (c)

Fig. 2. Example for deciding on triplet formation tolerance. From the top left corner
of a perfect QR code, the other two FIPs are enclosing 90 degrees and distance of FIP
centers is $a + b$ (a); Considering two scenarios of distortion where FIPs are shifted
inwards (b) and outwards (c) with a, distances and angle tolerances for acceptance can
be calculated using basic geometry.

While classifiers trained to the whole code area need no post-processing,
FIP-trained ones require the formation of a distance matrix for all FIP candidate pairs, and a direction matrix that stores the angle of the line segment
defined by all FIP pairs. After that, reading through n FIP candidates still takes
$\mathcal{O}(n^3)$ time, which is a bottleneck since a FIP-trained classifier can produce high
amount of FIP candidates (Fig. 3).

3   Evaluation and Results

The classifiers have been trained using OpenCV on the discussed training
database. Training time for Haar features took cca. 15 hours on a Core 2 Duo

(a)   (b)

Fig. 3. Example QR code and result of a Haar classifier trained on FIPs. Original image (a); feature image (b) with numerous FIP candidates (gray square), and marked candidates (white circle) that have passed post-processing. Circles close to each other means that a FIP candidate is participating in formation of more than one probable QR code.

3.00 GHz CPU, while LBP training took about 1.5 hours, and HOG-training was the fastest, taking only about 30 minutes. Processing of test images with the trained classifiers has no significant difference respecting detection time, and each one is fast enough for real-time application. Detection time mostly depends on the scaling parameter in multi-scale detection. The default scaling factor is 1.1 in OpenCV, in which case detection takes cca. 100–200 ms for 512×512 px images on an Intel Core 2 Duo 3.00GHz CPU.

Table 1 shows performance measures of the examined cascade classifiers. HAAR–FIP, as stated by authors of [4], has a hit rate above 90 %, and represents a good solution for FIP-training. However, all FIP-based classifiers have poor precision compared to the ones trained for full code region, and they can cause serious overhead for the next, decoding step of the QR code recognition process. Classifiers based on LBP and HOG do not reach the hit rate of the one with Haar features. HOG–FIP shows a noticeably higher precision than its siblings, but still cannot be considered as an effective classifier according to its hit rate. Performance measures are made by a 90 % minimum required overlap of detected bounding box to the ground truth for a true positive.

Table 1. Test results of the proposed cascade classifiers based on Haar-like features, LBP and HOG, both trained for finder patterns (–FIP) and whole code objects(–FULL)

	Precision	Hit rate	F-measure
HAAR-FIP [4]	0.1535 ± 0.0920	0.9436 ± 0.0753	0.2640 ± 0.1125
LBP-FIP	0.1686 ± 0.0530	0.7356 ± 0.1112	0.2743 ± 0.0773
HOG-FIP	0.4753 ± 0.2466	0.7885 ± 0.1960	0.5931 ± 0.1947
HAAR-FULL	0.4208 ± 0.2404	0.9995 ± 0.1092	0.5923 ± 0.1050
LBP-FULL	0.9050 ± 0.1312	0.9999 ± 0.0857	0.9501 ± 0.0721
HOG-FULL	0.5390 ± 0.2549	0.9975 ± 0.1001	0.6999 ± 0.1221

For classifiers with the whole code object as their target, results are much more spectacular. Both HAAR–FULL, LBP–FULL and HOG–FULL show outstanding hit rate and acceptable precision. The LBP–FULL classifier was able to detect all codes of the test database with a very low amount of false positives, having an F-measure over 0.95.

Table 2 shows results of the trained classifiers for the public database of Sörös et al. [11]. HAAR–FULL, LBP–FULL and HOG–FULL are the same classifiers like in Table 1, they are trained only in our training database and were evaluated with no modifications. The last three classifiers, HAAR–SOROS, LBP–SOROS and HOG–SOROS are classifiers using full code object, trained on their database which consists of about 100 arbitrarily acquired images taken with iPhone camera. The main difference between the two databases besides one being synthetic and the other real, is the higher variability in size and orientation of QR codes for the latter. As expected, each classifier has noticeably lower hit rate, since they were trained using another database with different constraints, however, results still prove that cascade classifiers are a reasonable approach for the selected task, even when they are evaluated on a significantly different test set.

We also experimented with training cascade classifiers on the Sörös data set, however, training had only 85 samples as input and 21 for evaluation, which is too few for making strong statements in a machine learning context. HAAR–SOROS and HOG–SOROS had no false positives at all, but they were also unable to detect all instances. LBP could be trained well for the database with respect to hit rate, but probably due to the low count of training samples, shows poor precision.

Table 2. Classifier performances for the database of Sörös et al. [11]. The ones ending with –FULL are the same classifiers trained on our synthetic database, while –SOROS classifiers are trained on their public database.

	Precision	Hit rate	F-measure
HAAR-FULL	0.2366 ± 0.2325	0.9060 ± 0.2192	0.3752 ± 0.1285
LBP-FULL	0.3663 ± 0.3265	0.7607 ± 0.1847	0.4944 ± 0.1430
HOG-FULL	0.7817 ± 0.2842	0.9487 ± 0.2871	0.8571 ± 0.2141
HAAR-SOROS	0.9999 ± 0.4220	0.7619 ± 0.2587	0.8649 ± 0.2937
LBP-SOROS	0.3684 ± 0.2082	0.9999 ± 0.1640	0.5385 ± 0.0973
HOG-SOROS	0.9999 ± 0.2127	0.9524 ± 0.1063	0.9756 ± 0.1347

In conclusion, the most efficient classifier disposes of the following parameters: LBP of 32×32 sample size used for feature extraction in cascade topology, boosted by Gentle AdaBoost, and a 10 stage learning phase with 0.995 hit rate and 0.5 false alarm rate, with no splits or tree structure. In cases where orientation variability is high for the expected codes, we recommend training two separate LBP–FULL classifiers with two training sample databases, with sample orientations around $0°$ and $45°$, respectively.

4   Concluding Remarks

QR codes became common for the past few years and their wide use made automatic reading desirable. We presented various cascade classifiers based on different features and training target, and studied their performance and capability for QR code localization. Our approach can be used in real-time applications with high hit rate and a moderate false positive rate that depends mainly on training parameters that can be tuned for the requirements of each end-user application, from postal services to smartphone camera software.

References

1. Parikh, D., Jancke, G.: Localization and segmentation of a 2D high capacity color barcode. In: IEEE Workshop on Applications of Computer Vision, WACV 2008, pp. 1–6 (2008)
2. Chu, C.H., Yang, D.N., Pan, Y.L., Chen, M.S.: Stabilization and extraction of 2D barcodes for camera phones. Multimedia Systems **17**, 113–133 (2011)
3. Ohbuchi, E., Hanaizumi, H., Hock, L.A.: Barcode readers using the camera device in mobile phones. In: 2004 International Conference on Cyberworlds, pp. 260–265 (2004)
4. Belussi, L.F.F., Hirata, N.S.T.: Fast QR code detection in arbitrarily acquired images. In: 2011 24th SIBGRAPI Conference on Graphics, Patterns and Images (Sibgrapi), pp. 281–288 (2011)
5. Viola, P., Jones, M.: Rapid object detection using a boosted cascade of simple features. In: Proceedings of the 2001 IEEE Computer Society Conference on Computer Vision and Pattern Recognition, CVPR 2001, vol. 1, pp. I-511–I-518 (2001)
6. Lienhart, R., Kuranov, A., Pisarevsky, V.: Empirical analysis of detection cascades of boosted classifiers for rapid object detection. In: Michaelis, B., Krell, G. (eds.) DAGM 2003. LNCS, vol. 2781, pp. 297–304. Springer, Heidelberg (2003)
7. Bodnár, P., Nyúl, L.G.: A novel method for barcode localization in image domain. In: Kamel, M., Campilho, A. (Eds.) ICIAR 2013. LNCS, vol. 7950, pp. 189–196. Springer, Heidelberg (2013)
8. Ojala, T., Pietikainen, M., Harwood, D.: Performance evaluation of texture measures with classification based on kullback discrimination of distributions. In: Proceedings of the 12th IAPR International Conference on Pattern Recognition, Conference A: Computer Vision and Image Processing, vol. 1, pp. 582–585 (1994)
9. Dalal, N., Triggs, B.: Histograms of oriented gradients for human detection. In: IEEE Computer Society Conference on Computer Vision and Pattern Recognition, CVPR 2005, vol. 1 pp. 886–893 (2005)
10. Wang, X., Han, T., Yan, S.: An HOG-LBP human detector with partial occlusion handling. In: 2009 IEEE 12th International Conference on Computer Vision, pp. 32–39 (2009)
11. Sörös, G., Flörkemeier, C.: Blur-resistant joint 1D and 2D barcode localization for smartphones. In: Proceedings of the 12th International Conference on Mobile and Ubiquitous Multimedia, MUM 2013, pp. 11:1–11:8. ACM, New York (2013)

Document Image Analysis

Using Scale-Space Anisotropic Smoothing for Text Line Extraction in Historical Documents

Rafi Cohen[1]([⊠]), Itshak Dinstein[2], Jihad El-Sana[1], and Klara Kedem[1]

[1] Department of Computer Science, Ben-Gurion University, Beer-Sheva, Israel
{rafico,el-sana,klara}@cs.bgu.ac.il
[2] Department of Electrical and Computer Engineering,
Ben-Gurion University, Beer-Sheva, Israel
dinstein@ee.bgu.ac.il

Abstract. Text line extraction is vital pre-requisite for various document processing tasks. This paper presents a novel approach for text line extraction which is based on Gaussian scale space and dedicated binarization that utilize the inherent structure of smoothed text document images. It enhances the text lines in the image using multi-scale anisotropic second derivative of Gaussian filter bank at the average height of the text line. It then applies a binarization, which is based on component-tree and is tailored towards line extraction. The final stage of the algorithm is based on an energy minimization framework for removing spurious text line and assigning connected components to lines. We have tested our approach on various datasets written in different languages at range of image quality and received high detection rates, which outperform state-of-the-art algorithms. Our MATLAB code is publicly available. (http://www.cs.bgu.ac.il/~rafico/LineExtraction.zip)

Keywords: Historical document processing · Text lines extraction

1 Introduction

Many of the document analysis algorithms, such as indexing, word retrieval and text recognition, expect extracted text lines, as an input. Thus, text line extraction is an essential operation in document processing and a substantial number of related algorithms have been published. Most of these algorithms expect binary images and some are designed to handle gray scale images.

Smearing based methods [4,10,15] apply Gaussian based filtering and binarization to enhance line structure. These approaches yield good results and became popular methods for text line extraction (ranked 1st in ICDAR 2009 and ICFHR 2010 contests [8,9], and 3rd in ICDAR 2013 contest [16]). However, the performance of these methods depends on choosing the correct scale of the Gaussian based filter. Most authors do not provide an algorithm for choosing the correct scale [10,15] or choose the scale based on ad-hoc heuristics [4]. The binarization phase also inherits the limitations of the adapted binarization algorithm which is either ad-hoc binarization [15] or based on active-contours [4,10]

A. Campilho and M. Kamel (Eds.): ICIAR 2014, Part I, LNCS 8814, pp. 349–358, 2014.
DOI: 10.1007/978-3-319-11758-4_38

which are computationally slow. Seam-based line extraction algorithm compute an energy map, which is used to guide the progress of the seam that determine the text lines or their boundaries. The algorithm is required to determine the boundary seams of the detected text-lines, which is done using ad-hoc heuristics [14].

In this paper we present a novel method designed to detect text lines. Our algorithm is based on robust theoretical background, i.e., scale space theory [11] and our binarization method is fast, and tailored towards line extraction in documents. In an initial step our approach enhances the text lines in the image using multi-scale anisotropic second derivative of Gaussian filter bank at the average height of the text line. It then applies a binarization, which is based on component-tree and utilizes the structure of smoothed text line.

In the rest of the paper we overview closely related work and background literature. We then present our algorithm and its experimental evaluation. Finally we conclude and draw directions for future work.

2   Related Work

Text line extraction algorithms could be categorized into projection-based methods [2], grouping methods [7,13], seam-based algorithm [14] and smearing methods [4,10,15].

Projection-based algorithms divide the document image into vertical strips and horizontal projections are calculated within the stripes. The resulting projections are combined in order to extract the final text lines. Bar-Yosef et al. [2] applied an oriented local projection profiles (LPP) inside a sliding stripe. The average skew of the current stripe is calculated and the next stripe is projected along that skew direction. Grouping methods extract text lines by aggregating units in a bottom-up strategy. The units may be pixel or higher level representation, such as connected components, blocks or other features such as interest points. Rabaev et al. [13] used a sweep-line to aggregate connected components, that correspond to characters, into text lines. A seam-carving-based approach has been developed recently. Saabni et al. [14] used two types of seams, medial and separating. Both types of seems propagate according to energy maps, which are defined based on the distance transform of the gray scale image. The seams tend to diverge when big gaps between words or holes in the document are present.

Smearing approaches enhance line structure and then apply binarization to extract text lines. Shi et al. [15] converted an input image into an adaptive local connectivity map (ALCM), where the value of each pixel is defined as the cumulative intensity of the pixel inside a window of a predefined size. Finally the ALCM image is binarized to extract text line patterns. The method do not contain a mechanism for determining the appropriate scale of the filter for degraded grayscale historical documents and the binarization algorithm is not tailored towards lines extraction. A popular variant of the smearing method [4,10] is based upon convolving the image with an anisotropic Gaussian (or a bank or Gaussians) followed by segmentation of text lines using active contours. Bukhari *et al.* [4] suggest to choose the scales of the Gaussians by binarizing the document and inspecting its height histogram, which is susceptible to noise in degraded documents, see Fig. 1(a). Another drawback for the level-set based active contours methods [10] is their complex and slow computation.

Despite considerable progress over the last decade, automatic text line segmentation of historical documents, as those presented in Fig. 1, remains an open problem.

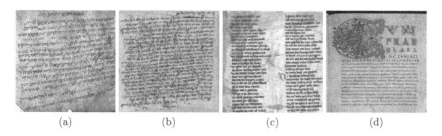

| (a) | (b) | (c) | (d) |

Fig. 1. Samples of the documents on which we perform our tests. (a) Genizah handwritten manuscript; (b) Pinkasim handwritten cursive manuscript; (c) German manuscript from Parzival dataset; (d) Latin manuscript from Saint Gall dataset.

3   Notations and Definitions

Our approach relies on scale space scheme and utilize component tree to extract text lines. To simplify the presentation of our algorithm we briefly overview these two topics.

3.1   Scale-Space Overview

Scale space can be intuitively thought of as a collection of smoothed versions of the original image. Formally, given an image $I : \mathbf{R}^2 \to \mathbf{R}$, its linear scale-space representation $L : \mathbf{R}^2 \times \mathbf{R}^2_+ \to \mathbf{R}$ can be defined by convolution with anisotropic Gaussian kernels of various lengths $\sqrt{t_x}$ and $\sqrt{t_y}$ in the coordinate directions, defined as $L(x, y; t_x, t_y) = g(x, y; t_x, t_y) * I(x, y)$, where $g : \mathbf{R}^2 \times \mathbf{R}^2_+ \to \mathbf{R}$ is an anisotropic Gaussian defined in Eq. 1. We define a multiplication factor η as $\frac{\sigma_x}{\sigma_y}$, where σ_i is related to t_i by $\sigma_i = \sqrt{t_i}$.

$$g(x, y; t_x, t_y) = \frac{1}{2\pi\sqrt{t_x t_y}} e^{-\left(\frac{x^2}{2t_x} + \frac{y^2}{2t_y}\right)}. \tag{1}$$

We denote by $\partial_{x^\alpha} L(x, y; t_x, t_y)$ the partial derivative of L with respect to x, where L is differentiated α times. Lindeberg [11] showed that the amplitude of spatial derivatives, $\partial_{x^\alpha} \partial_{y^\beta} L(x, y; t_x, t_y)$, in general *decrease with scale*, i.e., if an image is subject to scale-space smoothing, then the numerical values of spatial derivatives computed from the smoothed data can be expected to decrease.

If two signals f and f' are related by scale, i.e., $f(x) = f'(sx)$, then it is possible to normalize that spatial derivative of the scale-space such that the normalized derivatives are equal [11]. More formally, Let the scale space representation of f and f' be given as $L(x;t) = g(x,t) * f$ and $L'(x';t') = g(x',t') * f'$, where the spatial variables and the scale parameters are transformed according $x' = sx$ and $t' = s^2t$. Then, if γ-normalized function of the derivatives is defined as $\partial_\xi = \sqrt{t}\partial_x$ and $\partial'_\xi = \sqrt{t'}\partial_{x'}$ then $\partial_{\xi^\alpha}L(x;t) = \partial_{\xi'^\alpha}L'(x';t')$. That is, the γ-normalized function of the derivatives are *scale invariant*.

3.2 Component-Tree

The level sets of a map are the sets of points with level above a given threshold. The inclusion relation enables connected components of the level sets to be organized in a tree structure, which is called the *component tree* [12]. We denote the threshold set obtained by thresholding a map with threshold t by $\mathcal{B}_t$ and the set of connected components in $\mathcal{B}_t$ by $\mathcal{C}_t$. The nodes in a *component-tree* correspond to the components in $\mathcal{C}_t$ for varying values of the threshold t. The root of the tree is the member of $\mathcal{C}_{t_{\min}}$, where $t_{\min}$ is chosen such that $|\mathcal{C}_{t_{\min}}|=1$. The next level in the tree correspond to $\mathcal{C}_{t_{\min}+d}$, and in general the nodes in the tree that belong to level ℓ correspond to $\mathcal{C}_{t_{\min}+\ell d}$, where d is a parameter that determines the step size for the tree. There is an edge between $C_i \in \mathcal{C}_t$ and $C_j \in \mathcal{C}_{t+1}$ if and only if $C_j \subseteq C_i$. The maximal threshold $t_{\max}$ used in tree construction is simply the maximal value in the map.

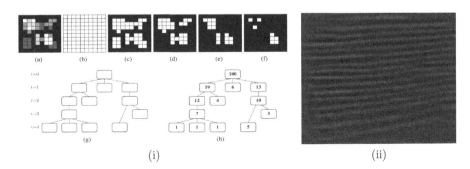

Fig. 2. (i)(a) A gray-level image F and its successive threshold sets $B_t(F)$ for t from 0 (b) to 4 (f), where $d = 1$; (g) The component-tree of F. (h) The same tree, enriched by an attribute (the size of the connected component of each node), courtesy of [12]. (ii) Lines enhancement result.

4   Our Approach

In this paper we describe a text line segmentation approach for handwritten documents, which is based on Gaussian scale space and component-tree traversal.

The method starts by enhancing lines in the image, using multi-scale anisotropic second derivative of Gaussian filter bank. The resulting image is binarized using component-tree traversal that is tailored towards line extraction. At the final step, spurious detected lines that do not correspond to text lines are removed.

4.1 Lines Enhancement

The pixels in an image can be regarded as two dimensional random variables. They are generated by an unknown Probability Distribution Function (PDF), which represents the distribution of text lines. Specifically, the PDF is continuous and has smaller values (dark) in the text line area, while there are larger values (bright) in the gap and marginal area [10]. Valleys on the probability map represent text lines, while peaks are the boundary between neighboring text lines. As a result of this structure, a convolution of text line with a second derivative of an anisotropic Gaussian, elongated along the horizontal direction generates ridges along text lines and valleys along the gaps between text lines [5]. Making it an appropriate filter for enhancing the lines structure in a document.

The Appropriate scale for this filter correspond to the text line height, which varies along the text line itself, due to ascenders and descenders, and along different text lines. We use a multi-scale filtering and detect the optimal scale for each point using the scale-space framework [11]. We construct a scale space representation of the images by convolving the image with the γ-normalized function of g_{xx} from Eq. 1 with $\eta > 1$, and choosing for each pixel the strongest response along the scale-space. The scales at which the image is convolved with corresponds to the height range of the characters in the document. A robust estimate of character height range in gray-scale images is obtained using the evolution map (EM) tool introduced by Biller $et\ al.$ [3]. The EM supplies details about the height range of the characters in the document, without binarization. For binary images the range is taken as $(\mu, \mu + \sigma/2)$, where μ and σ are the average and standard deviation of the heights of the connected components in the document. Fig. 2(ii) illustrates the result of lines enhancement on a document from Fig. 1(a).

4.2 Text Line Extraction Using Component-Tree

To extract the text lines we need to binarize the gray scale image, $\mathcal{R}$, resulting from applying the Gaussian scale space on the original image (Section 4.1). Off-the-shelf general binarization algorithm do not take into account the properties of the resulting image, require tuning parameters, and often introduce noise and artifacts. Instead, we apply a binarization procedure, which is based on $component\text{-}tree$ scheme and geared toward the structure of $\mathcal{R}$.

A connected component that represents a text line resembles a thick simple polyline that covers the entire text line (the thickness is not uniform). Motivated by this observation, we build a component-tree of $\mathcal{R}$ and for each connected component, C_i (represented by the node, $node(C_i)$, in the tree) we measure how well C_i can be represented by a simple piecewise linear approximation. Let us refer to this measure as $F(C_i)$. One could compute $F(C_i)$ by detecting the skeleton of the component and measuring its linearity, but skeleton structure is not robust and sensitive to noise. Instead, we fit a simple piecewise linear approximation from the left end to the right end of the component and measure quality of the fit. We chose to implement that by fitting a uniform least squares spline of order 1 with k knots for the connected component, C_i. The first and last points correspond to the left and right end of the component and the $k - 2$ remaining points are distributed uniformly along the line connecting the two end points, as depicted in Fig. 3(b). The fit quality is computed based on two terms: (a) the average distance of each pixel from the spline, and (b) the difference between the area of the component and the sum of the distances of the contour pixels from the spline. The average distance is compared with the average letter height to detect and refine component that include two consecutive lines. The second term is used to detect partial merge of adjacent text lines that form a non-convex component.

To extract the text lines we traverse the component-tree top-down and at each node, $node(C_i)$ we measure its fitness, $F(C_i)$, and based on that we determine whether it represents a text line or not. If C_i represent a text line we output this text line and the search along this branch is complete, otherwise we refine the component by recursively processing the children of the $node(C_i)$. Fig. 3(a) presents the pseudo-code of the traversal procedure.

```
 1: Ouput = φ.
 2: Enqueue the root node v into a queue Q
 3: while Q is not empty do
 4:     C_i ← Q.dequeue()
 5:     if F(C_i) represents a text line then
 6:         Ouput = Ouput ⋃ C_i.
 7:     else
 8:         Enqueue all children of C_i into Q.
 9:     end if
10: end while
11: return Output.
```

(a)   (b)

Fig. 3. (a) Traversal Algorithm; (b) a synthetic blob with an approximating spline (in red) that uses 6 knots (k=6)

4.3   Post-Processing

Our algorithm usually extracts the correct text line efficiently. However, in some cases it includes spurious lines that do not correspond to text lines or split a text lines into disconnected segments, as shown in Fig. 4(c). We overcome these limitations by detecting and removing spurious text lines and connecting segments that belong to the same text line. This stage involves minimizing an energy function on a binarized version of the document.

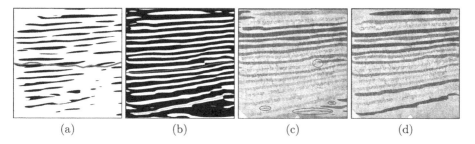

(a)	(b)	(c)	(d)

Fig. 4. The various stages of the component tree traversal, where splines used to evaluate piecewise linearity are depicted in red (unsuccessful fit) or cyan (successful fit), (a) the root of the component tree, at $\mathcal{C}_{-17}$, (b) the components at $\mathcal{C}_{13}$, (c) the result before discarding spurious lines (disconnected segments are encircled in red, and some spurious lines are encircled in blue) and (d) the final result.

Our approach relies on multi-label graph cut minimization [6] where graph cuts are used to approximate energy minimization of arbitrary functions. Let $\mathcal{L}$ be the set of lines (labels and lines are interchangeable throughout this section) that were extracted in Section 4.2 (Fig. 4(b)) and let $\mathcal{C}$ be the set of connected component in the document. The goal is to find a labeling f that assigns each component $c \in \mathcal{C}$ a label $\ell_c \in \mathcal{L}$, where f is consistent with the observed data, spatial coherent and uses a minimal set of labels (i.e., lines). The energy function, $E(f)$ defined in Eq. 2, consists of three terms: the data cost, the smoothness terms and the label cost. Minimizing the energy function, $E(f)$, produces an appropriate labeling.

$$E(f) = \sum_{c \in \mathcal{C}} D(c, \ell_c) + \sum_{\{c,c'\} \in \mathcal{N}} d(c, c') \cdot \delta(\ell_c \neq \ell_{c'}) + \sum_{\ell \in \mathcal{L}} h_\ell \cdot \delta_\ell(f) \qquad (2)$$

The cost term, $D(c, \ell_c)$, expresses the cost of assigning c the label ℓ_c and is defined as the Euclidean distance between the centroid of c and the line represented by ℓ_c. The smoothness term determines the coherence of the labels ℓ_c and $\ell_{c'}$ with the spatial relation of the components c and c'. That is, the closer the components are the higher is the chance that they got assigned the same label. Let $\mathcal{N}$ be the set of adjacent component pairs. We set $|\mathcal{N}| = 2$ and define the distance $d(c, c')$ in Eq. 2 according to $d(c, c') = \exp(-\alpha \cdot d_e(c, c'))$ (the spatial coherence strength decays exponentially with Euclidean distance). The term $d_e(c, c')$ is the Euclidean distance between the centroids of components c and c', and the constant α is defined as $(2 \langle d_e(c, c') \rangle)^{-1}$, where $\langle \cdot \rangle$ denotes expectation over all pairs of adjacent elements [5]. The term $\delta(\ell_c \neq \ell_{c'})$ is Kronecker's delta. The label costs penalize each unique label that appears in f, where h_ℓ is the nonnegative label cost of label ℓ, and $\delta_\ell(f)$ is an indicator function that is assigned 1, when the label ℓ appears in f and 0 otherwise. We define the *density* of a line ℓ as the number of foreground pixels in the binarized document overlapping with ℓ, and r_ℓ as the the ratio between the density of ℓ and the maximal density in $\mathcal{L}$. The label cost h_ℓ is defined as $\exp(-\beta \cdot r_\ell)$, where β is a constant we set experimentally.

Finally, we merge broken line segments. For each segment we extract its left and right endpoints and define the direction of a component as the vector connecting the left endpoint to the right endpoint. Two adjacent component are merged if (a) the direction of the vector connecting the two components (the right of the first component to the left of the second one) falls between the direction of the two components and (b) their vertical distance is less than the average letter height.

5   Experimental Results and Discussions

We evaluated our text line detection on various datasets and received encouraging results. The test datasets include documents written by different writers and in various languages. Hence, the presented methodology is script and writer independent and copes nicely with noise. the datasets are ICDAR 2013 [16], ICDAR 2009 [8], Hebrew [13], Saint Gall [7] and Parzival [1] datasets. ICDAR 2013 contains 150 pages written in English, Greek and Bangla. ICDAR 2009 contains 200 pages written in English, French, German and Greek. The Hebrew dataset contains 58 degraded pages from Cairo Genizah collection and 6 pages from the Pinkasim collection. The Saint Gall database contains 60 pages of a Latin manuscript from the 9th century. The Parzival includes 47 pages of a German manuscript from the 13th century. For Parzival we used the ground-truth generated by [13].

The performance evaluation is based on a MatchScore [16] that computes the maximum overlap of a text region with the ground truth region. If this score is above a given threshold T_α, the text line is considered as correct (one-to-one match, o2o). Based on this MatchScore, the Detection Rate (DR), the Recognition Accuracy (RA) and the Performance Metric (FM) are defined using Eq. 3, where N and M are the number of text lines in the ground truth and the number of text lines detected by the algorithm, respectively. In our experiments we set T_α as 95% for datasets of binary images, and 90% for datasets of gray-scale images. For all datasets and all algorithms the performance evaluation is based on a binarized version of the datasets. For Saint Gall and Parzival we measure the performance by means of the Pixel-Level Hit Rate (PHR) and the FM (also called Line Accuracy Measure) as in [1,7]. The results of the presented algorithm are reported in Table 1, we also mention for each dataset whether it consists of binary pages (B) or gray-scale pages (G). Throughout the experiments we have used the 15 knots (k=15) to measure the linearity of the components, the scale space is defined based on $d = 1$ and $\eta = 3$.

$$DR = \frac{o2o}{N}, RA = \frac{o2o}{M}, FM = \frac{2 \times DR \times RA}{DR + RA} \tag{3}$$

Although the algorithm achieves high detection rates, it suffers some limitations. For example, if salient objects in the image, such as holes and drawings,

Table 1. Results on different datasets compared with known state-of-the-art algorithms. Each dataset contains either binary (B) or gray-scale documents (G).

	Our Method					state-of-the-art
	M	o2o	DR	RA	FM	FM
ICDAR 2013 [16](B)	2651	2621	98.94%	98.86%	**98.90%**	98.66%
ICDAR 2009 [8](B)	4033	4021	99.67%	99.70%	**99.69%**	99.53%
Hebrew [13](G)	1257	1154	89.04%	91.88%	**90.44%**	86.10%
	PHR		FM		PHR	FM
Saint Gall [7](G)	**99.08%**		**99.22%**		98.94%	99.03%
Parzival [1](G)	**98.31%**		**97.88%**		96.30%	96.40%

| (a) | (b) | (c) | (d) |

Fig. 5. (a)-(c) Selected result samples of the algorithm: (a) Pinkasim ; (b) Genizah ; (c) Parzival. (d)(upper) The drawing causes the line above it to be missed; (d)(lower) two partial lines accidentally merged together.

are in close vicinity with a text line the result of the algorithm may produce incorrect results, as shown in Fig. 5(d).

6   Conclusions and Future Directions

In this paper, we presented a text line segmentation method for handwritten historical documents. Our approach applies smearing at different scales using a Gaussian scale-space, while utilizing the average height of the characters, followed by a dedicated binarization technique that is based on component-tree and utilize the structure of text lines. In future research we plan to upgrade the proposed method in two directions: (1) refine the use of the evolution maps (EM) to obtain a more reliable range of character heights in the document, and (2) find a more robust procedure for estimating whether a segment refers to a text line or not.

Acknowledgments. This research was supported in part by the DFG-Trilateral grant no. FI 1494/3-2, the Ministry of Science and Technology of Israel, the Council of Higher Education of Israel, the Lynn and William Frankel Center for Computer Sciences and by the Paul Ivanier Center for Robotics and Production Management at Ben-Gurion University, Israel.

References

1. Baechler, M., Liwicki, M., Ingold, R.: Text line extraction using dmlp classifiers for historical manuscripts. In: ICDAR, pp. 1029–1033 (2013)
2. Bar-Yosef, I., Hagbi, N., Kedem, K., Dinstein, I.: Text Line Segmentation for Degraded Handwritten Historical Documents. In: ICDAR, pp. 1161–1165 (2009)
3. Biller, O., Kedem, K., Dinstein, I., El-Sana, J.: Evolution maps for connected components in text documents. In: ICFHR, pp. 403–408 (2012)
4. Bukhari, S.S., Shafait, F., Breuel, T.M.: Script-independent handwritten textlines segmentation using active contours. In: ICDAR, pp. 446–450 (2009)
5. Cohen, R., Asi, A., Kedem, K., El-Sana, J., Dinstein, I.: Robust text and drawing segmentation algorithm for historical documents. In: HIP, pp. 110–117 (2013)
6. Delong, A., Osokin, A., Isack, H.N., Boykov, Y.: Fast approximate energy minimization with label costs. IJCV **96**(1), 1–27 (2012)
7. Diem, M., Kleber, F., Sablatnig, R.: Text line detection for heterogeneous documents. In: ICDAR, pp. 743–747 (2013)
8. Gatos, B., Stamatopoulos, N., Louloudis, G.: ICDAR2009 handwriting segmentation contest. IJDAR **14**(1), 25–33 (2011)
9. Gatos, B., Stamatopoulos, N., Louloudis, G.: ICFHR 2010 handwriting segmentation contest. In: ICFHR, pp. 737–742 (2010)
10. Li, Y., Zheng, Y., Doermann, D., Jaeger, S.: Script-independent text line segmentation in freestyle handwritten documents. IEEE TPAMI **30**(8), 1313–1329 (2008)
11. Lindeberg, T.: Feature detection with automatic scale selection. IJCV **30**(2), 79–116 (1998)
12. Naegel, B., Wendling, L.: A document binarization method based on connected operators. Pattern Recognition Letters **31**(11), 1251–1259 (2010)
13. Rabaev, I., Biller, O., El-Sana, J., Kedem, K., Dinstein, I.: Text line detection in corrupted and damaged historical manuscripts. In: ICDAR, pp. 812–816 (2013)
14. Saabni, R., Asi, A., El-Sana, J.: Text line extraction for historical document images. Pattern Recognition Letters **35**, 23–33 (2014)
15. Shi, Z., Setlur, S., Govindaraju, V.: A steerable directional local profile technique for extraction of handwritten arabic text lines. In: ICDAR, pp. 176–180 (2009)
16. Stamatopoulos, N., Gatos, B., Louloudis, G., Pal, U., Alaei, A.: ICDAR 2013 handwriting segmentation contest. In: ICDAR, pp. 1402–1406 (2013)

Multi-script Identification from Printed Words

Saumya Jetley(⊠), Kapil Mehrotra, Atish Vaze, and Swapnil Belhe

Centre for Development of Advanced Computing (C-DAC), Pune, India
{saumyaj,kapilm,atishv,swapnilb}@cdac.in

Abstract. In today's multi-script scenario, documents contain page, paragraph, line and up to word level intermixing of different scripts. We need a script recognition approach that can perform well even at the lowest semantically-valid level of words so as to serve as a generic solution. The present paper proposes a combination of Histogram of Oriented Gradients (HoG) and Local Binary Patterns (LBP), extracted over words, to capture the unique and discriminative structural formations of different scripts. Tested over MILE printed-word data set, this concatenated feature descriptor yields a state-of-the-art average recognition accuracy of 97.4 % over a set of 11 Indian scripts.

In an end-to-end document recognition system it is correct to assume a skew correction unit prior to script identification. Depending on the amount of skew, the skew correction unit can either yield a correctly aligned document or an inverted one. For script identification in such scenarios, we introduce novel modifications over existing HoG and LBP features to propose - Inversion Invariant HoG (II-HoG) and Inversion Invariant LBP (II-LBP) in order to achieve text inversion invariance. Once the script is recognized, script-specific HoG and LBP feature combination can be used to find the text alignment i.e. 0° or 180° for correction. For the MILE database, first-level inversion-invariant script-identification accuracy for 11 script-set is 95.8 % (1 % gain over the existing best) while the second-level script-specific orientation-detection accuracy is averaged at 97.7 %.

1 Introduction

In today's multi-lingual and multi-script setting, script identification has become a necessity for document analysis. A single document commonly contains two or even three distinct scripts. In the Indian context, this bi-script and tri-script scenario is well presented by Pati and Ramakrishnan [1]. State local script and Roman, with Devanagari as an extra addition, are common combinations. Research works have also dealt with script pairs such as Farsi and Latin [2], Han and Roman [3], and Persian and Roman [4].

If a character-recognition engine were to work for even two scripts together, number of classes would be prohibitively large, not to mention the inefficiency in terms of performance. Thus, it becomes important to identify a priori the script

© Springer International Publishing Switzerland 2014
A. Campilho and M. Kamel (Eds.): ICIAR 2014, Part I, LNCS 8814, pp. 359–368, 2014.
DOI: 10.1007/978-3-319-11758-4_39

from the known set and accordingly send the text for character-recognition. Also, pre-processing tasks like morphological de-noising, text-line/word/character segmentation tend to show script-biased behavior. With knowledge of the script, pre-processing modules tailored to the script can be called for an improved performance.

Script recognition has matured from its primitive role as a pre-cursor to document recognition. It is now also being used for document retrieval based on script similarity [5]. Particularly in this context, multi-script identification becomes relevant. The recognition unit should be equipped to identify more than 2 or 3 different scripts at a time.

Having discussed the need for bi-script, tri-script as well as multi-script recognition, we must identify the level at which the approach should function. In [6], the authors handle multi-script printed documents but assume page level script uniformity. The work in [7–11] again assumes text-block or line-level script uniformity. Only the methods presented in [1–3,12] perform script identification at word or character level, but none of these tackle possible text-skew or inversion. Basically, these methods work for a fixed script-set and/or assume particular level of script uniformity (block, line or page level) and thus lack generality.

Our present work aims to address this very lacuna. The novelty of our work is fourfold - (a) our script identification approaches work successfully even for the lowest semantically-valid level of words, (b) given an adequate database our approaches can be easily extended to any given script set, (c) our novel set of inversion invariant features - II-HoG and II-LBP is capable of identifying the script despite text inversion, and finally (d) we propose a complete module to identify the script, even for inverted text, and then find its orientation i.e. $0°$ or $180°$ for correction before further processing.

For a comparative experimental analysis, we test our approaches on word-level MILE database for 11 Indian scripts [1]. Using our gradient plus texture feature combination (HoG and LBP), the 11-script recognition accuracy of 97.4% is the new state-of-the-art. For inversion-invariant script identification, our novel feature combination of II-HoG & II-LBP achieves an accuracy of 95.8% (1% accuracy gain over the existing best).

The complete paper is organized as follows: Section 2 discusses the related works and existing approaches, Section 3 and 4 present the proposed approaches, Section 5 provides the experimental results and analysis, and Section 6 concludes the work.

2   Related Works and Existing Approaches

The task of script identification has been attempted at different levels – text block, text line, word and even at the component level.

Script identification at text block level is a commonly used idea. In [7], bi-dimensional empirical mode decomposition (BEMD) is followed by extraction of local binary patterns (LBPs) to identify between English, French, Chinese, Japanese, Russian and Korean scripts using 128x128 sized text blocks. In [11], wavelet energy based histogram moments are used with an SVM classifier to identify between 6 different scripts – Arabic, Chinese, English, Hindi, Thai and Korean. In [13], the authors extract texture features from co-occurrence histograms of wavelet decomposed images and use KNN classifier for block level recognition of 8 different Indian scripts.

In [8–10], the works propose script recognition at line level with the help of handcrafted structural and statistical features. Ghosh and Chaudhuri [8] introduce the idea of inversion-invariant script identification followed by script-specific orientation detection. However, their approach assumes line level script uniformity and employs a hierarchical classification setup that is customized for the given script set. Aithal et al. [9] use line level horizontal-projection profile and its statistical details to distinguish between Hindi, Kannada and English text in Trilingual documents. Gopakumar et al. [10] mark out horizontals, verticals, right diagonals and left diagonals in a given text line and carry out zone-based gradient analysis for identifying between 4 South Indian scripts of Kannada, Tamil, Telugu, Malayalam and English, and Hindi.

Word level approach adopted by Das et al. [12] shows the same hand-made feature and rule-based threshold trend, to distinguish between Telugu, Hindi and English. Huanfeng and Doermann [14] extract texture features using Gabor filter and apply them to a variety of bilingual dictionaries for word level script identification. Following suit, Pati and Ramakrishnan [1] employ a combination of Gabor filters to identify 11 Indian scripts, experimenting with both Nearest-neighbour and SVM classifier.

Another popular set of techniques makes use of component level script identification, with majority-vote based extension to word, line and page level script identification. In [2,3,5,6], the authors employ component level features and use SVM/KNN for classification. Khoddami and Behrad [2] present rotation and scale-invariant Curvature Scale Space features for identification of Farsi and Latin scripts. Chanda et al. [5] draw out a comparison between two distinct features – rotation-invariant Zernike moments and rotation-variant gradient features, to achieve the task of identifying amongst 11 Indian scripts. Wang et al. [6] make use of Downgraded Pixel Density features from skeletonized character for script identification. Pal et al. [3] use directional code based histograms for character level identification of Japanese, Korean, Chinese and Roman scripts.

To build a generic script recognition system we propose word-level implementation. Also, a close observation of the above approaches reveals one common idea. It is, the ability and hence wide use of texture and/or gradient features to successfully distinguish between different scripts. Building on this, we present a combination of both gradient and texture features for script identification. The first approach proposes concatenation of HoG and LBP descriptors for script recognition. The second approach introduces a novel modification in the form of Inversion-Invariant HoG and LBP (II-HoG and II-LBP) features and uses them for text-inversion invariant script identification.

Fig. 1. Structural highlights of 11 different Indian scripts

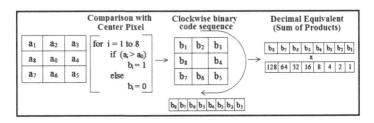

Fig. 2. Evaluation of Local Binary Pattern around a given pixel

3   Proposed Approach I - HoG and LBP

3.1   Histogram of Oriented Gradients (HoG)

For a task like script identification, important discriminative information lies in the relative proportion of different gradients. As shown in Figure 1(Top to Bottom/ Left to Right: Bangla(BE), Devanagari(HI), Roman(EN), Gujarati(GU), Kannada(KA), Malayalam(MA), Odiya(OD), Gurumukhi(PU), Tamil(TA), Telugu(TE) and Urdu (UR)), due to a necessary word headline (*shirorekha*) for Devanagari, Bangla and Gurumukhi, horizontal lines (or 0° gradients) are dominant in these scripts. It may depend on the font but as a general observation, the character-level joints become less curved and increasingly sharp from Devanagari to Gurumukhi to Bengali. Kannada script frequently shows a *horizontal line with an upward curl*, while Telugu has a highly common *tick* mark. Highlights of Oriya, Tamil and Malayalam are an *inverted U-shape*, *vertical lines*, and *right & left bracket shapes* respectively. Urdu is very different from any other Indian script. Majority of the lines have slope of 0° or other angles in the upper-half of 1st quadrant. These and many other unique structural properties of different scripts, as elaborated in [1], motivate the use of gradient proportions for script identification.

We employ histogram of oriented gradients [15] for script recognition at word level. The position of gradients within the text unit is not important, and HoG is applied at the complete word level without considering any overlapping sub-blocks. Angles lie in the range of 0°-180° and are divided into 36 bins based on the empirically evaluated bin spread of 5°.

3.2   Local Binary Patterns (LBP)

Local binary patterns capture image texture present as gray level variations in the immediate neighborhood of each image pixel. Figure 2 shows the computation of local binary pattern around a particular pixel in an image. For an LBP-based image texture analysis [16], the count of each binary pattern value is summed up over the image to yield the LBP histogram. For a 3x3 window analysis, the 256 distinct binary pattern values yield a feature descriptor of the same length.

3.3   HoG and LBP Based Classification

The feature vectors extracted above are concatenated to yield the final feature descriptor for the word image. Total length of the descriptor adds up to 292 (36 HoG features and 256 LBP features). The features are independently normalized using the classical L1-norm [17]. This normalization makes the feature-set size independent. Change in font size may change the absolute count of gradients/texture but their relative proportion remains the same.

We use SVM [18] for the task of multi-class classification. In order to handle non-linear class boundaries, SVM uses radial basis function kernel. The approach works highly accurately on the word level MILE database. With minimal training, it yields state-of the-art results. However, these features are not invariant to text inversion.

4   Proposed Approach II - Inversion Invariant HoG (II-HoG) and Inversion Invariant LBP (II-LBP)

For an end-to-end printed document analysis system it would be correct to assume a skew-correction unit prior to the script identification module. Without the knowledge of script, the skew-correction module can make alignment errors. For acute angle skews, the skew-corrected text is properly aligned. However, for obtuse angle skews, the text may get inverted during de-skewing. To handle this scenario, we propose a system flow as presented in Figure 3.

Fig. 3. Proposed system flow

4.1   Skew Correction Unit

We experimented with the skew-correction module of Leptonica library based on the work by Bloomberg et al [19] . Skew-corrected outputs for 2 different

(Bangla) text orientations, as shown in Figure 4, confirm the idea behind the proposed flow. Text block with an acute skew of 20° (Figure 4a) gets correctly aligned after de-skewing, while the text block with an obtuse skew of 150° (Figure 4b) gets inverted.

We introduce inversion-tolerant modifications over HoG and LBP features for recognition of script despite text inversion. For a given text segment, despite the orientation the output feature vector is the same. Thus, inversion, if present, is ignored and the task becomes one of plain script discrimination.

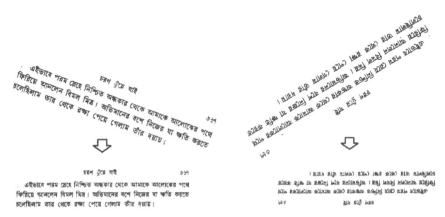

(a) Skew corrected output for a text block rotated by - (clockwise) 20° is correctly aligned

(b) Skew corrected output for a text block rotated by (anti-clockwise)150° is inverted

Fig. 4

4.2 Inversion Invariant HoG (II-HoG)

When the text is inverted, gradients in the 0°-90° range shift to the 90°-180° range and vice-versa. Inversion invariance can be achieved by either preventing this shift or staying independent of this shift. We have attempted to achieve invariance by staying independent. This is done by mapping all the gradients into the first quadrant i.e. 0°-90° range.

Gradient at a pixel is calculated as:

$$\vartheta = \arctan(dy/dx),$$

where dy is the vertical gradient and dx is the horizontal gradient at a given pixel point.

Following equation ensures that the gradients stay between 0°-90°:

$$
\begin{array}{ccc}
if\ (dx < 0) & & if\ (dy < 0) \\
dx = dx \times -1 & \& & dy = dy \times -1
\end{array}
$$

Thus, dx and dy values stay positive and as a result angles lie in the 0°-90° range. To keep the bin spread as 5° the number of bins is reduced to 18.

4.3 Inversion Invariant LBP (II-LBP)

For invariance to text inversion, we introduce a novel set of LBP features i.e II-LBP. Its evaluation is as shown in Figure 5. Re-assignment of weights makes the decimal-equivalent inversion tolerant. As is illustrated in Figure 5, the decimal value of the binary pattern for a given pixel remains the same despite the inversion of the pixel's neighborhood. Also, the 256 LBP values get reduced to a count of 31.

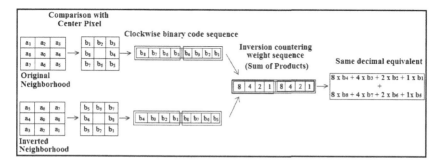

Fig. 5. Inversion Invariance - Evaluation of II-LBP

4.4 II-HoG and II-LBP

Final feature vector is a concatenation of the two features described above. Both the techniques are invariant to text inversion and so is their combination. The complete feature vector has a reduced length of 50 (31 II-LBP features and 19 II-HoG features). These features are learnt using a multi-class SVM based on radial basis function kernel.

5 Experimental Results and Analysis

For a comparative analysis, we tested our approaches on the printed-word MILE Database compiled by Pati and Ramakrishnan [1]. This database contains 20,000 printed word binary samples for 11 different Indian scripts (BE, HI, EN, GU, KA, MA, OD, PU, TA, TE, and UR). For suitability to texture as well as gradient analysis, we smoothen the binary images using a 3x3 averaging filter. For most practical purposes, we divide the database into 2,000 training samples and 18,000 testing samples respectively.

Table 1.

(a) 11-script test accuracy with increasing number of training samples
(b) Tri-script recognition accuracies evaluated using HoG & LBP feature set
(c) Script-specific orientation detection accuracies using HoG and LBP combination

No. of Training Samples	Test Accuracy (in %)
300	94.4
600	95.8
1000	96.6
2000	97.4

Local Script (with EN & HI)	Test Accuracy (in %)
BE	99.1
GU	99.2
KA	99.2
MA	98.3
OD	99.1
PU	97
TA	98.4
TE	99.3
UR	99.5
μ	98.8

Script	Test Accuracy (in %)
BE	99.3
HI	99.7
EN	95.4
GU	96.5
KA	98
MA	97.7
OD	98.3
PU	99.1
TA	95.6
TE	96.6
UR	98.4
μ	97.7

5.1   HoG and LBP Based Classification

For 11-script classification task, SVM classifier is trained on increasing number of training samples from 300 to 2,000. The test results on 18,000 sample-set are as compiled in Table 1a. *For just 600 training samples (<1/11th of the training samples assumed in [1]), the test accuracy becomes the new state-of-the-art with a gain of 1%.*

	HI	EN	GU	KA	MA	OD	PU	TA	TE	UR
BE	98.9	99.7	99.3	99.1	99.4	99.4	99.5	99.6	99.2	99.7
HI		99.6	99.3	99.5	99.3	99.6	96.2	99.5	99.5	99.8
EN			99.4	99.3	98.1	99	99.4	98.2	99.6	99.5
GU				99.2	98.5	97.6	99.5	98.6	99.1	99.3
KA					99	99.1	99.4	99.2	95.1	99.1
MA						97.8	98.8	97.2	98.8	99.3
OD							99.6	98.7	99	99.6
PU								98.6	99.5	99.7
TA									99.5	99.3
TE										99.2

Fig. 6. Recognition accuracies for the 55 bi-script scenarios evaluated using HoG & LBP feature set

Using the same 600 training samples and 18,000 test samples, the accuracy results for 55 bi-script scenarios are as shown in Figure 6. In [1], *the three lowest bi-script recognition results (by* their best configuration of Gabor features and SVM classifier*) are for Telugu-Kannada(91%), Urdu-Gurumukhi(93.7%), and Gurumukhi-Hindi(94.2%) script pairs. These are bettered by 4.1%, 6% and 2% respectively.* The average accuracy over the 55 bi-script scenarios is 99%, a gain of 0.6%.

For the 10 tri-script scenarios of Roman and Devanagari with 10 different local scripts, the recognition accuracies are presented in Table 1b. Our approach yields a *total accuracy gain of ˜5.1%* .

5.2   II-HoG and II-LBP Based Classification

As the feature vector length for inversion-invariant descriptor is only 50, we could experiment with an increased number of training samples. Thus, we trained the approach on a set of 6,000 word images and tested it on 14,000 word images, both containing a mix of inverted and non-inverted samples. An 11-script test accuracy of 95.8% is achieved. *Along with tolerance to text inversion, the feature set shows an average accuracy gain of 1% (against [1]) over 11 different Indian scripts. Given the high performance of this feature descriptor for the 11-script set and its similarity to HoG and LBP features, we are confident of top recognition results for the bi-script as well as the tri-script scenarios.*

The next level script-specific orientation detection is performed by HoG and LBP combination. Test accuracy figures are shown in Table 1c. For each script, two classes are considered. One for non-inverted text and other for inverted text. 600 word samples are used for training and 18,000 word samples for testing. *The average orientation detection accuracy over 11 scripts is 97.7%.*

6   Conclusion

The present work uses a combination of gradient (HoG) and texture (LBP) features to yield state-of-the-art recognition accuracies over 11 Indian scripts. It also introduces novel modifications to HoG and LBP features that makes them tolerant to image inversion. These inversion-invariant features (II-HoG and II-LBP) are combined together and used for script recognition in cases where the text may be inverted. They yield high recognition results, surpassing the existing best by approx. 1%. Both the proposed approaches perform at the word level and can quickly adapt to any new script given sufficient data samples. Thus, our approach is generic and can easily be integrated into various practical document recognition systems for an improved performance.

References

1. Pati, P.B., Ramakrishnan, A.G.: Word level multi-script identification. Pattern Recogn. Lett., 1218–1229 (2008)
2. Khoddami, M., Behrad, A.: Farsi and latin script identification using curvature scale space features. In: 2010 10th Symposium on Neural Network Applications in Electrical Engineering (NEUREL), pp. 213–217 (2010)

3. Chanda, S., Pal, U., Franke, K., Kimura, F.: Script identification: A han and roman script perspective. In: 2010 20th International Conference on Pattern Recognition (ICPR), pp. 2708–2711 (2010)

4. Roy, K., Alaei, A., Pal, U.: Word-wise handwritten persian and roman script identification. In: 2010 International Conference on Frontiers in Handwriting Recognition (ICFHR), pp. 628–633 (2010)

5. Chanda, S., Franke, K., Pal, U.: Identification of indic scripts on torn-documents. In: 2011 International Conference on Document Analysis and Recognition (ICDAR), pp. 713–717 (2011)

6. Wang, N., Lam, L., Suen, C.: Noise tolerant script identification of printed oriental and english documents using a downgraded pixel density feature. In: 2010 20th International Conference on Pattern Recognition (ICPR), pp. 2037–2040 (2010)

7. Pan, J., Tang, Y.: A rotation-robust script identification based on bemd and lbp. In: 2011 International Conference on Wavelet Analysis and Pattern Recognition (ICWAPR), pp. 165–170 (2011)

8. Ghosh, S., Chaudhuri, B.: Composite script identification and orientation detection for indian text images. In: 2011 International Conference on Document Analysis and Recognition (ICDAR), pp. 294–298 (2011)

9. Aithal, P., Rajesh, G., Acharya, D., Subbareddy, N.: Text line script identification for a tri-lingual document. In: 2010 International Conference on Computing Communication and Networking Technologies (ICCCNT), pp. 1–3 (2010)

10. Gopakumar, R., Subbareddy, N., Makkithaya, K., Acharya, D.: Zone-based structural feature extraction for script identification from indian documents. In: 2010 International Conference on Industrial and Information Systems (ICIIS), pp. 420–425 (2010)

11. Zhou, L., Ping, X., Zheng, E., Guo, L.: Script identification based on wavelet energy histogram moment features. In: 2010 IEEE 10th International Conference on Signal Processing (ICSP), pp. 980–983 (2010)

12. Das, M., Rani, D., Reddy, C.R.K.: Heuristic based script identification from multilingual text documents. In: 2012 1st International Conference on Recent Advances in Information Technology (RAIT), pp. 487–492 (2012)

13. Hiremath, P., Shivashankar, S., Pujari, J., Mouneswara, V.: Script identification in a handwritten document image using texture features. In: 2010 IEEE 2nd International Advance Computing Conference (IACC), pp. 110–114 (2010)

14. Ma, H., Doermann, D.: Word level script identification for scanned document images. In: Proc. of Int. Conf. on Document Recognition and Retrieval (SPIE), pp. 178–191 (2004)

15. Dalal, N., Triggs, B.: Histograms of oriented gradients for human detection. In: CVPR, pp. 886–893 (2005)

16. Ojala, T., Pietikäinen, M., Harwood, D.: A comparative study of texture measures with classification based on featured distributions. Pattern Recognition $29(1)$, 51–59 (1996)

17. Horn, R.A., Johnson, C.R.: Norms for Vectors and Matrices. In: Matrix Analysis. Cambridge University Press (1990)

18. Chang, C.-C., Lin, C.-J.: LIBSVM: A library for support vector machines. ACM Transactions on Intelligent Systems and Technology 2, 27:1–27:27 (2011)

19. Bloomberg, D.S., Kopec, G.E., Dasari, L.: Measuring document image skew and orientation. In: IS&T/SPIE's Symposium on Electronic Imaging: Science & Technology. International Society for Optics and Photonics, pp. 302–316 (1995)

Segmentation-Free Keyword Retrieval in Historical Document Images

Irina Rabaev[1](✉), Itshak Dinstein[2], Jihad El-Sana[1], and Klara Kedem[1]

[1] Department of Computer Science, Ben-Gurion University, Beer-Sheva, Israel
[2] Department of Electrical and Computer Engineering, Ben-Gurion University, Beer-Sheva, Israel
{rabaev,dinstein,el-sana,klara}@cs.bgu.ac.il

Abstract. We present a segmentation-free method to retrieve keywords from degraded historical documents. The proposed method works directly on the gray scale representation and does not require any pre-processing to enhance document images. The document images are subdivided into overlapping patches of varying sizes, where each patch is described by the bag-of-visual-words descriptor. The obtained patch descriptors are hashed into several hash tables using kernelized locality-sensitive hashing scheme for efficient retrieval. In such a scheme the search for a keyword is reduced to a small fraction of the patches from the appropriate entries in the hash tables. Since we need to capture the handwriting variations and the availability of historical documents is limited, we synthesize a small number of samples from the given query to improve the results of the retrieval process.

We have tested our approach on historical document images in Hebrew from the Cairo Genizah collection, and obtained impressive results.

Keywords: Historical document processing · Keyword retrieval · Segmentation-free · Bag-of-visual-words · Kernelized locality-sensitive hashing

1 Introduction

An ongoing considerable effort for digitizing historical manuscripts have produced huge datasets. Since the documents are represented as images, it is essential to provide a search and retrieve engine that simplify and accelerate accessing and processing the manuscripts. Current Optical Character Recognition (OCR) systems perform badly when applied to degraded historical documents, which leaves keyword spotting technique as a practical alternative [15]. In keyword spotting, the retrieval is performed on the image domain, and the aim is to locate regions in the image that are similar to the keyword query image.

The majority of word spotting approaches require the input to be segmented, at least to the text line level [6,10,13,15–17]. However, in addition to the physical degradations, many handwritten documents exhibit varying line slopes and

© Springer International Publishing Switzerland 2014
A. Campilho and M. Kamel (Eds.): ICIAR 2014, Part I, LNCS 8814, pp. 369–378, 2014.
DOI: 10.1007/978-3-319-11758-4_40

touching characters. Segmentation of such documents often results in united or split words, and loss of ascenders and descenders. This in turn influences the results of the subsequent search algorithms. We believe that the results of keyword retrieval can be improved by employing segmentation-free approach.

In this paper we present a segmentation-free scheme to efficiently retrieve keywords in gray scale historical documents. The scheme integrates bag-of-visual-words representation (BoVW) [4] with kernelized locality-sensitive hashing (KLSH) [11] and does not require any pre-processing image enhancement. While the BoVW with KLSH have been used for object retrieval in computer vision domain [11], this is the first time such scheme is applied for segmentation-free text retrieval in document images.

In an off-line stage each document image is (logically) subdivided into overlapping patches of several sizes. The patches are described by a BoVW model, and the obtained descriptors are hashed into several hash tables. The kernelized locality-sensitive hash functions ensure, with high probability, that descriptors of visually similar patches are placed into the same entry. Thus, we pre-compute the hash entries for all the patches in our input images.

To search for a given query keyword, we generate its BoVW descriptor and obtain the hash indices of the generated descriptor in each of the hash tables. The data items from the corresponding entries are retrieved as candidates and are searched to obtain the best matches. The search is fast due to the fact that the subset of candidate patches is relatively small. Since the availability of historical documents is limited and we need to capture the handwriting variations, we synthesize a small number of samples from the given query to improve the results of the retrieval process.

The presented scheme was tested on a set of Hebrew historical documents from the Cairo Genizah collection[1], which are highly degraded. Given that our input images are not binarized, slant corrected or segmented, the results we get are very impressive.

2   Related Work

Gatos and Pratikakis [7] presented a segmentation free word spotting approach that applies binarization and skew correction, and then computes block-based image descriptors for template matching. Rusinol *et al.* [18] introduced a patch-based framework, where each document is split into a set of equal size overlapping patches, and is represented by a feature-by-patch matrix. The patches are described using bag-of-visual-words model over the extracted SIFT descriptors. The feature-by-patch matrix is further refined by applying a latent semantic indexing technique. Dovgalecs *et al.* [5] also utilized patch-based framework. First, they evaluate a distance between the features of the query and each patch. Then, the best results are filtered using longest weighted profile algorithm.

---

[1] The Cairo Genizah (http://www.genizah.org/) is one of the largest collections of Hebrew medieval manuscripts in the world. It contains a huge amount of documents written between the 9th and 19th centuries AD.

Almazán *et al.* [1] represented documents with a grid of HOG descriptors, which are compressed with Product Quantization in order to save the memory space. Exemplar SVM is used to learn a better representation of the keyword queries, and the regions most similar to the query are located using sliding window.

Keyword retrieval usually deals with searching a large number of items. To make large-scale search efficient, commonly an approximate nearest-neighbor (ANN) search technique is applied. However, most of the ANN algorithms suffer from the curse of dimensionality. Indyk and Motwani [8] presented a locality-sensitive hashing (LSH) technique to implement an efficient NN search on a large collection of high dimensional items. The main idea of LSH is to use several hash functions (with their corresponding hash tables) that hash similar items to the same entry with high probability. The same hash functions are used to calculate entry indices for a query, and only the items from these entries are further searched. Kumar *et al.* [12] incorporated LSH for spotting words in a collection of printed documents. The preprocessed documents are segmented into words, which are represented by a combination of scalar, profile and structural features. A Discrete Fourier Transform is applied to feature vectors and the obtained final descriptors are hashed into the hash tables. Saabni and Bronstein [19] describe the segmented word parts by multi angular descriptors. They use the boost-map algorithm for embedding the feature space with the DTW measurement to a Euclidean space. This embedding allows subsequent use of LSH for finding k-nearest neighbors of a query image. Then, the candidate images are compared to the query using the DTW distance.

3   The Methodology

The schematic overview of the presented method is depicted in Fig. 1. For our input images we pre-compute a data structure of hash tables, where document patches are stored according to their descriptors. Given a query keyword q, initial candidates similar to q are retrieved from the data structure and are further processed to obtain the final results. To capture the handwriting variations and overcome the problem of limited available samples, we synthesize a small number of various instances from the given query to improve the retrieval process.

3.1   Extracting the Patch Descriptors

The presented method begins with calculating dense SIFT descriptors on a regular grid of 5 pixels imposed over the image, similar to [5,18]. At each grid vertex three descriptors, which correspond to three spatial sizes, are calculated. These sizes are chosen with respect to the font dimensions, which are automatically approximated using the technique developed in our lab [3]. Descriptors with low magnitude are ignored, as such descriptors usually correspond to non-text areas. Once the descriptors are calculated, they are quantized into n clusters using the k-means algorithm.

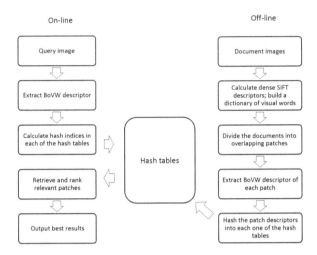

Fig. 1. The overview of the on-line and off-line stages of the presented scheme

Next, we subdivide each document into overlapping patches, sampled every p pixels in x and y directions. Previous approaches adopted equal size patches [5,18]. We chose to extract patches of several widths at each location, to take into account different word lengths. Each patch is represented by the bag-of-visual-words descriptors [4].

Let $D = \{w_1, w_2, \ldots, w_n\}$ be a dictionary of visual words. The BoVW representation is a vector $v = (v_1, v_2, \ldots, v_n)$, where v_i is the occurrence rate of w_i in the patch. Traditional BoVW representation does not take into account spatial distribution of visual words, and to overcome this limitation we impose 2×2 grid over the patch, resulting in 4 equal cells. The BoVWs of each cell are calculated and concatenated to generate the patch descriptor. This is similar to spatial pyramid matching technique presented by Lazebnik *et al.* [14], except that we use the highest pyramid level only.

3.2 Constructing the Data Structure

The aim of the data structure is to support fast search operations over a huge number of high dimensional descriptors. To accelerate the search, we use the LSH technique [8], which approximates k-nearest neighbors search on large collections of high dimensional datasets. LSH consists of l hash tables T_1, T_2, ..., T_l and l hash functions f_1, f_2, ..., f_l. Each hash function projects the objects onto randomly chosen low-dimensional Hamming space. The hash functions are constructed in such a way that the probability of the two objects to be hashed to the same entry is strictly decreasing with the distance between them. As the total number of entries may be large, to save memory space the non-empty entries are compressed using standard hashing; i.e., there are two levels of hashing: the locality-sensitive hash functions in the first level and standard hash functions in the second level. The main assumption of the LSH is that the data objects come from Euclidean space and the distance function is Euclidean distance. In our situation we are dealing with BoVW descriptors, which are histograms, and the χ^2 distance is an appropriate measure for comparing two histograms [2]. Kulis and Grauman [11] presented kernelized locality-sensitive hashing for k-nearest neighbors searches over arbitrary kernel functions. Similar to standard LSH, the hash functions are constructed using random projections, but the projections are calculated using the kernel function and the sparse set of examples from the collection itself. We use the KLSH with χ^2-kernel, K_{χ^2}, as formulated in Eq. 1, where V_1 and V_2 are two feature vectors and d is their dimension. Finally, the extracted patch descriptors are hashed to each of the hash tables. We actually store pointers to the descriptors and not the descriptors themselves.

$$K_{\chi^2}(V_1, V_2) = \exp\left(\frac{1}{2}\sum_{i=1}^{d}\frac{(V_1(i) - V_2(i))^2}{V_1(i) + V_2(i)}\right) \tag{1}$$

3.3   The Retrieval Process

To retrieve patches similar to a query image we obtain the descriptor of the query (in the same manner as described in Section 3.1), calculate the hash indices for the hash tables, and retrieve the items from the corresponding entries. The retrieved items are ranked according to their χ^2 distance from the query. Since there are overlapping patches, from each set of patches overlapping more than 20% we pick only the patch with the smallest χ^2 distance from the query, and discard the rest. Finally, the top results are returned to the user.

Handwritten text is characterized by variations in size, slant, noise, etc. In our previous research [16] we showed that employing multiple models for a query can improve retrieval results. However, it is not always possible to get sufficient number of samples for a given pattern in historical documents. Therefore, we synthesize additional samples from the original query by applying limited resizing, slant change, dilation, erosion, and adding noise (the noise is generated according to the degradation model [9]). After generating additional samples of the query, we proceed as is described above, except that we calculate indices for all the samples of the query in each hash table. We define the distance between a patch and the samples to be the average χ^2 distance between the patch and each of the samples.

4   Experiments and Results

The proposed method was tested on 12 document images from the Cairo Genizah collection, examples of which are presented in Fig. 2. The pages exhibit a variety of degradations, such as smeared characters, bleed through, and stains.

---

[2] Let H_1 and H_2 be two histograms with b bins. The χ^2 distance is defined to be:
$\chi^2(H_1, H_2) = \frac{1}{2}\sum_{i=1}^{b}\frac{(H_1(i) - H_2(i))^2}{H_1(i) + H_2(i)}$.

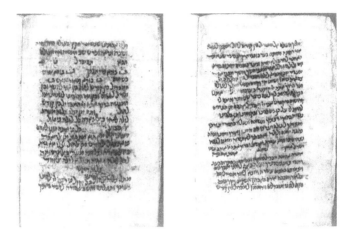

Fig. 2. Samples of the document pages on which we performed our tests

To build the dictionary, we used one of the pages and have experimented with dictionary sizes varying from 100 to 2000. The dictionary of sizes $400 - 500$ performed best on our document set. The patches were extracted every 25 pixels, and at each sample point we extracted patches of four sizes: 100×75, 135×75, 170×75 and 205×75 pixels (see Fig. 3a). The patches that did not contain any visual word were automatically detected and discarded. The total number of the extracted patches from all the 12 pages in our document set was 161952.

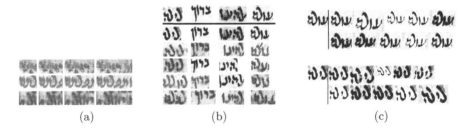

(a)   (b)   (c)

Fig. 3. (a) Examples of sampled patches; (b) The queries and corresponding retrieved results. The topmost image in each column is the query word; (c) The synthetically created images of two Hebrew words. The original image is the leftmost image in each group. The synthetic samples are created by re-sizing, adding noise, slant, dilating and eroding the original query.

The ground truth for the documents was manually built using the web-based system developed in our lab [2]. We randomly chose 50 queries, and the presented results were averaged over all the queries. The performance was evaluated in terms of Mean Average Precision (MAP). A retrieved patch is considered true

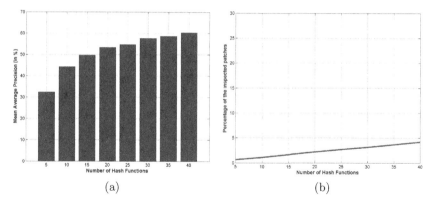

(a)   (b)

Fig. 4. (a) The performance of KLSH with varying number of hash functions and one sample per query. Percentage of the inspected patches versus the number of hash functions used. As we see, less than 5% of the patches from the database are inspected, even using 40 hash functions.

positive if it overlaps more than 50% with the bounding box of the relevant word in the document.

In the first set of experiments we analyzed how the number of hash function influences the retrieval results, when one sample per query is used. For this experiment, we varied the hash functions number from 5 to 40, and the corresponding MAPs are presented in Fig. 4a. The best being 0.6 for 40 hash functions. For comparison, the MAP of linear searches, which search over all patches, is 0.6818. As can be noted, the performance of the KLSH gets close to the results of linear search as the number of hash function increases. In contrast, the percentage of the inspected patches is less than 5% of the entire database, even when using 40 hash functions, as depicted in Fig. 4b. Due to the small fraction of inspected patches, our method (with 40 hash functions) is 10 times faster then the linear search. For comparison, we have downloaded the code provided by Almazán *et al.* [1] and used the same evaluation protocol. The results of [1] with the best configuration tuned for our documents is 0.5508. For the time being we do not compare run-time as our code still runs on Matlab and is not optimized.

Fig. 3b illustrates some retrieval results for four queries, using 30 hash functions and one query sample. The query is the topmost image in each column. As seen, the obtained results are promising for documents that have not undergone any image enhancement. Sometimes false positive words are retrieved (see the last two words in the leftmost column in Fig. 3b).

In the second set of experiments, we synthesized additional samples for each query and checked the influence of the number of samples on the performance. Fig. 3c illustrates examples of synthetic samples for two Hebrew words. The image on the left in each example is the original image, and to right of the original are its synthetically created samples. We ran experiments with 5, 10, 15

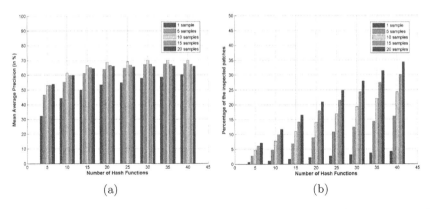

Fig. 5. (a) The performance results using 5, 10, 15 and 20 samples per query; (b) Percentage of the inspected patches for varying number of samples

and 20 samples. Fig. 5a illustrates the corresponding MAPs for varying number of hash functions. We can observe a significant improvement in precision rate from 5 samples (in comparison to using one sample). On the other hand, we do not observe further improvement when we increase the number of samples above 10. This might indicate that it is enough to use 10 samples. In addition, we noticed that using small number of samples per query can compensate for the need for a large number of hash tables. For example, the results with 10 samples and 10 hash tables even slightly better than the results with one sample and 40 hash functions. Finally, Fig. 5b illustrates the influence of the number of samples on the number of the inspected patches. As seen, the fraction of the inspected patches grows rapidly with the number of samples. However, it seems that 10 samples per query and 20 hash function give the reasonable trade-off between the accuracy and the number of searched patches, which is still less than 15% of the database.

5   Conclusions and Future Work

In this paper we presented a segmentation-free approach to spot keywords in degraded handwritten historical documents. The method does not require binarization or any other image enhancement. We integrate the BoVW representation with kernalized locality-sensitive hashing to create the input data structure of hash tables and descriptors for the patches of varying size in document images. We showed that, almost without compromising accuracy, we search less that 5% of the patches even when 40 hash functions are used. Furthermore, we demonstrated that additional synthetically generated samples of the query improve the retrieval results and reduce the need for a large number of hash functions. We found that 20 hash functions suffice when we use 10 samples of the query. While our experiments focus on Hebrew handwritten historical documents, the scheme is general and can be applied to historical documents in other languages. At future research we plan to inspect the influence of spatial pyramid co-occurrence [20] incorporated into BoVW and to perform tests on public document collections of handwritten historical documents.

Acknowledgments. This research was supported in part by the DFG-Trilateral grant no. FI 1494/3-2, the Ministry of Science and Technology of Israel, the Council of Higher Education of Israel, the Lynn and William Frankel Center for Computer Sciences and by the Paul Ivanier Center for Robotics and Production Management at Ben-Gurion University, Israel.

References

1. Almazán, J., Gordo, A., Fornés, A., Valveny, E.: Efficient Exemplar Word Spotting. In: British Machine Vision Conference, pp. 67.1–67.11 (2012)
2. Biller, O., Asi, A., Kedem, K., El-Sana, J., Dinstein, I.: WebGT: An Interactive Web-based System for Historical Document Ground Truth Generation. In: 12th International Conference on Document Analysis and Recognition, pp. 305–308 (2013)
3. Biller, O., Kedem, K., Dinstein, I., El-Sana, J.: Evolution Maps for Connected Components in Text Documents. In: International Conference on Frontiers in Handwriting Recognition, pp. 405–410 (2012)
4. Csurka, G., Dance, C., Fan, L., Willamowski, J., Bray, C.: Visual Categorization with Bags of Keypoints. In: Workshop on Statistical Learning in Computer Vision. vol. 1, pp. 1–2 (2004)
5. Dovgalecs, V., Burnett, A., Tranouez, P., Nicolas, S., Heutte, L.: Spot It! Finding Words and Patterns in Historical Documents. In: 12th International Conference on Document Analysis and Recognition, pp. 1039–1043 (2013)
6. Fischer, A., Keller, A., Frinken, V., Bunke, H.: Lexicon-free handwritten word spotting using character HMMs. Pattern Recognition Letters **33**(7), 934–942 (2012)
7. Gatos, B., Pratikakis, I.: Segmentation-free Word Spotting in Historical Printed Documents. In: 10th International Conference on Document Analysis and Recognition, pp. 271–275 (2009)
8. Gionis, A., Indyk, P., Motwani, R.: Similarity Search in High Dimensions via Hashing. In: VLDB, vol. 99, pp. 518–529 (1999)
9. Kieu, V., Visani, M., Journet, N., Domenger, J., Mullot, R.: A character degradation model for grayscale ancient document images. In: 21st International Conference on Pattern Recognition, pp. 685–688 (2012)
10. Kolcz, A., Alspector, J., Augusteijn, M., Carlson, R., Popescu, G.: A Line-Oriented Approach to Word Spotting in Handwritten Documents. Pattern Analysis and Applications **3**, 153–168 (2000)
11. Kulis, B., Grauman, K.: Kernelized Locality-Sensitive Hashing. IEEE Transactions on Pattern Analysis and Machine Intelligence **34**(6), 1092–1104 (2012)
12. Kumar, A., Jawahar, C.V., Manmatha, R.: Efficient Search in Document Image Collections. In: Yagi, Y., Kang, S.B., Kweon, I.S., Zha, H. (eds.) ACCV 2007, Part I. LNCS, vol. 4843, pp. 586–595. Springer, Heidelberg (2007)
13. Lavrenko, V., Rath, T., Manmatha, R.: Holistic Word Recognition for Handwritten Historical Documents. In: Workshop on Document Image Analysis for Libraries, pp. 278–287 (2004)

14. Lazebnik, S., Schmid, C., Ponce, J.: Beyond Bags of Features: Spatial Pyramid Matching for Recognizing Natural Scene Categories. In: IEEE Computer Society Conference on Computer Vision and Pattern Recognition, vol. 2, pp. 2169–2178 (2006)

15. Manmatha, R., Croft, W.: Word Spotting: Indexing Handwritten Archives. In: Intelligent Multimedia Information Retrieval Collection, pp. 43–64 (1997)

16. Rabaev, I., Biller, O., El-Sana, J., Kedem, K., Dinstein, I.: Case Study in Hebrew Character Searching. In: 11th InternationalConference on Document Analysis and Recognition, pp. 1080–1084 (2011)

17. Rath, T., Manmatha, R.: Word Image Matching Using Dynamic Time Warping. In: IEEE Computer Society Conference on Computer Vision and Pattern Recognition, vol. 2, pp. 521–527 (2003)

18. Rusinol, M., Aldavert, D., Toledo, R., Lladós, J.: Browsing Heterogeneous Document Collections by a Segmentation-free Word Spotting Method. In: 11th International Conference on Document Analysis and Recognition, pp. 63–67 (2011)

19. Saabni, R., Bronstein, A.: Fast Keyword Searching Using 'BoostMap' Based Embedding. In: International Conference on Frontiers in Handwriting Recognition, pp. 734–739 (2012)

20. Yang, Y., Newsam, S.: Spatial pyramid co-occurrence for image classification. In: IEEE International Conference on Computer Vision, pp. 1465–1472 (2011)

Character-Level Alignment Using WFST and LSTM for Post-processing in Multi-script Recognition Systems - A Comparative Study

Mayce Al Azawi[✉], Adnan Ul Hasan, Marcus Liwicki, and Thomas M. Breuel

German Research Center for Artificial Intelligence, University of Kaiserslautern,
67663 Kasierslautern, Germany
{ali,adnan,tmb}@iupr.com, liwicki@dfki.de

Abstract. In this paper, two new techniques to correct the OCR errors are proposed, recurrent neural networks with Long-Short Term Memory (LSTM), and Weighted Finite State Transducers (WFSTs) with context-dependent confusion rules. Both methods are applied on OCR results of Latin, and Urdu Script. Especially Urdu script is very challenging to OCR. For building an error model using context-dependent confusion rules, the OCR confusions which appear in the recognition outputs are translated into edit operations using Levenshtein edit distance algorithm. The new LSTM model avoids the calculations that occur in searching the language model and it also makes the language model eligible to correct unseen incorrect words. Our generic approaches are language independent. The proposed supervised LSTM model is compared with the context-dependent error model and state-of-the-art single rule-based methods. The evaluation on Latin script shows the error rate of LSTM is 0.48 %, error model is 0.68 % and the rule-based model is 1.0 %. The evaluation shows that the accuracy of LSTM model on the Urdu testset is 1.58 %, while the accuracy of the error model is 3.8 % and OCR recognition results is 6.9 % for Urdu testset. LSTM showed best performance on both Latin and Urdu script. As such, experiments show that LSTM performs very well in language techniques, especially, post-processing.

1 Introduction

Handwritten and printed text recognition research focuses more and more on challenging scripts and bad quality images, as these are difficult recognition tasks. Language modeling techniques are required to improve the recognition results. Dictionaries are built with finite vocabularies. However, a language model should be capable of efficiently creating infinite dictionary corrections. Therefore, a fast and accurate technique with a capability of predicting unknown tokens is needed. For language modeling in speech recognition [9], a general algorithm based on classical and new weighted automata algorithms is issued for computing exactly the edit distance between two string distributions given by two weighted automata. Another statistical language model technique is based

© Springer International Publishing Switzerland 2014
A. Campilho and M. Kamel (Eds.): ICIAR 2014, Part I, LNCS 8814, pp. 379–386, 2014.
DOI: 10.1007/978-3-319-11758-4_41

on n-grams [10]. These are widely used and considered as the state of the art for several application, such as, speech recognition, machine translation, and OCR. However, n-grams are not good enough to correct the unseen/unknown tokens even after a lot of efforts [10]. Another method of finding the correct form of a word, is to search through all dictionary entries to find the best candidate corrections. Such a method would be time consuming inefficient, and not eligible for unknown word forms. Error model is widely used in various applications such as spell-checkers and handwriting recognition. Hassan et al. [6] proposed an error model to aid the language model in a spell-checker to correct misspelling errors. They provided several suggestions using single rule-based error model. The error model consists of two-tape finite state automaton mapping of any string of the error model alphabet to at least one string of the language model alphabet. Llobet et al. [8] proposed a similar error model using OCR to improve the recognition results of handwritten Spanish in scanned forms. LSTM is used for normalizing historical orthography for OCR historical documents in Al Azawi et al. [1]. Frinken et al. [4] trained LSTM on word features, i.e. start-of-sentence and end-of-sentence tag.

1.1 Contributions

Building and evaluating a post-processing system for OCR corrections using two different language models: error model transducers in form of WFST and Character-Level alignment in LSTM is discussed.

C1 For WFST, an error model is built using context-dependent confusion rules. It is based on the confusion matrix that the OCR produces and is dependent on the context of the strings (OCR results). It was tested by implementing a finite state transducer from the Levenshtein edit distance relations. The context is a new idea instead of single character rules. This helps to fit the confusion rule in the proper string where it belongs and brings the string to the corrections. The language model can be as simple as a list of finite words compiled into finite state transducers. The frequencies of a token or rule in the corpus are converted to weights in the finite state transducer. In the error model approach, if multiple rules are applicable at the same position within a word, the rule that is ranked higher is applied.

C2 For the LSTM based approach, powerful LSTM networks were trained to learn corrections by themselves. LSTM is specifically designed to overcome limitations of RNN. LSTM has the ability to remember the target association between irrelevant input and target events even for very long time lags [5]. A new Character-Level alignment was proposed to normalize the strings length before the training of LSTM, as describe in Section 4.1. Both approaches are language independent. The experiments used Latin and Urdu script. The recognition and proposed approaches results examples of Urdu Nastaleeq are shown in Fig. 4. The improvement our methods brings over a correction algorithm using only the edit distance was evaluated. All approaches were implemented in C++, and Python under Linux. The experiment results show that our proposed LSTM model has better performance than the error model on the unknown data which were unseen during the training.

The paper is organized as follows. Section 2 describes the state-of-the-art single rule-based model. In Section 3 and 4, our new proposed context-dependent error model and LSTM networks are described. Section 5 contains the experimental results. Finally, Section 6 presents the conclusions.

2   Single Character Rules-Based Approach

The single character rules are extracted using Levenshtein edit distance algorithm [6]. The rules represent the primitive operations: insertions, deletion and substitution. These rules are used for constructing the transducers. Each transition in the transducer holds single rules. Insertion rule is used as $\varepsilon \to f$.

3   Context-Dependent Error Model Approach

In this section, extracting the context-dependent rules and constructing the error model transducer using those rules are described and the language model and alignment technique are explained.

3.1   Context-Dependent Confusion Rules Extraction

The purpose of an error model is to act as a filter to revert the mistakes of the recognition outputs. The error model typically provides a small selection of the best matches for the language model this means that when define the corrections, it is also necessary to specify their likelihood in order to rank the correction suggestions. The error model is built using the Levenshtein edit distance algorithm [7]. The misrecognition is assumed to be a number of operations applied to characters of a string: deletion, insertion and substitution with the neighbor characters on the leftmost and rightmost sides. We can also control the size of the context involved in the rule, as shown in Fig. 1. For example, the misrecognized word $Defnition$ which needs the rules $f\varepsilon n \to fin$ to be fixed. The misrecognized word $efect$ requires the rule $f\varepsilon e \to ffe$, as shown in Fig 1. The error model is a transducer and is constructed by aligning the misrecognized word of the OCR output with their corresponding ground truth. By using the outputs of the alignment, the OCR confusions are extracted in form of rules to be used in the error model with respect to their context in both misrecognized and ground truth wordforms.

3.2   Constructing Error Model Using Weighted Finite State Transducers (WFSTs)

The error model transducer is constructed using the extracted context-dependent rules in Section 3.1. The error model transducer is a weighted finite state transducer that maps the misrecognized words into correct strings. Each of these

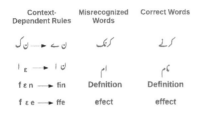

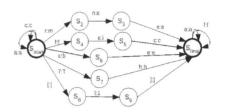

Fig. 1. Shows the context-dependent rules which are required to fix the misrecognized words and their correspondence correct words. ε corresponds to insert a character in this position

Fig. 2. Sample of the Latin context-dependent Confusion rules in error model transducer

OCR	Rule-Based	LSTM	Ground Truth
کروی	کروی	کروی	کروی
علی	علی	علی	علی
کربی	کری	کری	کری

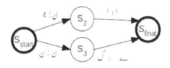

Fig. 3. Sample of the Urdu context-dependent confusion rules in error model transducer

Fig. 4. Sample Result of LSTM and Rule-based models with the correspondence OCR and Ground Truth

context-dependent rules can be assigned a probability. The probability is derived from the confusion matrix of the OCR classifier. The context-dependent rules consist of two parts, the left part is the OCR confusions and the right part is the corresponding ground truth. The rules are translated into a WFST, where the left part represents the input label of the transducer and the right part of the rule represents the output label. Therefore, the error model transducer is able to map the OCR error by matching the output label of the OCR transducer with the input label of the error model. The output label of the error model is matched to the corresponding input label of the dictionary and maps the OCR error to it's correspondence correction. Part of the constructed error model transducer for Urdu is shown in Fig. 3 and Fig. 2 for English. The open-source OpenFST library [3] was used which has achieved a competitive performance for building and applying WFSTs [2].

3.3 Alignment Technique

The standard WFSTs framework to include estimated probability were used. The formula for converting the frequencies f of a token or rule in the corpus to a weight in the finite state error transducer is $W_s = -log\ (f_s\ /\ C)$, where C is the size of the corpus. Three transducers were aligned. First, the OCR outputs were aligned with the error model to generate composed Levenshtein transducer with OCR confusions of OCR output. The alignment technique is described

Table 1. The Table shows the error rate of our LSTM model and Context-Dependent EM compare to the original OCR recognition results and Single Rules-Based model. We trained the LSTM 100 times and report the mean of the error rate from different training models. The Rule-Based is skipped from Urdu dataset because of low performance amongst other approaches

Dataset	OCR	Rule-Based	Context-Dependent	LSTM
English Testset	1.14%	1.0%	0.68%	**0.48%**
Urdu Testset	6.9%	-	3.8%	**1.58%**

in [2]. It contains all the possible and appropriate candidate corrections of the misrecognized tokens and provides the suggestions to the language model to decide which token is the best candidate correction. Both the OCR output and the error model are represented in finite state transducers. After aligning the input with the error model transducer, the results of WFST are aligned with the dictionary to filter out words that do not exist in the language. The aligned WFST has many paths depending on the compositions with the correspondence rules in the error model. The best path with lowest cost is chosen from the second composition.

4   Character-Level Alignment and LSTM Neural Networks Approach

A new technique based on LSTM recurrent neural networks is proposed to solve the problem OCR corrections. Very little attention has been paid to it. Levenshtein edit distance technique is applied to align the training pairs. The alignment technique of two strings finds the similarities and differences between them and can be interpreted as point mutations. If they share common characters and mismatches, or gaps when it is insertion or deletion mutations introduced in one or both lineages in the time since they diverged from one another.

4.1   Character-Epsilon Alignment

In this section, a preprocessing method to allow insertion, deletion, and substitution operations in the wordforms is described. The Levenshtein alignment technique [7] is used to align two strings A and B and find an optimal alignment given a better score. To compute an alignment that actually gives this score, you start from the bottom right cell, and compare the value with the possible sources (Match, Substitution, Insertion, and Deletion) to see where it came from. If Delete, then A_i is aligned with a gap, and if Insert, then B_j is aligned with a gap. Otherwise A_i and B_j are aligned. In this technique, epsilon is inserted after each character of the misrecognized wordform, then we apply alignment using the Levenshtein edit distance between the misrecognized and groundtruth wordforms to obtain the optimal aligned character pairs. For example, $e\varepsilon f\varepsilon e\varepsilon c\varepsilon t\varepsilon$.

4.2 String Encoding and Feature Extraction

For encoding a string, we use a sequence of vectors where each vector has a length corresponding to the size of the character set. Each character in the string is mapped to its code point which is used in the binary feature representation. Misrecognized wordforms along with their transcriptions are fed to the network, which perform the forward propagation step first. Alignment of output with associated transcriptions is done in the next step and then finally backward propagation step was performed. Recurrent Neural Networks have been applied to many of the pattern recognition tasks and showed promising results. LSTM is like a computer memory cell providing three multiplicative gates namely input, output, and forget gate in order to simulate write, read, and reset operations. LSTM can be used to remember contexts over a long period of time. In order to be aware of the context in both directions a variant name BLSTM is introduced by [5]. Furthermore, a CTC layer has been introduced to overcome the limitation of data pre-segmentation. After each epoch, training and validation errors were computed and the best results were saved. When there was no significant change in validation errors for a pre-set number of epochs, the training was stopped. There are two parameters, which need to be tuned; namely number of hidden states and the learning rate.

5   Experimental Results

Our methods are language independent. To show that, we evaluate our approaches on two very different scripts. One is Latin script (English) and the second is Urdu Nastaleeq (Arabic).

5.1 OCR and Materials

Two datasets of recognized script have been used for our experiments, the first is based on English script and the second is based on Urdu. The English script dataset is extracted from the Ocred collected work which is freely avaibale from the web[1]. The Urdu script dataset is the UPTI (Urdu Printed Text Images)-dataset [11], which contains synthetic scanned image data. Various degradation techniques were applied to increase the size of dataset. In the recognition phase, two parameters namely the number of hidden states 100 and learning rate 0.0001 were evaluated for their respective effect on the recognition accuracies. Parameter selection was done for a case where the ligature shape variations (191 classes) were considered.

5.2 Experimental Setup and Results

In the experiments, the datasets are divided into training and testing sets as described in [11]. We used the OCR's output with their corresponding ground

---

[1] https://code.google.com/p/ocropus/

truth to build the LSTM and the error model. For the Urdu datasets (UPTI), we used 60,177 entries for training purposes and 8,376 entries for testing purposes. For training the LSTM model, the misrecognized word forms with their corresponding groundtruth wordforms were used as recognition target. The training pairs were prepared using alignment technique as described in Section 4.1 which is considered a pre-processing step. The context-dependent EM has 830 extracted context-dependent rules to build the error model. The rules are used to build the error model using WFST. The language model (LM) can be as simple as a list of finite words compiled into probabilistic finite state transducers. The words were extracted with their frequencies from text corpus from UPTI and English datasets. The standard WFSTs framework to include probability estimates for constructing a unigram model is used. The error rate is measured using edit distance to find the number of the edit operation on character level. The evaluation shows an effective performance of our LSTM model on the UPTI testset with 1.58% error rate, while error model has 3.8% and the original error rate of the OCR recognition results is 6.9%. Fig. 4 shows samples of the results of LSTM and rule-based models on both datasets. In the experiments using English script, 6,000 wordforms with their corresponding ground truth wordforms were used. In testing, 3,917 wordforms and their corresponding wordforms were tested in UTF-8 encoded text format were used as ground truth to evaluate the generated wordforms by the proposed approaches. Table 1 shows the evaluation of the approaches using the whole testset. The unknown wordforms is subset from testset. The evaluation shows an effective performance of the LSTM on the testset 0.48% error rate. The context-dependent EM approach has 162 rules. It performs on the on the whole testset with 0.68%. The rule-based approach has 237 rules and performs 1.0%. Result examples of the approaches, correcting misrecognized word "rnethod" to "method" and "artifcial" to "artificial". The configuration of the network and the number of weights mapping between and within layers is shown in [5]. Training of the network proceeds by choosing text input lines randomly from the training set, performing a forward propagation step through the LSTM and output networks, then performing forward-backward alignment of the output with the ground-truth, and finally performing backward propagation. We trained LSTM networks with hidden-states of different sizes 40, 60, 80, 100, 120, 140 and 160. The optimal error rates are obtained when the size of the hidden-states is in a range between 100 - 160 and it takes 782 - 1097 minutes for training respectively. When the size of the hidden-states is in a range between 40 - 80, it takes 251 - 594 minutes for training respectively. The time increases linearly with an increase in the number of the hidden-states. After the model has been trained, the predictions are very fast. The most appropriate number of hidden-states determined keeping learning rate constant at 0.0001.

6   Discussions

In this paper, two new methods to build a language model to correct OCR errors are proposed, one based on WFST, the other based on LSTM. The experimental results show that the proposed methods achieve improvements of the

OCR results when being compared to single rule-based models. The LSTM based method yields the best performance. There are several indications that the LSTM-based approach generalizes much better to unseen samples than WFST and other approaches proposed in the literature. The Wordlist approach, for example, is unable to process unseen samples. The rule-based approach might not be able to cover all the misrecognized variants when the OCR does recognition errors which did not appear during training. In summary, most existing approaches just pass unseen samples keeping them unchanged. Both our methods process all tokens in the testset. The LSTM model is able to predict all different misrecognized variants accurately and significantly better than WFST. Our approaches have no limitation on the word length and the number of errors that occur in the words. The approach is completely language independent, and can be used with any language that has a dictionary and text data to build a language model.

References

1. Al-Azawi, M., Afzal, M.Z., Breuel, T.M.: Normalizing historical orthography for OCR historical documents using LSTM. In: Proc. of the 2nd International Workshop on Historical Document Imaging and Processing, HIP 2013, pp. 80–85. ACM, New York (2013)
2. Al-Azawi, M.I.A., Liwicki, M., Breuel, T.M.: WFST-based ground truth alignment for difficult historical documents with text modification and layout variations. In: DRR Proc. SPIE (2013)
3. Allauzen, C., Riley, M.D., Schalkwyk, J., Skut, W., Mohri, M.: OpenFst: a general and efficient weighted finite-state transducer library. In: Holub, J., Žďárek, J. (eds.) CIAA 2007. LNCS, vol. 4783, pp. 11–23. Springer, Heidelberg (2007)
4. Frinken, V., Zamora-Martinez, F., Espana-Boquera, S., Castro-Bleda, M., Fischer, A., Bunke, H.: Long-short term memory neural networks language modeling for handwriting recognition. In: 21st ICPR, pp. 701–704 (November 2012)
5. Graves, A., Liwicki, M., Fernandez, S., Bertolami, R., Bunke, H., Schmidhuber, J.: A novel connectionist system for unconstrained handwriting recognition. IEEE Transactions on Pattern Analysis and Machine Intelligence **31**(5), 855–868 (2009)
6. Hassan, A., Noeman, S., Hassan, H.: Language independent text correction using finite state automata. In: International Joint Conference on NLP (2008)
7. Levenshtein, V.: Binary Codes Capable of Correcting Deletions, Insertions, and Reversals. Soviet Physics-Doklady **10**(8), 707–710 (1966)
8. Llobet, R., Navarro-Cerdan, J.R., Perez-Cortes, J.C., Arlandis, J.: Efficient OCR post-processing combining language, hypothesis and error models. In: Hancock, E.R., Wilson, R.C., Windeatt, T., Ulusoy, I., Escolano, F. (eds.) SSPR & SPR 2010. LNCS, vol. 6218, pp. 728–737. Springer, Heidelberg (2010)
9. Mohri, M.: Edit-distance of weighted automata. In: Champarnaud, J.-M., Maurel, D. (Eds.) CIAA 2002. LNCS, vol. 2608, pp. 1–23. Springer, Heidelberg (2003)
10. Mikolov, T., Deoras, A., Kombrink, S., Burget, L., Cernocky, J.: Empirical evaluation and combination of advanced language modeling techniques. In: Proc. of Inter. Speech Communication Association, Florence, Italy (2011)
11. Ul-Hasan, A., Bin Ahmed, S., Rashid, F., Shafait, F., Breuel, T.: Offline printed urdu nastaleeq script recognition with bidirectional LSTM networks. In: 12th Intern. Conf. on Document Analysis and Recognition, pp. 1061–1065 (2013)

Handwritten and Printed Text Separation: Linearity and Regularity Assessment

Sameh Hamrouni$^{(\boxtimes)}$, Florence Cloppet, and Nicole Vincent

LIPADE, University of Paris Descartes, 45 rue des Saint-Pères, 75006 Paris, France
{sameh.hamrouni,florence.cloppet,nicole.vincent}@mi.parisdescartes.fr

Abstract. In this paper, we address the issue of discerning handwriting from machine-printed text in real documents (This work is funded by the PiXL project, supported by the "Fonds national pour la Société Numérique" of the French State. http://valconum.fr/index.php/les-projets/pixl). We present a reliable method based on a novel set of features belonging to two different categories, linearity and regularity, invariant to translation and scaling. Specifically, a novel linearity measure derived from the histogram of straight line segment lengths is introduced. The resulting framework is independent of the document layout and supports any latin language used. Its performances are assessed on real documents dataset comprising heterogeneous administrative images. Experimental results demonstrate its accuracy, allowing up to 90 % recognition rate.

1 Introduction

In many real world documents the reader or the user, annotating the already printed text, wants to add manually some information or to emphasize some parts of the document with a drawn mark. The resulting document can then be seen as a two-layer document : the first layer being the native document and the second one being made of the added information. Automatic processing of the two different layers does not however belong to the same frameworks. In particular, an optical character recognition system (OCR) is heavily dependent on the nature of the data to be processed : OCR for printed text recognition is different from that for handwriting recognition. The prior distinction between the two layers is then a key issue to automate the selection of the appropriate OCR.

Several works have been done in this context[2,3], where in a classical way, four steps are involved to solve the problem : preprocessing, page segmentation, feature extraction and classification.

We present here a reliable approach based on novel features. The outline of this paper is as follows. Section 2 introduces the general framework of the

The authors would like to thank ITESOFT society for providing the dataset and for their help to carry out the comparison with Belaid et al. method [1].

A. Campilho and M. Kamel (Eds.): ICIAR 2014, Part I, LNCS 8814, pp. 387–394, 2014.
DOI: 10.1007/978-3-319-11758-4_42

proposed method and details its different steps. Section 3 focuses on the proposed features. The performances of the resulting framework for real administrative documents separation are quantitatively assessed in Section 4. Conclusions and perspectives are given in Section 5.

2   Handwritten and Printed Text Separation Framework

We propose a unified pixel-wise labeling approach for handwritten and printed text separation, involving especially multiple descriptors categories which may be associated with multiple classifiers. Three elements are characterizing our proposal : (i) observation scale step, based on elementary textual entities selection. Pixels of each entity will be assigned a unique label; (ii) representation space step which is deriving descriptors characterizing each textual entity; and (iii) decision step which is the labeling of each entity and its pixels.

Observation scale definition. An observation scale is handled as stable textual entities zones. specificaly, aggregating neighboring connected components (CC) by promoting the horizontal direction, we can reach groups of letters, words or even lines. This is handled using a horizontal RLSA algorithm [4], where distance between characters belonging to the same textual entity is controlled by a RLSA parameter, denoted hereafter by R. Textual entity areas increase with R: larger values of R owing to lines whereas smaller values lead to smaller textual entities, the smallest one being the CC.

Representation space. Several features highlighting the difference between handwritten and typed text were used in the literature [3,5,6]. In this work, we propose to combine multiple features in order to discriminate handwriting from printed text. Two descriptors categories are selected to this end : linearity and regularity and are detailed in Section 3.

Decision. Upon completion of this step, a unique label should be assigned to each text entity. In this work, we confine ourselves to two possible labels : handwriting and printed text. To handle labeling, we opt for a two-step straightforward technique, based on decision rules. In the first step, accurate decision rules allowing a first labeling are learned during a training phase. Possible classification errors are further corrected by means of a regularization process. We adopt here the technique of textual entity re-grouping proposed in [1]. It uses spatial proximity to smooth separation results. For each entity, k nearest neighbours (kNN) are found and its label is compared to the kNN ones. If more than 50 % of kNN share the same label, current textual entity is assigned this label.

3   Proposed Features for Handwritten and Printed Text Separation

3.1   Linearity

Using linearity features is motivated by the fact that printed text looks more linear as it contains more straight-line segments compared to more rounded writing in handwritten text.

Problem statement and related works. The need to look for straight line segments in an image is a very common problem occuring in several applications and leading to various works[7–9]. The most representative works in general document analysis context are based on a global vision of the image. They perform a study of the general orientation in the writing rather than a study of the presence of oriented segments. The linear property in a straight line is however local.

In this work, we propose to extract real straight lines in order to study their properties rather than to have a statistical observation of the locally computed directions. In fact, our aim is not to extract precise straight line segments but to define a measure based on these segments in order to quantify the property of the writing associated with the presence or not of significant straight line segments. This measure is a relative quantification computed relying on the histograms of straight line segment lengths.

Histogram of straight line segment lengths. The linearity feeling given when observing a document comes from the presence of straight line segments. In an alphabet such as the latin alphabet, the straight line segments are included in the models used during the writing learning phase. The lengths of these segments are of different sizes, the largest size can be associated with ascenders and descenders, whereas the straight line segments of letters such as m or n are smaller. The remaining part of writing is made of curves within the letters or belonging to ligatures. In order to extract straight lines and to minimize the number of parameters to be fixed in the method, we have chosen to process similarly the straight parts and the curved parts of the writing. Curved parts are then approximated by small segments generating a new length among the straight line segment lengths histogram of the document, denoted shortly by *SLH*. Depending on the text content and on the writer, the modes can be more or less visible and the number of clusters can increase according to the specific style of the writer and to its habits. Then, we will not consider a decomposition of the histogram using a GMM that needs to fix/approximate the number of gaussians but rather qualify the histogram using a measure.

Proposed linearity measure. The aim of the proposed linearity measure is to highlight the presence of well marked modes in the *SLH*. When the lengths are varying too much and due to letter shape nature, the reader do not get the feeling of a linear writing. Value evolution between two consecutive bins is more important when modes are significant. This motivated us to base the linearity measure, L_m, on a formula with general expression as :

$$L_m(H_T) = \sum_{l=1}^{L} \omega_l \Delta_l \tag{1}$$

where H_T denotes the *SLH* relative to the considered text entity T^1, Δ_l designates the evolution involved by the length l and L is the largest value in the distribution. The relative difference is considered :

$$\Delta_l = \frac{H_T(l+1) - H_T(l)}{H_T(l)} \cdot \mathbb{1}_{[0,+\infty[}(H_T(l+1) - H_T(l)) = \frac{d_l}{H_T(l)} \cdot \mathbb{1}_{[0,+\infty[}(d_l)$$

where $\mathbb{1}$ denoting the indicator function[2]. To robustly account for the number of straight line segments variability, the linearity measure should be normalized. Weights have then been built as a length normalized against a number of segments :

$$\omega_l = \frac{l}{\sum_{m=1}^{L} H_T(m)} \cdot H_T(l) \tag{2}$$

Substituting (2) in (1), the linearity measure then rewrites as :

$$L_m(H_T) = \frac{\sum_{l=1}^{L} l \cdot d_l \cdot \mathbb{1}_{[0,+\infty[}(d_l)}{\sum_{l=1}^{L} H_T(l)} \tag{3}$$

Let us focus now on the straight line segment computation technique. To minimize dependency on the writing tool and to avoid creating lines related to the stroke thickness, we have chosen to consider a polygonal approximation of contour segments. Polygonal approximation is done using the algorithm proposed in [10]. The latter requires a user defined parameter P that controls the accuracy of the approximation. Larger values of P induce fewer but longer segments than when using smaller values. Obviously, increasing P is done at the cost of character shape degradation.

Relying on (3), it is expected that L_m values for typed text are larger than those computed over handwritten text. Inspecting a typical polygonization approximation of a handwritten text compared to its printed counterpart (Figure 1 **(b)**) reveals as expected for printed text a more regular approximation with the expected benefit of overall less segments length variability; and mostly longer segments. These observations are corroborated by the visual inspection of the corresponding *SLH* (Figure 1 **(c)**, **(d)**). Machine-printed *SLH* shows irregularities at the tail of the distribution, leading to larger values of L_m.

---

[1] In order to build a measure for a general application setting, T could be the whole text document or any finer observation scale such as *CC*, word or text line.

[2] Note that we only consider the evolution when it is positive.

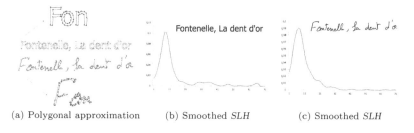

(a) Polygonal approximation   (b) Smoothed *SLH*   (c) Smoothed *SLH*

Fig. 1. Influence of text style on SLH shape and amplitude

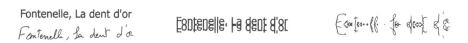

Fig. 2. Impact of axial symmetry on printed text compared to handwritten text

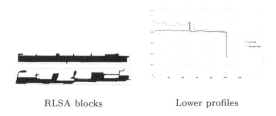

RLSA blocks   Lower profiles

Fig. 3. Regularity of machine printed text *vs.* handwritten text of Figure 2

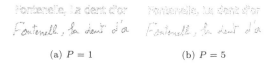

(a) $P = 1$ (b) $P = 5$

Fig. 4. Impact of increasing the value of P on polygonal approximation

Axial symmetry. We here introduce a transform that could enhance the linear property of printed text without having influence on handwritten text. Symmetry with respect to the perpendicular direction at end of a segment can do it. In printed text, most straight line segments are ending on the baseline. This has motivated us to define an axial symmetry. The axis is derived from the lower profile (see Section 3.2) as the horizontal axis containing the great majority of black pixels. In case of typed text, this axis coincides with the baseline. As shown on Figure 2, resulting symmetric image in case of non italic printed text enhances straight line segments whose lengths appear to be multiplied. This yields a multiplication of the *SLH* maximum length. This property is not verified in handwriting whose axial symmetric image bears a major difference from its printed counterpart due to the fact that handwritten straight parts, especially ascenders and descenders, are often not strictly vertical.

3.2 Regularity

In this section, we intend to study the regularity of the text. Regularity is tackled here as the uniformity of ascenders and descenders height. Printed text is then more likely to be regular than handwriting. This section presents a simple approach for text regularity evaluation. Starting from a binary textual entity image, we compute respectively upper and lower profiles. Upper profile is calculated as follows : for each column of the image, we retain the distance between the bounding box and its first (black) pixel. Inferior profile is defined along the same lines, whereas here we are seeking for the distance between the last black pixel and the upper part of the bounding box. Upper and lower profiles are normalized between 0 and 1. To emphasize the regularity gap between handwritten and typed text, we compute profiles over RLSA continuous black blocks rather than native text.

An example of lower profile computation is shown on Figure 3. As expected, profiles derived from printed text seem less dispersed. To quantify regularity, we propose then to compute the variance of each profile. higher variance values are associated with handwriting.

4 Experimental Results

4.1 Dataset and Performance Criteria

The proposed framework has been tested on an administrative dataset belonging to a real world industrial challenge. Images can be of various structures (forms, tables) or without any particular structure. We have used 40 images for training decision rules as well as different parameters, and 32 different images for test.

Separation results are systematically compared to a ground truth dataset built from a manual labeling of pixels. The efficacy of the proposed technique is then assessed along three well-defined performance criteria, precision, recall (recognition rate) and error rate, defined at the pixel level for each class c_k (c_k being handwriting or machine-printed).

4.2 Decision Rules and Method Parameters

Four different decision rules, two for each descriptor category, are presented in Table 1. As mentioned earlier, if polygonal approximation parameter P gets larger ($P = 5$ compared to $P = 1$), straight line segments get much longer in handwriting than in printed documents (Figure 4). This induces a population shift in the SLH with consequently a higher maximum length of the SLH and a higher linearity measure value. Relying on these assumptions, we get the C_1 decision rule. The three remaining decision rules can be readily deduced from the related descriptor definition in previous sections.

Method parameters values are learned during the training stage. RLSA parameter, R, was tuned experimentally by searching for a satisfying trade-off between separation accuracy and running time. Experiments showed that $R = 60$, allowing pseudo-word selection, is an appropriate choice. As for the regularization kNN process, we use a k-d tree for efficient nearest neighbors search. In practice, setting $k = 4$ yielded satisfying results.

Table 1. Decision rules

Linearity	L_m for $(P = 5)$ > $TL_1 \cdot L_m$ for $(P = 1)$	(C_1)
	Text axial symmetry SLH.length < $TL_2 \cdot$ original text SLH.length	(C_2)
Regularity	Lower profile variance > TR_1	(C_3)
	Upper profile variance > TR_2	(C_4)

Handwriting if C_1 AND C_2 AND (C_3 OR C_4)

4.3 Method Validation

An objective quantitative assessment of handwritten and machine-printed separation results (see Figure 5 for visual inspection) is summarized in Table 2. We also compared on the same dataset and with a similar validation protocol, our results with those obtained using Belaid et al. [1] method (Table 3). We gained 1% in recognition rate, but we can notice we used only 4 characteristics compared with 137.

Fig. 5. Handwritten and printed text separation results

Table 2. Evaluation of the proposed method. The statistics are evaluated on the measures computed for each document.

	Precision (%)			Recall (%)			Error rate (%)		
	Min	Max	Avg	Min	Max	Avg	Min	Max	Avg
Typewritten	59,93	100	95,41	42,08	100	92,85	0,0	57,92	7,14
Handwritten	0,0	100	79,60	0,0	100	80,02	0,0	100	19,98
Global	69,89	99,99	90,22	69,54	99,98	90,15	0,02	30,46	9,85

Table 3. Comparison with Belaid et al. [1] work

	Proposed method	Belaid et al. method [1]
Text entity	Pseudo-word	Pseudo-word
Descriptors	4	137
Classifiers	Decision rules	SVM
Regularization	kNN	kNN
Database	Industrial dataset	Industrial dataset
Recognition rate (%)	90,15	89,05

5   Conclusion

We have presented a method for handwritten and typed text separation involving novel linearity and regularity features. Specifically, we have derived a measure quantifying the linear aspect a written text may have. In the proposed approach, we do not refer to the orientation of the writing to evaluate the dominance of a specific direction, we are more interested in the length of the straight line segments and their regularity. This theoretical framework encompasses various possible observation scales, the smallest one being the CC whereas the biggest one is the text line. Tests carried at the pseudo-word level demonstrate the accuracy of the proposed method allowing up to 90% of recognition rate. Future work is directed towards separating touching mixtures of printed and handwritten text relying on pixel-wise features.

References

1. Belaïd, A., Santosh, K.C., D'Andecy, V.P.: Handwritten and printed text separation in real document. CoRR, abs/1303.4614 (2013)
2. Zagoris, K., Pratikakis, I., Antonacopoulos, A., Gatos, B., Papamarkos, N.: Handwritten and machine printed text separation in document images using the bag of visual words. In: International Conference on Frontiers in Handwriting Recognition (2012)
3. Peng, X., Setlur, S., Govindaraju, V., Sitaram, R.: Handwritten text separation from annotated machine printed documents using markov random fields. IJDAR **16**(1), 1–16 (2013)
4. Wahl, R., Wong, K., Casey, R.: Block Segmentation and Text Extraction in Mixed Text/Image Documents. IBM Research Lab, San Jose, California, Research Report RJ3356 (40312) (December 1981)
5. Zheng, Y., Li, H., Doermann, D.: Machine printed text and handwriting identification in noisy document images. University of Maryland, College Park, Technical Report (September 2003)
6. Shirdhonkar, M., Kokare, M.B.: Discrimination between printed and handwritten text in documents. IJCA **3**, 131–134 (2010). Special Issue on RTIPPR
7. Bilane, P., Bres, S., Emptoz, H.: Robust directional features for wordspotting in degraded syriac manuscripts. In: International Workshop on Content-Based Multimedia Indexing, CBMI 2008, pp. 526–533 (June 2008)
8. Berlemont, S., Aaron, B., Cloppet, F., Olivo-Marin, J.-C.: Detection of linear structures in biological images. In: Conference Record of the Forty-First Asilomar, Signals, Systems and Computers 2007, pp. 1279–1283 (November 2007)
9. Siddiqi, I., Vincent, N.: Text independent writer recognition using redundant writing patterns with contour-based orientation and curvature features. Pattern Recognition **43**(11), 3853–3865 (2010)
10. Wall, K., Danielsson, P.-E.: A fast sequential method for polygonal approximation of digitized curves. Computer Vision Graphics and Image Processing **28**(3), 220–227 (1984)

Parallel Layer Scanning
Based Fast Dot/Dash Line Detection Algorithm
for Large Scale Binary Document Images

Chinthaka Premachandra[1(✉)], H. Waruna H. Premachandra[2],
Chandana D. Parape[3], and Hiroharu Kawanaka[4]

[1] Department of Electrical Engineering, Graduate School of Engineering,
Tokyo University of Science
6-3-1 Niijuku, Katsushika-ku, Tokyo 125–8585, Japan
chinthaka@ee.kagu.tus.ac.jp
[2] ICT Center, Wayamba University of Srilanka, Makadura, Srilanka
[3] Graduate School of Engineering, Kyoto University, Kyoto, Japan
[4] Graduate School of Engineering, Mie University, Tsu, Mie, Japan

Abstract. A fast dot/dash line detection method suitable for large scale binary document images is proposed. The method works by reducing the number of scanned pixels used for the detection process. In the new method, pixels in vertical image layers with only a constant spacing are scanned. By using this technique, the computational time can be reduced because some of the uninteresting objects in the image can easily be omitted in the scanning stage. The new method is faster than the conventional method not only due to its scanning method but it also due to the simple process used for detecting dot/dash lines. A dot/dash line is detected by selecting a small defined image domain from the large scale image. We evaluated the new method against conventional methods on appropriate document images and found an improved processing time without any significant loss of line detection ability.

Keywords: Parallel layer scanning · Large scale image · Processing time reduction · Dot/dash line detection · Local image domain analysis

1 Introduction

Document image processing is a key research area in computer vision, and many studies can be found in the literature concerning document scanning, document structure comprehension, document computerization, and related topics [1]−[14]. Line detection is one of the main stages in document structure comprehension and analysis, as well as in character recognition. In this paper, images of documents in Japanese and English without figures are considered. Part of a target document image is illustrated in Fig. 1. It consists of characters, solid lines, dot/dash lines, and very few other objects, such as ellipses. Document images should be generated at a sufficiently high resolution to allow analyzing the information effectively; however, considerable time

© Springer International Publishing Switzerland 2014
A. Campilho and M. Kamel (Eds.): ICIAR 2014, Part I, LNCS 8814, pp. 395–402, 2014.
DOI: 10.1007/978-3-319-11758-4_43

is needed to process the large scale images that can result from a high resolution. In this paper, an image of at least 2480 × 3508 pixels is defined as a large scale image. Dozens of minutes are required to process such images. Therefore, it is important to find ways of effectively reducing the time to process large scale document images. Here, processing time reduction is achieved in the image scanning stage, as well as at the object detection stage.

Raster scanning is a major part of digital image processing. In raster scanning, all pixels in the image are scanned, starting from the top-left point. However, for large scale images, significant computational time is needed to detect desired objects when all pixels are scanned. We propose that limiting the pixels to scan to those necessary for processing will produce a less time-consuming object detection method for large scale binary images. In this study, pixels on vertical and horizontal layers with a constant spacing are scanned. This scanning approach will be called parallel layer scanning (PLS). Fig. 1 illustrates parallel vertical layer scanning (PVLS). Parallel horizontal layer scanning (PHLS) can be similarly defined by using horizontal layers. When there is a particular object detection target, some irrelevant objects can easily be skipped during PLS and, as a result, processing time can be reduced.

In this paper, the problem of detecting dot/dash lines in binary document images is considered. Objects, such as characters and lines in the document image, are assumed to be composed of black pixels and the background is assumed to be composed of white pixels. If a black pixel is found while scanning, the dot/dash line detection process is started by selecting a surrounding image domain (ID) of that pixel. Then, a dot/dash line model is developed from a limited area of the original image and, as a result, the processing time can be further reduced.

Many studies can be found in the literature regarding the line detection problem. Most of the detection methods are based on the Hough transform (HT), which is described in the next section, and are very time consuming. We propose a new and faster dot/dash line detection algorithm that does not depend on voting approaches as the HT does. The new algorithm uses the PLS and local ID analysis approach mentioned above. In tests with appropriate large scale document images, the new method showed a dot/dash line detection rate that was similar to that of the conventional method while reducing the occurrence of false positives. Furthermore, the new method required significantly less processing time.

This paper consists of five sections. Section 2 describes conventional line detection approaches. Section 3 details the new method, which is based on PLS and local ID processing. Section 4 describes the results of testing large scale document images and discusses possible applications of the proposed method. Finally, Section 5 concludes the paper and introduces some topics for future works.

2   Related Work

Line detection is one of the main stages in analyzing document images. Most studies of this interesting problem have approached the problem by using the HT [18][19][20]. The advantage of the HT is that it offers the ability to detect both solid and dot/dash lines simultaneously. However, the HT is a voting-based method, and due to the voting process it is expensive in both time and memory. Therefore, it is inefficient to use the HT for line detection in large scale images.

Some studies do not depend on the HT [15][17][23][24]. Leferve et al. [17] studied solid-line detection for scene modeling. Their objective is to detect horizontal and vertical lines in binary images. In their method, pixels are analyzed by creating an appropriate accumulator on a per-block basis to extract candidates for line segments. Kawanaka et al. [15] have conducted solid-line detection using connected component analysis: a connected component longer than a pre-defined threshold is detected as a line. These methods, however, do not work for detecting dot/dash lines because dot/dashes are not connected.

Adachi et al. [21] have proposed a fast method to find curved dot/dash lines in graphs. In that approach, dot/dash lines are detected by tracking the connected components. This method is effective for detecting dot/dash lines in a graph since a dot/dash line in a graph is isolated and no other objects are near the line. However, in the case of document images, many other components, such as characters, are likely to exist around the line; therefore, it is difficult to conduct effective connected component tracking in document images.

We overcome the above mentioned weaknesses of conventional approaches by scanning the image with PLS and analyzing an ID selected from the entire image.

3   Dot/Dash Line Detection

This section presents the proposed dot/dash line detection algorithm in detail.

3.1   Proposed Algorithm

Step 1: The document image is binarized by using discriminant analysis, as in the Otsu binarization method [22]. The LPP method [15] is then used for tilt correction.

Step 2: Either PVLS or PHLS is chosen for scanning. Image scanning using PVLS is illustrated in Fig. 1, where the scanned areas are indicated in red.

Step 3: Whenever a black pixel of an object is found while scanning, the same label is set to all black pixels of that object. However, labeling is automatically stopped when the number of labels exceeds a target threshold k (that is, when $(n_l) \geq k$), and the process moves to Step 9. If the threshold is not exceeded, the process moves to Step 4.

Step 4: The circumscribing rectangle of a labeled object (CR_l) is calculated. The aspect of CR_l $(w \times h)$ determines the next step:
  (i) When $w \times h \geq n \times n$ pixels, the process moves to Step 9.
  (ii) When $w \times h < n \times n$ pixels, the process moves to Step 5.

Step 5: The center of CR_l (G_0) is calculated, and a rectangular local ID is defined with G_0 as its center. The size of the ID is $w_{RA} \times h_{RA}$. The definition of an ID is illustrated in Fig. 1, and the enlarged ID is illustrated in Fig. 2. Then, the number of connected components (CC_i) having fewer than $n \times n$ pixels inside the ID are found.

If $CC_i \geq 5$, then we assume that part of a dot/dash line exists inside the ID, and the process moves to Step 6. Otherwise, process moves to Step 9.

Step 6: The middle points ($M_i, 1 \leq i \leq 5$) of CC_i are calculated, and then the 4 angles ($\alpha_i, 1 \leq i \leq 4$) between each pair of consecutive middle points are also calculated, as illustrated in Fig. 3. If the angles are approximately equal, then the process moves to Step 7. Otherwise, the process moves to Step 9.

Step 7: The average x and y coordinates of M_i (x_M, y_M) are determined from Equations 1 and 2, respectively. The average value of α_i (α_{AV}) is determined from Equation 3. The dot/dash line general equation can then be determined according to Equation 4. The process moves to Step 8.

$$x_M = \frac{1}{5}\sum_{i=1}^{5} x_i \tag{1}$$

$$y_M = \frac{1}{5}\sum_{i=1}^{5} y_i \tag{2}$$

$$\alpha_{AV} = \frac{1}{4}\sum_{i=1}^{4} \alpha_i \tag{3}$$

$$(x - x_M) = \tan \alpha_{AV}(y - y_M) \tag{4}$$

Step 8: All connected components having fewer than $n \times n$ pixels satisfying the derived general equation are classified as a dot/dash line.

Step 9: The process moves to Step 3, and the next (i, j) pixel is scanned.

In this algorithm, the processing time can effectively be reduced at the image scanning stage as well as at the dot/dash line detection stage. We evaluate the algorithm on appropriate large scale document images in the next section.

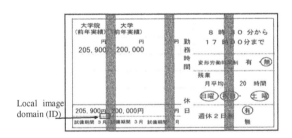

Fig. 1. Scanning the image on parallel vertical layers and defining an 1D

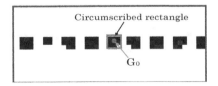

Fig. 2. Enlarged ID

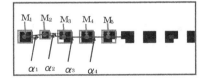

Fig. 3 Enlarged ID showing α_m and M_n

4   Experiment

4.1   Experimental Setup

Experiments were conducted using 40 large scale document images of size 2480 × 3508 pixels and a resolution of 300dps. We evaluated both the performance of the method according to dot/dash line detection rate and processing time. Furthermore, the results were compared with the performance of a conventional HT method on the same document images. In the experiments, dot/dash line detection was conducted and then detected lines were deleted by converting them to white pixels to clarify the results.

All of the experiments were conducted using a computer with an Intel® Core™ i7-2600 3.4 GHz CPU.

4.2   Experimental Results

Figures 4, 5, 6, 7, and 8 illustrate the dot/dash line detection results from the new method. These images are extracted from the large scale images to show the dot/dash line detection results clearly. Figures 4, 5, and 6 are extracted from Japanese document images, and Figs. 7 and 8 are extracted from English document images. In each figure, the upper image is the original image, and the lower image is the result after deleting detected dot/dash lines. Table 1 shows that the new method has almost the same dot/dash line detection rate as the conventional HT method. Furthermore, the new method has fewer false positives because it detects only dots and dashes. The HT approach sometimes detects character lines as dot/dash lines, which results in a higher false positive rate.

Table 2 shows the average time for processing 40 large scale images. The HT approach takes more than 10 minutes for processing; in contrast, the new method takes only a few seconds.

Overall, the experiments show that the new method can reduce both false positives and processing time while keeping the detection rate almost the same as that of the conventional method.

Table 1. Detection Rate Comparison

Method	Number of dot/dash lines	Detected lines	Detection rate	False positive rate
Proposed	300	291	97%	0%
HT	300	297	99%	8%

Table 2. Processing Time Comparison

Method	Processing time
Proposed	3 *s*
HT	620 *s*

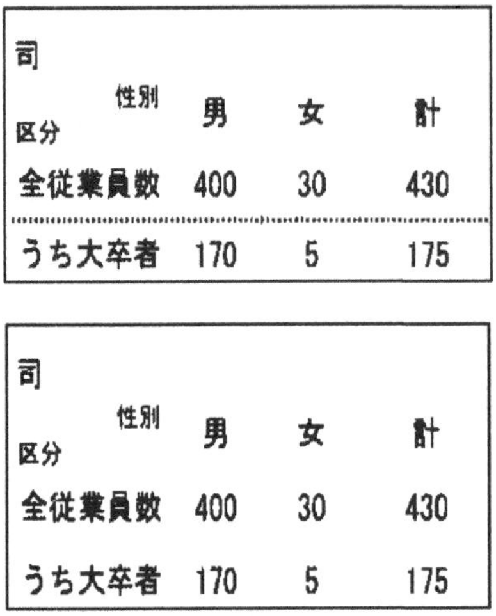

Fig. 4 Dot/dash line detection results

Fig. 5 Dot/dash line detection results

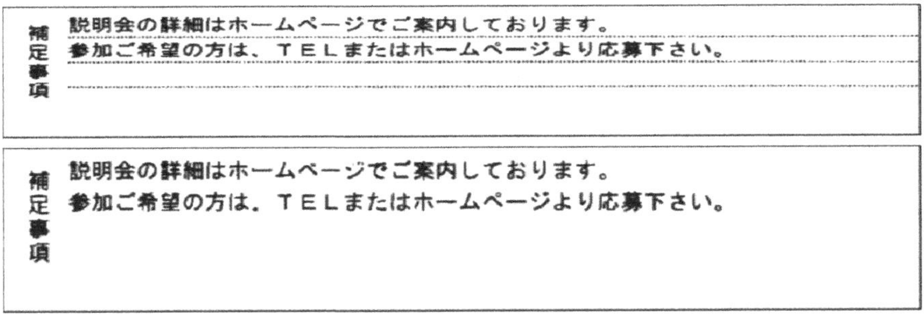

Fig. 6. Dot/dash line detection results

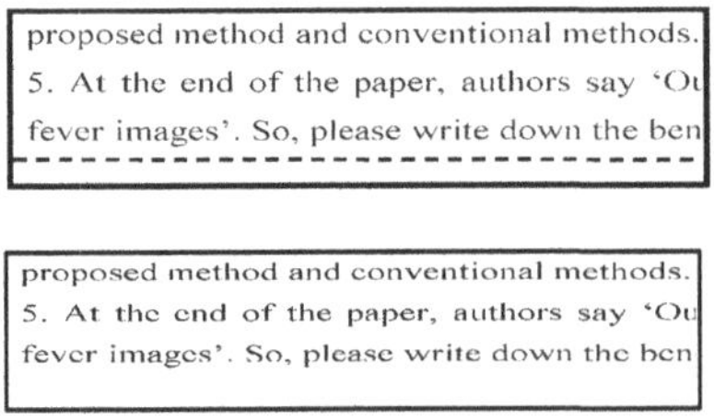

Fig. 7. Dot/dash line detection results

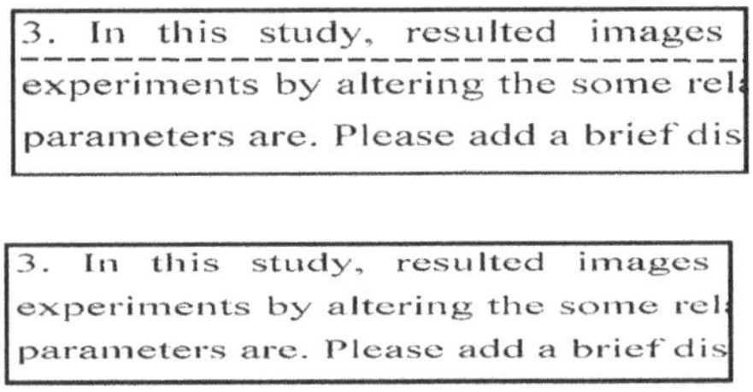

Fig. 8 Dot/dash line detection results

The new approach is able to handle scanning noise in all but a very few cases. If there are five noise dots inside a defined ID at Step 5 of the algorithm and those are smaller than $n \times n$ pixels, then there is a small possibility that they will be classified as a dot/dash line since our method proposes a line model when five dots or dashes are almost on a line. However, it is not easy for noise to fulfill the necessary conditions. We conducted experiments to evaluate dot/dash line detection in several noisy images and found that noise was not detected as dot/dashes.

4.3   Application

This new method has been applied in the development of a job-opening database at Mie University, Japan. In this database, students can search for desired company information by entering keywords that are matched against keywords extracted from job-opening document images. The images of the job announcements are stored in the database after an analysis of the document structure, which is determined by detecting lines on the sheets. The new method is used to detect dot/dash lines.

5   Conclusions

In this paper, we have introduced a fast object detection approach for use on large scale document images. Here, a dot/dash lines are considered as a target object to be detected. In the proposed method, the image is scanned on parallel vertical or horizontal layers, and dot/dash line detection is conducted by analyzing only a local ID selected from the image. Experiments were conducted to evaluate the new method using appropriate large scale images. The new method had almost the same dot/dash line detection rate as a well-known conventional method. Furthermore, the new method is much faster.

References

1. Jin, S., You, Y., Huafen, Y.: Scanned Document Image Processing Model for Information System. In: Proc. of Asia-Pacific Conf. on Wearable Computing Systems, pp. 198–201 (2010)
2. Wang, Q., Chi, Z., Zhao, R.: Hierarchical content classification and script determination for automatic document image processing. In: Proc. of 16th International Conference on Pattern Recognition, pp. 77–80 (2002)
3. Yip, S.K., Chi, Z.: Page segmentation and content classification for automatic document image processing. In: Proceedings of 2001 International Symposium on Intelligent Multimedia, Video and Speech Processing, pp. 279–282 (2001)
4. Manikandan, V., Venkatachalam, V., Kirthiga, M., Harini, K., Devarajan, N.: An enhanced algorithm for Character Segmentation in document image processing. In: IEEE International Conference on Computational Intelligence and Computing Research (ICCIC), pp. 1–5 (2010)
5. Yang Y., Yan, H.: A robust Document processing system combining image segmentation with content-based document compression. In: Proceedings of the 15th International Conference on Pattern Recognition, pp. 519–522 (2000)

6. Borges, P.V.K., Mayer, J., Izquierdo, E.: Document Image Processing for Paper Side Communications. IEEE Transactions on Multimedia 10(7), 1277–1287 (2008)
7. Shi, Z., Setlur, S., Govindaraju, V.: A Model Based Framework for Table Processing in Degraded Document Images. In: 12th International Conference on Document Analysis and Recognition (ICDAR), pp. 963–967 (2013)
8. Takasu, A., Satoh, S., Katsura, E.: A rule learning method for academic document image processing. In: Proc. of the Third International Conference on Document Analysis and Recognition, pp. 239–242 (1995)
9. Cao, R., Tan, C.L., Shen, P.: A wavelet approach to double-sided document image pair processing. In: Proc. 2001 Int. Conference on Image Processing, pp. 174–177 (2001)
10. Parodi, P., Piccioli, G.: An efficient pre-processing of mixed-content document images for OCR systems. In: Proc. of the 13th Int. Conf. on Pattern Recognition, pp. 778–782 (1996)
11. Baier, P.E.: Image processing of forensic documents. In: Proceedings of the Third International Conference on Document Analysis and Recognition, pp. 1–4 (1995)
12. Le, D.X., Thoma, G.R., Wechsler, H.: Document image analysis using integrated image and neural processing. In: Proc. of the Third Int. Conf. on Document Analysis and Recognition, pp. 327–330 (1995)
13. Li, Y., Lalonde, M., Reiher, E., Rizand, J.F., Zhu, C.J.: A knowledge-based image understanding environment for document processing. In: Proc. of the Fourth International Conference on Document Analysis and Recognition, pp. 979–983 (1997)
14. Rosner, D., Boiangiu, C.A., Stefanescu, A., Tapus, N., Olteanu, A.: Text line processing for high-confidence skew detection in image documents. In: IEEE International Conference on Intelligent Computer Communication and Processing (ICCP), pp. 129–132
15. Kawanaka, H., Sumida, T., Yamamoto, K., Shinogi, T., Tsuruoka, S.: Document Recognition and XML Generation of Tabular Form Discharge Summaries for Analogous Case Search System. Method Inf. Med. 46, 700–708 (2007)
16. Tsuruoka, S., Hirano, C., Yoshikawa, T., Shinogi, T.: Image-based Structure Analysis for a Table of Contents and Conversion to XML Documents. In: Proc. of Document Layout Interpretation and its Application, pp 59–62 (2001)
17. Lefevre, S., Dixon, C., Jeusse, C., Vincent, N.: A Local Approach for Fast Line Detection. In: IEEE International Conference on Digital Signal Processing, pp. 1109–1112 (July 2002)
18. Li, W.C., Tsai, D.M.: Defect Inspection in Low-Contrast LCD Images Using Hough Transform-Based Nonstationary Line Detection. IEEE Transactions on Industrial Informatics 7(1), 136–147 (2011)
19. Zhao, X., Liu, P., Zhang, M., Zhao, X.: A novel line detection algorithm in images based on improved Hough Transform and wavelet lifting transform. In: IEEE International Conference on Information Theory and Information Security (ICITIS), pp. 767–771 (2010)
20. Aggarwal, N., Karl, W.C.: Line detection in images through regularized hough transform. IEEE Transactions on Image Processing 15(3), 582–591 (2006)
21. Adachi, N., Omachi, S., Aso, H.: High-Speed Recognition of Line Graph Images In Documents by Simplified Interpolation Technique. Technical Report of Institute of Electronics, Information, and Communication Engineers Japan
22. Otsu, N.: Threshold Detection Method from Grey-Level Histograms. IEEE Trans. Systems, Man, and Cybernities 9(1), 62–66 (1979)
23. Chen, J., Lopresti, D.: Model-based ruling line detection in noisy handwritten documents. Pattern Recognition Letters 35(1), 34–45 (2014)
24. Zheng, Y., Li, H., Doermann, D.: A Parallel-Line Detection Algorithm Based on HMM Decoding. IEEE T-PAMI 27(5), 777–792 (2005)

A Hybrid CRF/HMM Approach
for Handwriting Recognition

Gautier Bideault[(✉)], Luc Mioulet, Clément Chatelain, and Thierry Paquet

Laboratoire LITIS - EA 4108, Université de Rouen, 76800
Mont-Saint-Aignan, FRANCE
{gautier.bideault,luc.mioulet,
clement.chatelain,thierry.paquet}@univ-rouen.fr

Abstract. In this article, we propose an original hybrid CRF-HMM
system for handwriting recognition. The main idea is to benefit from both
the CRF discriminative ability and the HMM modeling ability. The CRF
stage is devoted to the discrimination of low level frame representations,
while the HMM performs a lexicon-driven word recognition. Low level
frame representations are defined using n-gram codebooks and HOG
descriptors. The system is trained and tested on the public handwritten
word database RIMES.

1 Introduction

Handwriting Recognition (HWR) is a difficult problem due to the high variability of the data. Currently, the most widely used probabilistic models for
handwriting modeling are Hidden Markov Model (HMM) [12]. Multiple training
frameworks have been proposed to train these generative models. The original
generative framework relies on a Maximum Likelihood (ML) criterion [10], but
it has been shown that a discriminative framework based on a Maximum Mutual
Information (MMI) criterion [2] could lead to some improvement. Regardless of
the criterion, HMM rely on strong observation independence assumptions and
they perform poorly on high dimensional observations.

Conditional Random Fields (CRF) [16] became more and more popular models during the last decade for sequence modeling because they are discriminative
models and they do not rely on the same restrictive assumptions. The original CRF framework [16] was proposed to process symbolic data in the field of
automatic language processing [6]. A major drawback concerning CRF is there
inability to process numerical data, they only process discrete values. When fac-
ing numerical data, they are generally introduced at a second stage of the model
in order to model the dependency between classes, while raw numerical data
are analyzed through a classification stage such as Artificial Neural Networks
(ANN) for example in the field of Automatic Speech Recognition (ASR) [8,18].

Despite their ability to deal with symbolic data, CRF models are limited
to label the observation sequence, *i.e.* to provide a label to each frame of the
sequence. As a consequence, the CRF is not able to integrate high level knowledge

A. Campilho and M. Kamel (Eds.): ICIAR 2014, Part I, LNCS 8814, pp. 403–410, 2014.
DOI: 10.1007/978-3-319-11758-4_44

through the integration of lexicons and/or language models, as it is whith HMMs. A second limitation of CRF, as opposed to HMMs, is the requirement of having groundtruthed data at frame level in order to train the models, thus preventing using embedded training afforded within the HMM framework.

In this paper, we propose a hybrid model that takes advantage of both generative and discriminative models in order to tackle Off-Line omni-writer handwriting recognition. The paper is organized as follows: first a review of the related works is given in section 2, then we present the hybrid model devoted to handwriting modeling in section 3. Experimental setup and results reported using the RIMES database [5] are presented in section 4.

2   Related Work

In the early nineties, hybrid architectures have been proposed to combine the advantages of both discriminative and generative models. They were initially designed for ASR by combining ANN (mostly Multi Layer Perceptron) with HMM [15]. Such hybrid models have also been proposed for HWR [1].

In general, these models use the ANN discriminative stage to analyse and classify local observations at frame level, whereas the HMM generative stage is devoted to the integration of higher level information such as lexicon, language models, ... More precisely, the Gaussian Mixture Models (GMM) of the HMM stage are substituted for local posteriors computed by the ANN stage.

Recently, the Bilateral Long Short Term Memory (BLSTM) neural networks combined with a Connectionist Temporal Classification (CTC) stage [4] has proven to be a powerful alternative hybrid structure for sequence classification. Such a structure combines an efficient low level frame modeling stage with the ability to model long time dependencies, with a discriminative classification stage made of a simple logistic classifier. This structure has proven to perform extremely well for ASR and HWR [3].

CRFk [7] were originally formulated for language processing tasks, due to their interesting theoretical properties they have also been applied in fields in which the ability to process numerical data is important. Hence, in order to process this data the CRF model has been adapted to be applied to applications fields such as Gesture Recognition (GR) [9] or ASR [11].

In the field of HWR, some attempts have been reported on using CRF models. In [14], the authors introduce a CRF model to perform character sequences recognition. However, this method is applied on an already segmented character sequence consequently the segmentation is not modeled by the CRF stage. In order to perform both segmentation and recognition of characters [17] introduced a non linear HCRF model that consists in a Deep Neural Network (DNN) and a CRF. The deep structure improves the discrimination at the low level while the HCRF allows high level modeling.

Most of the previous works of the literature that have developed hybrid models introduce a discriminative stage that deals with the low level input observable raw data. Neural Networks such as MLP, BLSTM or DNN are suitable models that provide higher level informative features (e.g class conditional probabilities) to the second stage of the hybrid architecture. This second stage is most of the time devoted to the contextual analysis of the hypothesis given by the first stage. It is generally based on a generative model that can introduce constraints such as lexicons and/or language models. In most cases, HMMs are implemented, but dynamic programming stages, such as CTC, have proved to be a possible alternative architecture.

HCRF have the specificity to be discriminative at both low and high level stages. But they are limited to the task of sequence labelling they have been trained for. Moreover, they cannot embed higher level information such as lexicon or language model at decoding time.

The following section presents the proposed hybrid model.

3   A CRF-HMM Hybrid Approach

3.1   Overview of the Proposed Approach

The proposed CRF / HMM architecture has been chosen in order to take advantage of both generative and discriminative frameworks. As described on Figure 1, the CRF stage performs the discrimination of the low level frame representation. It extracts the local posterior probabilities of every character at every time using a forward-backward inference :

$$p(s_t = q_k | O^{(n)}) = \frac{\alpha_t(j)\beta_t(j)}{\sum_{i=1}^{N} \alpha_t(i)\beta_t(i)} \tag{1}$$

The forward $\alpha_t(j)$ and backward variable $\beta_t(j)$ are defined as :

$$\alpha_t(j) = P(O_1 O_2...O_t, q_t = S_i | \lambda) \tag{2}$$

i.e the probability of the partial observation sequence, $O_1 O_2...O_t$ and state S_i at time t, given the model λ.

The backward variable $\beta_t(j)$ is defined as :

$$\beta_t(j) = P(O_{t+1} O_{t+2}...O_T | q_t = S_i, \lambda) \tag{3}$$

i.e the probability of the partial observation sequence $O_{t+1} O_{t+2}...O_T$, given the state S_i and the model λ.

In order to use the discriminative and highly contextual information of the CRF, the GMM of the HMM stage are substituted for these local posteriors, as it is traditionally the case for hybrid Neuro-HMM structures. Doing this, we can use the HMM generative stage to analyze the information in context with the possibility to introduce lexical and language constraints.

As CRFs are not able to cope well with numerical data, we propose an unsupervised classification stage based on k-means devoted to the discretization of the numerical Histograms of Oriented Gradient (HOG) feature vector (for further details see section 3.3 and 4.1).

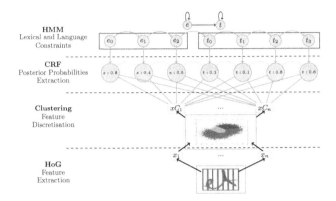

Fig. 1. Hybrid structure CRF/HMM : Detail of every step of the whole hybrid structure from feature extraction to word recognition for the word **et**

3.2 CRF-HMM Training

In order to train our hybrid CRF/HMM structure, we have to train both CRF stage and the transition probabilities of the HMM stage. An important issue when training a discriminative model, such as CRF, is that it requires a labelled training set at the frame level, whereas the groundtruth of handwriting databases is generally given at the word level. In order to get this frame level segmentation, we need to use first a standard HMM model trained on the same learning dataset, and used in a forced Viterbi alignment mode of the frame data on the word character sequence groundtruth. Following this frame labelling stage, the CRF is trained using Stochastic Gradient Descent (SGD). The convergence and the overfit of the training is controlled on a validation dataset during training. The HMM parameters (the conditional transition probabilities) are also computed on the labelled dataset.

3.3 N-gram Data Representation

CRF have been originally proposed to deal with high dimensional discrete symbolic features (words) for automatic language processing tasks. Therefore, HCRF have been introduced to deal with real valued raw data, in a way similar to neural networks or deep neural networks can do. Deep architectures have the ability to learn high level features from the raw numerical data an unsupervised training, whereas HCRFs introduce a fixed number of hidden states that act as sequentially structured features optimized during training.

The drawback of these architectures is their very long training time and their sensitivity to the initial conditions, which make them difficult to optimize with standard computational resources. The use of GPU is recommended to learn the model under a reasonable time.

Taking advantage of the ability of CRFs to deal with very large discrete features (several thousands in the case of language processing), which can even be extended to n-gram features as a result we use n-gram feature codebooks. In a way similar to the pre-training stage of a DNN, feature codebooks are trained in an unsupervised manner, so as to minimize the mean square error of the training set, using k-means, or LindeBuzoGray clustering for example.

This stage provides a high dimensional symbolic feature codebook representation of the data (see Fig. 2). In the experiments described below, we explore the use of uni-gram, bi-gram and tri-gram feature codebooks.

4   Experiments

4.1   Discretization of Frame Level Numerical Features

An initial 70 continuous feature set has been designed, based on Histograms of Oriented Gradient (HOG) [13] extracted from each frame using a 8-pixels width sliding window. It is composed of 64 HOG features (8 directions from the frame divided into 2 columns × 4 rows), and 6 high level information features: the position of the vertical and horizontal centroids, the position of the highest and lowest black pixels in the frame, the distance between them, and the number of black pixels in the frame. This continuous representation is fed to the unsupervised clustering stage allowing the definition of a discrete codebook. In our experiments, we explore the use of uni-gram, bi-gram and tri-gram codebooks extracted respectively from 1, 2 and 3 consecutive frames. Using KMeans clustering, three different codebooks are generated, providing three discrete representation levels of the input numerical data (see Fig. 2). After a validation step, 1000, 2000 and 5000 clusters has been determined to be the optimal size for 1, 2 and 3 consecutive frames.

Finally, the CRF is fed with uni-gram, bi-gram and tri-gram codebooks in context:

- The unigram representation is composed of 9 cluster numbers (symbols): the current symbol and its 4 previous and next neighbours (I)
- The bigram representation is composed of 3 cluster numbers (symbols) computed from frames $[t, t + 1]$ and frames $[t - 1, t]$ (II)
- The trigram representation is composed of 1 cluster numbers (symbols) computed from frames $[t - 1, t, t + 1]$ (III)

We evaluated the following configurations: (I), (I+II) and (I+II+III) (see Table 1).

4.2   Results and Discussion

The CRF training converged in 80 iterations of 135s each (average value). We carried out the experiments on the public RIMES 2009 database of isolated words [5]. The participants were given about 43000 words snippets to train their system, and a validation database of more than 7000 words to test them. The unknown test dataset is composed of 7464 snippets. The system is evaluated on this test dataset with a lexicon of 1600 entries. The results of our experiment are summarized in Table 1. We provide the frame error rate (FER) in Top 1, and the word error rate (WER) in Top 1, Top 2, Top 3 and Top 5 of the whole system.

Table 1. Results on Rimes database

Features	FER Top 1	WER Top 1	WER Top 2	WER Top3	WER Top5
HMM (standard HOG)	88.6 %	36 %	32 %	30 %	25 %
CRF-HMM (I)	53.8 %	38 %	33 %	29 %	21 %
CRF-HMM (I+II)	52.5 %	34 %	29%	25 %	18 %
CRF-HMM (I+II+III)	51.2 %	31 %	29%	23 %	18 %
BLSTM-HMM [4]	33.93	12.19%	x	x	x

It can be seen that the multi-scale feature set improves the performance of our system at frame and word level. We observe an enhancement of 1.6% at frame level and 6% at word level between the set of features without multi-scaling information (I) and the set of features adding the bi-grams and tri-grams information. Figure 3 presents an example showing the ability of the model to perform a frame level recognition, and to retrieve the correct character alignment (shown in red) thanks to the HMM lexicon-driven decoding. Our best system achieves 69% word recognition (Top 1) which is under the best performance reported on this database. However, these are promising results if we look at the potential improvements of the method. From our point of view, one of the main limitation of the system is that the CRF is trained on a frame-labelled dataset obtained from an initial Viterbi forced-alignment using an initial trained HMM. This means that the CRF is trained to recognize characters, but not to

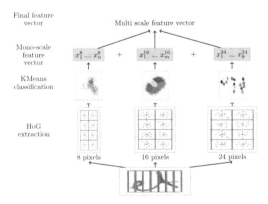

Fig. 2. Feature Extraction : Detail of every step during the feature extraction from the initial image to the final feature vector with multi-scale information of the word et

segment them. Some improvements are expected by introducing a lexicon-based training procedure of the proposed hybrid architecture. As a result, recognition and segmentation could be trained in conjunction. In addition, such scheme would allow to avoid training an initial HMM.

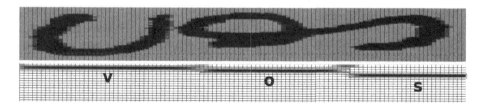

Fig. 3. Posteriors probabilities given by the CRF on the word "vos" and the alignment provide by the HMM

In order to avoid similar wrong recognition events, we have to keep working on our features, try to find a better representation of our data. A major uncertainty we are faced with, is that we do not know if the segmentation performed by the HMM is suitable for the CRF. This is why we intend to design a system in which the CRF could impact the labelling processing of each frame during the learning stage.In order to achieve this we could introduce a joint training of the whole system CRF/HMM. After training the CRF a first time, the HMM produces a new alignment on the learning database using the CRF outputs. This new labelled database is used to retrain a new CRF. This two step learning method is repeated until the system stops improving the word recognition rate. By using this training method, the CRF outputs impact the global result of the system, and are not a simple byproduct of it, therefore improving the recognition of the CRF/HMM system.

Last but not least, in our CRF training the criterion is based on frame recognition rate, they are not trained to perform word recognition directly. To infer this information we have to add the word level information of the HMM stage in the training criterion of the standard CRF.

5   Conclusion and Future Work

In this paper, we have proposed a hybrid CRF/HMM model to perform off-line omni-writer handwriting recognition. We showed the architecture has promising performance even if the recognition rate is still below the best performance of the literature obtained on the same database.

Further improvements are expected by introducing embedded training of the hybrid model allowing joint training of the CRF and the HMM stage to perform both segmentation and character recognition, bypassing the need of an initial labelling.

Another expected improvement lies in the optimization of the HMM structure including character duration.

References

1. Bengio, Y., LeCun, Y., LeRec, Y.: Ann/hmm hybrid for on-line handwriting recognition. Neural Computation **7**(6), 1289–1303 (1995)
2. Gauvain, J., Lee, C.-H.: Maximum a posteriori estimation for multivariate gaussian mixture observations of markov chains. In: Speech and Audio Processing, pp. 291–298 (April 1994)
3. Graves, A., Liwicki, M., Fernandez, S., Bertolami, R., Bunke, H., Schmidhuber, J.: A novel connectionist system for unconstrained handwriting recognition. PAMI, 855–868 (May 2009)
4. Graves, A., Fernández, S., Liwicki, M., Bunke, H., Schmidhuber, J.: Unconstrained online handwriting recognition with recurrent neural networks. In: NIPS (December 2007)
5. Grosicki, E., El Abed, H.: Icdar 2009 handwriting recognition competition. In: ICDAR (2009)
6. Gunawardana, A., Mahajan, M., Acero, A., Platt, J.C.: Hidden conditionnal random fields for phone classification. In: InterSpeech (2005)
7. Lafferty, J., McCallum, A., Pereira, F.C.N.: Conditional random fields: Probabilistic models for segmenting and labeling sequence data. In: ICML (June 2001)
8. Mohamed, A.-R., Dong, Y., Deng, L.: Investigation of full-sequence training of deep belief networks for speech recognition. In: InterSpeech (2010)
9. Morency, L.-P., Quattoni, A., Darrell, T.: Latten-dynamic discriminative models for continuous gesture recognition. In: CVPR (2007)
10. Nefian, A.V., Hayes III, M.H.: Maximum likelihood training of the embedded hmm for face detection and recognition. Image Processing **1**, 33–36 (2000)
11. Quattoni, A., Collins, M., Darrel, T.: Conditional random fields for object recognition. In: NIPS (December 2005)
12. Rabiner, L.R.: A tutorial on hidden markov models and selected applications in speech recognition. Proceedings of the IEEE **77**(2) (February 1989)
13. Rodriguez, J.A., Perronin, F.: Local gradient histogram features for word spotting in unconstrained handwritten documents. In: ICFHR (2008)
14. Shetty, S., Srinivasan, H.: Handwritten word recognition using conditional random fields. In: ICDAR, pp. 1098–1102 (September 2007)
15. Stephenson, T.A., Bourlard, H., Bengio, S., Morris, A.C.: Automatic speech recognition using dynamic bayesian networks with both acoustic and articulatory variables. In: ICSLP, vol. 2, pp. 951–954 (October 2000)
16. Sutton, C., McCallum, A.: Introduction to conditional random fields for relational learning. In: Introduction to Statistical Relational Learning, pp. 94–126 (2006)
17. Vinel, A., Do, T.M.T., Artieres, T.: Joint optimization of hidden conditional random fields and non linear feature extraction. In: ICDAR, pp. 513–517 (September 2011)
18. Zweig, G., Nguyen, P.: A segmental crf approach to large vocabulary continuous speech recognition. In: Automatic Speech Recognition & Understanding, pp. 152–157 (December 2009)

Image and Video Retrieval

Exploring the Impact of Inter-query Variability on the Performance of Retrieval Systems

Francesco Brughi[1]([✉]), Debora Gil[1], Llorenç Badiella[2], Eva Jove Casabella[3], and Oriol Ramos Terrades[1]

[1] Department Ciències de la Computació, Computer Vision Center,
Univ. Autónoma de Barcelona, Barcelona, Spain
fbrughi@cvc.uab.es
[2] Servei de Estadística Aplicada, Univ. Autónoma de Barcelona, Barcelona, Spain
[3] Department História i História de l'Art, Univ. de Girona, Girona, Spain

Abstract. This paper introduces a framework for evaluating the performance of information retrieval systems. Current evaluation metrics provide an average score that does not consider performance variability across the query set. In this manner, conclusions lack of any statistical significance, yielding poor inference to cases outside the query set and possibly unfair comparisons. We propose to apply statistical methods in order to obtain a more informative measure for problems in which different query classes can be identified. In this context, we assess the performance variability on two levels: overall variability across the whole query set and specific query class-related variability. To this end, we estimate confidence bands for precision-recall curves, and we apply ANOVA in order to assess the significance of the performance across different query classes.

1 Introduction

An effective performance measure is of essential importance in the development of new learning algorithms. In the case of content-based image retrieval (CBIR), the standard evaluation protocol consists of defining an image query set, computing a performance score for each single query, and finally aggregating - usually averaging - them to obtain a global score. Whereas this is a very compact way to represent and compare algorithm performances, it might not be fully informative since the single global score does not take into account performance variability. In order to estimate if there are significant differences in evaluation scores, a usual practice is to compute confidence intervals for the achieved score. In the context of classification problems, the usage of *bootstrapping* has been advocated [1]. The application of this technique to precision-recall (PR) curves and receiver operating characteristic (ROC) curve is discussed in [2] and [3], respectively. Bootstrapping basically consists in repeatedly taking random samples, with replacement, from the data points (images from the test sets, in our case).

A. Campilho and M. Kamel (Eds.): ICIAR 2014, Part I, LNCS 8814, pp. 413–420, 2014.
DOI: 10.1007/978-3-319-11758-4_45

Fig. 1. Examples of four different motive classes

From each sample, a curve will be generated. Alternatively, cross-validation can be used to repeatedly split the dataset into a training and a test set. This produces a curve for each split. Once multiple curves are obtained from the data, several methods exist in order to generate confidence bands for each curve [4]. The variability caught by this approach is entirely associated to the search space, as it depends on the test dataset images. In the context of CBIR, aside from the variability associated to the whole search space [2], there are specific variability factors associated to each query. As a matter of fact, this variability is lost when averaging the individual query scores in order to obtain an overall measure (such as mean average precision).

Variability is particularly critical in the case of a very heterogeneous set of queries, given that the algorithm performances is prone to vary significantly across the query set. This is the case, for instance, of artistic motive retrieval from ancient Greek pottery digital repositories [5], [6]. In this context, we have a set of queries divided into several classes (some examples in Figure 1) which, as discussed in [5], show high inter-class variability. The exploratory study presented in [5] also showed that the method that best performs on a certain query class, might not be as effective on the others. In this context, evaluating a system with an overall score which aggregates the individual query results does not provide enough information to select the best solution. Since the interest is to assess the robustness of the tested methods, this motivates to produce an evaluation metrics capable to capture the method average performance as well as its variability when applied to different query classes. In this direction, besides the context of image processing, a large amount of work has been published in the field of test diagnostics concerning the estimation of test scores - such as the area under the receiver operating characteristic curve (AUC) - and their variability when comparing different scores. Both non-parametric [7], [8] and parametric approach, based on normality assumption [9], have been proposed in the literature. A common concern is the impossibility of these methods to analyse the sources of variability and the factors influencing the performance of a system.

This paper presents a statistical framework that allows us to evaluate and compare different CBIR methods, in terms of the factors that most influence their performances. Our evaluation scheme is focused on studying the performance variability associated to the different classes of query as well as allowing for a class-wise comparison. Our comparison framework has been applied to 2 standard methods and experiments show the influence of the query type in their performances.

2   Assessment of Inter-query Variability

The common evaluation protocol for CBIR, inherited from information retrieval [10], is based on the notions of *relevant* and *non-relevant* retrieved images for a certain query. Given a test set and a set of query images, for each query a CBIR system is asked to output a number of ranked list of the test set images, according to a relevance measure of the images to the query. The quality of the ranked lists is evaluated based on whether the first k retrieved images are actually relevant or not for the given query. Whereas in binary classification problems *true positive rate* (TPr) and *false positive rate* (FPr) are commonly used, the standard evaluation metrics in CBIR are *precision* and *recall* (also known as *sensitivity*) since they better deal with unbalanced class distributions, which are typical in retrieval tasks [11]. Precision $p(k)$ and recall $r(k)$ for the first k elements of the output ranked list are defined as

$$p(k) = R(k)/k \qquad \text{and} \qquad r(k) = R(k)/N_{rel}, \tag{1}$$

where $R(k)$ is the number of relevant documents contained in the top k ranked elements and N_{rel} is the total number of relevant documents contained in the test set. Precision measures how many of the retrieved documents are actually relevant for the query, whereas recall estimates how many of the relevant documents have been retrieved. The plot given by precision and recall values obtained for each query, called *precision-recall* (PR) *curve*, is commonly used to visually assess the CBIR systems. For each query, the area under the PR curve, known as average precision (AP), is the usual evaluation score of the single query retrieval, and it is given by $AP = \frac{1}{2} \sum_{k=2}^{N} [p(k) + p(k-1)][r(k) - r(k-1)]$. The overall system performance score is then computed by averaging the AP values obtained for each query. This score is known as *mean average precision* (mAP), and it is normally used to compare the performances of different algorithms, given a query set and a test set.

As pointed out in Section 1, mAP comparisons might yield unfair results and cannot detect the sources of error and variability in performance. The PR curves and the corresponding APs will be used in the following for our study on CBIR system evaluation. As introduced in Section 1, we are interested in estimating the performance variability within query sets (or subsets such as classes) in order to achieve a more informative evaluation of a retrieval system. Quantifying the variability of the performance for different queries within a set can be useful to assess the method robustness for that set. Such variability can be obtained by exploring the differences on PR curves and APs across a given set. Variability of PR curves will be assessed by computing confidence bands for curves sampled over a given population group. Confidence bands will be computed using *vertical averaging* (VA) [4]. VA consists of stacking precision values from the different samples that correspond to the same recall values. Therefore, the precision has to be expressed directly as a function of the recall. This can be done by obtaining k from (1) as $k(r) = R^{-1}(rN_{rel})$. It must be noted that R is monotonically increasing within its domain, which guarantees the existence of its inverse R^{-1}. By substitution, we find $p(r) = rN_{rel}/R^{-1}(rN_{rel})$. In practice, $p(r)$ is only defined for a discrete set of recall values within $[0,1]$, which vary across different queries. Therefore, we linearly interpolated the function in $[0,1]$ and we sampled the recall with step $1/(N_P - 1)$, where N_P is the number of quantiles. For each sampled quantile, the average defining the confidence band is computed from a given a set of N_Q query images, thus, N_Q PR curves, as follows. Let $p_j^q = p^q(r_j)$ be our precision observations for the j-th quantile, $j = 1, \ldots, N_P$, and the q-th query image, $q = 1, \ldots, N_Q$. If μ_{p_j}, σ_{p_j} are, respectively, the unbiased sample "vertical" mean and variance for the j-th quantile, then the interval for μ_{p_j} at confidence level $1 - \alpha$ is:

$$\left[\mu_{p_j} - t_{\alpha/2}^{N_Q-1} \frac{\sigma_{p_j}}{\sqrt{N_Q}}, \quad \mu_{p_j} + t_{\alpha/2}^{N_Q-1} \frac{\sigma_{p_j}}{\sqrt{N_Q}} \right], \tag{2}$$

where $t_{\alpha/2}^{N_Q-1}$ is the value of a t-Student distribution with $N_Q - 1$ degrees of freedom. Joining the confidence intervals computed for all the N_P quantiles, we obtain the confidence band of the overall curve.

Confidence bands already provide visual assessment for significance difference in performance for 2 CBIR systems. In order to numerically check whether a method performance significantly differs across query classes, we will use *analysis of variance* (ANOVA) [12]. ANOVA is a statistical tool used to test data when it consists of a quantitative response variable and one or more categorical explanatory variables (or factors). In its simplest form, it allows to check the hypothesis that all the groups (corresponding to the different factors) have the same population mean. In our case, we want to study the different performances between different query classes as well as between different methods. Therefore our factors will be all possible method-query class pairs, whereas an intuitive choice for the response variable is constituted by the AP. We will denote by N_C the number of query classes, and by n_c the number of images belonging to the c-th query class, being $c = 1, \ldots, N_C$. Assuming that we want to compare 2 methods, A and B, our factors are defined as $X^{c,m}$, where m is either A or B. The response variable, i.e. the AP score for the q-th query and the method m, will be represented by $Y^{c,m}$. This way, for each ANOVA group - defined by the factor $X^{c,m}$ and the response variable $Y^{c,m}$ - we have n_c observations $\{\hat{Y}_q^{c,m} : q \in \mathcal{C}_c\}$, being $\mathcal{C}_c$ the set of all subscripts q that belong to the c-th class. Then, we can express the ANOVA null hypothesis as

$$H_0 : \mu_{Y^{1,A}} = \ldots = \mu_{Y^{N_C,A}} = \mu_{Y^{1,B}} = \ldots = \mu_{Y^{N_C,B}}, \tag{3}$$

which states that the precision observations obtained for the N_C query classes and the 2 different methods come from distributions with the same mean.

The ANOVA outcome indicates whether it is possible to reject the null hypothesis or not. Yet, what we are interested to know is, for instance, which is the best performing method-class combination, or whether there is a significant difference between two specific performances. We can answer these questions by applying pairwise comparison to the ANOVA outcome. In particular, we have used Tukey's *honestly significant difference test* (HSD) [13], which compares the difference between each pair of factors with appropriate adjusting for multiple testing. HSD is similar to a t-test, except that it takes into account the fact that when there are multiple comparisons being made, the probability of making a type I error increases [13]. Given a pair of factors, after estimating their $1 - \alpha$ confidence intervals, the test considers them significantly different if their intervals are disjoint, and not significantly different otherwise.

3   Experimental Set-Up

The goal of these experiments is to assess the impact of variability in performance evaluation of retrieval systems using the methods described in Section 2. We have chosen the well known Oxford 5k dataset[1], which contains 5062 images of building "landmarks" from different viewpoints. A landmark is intended to be a particular of a building. The landmarks are divided into 11 classes. Ground truth is provided as follows. For each class, 5 images are annotated as queries. The remaining images are annotated as: *good* if the landmark is clearly visible, *ok* if more than the 25% of the landmark is clearly visible or *junk* if less than the 25% of the landmark is visible or distortions are present, *absent* when the landmark does not appear. Given that the number of images for the different classes is highly variable (considering together *good* and *ok*, it ranges from 7 to 220), we selected a subset with balanced number of elements per class, since we do not want the dataset imbalance to affect our statistical analysis. Our subset of the Oxford 5k was created as follows. We picked the 5 classes that have the highest numbers of elements (Fig. 2), among the *good* and *ok* annotated images. Using the minimum of these numbers, we randomly sampled each class, without replacement, until obtaining 5 subclasses with the same number of images. Then, we added 300 distractor images, randomly sampled among the ones labelled as *absent* for the picked 5 classes. Our final balanced dataset consists of 475 images.

In order to carry out our experiments, we implemented two CBIR systems that have been evaluated on the dataset obtained as previously described: a feature-level matching system and a local feature-based bag-of-words pipeline. Both systems rely on SIFT [14] for local feature extraction, which has been extensively used in literature for retrieving images of the same objects from different viewpoints [15], [16], [17]. For the sake of compactness, from now on we will refer to the first method as SIFT and to second method as BOW.

Following [14], our SIFT system matches features according to minimum Euclidean distance. Moreover, a query feature is matched to a dataset feature only if their distance - multiplied by a threshold - is less than the distance between the query and all the other database features. The obtained matching are then refined by checking for spatial consistency using RANSAC [18]. The implementation of our BOW system follows the works of [15] and [16]. We tried

---

[1] http://www.robots.ox.ac.uk/~vgg/data/oxbuildings/.

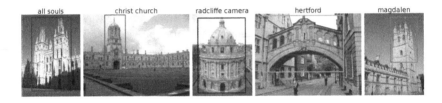

all souls   christ church   radcliffe camera   hertford   magdalen

Fig. 2. Examples from the 5 query classes we chose to build our dataset

different vocabulary sizes and we found that 50 was the best performer, thus it has been used for the presented experiments. Moreover, 3% most and least frequent visual words are clipped from the vocabulary and not used for image representation and we applied the commonly used *tf-idf* weighting [15].

For each method, PR confidence bands were computed using all query classes and $N_P = 10$ quantiles, according to (2). ANOVA was computed for the APs obtained for each query class and method, resulting in $5 \times 2 = 10$ ANOVA groups, with 5 samples each. All statistics were computed at a significance $\alpha = 0.05$.

4   Results and Discussion

Computing the traditional AP scores for the two methods under test, we obtain a value of 0.25 for SIFT and 0.30 for BOW. This would suggest that BOW globally outperforms SIFT on this test set. However, the confidence bands obtained for the PR curves of the two methods (Fig. 3(a)) show that, in both cases, the performances are notably variable and the bands consistently overlap. Therefore, we cannot find statistical evidence of the difference between the performances, and even though the AP score is favourable to BOW, it does not necessarily imply that this method is to be preferred for every query class.

Further evidences are brought by the ANOVA multiple comparison experiment, whose outcome is illustrated in Figure 3(b). The figure represents the confidence intervals for the different method-query class factors. As a general comment, SIFT seems more stable showing a slightly smaller variance across the query set. Considering differences across queries, the test does not find a significant difference between the methods for 4 out of 5 classes. The intervals for the classes *all souls* and *christ church* are completely overlapped so it is not possible to make considerations in favour of either one or the other method. Concerning *magdalen* class, we cannot observe a significantly best performance, from a statistical point of view, even if SIFT seem to be slightly preferable. Visually, this class does not particularly differ from *all souls* and *christ church*, sharing with them many local recurring patterns. We suspect that spatial consistency played an important role in discriminating this class from the others, and it determined the success of SIFT method. On the other hand, BOW is significantly better in dealing with *hertford* class, which is the best case for both methods. This class collects images of a building whose structure is sensibly different from the

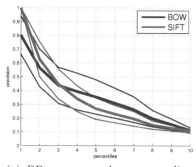
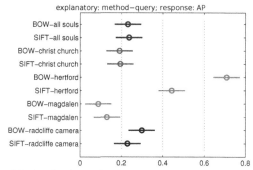
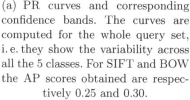

(a) PR curves and corresponding confidence bands. The curves are computed for the whole query set, i. e. they show the variability across all the 5 classes. For SIFT and BOW the AP scores obtained are respectively 0.25 and 0.30.

(b) ANOVA multiple comparison outcome. Explanatory variables are method-class pairs. The response varible is the AP score. If two intervals are disjoint, two estimates are significantly different. They are not significantly different if the intervals overlap.

Fig. 3. Results from the performed experiments

buildings of other classes. So, we might argue that the presence of very distinguishable features made the task easier for the algorithms, especially favouring the generalization properties of the BOW approach. This consideration can be extended to the *radcliffe camera* class. Even though the test outcome has no statistical significance we can practically observe an important difference between the estimated mean values.

5   Conclusion

In this paper we present a study of a new evaluation framework for a better understanding of the performance scores in image retrieval. This is particularly useful when different query classes can be found in the dataset, such as in the case of the Oxford 5k dataset, or in Greek pottery datasets. We proposed the usage of statistical tools in order to estimate the performance variability, both overall and with respect to the different query classes. This variability, usually neglected by the traditional performance metrics (e. g. mAP score), can reflect the method robustness and allows for a more informed comparison between methods, especially when the query set is particularly heterogeneous.

A main concern for the proposed approach is the number of samples (individuals) for each ANOVA factor, which, being as low as in the current case, it drops ANOVA discriminative power. This implies that less difference might be detected, even though it was possible to observe important differences between the performances for some query classes. This validates our variability study and encourages searching for alternative statistical tools. In particular we plan to apply mixed model with random effects [19] to increase the discriminative power. Such models are more flexible than ANOVA and allow to to identify explanatory variables for complex designs.

Acknowledgments. Work supported by Spanish projects TIN2012-33116 and TIN2012-37475-C02-02.

References

1. Everingham, M., Ali Eslami, S.M., Van Gool, L., Williams, C.K.I., Winn, J., Zisserman, A.: Assessing the significance of performance differences on the pascal voc challenges via bootstrapping. Tech. rep. (2013)
2. Bertail, P., Clemencon, S., Vayatis, N.: On bootstrapping the roc curve. In: NIPS, pp. 137–144. Curran Associates Inc. (2008)
3. Clémençon, S., Vayatis, N.: Nonparametric estimation of the precision-recall curve. In: ICML, pp. 185–192 (2009)
4. Macskassy, S.A., Provost, F.J.: Confidence bands for roc curves: Methods and an empirical study. In: ROCAI, pp. 61–70 (2004)
5. Brughi, F., Gil, D., Ramos Terrades, O.: Artistic heritage motive retrieval: an explorative study. Tech. rep. (2013)
6. Crowley, E.J., Zisserman, A.: Of gods and goats: Weakly supervised learning of figurative art. In: BMVC (2013)
7. Bamber, D.: The area above the ordinal dominance graph and the area below the receiver operating characteristic graph. J. Math. Psy. **12**, 387–415 (1975)
8. DeLong, E.R., DeLong, D.M., Clarke-Pearson, D.L.: Comparing the Areas under Two or More Correlated Receiver Operating Characteristic Curves: A Nonparametric Approach. Biometrics **44**, 837–845 (1988)
9. Wieand, S., Gail, M.H., James, B.R., James, K.L.: A family of nonparametric statistics for comparing diagnostic markers with paired or unpaired data. Biometrika **76**(3), 585–592 (1989)
10. Manning, C.D., Raghavan, P., Schütze, H.: Introduction to Information Retrieval. Cambridge University Press (2008)
11. Davis, J., Goadrich, M.: The relationship between precision-recall and roc curves. In: ICML, pp. 233–240 (2006)
12. Casella, G., Berger, R.: Statistical inference. Duxbury Press (1990)
13. Hochberg, Y., Tamhane, A.C.: Multiple Comparison Procedures. John Wiley & Sons Inc. (1987)
14. Lowe, D.G.: Distinctive image features from scale-invariant keypoints. IJCV **60**(2), 91–110 (2004)
15. Sivic, J., Zisserman, A.: Video google: A text retrieval approach to object matching in videos. In: ICCV, pp. 1470–1477 (2003)
16. Philbin, J., Chum, O., Isard, M., Sivic, J., Zisserman, A.: Object retrieval with large vocabularies and fast spatial matching. In: CVPR (2007)
17. Philbin, J., Chum, O., Isard, M., Sivic, J., Zisserman, A.: Lost in quantization: Improving particular object retrieval in large scale image databases. In: CVPR, pp. 1–8 (2008)
18. Lebeda, K., Matas, J., Chum, O.: Fixing the locally optimized ransac. In: BMVC, pp. 1–11 (2012)
19. Badiella, L., Puig, P., Leton, E.: Evaluacion diagnostica mediante curvas roc. Tech. rep. (2010)

Relevance Assessment for Visual Video Re-ranking

Javier Aldana-Iuit[⊠], Ondřej Chum, and Jiři Matas

Department of Cybernetics, Faculty of Electrical Engineering, Center for Machine Perception,
Czech Technical University in Prague, Karlovo nam. 13, 121 35 Prague 2, Czech Republic
{aldanjav,chum,matas}@cmp.felk.cvut.cz

Abstract. The following problem is considered: Given a name or phrase specifying an object, collect images and videos from the internet possibly depicting the object using a textual query on their name or annotation. A visual model from the images is built and used to rank the videos by relevance to the object of interest. Shot relevance is defined as the duration of the visibility of the object of interest. The model is based on local image features. The relevant shot detection builds on wide baseline stereo matching. The method is tested on 10 text phrases corresponding to 10 landmarks. The pool of 100 videos collected querying You-Tube with includes seven relevant videos for each landmark. The implementation runs faster than real-time at 208 frames per second. Averaged over the set of landmarks, at recall 0.95 the method has mean precision of 0.65, and the mean Average Precision (mAP) of 0.92.

Keywords: Video re-ranking · Object detection · Wide-baseline stereo matching

1 Introduction

In this paper we address an application of acquiring videos containing a user specified object. The user provides a text identification of the object of interest, possibly also an image – for example from a Wikipedia page. The text description is used to query some external image and video sharing sites. From the relevant images of additional views of the object, a visual model is built. The model is then used to efficiently identify shots in videos depicting the object of interest and consequently to re-rank the videos.

An example of the use of our solution is the following: During a holiday trip in Paris we took a set of images from the Notre Dame cathedral from different points of view, then we may want to search on YouTube videos related to the same landmark, in order to learn more about it or getting tour guide videos with information about surrounding venues. It would be annoying to check manually the retrieved videos for finding the shots where the landmark appears in case it does so.

In the proposed method, we are not interested in indexing a fixed corpus of videos, but we relay on text based search capabilities provided by, for example, You Tube. Through the text search, possibly relevant, but likely noisy, a short-list of videos is obtained. An efficient visual content based matching is applied to verify and re-rank the initial short-list. The paper focuses on the object model building from a set of images and on efficient online detection of the object in videos. The method is summarized in Fig. 1.

© Springer International Publishing Switzerland 2014
A. Campilho and M. Kamel (Eds.): ICIAR 2014, Part I, LNCS 8814, pp. 421–430, 2014.
DOI: 10.1007/978-3-319-11758-4_46

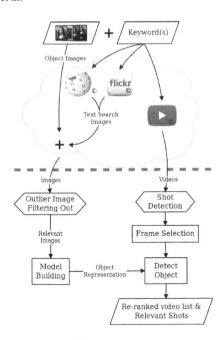

Fig. 1. The workflow of relevant shot detection. The part below the dashed red line is automatic and the focus of the paper, the text-based search has been done manually.

The applicability of the proposed system ranges from individual user searches for relevant videos to systematic augmentation of Wikipedia (or similar) pages with relevant video documents.

Relevant work. Visual content based searching of videos and large image collection has become very popular with Video Google [16] by Sivic and Zisserman. In this work, as well as in other image retrieval publications [6,11,14], it is assumed that the video or image collection is going to be sought repeatedly for different query objects. Therefore an offline stage of indexing of the videos or image collection takes place. On the contrary, we assume that each video is unlikely to be needed multiple times. In fact, most of the videos will never be accessed, and therefore we leave the initial retrieval of the short list on text search facilities of the video sharing site, YouTube in our experiments.

The concept of matching multiple views of a single object to obtain a visual model with stable local features has been used in a number of applications. In query expansion [4], a generative model of the object is built from a small number of geometrically consistent retrieved result images. In [17], the database features are reduced by matching the images within the dataset, resulting in more compact representation without hurting the search performance.

Text-based search works as mechanism for collecting input data, likewise [1]. In video analysis, features that are repeatedly detected over a number of consecutive frames are reliable [15] and are kept for further computation.

2   The Method

The paper focuses on two aspects of the problem: the object model building and efficient online detection of the object in videos.

The object model is built from a set of pre-filtered, but still possibly contaminated, images of an object of interest. We take such a collection of images as an input and call it *the pool of images*. To pre-filter the images obtained from image sharing site by a text query, user provided images or Wikipedia images are used. All images are used jointly to build a representation of the object based on local features. Detailed description follows in Sec. 2.1.

Another input to our method is a short-list of videos, retrieved by a text query to You Tube. Videos from the short-list are represented as sequences of shots, each shot is represented by its key frames. A relevance of a key-frame to the object is given by the number of geometrically consistent image features found after a wide-baseline stereo matching to the object model. The videos are finally ranked w.r.t. the number of relevant frames. Detailed description of the object detection is given in Sec. 2.3.

2.1   Object Model

In this section, the process of the object model construction is described. The model is a collection of local affine covariant image features localized in an image coordinate frame. Rather than using a single image to obtain the model, we use a small set of images (sets of 7 images were used in our experiments). Using multiple images provides richer description, as some parts of the object may not be well represented in a single image due to noise, (self-)occlusion, etc.

Local features. Local affine covariant features are extracted in images from the pool of images, using *Hessian Affine* detector [10]. The image features are described with the SIFT [8] descriptor.

Model coordinate system. We identify the model coordinate system with one of the images. The Iconoid shift [18] is applied to select the reference image, which is used to define the coordinate system of the model. The Iconoid shift is seeded from each image in turn and the image selected as a mode the most often is selected as the reference image. Unrelated images are filtered out from the pool of images preserving the top K images from the mode support scored by the Homography Overlap Distance (HOD) defined in [18] only. We used $K = 7$ in our experiments. Fig. 2 (a) shows three pools of images, the green rectangles indicates the reference images.

Features from other images are back-projected to the model based on image-to-image homography robustly estimated [3] between the images and the reference image.

Feature selection. In the local feature matching state, the descriptors of the features are compared. Pairs of features (one feature from each image) with similar descriptors are considered as tentative correspondences. It has been suggested in [8] that a distance between descriptor of the same surface patch in different images also depends on the

(a)   (b)

Fig. 2. (a) Three examples of set of images used for building the object models, each set is known as the *Pool of images*. (b) Local features found in multiple images in the image pool, called *salient* features. The color scale indicates the number of images where the feature were recognized, and the ellipses indicate the shape of the feature.

appearance of the patch itself, therefore it is better to use the ratio of the distance to the nearest and the second nearest descriptor in the other image.

Since our model is a collection of back-projected features from multiple images, one physical patch can be represented by a number of descriptors. If the distance ratio approach [8] is adopted, the distance ratio can be close to 1 even for a good tentative correspondence, because the first and second nearest descriptor may belong to two different instances of the same physical scene patch. We compare two approaches avoiding this phenomenon.

The first approach is based on a recent idea from [12], called *1st Geometrical Inconsistent* strategy. Some detectors, especially those using synthetic image warping to improve feature detection, have multiple detections of very similar features. To avoid dropping correct tentative correspondences, authors of [12] suggest to compute the distance ratio to the nearest descriptor that comes from feature that is sufficiently far away (i.e. geometrically inconsistent) from the tentatively corresponding one.

The second approach tries to reduce the number of features in the model by joint clustering in the SIFT and image domain. For each feature back-projected into the model, 130D SIFT-XY descriptor is created by concatenating the SIFT descriptor with the feature coordinates (multiplied by a normalizing constant). The features are clustered by applying DBSCAN [5] algorithm to the SIFT-XY descriptors. In order to drop randomly detected features that are not repeatable, features from singleton clusters are dropped. An average feature (in SIFT and XY) is kept in the model for each of the feature clusters. The average model features for different landmarks are shown in Fig. 2 (b). A similar approach for computing mid-level features is proposed in [7]. The full algorithm to compute the set of salient features is summarized in Alg. 1.

2.2   Video Representation

The set of videos collected from the text retrieval are represented by a subset of keyframes (Intra-coded frames or I-frames) concerning the CODEC. Local affine covariant features are detected and described on every selected key-frame. This stage avoids the wide-baseline stereo matching over all frames of the video, rather than that, we match the object model against up to 1% of the total number of frames. For shot boundary detection, we apply a simple detector [2], that thresholds the sum of pixel-wise

Algorithm 1. Salient features

Require: Pool of images (P), reference image (I_{ref})
Ensure: Set of salient features (SF)
    $N \leftarrow |P|$
    // Detect and describe image features
    for $i = 1$ to N **do**
        $f_i \leftarrow$ hessian_affine_detection(p_i)
        $d_i \leftarrow$ SIFT_description(f_i)
    end for
    $D = \{d_1, ..., d_N\}$
    // Features in images of the pool without the reference
    $C \leftarrow D \setminus \{d_{ref}\}$
    $c_i \in C, i = 1, ..., N - 1$
    // Set of reprojected features (RF)
    $RF \leftarrow \{f_{ref}\}$
    for $j = 1$ to $N - 1$ **do**
        $H_j \leftarrow$ wbs_match(d_{ref}, c_j)
        $RF \leftarrow \{RF \cup$ reproject_features(H_j, c_j)$\}$
    end for
    $CL \leftarrow$ DBSCAN_clustering(RF)
    // Salient features are described by average SIFT
    $SF \leftarrow$ average_SIFT(CL, RF)
    return SF

---

absolute differences. To reduce the number of selected key-frames, we drop key-frames close to the shot boundary, as these are typically corrupted by the shot transition.

2.3 Object Detection in Video Frames

A shot is regarded as relevant if the object or landmark appears on at least one of its selected frames. The object recognition is addressed as a *Wide-Baseline Stereo Matching* problem, as proposed in e.g. [9]. To efficiently detect the nearest neighbor SIFT descriptors, approximate nearest neighbor search is used [13]. Global geometric model and supporting tentative correspondences are robustly estimated using LO-RANSAC [3]. The geometric model of homography or affine transformation are compared.

    The relevance of the video the object model is given by the number of relevant frames that appear in the video.

3 The Dataset

The relevant shot detection algorithm was applied to a dataset of images and videos collected from 10 different queries: *Petra city* in Jordan, *Notre Dame cathedral* in France, *Taj Mahal palace* in India, *The Mona Lisa* painting in France, *The Merida's Monumento a la Patria* in Mexico, *Christ The Redeemer* in Brazil, the Coca-Cola logo, the Lola perfume container, Starbucks logo and Virgin Mary painting.

The image pools contain 7 images (top 7 images in the mode support ranked by the HOD) per query object with a fixed width of 640 pixels and keeping the aspect ratio. All images were stored in JPEG format. The number of local affine covariant features detected on the images are presented on Tab. 1.

The video set contains 100 videos downloaded from You Tube. Every object of interest has 10 videos, 7 of them actually depict the object and 3 of them works as confusers (videos were retrieved by querying You-Tube with the same text search but the object never appears on scene).

The videos have an average duration of 3 minutes, the frame rate is fixed 25 fps, the size of the frames is 640x480 pixels. All videos are stored with the codec H.264, which inserts a keyframe (Intra-coded picture) every 60 frames. Notice that only keyframes are processed.

4   Experiments

4.1   Object Model Construction

The effectiveness of the object representation is tested in the experiments comparing the results using 2 types of representation. The first one is called *Union* which is the set of reprojected features on the reference image with no filtering stage. The second one is the set of salient features (described in Sec. 2.1) and it is called *Salient*.

Tab. 1 contains the number of features in the two object representations and the reference image itself. The average size of the *salient* representation is 3% of the whole features detected on the pool of images (union) and 18% of the features detected on the reference image. The significant reduction in the cardinality of the feature sets is reflected in memory allocation and the complexity of matching task. The average time for building a *salient* model is 4.1 sec. for a single image pool. Construction time of Union models (1.27 sec) is obtained subtracting the mean-shift clustering step. The percentages of processing time for each step of the model computation are shown in Fig. 5.

4.2   Comparison of Different Approaches

In this section we compare different combination of choices of model construction (Union vs. Salient), tentative correspondence establishment (2NN vs. 1GI) and global geometry model type used in RANSAC (homography vs. affine transformation).

For this task, one video per landmark (6 videos) were annotated manually fixing the subsampling factor $s = 50$ (0.5fps). The Fig. 4.2 (a) shows the recall/precision curves obtained from 6 different method combinations. A number of observation can be made from the plot: (1) better matching results are obtained with more restrictive affine transformation than with full planar homography model; (2) the union representation of the object is slightly more accurate than the salient representation; (3) the 1GI brings almost no advantage for the salient model since similar features have been locally unified in the clustering step.

Two single-frame examples of the matching results with the object model are shown in Fig. 4. Figure 4 (a) corresponds to a frame with the object of interest, the system

Table 1. The *number of features* in the object representations is shown: *Ref. image* column for features on the reference images, *Union* column for features detected in the whole pool of images and *Salient* column for selected features only. In addition, Kendall tau rank correlation coefficients between the ground truth video ranked list and both retrieved ranked lists, regarding the *Text search* list and the *Re-ranked* list by relevance assessment, are shown as *Ranking Quality*. Best ranked lists are highlighted with bold font.

Query object	Number of features			Ranking Quality	
	Ref. image	Union	Salient	Text Search	Re-ranked
Taj Mahal	1368	11363	585	**0.78**	0.47
Petra city	3484	28109	1002	0.60	**0.78**
Notre Dame	5981	30611	2962	0.56	**0.60**
Monumento Patria	2764	14758	739	0.47	**0.60**
Mona Lisa	2303	17243	2449	0.47	**0.73**
Christ Reedemer	3771	10965	477	0.51	**0.69**
Coca Cola	834	8466	315	0.51	**0.51**
Starbucks	1408	12345	1017	0.33	**0.56**
Virgin Mary	6594	66675	5589	0.69	**0.73**

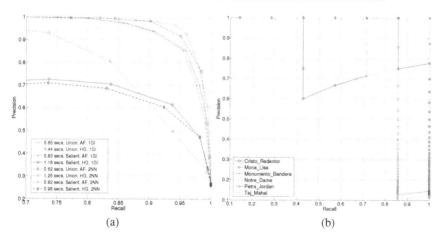

Fig. 3. (a) Recall/Precision curves on training data for the "Union of feature sets" and "the set of salient features". The mean processing time per frame is shown in the legend. (b) Recall/Precision curves for the "Salient, AF, 1GI" method applied to the 10 landmarks.

found 39 correct feature matches with an inlier ratio of 40%. The Fig. 4 (b) shows the result of matching a frame without the object, the system found 6 inliers with a ratio of 11%, even though all matches are actually incorrect. The number of inliers of matched features is significantly higher when the object is present in the frame.

The best performance concerns to the *Union* model, AF geometric model for RANSAC and 1GI as matching strategy. The later configuration has the second shortest mean processing time per frame. The fastest results comes from the *Salient* model, AF and 2NN, the counter part is a 8% lower precision. The mean processing time per frame in this configuration is 83.1 sec, see Fig. 5 for percentages of time per processing

(a)   (b)

Fig. 4. Matching of the object model against a frame containing the object (a) and a frame where the object does not appear (b)

stage. The processing time for 1GI and 2NN are not significantly different because of the previous *SIFT-XY* filtering that suppresses multiple instances of the same feature which hurts the 2NN matching strategy.

For verification, an additional set of experiments were performed with the parameter setting: AF and 1GI and the Union features representation. Based on the recall/precision curve for the training stage, we fixed the detection threshold to 6 inliers which corresponds to a recall of 0.96 and precision of 0.93. The relevant frames are detected with an average recall of 0.88 and average precision of 0.94 over 20 prelabeled videos. The mean processing time per frame is 0.49 secs. The precision and recall fall 0.05 and 0.02, respectively, from training to testing stage. In application such as determining whether the object is present in the video sequence is enough to tune the system for a high ($> 95\%$) recall even that the precision is lower than $30\% - 20\%$, since with only one frame detected correctly, the whole video would be classified as positive.

Relevance-Shot and Re-ranking

In the shot-level detection, *salient* models and video representation are used for ranking the list of retrieved videos. For the experiments with short-lists of 10 videos and 30% of confusers for each landmark, we obtained for recall 1, a precision of 1. Then, we propose to measure the improvement of the re-ranking method over the text search ranked lists by means of the Kendall tau rank correlation coefficients wrt the ground truth of video ranked list by relevant content. The re-ranking method improved the quality of the retrieved ranked lists in 90% of the landmarks (see Table 1).

A set of more challenging experiments were done over all landmarks with short-list of 60 videos and 88% of confusers. The performance of the algorithm on precision and recall is shown in the graphs of Fig. 4.2 (b). Querying the *salient* model at recall 0.95, the average precision is 0.67 and the mean Average-Precision (mAP) is 0.92. For the *Union* model, at recall 0.95, the average precision is 0.64 and the mAP is 0.9. In our experiments, the landmark *Christ, The redeemer* (Cristo Redentor in Portuguese) gets the lowest performance because the image features depends in the light conditions since the statue has the same color everywhere so the shape of the features is strongly dependent of shadows and shadings. Besides, most of the related videos capture the object under extreme point of view (from helicopter) hard to recognize even for the human eye.

The frame selection (video subsampling) is performed in 454.5 fps, and the percentage of time spent in each step of this task is shown in Fig. 5.

Once the object representation is built and the videos are subsampled, the relevance shot detection is done on 208 fps (faster than real-time). The matching task for building the model is the most expensive stage in time and computation resources but it is independent on the length of the short-list and frame selection, moreover the geometric relationship between views (pool of images) are computed during the Iconoid shifting for finding the reference image.

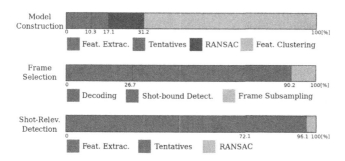

Fig. 5. The fraction of the time spent in the main steps of the relevance-shot detection (in %): building the object representation (top), the frame selection (middle) and the detection task (bottom)

5 Conclusions

In the paper, we have considered the following problem. Given a set of images that includes images of an object of interest and possibly outliers and a pool of videos, re-rank the videos by relevance to the object of interest. Further, the videos are augmented with a list of shots depicting the object of interest. The proposed approach first builds a visual model of the object of interest based on local image features. The relevant shot detection builds on wide baseline stereo matching. Shot relevance is defined as the recording time spent capturing the object of interest reflected in the number of frames depicting it. A number of algorithmic options have been experimentally evaluated. The experiments were carried out on a set of 100 videos collected querying You-Tube with 10 different text phrases.

The best performing method builds the model as a union of features from all example images and constructed the tentative correspondences using the 1st geometrically inconsistent rule. Averaged over the 10 landmarks, mAP is 0.92 querying the object model based on salient features that turns out to outperforms the union model by 2% on mAP. The implementation runs faster than real-time at 208 fps.

Acknowledgments. Javier Aldana-Iuit was supported by CONCIYTEY-CONACYT-Mexico PhD scholarship 216786, DGRI-SEP and Project SGS13/142/OHK3/2T/13. Ondřej Chum was supported by the project GACR P103/12/2310. Jiři Matas was supported by the Czech Science Foundation project GACR P103/12/G084.

References

1. Arandjelović, R., Zisserman, A.: Multiple queries for large scale specific object retrieval. In: British Machine Vision Conference (2012)
2. Boreczky, J.S., Rowe, L.A.: Comparison of video shot boundary detection techniques. In: Storage and Retrieval for Still Image and Video Databases IV, pp. 170–179 (1996)
3. Chum, O., Matas, J., Kittler, J.: Locally optimized ransac. In: Michaelis, B., Krell, G. (eds.) DAGM 2003. LNCS, vol. 2781, pp. 236–243. Springer, Heidelberg (2003). http://dx.doi.org/10.1007/978-3-540-45243-0_31
4. Chum, O., Philbin, J., Sivic, J., Isard, M., Zisserman, A.: Total recall: Automatic query expansion with a generative feature model for object retrieval. In: ICCV (2007)
5. Ester, M., Kriegel, H.-P., Sander, J., Xu, X.: A density-based algorithm for discovering clusters in large spatial databases with noise, pp. 226–231. AAAI Press (1996)
6. Jegou, H., Douze, M., Schmid, C.: Hamming embedding and weak geometric consistency for large scale image search. In: Forsyth, D., Torr, P., Zisserman, A. (eds.) ECCV 2008, Part I. LNCS, vol. 5302, pp. 304–317. Springer, Heidelberg (2008)
7. Koniusz, P., Yan, F., Mikolajczyk, K.: Comparison of mid-level feature coding approaches and pooling strategies in visual concept detection. Computer Vision and Image Understanding **117**(5), 479–492 (2013). http://www.sciencedirect.com/science/article/pii/S1077314212001725
8. Lowe, D.G.: Object recognition from local scale-invariant features. In: ICCV, pp. 1150–1157 (1999)
9. Matas, J., Obdrzlek, S., Chum, O.: Local affine frames for wide-baseline stereo. In: ICPR (4), pp. 363–366 (2002), http://dblp.uni-trier.de/db/conf/icpr/icpr2002-4.html#MatasOC02
10. Mikolajczyk, K., Tuytelaars, T., Schmid, C., Zisserman, A., Matas, J., Schaffalitzky, F., Kadir, T., Gool, L.V.: A comparison of affine region detectors. Int. J. Comput. Vision **65**(1–2), 43–72 (2005). http://dx.doi.org/10.1007/s11263-005-3848-x
11. Mikulík, A., Perdoch, M., Chum, O., Matas, J.: Learning a fine vocabulary. In: Daniilidis, K., Maragos, P., Paragios, N. (eds.) ECCV 2010, Part III. LNCS, vol. 6313, pp. 1–14. Springer, Heidelberg (2010)
12. Mishkin, D., Perdoch, M., Matas, J.: Two-view matching with view synthesis revisited. In: IVCNZ, pp. 436–441 (2013)
13. Muja, M., Lowe, D.G.: Fast approximate nearest neighbors with automatic algorithm configuration. In: International Conference on Computer Vision Theory and Application (VISSAPP 2009), pp. 331–340. INSTICC Press (2009)
14. Philbin, J., Chum, O., Isard, M., Sivic, J., Zisserman, A.: Object retrieval with large vocabularies and fast spatial matching. In: CVPR (2007)
15. Sivic, J., Schaffalitzky, F., Zisserman, A.: Object level grouping for video shots. In: Pajdla, T., Matas, J.G. (eds.) ECCV 2004. LNCS, vol. 3022, pp. 85–98. Springer, Heidelberg (2004)
16. Sivic, J., Zisserman, A.: Video Google: A text retrieval approach to object matching in videos. In: ICCV (2003)
17. Turcot, P., Lowe, D.G.: Better matching with fewer features: The selection of useful features in large database recognition problems. In: ICCV Workshop LAVD (2009)
18. Weyand, T., Leibe, B.: Discovering favorite views of popular places with iconoid shift. In: Metaxas, D.N., Quan, L., Sanfeliu, A., Gool, L.J.V. (eds.) ICCV, pp. 1132–1139. IEEE (2011), http://dblp.uni-trier.de/db/conf/iccv/iccv2011.html#WeyandL11

Remote Sensing

Delineation of Martian Craters Based on Edge Maps and Dynamic Programming

Jorge S. Marques[1] and Pedro Pina[2(✉)]

[1] ISR, Instituto Superior Técnico, Av. Rovisco Pais, 1049–001 Lisboa, Portugal
[2] CERENA, Instituto Superior Técnico, Av. Rovisco Pais, 1049–001 Lisboa, Portugal
jsm@isr.ist.utl.pt, ppina@tecnico.ulisboa.pt

Abstract. The delineation of impact craters is performed with a novel algorithm working in polar coordinates. The intensity transitions are determined along radial lines intersecting the center of the crater (Edge Map) being the optimal path, which corresponds to the minimization of an energy functional, computed by Dynamic Programming. The approach is tested on 8 HiRISE scenes on Mars, achieving a performance of 95 % of correct delineations.

Keywords: Crater rim · Edge map · Dynamic Programming · Mars

1 Introduction

The detection of impact craters on remotely sensed images from planetary surfaces is being done with an increasing number of automated approaches. A consistent evolution is observed in the last decade [1–9] with significant improvements that permit their use in the creation of crater catalogues [10–12]. Nevertheless, all these detections are represented in a simplified manner: each crater is described by a dimension (average diameter) and a location (coordinates of its centre), that is, by a perfect circular shape. The assimitries and irregularities of contours are thus not taken into account. Although these features are not fundamental for establishing surface chronologies [13], their availability at large scale is crucial to a better understanding of the resurfacing history and of the past climates on Mars [14]. The automated delineation of impact craters has only been done so far on two approaches: one based on a judicious sequence to find and link the crater edges in polar coordinates [15], the other based on the watershed transform and other mathematical morphology operators [16]. The initial results achieved a very good degree of success, but faced some difficulties when the datasets were enlarged, being not able to estimate a contour in a large amount of the samples and being too sensitive to local textural variations. Since there was an evident degradation of the performance in the most difficult examples, there still exists enough space for improvements. Therefore, we propose a novel algorithm to overcome those difficulties which is built into two main steps: edge enhancement in polar coordinates and crater delineation.

© Springer International Publishing Switzerland 2014
A. Campilho and M. Kamel (Eds.): ICIAR 2014, Part I, LNCS 8814, pp. 433–440, 2014.
DOI: 10.1007/978-3-319-11758-4_47

2   Algorithm

2.1   Overview

We assume that, to estimate the crater boundary contour, we know the location and radius of each crater. Even though we know this information in advance, crater delineation is a chalenging task since crater images often present low contrast between the crater rim and surrounding terrains making the detection of the rim very subtle.

The first step of the algorithm relies on intensity variation and tries to detect the intensity changes associated with the crater rim, while the second step tries to link the edges using geometric information.

Unfortunately, simple edge detection and linking approaches fail in this kind of images. Edge detection algorithms provide unreliable edges most of them associated to the terrain irregularities. To circumvent this difficulty, this paper defines a continuous edge map, $e(\mathbf{x}) \in [0, 1]$, which measures the amount of directional intensity variation in the vicinity of each point $\mathbf{x}$. A value $e(\mathbf{x}) = 0$ is assigned to a pixel $\mathbf{x}$ if there is strong intensity variation in the vicinity of $\mathbf{x}$ in a direction orthogonal to the crater contour. On the contrary, a value $e(\mathbf{x}) = 1$ is assigned if the image is constant in such direction. In the second step, we compute a closed contour, $\mathbf{x}(s)$, that minimizes an energy functional

$$E = \int e(\mathbf{x}(s))ds + E_{int}(\mathbf{x}) , \qquad (1)$$

similar to the one used in the snake algorithm [17,18]; $E_{int}(\mathbf{x})$ denotes the internal energy which measures deviations of the crater contour, $\mathbf{x}(s)$, with respect to a circle and s denotes the arc length parameter of the curve.

It should be stressed that both operations become simpler and more effective if the image is converted from Cartesian to polar coordinates. This conversion is performed according to the procedure presented in [15].

2.2   Edge Map

We wish to define an edge map in polar coordinates $e(r, \theta)$. This map should assign a low value to points which are likely to be edges and high values to points which are not. We will assume that edges are associated to intensity transitions along radial lines intersecting the crater center, $\mathbf{c}$ (θ constant).

The radial gradient is defined as

$$g(r, \theta) = |P(r, \theta) * h(r)| , \qquad (2)$$

where $|.|$ is the absolute value, $P(r, \theta)$ is the input image in polar coordinates (r, θ), $*$ denotes the convolution operation along the columns of P and $h(r)$ is the impulse response of a highpass filter, defined by $h(r) = -u(r - T) + 2u(r) - u(r + T)$ where $u(r)$ is the unit step function. This convolution can be computed extremely fast if we compute the integral image along the columns of P [20].

After computing the gradient, the edge map is obtained using the logistic function

$$\epsilon(r,\theta) = \frac{2}{1 + e^{sg(r,\theta)}} \,, \tag{3}$$

which is often used to map the gradient intensity $g \in [0, +\infty[$ into an edge confidence $\epsilon \in [0, 1[$; s is a scale parameter. Since we have a good estimation of the radius of the crater, R, we will restrict r to an interval $[r_{min}, r_{max}]$ centered on R.

Fig. 1 shows the conversion from Cartesian to polar coordinates, assuming that $r_{min} = 0.8R, r_{max} = 1.2R$, and the corresponding edge map (right). The first and last rows of the edge map are padded with high intensity values since the highpass filtering results are unreliable.

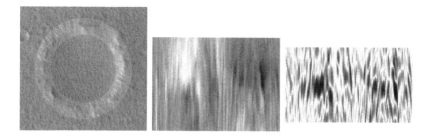

Fig. 1. Image transformation: original image and sampling points (left), polar image (centre) and edge map (right)

2.3 Crater Delineation

The second step concerns crater delineation. We will assume that the edge map, ϵ, has M lines and N columns. The crater boundary is characterized by a sequence of row indices $\mathbf{r} = (r_1, r_2, \ldots, r_N)$ such that $r_t \in \{1, \ldots, M\}$. These indices represent the crater radius for each direction. If the crater boundary was a circle centered at $\mathbf{c}$, then the index sequence would be constant. In practice, the radius r_t changes slowly and must obey the boundary condition $r_1 = r_N = k$ (k unknown), since it represents a closed contour. Fig. 2 shows the edge map and the estimated countour in polar and Cartesian coordinates.

The contour sequence, $\mathbf{r}$, is chosen to minimize an energy functional

$$E(\mathbf{r}) = \epsilon(1, r_1 = k) + \sum_{p=2}^{N} \epsilon(p, r_p) + c(r_{p-1}, r_p) \,, \tag{4}$$

where $\epsilon(p, r_p)$ is the edge map and $c(r_{p-1}, r_p)$ denotes the cost associated to the transition from r_{p-1} to r_p. For the moment, we assume that r_1 is known ($r_1 = k$). In addition, we also assume that $|r_p - r_{p-1}| \leq 1$ to enforce smooth transitions and the transition cost is defined by

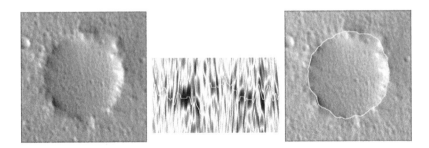

Fig. 2. Contour delineation: original image (left), edgemap and optimal contour (centre) and transformed contour (right)

$$c(r_{p-1}, r_p) = \begin{cases} 0 & \text{if } |r_p - r_{p-1}| = 0 \\ \alpha & \text{if } |r_p - r_{p-1}| = 1 \\ +\infty & \text{otherwise} \end{cases} . \tag{5}$$

The minimization of $E(r)$ under the constraint $r_1 = r_N = k$ can be solved by Dynamic Programming [21,22]. Dynamic Programming minimizes $E(r)$ in two steps. The first step computes the optimal costs to go from column 1 and line k to column t and line j, $E_t(j)$,

$$E_t(j) = \min_{r_2, \dots, r_t : r_t = j} \left[\epsilon(1, r_1 = k) + \sum_{p=2}^{t} \epsilon(p, r_p) + c(r_{p-1}, r_p) \right] . \tag{6}$$

The optimal costs are computed by a forward recursion

$$E_t(j) = \epsilon(t, j) + \min_i \left[E_{t-1}(i) + c(i, j) \right] . \tag{7}$$

Since we want to retrieve the optimal path, it is important to store which value of i minimizes $[E_{t-1}(i) + c(i, j)]$ in (7). This information can be stored using a set of a pointers

$$\psi_t(j) = \arg\min_i \left[E_{t-1}(i) + c(i, j) \right] . \tag{8}$$

After computing the optimal costs $E_t(j), t = 1, \dots, N, j = 1, \dots, M$, we know what is the minimum energy associated to an optimal path $r_1^*, \dots, r_N^*$ ending in $r_N^* = k$. The optimal path $\mathbf{r}^* = (r_1^*, r_2^*, \dots, r_N^*)$ such that $r_N^* = k$, can be obtained by backtracking

$$r_{t-1}^* = \psi_t(r_t^*) \qquad t = N, \dots, 2 . \tag{9}$$

The Dynamic Programming algorithm under the restriction $r_1 = r_N = k$ is summarized in Table 1. It provides the optimal path assuming that we know the boundary conditions k. Since the optimal k is unknown we repeat this procedure for all possible values of $k \in \{1, \dots, M\}$ and choose the one which minimizes the energy.

Table 1. Dynamic Programming algorithm with boundary conditions $r_1 = r_N = k$

Forward recursion: computation of the optimal energies

$$E_1(j) = \begin{cases} \epsilon(1,k) & \text{if } j = k \\ +\infty & \text{otherwise} \end{cases}$$

$$E_t(j) = \epsilon(t,j) + \min_i \left[E_{t-1}(i) + c(i,j) \right], \qquad t = 2, \ldots, N$$

$$\psi_t(j) = \arg\min_i \left[E_{t-1}(i) + c(i,j) \right], \qquad t = 2, \ldots, N$$

Backward recursion: computation of the optimal contour

$$r_N^* = k$$

$$r_{t-1}^* = \psi_t(r_t^*) \qquad t = N, \ldots, 2 .$$

---

3   Experimental Results

We tested the algorithm on the highest resolution images presently available from the surface of Mars, that is, those captured by the HiRISE camera onboard the Mars Reconnaisance Orbiter in the two commonly provided resolutions, 0.25 and 0.50 m/pixel, in a map projected product. Thus, we selected regions in both hemispheres, with noticeable differences in the amount of craters, also exhibiting a wide variety of erosions rates, from pristine craters (with sharp rims) to degraded structures (with irregular, faint or missing parts of the rim), and also some examples with craters hardly noticeable. The testing datasets are constituted by 8 HiRISE images and a total of 805 craters depicted from them. The following parameters were heuristically chosen: $N = 61$, $M = 360$, $T = 6$ and $\alpha = 0.02$.

We evaluate the performance of the algorithm through the comparison of the delineated contour with a manually created contour (ground-truth contour) for each and every crater of the dataset. Each crater was manually delineated, also estimating a contour in regions where the crater rim was absent, that is, creating always one single closed contour for each impact structure. The distortion between those pairs of contours was measured by the percentage of correct points (cp), small errors (se) and gross errors (ge), as defined in [15,16].

Each crater of the 8 images was individually analysed and a closed contour estimated by the current algorithm ('Dynamic Programming') and by one of the previous approaches ('Morphologic') [16]. In many pratical applications, like in this crater delineation problem, small errors are acceptable, so we focus mainly our attention on gross errors (those whose distance between contours is superior to 0.05 of the crater diameter).

The average performances obtained by both methods are shown in Table 2. The Dynamic Programming algorithm performs very well and leads to an overall error of only 5% of incorrect delineations. In comparison, the 'Morphologic' algorithm obtained a lower performance with an overall error of 10.5%.

Table 2. Average performances (%) of automated crater delineation (*cp*-correct points, *ge*-gross errors, *se*-small errors)

Dataset	Craters	Dyn. Prog.			Morphologic		
	(#)	*cp*	*se*	*ge*	*cp*	*se*	*ge*
8 images	805	60.1	34.9	5.0	45.8	43.7	10.5

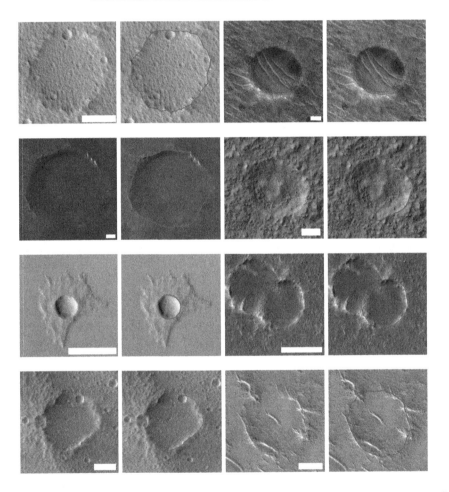

Fig. 3. Successful crater delineation examples (the white scale bars correspond to 50m) [image credits: NASA/JPL/University of Arizona]

The images of positive and negative examples, provided respectively in Fig. 3 and Fig. 4, are also a comprehensive illustration of the performances achieved by the algorithm. The proposed algorithm manages to delineate very difficult examples with high texture and missing rims. The number of failures is small and usually associated to strong geometric deformations of the crater rim in which the circular shape can no longer be assumed. These cases are very rare.

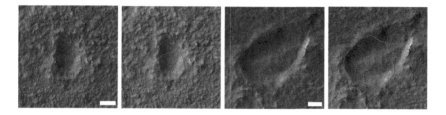

Fig. 4. Incorrect crater delineation examples (the white scale bars correspond to 50m) [image credits: NASA/JPL/University of Arizona]

4   Conclusions

In this study we presented a novel algorithm to delineate the boundary of impact craters previously detected on the surface of Mars. The proposed algorithm achieves very high performances (average error of 5%) in a diversified dataset of 805 craters and clearly outperformed the best available algorithm.

We consider that the exploitation of the *a priori* knowledge about the problem, like the circular geometry and image intensity patterns of the craters, and its integration into an optimization procedure, are the key features for the robustness and high success achieved by this novel algorithm. In particular, the geometry of the craters permits to adequately define a region of interest around its rim and hugely constrain the space of search for edges of interest. Moreover, the improved detection of the crater edges synthesized on the Edge Map and the detection of the optimal path (the crater contour) with the Dynamic Programming algorithm are also strong points. Finally, converting and processing the crater images into polar coordinates also greatly simplifies the processing and turns it into an additional advantage of the approach.

Acknowledgments. This work was developed in the frame of the projects PTDC/CTE-SPA/110909/2009 and PEst-OE/EEI/LA0009/2013, both funded by FCT-Fundação para a Ciência e a Tecnologia, Portugal.

References

1. Michael, G.: Coordinate registration by automated crater recognition. Planetary and Space Science **51**, 563–568 (2003)
2. Bue, B.D., Stepinski, T.F.: Machine detection of Martian impact craters from digital topography data. IEEE Trans. Geoscience & Remote Sensing **45**, 265–274 (2007)
3. Bandeira, L.P.C., Saraiva, J., Pina, P.: Development of a methodology for automated crater detection on planetary images. In: Martí, J., Benedí, J.M., Mendonça, A.M., Serrat, J. (eds.) IbPRIA 2007. LNCS, vol. 4477, pp. 193–200. Springer, Heidelberg (2007)
4. Bandeira, L., Saraiva, J., Pina, P.: Impact crater recognition on Mars based on a probability volume created by template matching. IEEE Trans. Geoscience & Remote Sensing **45**, 4008–4015 (2007)

5. Martins, R., Pina, P., Marques, J.S., Silveira, M.: Crater detection by a boosting approach. IEEE Geoscience and Remote Sensing Letters **6**, 127–131 (2009)
6. Urbach, E.R., Stepinski, T.F.: Automatic detection of sub-km craters in high resolution planetary images. Planetary and Space Science **57**, 880–887 (2009)
7. Bandeira, L., Ding, W., Stepinski, T.F.: Detection of sub-kilometer craters in high resolution planetary images using shape and texture features. Advances in Space Research **49**, 64–74 (2012)
8. Vijayan, S., Vani, K., Sanjeevi, S.: Crater detection, classification and contextual information extraction in lunar images using a novel algorithm. Icarus **226**, 798–815 (2013)
9. Jin, S., Zhang, T.: Automatic detection of impact craters on Mars using a modified adaboosting method. Planetary and Space Science (in press, 2014)
10. Salamunićcar, G., Lončarić, S., Pina, P., Bandeira, L., Saraiva, J.: MA130301GT catalogue of Martian impact craters and advanced evaluation of crater detection algorithms using diverse topography and image datasets. Planetary and Space Science **59**, 111–131 (2011)
11. Salamunićcar, G., Lončarić, S., Mazarico, E.: LU60645GT and MA132843GT catalogues of Lunar and Martian impact craters developed using a Crater Shape-based interpolation crater detection algorithm for topography data. Planetary and Space Science **60**, 236–247 (2012)
12. Salamunićcar, G., Lončarić, S., Pina, P., Bandeira, L., Saraiva, J.: Integrated method for crater detection from topography and optical images and the new PH9224GT catalogue of Phobos impact craters. Advances in Space Research **53**, 1798–1809 (2014)
13. Hartmann, W.K., Neukum, G.: Cratering chronology and the evolution of Mars. Space Science Reviews **96**, 165–194 (2001)
14. Boyce, J.M., Garbeil, H.: Geometric relationships of pristine Martian complex impact craters, and their implications to Mars geologic history. Geophysical Research Letters **34**, L16201 (2007)
15. Marques, J.S., Pina, P.: An algorithm for the delineation of craters in very high resolution images of mars surface. In: Sanches, J.M., Micó, L., Cardoso, J.S. (eds.) IbPRIA 2013. LNCS, vol. 7887, pp. 213–220. Springer, Heidelberg (2013)
16. Pina, P., Marques, J.S.: Delineation of impact craters by a mathematical morphology based approach. In: Kamel, M., Campilho, A. (eds.) ICIAR 2013. LNCS, vol. 7950, pp. 717–725. Springer, Heidelberg (2013)
17. Kass, M., Witkin, A., Terzopoulos, D.: Snakes: Active contour models. International Journal of Computer Vision **1**, 321–331 (1988)
18. Blake, A., Isard, M.: Active Contours. Springer (1998)
19. Szeliski, R.: Computer vision: algorithms and applications. Springer (2011)
20. Viola, P., Jones, M.: Robust real-time object detection. International Journal of Computer Vision (2002)
21. Bellman, R.E.: The Bellman Continuum. A collection of the works of Richard E. Bellman, Robert S. Roth (ed.) World Scientific (1986)
22. Bertsekas, D.: Dynamic Programming and optimal control. Athena Scientific (2005)

Automatic Interpretation of Remotely Sensed Images for Urban Form Assessment

John Mashford[1]([✉]), Felix Lipkin[1], Charlelie Olie[2],
Mailys Cuchennec[2], and Yong Song[1]

[1] Commonwealth Scientific and Industrial Research Organisation (CSIRO),
Melbourne, Australia
john.mashford@csiro.au
[2] Université de Technologie de Compiègne, Compiègne, France

Abstract. A system for generating information for an urban inventory by analysing remotely sensed or ground based sensed images is described. The urban inventory contains information about all land parcels in an urban area and the information is stored in a GIS database. The analysis system uses the semi-hierarchical multiresolution MCV image labeling algorithm and ensemble SVM classifiers to detect building footprints, trees and other urban land cover classes. The system has high accuracy for building footprint and tree detection on the data on which it has been tested.

1 Introduction

Urban form assessment through the automatic processing of remotely sensed data has wide application in areas such as cartography, urban planning, military intelligence, disaster (e.g. flood or bushfire) management and environmental modelling. Despite the value of this information, automated extraction of reliable urban form remains an extremely challenging field of research. Urban form assessment involves the determination of building footprints, identification of features such as trees, roads parks and so on. It may also involve 3-D building reconstruction and building material determination.

The ability to determine building footprints requires the ability to distinguish building objects from non-building objects such as trees, natural ground and artificial ground. The problem is a special case of the general problem of land cover classification. Data for such problems can be in the form of multispectral images obtained by satellite, aerial photography images, light detection and ranging (lidar) images, synthetic aperture radar (SAR) images or a combination of two or more of these. Lidar images can be in the form of point clouds derived from the processing of single laser echoes (first echo or last echo), multiple echoes (ME) images or full waveform (FW) images.

There are at least four general approaches to building detection. These are the pixel-based approach, the structural approach, the object-based approach

© Springer International Publishing Switzerland 2014
A. Campilho and M. Kamel (Eds.): ICIAR 2014, Part I, LNCS 8814, pp. 441–449, 2014.
DOI: 10.1007/978-3-319-11758-4_48

and the stochastic geometry approach. In the pixel-based approach features are extracted for each pixel in a remotely sensed image or a collection of georeferenced multisource remote sensing data and the feature vector is classified by a classifier such as an artificial neural network (ANN), a support vector machine (SVM) or a decision tree classifier (e.g. see[1]). In the stochastic geometry approach stochastic processes are used to generate geometric elements (e.g. see [2]). In the commonly used structural approach building elements are generated in a bottom up fashion from line, corner and other elements (e.g. see [3]). In the object-based approach the image is first partitioned (segmented) into regions comprising objects or parts of objects and then the regions are classified and analysed [4,5].

Applications of urban form assessment are aligned with areas of strategic national importance such as improved infrastructure planning and failure prediction, understanding trends in urban design with relevance to energy efficiency and carbon footprints, and estimation of bushfire vulnerability in peri-urban environments. A major research area is the analysis of risk exposure and developing implementable adaptation options for responding to extreme weather events such as bushfires, inundation, wind gusts and heat waves as well as less severe but more frequent events that impact people in their built environments. Information about urban form including building footprint, 3-D building model, building material and pervious/impervious surface distinction is very important for such analysis.

We have developed a system for the automatic generation of an urban inventory. The Urban Inventory project has the goal of populating a GIS database with information about houses or other buildings in a region such as building footprint, nearby trees, nearby roads, pervious/impervious surface classification and other useful properties. The Urban Inventory database has information about each parcel of land obtained from local government. It also has a number of images of each house or building such as 3 Google Street View images and 3 Google Earth images. The principal goal of the Urban Inventory project is to process these images using computer vision techniques to obtain information about the buildings.

We have pursued an object-based approach utilizing an effective image labeling algorithm called MCV.

2   MCV (Markov Concurrent Vision)

Computer vision systems typically operate in a number of stages or modules, these being, image segmentation, image classification, image analysis and high-level systems such as rule-based systems. Mashford [6,7] proposed that the first two of these stages can be carried out concurrently and MCV has some aspects of this concurrency. MCV is a method for image segmentation or, more generally, image labeling.

Image segmentation is the process of partitioning an image up into a number of regions corresponding to physical objects or other significant or meaningful

Fig. 1. Google Street View image

components. An intermediate step towards this goal is to partition an image into regions over which the image is homogeneous or at least locally homogeneous. To carry this out we must have a precise definition of what we mean by homogeneous and locally homogeneous. Intuitively, a region of an image is homogeneous if properties of a pixel at any point in the region are the same as or similar to properties of a pixel at any other point. Such properties may be pixel values or features computed from a neighbourhood of the pixel under consideration. A region is locally homogeneous if nearby pixels have similar properties.

MCV produces more than a simple segmentation partition, it produces a sequence of partitions. It is a semi-hierarchical algorithm commencing with a partition made up of single pixel regions. Regions are partially merged at any level of the process if they have a common boundary point such that the image over a certain window centred on that point is homogeneous according to a Markov random field (MRF) criterion [8]. An image over a region can be declared to be homogeneous if its probability of formation by the MRF stochastic process is sufficiently large. This condition can be recast in terms of the condition that a certain energy value associated with the image over the region is less than a certain Markovian threshold. If a Gaussian MRF is used and multiresolution image pyramids are used to relate the image evaluation at different levels then the evaluation of a region for homogeneity can be effected by a hard-wired neural network. MCV in this form is a fully automatic and unsupervised algorithm with

Fig. 2. Result of MCV algorithm applied to image of Figure 1 (objects identified)

only two adjustable parameters or functions, Markov threshold and number of levels [9].

Let $X = \{1, \ldots, m\} \times \{1, \ldots, n\}$ be the image lattice. Let V be the set of values taken by pixels. Then an image can be considered to be a map $\omega : X \to V$. For greyscale images $V = \{0, \ldots, d - 1\}$ for some $d \geq 2$ (e.g. $d = 256$), while for color images $V = \{(v_1, v_2, v_3) : 0 \leq v_1, v_2, v_3 \leq d - 1\}$ for some $d \geq 2$ is the set of RGB triples. More generally, V may be a set of vectors of multispectral components or feature vectors.

Define a point $x \in X$ to be a boundary point of a region $R \subset X$ if

$$(x + W_0) \cap R \neq \emptyset \text{ and } (x + W_0) \backslash R \neq \emptyset, \tag{1}$$

where $W_0 \subset \mathbf{Z}^2$ is the fundamental neighbourhood of the origin e.g. the usual 9-neighbourhood. The MCV algorithm is a semi-hierarchical algorithm which operates iteratively at a number of levels from level $= 1$ to level $= N$. In general, one needs to specify

1. a sequence $W_1 \subset W_2 \subset \ldots \subset W_N \subset \mathbf{Z}^2$ of evaluation windows
2. a sequence $\Psi_1 \subset \Psi_2 \subset \ldots \Psi_N \subset \mathbf{Z}^2$ of merge windows
3. evaluation functions $E_i : \Omega(R) \to \{0, 1\}$ for all $i = 1, \ldots, N$ and $R \subset W_i$
4. a permutation π of X e.g. raster scan

The MCV algorithm generates a sequence of partitions of X as follows.

Fig. 3. Google Earth image

1. initialize $\Pi = \{\{x\} : x \in X\}$
2. for $i = 1, \ldots N$
    for $j = 1 \ldots mn$
    (a) if $\pi(j)$ is a boundary pixel evaluate ω in the window $(\pi(j) + W_i) \cap X$
    (b) if it is homogeneous then compute the region $M_1(x, \Pi)$ and the collections of regions $M_2(x, \Pi)$ and $M_3(x, \Pi)$ and update Π according to
    $\Pi := \{M_1(x, \Pi)\} \cup M_2(x, \Pi) \cup M_3(x, \Pi),$

where

$$M_1(x, \Pi) = \cup\{R \cap (x + \Psi) : R \in \Pi, R \cap (x + W_0) \neq \emptyset\}, \tag{2}$$

$$M_2(x, \Pi) = \{R \in \Pi : R \cap (x + W_0) = \emptyset\}, \tag{3}$$

$$M_3(x, \Pi) = \{R \backslash M_1(x, \Pi) : R \in \Pi, R \cap (x + W_0) \neq \emptyset\}. \tag{4}$$

In the MCV algorithm sub-images $\omega : R \to V$ are evaluated for homogeneity by computing the probability $p(\omega)$ that the image was generated by a given Markov random field (MRF) model (e.g. a Gaussian MRF). Thus in the current implementation

$$p(\omega) = \frac{1}{Z(T)} \exp(-U(\omega)/T), \tag{5}$$

$$U(\omega) = \sum_{x \in R} d(\omega(x), \sum_{y \in G_x} \theta_x(y)\omega(y))^2, \tag{6}$$

Fig. 4. Result of MCV algorithm applied to image of Figure 3

$$d(u, v) = \sum_{i=1}^{b} ((v_i - u_i)^2)^{\frac{1}{2}}, \tag{7}$$

where $\{G_x : x \in X\}$ is the neighbourhood system, $\{\theta_x : x \in X\}$ is the neural weight system, b is the number of bands i.e. $V = \mathbf{R}^b$ and $Z(T)$ is a normalising factor.

MCV will be extensively compared with other methods (state of the art) and the results will be presented in a forthcoming paper. MCV has been tested on images from the Berkeley segmentation database with some good results and some poor results. The Berkeley segmentation databas is tailored to favour algorithms based on edge detection so it may not be a fair comparison. It is to be expected that extensions of MCV utilising MRFs other than GMRF and involving true concurrency will perform better, even on the biased Berkely segmentation database. MCV has also been tested on street scenes (Bourke Street, Melbourne, Australia) with good results.

3   Ensemble SVM Learning for Blob Classification

At each level of the MCV algorithm the image is partitioned up into a number of blobs. Blob classification is effected by a form of ensemble learning. A literature survey relating to methods of ensemble learning will be presented in

Table 1. Performance of the ensemble classifier for different thresholds

Threshold	True positives	False Positives	False Negatives	True Negatives
0.05	99.75	0.25	39.01	60.99
0.1	99.75	0.25	39.01	60.99
0.15	98.48	1.52	16.34	83.66
0.2	98.48	1.52	16.34	83.66
0.25	98.48	1.52	14.46	85.54
0.3	94.67	5.33	5.05	94.95
0.35	94.67	5.33	5.05	94.95
0.4	88.07	11.93	1.81	98.19
0.45	80.46	19.54	1.36	98.64
0.5	80.20	19.80	1.13	98.87
0.55	56.85	43.15	0.15	99.85
0.6	56.85	43.15	0.15	99.85
0.65	38.58	61.42	0.00	100.00
0.7	26.14	73.86	0.00	100.0

a forthcoming journal paper. The blobs merge (and sometimes break up) as the algorithm proceeds. It is observed that at some level a blob represents well an object such as a rooftop (for Google Earth images) or a tree (for Google Street View images) but then at a higher level it might merge with another object (e.g. a rooftop might merge with a nearby tree, or a tree might merge with the vertical face of a house) or a shadow. Also using different Markov thresholds results in different sequences of partitions. There seems to be an optimal level and/or threshold for any given object.

In a fully concurrent system the blob classification would occur in concert with the iterative image labeling process. However, in our present implementation, we carry out blob classification in a *post factum* fashion in which all the blobs associated with various levels and Markov thresholds of the MCV algorithm are saved to the GIS database and the blobs in the database are then processed using an ensemble of support vector machines (SVMs). Each of the SVMs acts on a feature vector derived from each blob input to it. The features computed for a blob which are then fed into various SVMs are

1. multiscale blob boundary curvature features
2. Hough features
3. Gabor features
4. blob area, perimeter
5. color features
6. features relating to location of blob within associated land parcel

Each SVM outputs a probability [10] and a total score of the ensemble classifier is computed by taking the weighted sum of the outputs of the various dedicated SVMs weighted by their training accuracies over a number of iterations of a bootstrap aggregation (bagging) procedure [11].

4 Results

One can declare a blob to be classified as a building if its total score as output by the ensemble classifier exceeds some threshold. Different thresholds result in different performance accuracies with a trade off between overall accuracy, false positives and false negatives as is shown in Table 1. This table describes performance of the system on a large collection of images obtained from Google earth images of Parramatta, Sydney, Australia.

There is a tradeoff between false positives and false negatives. Excellent results seem to be achieved with a threshold of 0.3. The results would be different with different SVM design (e.g. non-RBF kernel) and different ensemble learning algorithm (e.g. non-bagging).

5 Conclusion

The results of this work will have wide application in urban sustainability and adaptive capacity research with high definition 4-D urban forms (time series of building footprint, height and material information). Subsequent work may involve further development of rule-based approaches. Other AI techniques such as fuzzy logic or Bayesian reasoning may be useful for the purpose of data fusion which is necessary to integrate all the information which is available about each house or other building in a region. Thus, for example, computer vision techniques can be applied to different images of a house resulting in different symbolic high-level descriptions. Data fusion can be used to combine these high-level descriptions into one overall description which may be probabilistic or fuzzy, e.g. statements may have associated certainty factors. Alternatively, data fusion can be applied at a lower level of the vision system, e.g. at the level of image classification.

Acknowledgments. The authors thank Stewart Burn and Xiaoming Wang for supporting this work. The work was funded by the then CSIRO Water for a Health Country and Climate Adaptation Flagships.

References

1. Guo, L., Chehata, N., Mallet, C., Boukir, S.: Relevance of airborne lidar and multispectral image data for urban scene classification using Random Forests. ISPRS Journal of Photogrammetry and Remote Sensing **66**, 56–66 (2011)
2. Ortner, M., Descombes, X., Zerubia, J.: A marked point process of rectangles and segments for automatic analysis of digital elevation models. IEEE Transactions on Pattern Analysis and Machine Intelligence **30**(1), 105–119 (2008)
3. Wang, Q., Jiang, Z., Yang, J., Zhao, D., Shi, Z.: A hierarchical connection graph algorithm for gable-roof detection in aerial image. IEEE Geoscience and Remote Sensing Letters **8**(1), 177–181 (2011)
4. Zhou, W., Troy, A.: An object-oriented approach for analysing and characterizing urban landscape at the parcel level. International Journal of Remote Sensing **29**(11), 3119–3135 (2008)

5. Hu, Q., Wu, W., Xia, T., Yu, Q., Yang, P., Li, Z., Song, Q.: Exploring the use of Google Earth imagery and object-based methods in land use/cover mapping. Remote Sensing **5**, 6026–6042 (2013)
6. Mashford, J.S.: A method for the development of parallel concurrent machine vision systems. In: Proc. ICCIMA 1998 (International Conference on Computational Intelligence and Multimedia Applications 1998), World Scientific, pp. 378–383 (February 1998)
7. Mashford, J., Dai, W., Drogemuller, R., Marksjö, B.: Image classifier and scene understanding systems of multi-agent teams. In: Proc. 2000 IEEE International Conference on Systems, Man and Cybernetics, Nashville, Tennessee, USA, pp. 1460–1465 (October 2000)
8. Mashford, J.S.: A neural Markovian concurrent vision system for object identification and tracking. In: Proc. 2004 International Conference on Computational Intelligence for Modelling, Control and Automation, Gold Coast, Australia (2004)
9. Mashford, J.: Image segmentation using the MCV image labeling algorithm. In: Proc. 2013 International Conference on Image Processing, Computer Vision and Pattern Recognition, Las Vegas, USA, pp. 728–732 (2013)
10. Platt, J.: Probabilistic outputs for support vector machines and comparison to regularized likelihood methods. In: Smola, A.J., Bartlett, P.L., Schölkopf, B., Schuurmans, D. (eds.) Advances in Large Margin Classifiers. MIT Press, Cambridge (2000)
11. Brown, G., Wyatt, J., Harris, R., Yao, X.: Diversity creation methods: a survey and categorisation. Information Fusion **6**(1), 5–20 (2005)

Image Mosaicing by Camera Pose Estimation Based on Extended Kalman Filter

Alper Yildirim and Mustafa Unel[(✉)]

Faculty of Engineering and Natural Sciences, Sabanci University, Istanbul, Turkey
{alperyildirim,munel}@sabanciuniv.edu

Abstract. We develop a sequential image mosaicing approach for aerial images of pseudo-planar scenes which is based on the estimation of camera pose from images. We use Extended Kalman Filter (EKF) to update the camera pose and scene parameters with every new image which improves the global consistency of the mosaic. Proposed approach is tested on aerial images where visually appealing results are obtained and residuals are quantified.

1 Introduction

Image mosaicing is the process of combining sets of images captured from a scene and creating a large composite image which provides a better understanding of the scene than the separate images. It can be beneficial for many different areas such as personal, medical and remote sensing applications.

It is possible to create panoramas of natural scenes [3] with the images captured from an inexpensive camera. For medical applications, satisfying results are obtained for mosaicing of tissues [18], retinal images [7]. Image mosaicing also come into use in microscopic [6] and fingerprint [8] imaging. For remote sensing applications, it is used in aerial [13] and underwater [15] applications.

Different methods are proposed for mosaicing applications. One method is to approach the problem using graph theory tools. For example, Kang et al. use optimal paths in a graph to improve global consistency where graph represent the image connections [12]. Elibol et al. use Minimum Spanning Tree (MST) algorithm to infer structure of the mosaic [10]. Another possible strategy is to attack the problem by using a filtering framework. Using Simultaneous Localization and Mapping (SLAM) to create image mosaics is proposed by Civera et al. [9] for pure-rotational camera. They propose an EKF based SLAM approach for real time operation. Another EKF based approach is proposed by Caballero et al. [5] for aerial localization and image mosaicing. In their work, homograpy parameters are stored in the state vector and updated by EKF when loops are detected in the mosaic.

In this paper, we develop a new EKF based image mosaicing algorithm for aerial images captured from pseudo-planar scenes. Proposed method uses EKF to update the camera pose and scene normal parameters, and it is computationally more efficient than similar methods in the literature. It uses camera pose

© Springer International Publishing Switzerland 2014
A. Campilho and M. Kamel (Eds.): ICIAR 2014, Part I, LNCS 8814, pp. 450–457, 2014.
DOI: 10.1007/978-3-319-11758-4_49

parameters of all the images and a two parameter plane model for the scene instead of using homographies in the estimation.

The paper organization is as follows: Image mosaicing is outlined in Section 2. Proposed algorithm is presented in Section 3. Experimental results are provided in Section 4. Finally the paper is concluded with some remarks in Section 5.

2   Image Mosaicing

Image mosaicing involves merging the images captured from different camera poses after they are properly transformed. When the scene is assumed to be planar, coordinates of the scene points in different cameras can be mapped to each other by 3×3 homogeneous transformations. For cameras observing a common scene area, we can estimate the relative motion between two cameras by utilizing a homography estimation with the distinctive feature matches between images. For two images of different scene areas, homography can be calculated by combining homographies of the pairwise images linking these images to each other. However, small registration errors between pairwise images tend to accumulate over time. As a result, when images are aligned on a common reference frame by using this method, misregistrations occur at loop-closing regions because of the drift since local estimations are performed. It can be beneficial to use a tool which considers the global consistency of the mosaic during the estimations. For planar scene mosaicing, an EKF based approach is proposed by Caballero et al. [5] where EKF is used to propagate the feature errors through the mosaic by using the misregistrations at the loop closing regions of the mosaic to enhance global consistency.

In the next section, we propose a new algorithm where camera rotation and scaled translations extracted from the pairwise homographies are used in the estimation. We also include plane normal parameters of the dominant scene in the estimation. Extraction of these parameters from a pairwise homography is detailed in [14].

3   Proposed Approach

We use classical EKF loop to update the mosaic with every new image. In the state vector of the EKF, global rotation and translation parameters for every image and parameters of the dominant plane in the scene with respect to the first camera frame are concatenated. Rotations are parameterized by Euler angles ($E_i = \begin{bmatrix} \phi_i \ \theta_i \ \psi_i \end{bmatrix}$ for image i) which are defined as:

$$R_i = {}_1^i R = \begin{bmatrix} \cos \psi_i & -\sin \psi_i & 0 \\ \sin \psi_i & \cos \psi_i & 0 \\ 0 & 0 & 1 \end{bmatrix} \begin{bmatrix} \cos \theta_i & 0 & \sin \theta_i \\ 0 & 1 & 0 \\ -\sin \theta_i & 0 & \cos \theta_i \end{bmatrix} \begin{bmatrix} 1 & 0 & 0 \\ 0 & \cos \phi_i & -\sin \phi_i \\ 0 & \sin \phi_i & \cos \phi_i \end{bmatrix} \quad (1)$$

Plane normal vector is parameterized by a two parameter model (α, β) which is given as:

$$n = {}^1 n = \begin{bmatrix} \sin \alpha \sin \beta, \ \sin \alpha \cos \beta, \ \cos \alpha \end{bmatrix}^\mathsf{T} \quad (2)$$

For instance, after image I_i is included into the estimation, the state vector is given as:

$$x = \left(\alpha, \beta, E_2^\mathsf{T}, t_2^\mathsf{T}, E_3^\mathsf{T}, t_3^\mathsf{T}, \dots E_i^\mathsf{T}, t_i^\mathsf{T}\right)^\mathsf{T} \tag{3}$$

where t_i denotes the translation of the first camera frame in the ith camera frame. Our algorithm can be summarized as follows:

1. When a new image is captured, homography estimation is performed between new and the previous image(H_{ij} for new image i and previous image j. Relative rotation $\left(_j^i R\right)$ and scaled translation $\left(^i t_{ij}\right)$ are extracted from this homography and used to initialize new state vector variables (E_i, t_i).
2. Previous images intersecting with the new image are detected geometrically by using Separating Axis Theorem (SAT) and pairwise homography estimation is performed between the new and each of the previous images which are used as the measurements of the EKF.
3. State vector is updated by the update equations of the filter.

3.1   Prediction

When a new image is captured, its pairwise homography estimation is performed with the previous image. Relative camera pose is extracted as $_j^i R$ and $^i t_{ij}$ from this homography (H_{ij}). Since we know the pose of the previous camera frame and relative pose between the new and previous camera, new camera pose can be obtained. To find the covariances of the new parameters (E_i and t_i), we calculate the Jacobian of these parameters with respect to the state vector and relative pose parameters between images (E_{ij} and $^i t_{ij}$). Jacobian can be given as:

$$J = \frac{\partial \left[E_i \; t_i\right]}{\partial \left[x_{\text{old}} \; E_{ij} \; ^i t_{ij}\right]} \tag{4}$$

where E_{ij} is the Euler angle parameters obtained from $_j^i R$. New covariance matrix can be calculated as:

$$P_{\text{k}} = \begin{bmatrix} I & | & 0 \\ \hline & J & \end{bmatrix} \begin{bmatrix} P_{\text{k,old}} & 0 \\ 0 & C_{ij} \end{bmatrix} \begin{bmatrix} I & | & 0 \\ \hline & J & \end{bmatrix}^\mathsf{T} \tag{5}$$

where C_{ij} denotes the covariance matrix of the relative camera pose $\left[E_{ij} \; ^i t_{ij}\right]$. In this work, this covariance matrix is assumed to be a multiple of the identity matrix, i.e λI.

3.2   Measurement

New images are initialized by using its pairwise homography with the previous image. However, it is possible that new images also have common scene features with some of the other images in the mosaic. We can get better estimates of parameters by using all the previous images which have common features with the new image. As a result, during the measurement step, we propose to update the initialized estimates by using all the previous images which have common image features with the new image. This provides a better global consistency to our algorithm since we consider all the available data in the mosaic. To obtain the the previous images which have common features with the new image efficiently, we propose to use the Separating Axis Theorem (SAT).

Separating Axis Theorem. This theorem is used in computer graphics applications to detect collisions between objects [16]. Theorem simply states that if there exist a line for which the intervals of projection of the two objects onto that line do not intersect, we can conclude that the objects are separated. Since our images becomes 2D quadrilaterals when aligned to the mosaic and we know the rough alignment of the new image on the mosaic from the initialization procedure, we can detect which of the previous images intersect with the new image by this theorem. After all the intersecting images are detected, feature matching procedure is employed between the new image and the intersecting previous images to estimate the pairwise homographies between these images. These homographies are used to create measurements.

Measurement Function and Its Covariance. We first normalize the homographies to get a unique representation of estimations since an arbitrary multiple of a homography represent the same transformation. This is done by dividing the homographies to its Frobenius norm. Covariance matrices of the homographies are also required for estimation. However, these matrices are not invertible because of the redundant nature of the homography which cause problems during the inversion of the innovation covariance. As a result, we propose to perform a linear transformation on h_{ij} to construct measurements for which covariance matrix is invertible. We choose the measurements as:

$$z_{ij} = A_{ij} h_{ij} \tag{6}$$

where A_{ij} is a 8×9 matrix whose rows are orthogonal to h_{ij} and each other. To obtain the covariance matrix for the measurement H_{ij}, we use the procedure explained in [11]. Estimation is performed using the following steps:

1. Jacobian of the feature matches (J_i) are calculated with respect to the measurement parameters $(\frac{\partial x'}{\partial z_{ij}})$ and J matrix is formed as the vertical concatenation of these individual Jacobians.
2. Covariance matrix of the measurement is given as:

$$\Sigma_{z_{ij}} = \left(J^\mathsf{T} \Sigma_{x'}^{-1} J\right)^{-1} \tag{7}$$

where $\Sigma_{x'}$ is a block diagonal matrix whose diagonal elements are the covariance matrices of the feature coordinates. We take this matrix as identity.

3.3   Update

Measurements are used to update our state variable estimates (x_k) obtained from the image initialization step. Assume that there are n measurements obtained from the pairwise homographies. We construct a measurement vector (z) by concatenating all of the individual measurements. Covariance matrix of this measurement vector(R_z) is given with a block diagonal matrix where diagonal elements are the individual covariance matrices of the measurements. Predicted homographies are transformed by the same transformation matrices previously obtained for pairwise homographies. Update equations for the Kalman filter are given as:

$$S_k = Z_k P_k Z_k^\mathsf{T} + R_z \tag{8}$$

$$K_k = P_k Z_k^\mathsf{T} S_k^{-1} \tag{9}$$

$$x_{k+1} = x_k + K_k (z - \hat{z}) \tag{10}$$

where Z_k is the jacobian of the measurement function with respect to the state variables calculated at $x = x_k$.

4   Results

We implemented our algorithm on 'Cadastre in Switzerland' [1] and 'Gravel Quarry'[2] datasets. After the EKF estimations were completed, homographies between the images were calculated from the camera poses and the images were warped on a reference plane. We used SIFT features during our experiments. 58 sequential images were used for 'Cadastre in Switzerland' and 125 images were used for 'Gravel Quarry' dateset. Because of the seams caused by the illumination differences and small misregistrations in the mosaic, results were blended by using multi-band blending [4].

Image mosaic obtained from Cadastre is shown in Fig. 1. Since images are captured from an aerial vehicle which follows loopy trajectories, many loop closings appear during the estimations. Because of the EKF, it is expected that errors at these loop closings will be propagated through the mosaic. As a result, we expect a short tailed distribution cumulated around a mean value for the x-axis ant y-axis components of the residual vectors. Probability density functions (pdf) of the components of the residual vectors for Cadastre sequence are given in Fig. 2. It can be inferred from the figure that error is roughly cumulated around the zero mean for both components of the residual vectors and distributions have relatively short tales when it is considered that images are size of 1152×864. For comparison purposes, we also implemented a bundle adjustment algorithm [17] for the same image sequence. This was done by minimizing the sum-of-squares of the feature projection errors between matching images via Levenberg-Marquard algorithm where homographies of all the images are computed. As a quantitative evaluation of the error, root mean square (RMS) values of the feature projection errors calculated from 110257 feature matches

Fig. 1. Mosaic image of the Cadastre

are given in Table 1. Since image sizes (1152 × 864) are very large when compared to RMS values in the Table, visual differences between these two methods are almost negligible. Mosaic result for 'Gravel Quarry' is given in Figure 3. Bundle

Table 1. RMS values for Cadastre

Case	Total Matches	RMS(pix)
Proposed Algorithm	110257	8.8500
Bundle Adjustment	110257	2.4414

adjustment results are also obtained for this dataset. RMS values of the residual error in the mosaic are given in the Table 2. Again because of the large image sizes (1152 × 864), differences between the RMS values for both methods imply negligible visual seams.

Table 2. RMS values for Gravel Quarry

Case	Total Matches	RMS(pix)
Proposed Algorithm	564900	8.1588
Bundle Adjustment	564900	4.9318

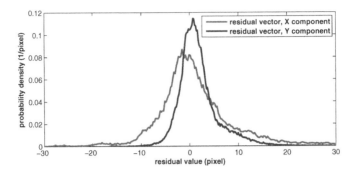

Fig. 2. PDFs for X and Y components of the residual vectors for Cadastre

Fig. 3. Mosaic image of the 'Gravel Quarry' dataset

5   Conclusions

We have now presented a new image mosaicing algorithm which works sequentially and is capable of creating image mosaics of pseudo-planar scenes. Extended Kalman Filter (EKF) has been used to update the camera pose and scene normal parameters with the new images that improves the global consistency of the mosaic. Results are both visually and numerically promising. More experimental work has to be done to see further potential of the proposed method.

Acknowledgments. Authors would like to acknowledge Pix4D for the test images and a trial version of Pix4Dmapper software.

References

1. http://www.pix4d.com (accessed: February 01, 2014)
2. https://www.sensefly.com/examples-of-postflight-processing.html (accessed: June 18, 2014)
3. Brown, M., Lowe, D.G.: Automatic panoramic image stitching using invariant features. Int. J. Comput. Vision **74**(1), 59–73 (2007). http://dx.doi.org/10.1007/s11263-006-0002-3
4. Burt, P.J., Adelson, E.H.: A multiresolution spline with application to image mosaics. ACM Trans. Graph. **2**(4), 217–236 (1983). http://doi.acm.org/10.1145/245.247
5. Caballero, F., Merino, L., Ferruz, J., Ollero, A.: Homography based kalman filter for mosaic building applications to uav position estimation. In: ICRA 2007, pp. 2004–2009 (2007)
6. Carozza, L., Bevilacqua, A., Piccinini, F.: Mosaicing of optical microscope imagery based on visual information. In: 2011 Annual International Conference of the IEEE Engineering in Medicine and Biology Society, EMBC, pp. 6162–6165 (2011)
7. Choe, T.E., Cohen, I., Lee, M., Medioni, G.: Optimal global mosaic generation from retinal images. In: Proceedings of the 18th International Conference on Pattern Recognition, ICPR 2006, vol. 3, pp. 681–684. IEEE Computer Society, Washington, DC (2006), http://dx.doi.org/10.1109/ICPR.2006.910
8. Choi, H., Choi, K., Kim, J.: Mosaicing touchless and mirror-reflected fingerprint images. IEEE Trans. Information Forensics and Security **5**(1), 52–61 (2010)
9. Civera, J., Davison, A.J., Magallón, J.A., Montiel, J.M.: Drift-free real-time sequential mosaicing. Int. J. Comput. Vision **81**(2), 128–137 (2009)
10. Elibol, A., Gracias, N., Garcia, R.: Fast topology estimation for image mosaicing using adaptive information thresholding. Robot. Auton. Syst. **61**(2), 125–136 (2013). http://dx.doi.org/10.1016/j.robot.2012.10.010
11. Hartley, R.I., Zisserman, A.: Multiple View Geometry in Computer Vision, 2nd edn. Cambridge University Press (2004), ISBN: 0521540518
12. Kang, E.Y., Cohen, I., Medioni, G.: A graph-based global registration for 2d mosaics. In: Proceedings of the 15th International Conference on Pattern Recognition, vol. 1, pp. 257–260 (2000)
13. Lin, Y., Medioni, G.: Map-enhanced uav image sequence registration and synchronization of multiple image sequences. In: IEEE Conference on Computer Vision and Pattern Recognition, CVPR 2007, pp. 1–7 (2007)
14. Malis, E., Vargas, M., et al.: Deeper understanding of the homography decomposition for vision-based control (2007)
15. Prados, R., Garcia, R., Gracias, N., Escartin, J., Neumann, L.: A novel blending technique for underwater gigamosaicing. IEEE Journal of Oceanic Engineering **37**(4), 626–644 (2012)
16. Schneider, P.J., Eberly, D.: Geometric Tools for Computer Graphics. Elsevier Science Inc., New York (2002)
17. Triggs, B., McLauchlan, P.F., Hartley, R.I., Fitzgibbon, A.W.: Bundle adjustment – a modern synthesis. In: Triggs, B., Zisserman, A., Szeliski, R. (eds.) ICCV-WS 1999. LNCS, vol. 1883, pp. 298–372. Springer, Heidelberg (2000)
18. Vercauteren, T., Perchant, A., Malandain, G., Pennec, X., Ayache, N.: Robust Mosaicing with Correction of Motion Distortions and Tissue Deformation for In Vivo Fibered Microscopy. Medical Image Analysis **10**(5), 673–692 (2006). http://hal.inria.fr/inria-00163961

Applications

A Fast Plain Copy-Move Detection Algorithm Based on Structural Pattern and 2D Rabin-Karp Rolling Hash

Kuznetsov Andrey Vladimirovich[1,2(✉)], and Myasnikov Vladislav Valerievich[1,2]

[1] Samara State Aerospace University (SSAU), Samara, Russia
[2] Image Processing Systems Institute of the Russian Academy of Sciences (IPSI RAS),
Samara, Russia
kuznetsov@outlook.com, vmyas@rambler.ru

Abstract. Image forgery detection problem is challenging and important for many years. One of the most frequently used type of forgery is copying and pasting content within the same image or copy-move. Copy-move forgery detection has become one of the most actively researched topics in blind image forensics. We propose a novel plain copy-move detection algorithm using structural pattern and two-dimensional Rabin-Karp rolling hash. The novelty of proposed method is zero false negative error and high execution speed for large images. We also present the results of quality and speed investigations of the proposed algorithm, which depend on structural pattern construction type.

Keywords: Forgery · Copy-move detection · Structural pattern · Rabin-Karp rolling hash

1 Introduction

A digital image is an important way to present visual information. Images are used for research, commercial and military purposes. Regardless of the field of use of digital images the end user must be sure that the data they contain is original and hasn't been changed. When we speak about original image, we mean that its data wasn't changed to improve quality, to preprocess for specific applied algorithms, to compress data, etc. These changes do not harm the end user, so their detection is not very significant. But it is much more important to detect changes that hide or replace information, stored in an image.

The first papers on developing algorithms for forgery or image tampering detection appeared in 2004-2005 [1, 2]. There have been analyzed several types of forgeries: resampling, copy-move, splicing, etc. The most frequently used type of image tampering is copying image fragment from one place and pasting it in another place of the same image (copy-move forgery). Thus between copying and pasting the fragment it can be geometrically transformed (scaling + rotation). Otherwise pasting is made after simple region translation (the so-called plain copy-move).

Actually researchers have achieved certain results in developing algorithms for transformed [3, 4, 5] and plain copy-move detection [6, 7] in the sense of tampering

© Springer International Publishing Switzerland 2014
A. Campilho and M. Kamel (Eds.): ICIAR 2014, Part I, LNCS 8814, pp. 461–468, 2014.
DOI: 10.1007/978-3-319-11758-4_50

detection quality criteria. These algorithms can be divided into two main groups: block-based [3, 4] and keypoint-based [5], which were analyzed in [8]. Experimental results showed that none of the existing plain copy-move detection algorithms [8] guarantees zero false negative error. It is caused by the standard of constructing copy-move detection algorithms [8], which proposes dividing image into overlapping blocks and calculating one or more features for each block. Furthermore this approach does not allow to use sliding window technique, because of high computational complexity – this is another reason for non zero false negative error. In addition there is a problem of non zero false positive error, which appears due to significant deviation of the analyzed image size from copy-move region size [8].

In this paper we propose a new plain copy-move detection algorithm with the following key features:

— guarantee of zero false negative error;
— high execution speed (provides real-time image analysis) and low computational complexity;
— mean value of false positive error is $10^{-5}\%$.

The proposed algorithm is based on several key points. First, we use sliding window approach instead of dividing image into non-overlapping blocks during analysis. It helps to analyze all possible image fragments. Second, we use a special structural pattern, which consists of several rectangular fragments. For all these fragments within a pattern we calculate values (characteristics) of a specific hash function. We propose a two-dimensional generalization of Rabin-Karp rolling hash algorithm for calculating these characteristics. We have also developed a recursive algorithm for hash value calculation. This is the key to reduce computational complexity and to provide an ability to use the proposed algorithm for large image analysis (5000×5000 pixels and more) in real-time mode.

2   Structural Pattern

Let $f(m,n)$ be an analyzed image. Under a structural pattern we mean a finite quadruply connected set of coordinates $\{(0,0),\hbar ,(m,n)\}$.

Let us consider a special *structural pattern* $\aleph(\Lambda,a,b)$ defined as follows:

$$\aleph(\Lambda,a,b) \equiv \underset{(m,n)\in\Lambda}{\hbar} \Pi(a,b,m,n) \qquad (1)$$

where the set of coordinates $\Pi(a,b,m,n)$ is defined as

$$\Pi(a,b,m,n) \equiv \hbar \left\{ \begin{array}{l} (m,n),(m,n+1),\hbar ,(m,n+b-1), \\ \\ (m+a-1,n),\hbar ,(m+a-1,n+b-1) \end{array} \right\} .$$

Parameter Λ defines pattern's structure. Let us say, that there are *duplicates by a pattern* $\aleph(\Lambda,a,b)$, if there are at least 2 pairs of coordinates (m',n') and (m'',n''), which satisfy the following equalities:

$$f(m'+m,n'+n)=f(m''+m,n''+n),$$
$$\forall(m,n)\in \aleph(\Lambda,a,b).$$

Searching a duplicate by a pattern $\aleph(\Lambda,a,b)$ is a task of determination for each image sample (m,n), which defines the upper left point of an image fragment with a form defined by a pattern $\aleph(\Lambda,a,b)$, a unique number $t(m,n)\in \mathbf{N}$, which characterizes an image fragment in the following way:

$$t(m,n)\equiv \begin{cases} 0, & no\ copy-move \\ >0, & copy\text{-}move\ type\ number \end{cases}.$$

We will also use a simplified form of a structural pattern further – an analysis window of size $a\times b$, which corresponds to the structural pattern $\aleph(\{(0,0)\},a,b)$ use.

It should be noted that structural pattern representation may not be unique. This ambiguity is the basis for experiments presented in Section 5.

Let us consider a *hash function* T of an image fragment with a form defined by a pattern $\aleph(\Lambda,a,b)$. This function converts intensity values of an image fragment to an integer nonnegative value in the range $[0,L-1]$.

3   Two-Dimensional Rabin-Karp Rolling Hash

3.1   Proposed Hash Function

Let there be given a structural pattern $\aleph(\{(0,0)\},a,b)$ and an image f, where $f(m,n)\in [0,2^q-1]$. Then a hash value for an image fragment will be calculated as a 2D generalization of Rabin-Karp rolling hash:

$$\begin{aligned} H(m,n,f)&\equiv f(m,n)\cdot 2^{q(ab-1)}+f(m,n+1)\cdot 2^{8(ab-2)}+... \\ &...+f(m,n+b-1)\cdot 2^{q(ab-b)}+...+f(m+a-1,n)\cdot 2^{q(b-1)}+ \\ &+f(m+a-1,n+1)\cdot 2^{q(b-2)}+...+f(m+a-1,n+b-1)\cdot 2^0. \end{aligned} \tag{2}$$

It is quite difficult to store such values in internal memory of a workstation because of the following problems:

— absence of standard numeric types for operating with large numbers;
— no possibility to allocate memory to store hash table of required size (hash table use will be described further).

To solve these problems we propose the following solution. According to Chinese remainder theorem (CRT) R modular representations of (2) can be defined in the following way:

$$H_r(m,n,f) \equiv H(m,n,f) \bmod b_r, \tag{3}$$

where b_r are coprime numbers. Moreover a system of R functions (3) guarantees one-to-one correspondence of an analyzed image fragment to a hash value. This fact allows to use any of remainders (3) as a hash value. We will take $b_r \gg 2^q - 1$ further.

3.2   Recursive Algorithm for Hash Value Calculation

Let us consider a standard form of function $H_r(m,n,f)$:

$$H_r(m,n,f) \equiv \begin{pmatrix} \left(f(m,n) \bmod b_r \cdot 2^{q(ab-1)} \bmod b_r\right) \bmod b_r + \\ +\left(f(m,n+1) \bmod b_r \cdot 2^{q(ab-2)} \bmod b_r\right) \bmod b_r + \dots \\ \dots + f(m+a-1,n+b-1) \bmod b_r \end{pmatrix} \bmod b_r. \tag{4}$$

Let us also consider the following simplifications to calculate the value of expression (4):

- $f(m,n) \bmod b_r = f(m,n)$ due to assumptions, that $f(m,n) \in \left[0, 2^q - 1\right]$ and $b_r \gg 2^q - 1$;
- $p_r^i = 2^{qi} \bmod b_r$, $i \in [1, b-1]$ can be calculated once before image analysis (no need to calculate these values for every sliding window position);
- $\bmod b_r$ calculation for every summand can be discarded, because the computable sum will not exceed a bit grid dimension (let us consider, that $b_r = 2^{31} - 1$, then the order of (4) equals $ab \cdot 2^q 2^{31}$, so the value of (4) can be stored in *LONG* numeric type if $ab < 2^{24}$).

In consideration of these simplifications, expression (4) is changed to the following:

$$H_r(m,n,f) = \begin{pmatrix} f(m,n)p_r^{ab-1} + \\ + f(m,n+1)p_r^{ab-2} + \dots \\ + f(m+a-1,n+b-1) \end{pmatrix} \bmod b_r. \tag{5}$$

It is convenient to use $b_0 = 2^{31} - 1$. For $b_i, i > 0$ we suggest to take prime numbers less than b_0.

Hash value (2) can be calculated recursive for a structural pattern $\aleph(\{(0,0)\},1,b)$ both for initial and modular representations as following:

$$H(m,n,f) = 2^q \left(H(m,n-1,f) - 2^{q(b-1)} f(m,n) \right) + f(m,n+b-1).$$

For a 2D structural pattern the recursive algorithm will be as following (for rows and columns correspondingly):

$$H(m,n+1,f) = 2^q H(m,n,f) -$$

$$- 2^{qab} f(m,n) + \sum_{i=1}^{a-1} 2^{qb(a-i)} \left(f(m+i-1,n+b-1) - f(m+i,n) \right) +$$

$$+ f(m+a-1,n+b-1),$$

$$H(m+1,n,f) = 2^{qb} \left(H(m,n,f) - \sum_{i=0}^{b-1} 2^{q(ab-i-1)} f(m,n+i) \right) + \sum_{i=1}^{b} 2^{q(b-i)} f(m+a,n+i).$$

Multiplication by powers of "2" are computed effectively using register shift operations. This simplification reduces hash value calculation time.

4   Plain Copy-Move Detection Algorithm

The proposed algorithm involves sequential analysis of all possible positions of image fragments $\Pi(a,b,m,n)$ using sliding window approach. It means that for every position (m,n) a hash value is calculated using pixels $f(m',n')|_{(m',n') \in \Pi(a,b,m,n)}$. This hash value is used:

- to update hash table $Ht(t)$ (hash table contains absolute frequencies of hash values t);
- to update an image of potential duplicate types $T(m,n)$.

It is obvious, that as the structural pattern $\aleph(\Lambda,a,b)$ consists of several rectangular patterns $\Pi(a,b,m,n)$, analyzed image fragment in (m',n') position will be a duplicate only if all of the fragments $\Pi(a,b,m'+m,n'+n)$, $(m,n) \in \Lambda$ are duplicates. As a result, the decision rule for duplicate type detection using selected structural pattern looks like

$$t(m',n') \equiv \begin{cases} 0, & \exists (m,n) \in \Lambda \quad H(T(m'+m,n'+n)) \le 1; \\ T(m',n')+1, & \text{else.} \end{cases}$$

It can be noticed that due to the ambiguity of constructing a representation (1) for a particular structural pattern $\aleph(\Lambda,a,b)$ the proposed algorithm is ambiguously determined. For this reason there are examined several issues in Section 5, which are related to the construction of optimal (in the sense of the quality value) representation (1) for a particular structural pattern.

It has been already mentioned, that one of the main advantages of the proposed algorithm is zero false negative error. This statement is proved according to the following statements:

— the analysis is made using sliding window approach;
— hash values are calculated for every sliding window position (the same image fragments correspond to the same hash values);
— an image fragment is identified as a duplicate, if its absolute frequency is greater than 1.

An example of the proposed algorithm work is shown in Figure 1 (there have been detected 2 duplicate types on the Geoeye-1 satellite image).

Fig. 1. Initial image (left) and detection result (right)

5   Experimental Results

We used 50 SPOT-4 and 50 Geoeye-1 images without duplicates as initial data for experiments. Analysis of each image takes 10 seconds on a workstation with Intel Core i5 3470, 4GB RAM.

Let us use a number of false detected duplicates (collisions) as a *quality parameter K*.

There are considered two main issues for experimental investigations:

— calculate an optimal number of rectangular patterns in (1);
— determine the best representation type of (1). In other words there will be investigated 2 alternative representation types of (1): for maximum possible pairwise intersection of $\Pi(a,b,m,n)$, $(m,n) \in \Lambda$, forming part of $\aleph(\Lambda,a,b)$, and for minimum.

Let us consider two different sliding windows for image analysis: 11×11 ($|\Lambda| = 4$) и 18×18 ($|\Lambda| = 9$). The size $a \times b$ of a structural pattern will be varying from minimum (for minimum intersection) to maximum. Then the number of collisions of the proposed detection algorithm will change as it is shown in Figures 2 and 3.

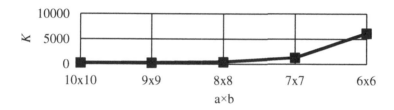

Fig. 2. Relationship of K from the pattern's size $a \times b$ for window size 11×11

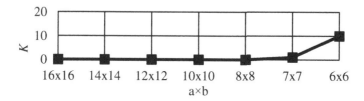

Fig. 3. Relationship of K from the pattern's size $a \times b$ for window size 18×18

It can be seen, that the number of collisions increases exponentially while the intersection part of $\Pi(a, b, m, n)$, $(m, n) \in \Lambda$ decreases. So the optimal structural pattern's size is from 8×8 to 10×10. It can be noted that the number of collisions decreases with the power of set $|\Lambda|$ increase.

The result obtained for a sliding window with size 19×19, $|\Lambda| = 4$ is shown in Figure 4.

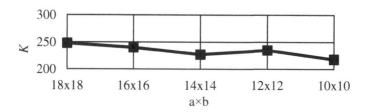

Fig. 4. Relationship of K from the pattern's size $a \times b$ for window size 19×19

Figure 4 shows a slight decrease of collisions by reducing the size of a structural pattern. In comparison with results shown in Figures 2 and 3, in this case (structural pattern size $a \times b$ is greater than 10×10) the number of collisions can be considered constant. When the power of set $|\Lambda|$ increases, the number of collisions tends to 0.

According to the experimental results, the following conclusions can be made:

— the best value of a structural pattern's size is greater than 8×8 ;
— the power of set $|\Lambda|$ should not be less than 6 (9 recommended);

− the value of intersection part in a structural pattern doesn't have a reasonable effect on the processing result, if 2 previous objectives are gained.

6   Conclusion

In this paper, we proposed a new structural pattern based algorithm for plain copy-move detection with zero false negative error. The proposed algorithm is fully automatic and allows to perform image analysis in real time due to low computational complexity. We determined optimal parameters of a structural pattern, which is used to achieve minimum false positive error. The proposed algorithm is also shown its effectiveness during analysis of high resolution satellite images received at the remote sensing data receiving station of Samara State Aerospace University.

Acknowledgements. This work was supported by the Russian Foundation for Basic Research (RFBR) grant №12-07-00021-a and by the Ministry of education and science of the Russian Federation in the framework of the implementation of the Program of increasing the competitiveness of SSAU among the world's leading scientific and educational centers for 2013-2020 years.

References

1. Popescu, A.C., Farid, H.: Statistical tools for digital forensics. In: Fridrich, J. (ed.) IH 2004. LNCS, vol. 3200, pp. 128–147. Springer, Heidelberg (2004)
2. Fridrich, J., Soukal, D., Lukas, J.: Detection of copy–move forgery in digital images. In: Proceedings of Digital Forensic Research Workshop, pp. 55–61 (2003)
3. Mahdian, B., Saic, S.: Detection of copy-move forgery using a method based on blur moment invariants. Forensic Science International **171**(2), 180–189 (2007)
4. Zhang, J., Feng, Z., Su, Y.: A new approach for detecting copy-move forgery in digital images. In: Proceedings of the International Conference on Communication Systems, pp. 362–366 (2008)
5. Dybala, B., Jennings, B., Letscher, D.: Detecting filtered cloning in digital images. In: Proceedings of the Workshop on Multimedia and Security, pp. 43–50 (2007)
6. Huang, H., Guo, W., Zhang, Y.: Detection of copy-move forgery in digital images using SIFT algorithm. In: Proceedings of the Pacific-Asia Workshop on Computational Intelligence and Industrial Application, pp. 272–276 (2008)
7. Pan, X., Lyu, S.: Region duplication detection using image feature matching. IEEE Transactions on Information Forensics and Security **5**(4), 857–867 (2010)
8. Christlein, V., Riess, C., Jordan, J., Riess, C., Angelopoulou, E.: An evaluation of popular copy-move forgery detection approaches. IEEE Transactions on Information Forensics and Security **7**(6), 1841–1854 (2012)
9. Cormen, T.H., Leiserson, C.E., Rivest, R.L.: Introduction to Algorithms (1990)

Automatic Annotation of an Ultrasound Corpus for Studying Tongue Movement

Samuel Silva$^{(\boxtimes)}$ and António Teixeira

DETI/IEETA, University of Aveiro, 3810–193 Aveiro, Portugal
{sss,ajst}@ua.pt

Abstract. Silent speech interfaces can work as an alternative way of interaction in situations where the acoustic speech signal is absent (e.g., speech impairments) or is not suited for the current context (e.g., environmental noise). The goal is to use external data to infer/improve speech recognition. Surface electromyography (sEMG) is one of the modalities used to gather such data, but its applicability still needs to be further explored involving methods to provide reference data about the phenomena under study. A notable example concerns exploring sEMG to detect tongue movements. To that purpose, along with the acquisition of the sEMG, a modality that allows observing the tongue, such as ultrasound imaging, must also be synchronously acquired. In these experiments, manual annotation of the tongue movement in the ultrasound sequences, to allow the systematic analysis of the sEMG signals, is mostly infeasible. This is mainly due to the size of the data involved and the need to maintain uniform annotation criteria. Therefore, to address this task, we present an automatic method for tongue movement detection and annotation in ultrasound sequences. Preliminary evaluation comparing the obtained results with 72 manual annotations shows good agreement.

1 Introduction

Silent speech interfaces [1] can be an alternative way of interaction in situations where users are unable to use speech, whether due to speech impairments (e.g., as a result of a laryngectomy) or due to environmental noise or privacy concerns. In these contexts, external data might be used to infer about the speech contents or even improve speech recognition. Surface electromyography (sEMG) is one of the modalities used to gather such data, but its applicability still needs to be further studied as evidenced, for example, by the lack of information regarding how it can be used to detect tongue movements. To gather additional insight over this matter, experimental studies must be conducted collecting both sEMG and tongue movement data. The technology used for tongue movement assessment, which will provide grounds for the analysis, should fulfil some requirements: a) provide data at a high enough sample rate to allow observation of the movement; b) do not generate electromagnetic fields/noise

© Springer International Publishing Switzerland 2014
A. Campilho and M. Kamel (Eds.): ICIAR 2014, Part I, LNCS 8814, pp. 469–476, 2014.
DOI: 10.1007/978-3-319-11758-4_51

that affect sEMG collection; and c) allow simultaneous (synchronous) acquisition of other modalities used to assess related aspects such as lip movement. Approaches using asynchronous acquisition of different modalities are possible, followed by offline synchronization, but require a greater effort to ensure proper matching between the multiple modalities [2]. Considering these requirements, modalities such as real-time MRI [7] and electromagnetic midsagittal articulography (EMMA) [4], that could provide tongue movement data, are not suitable. One alternative that matches the requirements, and has been widely used to study the movements of the tongue [5], is ultrasound imaging.

The rationale is to acquire synchronized sEMG and ultrasound (US), annotate tongue movements using the latter, and then perform an exploratory analysis over the sEMG signals. The manual annotation of large sets of ultrasound sequences of the tongue is a tiresome task that entails visual inspection of the video, frame-by-frame, and an identification of the instants for tongue movement start and stop. This is prone to some degree of subjectivity (regarding when to set the start and stop of the movement) and to some variation of the criteria (due to noisy frames) used by the human annotator along the sequences. The variability resulting from these aspects might, to some extent, influence subsequent analysis and, therefore, the use of uniform criteria is desirable.

To tackle the tongue movement annotation task from US sequences, part of a multimodal dataset [2] used to explore the applicability of sEMG to tongue movement detection, a method is proposed that performs automatic detection and annotation of tongue movements. The direction of the movement is also provided for the movement events occurring during relevant segments. A preliminary comparison of the annotations provided by the presented method with manual annotations of multiple sequences was performed, yielding a good match between both sets of annotations.

The remainder of this article is organized as follows: section 2 briefly presents the setup used for data acquisition; section 3 describes the methods used for tongue movement annotation in US video sequences; section 4 presents a preliminary evaluation comparing manual and automatic tongue movement annotations; finally, section 5 presents some conclusions and ideas for further work.

2   Ultrasound Data Acquisition

The experimental setup includes the acquisition of data for multiple modalities (sEMG, 3D video, ultrasonic Doppler). For the sake of simplicity, since it has no influence on the described methods, only the ultrasound setup and acquisition are described. Additional details regarding the different aspects of the multimodal setup can be found in [2].

2.1   Corpus

The main purpose was to record sequences that included several tongue position transitions. Since it was also important to favour tongue movements over movements of the lips and jaw, the corpus was also defined having that in mind. The selected sequences include transitions between vowels, in the form of $/V_1V_2V_1/$ (e.g., [iui], [eoe]), and consonants ([k, l, ʎ, t, s]) in different /vCv/ contexts (e.g., [aka, itu, eʎe]). To ensure a clear distinction of the tongue position transitions, the speakers were asked to sustain each vowel sound for around one second. For example [iui] was uttered "iiiiiiiiiiuuuuuuuuuuiiiiiiii".

2.2   Ultrasound Acquisition

The ultrasound setup comprises: a Mindray DP6900 ultrasound system with a 65EC10EA transducer; an Expresscard|54 Video capture card, to capture the ultrasound video; a microphone, connected to a Roland UA-25 soundcard; and a SyncBrightUp unit, which allows synchronization between the audio and ultrasound video, recorded at 30 frames per second. To ensure that the relative position of the ultrasound probe towards the head is kept during acquisition, a stabilization headset is used [5], securing the ultrasound probe below the participant's chin (figure 1).

At the start of each recording the SyncBrightUp unit inserts several trigger pulses in the audio and white squares in the corresponding video frames. The synchronization between the audio and video is tuned after acquisition, using Articulate Assist Advanced (www.articulateinstruments.com), by checking proper alignment between corresponding trigger pulses and video frames.

The audio signal is shared between the US setup and the remaining acquired modalities and thus serves to ensure synchronization throughout the dataset. Therefore, by having the audio signal as a time reference, when performing the annotations, ensures their synchronization with the remaining data.

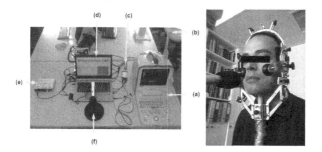

Fig. 1. To the left, ultrasound acquisition setup: a) ultrasound equipment; b) ultrasound probe; c) Audio-video synchronization unit; d) laptop, running Articulate Assist software, showing the prompts; e) external soundcard for sound recording; f) microphone. To the right, the head stabilization headset with the ultrasound probe attached below the speaker's chin.

At this stage, three volunteer European Portuguese male speakers, aged 29-33, have already participated in the experiment. Each participant was given an explanation regarding the ultrasound setup and its different components and informed that the session could be interrupted at any time on his/her request.

The probe stabilization headset was placed on the participant's head and adjusted to a comfortable fit with the help of an assistant. The probe was mounted next, while the ultrasound output was monitored, to ensure that that probe position yielded acceptable images.

For each stimuli in the corpus, the participant was presented with a prompt and asked to repeat it twice, per recording. The full corpus was repeated three times in random orders, for each speaker, resulting in 81 recordings per participant. Since, for each recording, four transitions between phonemes are expected (not including tongue movements at the beginning and end of each prompt), at least around 1000 tongue movement segments need to be annotated (3 participants × 81 recordings × 4 movements).

3   Methods

The following sections describe the most important steps of the method proposed for automatic annotation of tongue movement in US image sequences.

3.1   Audio Segment Identification

The audio recordings, even within each recording session, have varying durations and different noise and speech levels resulting from changes in the participant's position towards the microphone. Each recorded sequence comprised two repetitions of a prompt (e.g., "iiiuuuiii <pause> iiiuuuiii").

The first processing step is the identification of the audio segments corresponding to each repetition as this provides the segments of interest on which to focus for tongue movement analysis. After filtering the audio signal, to remove frequency components above 2 kHz, the Hilbert transform [3] is used to extract its envelope, $E(i)$. Envelope analysis is performed to find the start and stop times for each repetition. The threshold level, L_{Th}, determined empirically, to distinguish between speaker utterances and silence, is obtained by $L_{Th} = 1.4 \times \min(E(i)), i \in [0.15 \times N, 0.85 \times N]$, where N is the total duration of $E(i)$, and basically targets the silence between repetitions.

In order to cope with utterances including plosives (e.g., [aka]), resulting in no sound being produced, which might be mistaken by the silence between repetitions, a minimum duration for each repetition is considered.

3.2   Tongue Movement Detection

Given the noisy nature of the US image sequences (figure 2), pre-processing is applied to reduce noise. Since it is important to preserve the edge corresponding to the tongue, anisotropic diffusion is used [8]. Due to the fact that the images resulting from US acquisition show regions with no relevance, above and below the tongue, a region-of-interest is selected, discarding them.

One possible approach could be tongue segmentation [6], but the complexity associated with the task (image noise, incomplete tongue edges, etc.) precluded

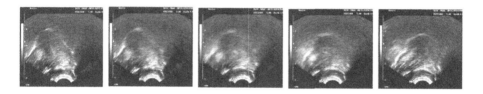

Fig. 2. Selected ultrasound frames along the transition from [i] to [u] in sequence [iui]

its use, at least for these first stages of exploratory studies. In alternative, a much more direct approach is used. The tongue movement is inferred by computing the pixelwise inter-frame difference, $D(i) = \sum_{x=1}^{N_x} \sum_{y=1}^{N_y} |F_i(x,y) - F_{i-1}(x,y)|$, where N_x and N_y are the number of pixels in each image dimension, and $F_i(x,y)$ is the value for pixel in position (x,y) in frame i. When the tongue moves, the inter-frame difference is higher, originating local maxima in $D(i)$. The inter-frame difference curve, $D(i)$, is then masked using the detected segments of interest (repetitions), and the two highest peaks are determined for each repetition, analysing the signal and its first derivative. The interval corresponding to movement, around each peak, is determined considering the second derivative zero-crossings. Figure 3 depicts an example of the distance curve used to detect tongue movements and identified movement segments for the sequence recorded for prompt [iɛi].

After identifying the movements within each repetition, the remaining segments of the sequence are considered to identify additional tongue movements. These are mostly limited to those appearing at the beginning and end of each repetition, as depicted in figure 3.

The detection of these movements is important to provide further data for exploratory analysis of different sEMG channels. For example, these annotations can be used to discard the corresponding sEMG segments while training a "no tongue movement" classifier.

3.3   Tongue Movement Annotation

Besides identifying the segments presenting tongue movement, it is also possible to add annotations to provide extra data regarding each movement. Two different situations are considered: the movements corresponding to the transitions between phones and the remaining tongue movements. For the latter, at this moment, the annotation only comprises the interval for which movement was detected. For the former, based on the tongue movement segments identified within each repetition, each of the tongue movements is associated with the corresponding transition. For the sequences only including vowel sounds, e.g., [ɛɔɛ], the identified movements correspond to the transition between vowels: ɛ to ɔ and ɔ to ɛ. For the sequences including a consonant, e.g. [aka], the two movement segments correspond to the vowel-consonant transition ([a] to [k]) and to the consonant-vowel transition ([k] to [a]).

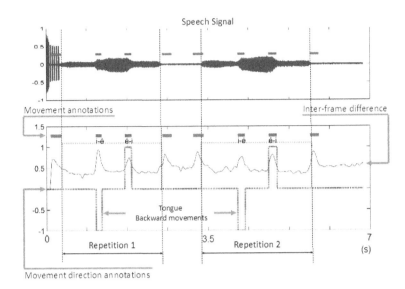

Fig. 3. Data generated for sequence [iEi], uttered by speaker JF: identification of each repetition; the inter-frame difference curve; the automatic annotations of tongue movements, within and outside the repetitions; and the corresponding movement direction, where possible

By annotating the tongue movements, with the corresponding inter-phone transitions, it is possible to perform selections of the data based on the characteristics of the movements. For example, all occurring transitions can be grouped according to the direction of movement: front-back (e.g., [i] to [u]) or back-front (e.g., [o] to [e]). Figure 3 shows an example of annotation depicting these two types of movements: -1 for backward movement (from [i] to [ɛ]) and 1 for forward movement (from [ɛ] to [i]). Other possible annotations could distinguish variations in tongue height (e.g., [ɔ] to [ɛ]).

4   Evaluation

To assess the performance of the proposed method, an evaluation comparing the automatic tongue movement annotations with annotations performed manually, by an observer, has been carried out.

4.1   Methods

The first six sequences recorded for each speaker, including different vowels and consonants (and not including sequences used during development), were manually annotated to identify segments where the tongue was moving, yielding a total of 72 tongue movement segments. This annotation was performed in Articulate Assistant Advanced by analysing the captured image frames and considering only the tongue movements during the relevant speaker utterances, i.e., the transitions between phones. These same sequences were also processed using the proposed automatic annotation method.

To compare the annotations, resulting from the manual and automatic methods, two measures were used: the Dice coefficient, to provide a measure of similarity between the two intervals, $D = \frac{2|X \cap Y|}{|X|+|Y|}$; and the overlap coefficient, $Ov(X,Y) = \frac{|X \cap Y|}{min(|X|,|Y|)}$. For both, X and Y denote the two intervals being compared.

For each pair of corresponding manual and automatic annotations, the difference between starting times and between ending times was also computed, always subtracting the manual times from the automatic times. This means that a positive difference, in the starting time, corresponds to a late start for the automatic annotation, and a negative difference, between the ending times, corresponds to an early stop for the automatic annotation.

4.2   Results

Table 1 shows the overall results obtained for the evaluation and box plots of the different measures. Notice that the overlap is close to 0.95 (where 1.0 means one interval is a subset of the other), the Dice coefficient is high, and the start and stop displacements show that the automatic annotation is mostly contained within the interval defined by the manual annotation (i.e., positive start displacement, negative stop displacement). The box plots depict additional detail for each of the measures. Regarding start and stop displacements, for example, they clearly show a prevalence of positive start displacements and negative stop displacements. Notice that the sequences have a framerate of 30 frames/s, yielding an inter-frame time of 33 ms which is similar to the median displacements observed towards the manual annotations. In practice, this means a variation of one frame in the manual annotation which is, given the subjective nature of the criteria used, quite good.

Table 1. Overall values obtained by comparing manual tongue movement annotations with corresponding automatic annotations obtained using the proposed method

	Dice	Overlap	Displacement (s)	
			start	stop
Mean	0.7358	0.9315	0.0146	0.0007
Median	0.7705	0.9991	0.0338	-0.0218

5   Conclusions

This article presents an automatic method for tongue movement annotation in US image sequences. It identifies the time ranges for which the tongue is moving, in each sequence, and allows further categorization of the movements (e.g., direction) for those corresponding to the transitions between sounds. Comparison of the obtained results with a set of manual annotations was performed yielding good results.

The annotations generated using the proposed method are being used to assess the applicability of a set of five sEMG sensors to the detection of tongue movement and its direction.

The proposed method can still be further improved to support the US+sEMG studies. For example, methods should be explored to detect tongue movement direction directly from the image sequences to make it more versatile.

Due to its computational weight, the amount of data involved (also considering that this is part of a multimodal set), and the possibility to perform parallel processing of different sequences, the proposed method would profit from an implementation in a cloud computing scenario.

Acknowledgments. Research partially funded by FEDER through IEETA Research Unit funding FCOMP-01-0124-FEDER-022682 (FCT-PEst-C/EEI/UI0127/2011), project Cloud Thinking (QREN Mais Centro, ref. CENTRO-07-ST24-FEDER-002031) and Marie Curie Actions IRIS (ref. 610986, FP7-PEOPLE-2013-IAPP).

References

1. Denby, B., Schultz, T., Honda, K., Hueber, T., Gilbert, J.M., Brumberg, J.S.: Silent speech interfaces. Speech Communication **52**(4), 270–287 (2009)
2. Freitas, J., Teixeira, A., Dias, M.S.: Multimodal corpora for silent speech interaction. In: Proc. LREC, Reykjavik, Iceland (2014)
3. Hahn, S.L.: Hilbert Transform in Signal Processing. Artech House (1996)
4. Rossato, S., Teixeira, A., Ferreira, L.: Les nasales du portugais et du français: une étude comparative sur les données EMMA. Journées d'Études sur la Parole (JEP), 143–146 (Juin 2006)
5. Scobbie, J., Wrench, A., van der Linden, M.: Head-probe stabilization in ultrasound tongue imaging using a headset to permit natural head movement. In: Proc. 8th Int. Seminar on Speech Production, pp. 373–376 (2008)
6. Tang, L., Bressman, T., Hamarneh, G.: Tongue contour tracking in dynamic ultrasound via higher-order MRFs and efficient fusion moves. Medical Image Analysis **16**(8), 1503–1520 (2012)
7. Teixeira, A., Martins, P., Oliveira, C., Ferreira, C., Silva, A., Shosted, R.: Real-time MRI for Portuguese: database, methods and applications. In: Caseli, H., Villavicencio, A., Teixeira, A., Perdigão, F. (eds.) PROPOR 2012. LNCS, vol. 7243, pp. 306–317. Springer, Heidelberg (2012)
8. Weickert, J.: Anisotropic Diffusion in Image Processing. ECMI Series. Teubner-Verlag (1998)

Improving Fire Detection Reliability by a Combination of Videoanalytics

Rosario Di Lascio, Antonio Greco, Alessia Saggese$^{(\boxtimes)}$, and Mario Vento

Department of Information Engineering, Electrical Engineering and Applied Mathematics, University of Salerno, Salerno, Italy
{rdilascio,agreco,asaggese,mvento}@unisa.it

Abstract. In this paper we propose a novel method for detecting fires in both indoor and outdoor environments. The videos acquired by traditional surveillance cameras are analyzed and different typologies of information, respectively based on color and movement, are combined into a multi expert system in order to increase the overall reliability of the approach, making it possible its usage in real applications. The proposed algorithm has been tested on a very large dataset acquired in real environments and downloaded on the web. The obtained results confirm a consistent reduction in the number of false positive detected by the system, without paying in terms of accuracy.

Keywords: Fire detection · Multi expert system

1 Introduction

In the last years a wide attention has been devoted to the prevention of fires, which can generate smoke pollution, release greenhouse gases, as well as unintentionally degrade ecosystems. A prompt detection and then an immediate intervention could be very important in order to save the environment or, at least, to reduce the damages caused by the fire.

A solution to this problem can be found by analyzing visual data acquired by surveillance cameras, and in the last years several solutions have been proposed [3][11]. For instance, in [2] a color based approach has been used: fire pixels are recognized by an advanced background subtraction technique and a statistical RGB color model. In [10] such strategy is improved by a multi resolution two-dimensional wavelet analysis, which evaluates energy variation to detect the motion of flames, and a disorder feature to decrease the number of false positive events. Wavelet transform has been also used in [13] for detecting the flame flicker. However, the main limitation in this kind of approach is related to the frame rate: in fact, for evaluating the flicker, the acquisition device should work at least at 20 fps, and then also the algorithm for detecting events on line should work at the same frame rate. Furthermore, a common limitation lies in the fact that RGB color makes the proposed methods sensitive to changes in brightness

© Springer International Publishing Switzerland 2014
A. Campilho and M. Kamel (Eds.): ICIAR 2014, Part I, LNCS 8814, pp. 477–484, 2014.
DOI: 10.1007/978-3-319-11758-4_52

and then can cause a high number of false positive, due to the presence of shadows or to different red colors.

In [14] both fire and smoke are detected by color evaluation: in particular, HSI and RGB color spaces have been used for detecting respectively fire and smoke. A similar approach has been used in [9], where flicker detection is performed by using a cumulative time derivative matrix of luminance and fire color detection through RGB and HSV thresholding. In [1] the limitation or RGB based approach is overcome by using YUV statistical color model to separate the luminance from the chrominance more effectively than RGB, then reducing the number of false positive detected by the system (from 66% [2] to 31%).

Although the promising performance in terms of accuracy of the state of the art approaches, two main limitations can be highlighted: on one side, the number of false positive is still too high for using such methods in real applications [1][2][13]. On the other side, the reduction in the number of false positive is often paid in terms of computational cost, so making critical their usage on embedded platforms or on general purposes systems combined with other video analysis applications [10][14].

In order to face the above mentioned problems, we propose a novel method able to properly combine different typologies of information, respectively related to color and motion. Color decision is evaluated in the YUV space: although providing an high accuracy, the color evaluation is not robust with respect to other *red* objects moving in a scene. On the other hand, motion decision is based on a SIFT tracker: the rationale is that a set of given keypoints in a moving object (such as a person or a vehicle) follows the same direction, while in the fire their movement is much more disordered. The results are finally combined by a multi expert system: the main advantage deriving from this choice lies in the fact that the decision systems (color and motion based) consider different but complementary aspects of the same decision problem, and their combination provides better performance if compared with any single system.

2   Proposed Method

An overview of the proposed approach is presented in Figure 1: the pixels corresponding to moving objects are extracted (*Foreground Mask Extraction* and *Background Updating*) by using the detection algorithm that we recently proposed in [5]. The main novelty lies in the fact that two different kind of information, respectively based on the color (*Color Threshold*) and on the movement (*Connected Component Filter* and *Disorder Evaluation*), are properly combined by a multi expert system (*MES classifier*), so significantly increase the overall reliability of the system.

2.1   Color Evaluation

The proposed algorithm is based on the YUV color space, which separates the luminance from the chrominance and is less sensitive to changes in brightness

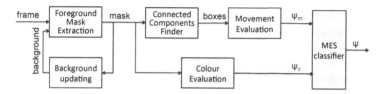

Fig. 1. Overview of the proposed approach: once extracted the foreground mask, a multi expert system is used to combine information respectively based on color and motion

than the RGB color space. In particular, the four rules based on the statistical color model proposed in [1] have been exploited. The first two rules r_1 and r_2 are based on the consideration that in flame pixels the Red channel value is greater than the Green channel value, as well as the Green channel value is greater than Blue channel value. Such consideration, transformed in the YUV color space, becomes for the generic pixel (x,y) of the image:

$$r_1 : Y(x,y) > U(x,y); \quad r_2 : V(x,y) > U(x,y) \tag{1}$$

The third rule r_3 can be obtained by considering that the flames' brightness is higher than other areas of the frame. This consideration suggests that a fire pixel has the Y and V components higher than the average Y and V value in the frame, while the U component lower than the average U value in the frame:

$$r_3 : Y(x,y) > \frac{1}{N} * \sum_{k=1}^{N} Y(x_k, y_k), \tag{2}$$

$$U(x,y) < \frac{1}{N} * \sum_{k=1}^{N} U(x_k, y_k), \quad V(x,y) > \frac{1}{N} * \sum_{k=1}^{N} V(x_k, y_k)$$

Moreover, the previous consideration allows to conclude that there is a considerable difference between U and V components of the fire pixels. Then, the fourth rule can be defined as: $r_4 : |V(x,y) - U(x,y)| \geq \tau$, being $\tau = 40$ as suggested in [1]. The main novelty with respect to [1] lies in combination of the above mentioned rules; in particular, the reliability ψ_c is computed by a weighted combination of such rules:

$$\psi_c = \frac{\gamma_1 * r_1 + \gamma_2 * r_2 + \gamma_3 * r_3 + \gamma_4 * r_4}{\gamma_1 + \gamma_2 + \gamma_3 + \gamma_4}, \tag{3}$$

In our experiments, $(\gamma_1, \gamma_2, \gamma_3, \gamma_4)$ have been set to $(1, 1, 1, 1)$ for equally weigh the considered contributions.

2.2 Movement Evaluation

In sterile environments, the color could be sufficient alone to correctly recognize fire events without generating too many false alarms. On the other side, this consideration is not completely true in common video surveillance environments, where several false alarms could be generated: think, as an example, to a person with a red shirt walking in a street, which could be detected as fire by a traditional color-based approaches. The introduction of a motion based information is then fundamental to recover these kinds of situations.

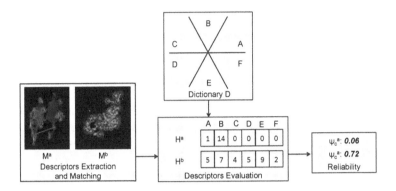

Fig. 2. Motion evaluation: for each box, the descriptors' matching M^a and M^b, associated respectively to the boxes a and b, are evaluated according to the dictionary D previously defined. The occurrences of the angles H^a and H^b are computed and the reliability ψ_c^a and ψ_c^b is obtained: 0.06 for a and 0.72 for b.

At the light of the above considerations, in this paper we propose to represent the motion as a high level feature vector. The main idea is that the most discriminant feature able to distinguish a common moving object (a person or a vehicle) from the fire is related to the shape variation: in fact, the shape of an object varies in a very slow way while the fire changes it instantaneously. It means that tracking and analyzing the movement of some keypoints could help to distinguish the fire from other moving objects.

An overview of the proposed approach is shown in Figure 2: the keypoints extracted in two consecutive frames are evaluated according to a dictionary previously defined and the occurrences of angles associated to the movement are properly evaluated.

In particular, an approach based on Scale Invariant Feature Transform (SIFT) [7] has been used: the set of corners $C_t = \{c_t^1, ..., c_t^{|C_t|}\}$, being $|C_t|$ the cardinality of the set, are extracted from the foreground mask at time instant t by using the Shi-Tomasi corner detection algorithm [12], an enhanced version of traditional Harris corner detector which proved its effectiveness in several application domains. Each corner is then represented by measuring the local image gradients in the region around it, so obtaining the set of corresponding feature vectors $V_t = \{v_t^1, ..., v_t^{|V_t|}\}$, being $|V_t| = |C_t|$.

Given the feature vectors V_t and V_{t-1} the 1:1 matching $M(V_t, V_{t-1})$ is performed inside each box by minimizing the distance, so that the generic matching m_j is given by: $m_j = \arg min \quad distance(v_t^a, v_{t-1}^b), a = \{1, ..., |V_t|\}, b = \{1, ..., |V_{t-1}|\}$. Note that the maximum size of M depends on the dimensionality of the descriptors and then can be computed as follows: $|M| \leq min(|v_t|, |v_{t-1}|)$.

For each matching m_j, the angle ϕ_j associated to the movement is evaluated: $\phi_j = \arctan\left(\frac{m_j|_y}{m_j|_x}\right)$, being $m_j|_x$ and $m_j|_y$ the horizontal and the vertical component of m_j, respectively. ϕ_j is then quantized according to a dictionary D manually defined by uniformly partitioned the round into a fixed number of $|D|$ sectors: $D = \left\{d_k \in \left] k\frac{2\pi}{|D|}, (k+1)\frac{2\pi}{|D|}\right]\right\}$. $|D|$ has been experimental set in this paper to 6. In particular, ϕ_j is associated to the sector s_j it belongs to, among the $|D|$ available: $s_j = d_k | \phi_j \in d_k$.

For each box, the angles $\phi = \{\phi_1, ..., \phi_{|M|}\}$ are computed and its high level representation is built by evaluating the occurrences of angles. The obtained vector $H = \{h_1, ..., h_{|D|}\}$ can be computed as follows: $h_i = \sum_{m=1}^{|M|} \delta(s_m, i)$, $j = 1, ..., k$, being $\delta(\cdot)$ the Kronecker delta.

Finally, the reliability ψ_m associated to the object is evaluated as: $\psi_m = 1 - max(H)/\sum_{k=1}^{|H|} h_k$. It means that, as shown in Figure 2, the corner points associated to people (box a) move approximatively in the same direction, and the high level representation is polarized toward one or just a few angles (angle B in the example). On the other side, the angles extracted by movement's fire are much more spread, so implying that the reliability is higher (0.72 against 0.06 in the example).

2.3 Multi Expert Evaluation

The information obtained by evaluating color and movement are finally combined in an *intelligent* way by using a Multi Expert System (MES). In particular, the classification reliability ψ is evaluated by a weighted voting rule which combines ψ_c and ψ_m: $\psi = (\alpha_c * \psi_c + \alpha_m * \psi_m)/(\alpha_c + \alpha_m)$.

The weights α_c and α_m are dynamically evaluated during the training step, depending on the overall reliability of the single expert module. In particular, given the misclassification matrix $C^{(k)}$ computed by the expert module e_k on the training step, such values can be determined by evaluating the probability that the pattern x under test, belonging to the class i, is assigned to the right class by the expert module e_k, being $k = \{c, m\}$ [6]:

$$\alpha_k = P(x \in i | e_k(x) = i) = C_{ii}^{(k)}/\sum_{i=1}^{M} C_{ij}^{(k)}, \tag{4}$$

being M the number of classes (two in the proposed approach, *fire* and *non fire*) and $C_{(ij)}$ the value of the misclassification matrix in the position (i, j).

Finally, the decision is taken according to a threshold β: if $\psi \geq \beta$ for at least one box, then a fire event is detected and an alert is sent to the human operator.

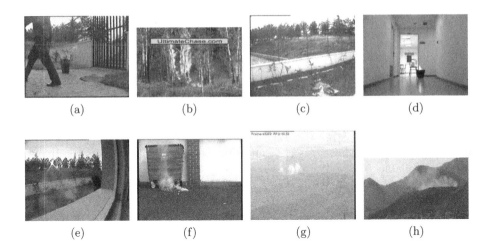

Fig. 3. A few images extracted from the videos used for testing the method: (a) *fire1*, (b) *fire4*, (c) *fire6*, (d) *fire13*, (e) *fire14*, (f) *fire15*, (g) *fire17*, (h) *fire21*

3   Experimental Results

Although several methods have been recently proposed, no standard datasets for benchmarking purposes have been made available up to now. For this reason, in order to test the proposed method we collected 28 videos in indoor and outdoor conditions, resulting in 53.808 frames to be evaluated. The videos have been both acquired in real environments and downloaded from the web [4]. More information are reported in [8], while some visual examples are shown in Figure 3. The dataset can be partitioned into two main folders: the first 13 videos contains fires and the last 15 videos does not contain fire but instead smoke, clouds or simply moving objects. Such composition allows us to stress the system and then to test it in several real conditions. It is worth pointing out that each video stresses a particular situation: Figures 3c and 3f, for instance, show several red objects, whose color is very similar to the one of the fire; a similar situation happens in Figure 3e, due to the reflection introduced by the window; finally, several objects (persons, smoke or clouds) move inside the scene, as shown in Figures 3a and 3g.

The dataset has been partitioned in order to fix the parameters: in particular, 20% of it has been used to validate the system for the multi expert evaluation while the remaining 80% has been used to test it.

The results achieved by the proposed approach on the test set are reported in Table 4: on the left the ROC curve is obtained by varying the β parameter while on the right the misclassification matrix is reported by optimizing the performance on the training set ($\beta = 0.7$). In order to further confirm the effectiveness of the proposed approach, compared with state of the art ones, a deep comparison has been performed.

The results are summarized in Figure 1. We can note that in general YUV based approach strongly outperforms RGB based ones, both in terms of accuracy and false positive. This consideration confirms our choice to exploit a YUV based strategy for the evaluation of the color. Furthermore, the results obtained by the proposed MES based on YUV and movement evaluation (accuracy = 92.59% and false positive = 6.67%) outperforms the other considered approaches, so confirming the effectiveness of the proposed methodology.

Finally, we also evaluate the computational cost of the proposed approach. In particular, we used a traditional computer, equipped with an Intel dual core processor T7300 and with a RAM of 4GB. The proposed method is able to work, on average by considering 1CIF videos, with a frame rate of 70 frame per seconds over the above mentioned platform, so making it especially suited for low-cost real applications.

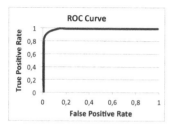

		Predicted Class	
		Fire	No Fire
GT	Fire	91.67%	8.33%
	No Fire	6.67%	93.33%

Fig. 4. Results obtained by the proposed system in terms of ROC Curve, on the left, and misclassification matrix, on the right, computed with $\beta = 0.70$

Table 1. Comparison of the proposed approach with state of the art methodologies

		Accuracy	False Positive
Color	RGB [2]	48.15 %	93.33 %
	YUV [1]	88.89 %	20.00 %
Combination	RGB + Movement	66.67 %	60.00 %
	Proposed (YUV + Movement)	**92.59 %**	**6.67 %**

4   Conclusions

In this paper we proposed a method for detecting fires in both indoor and outdoor environments. The main advantage of the proposed approach lies in the fact that the chosen combination significantly reduces the number of false positive detected by the system. Furthermore, the introduction of a similar application on existing video surveillance systems only slightly improves their cost: in fact, on one side, no additional cameras needs to be installed and the existing ones can be still used, since the proposed method does not require an ad hoc setup. On the other side, the obtained performance, both in terms of accuracy and computational cost, confirms its applicability in real applications.

Acknowledgments. This research has been partially supported by A.I.Tech s.r.l. (http://www.aitech-solutions.eu).

References

1. Celik, T., Demirel, H.: Fire detection in video sequences using a generic color model. Fire Safety Journal **44**(2), 147–158 (2009)
2. Celik, T., Demirel, H., Ozkaramanli, H., Uyguroglu, M.: Fire detection using statistical color model in video sequences. J. Vis. Comun. Image Represent. **18**(2), 176–185 (2007). http://dx.doi.org/10.1016/j.jvcir.2006.12.003
3. Cetin, A.E., Dimitropoulos, K., Gouverneur, B., Grammalidis, N., Gunay, O., Habiboglu, Y.H., Toreyin, B.U., Verstockt, S.: Video fire detection: a review. Digital Signal Processing **23**(6), 1827–1843 (2013)
4. Cetin, E.: Computer vision based fire detection dataset (May 2014), http://signal. ee.bilkent.edu.tr/VisiFire/
5. Conte, D., Foggia, P., Petretta, M., Tufano, F., Vento, M.: Meeting the application requirements of intelligent video surveillance systems in moving object detection. In: Singh, S., Singh, M., Apte, C., Perner, P. (eds.) ICAPR 2005. LNCS, vol. 3687, pp. 653–662. Springer, Heidelberg (2005)
6. Lam, L., Suen, C.Y.: Optimal combinations of pattern classifiers. Pattern Recognition Letters **16**(9), 945–954 (1995)
7. Lowe, D.G.: Distinctive image features from scale-invariant keypoints. Int. J. Comput. Vision **60**(2), 91–110 (2004)
8. Mivia: Mivia fire detection dataset (May 2014), http://mivia.unisa.it/
9. Qi, X., Ebert, J.: A computer vision-based method for fire detection in color videos. International Journal of Imaging **2**(9 S), 22–34 (2009)
10. Rafiee, A., Tavakoli, R., Dianat, R., Abbaspour, S., Jamshidi, M.: Fire and smoke detection using wavelet analysis and disorder characteristics. In: IEEE ICCRD, vol. 3, pp. 262–265 (March 2011)
11. Ravichandran, A., Soatto, S.: Long-range spatio-temporal modeling of video with application to fire detection. In: Fitzgibbon, A., Lazebnik, S., Perona, P., Sato, Y., Schmid, C. (eds.) ECCV 2012, Part II. LNCS, vol. 7573, pp. 329–342. Springer, Heidelberg (2012)
12. Shi, J., Tomasi, C.: Good features to track. In: IEEE CVPR, pp. 593–600 (1994)
13. Töreyin, B.U., Dedeoğlu, Y., Güdükbay, U., Çetin, A.E.: Computer vision based method for real-time fire and flame detection. Pattern Recogn. Lett. **27**(1), 49–58 (2006)
14. Yu, C., Mei, Z., Zhang, X.: A real-time video fire flame and smoke detection algorithm. Procedia Engineering **62**, 891–898 (2013). asia-Oceania Symposium on Fire Science and Technology

Automatic Method for Visual Grading of Seed Food Products

Pierre Dubosclard[1,2]([⊠]), Stanislas Larnier[1,2], Hubert Konik[3],
Ariane Herbulot[1,2], and Michel Devy[1,2]

[1] CNRS, LAAS, 7 Avenue du Colonel Roche, 31400 Toulouse, France
pierre.dubosclard@laas.fr
[2] Univ de Toulouse, UPS, LAAS, 31400 Toulouse, France
[3] Laboratoire Hubert Curien, Saint-Etienne, France

Abstract. This paper presents an automatic method for visual grading,
designed to solve the industrial problem of evaluation of seed lots. The
sample is thrown in bulk onto a tray placed in a chamber for acquiring
color image. An image processing method had been developed to separate
and characterize each seed. The approach adopted for the segmentation
step is based on the use of marked point processes and active contour,
leading to tackle the problem by a technique of energy minimization.

1 Introduction

In agriculture, the global grain harvest reached several billion tons each year.
Seed producers exchange their crops at a price determined by the quality of
their production. This assessment, called grading, is performed for each set on
a representative sample. The difficulty of this assessment is to fully characterize
the sample. To do so, it is necessary to qualify each of its elements. Historically,
this has been performed manually by an operator. This method is exposed to
various problems and the results can vary from one operator to another.

Alpha MOS company [2] develops systems for quality control of food products. It proposes a visual sensory system to provide an alternative to human
evaluation. The assessment should be simple to implement and at least as fast
as the human evaluation.

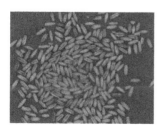

Fig. 1. Image of wheat seeds in bulk

Fig. 2. Acquisition system

© Springer International Publishing Switzerland 2014
A. Campilho and M. Kamel (Eds.): ICIAR 2014, Part I, LNCS 8814, pp. 485–495, 2014.
DOI: 10.1007/978-3-319-11758-4_53

The seed samples are presented in bulk, without any arrangement, but they are spread over a tray in such way that there is no overlapping between the objects to avoid occlusion (Figure 1).

The evaluation by the instrument is composed of three steps. The first step is the **acquisition**: the operator places the samples on the tray in the instrument and takes an image. Then the **detection** step consists in finding each object in the image, to finally classify them in different quality classes regarding several criteria (shape, color, spot) during the **classification** step.

The quality of the sample can then be deduced from the result of the classification. The detection step is the main difficulty. It is necessary to develop a segmentation method to isolate each object under the following constraints:

- the number of seeds is unknown (an approximative estimation can be done);
- the objects have quite generical geometric and chromatic features;
- they are randomly placed, without arrangement and with no overlapping.

In Section 2, a state of the art around the visual grading problem is presented. Section 3 describes the data acquisition system. The notion of marked point processes is introduced in Section 4. The segmentation steps are detailed in Section 5. Numerical results are presented in Section 6.

2   State of the Art

Several studies have been conducted on the cereal seeds grading. Augustin et al. [1] focused on the quality control of grain of rice, regarding different criteria of shape and color. From these criteria, a classification method based on neural network is used to qualify each grain. This approach gives good results for the classification of complete, broken and colors defect rice grain. However this method is applied on images with separated grain. The segmentation issue is then simplified by an operator or a mechanical system (vibrating bowl or slot) to separate the grain in front of the camera.

Other studies have been conducted on the cereal segmentation topic, mainly on wheat and rice. Yao et al. [12] and Faessel et al. [8] focused on detection and separation of rice grain. They both address the problem by working on a binary image obtained by a threshold to separate the objects from the background. Yao et al. [12] then work on the contours and search the concaves angles to connect them two at a time in order to detect objects boundaries. Faessel et al. [8] used a mathematical morphology method on the binary image: a skeleton operation on the background. The open lines of the skeleton, without ending, are then combined under some constraints to obtain the objects boundaries. These two methods give good results on image of touching grain with low density of objects. The computation times are short, but these methods are not adapted for images with heaps and high density of seeds.

3   Acquisition System

The acquisitions are made in a cabin (Figure 2) which integrates a camera and a lighting system. This cabin offers stable and reproducible acquisition condition, independently from the external lighting.

Some improvements have been made on the existing system available at Alpha MOS. The lighting system and the camera have been replaced by new material to improve the quality and the stability of the color image acquisition. The lighting source retained is composed of white LEDs. These LEDs have a continuous spectrum in the visible range and were chosen for their stability over time in term of luminous intensity. As LEDs are punctual sources, a diffuser is placed downstream to ensure the lighting homogeneity in the acquisition area. The image acquisition is performed at a distance of 400 mm from the object plan by a CMOS mono sensor color camera of 5 megapixel with a 5 mm lens. The chosen camera was a Basler acA2500-14gc. It offers a resolution on the object plan around 6 pixels per millimeter, which is important for our application as the objects have a size of only few millimeters. The image acquisitions presented in this paper were obtained with this system.

4   Marked Point Processes

The notion of marked point processes has widely been used to represent stochastic phenomena such as waiting queue. More recently, this approach was used to extract objects in image processing with for example, the detection of roads [9] or to count trees [11] on satellite and aerial images.

4.1   Introduction to the Marked Point Processes

Figure 1 presents an example of seeds. The chosen approach to modelize and extract the seeds is based on the marked point processes. Indeed, the seeds can be represented by a generical simple shape and there is no arrangement between them, they are randomly disposed. These objects are defined by their positions and their geometric attributes or marks. Let χ be the space of objects such as $\chi = P \times M$, with P the space of the position and M the space of the geometric attributes describing the object. A configuration of objects from χ, noted $\mathbf{x}$, is a non-arranged list of objects: $\mathbf{x} = \{x_1, \ldots, x_n\}, n \in \mathbb{N}, x_i \in \chi, i = 1, \ldots, n$.

The objects to detect can be approximated by an ellipse characterized by its marks, for example its orientation, its minor axis and its major axis (Figure 3).

For each object x_i of the configuration $\mathbf{x}$, an energy $U(x_i)$ composed of two terms is associated. The first term is a *data term* noted $U_d(x_i)$, which represents the likelihood of the marked point process regarding the data (the image in our case). This term is defined by the data of the object itself. The second term is an *a priori* term, noted $U_p(x_i)$, which imposes condition on the overall configuration.

In the context of object detection inside an image, the aim is to find the most likely object configuration. This research is based on the two energies terms that are defined in the next section.

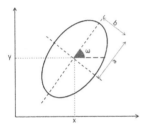

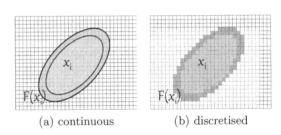

(a) continuous   (b) discretised

Fig. 3. Position and marks of an ellipse

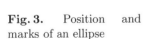

Fig. 4. Object x_i and its crown $\mathcal{F}(x_i)$ (a), and their equivalent disretized (b)

4.2   Energy U(x)

The energy associated to an object x_i, noted $U(x_i)$, is the sum of the data term $U_d(x_i)$ and a priori term $U_p(x_i)$. The energy for the configuration $\mathbf{x}$ is then:

$$U(\mathbf{x}) = U_d(\mathbf{x}) + \gamma U_p(\mathbf{x})$$

with γ a weight coefficient which is determined empiricaly.

The term $U_d(\mathbf{x})$ takes into account the image data for each object of $\mathbf{x}$. It is computed by using the Bhattacharyya distance, noted d_B, defined in [6]:

$$d_B(x_i, \mathcal{F}(x_i)) = \frac{(\mu_1 - \mu_2)^2}{4\sqrt{\sigma_1^2 + \sigma_2^2}} - \frac{1}{2} \log \left(\frac{2\sigma_1 \sigma_2}{\sigma_1^2 + \sigma_2^2} \right)$$

with an object $x_i \in \chi$ and $\mathcal{F}(x_i)$ the object crown (Figure 4), (μ_1, σ_1) and (μ_2, σ_2) respectively the means and the variances of the radiometric values of the object and its crown.

The computation of this distance provides a criterion that highlights area with important contrast between the object and its crown. It also takes into account the homogeneity of the area. Finally, the term $U_d(\mathbf{x})$ is defined as follows:

$$U_d(\mathbf{x}) = \sum_{x_i \in \mathbf{x}} U_d(x_i) = \sum_{x_i \in \mathbf{x}} \mathcal{Q}(d_B(x_i, \mathcal{F}(x_i)))$$

with $\mathcal{Q}(d_B) \in [\text{-}1,1]$ a quality function which favorizes or penalizes the objects considering a given threshold d_0:

$$\mathcal{Q}(d_B) = (1 - \frac{d_B}{d_0}) \text{ if } d_B < d_0, \quad \mathcal{Q}(d_B) = \exp \left(-\frac{d_B - d_0}{100} \right) - 1 \text{ if } d_B \geq d_0.$$

The objects having an important contrast with their crown ($d_b ¿ d_0$) are then favored and their associated data energy is negative.

The $U_p(\mathbf{x})$ term gives information on the a priori knowledge on the target configuration, like the interactions between the objects. In the context of seed segmentation, $U_p(\mathbf{x})$ is a repulsive term that penalizes the objects overlapping.

For each object $x_i \in \chi$, $U_p(x_i)$ is the sum of repulsive strengths emitted by the objects in interaction with x_i, that are in overlapping with x_i. These repulsive strengths are computed by counting the number of pixels that belong to the object x_i and to its neighbouring objects noted $\mathcal{V}(x_i)$:

$$U_p(\mathbf{x}) = \sum_{x_i \in \mathbf{x}} U_p(x_i) \quad \text{with} \quad U_p(x_i) = \sum_{x_j \in \mathcal{V}(x_i)} \mathcal{A}(x_i \cap x_j)$$

and $\mathcal{A}(x_i \cap x_j)$ the common area of x_i and x_j objects.

5   Segmentation

The presented segmentation method is inspired by the multiple Birth-and-Death algorithm described by Descombes et al. in [7]. This approach involved the marked point processes in an optimization framework. But we adapt this approach to treat our segmentation topic by adding a detection step between the birth step and the death step. The difference with the approach of Descombes et al. is that we do not consider the optimization on the entire configuration but on specific objects. We use this Birth-and-Death dynamic as a sampler, the optimization part is realized by an active contour method detailed later. First, the initialization of the method is presented, then the different steps of the method are described.

5.1   Initialization

Birth map. The first initialization step consists of computing an image that is named birth map. This image has the same size as the input image and it associates to every position p a probability $B(p)$ that there is an object centered at this position.

This image is computed in two steps. The first step consists in a binarization of the input image to separate the objects from the background, pixels of the background are set to zero and the probability associated is null. The second step is the computation of the Euclidean distance to the contours.

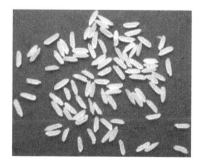 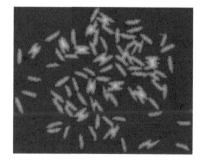

Fig. 5. From left to right : input image and birth map corresponding

Fig. 6. Example of three orientation maps

Orientation maps. The orientation maps are a set of images that associate to every position different probabilities on the possible orientations of an object in this point. To obtain them, mean filters which have a geometrical shape and different orientations are used on the binary image. The geometrical shape is the mean of the possible shapes which approximate the seeds.

For example, the ellipse had been chosen in the case of rice seeds. Figure 6 presents three orientation maps obtained from the input image in Figure 5.

5.2   Active Contour

The objects created in the context of the marked point processes have only simple shapes like ellipses with a limited range of axes sizes. The computational time is the main reason. But to accurately detect every object in the image, we need to obtain the most precise boundaries.

As the objects to detect have a generical shape, we decided to use the method based on an active contour with a geometric shape prior proposed by Bresson et al. [3]. This method follows the well-known energy functionnal model of Chen et al. [5] where the shape prior of Leventon et al. [10] is integrated. Finally, to improve the robustness of the method, Bresson et al. add a region-based energy term based on the Mumford-Shah functionnal (Vese and Chan [4]). This method is then based on three complementary terms dedicated to shape, boundary and region inside the contour.

5.3   Birth-and-Death Dynamic

The method adapted for the Birth-and-Death algorithm is composed of three steps that are done iteratively. We added a detection step to the original approach in order to detect the object boundary with more accuracy, but also to be able to segment the heaps progressively from their boundaries to their cores.

Birth step. The first step consists of objects birth and is illustrated on Figure 7. For each point p of the input image, if there is not already an object at this position, the birth probability $\delta B(p)$ is computed from the birth map, with δ

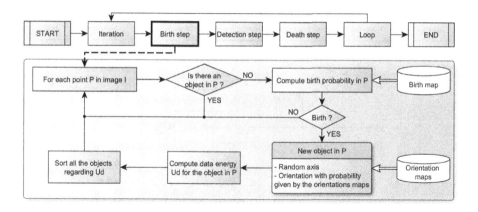

Fig. 7. Birth step

a regularization coefficient that handles the approximative number of objects. If an object x_i is created, its axes are randomly chosen and its orientation is obtained from the set of orientation maps. For a given number of angles, the set of orientation maps provides the probability that an object has this angle. Then the data energy $U_p(x_i)$ of the object x_i is computed and the object is placed in the configuration $\mathbf{x}$ by sorting them regarding their data energy. Once all the image is scanned, the algorithm goes to the next step.

Detection step. The aim of the detection step is to validate the objects of the configuration $\mathbf{x}$. Figure 8 described this step. For each object x_i of the configuration taking by their data energy classement order, their data energy is compared to a threshold. If their energy is inferior to this threshold, they may be correctly placed. Then the active contour approach detailed previously is use to validate this hypothesis on one hand, and to get an accurate boundary if the object is correct on the other hand. The result of the active contour is analyzed to determine different criteria like area or roundness. From these criteria the object is then validated or not. If the object is validated, the object is removed from the configuration $\mathbf{x}$, the birth map is updated by affecting the probability to create an object in this area at zero. The input image is also updated by turning the pixels values of the correct object to zero, so the heaps can be progressively processed from their boundaries to their cores. If the object is not correct, we only remove it from the configuration $\mathbf{x}$.

Death step. The death step consists of cleaning the configuration $\mathbf{x}$ and is illustrated on Figure 9. If some object have been validated during the detection step of the current iteration, we compute the new data term of all the objects from the updated input image. We then compute the a priori energy and the death probability of each object in the configuration:

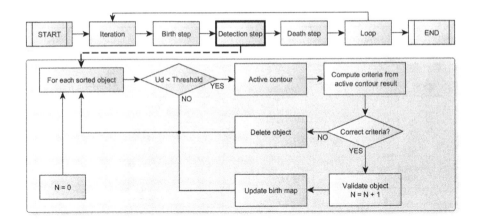

Fig. 8. Detection step

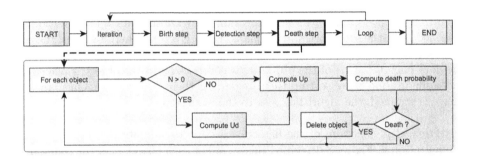

Fig. 9. Death step

$$D(x_p) = \frac{\delta a_\varphi(x_p)}{1 + \delta a_\varphi(x_p)} \mathbf{x}$$

with $a_\varphi(x_p) = \exp(-\varphi U(x_p))$. The object is then remove from the configuration with the probability $D(x_p)$.

6   Numerical Results

Figure 10 illustrates the behaviour of the detection step in the cases of bad starting contour (a) and a good one (b). The first leads to a final contour with a shape distant from an ellipse and is rejected. The second leads to a final contour with a shape similar to an ellipse and is accepted.

Figure 11 and Figure 12 presents the final segmentation. The green color represents the contours. For the greater part, rice seeds and oats are well detected.

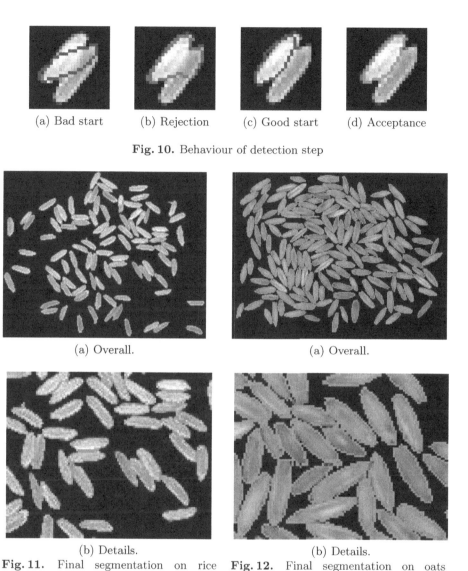

(a) Bad start   (b) Rejection   (c) Good start   (d) Acceptance

Fig. 10. Behaviour of detection step

(a) Overall.   (a) Overall.

(b) Details.   (b) Details.

Fig. 11. Final segmentation on rice sample

Fig. 12. Final segmentation on oats sample

Some improvements could be made. Further development is under consideration especially in the algorithm parameters selection. This selection could be made thanks to an automatic learning on separated seed.

7   Conclusion

This paper proposes an approach to perform the visual quality control of cereal seeds samples. This operation called visual grading can be treated in three steps: acquisition, segmentation and classification. An acquisition system of color images has been created to collect the data. A new segmentation approach has been developed, based on the marked point processes. The Birth-an-Death dynamic has been modified to integrate a new detection step based on an active contour with a shape prior term. The results on rice seeds are promising.

Experiments with higher density and with other type of seeds (barley, pea, wheat) are in progress. Other tests like comparison with human operator and reproductibility on the same sample in different configurations are also underway.

In the future, some algorithm parameters will be automatically learnt on simple images with a representation sample of separated seeds. The shape parameters would be extracted from statistics on the binarized image. The integration of a 3D data acquisition system like stereovision with two cameras is under consideration. Despite the hardware cost, such data might be useful in particular to enrich the birth map but also to provide criteria for the classification stage.

Acknowledgments. This CIFRE thesis work was made possible thanks to the involment of Alpha MOS company.

References

1. Agustin, O.C., Oh, B.-J.: Automatic milled rice quality analysis. In: Second International Conference on Future Generation Communication and Networking, FGCN 2008, vol. 2, pp. 112–115 (December 2008)
2. Alpha MOS, http://www.alpha-mos.com
3. Bresson, X., Vandergheynst, P., Thiran, J.-P.: A variational model for object segmentation using boundary information and shape prior driven by the mumford-shah functional. International Journal of Computer Vision **68**(2), 145–162 (2006)
4. Chan, T.F., Vese, L.A.: Active contours without edges. IEEE Transactions on Image Processing **10**(2), 266–277 (2001)
5. Chen, Y., Tagare, H.D., Thiruvenkadam, S., Huang, F., Wilson, D., Gopinath, K.S., Briggs, R.W., Geiser, E.A.: Using prior shapes in geometric active contours in a variational framework. International Journal of Computer Vision **50**(3), 315–328 (2002)
6. Descamps, S., Descombes, X., Bechet, A., Zerubia, J.: Automatic flamingo detection using a multiple birth and death process. In: IEEE International Conference on Acoustics, Speech and Signal Processing, ICASSP 2008, Las Vegas, USA, pp. 1113–1116 (March 2008)
7. Descombes, X., Minlos, R., Zhizhina, E.: Object extraction using a stochastic birth-and-death dynamics in continuum. Journal of Mathematical Imaging and Vision **33**, 136–139 (2009)
8. Faessel, M., Courtois, F.: Touching grain kernels separation by gap-filling. Image Analysis and Stereology **28**(3), 195–203 (2011)
9. Lacoste, C., Descombes, X., Zerubia, J.: Point processes for unsupervised line network extraction in remote sensing. IEEE Transactions on Pattern Analysis and Machine Intelligence **27**(10), 1568–1579 (2005)
10. Leventon, M.E., Grimson, W.E.L., Faugeras, O.: Statistical shape influence in geodesic active contours. In: IEEE Conference on Computer Vision and Pattern Recognition, vol. 1, pp. 316–323 (2000)

11. Perrin, G., Descombes, X., Zerubia, J.: A marked point process model for tree crown extraction in plantations. In: IEEE International Conference on Image Processing (ICIP), vol. 1 (September 2005)
12. Yao, Q., Zhou, Y., Wang, J.: An automatic segmentation algorithm for touching rice grains images. In: International Conference on Audio Language and Image Processing (ICALIP), pp. 802–805 (November 2010)

Weight Estimation of Pigs
Using Top-View Image Processing

Mohammadamin Kashiha[1], Claudia Bahr[1], Sanne Ott[2,3], Christel P.H. Moons[2], Theo A. Niewold[3], Frank O. Ödberg[2], and Daniel Berckmans[1]

[1] M3-BIORES - Measure, Model and Manage Bioresponses, Department of Biosystems, KU Leuven, Kasteelpark Arenberg 30, 3001, Leuven, Belgium
amin.kashiha@biw.kuleuven.be
[2] Department of Animal Nutrition, Genetics, Breeding and Ethology, Ghent University, Heidestraat 19, 9820, Merelbeke, Belgium
[3] Division of Livestock-Nutrition-Quality, Department of Biosystems, KU Leuven, Kasteelpark Arenberg 30, 3001, Leuven, Belgium

Abstract. Good health is a key element in pig welfare and steady weight gain is considered an indicator of good health and productivity. Therefore, continuous weight monitoring is an essential method to ensure pigs are in good health. The purpose of this work was to investigate feasibility of an automated method to estimate weight of pigs by using image processing.

The weight estimation process developed as follows: First, to localize pigs in the image, an ellipse fitting algorithm was employed. Second, the area the pig was occupying in the ellipse was calculated. Finally, the weight of pigs was estimated using dynamic modelling. This method can replace the regular weight measurements in farms that require repeated handling and thereby causing stress to the pigs.

Overall, video imaging of fattening pigs appeared promising for real-time weight and growth monitoring. In this study the weight could be estimated with an accuracy of 97.5% (± 0.82 kg). This result is significant since the existing automated tools currently have a maximum accuracy of 95% (± 2 kg) in practical setups and 97 % (± 1 kg) in walk-through systems (when pigs are forced to pass a corridor one by one) on average.

Keywords: Top-view body area · Pig weight estimation · Automated Image Processing · Transfer function modelling · Ellipse fitting

1   Introduction

At present, there are over 60 billion animals slaughtered yearly for food production [1]. While today's systems entail efficient use of land and labor, the increased number of animals per farm has resulted in new welfare problems because time is too limited to provide individual animal care [2]. Nowadays technologies are available that even monitor animals automatically at 24 hours a day. Research reported by [3] identified over 90 potential applications for image analysis in pig production. Of these, estimation of pig weight was identified as a primary application for the development of

© Springer International Publishing Switzerland 2014
A. Campilho and M. Kamel (Eds.): ICIAR 2014, Part I, LNCS 8814, pp. 496–503, 2014.
DOI: 10.1007/978-3-319-11758-4_54

image analysis techniques for use in livestock production. Accurate monitoring of weight gain performance and the use of weight data to make effective management decisions is also crucial for efficient pork production.

Automatic monitoring of animals based on video analysis is a novel approach, which has been proven useful to farm managers [3]. Weight measurement is an important variable in farm management that nonetheless suffers from a number of drawbacks when performed manually since this is labor intensive and stressful for both animals and workers. Machine vision-based weighing of pigs is a non-intrusive, fast and accurate approach, which could deal with above issues during the weighing process [4].

Recently, visual image analysis (VIA) has been proposed as a method for real-time and continuous monitoring of pig weight gain performance, thereby allowing quicker detection of problems and more effective management decisions [5]. The VIA technique uses aerial-view images of animals provided by cameras to determine body surface dimensions and may be used for real-time monitoring of pig weight. Camera technology can be used to determine the area of the aerial view of a pig's body. Using information on the relationship between area and Body Weight (BW), VIA systems have been developed and have been found to be accurate enough to estimate live BW within 5% [6], but to date, this technology has required that pigs were separated from a group to be measured.

Other researchers previously investigated different approaches to estimate weight of pigs using image analysis. Brandl and Jørgensen [7] used spline functions to express the relationship between the body area of the pig measured by image analysis and the live weight of the pig. Marchant, et. al. [5] developed automated algorithms that could find the plan view outline of pigs in a normal housing situation, measure major body components and predict the weight of the group of pigs at 34 kg with standard errors of 7.3% while using manual weighing to calibrate the system. Schofield, et. al. [8] developed prototype imaging systems to record the weight-related areas of pigs by fitting linear regression coefficients. Craig and Schinkel [9] proposed a mixed effects model[1] to estimate pig weight. Wang, et. al. [4] developed an image-based walk-through system for pig live weight approximation. They employed artificial neural network technique to correlate physical features extracted from the walk-through images to pig live weight in order to improve the accuracy of live weight approximation and could estimate pig weight with an average relative error of 3%.

Some suggest that BW and top-view body area have a linear relationship [8] and use a single linear regression equation to estimate the live BW of animals from the body area based on the interpretation of individual images. Schofield, et. al. [8] suggested that different breeds may require different algorithms for BW prediction. Also Fisher, et. al. [11] suggested a need for unique algorithms for specific breeds or lines of pigs. More recently, researchers have been highlighting the benefits of mixed

---

[1] Mixed-effects models, like many other types of statistical models, describe a relationship between a response variable and the covariates that have been measured or observed along with the response. For further information reader is referred to 10. Pinheiro J, Bates D. Mixed Effects Models in S and S-Plus: Springer; 2000.

effects models [12] and justify their argument that mixed effects model is easily adaptable to stochastic modelling. However, despite the advantages of mixed effects models compared to fixed effects models, it is important to note that there is a large amount of variation in the accuracy of different mixed effects models.

In this work, dynamic data based (transfer function: TF) models were used. Such modelling techniques are compact and allow accurate prediction of the time-variant process response, which makes them suitable for model-based predictive monitoring purposes [13].

In this paper, an approach was presented to monitor pigs weight in a fully automated way based on continuous image analysis. The hypothesis in this work was that combining TF modelling and top-view pig body area calculation using image processing could lead to a more accurate weight estimation.

2   Materials and Methods

2.1   Animals and Housing

Two experiments, identical in setup, were carried out in February and June 2011, whereby data from the former were used to develop the model while the latter was a validation experiment. Experiments were carried out in Agrivet research farm, Merelbeke, Belgium and lasted three weeks each. Details of the experiment are explained in [14]. Figure 1a shows a floor plan of the experimental pens including the location of the cameras, feeders and water outlets.

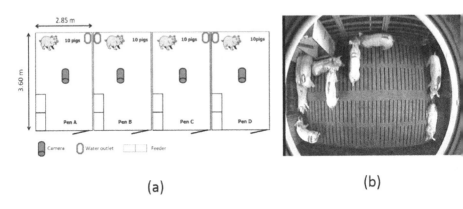

(a)   (b)

Fig. 1. a. Ground plan of the 4 pens in the research barn.; b. A frame of a video showing a top view of one of the four pig pens in the research barn

2.2   Equipment and Data Collection

Top-view video images of the pigs in the four pens were captured by cameras installed in the rafters of the barn. Video images from top view Panasonic WV-BP330 cameras were collected for all pens during 13 days for 12 hours a day (07:00 to

19:00h) resulting in 156 hours of video recordings per experiment. Videos were recorded in MPEG-1 format, with a frame rate of 25 frames per second, a frame width of 720 pixels, a frame height of 576 pixels and a data rate of 64 kbps. Figure 1b shows a frame of the videos recorded in the experiments.

Above experiment was repeated identically for validation purposes. In this validation experiment, pig body weight was measured twice a week using MS Schippers MS-100 weighing scale. These measurements served as the gold standard reference to which the estimated weights obtained from image analysis and modelling were compared. Average weight obtained from image on the hand weighing days was compared with real measured weights to evaluate performance of the system.

2.3   Image Segmentation

The captured video images were subsequently processed offline in MATLAB 2010A environment to extract the outline of the body area, which consisted of a two-step process. First, pigs were localized and segmented in the image using an ellipse fitting algorithm. Second, head and neck in the image were separated from the body to maximize correlation to BW [6].

2.3.1   Localizing and Segmenting Pigs Image by Ellipse Fitting

To localize pigs within the pen, an ellipse fitting algorithm using Generalized Hough Transform as introduced by Davies [15] was adapted. In the next step, the corpus image was separated from the head by using the same ellipse fitting algorithm. Here, the algorithm gave two ellipses as shown in figure 2.a. The bigger ellipse represents the corpus and the smaller one the head. The corpus area of the pig surrounded by the corpus ellipse, namely "A" in figure 2.b was calculated once a minute and used for BW estimation. In order to limit processing to standard standing positions of pigs in weight estimation, 2700 area pixels (for camera height of 2.2 m) were regarded as a minimum of "A".

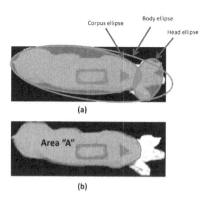

Fig. 2. a. Extracted pig body using ellipse fitting; corpus and head separation by repeating ellipse fitting algorithm; b. The resulting body area "A" used for BW estimation

2.4   Weight Estimation Using the TF Model

The objective of the next step was to quantify the dynamics of body area (A) and to relate it to the golden standard BW. A single-input, single-output (SISO) TF model was used. The model structure used could be described by equation 1 [16].

$$BW(t) = \frac{a(z^{-1})}{b(z^{-1})} A(t - nt_T) \tag{1}$$

In the above equation BW(t) is the body weight, t represents the discrete-time instants for weight estimation and measurement; A(t) represents the input of the model, namely Body Area; nt_i is the number of time delays between each input i and their first effects on the output; $a(z^{-1})$ is the nominator polynomial and equals $1 + a_1 z^{-1} + a_2 z^{-2} + \cdots + a_{n_a} z^{-n_a}$; $b_i(z^{-1})$ is the denominator polynomials linked with the inputs i and is equal to $b_0 + b_1 z^{-1} + b_2 z^{-2} + \cdots + b_{n_b} z^{-n_{bi}}$; a_j, b_i are the model parameters to be estimated; z^{-1} is the backward shift operator, defined as $z^{-1}.y(k) = y(k-1)$; n_a, n_b are the orders of the respective polynomials.

The model parameters were estimated using a refined instrumental variable approach with the Captain toolbox in Matlab [16]. In order to build the model, different combinations for n_a, n_b and nt_T were calculated. More specifically, in the SISO model which has only one input, n_a ranged from 1 to 3, n_b from 1 up to 3 and nt_T from 0 to 2. Therefore, to identify the best fitting TF model parameters of a total of 48 (4x4x3) possible models were calculated. The resulting models were evaluated by the coefficient of determination R_T^2 [17] and an identification procedure was used to select the most appropriate model order based on the minimization of the Young Identification Criterion (YIC) explained by Young and Lees [17]. The smaller the variance of the model residuals in relation to the variance of the measured output, the more negative this term becomes.

Weight measurements in the development experiment were used to design the model. The developed model was then used to estimate the BW in a validation experiment, which was methodologically identical.

Finally, results of TF modelling were compared against a linear regression model [8] and a non-linear mixed effects model [12].

3   Results

When applying the modelling approach to the data of the whole experiment (240 measurements) the YIC criterion selected models which were predominantly second order (equation 2) and without delay, stable (YIC = -7.294) and with the highest R_T^2 (0.975). The optimal model structure was described by $n_a=2$, $n_b = 1$ and $nt_T= 0$ based on parameters demonstrated in equation 1.

$$BW(t) = \frac{b_0 + b_1.z^{-1}}{1 + a_1.z^{-1} + a_2.z^{-2}} A(t) \tag{2}$$

Where: a_1 = -0.0768 ($\pm$0.0061), a_2 = 0.9609 ($\pm$0.0093); b_1= 0.289 ($\pm$0.0014); b_0 = 0

Figure 3 illustrates the adapted model with the optimal parameters presented above and figure 4 shows the measured actual weights versus the estimated weights over six days of measurements for all four pens and ten pigs per pen (240 data points). The ideal case was that all of the data points align with the identity line (R^2 of 100% which means for every data point, estimated weight would equal the measured weight). This means the more erratic the points are, the less R^2 and accuracy of weight estimation will be. In total, using TF modelling of top-view pig body area, pigs weight could be estimated with an accuracy of 97.5% at group[2] level.

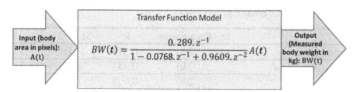

Fig. 3. The TF model adapted to estimate BW (in kg) using body area (in pixels) as input

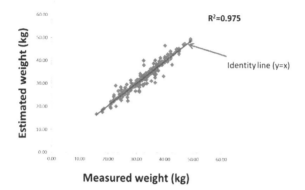

Fig. 4. Measured weights versus estimated weights over six measurement days of all four pens with ten pigs per pen (240 data points) in the validation experiment

4   Discussion

The proposed image processing and modelling method proved the ability to work unattended in a piggery environment with the pigs increasing in weight from a mean of 23 to 45 kg. The system calculated an average of one area measurement every one minute. Subsequently, the body area calculated by the image processing was used to design a TF model with weight measurements as output. The resulting model was evaluated in a validation experiment in which the body area was the input of the model. The model output, namely the estimated weight, was subsequently compared against conventional weight measurements. Average weight of individuals in a group (group level) was estimated using the developed model. Taking all four pens into account R^2 was as high as 0.975 for group weight. These results prove that the mean

---

[2] Group level weight estimation is derived from calculating an average of individuals weight.

weight of the pigs can be estimated with a deviation of 2.5% in a weight range of 23 to 45 kg.

The results obtained using TF model were compared with previous work on this topic, namely linear regression models [8] and mixed effects (non-linear) models [12]. Table 1 compares the results of these three methods applied to the group level data of the validation experiment while data of the first experiment were used to develop the models.

Table 1. Comparison of results of applying "Linear regression", "Mixed effects (non-linear)" and TF models to body area data in group level

Model	Data points	R^2	SE^3 (%)	SE (kg)
Linear regression	240	0.871	10.04	4.52
Mixed effects (non-linear)	240	0.943	5.95	2.68
TF	240	0.975	1.82	0.82

The data presented in table 1 indicate that the TF model yields a higher R^2 and a lower SE, which means this method can estimate BW with a higher accuracy and reliability.

In terms of practical application of this method, problems should be solved as a number of pitfalls have been identified for this study. The first pitfall was that there were occasions where certain pigs stood on their back feet and therefore presented a reduced area for image capturing and analysis. These cases were automatically excluded by thresholding the minimum body area. Another pitfall was in illumination conditions, which are also important for segmentation of the images. A dim illumination could make pig segmentation against dark backgrounds more difficult. In the experiments of this work, it was found that a range of light intensity of 40 to 150 lux would be optimal.

5   Conclusion

A technique has been introduced that offers fully automated weight estimation of pigs. The results show that by measuring of top view body area and adapting a TF model, it is possible to estimate BW with an accuracy of 97.5% (± 0.82 kg) on group level overcoming competing linear and non-linear modelling methods. In conclusion, application of the introduced method can bring important profits for livestock enterprises since continuous information on daily weight would allow producers to optimize nutritional management practices, predict and control shipping weights, and potentially assist in monitoring herd health.

Acknowledgements. This project was funded by Agentschap voor Innovatie door Wetenschap en Technologie (IWT). (project number: 080530/LBO)

---

[3] Standard Error.

References

[1] Prakash, A., Stigler, M.: FAO Statistical Yearbook. Food and Agriculture Organization of The United Nations (2012), http://faostat.fao.org/

[2] HSUS: The Welfare of Animals in the Pig Industry. The Humane Society of the United States (HSUS) (2010)

[3] DeShazer, J.A., Moran, P., Onyango, C.M., Randall, J.M., Schofield, C.P.: Imaging systems to improve stockmanship in pig production. AFRC Institute of Engineering Research (1988)

[4] Wang, Y., Yang, W., Winter, P., Walker, L.: Walk-through weighing of pigs using machine vision and an artificial neural network. Biosyst. Eng. **100**(1), 117–125 (2008)

[5] Marchant, J.A., Schofield, C.P., White, R.P.: Pig growth and conformation monitoring using image analysis. J. Anim. Sci. **68**, 141–150 (1999)

[6] Schofield, C.P.: Evaluation of image analysis as a means of estimating the weight of pigs. Journal of Agricultural Engineering Research **47**, 287–296 (1990)

[7] Brandl, N., Jørgensen, E.: Determination of live weight of pigs from dimensions measured using image analysis. Comput. Electron. Agric. **15**(1), 57–72 (1996)

[8] Schofield, C.P., Marchant, J.A., White, R.P., Brandl, N., Wilson, M.: Monitoring Pig Growth using a Prototype Imaging System. Journal of Agricultural Engineering Research **72**(3), 205–210 (1999)

[9] Craig, A.B., Schinkel, A.P.: Nonlinear mixed effects model for swine growth. Prof. Anim. Sci. **17**, 256–260 (2001)

[10] Pinheiro, J., Bates, D.: Mixed Effects Models in S and S-Plus. Springer (2000)

[11] Fisher, A.V., Green, D.M., Whittemore, C.T., Wood, J.D., Schofield, C.P.: Growth of carcass components and its relation with conformation in pigs of three types. Meat Sci. **65**(1), 639–650 (2003)

[12] Schinkel, A.P., Einstein, M.E., Jungst, S., Booher, C., Newman, S.: Evaluation of different mixed model nonlinear functions to describe the body weight growth of pigs of different sire and dam lines. Prof. Anim. Sci. **25**, 307–324 (2009)

[13] Aerts, J.M., Wathes, C.M., Berckmans, D.: Dynamic Data-based Modelling of Heat Production and Growth of Broiler Chickens: Development of an Integrated Management System. Biosyst. Eng. **84**(3), 257–266 (2003)

[14] Kashiha, M.A., Bahr, C., Ott, S., Moons, C.P.H., Niewold, T.A., Tuyttens, F., et al.: Automatic Monitoring of Pig Locomotion Using Image Analysis. Livest Sci. **159**, 141–148 (2014)

[15] Davies, E.R.: Finding ellipses using the generalised Hough transform. Pattern Recognition Letters **9**(2), 87–96 (1989)

[16] Young, P.C.: Recursive Estimation and Time-Series Analysis, 2nd edn. XVIII. Springer (2011)

[17] Young, P.C., Lees, M.: The active mixing volume: a new concept in modelling environmental systems. In: Barnet, V., Turkman, R., Feridun, K. (eds.) Statistics for the Environment. Wiley, Chichester (1993)

An Efficient Image Self-recovery and Tamper Detection Using Fragile Watermarking

Sajjad Dadkhah[1]($\boxtimes$), Azizah Abd Manaf[2], and Somayeh Sadeghi[3]

[1] Faculty of Computing, Universiti Teknologi Malaysia,
54100 Kuala Lumpur, Malaysia
dsajjad2@live.utm.my
[2] Advanced Informatics School, Universiti Teknologi Malaysia,
54100 Kuala Lumpur, Malaysia
azizah07@ic.utm.my
[3] Faculty of Computer Science and Information Technology, University of Malaya,
Kuala Lumpur, Malaysia
ssomayeh@siswa.um.edu.my

Abstract. Fragile watermarking is one of the most effective approaches to insure the integrity of digital images. In this paper, an efficient self-recovery and tamper localization scheme using fragile watermarking is proposed. The proposed method generates 12-bit tamper detection data and 20-bit self-recovery data for each 4×4 block. The generated tamper detection and self-recovery features are encrypted by utilizing user secrete key. A random block mapping scheme is used to embed the encrypted block features into its mapping block. The proposed two-level tamper detection creates high capacity for tamper detection data which improves the security and tamper localization. The performance of the proposed scheme and its robustness against famous security attacks is analyzed. The experimental results demonstrate the high efficiency of the proposed scheme in terms of tamper detection rate, tamper localization and self-recovery. This method is robust against security attacks such as collage attack and constant average attack.

Keywords: Tamper detection · Tamper localization · Self-recovery · Fragile watermarking · Image security

1 Introduction

The integrity and authenticity of the digital images can be assured by utilizing the tamper detection algorithms that use watermarking techniques . Fragile watermarking is one of the most effective methods to be used for tamper detection and tamper localization [1]. In recent years, various fragile watermarking schemes for tamper detection and self-recovery have been proposed [2–7]. Generally, the digital images that are watermarked by these schemes are partitioned into non-overlapping blocks of pixels. The generated watermark feature for tamper detection and recovery is embedded into blocks with different locations which

© Springer International Publishing Switzerland 2014
A. Campilho and M. Kamel (Eds.): ICIAR 2014, Part I, LNCS 8814, pp. 504–513, 2014.
DOI: 10.1007/978-3-319-11758-4_55

makes them robust against certain malaciouse attacks. However, these tamper detection and self-recovery methods struggle with a few more problems.

1. **Lack of tamper localization precision**
   Tamper detection schemes with self-recovery capability embed the generated watermark information into blocks with different locations. Therefore, if a mapping block that contains watermark information of a different block is destroyed, two blocks will be detected as tampered. To address this issue, Lin et al. [2] proposed a hierarchical tamper detection algorithm with self-recovery capability. The tamper detection data generated by Lin's algorithm is embedded as watermark payload into the same block and self-recovery data is embedded into a different block. The embedding procedure proposed by Lin has been adopted by several researchers [2,3,5–9].
2. **Insufficient embedding capacity**
   Because of the insufficient embedding capacity, certain constant information such as average intensity of the block or certain features of discrete cosine transform (DCT) coefficients are used by the fragile tamper detection schemes. These methods [2,3,8,9] are incapable of detecting tampering attacks that do not modify their designated feature. The dual watermarking algorithm proposed by Lee and Lin [3] suffer from this problem. Their proposed algorithm offers a second chance of recovery survival, but in contrast any modification that alters bits in 5 MSB (most significant bit) or higher positions cannot be detected by their algorithm.
3. **Lack of security for embedding procedure**
   The blockwise dependency ensures the robustness of self-recovery algorithm [6–8,10] against common security attacks such as vector quantization (VQ) [11]and collage attack [12]. However, these schemes are vulnerable against tampering attacks which use the same block mapping scheme to locate the generated watermark data. Several tamper detection algorithms suffer from lack of sufficient security measurement such as secret key for encrypting in the embedding procedure.

To resolve the tamper localization and security problems that are mentioned above, this paper proposes an efficient tamper detection and self-recovery algorithm based on fragile watermarking with following characteristics:

1. Generate 12-bit tamper detection based on block binary feature and 20-bit average intensity for self-recovery.
2. Generate encrypted block-mapping algorithm based on security key and encrypt the inserted information of each block 4×4 pixels.
3. Apply a second-level of tamper detection by generating new 20-bit tamper detection keys, which are embedded in different block to eliminate security attacks, such as a VQ counterfeiting and collage attack.

The remainder of this paper is organized as follows. In section 2, the proposed fragile watermarking for tamper detection and self-recovery is described. Section 3 presents the performance analysis and experimental results. The paper's conclusions are presented in section 4.

2   The Proposed Algorithm

The proposed fragile tamper detection and self-recovery scheme is explained in three phases : watermark generation and embedding, tamper detection and localization, self-recovery.

2.1   Watermarking Scheme

The proposed watermarking scheme is encrypted by using a user secret key. For digital images which have more than one color space such as RGB images, all color channels (red, green and blue) are watermarked by the proposed algorithm. The proposed watermarking procedure consists of the following steps:

Step 1. Preprocessing.The original image O is divided into M 4×4 blocks F_i, and F_i is divided to four 2×2 blocks G_i. The two least significant bit of each pixel is converted to zero.

Step 2. Tamper Bit Generation. Each 4×4 block F_i is decomposed as $F_i = R_i^+||C_i^+$, where R_i^+ is the addition result of pixels in each row, and C_i^+ is the addition result of pixels in each column of 4×4 blocks, and $||$ is bitwise concatenation. As following equations illustrate, the $12_{bit}TDK$ is the tamper detection key for each block of 4×4 pixels.

$$12_{bit}TDK = 8_{bit}(A_{avg})||4_{bit}(F_n) \tag{1}$$

$$K_i = mod(R_i^+, 2) + mod(C_i^+, 2), i = (1, ..., 4) \tag{2}$$

$$4_{bit}(F_n) = \begin{cases} 1 \ \ if \ mod(CO(K_n, 1), 2) = 0, (n = 1, ..., 4) \\ \\ 0 \ \ if \ mod(CO(K_n, 1), 2) = 1, (n = 1, ..., 4) \end{cases} \tag{3}$$

$$8_{bit}(A_{avg}) = mod(Av_{F_n}/2^{j-1}, 2), j = (1, ..., 8) \tag{4}$$

where K_i is the total binary summation of each row pixel addition R_i^+ with column pixel addition C_i^+ for the same i value. Moreover, for each 4×4 block , four R_i^+ and four C_i^+ value are generated, and as i in equation 2 illustrated, four value of K_i are generated for each 4×4 block. The $CO(K_n, 1)$ in equation 3 presents the total number of 1's in binary form of $K_n(n = 1, ..., 4)$. As illustrated in equation 3, four $F_n(n = 1, ..., 4)$ value is generated for each 4×4 block. However, if the value of $CO(K_n, 1)$ is even, F_n will be set to 1, otherwise, F_n will be set to 0. Av_{F_n} in equation 4 present the average intensity of 4×4 blocks, and $8_{bit}(A_{avg})$ is the 8-bit binary form of average intensity.

Step 3. Self-recovery Bit Generation. The self-recovery data generated by the proposed scheme, is 20-bit key RCK, which consists of the five most significant bits (5MSB) of each average intensity of 2×2 blocks G_i.(20_{bit} $(RCK) = G_i^1||G_i^2||G_i^3||G_i^4)$

Step 4. Encryption. The 32-bit watermark data which is decomposed as $32Wt_{bit} = 12_{bit}(TDK) \| 20_{bit}(RCK)$, is encrypted with the following equation,

$$E(Wt_{bit}) = 32Wt_{bit} \oplus K_s \tag{5}$$

where K_s is user secret key and $\oplus$ is the exclusive or (XOR). The user key K_s will be obtained by user in the beginning of each watermarking and tamper detection procedure. However, as equation 5 illustrated, the generated 32-bit watermark data $32Wt_{bit}$ for each 4×4 block will be encrypted by user key K_s which is only known to user. The optimization conducted in this step secures the proposed scheme against famous security attacks such as four-scanning attack.

Step 5. Embedding and Block-mapping. The generated $12_{bit}(TDK)$ is embedded into the least significant bit of each pixel inside 4× 4 block F_i. However, as Fig.1 demonstrates, the $20_{bit}(RCK)$ is embedded into first and second least significant bit of a random selected mapping block. Fig.1 shows that the proposed block-mapping algorithm selects a random block with the most distanced location from the original block.

```
1:  b = (Block.no ÷ 2) + (width ÷ 4)
2:  d = (Block.no ÷ 2) + 1
3:  Process
4:      for all (rand(i) ∈ b) ⊆ d do
5:          if i ≤ d then
6:              for all ee ∈ {1 − 20} do
7:                  if ee < 16 then
8:                      2LSB {A_i^block(1, ee)} ← ∀ Get.Bit_i^TDK(1, ee)
9:                  else
10:                     1LSB {A_i^block(1, ee)} ← ∀ Get.Bit_i^RCK(1, ee)
11:                 end if
12:             end for
13:             b ⇐ b + (width ÷ 4)
14:             d ⇐ b − (width ÷ 4) + 1
15:             decrement i by one
16:         end if
17:     end for
18: end Process
```

Fig. 1. Embedding and block-mapping algorithm

2.2   Tamper Detection and Localization Algorithm

The proposed tamper detection and tamper localization algorithm locates the manipulated regions of the watermarked image $Wt_i, (i = 1, ..., n)$, and marks the suspicious block as either valid $v_i = 1$ or invalid $v_i = 0$. However, the optimization proposed in this section creates a blockwise dependency which secures the proposed scheme against tamper attack such as the collage attack. The details of the proposed tamper detection method are explained as follows.

Step 1. Block partitioning. The same procedure as Step 1 in Section 2.1 will be conducted.

Step 2. Retrieve watermark. Extract the $12_{bit}(TDK)$ from each 4×4 block F_i and $20_{bit}(RCK)$ from mapping blocks. The mapping block location is determined with the same procedure presented in Step 5 of Section 2.1.

Step 3. Tamper detection. In this step, the 12-bit tamper detection data TDK^n and 20-bit self-recovery RCK^n is reconstructed with the same procedure presented in Steps 1 and 2 of Section 2.1. The extracted detection key TDK and new generated key TDK^n are compared as:

$$v_1^i = \begin{cases} 1 & if\ 12_{bit}(TDK) = 12_{bit}(TDK^n) \\ 0 & if\ 12_{bit}(TDK) \neq 12_{bit}(TDK^n) \end{cases} \tag{6}$$

where the new generated self-recovery information RCK^n will be used for tamper detection purpose and the tampered blocks will be marked as tamper $v_1^i = 0$. Moreover, the following expressions secure the proposed scheme against malicious attack such as collage tampering.

$$v_2^i = \begin{cases} 1 & if\ v_1^i = 1\ and\ 20_{bit}(RCK) = 20_{bit}(RCK^n) \\ 0 & if\ v_1^i = 1\ and\ 20_{bit}(RCK) \neq 20_{bit}(RCK^n) \end{cases} \tag{7}$$

Step 4. Tamper localization. The 4×4 blocks F_i with $v_1^i = 0$ or $v_2^i = 0$ will be presented as tampered regions.

2.3   Recovery Algorithm

The proposed tamper localization scheme distinguishes the tampered blocks by marking them as valid or invalid. However, to identify the blocks that need to be recovered, the array $N_i^R, i = (1, .., N)$ is generated by the following expression:

$$N_i^R = \begin{cases} 1 & if\ v_1^i = 1\ \&\ v_2^i = 1 \\ 0 & if\ v_1^i = 0\ \&\ v_2^i = 0 \end{cases} \tag{8}$$

The 20-bit self-recovery features RCK_i^n is extracted from its mapping block by Step 2 of Section 2.2. The 20-bit RCK_i^n consist of four 5-bit values which are extracted from 5MSB of the average intensity of the 2×2 blocks G_i^n. Moreover, if $N_i^R = 1$ the tampered block F_i^R will be recovered by substituting the extracted self-recovery information RCK_i^n with the destroyed pixels in F_i^R. Since the proposed self-recovery information is constructed based on 2×2 blocks, the quality of the recovered image will be improved after self-recovery procedure.

3   Experimental Results

To evaluate the performance of the proposed tamper detection and self-recovery algorithm, two distinct measurements are introduced in this section. Generally, different quality measurements such as signal to noise ratio (SNR), peak signal to noise ratio (PSNR), Mean square error (MSE) and Watson distance (WD) will be used to evaluate the quality of watermarked image and self-recovery scheme. In this paper MSE and PSNR are used as follows :

$$\text{MSE} = \frac{1}{mn} \sum_{j=0}^{m-1} \sum_{j=0}^{n-1} [I(i,j) - K(i,j)]^2, \tag{9}$$

$$\text{PSNR} = 10.Log_{10}(\frac{b}{\text{MSE}}), \tag{10}$$

where b is the square of the maximum value of the signal, and m × n denotes the dimensions of the monochrome image of I and K. In this paper, i.e., image intensity is of 8 bits format, so b= 255^2. The second performance measurement which is used for evaluation, is tamper detection rate T_{dt}.

$$T_{dt} = (1 - (FP_r + FN_r)/(1 + P)) \times 100 \tag{11}$$

where FP_r is false positive rate and FN_r is false negative rate and P is the number of regions which have been manipulated.

3.1 Malicious Tampering Attacks

To evaluate the security robustness of the proposed scheme, several malicious attacks such as collage attack, constant-average attack(CAA) [13] and VQ attack are examined. In addition, several general tampering such as deletion attack and drawing attack are also examined. Fig. 2 shows the visual experimental results of the proposed scheme against several malicious tampering attacks. The Blond, Color Lena, Pirate and Barbara images with size of 512 × 512 are selected. The Magazine and Soldier images with size of 512 × 512 and 400 × 290 are collected from [14]. All test images in this experiment are watermarked with the same secret key. Thus, it is assumed that the attacker has knowledge about the contents of the secret key and proposed scheme structure.

As seen in Fig.2a,the watermarked Blond, color Lena and Pirate images generated by the proposed watermarking algorithm, 2e and 2i, has the PSNR of 43.21, 43.87 and 43.70 dB, respectively. Fig.2b is the tampered image with tamper ratio less than 20 %. As shown in Fig. 2d, the recovered image produced by the proposed algorithm, has the PSNR of 38.42 dB. Fig. 2f, represents three type of distinct tampering attacks:(1) Square deletion and rectangle deletion, (2) VQ tampering attack: copy woman and nightstand lamp from watermarked room image and place it on different spatial locations inside Lena image. The room image has been watermarked by the proposed scheme with the same secret key used for watermarked Lena image, and (3) Writing tampering: some letters "UTM" with red color is placed in Lena image. The tamper ratio for the multi region tampering attack in 2f is more than 30 %. Fig.2k is the collage tampered Pirate image, in which more than 40% of the watermarked Barbara image is copied and pasted into watermarked Pirate. Moreover, in this attack, the spatial

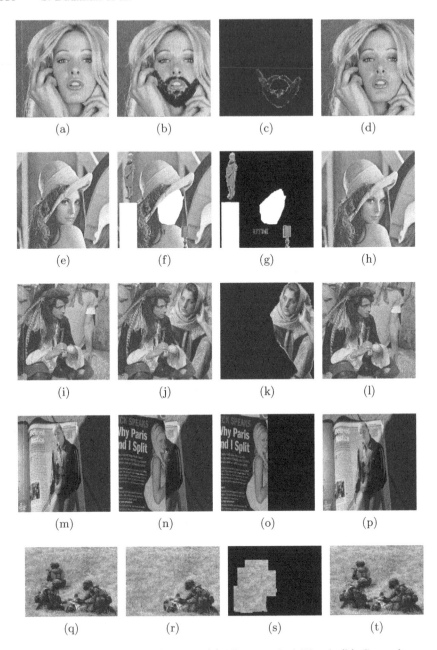

Fig. 2. Malicious Tampering Attacks. (a) Watermarked Blond ,(b) General tampering, (c) Tampered located, (d) Recovered image (PSNR= 38.42 dB), (e) Watermarked Color Lena(PSNR= 43.87 dB), (f) Multi Tampering , (g), Tampered located, (h) Recovered image (PSNR= 34.22 dB),(i) watermarked pirate, (j) Collage attack , (k) Attack detected ,(l) Recovered image (PSNR= 33.44 dB),(m) Watermarked magazine, (n) Collage attack 50 % , (o) 50 % CA attack detected ,(p) Recovered image ,(q) Watermarked soldiers, (r) CAA and VQ attack , (s) Attack detected ,(t) Recovered image

locations of the copied watermarked Barbara image is preserved in the water-marked pirate image.

As illustrated in Fig. 2c, 2g and 2k, the proposed tamper detection algorithm accurately located all the tampered regions, the black color regions are the authentic part of the tested images. The proposed tamper detection algorithm is very efficient in indicating the tampered and original 4 × 4 blocks. As shown in , Fig. 2d, 2h and 2l, the self-recovery scheme completely recovered all the tampered regions. The recovered Blond,Lena and pirate images, have the PSNR of 38.42, 34.22 and 33.44 dB, respectively. As Fig.2m, 2n, 2o and 2p demonstrated, the 50 % CA attack is completely detected and recovered. Different pixels of block 4 × 4 in Fig.2r are modified with CAA attack and multiple regions of the images are replaced with VQ attack. As 2s and 2t illustrated, all the tampered areas are completely detected and recovered. As the experimental results demonstrate in Fig. 2, the proposed scheme is able to efficiently locate and recover different types of tampering such as general tampering, VQ attack, Collage Attack and multi region tampering attack with a satisfying PSNR values. However, the proposed self-recovery algorithm is efficient in recovering the tampered region because of the selected recovery block size, which is 2×2 pixels.

3.2   Performance Analysis and Evaluations

In this section, the performance of the proposed tamper detection and self-recovery scheme is analyzed. Fig. 3 shows the PSNR and Fp_r value of the recovered images by the proposed scheme, for different tamper ratios. As seen in Fig. 3a , the PSNR of the recovered image for tampering attack with tamper ratio less than 10 % is fairly high. However, Fig.3a shows that the proposed self-recovery algorithm achieve the satisfying PSNR value of 31.00 dB for tamper ratio of 50 %.

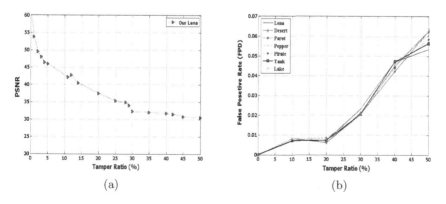

Fig. 3. Performance Analysis.(a)Recovered image PSNR (b) FP_r values

Fig. 3b shows that the false positive rate of the proposed algorithm is slightly increased with increase of tamper ratio. However, with the increase of FP_r, tamper detection rate T_{dt} will be degraded. It can be seen from Fig. 3b, that the FP_r of the proposed tamper detection algorithm is always less than 0.1 for different tamper ratios, and the FP_r of the different images are almost the same. The similarity of the false positive rate value for different images shows that, the images with different complexity does not have any degrading effect on the performance of the proposed tamper localization scheme. Moreover, after examining several digital images, the value of FP_r for different tamper ratio remained less than 0.1, and the value of false negative rate FN_r is very low. The tamper detection rate T_{dt} of the proposed scheme, which is obtained by equation 11, is higher than 99 % for general tampering attacks.

Table 1 presents the performance comparison of the proposed tamper detection and self-recovery algorithm against different malicious attacks such as collage attack. The 512×512 Lena image is used for performance analyses in Table 1. Table 1 shows the good recovery quality of Lee' s algorithm [3] for tamper ratio higher than 30 %, but his algorithm is not robust against any of malicious attacks. Patra [5] and Tong's [6] scheme generate PSNR lower than 31.00 dB for recovered image and their algorithms are not robust against all the malicious attacks mentioned in Table 1. However, as Table 1 demonstrates, the proposed method outperform other algorithms in security robustness and self-recovery.

Table 1. Performance Comparison of Self-recovery and Security robustness

Methods	Watermark PSNR (dB)	Recovered 30% tamper PSNR (dB)	Collage attack	VQ	CAA
Lee [3]	40.68	36.39	No	No	No
Patra [5]	43.94	31.41	Yes	Yes	No
Tong [6]	40.73	27.30	No	Yes	Yes
Proposed	43.87	37.23	Yes	Yes	Yes

4   Conclusions

In this paper, an efficient tamper detection and self-recovery scheme using fragile watermarking is proposed. The proposed tamper detection scheme generates 12-bit tamper detection based on block binary feature and 20-bit average intensity for self-recovery. The proposed tamper localization algorithm accurately locates the tampered blocks of size 4×4 pixels and the self-recovery scheme recovers the four blocks of size 2×2 pixels within the tampered block. The proposed random block-mapping algorithm creates robustness against security attacks such as collage attack CAA and VQ attack. However, the performance analysis and experimental results clearly demonstrate the efficiency of the proposed scheme in terms of tamper localization, security robustness and recovery quality. Future research include utilizing block-neighboring characteristic to recover the tampered blocks whose recovery information is destroyed.

Acknowledgments. The authors would like to thank Universiti Teknologi Malaysia for its educational and financial support.This work is funded by the FRGS grant under Vote No. 4L043 which is supported by Universiti Teknologi Malaysia (UTM) and the Ministry of Higher Education (MOHE).

References

1. Dadkhah, S., Manaf, A.A., Sadeghi, S.: Efficient digital image authentication and tamper localization technique using 3lsb watermarking. International Journal of Computer Science Issues (IJCSI) **9** (2012)
2. Lin, P.L., Hsieh, C.-K., Huang, P.-W.: A hierarchical digital watermarking method for image tamper detection and recovery. Pattern Recognition **38**(12), 2519–2529 (2005)
3. Lee, T.-Y., Lin, S.D.: Dual watermark for image tamper detection and recovery. Pattern Recognition **41**(11), 3497–3506 (2008)
4. Yang, C.-W., Shen, J.-J.: Recover the tampered image based on vq indexing. Signal Processing **90**(1), 331–343 (2010)
5. Patra, B., Patra, J.C.: Crt-based fragile self-recovery watermarking scheme for image authentication and recovery. In: IEEE International Symposium on Intelligent Signal Processing and Communication Systems (ISPACS), pp. 430–435 (2012)
6. Tong, X., Liu, Y., Zhang, M., Chen, Y.: A novel chaos-based fragile watermarking for image tampering detection and self-recovery. Signal Processing: Image Communication **28**(3), 301–308 (2013)
7. Chang, C.-C., Chen, K.-N., Lee, C.-F., Liu, L.-J.: A secure fragile watermarking scheme based on chaos-and-hamming code. Journal of Systems and Software **84**(9), 1462–1470 (2011)
8. Zhu, X., Ho, A.T., Marziliano, P.: A new semi-fragile image watermarking with robust tampering restoration using irregular sampling. Signal Processing: Image Communication **22**(5), 515–528 (2007)
9. Wang, L.-J., Syue, M.-Y.: A wavelet-based multipurpose watermarking for image authentication and recovery. International Journal of Communications **2**(4) (2013)
10. Qian, Z., Feng, G., Zhang, X., Wang, S.: Image self-embedding with high quality restoration capability. Digital Signal Processing **21**(2), 278–286 (2011)
11. Holliman, M., Memon, N.: Counterfeiting attacks on oblivious block-wise independent invisible watermarking schemes. IEEE Transactions on Image Processing **9**(3), 432–441 (2000)
12. Fridrich, J., Goljan, M., Memon, N.: Cryptanalysis of the yeung-mintzer fragile watermarking technique. Journal of Electronic Imaging **11**(2), 262–274 (2002)
13. Chang, C.-C., Fan, Y.-H., Tai, W.-L.: Four-scanning attack on hierarchical digital watermarking method for image tamper detection and recovery. Pattern Recognition **41**(2), 654–661 (2008)
14. Ng, T.-T., Chang, S.-F., Hsu, J., Pepeljugoski, M.: Columbia photographic images and photo realistic computer graphics dataset, Columbia Univ., New York, ADVENT Tech. Rep., 205–2004 (2005)

Author Index

Printed in the United States
By Bookmasters